# Daily Mail

# modern BRITISH COOKBOOK

**Daily Mail**

# modern
# BRITISH
# COOKBOOK

## OVER 500 RECIPES, ADVICE & KITCHEN KNOW-HOW

# ALASTAIR LITTLE
# & RICHARD WHITTINGTON

DRAWINGS BY BRIAN MA SIY
PHOTOGRAPHY BY JOHN LAWRENCE JONES

FOURTH ESTATE · *LONDON*

*For Lewis Esson, in appreciation of his skills as an editor, a friend who always makes sure the eggs stay on the plate and off the author's face.*

Both metric and imperial quantities are given. Use either all metric or all imperial, as the two are not necessarily interchangeable.

Editor & Project Manager: Lewis Esson
Design: Siân Keogh at Axis Design and the Senate
Drawings: Brian Ma Siy
Photography: John Lawrence Jones
Food and Styling for Photography: Linda McLean

First published in Great Britain in 1998 by
Fourth Estate Ltd
6 Salem Road
London W2 4BU

Cataloguing-in-Publication Data: a catalogue record for this book is available from the British Library.

ISBN 1-85702-772-8

Colour separations by Rapida Group plc, London
Printed and bound in Great Britain by the Bath Press, Bath

# contents

# preface

In July 1992, the photographer Angus Forbes was having a drink with Alastair Little in The Groucho, the club just round the corner from Alastair's restaurant in Soho. Over the years, Alastair had been approached by about 14 publishers anxious to publish a cookbook about his then uniquely multinational approach to cooking. He was wondering who might write it and with whom he would enjoy working on the project. Angus suggested me.

Alastair and I had known each other since 1974, when we met during his time at The Old Compton Wine Bar. Since then we had often eaten together and were — in that Soho fashion — friends who did not live in each other's pockets but who always enjoyed each other's company and shared a passion for food and cooking. I worked only briefly as the chef of The Studio in Swallow Street in 1982, an experience which confirmed that I could satisfy paying customers but proved to me that the restaurant kitchen was not where I wanted to spend my life. At the time Angus suggested me to Alastair as the collaborator on his book, I was earning my living as a script-writer and doing all my cooking at home and for friends. *Keep It Simple*, as we decided to call the book, was to change my life and my career and this is my third collaboration with Alastair and the sixth book I have written about food and cooking. A seventh is nearing completion and an eighth is waiting in the wings.

*Keep It Simple* was a success both critically and financially. We worked together on it at my house, where all the recipes were cooked in what is an ordinary domestic kitchen, the only concession to the work-load with which it now copes being three ovens. At that time, domestic reworking of a chef's recipes was not much done, though its value is no longer in question. We went on to collaborate on more books but also on The Cookery Doctor, a weekly column in the *Daily Mail's Weekend magazine*, in which reader's questions are addressed and answered. *The Daily Mail's Modern British Cookbook* is based on that five-year interaction. It covers dishes from all over the world because that is what contemporary eating in this country is increasingly about.

As our correspondents demonstrate with literally hundreds of letters each month, their concerns are truly international. More people travel, more eat out or take out on a regular basis. Ethnic restaurants dominate the British restaurant scene and have stimulated an interest in cooking at home with the spices and ingredients that are at the very roots of their food cultures. What was once alien and foreign is now assimilated, stimulating changes in the things people want to buy. Partly in response to this demand for different ingredients, the big supermarkets have become global larders. Five years ago, few people had heard of coriander, galangal and lemon grass. Now they can buy them round the corner. The thought of eating alligator or ostrich was an unlikely one in 1992. In 1998 they are just another low-fat meat option.

As we prepare to move into another century, the food we eat is light years away from what it was only a decade or so ago, when we British were still largely insular in our tastes — and certainly very limited in our home cooking aspirations. By addressing the changing interests of our *Weekend* readers we have arrived at a 'modern British cookbook', a reflection of where eating in this country is today. That is, anywhere and everywhere.

Richard Whittington, London, June 1998

# GLOBAL KITCHEN GLOSSARY

**T**he way our cooking changes to embrace other cultural styles and the ingredients we buy from an increasingly global larder make our kitchens more international by the day. Things most of us had never heard of four or five years ago are now commonplace on supermarket shelves. A glossary that attempts to deal not only with the huge diversity of ingredients now available to us but also with every aspect of the kitchen inevitably grows like Topsy and can easily expand to book length. The most difficult thing about this process is what to leave out. Compiling this list was made easier as most of the subjects were raised by readers' questions over the years.

## A

### Ackee
The fruit of a West-African tree, *Blighia sapida*, the edible part of which looks a lot like scrambled eggs. It is perhaps best known for its inclusion in the traditional Jamaican dish saltfish and ackee.

### Agar-agar
Agar-agar is a vegetarian gelling agent made from a red seaweed. Not as powerful as **gelatine**, you can buy it in powder, stick and flake forms from Oriental markets. In its stick form, agar-agar is also often eaten in the Far East as a salad ingredient, after it has been softened in warm water for just long enough to make it **al dente** (left to soak too long, it will dissolve completely). Store agar-agar in zip-lock bags in the fridge.

### Ageing Meat
Hanging whole carcasses is the traditional method of ageing meat, poultry and game. Today a lot of meat is stored as vacuum-wrapped joints and cuts, at low controlled temperatures. The meat is tenderized over 4–6 weeks by naturally occurring enzymes that break down muscle fibres.

### Aiguillettes
This French term describes meat cut into thin strips. It implies a good-quality lean cut needing only brief cooking and is typically applied to duck breast or beef fillet.

### Al Dente
Italian for 'to the teeth', this term literally describes the precise stage when pasta is cooked but retains a residual firmness, discernible when you bite into it.

8

### Allspice

Allspice is the definitive Jamaican spice, a pungent brown berry the size of a large peppercorn that is dried in the same way. It is a common misunderstanding to think of it as a spice mixture, as in its complex aroma one can detect subtle shades of **mace**, cinnamon and cloves. Allspice is one of the principal flavourings in **jerk** dishes, Jamaican marinated and barbecued chicken and pork, though it is also used in baking. The vigour of ready-ground allspice declines rapidly. Seek out whole berries and grind them fresh in a coffee grinder or pepper-mill that you keep exclusively for spices. The difference is as profound as that between ready-ground pepper and freshly milled.

### Andouillette

Andouillettes are sausages made from the chopped small intestines of pigs mixed with bits of beef stomach stuffed into more small intestines of pigs. The flavour is as forceful as you might expect and what one might call an acquired taste, indeed a taste that some people just plain refuse to get acquainted with at all. There are two distinct styles of andouillettes: the northern ones from Champagne, which are moist and rather slippery; and the drier, stronger-tasting sort which come from Normandy. All are sold cooked, so all you need do is grill them briefly to heat them through before serving them with mashed potatoes and fried onions. A good Dijon **mustard** on the side is obligatory.

### Anise Pepper, see Szechuan Pepper

### Annatto

This very common yellow food dye is made from the pulp surrounding the seeds of a small flowering tree indigenous to tropical South America. It is often used in dairy products like cheese, butter and margarine, and to colour so-called 'smoked' fish.

### Antipasto

Literally meaning 'before the pasta course', this term denotes the first course of a traditionally constructed Italian meal. An assortment of *antipasti* usually consists of mixed preserved meats, sausages and pickled vegetables.

### Arrowroot

A white starchy powder extracted from the root that is generally used to thicken sauces. It is favoured for its complete lack of flavour and its clarity.

### Arugula, see Rocket

### Asafetida or Asafoetida

A yellowish-brown hardened root extract from India, asafetida has a peculiar and rather off-putting smell, but imparts an intriguing flavour when used in small amounts. It is available either in lump form or as a powder. The former is superior and keeps for a long time in a jar without losing its strong flavour. Powder the pieces in a coffee grinder or smash them with the flat of a heavy knife.

# B

### Baccalà, Bacalao, Bacalhau, see Salt Cod

### Bacon

Many readers complain that the bacon they buy ready-sliced in packets is of a very poor quality and that it exudes a grey watery scum in the frying pan. This is because industrial bacon producers immerse sides of pork in **brine** and also inject brine into the meat rather than use the dry salt and nitrite of artisanal cures. They do so since this is a cheap and rapid method which takes days rather than weeks, while the inclusion of water is legal and means the bacon can be marketed at an apparently lower price by weight.

The inclusion of water must be stated on the label by law, though many people do not read this small print and will not be aware of just how much water they are paying for, or what this does to the way the bacon cooks and tastes. Furthermore, the first 10 per cent of water doesn't even need to be declared on the label, so 10 per cent on the label can actually mean 20 per cent water in the bacon.

Supermarkets do respond to customer demands and are now selling bacon which is labelled as 'traditionally dry-cured' (at a higher price). The word 'traditional' on packets of bacon may describe a largely cosmetic process in the mass-production context, while 'smoked' probably means the use of smoke flavour dissolved in the curing brine.

9

### Bagel

This robust round roll with a hole through the middle is distinguished by a good crust and a chewy interior. The differentiating element in the preparation of bagels is a brief scalding of the dough in boiling water prior to baking. They are often topped with poppy, caraway or **sesame seeds**, but these are entirely optional. Once uniquely Jewish fare, bagels now enjoy a wider popularity, though they are not yet as common here as they are in the USA. There they have become a standard brunch item, most frequently partnered with smoked salmon, which they call **lox**, and cream cheese.

### Bagna Cauda

You do not actually cook in the *bagna cauda* (literally, hot bath), a round earthenware dish glazed only on the inside and with a space underneath for a candle, the function of which is keeping the contents of the dish warm. The *bagna cauda* is used in Piedmont in the autumn for an anchovy and garlic sauce into which pieces of raw vegetable are dipped at the table. This is washed down with plenty of Barolo, the powerful full-bodied red wine of the region. Anything less robust would not stand up to the experience.

### Bain-marie

This is a large shallow container half-filled with water into which dishes are placed to help moderate temperature during cooking. This may be in the oven – as for baked custard or a terrine – or on the hob when making egg-based custards and sauces.

### Baking Powder, see Raising Agents

### Balsamic Vinegar

Balsamic vinegar is the ultimate vinegar, dark and potent with an incredible sweet intensity. Real balsamic vinegar comes exclusively from Modena and the surrounding area of Italy and is made from grape juice which is first boiled to reduce its volume by two-thirds before being put into oak barrels and matured for years. At intervals, as further volume is lost by evaporation and soaking into the wood, the vinegar is put into smaller and smaller barrels until reduced by a further six times.

The finest, *Aceto Balsamico Tradizionale di Modena*, is barrel-aged for more than 20 years, which goes some way to explaining its retail price of £60 and upwards per litre. By the time it has been put into small bottles with fancy labels the price can exceed £100 a litre. In the past, grand families in Modena would have barrels of *balsamico* laid down on the birth of a daughter as part of her dowry, rather as smart people have port laid down if a good vintage coincides with the birth of a son.

The flavour and intensity of good balsamic vinegar is extraordinary and only a few drops will impart a fragrant edge to a sauce or vinaigrette. Supermarkets now sell own-label bottles of balsamic vinegar which may be as young as 12 years or perhaps, with market forces, even less – but, then, it does not cost £60 a litre.

Because it is so special and so expensive balsamic vinegar is mostly used uncooked and undiluted in dressings like vinaigrettes, in which it should be mixed with 4 or 5 parts **extra-virgin olive oil** and seasoned with only a little sea salt and pepper. It is sometimes used on its own, dribbled over a plate of *bollito misto*, that splendid Italian dish of different boiled meats, the richness of which is perfectly balanced by the vinegar's aromatic fragrance. It may also be added to some cooked dishes to impart an unusual extra dimension. A tablespoon or two of balsamic vinegar in a slow-cooked stew, for example, delivers a hint of fascinating complexity to the completed dish.

### Balti

In the last 15 years, Birmingham curry-houses have developed a style of cooking and presenting curries in small **woks** called **karhai**. Claims that this cooking originated in part of Pakistan called Baltistan are fanciful. Balti is Birmingham, through and through.

### Banderillo

*Banderillas* are just another form of *tapas*, the bar food that turns drinking in Spanish bars into as much of a meal as you choose to make it. Technically, *banderillas* are simply snacks skewered on cocktail sticks, which means they can be pretty much anything you like as long as the ingredients are fairly traditionally Spanish.

### Barding

This is the practice of placing sheets of pork back fat over game birds, or other very lean meat or poultry with virtually no fat, in order to baste their flesh during cooking and prevent it drying out. The fat melts continuously as the bird cooks, effectively basting it. Although game dealers and butchers favour back fat, green streaky bacon is nicer and has the advantage of being edible at the end of cooking.

### Bath Chap

This is a pig's cheek simmered in a well-salted broth with herbs, including sage, for 2–3 hours until tender. It is then put into a shallow dish and left to cool. When cold, it is egged and crumbed and shallow-fried, a dish that is gelatinous within and crisp without. A **sauce gribiche** or **rémoulade** would go well with it, the sharp taste cutting the rich fattiness of the Bath chap.

### Baton

From the French for 'stick', this term is used for vegetables cut into neat strips.

### Battery Farming

Batteries are large sheds used for the intensive rearing of chickens, a process which produces cheap protein but meat of poor flavour and texture. It is a grim business, for the birds are raised in vile conditions, crammed in cages the size of an A4 piece of paper and stacked in tiers from floor to ceiling. They do nothing except eat processed food and are kept in bright light 24 hours a day, so they never sleep. If the air-conditioning is not working, the ammoniacal stench defies description, while the din from the birds is deafening. At eight weeks they are jammed into crates to be transported to the abattoir, many arriving with broken legs and wings, some arriving dead. Slaughter involves being slung upside down on conveyor belts, which first dip their heads in electrically charged water to stun them before their necks are cut.

### Bavette

A juicy cut from the lower rib of beef, similar to **skirt steak**, this has well-distributed fat and connective tissue.

### Beancurd

This high-protein, soft and virtually flavourless material, similar in texture to a firm custard, is hydrogenated from soya milk and is available in firm, medium-firm and hard versions. Ideally use beancurd, or tofu as it is known by the Japanese, on the day of purchase, though it will keep in the fridge for weeks. With the growth of vegetarianism, consumption has increased dramatically in the West over the past decade, though it has been eaten in the East for nearly 2,000 years. It readily absorbs flavours from the seasonings and aromatics in which it is **marinated** or cooked.

### Beignet

A sweet or savoury fritter, more often sweet than savoury, the former typically containing fruit and the latter cheese. Also in Louisiana, a doughnut.

### Belacan or Blacan

An important Southeast Asian ingredient, this compressed shrimp paste is available from Oriental and Asian markets. It is made from partially decomposed salted shrimps and has an unfortunate smell which, on first acquaintance, is not very appealing; this vanishes during cooking. Belacan is invariably first dry-roasted before use. Wrap the amount you need in foil and put in an oven preheated to 180°C/350°F/gas 4 for 6–8 minutes. Let it cool before using it. Keep the unused paste wrapped and in a screw-top jar in the fridge.

### Bellini

A delicious combination of **prosecco** and fresh peach juice, which was first served in Venice's famed Harry's Bar.

### Besan, see Gram Flour

### Beurre Manié

A paste of equal parts flour and butter that is whisked into a sauce towards the end of cooking to thicken it.

### Beurre Noisette

Butter cooked over a high heat for a few seconds until just browned (*noisette* meaning 'nut'); it is always made and used at the last minute, generally as a dressing for fish.

### Bicarbonate of Soda, see Raising Agents

### Biscotte

A rusk, that is a biscuit-sized piece of bread, baked a second time in a very low oven until crisp and dry.

### Biscotti

Italian hard dry sweet biscuits, usually flavoured with almonds, traditionally served with vin santo but now often served here to accompany coffee.

### Bistro or Bistrot

This French name for a small informal restaurant dates back to the time of the Napoleonic wars when invading Russian soldiers demanded of innkeepers in their own language that they be served quickly, the word bistro meaning 'be quick' in Russian. Russian fast-food outlets are called *bistros* today.

### Black Bean

Chinese black beans are used as a flavouring and can be bought canned, bottled or dried from Oriental supermarkets and some health-food shops. They are heavily salted and need to be thoroughly rinsed before use. Even then, care should be taken before adding any more salt to the dish in which they are cooked.

### Blanching

The partial cooking of food, generally vegetables, in rapidly boiling water to help fix colour or facilitate the removal of skins (as with tomatoes). It is often followed by the process of refreshing in cold water to arrest the cooking process. Restaurant practice often blanches vegetables to hold them almost cooked so that brief immersion in boiling water will get them ready for service.

Vegetables are also often blanched prior to freezing. Salty foods, like bacon, may be blanched to remove excess salt and some offal, notably sweetbreads, is blanched to remove impurities prior to any further cooking.

The term is also used of the horticultural practice of growing vegetables, like asparagus and chicory, in the dark to produce pale specimens.

### Boiling

Because we know bubbling water is at a temperature of 100°C without using a thermometer we need to differentiate between this state and very hot water when describing cooking in water, hence words like 'simmering' and 'poaching'.

To be accurate, it is only right to say that water boils at 100°C if you qualify the statement with the words 'at sea level'. Every 300 metres (1,000 feet) you go up, the boiling point reduces by 1°C because the atmospheric pressure on the surface of the water gets less. Mountaineers know that over about 1,500 metres (5,000 ft) their cup of tea is going to be insipid, rather like the cup which fails to cheer abroad when hot water is brought to the table for you to dunk a tea bag. The higher the pressure, the more energy needed by water molecules to vaporize and escape from the surface. It is this principle which is utilized in pressure cookers, which boil water in an airtight container, preventing steam from escaping and thereby increasing the cooking temperature.

For those of us who do not live in the high Alps, the temperature of bubbling water can be assumed to be 100°C. The difference between poaching and simmering from boiling is therefore not simply a matter of temperature. Water at a fast rolling boil is used for cooking pasta and when blanching green vegetables, where their brief exposure is made more effective by the water's aggressive agitation which tumbles them about like a giant washing machine. They don't stay in the water long enough for this violent movement to damage them.

Potatoes should be cooked with the water bubbling but not too hard or the tumbling action produces friction between the potatoes, and their surfaces break down. If you bubble stock rapidly for more than a few minutes you will encourage albumen and calcium in the bones to exude, giving the liquid an unpleasant gluey flavour. There is, however, a difference between boiling and simmering that is more than just agitation – the agitation causes a more rapid transfer of heat to the object being cooked, so it does cook faster.

For some mysterious reason a stew is always better if cooked below boiling point at around 90°C, with effective cooking taking place over a long period as low as 82°C. To boil or not to boil, that is the question. Whether 'tis more effective in the mind to poach or simmer...

### Bok Choy

Bok choy is a dark-leafed Asian brassica with crisp white stems that is used extensively in the cooking of China and Southeast Asia. It is lightly cooked as you would spinach and may be briefly **blanched** in boiling water, stir-fried or wilted in very hot oil.

### Bonito Flakes

Bonito is a large game fish, somewhere between a tuna and a mackerel, that is much loved by the Japanese. The fish is usually dried and grated to produce fine strong-flavoured flakes. These are used with **konbu** seaweed to produce **dashi**, the ubiquitous broth which has a taste that says Japan as loudly as Kikkoman **soy sauce**. A good Japanese restaurant will always grate its bonito fresh for each application, but the rest of us can buy it in packets from Oriental markets.

### Bottled Sauces

**Ketchups**, catsups and British brown sauces should not be sneered at. They have a long and distinguished pedigree dating back to the sixteenth century and are very useful weapons in the kitchen armoury of flavours, where they can be used to good effect in stews and marinades. The ingredients hint at their Eastern origins, with exotic spices like cardamom and cloves in combination with vinegar, anchovies, molasses and sultanas to deliver a heady and complex taste. A tablespoon of a good-quality brown sauce, like HP, will do wonders for a beef stew. See also **Worcestershire Sauce**.

### Botulism

While fortunately rare in these days of better hygiene and public health, *clostridium botulinum* is an anaerobic bacterium – meaning it can grow even when oxygen is not present, for example in cans – which produces a deadly nerve toxin. It can, however, be killed by relatively brief exposure to a sterilizing or boiling temperature of 100°C/212°F, but its spores are more resilient and can only be killed at much higher temperatures over a prolonged period. Foods which have low acid levels, like meat, poultry, fish and fresh vegetables, are the most susceptible to bacterial contamination, while fruits such as tomatoes, which have high acid levels, are the least susceptible. For this reason, those intending to flavour oils with aromatics like herbs, **chillies** or garlic should first toss these flavouring elements in vinegar or lemon juice before immersing them in the oil.

### Bouillon

Properly, in the professional kitchen, this term describes a reduced unclarified beef or lamb bone-based stock, though it is sometimes incorrectly used to describe consommé. Stock cubes are made to sound grander by calling them bouillon cubes.

### Bouquet Garni

A bundle of fresh herbs, classically parsley, thyme and bay leaves, tied with string (often contained within a celery stalk), or dried herbs in a muslin bag, which is removed after cooking.

### Brandy Butter

Brandy butter, also called hard sauce, is the classic accompaniment to steamed puddings, particularly the traditional Christmas pud. It is also one of those items where easy-to-produce equates with delicious and it can be made ages in advance. Cream 115 g / 4 oz unsalted butter with 150 g / 5 oz icing or granulated sugar, then gradually beat in 3 tablespoons of brandy and chill. If butter is excessively rich for your diet, then try beating crème fraîche with a couple of tablespoons of rum and two or three tablespoons of icing sugar. Chill well. You can use rum or whisky in place of the brandy, and there are even versions flavoured with vanilla.

### Bresaola, see Italian Cured Meats and Sausages

### Brine

Brine describes a salt water solution, which may also contain saltpetre and aromatics. Brines are used to modify flavour and for pickling and preserving meat, fish and vegetables.

### Broiling

The term used in the USA for grilling. It differs from our understanding of the process in that it means exposing food to a high heat from above and below simultaneously. You can buy electric broilers, but will achieve the same effect on a piece of fish, for example, by putting it skin side down into a smoking hot pan briefly before transferring the pan to under a preheated grill.

### Brunoise

Food, usually a mixture of vegetables, that has first been thinly sliced, then cut into matchstick shreds and possibly then across into uniform dice, for use as a flavouring base to sauces, soups and stuffings.

### Bruschetta

Bruschetta and crostini have enjoyed huge restaurant popularity in recent times. As the names suggest, they emanate from Italy and are basically open sandwiches, the principal difference being that crostini are slices of bread brushed with olive oil before being crisped and browned in a hot oven, while bruschetta are pieces of grilled bread (OK, toast) which are first rubbed with raw garlic then dribbled with extra-virgin olive oil. You then add whatever you want in the way of toppings, which can be as crude or as elegant as your fancy, pocket and imagination dictate. At the risk of stating the obvious, the better the bread and the olive oil, the better the bruschetta or crostini. **Rocket**, shaved Parmesan, anchovies, olives, prosciutto and salami, individually or in the combination of your choice, all have an authentic place on top of the bread, which should be rough country stuff. Bean purées are also nice spread thickly on the bread and scattered with fresh herbs.

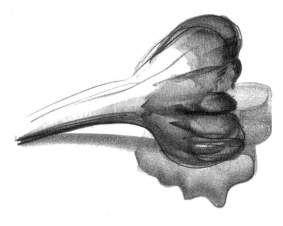

### BSE

The current abattoir practice of removing the brain and spinal cord material – the elements in a carcass where Bovine Spongiform Encephalopathy is primarily manifested – is not particularly sophisticated. Whatever reassurances are given by Government and meat industry spokespersons, the speed at which sawing and cutting must take place means the procedure cannot be foolproof, since individual skills vary and you do not have to be a scientist to wonder about contamination of tissue in immediate proximity to the potentially infected elements *post mortem* or about the role of blood and lymph in transporting viral material throughout a beast's system while it is alive.

The believed original cause of BSE, feeding livestock protein supplements the source material of which included flesh from sheep that had died from scrapie (a similar brain disease in that mammal), was always a horrible and unnatural thing to do and it has now been scientifically proved that animals of other species, including goats, mice, mink and sheep, fed with BSE-infected offal have contracted the disease. The Government's recent decision to ban the sale of calves' sweetbreads and intestines – and even more recently the questionable ban on beef on the bone – makes one wonder what parts they will next consider unsafe.

The long incubation period of Creutzfeld-Jakob Disease, (CJD), the disease in humans very like BSE, suggests that more time is needed before a causal link can be completely ruled out.

Beef sales have understandably taken a dive as the increasingly nervous public switches to eating more poultry and lamb, but this already seems probably only a temporary effect – the public memory in these matters is always very short. If you are still worried you could turn to organic beef, which has been raised naturally to strict standards laid down by the Soil Association, the largest of the organizations representing organic producers and ratified by UKROF, the Government register of organic food standards which also polices registered producers in the area. Organic beef is more expensive and does not automatically taste better, but at least you can be confident that it is unlikely to be BSE-contaminated and that the animals have had a reasonably natural life.

As yet organic butchers are few and far between, but you can obtain organic meat direct from producers, a list of whom can be had from The Soil Association, 86 Colston Street, Bristol BS15 5BB, if you send them an A4 self-addressed envelope with a 36p stamp on it.

### Burghul or Bulgur

This grain is made from wheat kernels that have been steamed, dried, then crushed. Often confused with cracked wheat, which consists of the broken uncooked kernels, burghul needs no further cooking, but is usually first soaked in water before being added to salads such as tabbouleh.

# C

### Caffeine

In small quantities, caffeine is good for you. It is a drug which occurs naturally in coffee, tea and cocoa, and is put into many soft drinks. It is a vasodilator; that is, it opens blood vessels and has a stimulant effect on the heart and brain cortex, where it improves concentration. Caffeine wakes you up and combats tiredness. It is a diuretic, increasing water passage through the kidneys. All in all, it is as miraculous in its multiple effects as aspirin. The trouble begins when it is taken in ever-larger doses, when it has a wide range of negative effects, including heart arrhythmia and palpitations, irritability, insomnia and trembling hands.

The increased popularity of decaffeinated coffee is an expression of the growing awareness of caffeine's negative effects. People have been encouraged to perceive themselves as caffeine addicts, who seek their fix at ever more regular intervals. The British passion for drinking tea all day is well known, while most Americans automatically drink coffee in much the same way, with an average cup of coffee containing about 50 per cent more caffeine than the same size cup of tea.

Decaffeination can be done in one of two ways: in the first, unroasted beans are steam-treated with a solvent which is poisonous and has to be carefully washed off; in the alternative method the beans are water-steamed, which brings the caffeine to the surface, and they are then tumbled and rubbed to remove the outer layers. Both these treatments inevitably destroy some of the flavour components.

### Cajun

In culinary terms, this means the spicy cooking style developed in Louisiana. The Cajun people emigrated to Nova Scotia from South-Western France and their colony was called Acadia. Driven out by the British, many of them moved to the largely French settlement of Louisiana, where they became known as Cajuns, developing a spicy cooking style which bears the same name. It is often confused with the other cooking style of the region, **Creole**.

### Callaloo

The young leaf of the dasheen tuber and various members of the same family that includes eddoe and taro, callaloo has a flavour rather like strong spinach. You are most likely to find it in West Indian markets. The dish called callaloo is probably the best known of all the Island soups, the Trinidadian version of which traditionally includes salt pork, blue crab and **okra**, the latter giving it a similar glutinous texture to the **gumbos** of Louisiana.

The leaf is also served as sahina, callaloo leaf fritters. Blanched leaves are squeezed dry, chopped and combined with coarsely mashed cooked **lentils**, chickpea flour, baking powder, turmeric and salt. This is mixed to a thick batter with water and deep-fried in spoonfuls.

### Canary Island Potatoes, see Gran Canarian Potatoes

### Cantucci

Hard almond biscuits, usually served with the sweet Italian dessert wine vin santo. The biscuits are dunked in the wine to soften them. See also **Biscotti**.

### Caper Berry

Caper berries are the fruit of the caper bush and a speciality of Andalucia, where they are most often lightly pickled in sherry vinegar and **brine**. The caper bush grows wild in arid volcanic soil or, as often happens, in crumbling walls, having the same ability to grow in the most inhospitable habitats as our native buddleia. The berry is the false fruit, containing the seeds – its true fruits. The best way to eat caper berries is uncooked and straight from the brine as a nibble with a glass of chilled fino, a delicious combination.

The caper, as opposed to the caper berry, is the unopened bud of the caper flower. These were apparently eaten fresh by the Ancient Greeks and Romans but are now generally sold either salt-packed or brined, the former of these treatments producing capers of much better flavour and quality than the latter – and accordingly significantly more expensive.

### Capon

A hand-castrated cock, fed on cereals and fattened to twice the size of an average chicken, usually weighing 3–3.5 kg / 6½–7½ lb.

### Cappuccino

A cappuccino is properly made with a very strong cup of **espresso** and 125 ml / 4 fl oz of frothed milk. It is served in a standard 175 ml / 6 fl oz coffee cup. The froth should stand proud of the rim and have a white centre surrounded by a discernible ring of brown coffee cream.

To get the best results when frothing milk, always use low-fat milk. As a general rule, the lower the fat content the thicker the froth, but with technical improvements in frothing attachments (*vapore*) this is no longer as significant as it used to be.

### Carambola

Unless perfectly ripe (a rare event outside the tropics), a pointless fruit which, when cut across, produces star-shaped slices – hence 'star fruit', its alternative name, and why those who should know better use it to decorate desserts.

### Caramelization

When sugar is boiled it browns, hence 'caramel' and 'caramelization'. The latter term is also used to describe the browning that occurs when meat or vegetables are exposed to a high temperature. The changes that occur in both the colour and the flavour are caused by the burning of natural sugars in the raw foods.

### Carbonnade

A traditional Flemish dish of beef and **caramelized** onions braised in beer.

### Cardamom

Cardamom is used in both savoury and sweet Indian dishes. When fresh, cardamom pods are green, the shade growing less pronounced as they dry and age. The seeds held within these pods are the true fruits, which can be bought separately, either whole or ground. The flavour of cardamom is very strong and complex, a mixture of eucalyptus, orange, lemon and camphor, and use should therefore be restrained or it can be too dominant.

Cardamom seeds are one of the principal elements of **garam masala**, the aromatic spice mix that is added to curries towards the end of cooking. When flavouring dishes like curry stews or rice pilaffs, the pods can be added whole and discarded before serving. They also feature in *paan*, the small packets of betel nut and aromatics chewed throughout India to freshen the mouth and breath after eating strongly flavoured food.

### Carpaccio

Invented in Venice's Harry's Bar, this modern classic of Italian cooking consists of thinly sliced raw beef fillet pounded out even more thinly and dressed with a Tabasco and mustard mayonnaise. It is often confused with *carne all'albese*, a more traditional dish of similarly treated beef with lemon juice, olive oil and shaved truffle or Parmesan.

### Cast-iron Pans

After copper and aluminium, cast iron is one of the best heat conductors and its thickness and weight give an even distribution of that heat through the sides and base, which means food cooks uniformly without hot spots to cause burning. So called 'seasoning' prevents rusting, and the slow heating of empty pans with a thin coating of oil actually builds up a hard surface layer which makes them less prone to food sticking during cooking.

To prevent removal of this protective layer you should never use harsh detergents or scouring pads when cleaning. You must wash the pans thoroughly before starting the seasoning process, to get rid of the heavy protective coating of industrial oil with which they come from the foundry. Failure to do so may cause food discoloration. A neutral cooking oil like sunflower or peanut is the best coating.

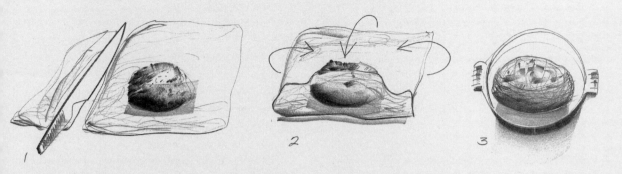

*Wrapping lean meat in caul fat*
*To prepare the sheets of caul fat for use, first soak them in a bowl of warm water to which a little vinegar has been added. This helps to soften the fat and makes it easier to peel away and separate the layers, and thus prevents the membrane from tearing.*

❶ Lay a sheet of caul on a flat surface and trim the edges to give a regular shape just big enough to wrap the meat well.
❷ Place the object to be wrapped in the centre of one side of the piece of caul and fold the sides in and over. Then roll it up to wrap with at least a double thickness.
❸ During baking the caul renders its fat, basting the object continuously and leaving next to nothing of itself behind.

### Caul Fat

The mesentery of a pig, that is, its stomach lining of lacy fat – looking rather like a lace shawl – is used to wrap faggots and other lean meats or pâtés to keep them moist and a coherent shape during cooking.

### Caviar

Caviar is the prepared roe of different types of sturgeon, including the Beluga, Oscietre and Sevruga, large shark-like fish found especially in the estuaries of rivers flowing into the Caspian and Black Seas, though they also exist to a lesser extent in China and in the USA. The eggs of other types of fish may be sold with the word caviar in their description, but only the roe of the sturgeon is held to be the real thing.

Since the collapse of the USSR and the end of state-controlled fishing, the sturgeon is being decimated there by pollution and unrestricted netting, while a booming black market has further damaged the quality of the former Republic's caviar. Unless a total ban is imposed on sturgeon fishing now, they will become extinct there. We may think of it as quintessentially Russian, but the majority of caviar legally imported into Britain today comes from Iran, which has a long history as a quality producer and where the same families who were involved in the business a century ago still run it today.

Fresh caviar is lightly salted and packed in round, flattish tins. A constant low temperature of between 0°C / 32°F and 5°C / 41°F is vital for it to keep a maximum of three months. Once opened, it should ideally be eaten the same day. Long-term storage, however, is unlikely to be an issue for most consumers.

The roe varies in the size of its eggs and in the depth of its grey colour. Caviar is brought into this country in large tins, then repacked for sale in smaller tins from 50 g (a portion size), then 125 g, 250 g and 500 g, with kilo tins the largest.

Beluga is widely regarded as the most desirable, with its large glistening, near-black eggs, and is thus the most expensive, currently retailing for up to £1,500 a kilo. Oscietre is about half the price and Sevruga is the least expensive, at around £450 a kilo, but still scarcely bargain-basement.

Connoisseurs tend to eat caviar by the spoonful, with the occasional bite of dry melba toast, but smaller amounts can be made to go further if served with the traditional Russian accompaniments of blinis (buckwheat **yeast** pancakes), a little sour cream, some chopped hard-boiled egg and finely chopped onion. While forever paired in most minds with Champagne, the Russians, of course, wash it down with shots of chilled vodka.

Those who love caviar are passionate about it, but when Hamlet remarked, ''twas caviar to the general,' he meant that it was an acquired taste and at the current prices – which can only continue to rise – perhaps it is one best left undeveloped.

### Cep, see Porcini

### Ceun Chai

Ceun chai is Thai celery. It has a much stronger flavour than European celery, is greener and has thinner stalks, with a greater proportion of leaves to stalk. The leaves, its main point, are used as a herb.

### Ceviche, see Marinate

### Chana Dal

Small, nutty-flavoured yellow split peas which are much used in Indian cooking.

### Chapati Flour

A fine low-protein wholemeal flour used to make the simple Indian unleavened breads of the same name.

### Chayote

Also called cho-cho and christophene, chayote is a pear-shaped squash covered with prickly hairs. They are often stuffed and baked or used raw in salads.

### Chiffonnade

A French culinary term used to describe a way of preparing leaves, like spinach or chard, which have been piled on top of each other, rolled up like the tobacco leaves in a cigar and cut across to produce fine ribbons.

### Chile con Carne

Chile con carne is a spicy meat dish from Texas and New Mexico. The phrase is Spanish for 'chillies with meat', a literal emphasis since the original dish probably contained more chillies than pork. When the Spaniards colonized Mexico they brought with them pigs, which quickly entered the heart of Mexican cooking. Indeed, lard is still used there extensively to this day and is preferred to vegetable or olive oils.

The original dish is carne con chile colorado, a stew of bite-sized pieces of pork cooked with mild dried red chillies and **coriander**, a relatively gentle spicing by Mexican standards. In its Tex-Mex reworking, the meat becomes beef, which is not minced but cut into pieces about the size of a little fingernail, then browned in oil before being stewed slowly in beer and stock or water with chopped onion, garlic, tomatoes and sweet peppers, hot chilli flakes or powder, ground toasted coriander and cumin seeds, oregano, salt and pepper.

There is no one recipe, individual variations giving rise to the chile cook-offs which take place at country fairs throughout the South Western USA, but we think it is improved by being a mixture of two parts beef to one of pork. The resulting red-brown stew is served with soft wheat-flour tortillas or boiled rice and with refried red kidney, black or pinto beans on the side. True chile never includes beans in the stew. Leaves of coriander – cilantro to Yanquis and Mexicanos alike – make the most authentic garnish.

### Chillies

The chilli is a vegetable, a member of the pepper family. When dried it is used as you would a spice, and people in the countries where they are grown value the chilli in its dried form just as much as when it is fresh.

All chillies are of the genus capsicum, therefore relatives of sweet peppers. Their vast diversity makes the subject confusing and there is no way to tell how hot chillies are just by looking at them. The usual colour thing of red being hot and green cool does not apply either. Chillies vary in size, appearance and intensity. As a general rule, the smaller they are – like the deceptively innocent-looking and tiny Thai

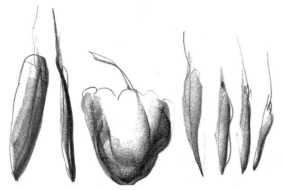

green chilli – the more vicious, but this is not a safe way of judging. In this country we tend to think of chillies as being intrinsically of the Far East, but this is inaccurate, since the *chile* – the same thing but note the Spanish spelling – originated in Mexico and made the journey to India and China via Africa.

The heat of the chilli is concentrated in the pale placenta or seed cluster, which can literally burn the skin so be careful when stripping them out (though injunctions to wear rubber gloves seem a bit over the top). The heat-producing element is called capsaicin and is measured in Scoville units, which range from zero for sweet peppers to 300,000 for the habanero. Automatically removing the seeds is not necessarily the right thing to do; if you are making something you want to be really hot then leave them in.

Always wash your hands after handling hot chillies and keep your fingers away from your eyes and all other sensitive parts as you are working with them. You can calm the hottest varieties by soaking them for 30 or 40 minutes in 300 ml / ½ pint of water mixed with 1 tablespoon of vinegar and 2 teaspoons of salt.

Ultimately the only way to test heat is to put a tiny piece on your tongue. As far as why and when you use fresh as opposed to dry, this is a question of flavour and texture; fresh being used like vegetables and dried like spices. Dried chillies are ground up for use in curry powders or can be used whole to infuse cooking oil.

The more you explore chillies, the more you will become aware of their complexity and the range of flavours. Just be circumspect. You will only really know what burning heat means the day you forget to wash your hands before rubbing an eye or some other sensitive part.

### Chinese Chives

Also called Cantonese onion or garlic chives, because of their flavour, these are larger and thicker-skinned than ordinary chives, with flat leaves. They are usually cooked rather than being used raw.

### Chinese Pepper, see Szechuan Pepper

### Chopping Boards

The news that wooden chopping boards may indeed be safer than plastic boards once the latter have been scarred does not amuse restaurateurs or chefs who have been forced by environmental health regulations to ban wooden surfaces from the professional kitchen and wholesale junking of hugely expensive butchers' blocks.

The most important factor in this aspect of good food hygiene is scrubbing the surface vigorously after use. There are anti-bacterial cleaning agents available that do not leave any taint on the wood, and malt vinegar is also an excellent disinfectant (and particularly good for wiping the insides of a fridge).

After cutting raw meat or fish, clean the chopping board carefully before putting cooked materials (or ingredients like salad leaves which need no cooking) on the same surface. Strongly flavoured foods, notably garlic and onions, will temporarily taint the board.

### Choy Sum

Choy sum is a Chinese brassica which has a fine taste somewhere between that of spring greens and Savoy cabbage, and looks like a smaller and paler green **bok choy**. It is sometimes sold in yellow flower, and all of it is edible.

### Christophene, see Chayote

### Clarified Butter

Butter from which the moisture and milk solids have been separated by heating, skimming and filtering. Their removal increases the temperature to which the butter may be heated without burning, thus facilitating its use as a cooking medium.

*Clementine, see Mandarin Orange*

## Coconut Milk

Coconut milk – really a thick cream – is an important ingredient in Southeast Asian cooking, which uses it extensively in both savoury and sweet dishes. You can make it yourself by pouring hot water over the frozen grated coconut or unsweetened coconut cream sold in packets. Both produce an excellent result and their use is a lot less arduous than removing the flesh from the coconut yourself. Packets and cans of coconut cream are best of all, though more expensive.

## Cocotte

The French term for a casserole, large or small, which in English more usually refers to small round ovenproof earthenware dishes used for everything from baked eggs to individual soufflés.

## Coeliac Disease

About one person in 50,000 in Britain suffers from coeliac disease, a severe allergic reaction to gluten, a substance both elastic and plastic formed by the natural proteins found principally in wheat flour but also present to a lesser extent in rye, oats and barley. It is wheat gluten's extraordinary properties that allow the carbon dioxide generated by **yeast** to be trapped in bubbles distributed uniformly throughout the dough, giving it a spectacular and sustained rise and a light-textured loaf.

In coeliacs, gluten does damage to the lining of the small intestine, causing malabsorption of nutrients, and this can lead to profound anaemia. There are now many gluten-free products on the market, including flour for baking gluten-free bread. All such products are available to diagnosed coeliacs on prescription, or they can be bought over the counter. If you want to bake a gluten-free loaf then you can, but be prepared to pay the chemist up to £6.50 for 500 g of bread mix, white or wholemeal, then follow the instructions on the packet.

For information on the dietary requirements of sufferers from coeliac disease, write to The Coeliac Society, PO Box 220, High Wycombe, Bucks HP11 2HY. For £2.50, they will send you an annually updated list of gluten-free products.

## Collagen

This is the technical name which describes the intramuscular connective tissue which softens and dissolves during slow cooking. It occurs more in some cuts than others, making them particularly suitable for stews and braises.

## Conch

A large shellfish, conch is much used in Caribbean soups, fish stews and salads. The flesh is very leathery and is traditionally tenderized by beating it on rocks.

## Confit

The French term for 'preserved', confit is most often used for a meat dish, usually goose or duck, poached and then preserved in its own fat. Slow-cooked, **caramelized** onions (onion 'jam') are just one of the other dishes you may find described on menus as *confit*.

## Consommé

A clear soup which is judged by its clarity and depth of flavour. Clarification of the cloudy stock from which it is made is classically achieved by means of added egg whites, though low-temperature poaching of the base ingredients and careful sieving largely obviate this clumsy and time-consuming process.

*Convection Ovens, see Fan-assisted Ovens*

## Copper Pans

Copper conducts heat more efficiently than any other metal, which is why it has always been popular in professional kitchens. Old unlined pans can be harmful, as copper ions leach into foods during cooking and the human body can only get rid of so many before they build up to toxic levels in the liver, causing damage. Old copper pans are lovely things anyway and are good in the kitchen purely for their decorative effect. Modern copper pans are lined with tin, which creates reasonably efficient cookware, though its relatively low melting point means you have to take care not to expose it to high heat for too long. If left empty on a high flame the cooking surface is ruined and no amount of oiling and seasoning will bring it back.

## Coquelet

A young cockerel killed at 4–6 weeks, it has more flavour than a **poussin**.

## Coriander

This classic herb of Asian and Latin American cooking, also known as Chinese parsley or cilantro, is becoming much more widely available fresh. The best place to buy coriander is in ethnic markets, where it is sold loose much more cheaply and with the added bonus of roots attached. Thai food makes extensive use of these roots, but supermarkets trim them off before packaging the leaves and stems. If you do manage to find a market selling loose coriander, wash it when you get it home because it will be very gritty. Cut off the roots, bag and freeze them, and put the leaves and stems in a plastic bag in the fridge where they will keep fresh for a week. Coriander with its roots intact may also be kept in a jug like flowers; this way the leaves last for some time and you can still freeze the roots after the leaves have wilted.

## Corn Syrup

Corn syrup, a starch extract from the corn kernels chemically treated to produce a sweet syrup, has been made in North America for 140 years or so. Food technologists can now do very sophisticated things and have ways of making corn syrup more or less sweet, but also – significantly – more or less viscous.

If you look on the wrappers of many sweets you will see corn syrup listed as an ingredient and this is because it gives that popular chewy texture. The viscous aspect of modified corn syrup can be produced without any sweetness at all, so giving confectioners the opportunity to have malleability and stretch without excessive sweetness. If you want to use corn syrup as a sweetening alternative to sugar, there are no particular benefits since it is synthesized glucose and **maltose**, the things we taste as sweet on the tongue – sugar, in other words.

## Cotechino, see Italian Cured Meats and Sausages

## Coulis

The term for a sieved sauce that is commonly served under the principal element of a dish. Its use was in the ascendant during the late '70s, when **nouvelle cuisine** held sway, then became omnipresent on menus during the '80s and died recently. RIP. Nowadays, thankfully, its use seems to be limited to thick purées, usually of uncooked fresh fruit, intended as sauces.

## Court-bouillon

An aromatic acidulated light stock for poaching fish and shellfish.

## Couscous

This pale yellow Moroccan and Tunisian staple is made from coarse-ground **semolina** and is traditionally cooked in a *couscousière*, a deep metal pot with an upper portion rather like a fine lidded colander in which the grain is cooked in the steam from the seven-vegetable stew bubbling underneath.

## Cracked Wheat, see Burghul

### Crème Fraîche

Made from double cream mixed with buttermilk heated to a constant 75°C for several hours until it thickens and stabilizes, crème fraîche acquires a distinctive tangy taste. It is used to thicken savoury sauces, is extremely resilient in a **reduction** and is excellent for taking excessive sweetness out of desserts as it has a flavour that is both astringent and rich at the same time.

### Creole

A New Orleans style of cooking fusing French, Spanish, Italian and West-African cooking styles with local ingredients. It is more complex and sophisticated than **Cajun** food.

### Crostini, see Bruschetta

### Curry Spices

It is a good idea to buy individual whole spices and make masalas (spice mixes, see **Garam Masala**) for curries rather than buying ready-made curry powders. This way, after toasting the spices to accentuate their aromatic quality, they can be ground fresh for every dish. You can also ring the changes by mixing them in different quantities or leaving one or two out, while you are free to use spices individually to good effect. One thinks of cumin and **coriander** particularly in this context.

Buy spices in small amounts, starting with cumin, **coriander**, black peppercorns, cloves, **fennel** and **mustard** seeds. Other spices to start with are cinnamon, **cardamom**, ground turmeric and **fenugreek**. Fresh additions, like **ginger root**, coriander leaf, garlic, shallots, mint and hot *chillies*, make all the difference and, as with the majority of ingredients in Indian cooking, they can be used in many dishes that are not Indian *per se*. The great thing is to use different spice combinations so you can make a number of dishes which have very different flavours and textures without going to any great trouble.

### Cutlet Bat

This heavy wooden implement is used to bat slices of raw meat, like veal escalopes, into paper-thin pieces, usually done between plastic sheets to avoid sticking and tearing.

# D

### Daikon

This large mild-flavoured white radish is also called mooli. It is normally served raw and finely shredded and is a classic accompaniment to many Japanese dishes.

### Darne

A thick slice or steak cut from a large round fish, like salmon.

### Dashi

A light Japanese stock made from **bonito** and **konbu**. Sachets of dashi-no-moto, instant soup granules with the addition of **monosodium glutamate**, are widely available. All you do is add hot water.

### Deglazing

Deglazing is a classic way of finishing a dish after the cooked item has been removed to a warm place to stand, whereby the residual bits left on the bottom of the pan after frying or roasting a piece of meat or fish are scraped off the pan where they have stuck and stirred into some wine or stock which has been added to the very hot pan. The wine or stock bubbles away quickly as it amalgamates with the tasty bits in the pan and within a minute or so you are left with a tablespoon or two of intensely flavoured, syrupy sauce or gravy.

This can be used as it is, poured over the meat or fish, but is usually finished by swirling in small pieces of cold unsalted butter. You then taste, season if necessary and your sauce is finished.

### Dégraisser

This is the French term for skimming fat and impurities from the surface of a cooking liquid or stock.

### Digestif

A term denoting a drink of neat spirits taken after a meal 'to aid digestion' – not a widely held theory in medical circles.

### Dolmades

These popular Greek or Turkish dishes consist of vine leaves rolled around a stuffing, usually of rice.

### Döner Kebab

*Döner*, a giant lamb kebab grilled on a vertical spit, is Turkey's most popular fast food and you find specialist cafés serving it throughout that country. There it is eaten only with flat pocket breads and some mint and flat-leaved parsley, invariably washed down with raki, the anise-based national spirit akin to a fiery pastis. The addition of shredded cabbage and tomato slices is an inauthentic British idea or, rather, a way of making the pitta sandwich look larger.

While *döner* is now common throughout Britain, it had a slow start, though it was a relatively early player in our burgeoning take-away culture. The very first *döner* take-out is thought to have been The Golden Horn, opened by Mr Arif in Wardour Street in Soho in 1971 (four years before McDonald's established its toehold in Greenwich) and sadly closed down some years ago. His formula was absolutely classic and used only the meat from the hindquarters of lambs. Few of today's *döneri* are made to such exacting standards, but his was undoubtedly as good as it was ever going to get.

The meat was trimmed of all obvious fat and sinews before being cut into long strips which were then beaten flat with a mallet. These were marinated in a mixture of olive oil, milk and finely chopped onion for 24 hours before the construction of the döner could begin, a painstaking, lengthy and difficult business that started in the early hours of the morning to ensure the beehive-shaped kebab – which could weigh as much as 32 kg / 70 lb – was cooking in time for the first customers at noon. The marinated meat was first drained, then painted with melted lamb fat and seasoned before being wound, one strip at a time, around the long spit, starting in the middle and working towards either end – with the finished shape thickest in the centre.

When finished, the spit of a *döner* is set vertically in front of an upright grill and slowly rotated so that an uncooked surface is always presented to the heat. As the outer meat browns and cooks, it is carved off with a long knife in thin slices, which fall into a special metal shoe held in the other hand. This goes on until the meat is finished. If any is left at the end of the day it should really be thrown away (an overnight sit cooling on the spit at room temperature for recooking the next day is a sure recipe for food poisoning).

A similar vertical kebab which we now see here increasingly is Syrian *shawarma*. This tends to be a rather more robust affair, using larger pieces of meat (which may be beef) and which is much more aggressively spiced with **coriander**, **fenugreek**, **cardamom** and garlic.

### Dried Mushrooms

All dried mushrooms must be soaked before cooking, but even so the stems tend to stay determinedly tough unless you simmer them for a prolonged period in liquid, as in, for example, a stew. They are best used in stocks.

Soak all dried wild mushrooms for 20–30 minutes in warm water or stock, then put them through a muslin-lined sieve, keeping the soaking liquid to add to stock or a stew. Rinse the reconstituted mushrooms thoroughly in a colander, then cut off the tough ends of the stems, using these in a stock. Cut the remaining flesh into strips before cooking.

Risotto is a particularly good way of using any dried mushrooms, since they benefit from being cooked with the rice in stock for about 20 minutes, or add a few reconstituted dried mushrooms when frying fresh mushrooms to give a greater depth of flavour.

### Duxelles

A classic restaurant **garnish** of chopped mushrooms, parsley, breadcrumbs and shallots or onions. It is also used to describe a stuffing made from the same ingredients, perhaps most notably used in beef *en croûte*.

# E

### Eggs

What is a 'free-range' egg, a 'farm' egg, an egg 'laid in a perchery'? Definitions of 'free-range' are not legal absolutes, while the description 'farm egg' simply means that the chicken lived in a battery cage on a farm, whatever a 'farm' might be. Ethical and emotional considerations aside, there is no nutritional difference between a battery egg and a free-range egg, but some would say they can tell the difference. Freshness is the most vital thing when cooking eggs.

Improved quality control means the eggs you buy from supermarkets will not be bad, but how fresh is fresh? A week or more may elapse between an egg being laid and its arrival on the shop shelf, perhaps even longer. The 'use-by' date stamps which are coming in are not as useful as a 'laid on' date. This problem may be compounded when people get their eggs home and transfer them into a container, often with eggs that have been sitting there for a week or even longer.

A quick and easy test if you are worried that your eggs are no longer fresh is to put them in a large tumbler and pour in cold water. Very fresh eggs will sit happily on the bottom; eggs that are less fresh develop a larger bubble of gas inside them and will sit up in the water or even rise from the bottom – if an egg should actually float to the top it is quite definitely off. See also Free-range Chicken.

### Emulsion

An emulsion is formed between two liquids that won't normally mix, when particles of one become suspended in the other. Everyday examples are milk (an emulsion of dairy fat in water) and mayonnaise (oil in egg yolk). Achieving and maintaining an emulsion are often helped by the addition of an emulsifier, such as the mustard in vinaigrette dressings or the natural lecithin present in egg yolk. An important tip in making any of the sauces that involve emulsions, such as mayonnaise and hollandaise, is to have all your utensils and ingredients at the same (ideally room) temperature.

### Espresso

Espresso means 'on the spur of the moment' and small domestic espresso machines work on exactly the same principle as the big professional ones, forcing water at 90°C / 195°F under pressure through individual portions of finely ground coffee for between 20 and 30 seconds.

Everything starts with the quality and blend of Arabica and Robusta beans, to produce the right balance between bitter, acid and sweet elements in the cup. The higher the proportion of the more expensive and superior Arabica beans, the better the espresso. Unless you buy the right coffee you will never make a good espresso and the success of subsequent milky variations is dependent on that perfect small cup of strong black coffee, with its nut-coloured creamy surface.

A classic espresso is made with 7 g / ¼ oz of finely ground coffee and 50 ml / 1½ fl oz water. It is served in a demi-tasse, that is a heavy 60 ml / 2 fl oz cup, which should be warmed before use. The characteristic hazelnut-coloured cream on the surface of an espresso is an indicator of how well-balanced the roast is and whether the setting on your grinder is correct.

WHY PUT LEMON PEEL IN AN ESPRESSO?
*This is an American invention but who first started it – or when – is unknown, though suspicion points the finger at California. The idea of adding aromatics like fig or cardamom to coffee is very Arab, so perhaps the inspiration came from the Middle East. A lemon twist will not make a good espresso taste better, but the citrus oil will mask the bitterness of a lousy espresso made from poor-quality beans or an inappropriate roast.*

### Estouffade

This term of *haute cuisine* is really only a grand word for a basic brown stew.

### Étuver

This French culinary term means cooking vegetables very gently, primarily in their own juices but usually starting with a little fat or oil to prevent them sticking. The English term for this is **sweating**.

# F

*Fagara, see Szechuan Pepper*

### Fajita
A Mexican stir-fried dish of chicken or beef and sweet peppers flavoured with cumin and **coriander** and served with wheat-flour tortillas.

### Falafel
These deep-fried patties, made from ground broad beans or chickpeas, are common in the Middle East.

### Fan-assisted Ovens
Neff was the first manufacturer to introduce fan, or convection, ovens at the end of the '70s as a solution to cooks wanting to batch-bake throughout the oven, and all the others followed suit. Circulating the air within the oven at high speed has two consequences: it improves cooking effectiveness by wrapping what is being cooked uniformly in hot air and at the same time delivers a consistent temperature throughout the oven space. There will always be some things which are better cooked without fan assistance and most fan ovens allow you to choose whether or not you use the fan. For example, you may want to start cooking with fan assistance at a high temperature, say when roasting beef, then switch off the fan and lower the temperature to finish.

One thing new users need to keep in mind is that convection effectively increases the temperature by 15–20°C above that when the fan is off. Our experience suggests you need to be flexible about when you use fan assistance and that it is very irritating to have an oven where you can't switch it off. Manufacturers' cookbooks are generally dire and don't always give the best advice. It is a case of being prepared to challenge assumptions based on years of using conventional ovens – never easy, but in this case essential.

### Fancy Meats, Variety Meats
These are euphemisms for offal, which includes glands like sweetbreads (the thymus), liver, heart, lungs, kidneys, tongues, tails and testicles. The French euphemism for the last named is *frivolités*.

### Fennel
The bulb of this plant is eaten as a vegetable, the feathery fronds as a herb and the dried seeds as a spice. All taste of aniseed.

### Fenugreek
The pale yellow aromatic seeds of fenugreek have a sweet complex aroma. Open a can of commercial curry powder and you will smell fenugreek overriding everything else.

### Feta
This crumbly, slightly sour goats' cheese is used extensively in Greek salads and cooked dishes. As most commercial feta is now made from cows' milk, Cypriot grocers are the places to buy the best goats'-milk feta.

### Filé Powder
This is the powdered dried sassafras leaves used as a flavouring in **gumbos** and as an additional thickening agent to the okra which gives such stews a thick and gelatinous texture.

### Filo or Phyllo
Paper-thin sheets of pastry used throughout the Middle East and North Africa for both savoury and sweet dishes, and available fresh and frozen. The sheets dry on exposure to the air and rapidly become unusable, so once the pack is opened keep the sheets covered with a damp cloth.

### Fines Herbes
Fines herbes usually include parsley, chives, chervil and tarragon, a mixture that is classic with fish or chicken.

### Fish Cake (Vietnamese)
Made from the pounded flesh of different kinds of fish, these are sold ready-cooked in rolls from the chill cabinets of Asian stores. All you do is cut these into slices and heat them through gently, usually in liquid dishes like soups.

### Fish Sauce
More than any other ingredient, fish sauce delivers the flavour which positions and differentiates the cooking of Southeast Asia. It is used as a sauce, like **soy sauce**, but also

in cooking, when exposure to heat moderates its intense and complex flavour to the point where its origins cannot be determined, only a subtle alteration to the overall taste – so you notice its absence almost more than its inclusion.

The most common fish sauces are *nam pla* from Thailand and *nuoc mam* from Vietnam. Both are made from small sea fish and squid, which are layered with sea salt in huge wooden tubs then left to ferment for several months. The liquid which this produces is drawn off into ceramic pots and left in the sun to mature for several weeks before being bottled; the first of several extractions, with the first being the lightest and finest. The result is a rich and mellow sauce which smells rather alarming to the uninitiated, but the taste of which is difficult to describe and certainly very different from what the strong odour leads you to expect.

Fish sauce is salty, and has affinities with soya sauce, but has a delicious and subtle fragrance on the palate that is quite unique. The use of fish in sauces to complement meat and vegetable dishes, as well as fish or shellfish, is both ancient and universal. The Greeks had *garon* and the Romans *garum*, a highly prized intense sauce made from salted mackerel and anchovy intestines fermented and matured in the sun in exactly the same way as *nam pla* and *nuoc mam*. It is interesting to note that, even in our own food culture today, anchovies are an essential ingredient of Worcestershire sauce and some brown sauces.

Supermarkets now sell Asian fish sauces and, despite their lengthy preparation and the cost of importation, they are not expensive. Although the production process sounds primitive and unhygienic, nobody has ever reported being made ill by eating fish sauce. In Laos, babies actually have a few drops added to their drinks as a tonic, so buy a bottle and experiment with impunity.

### Five-spice Powder

This is a Chinese aromatic ground spice mixture which has no absolute recipe but which usually includes cloves, cinnamon, **fennel** seeds, **schezuan pepper** and **star anise**. It may also contain powdered ginger, aniseed and nutmeg or mace.

It is most frequently used to flavour meats prior to roasting. Bought in powdered form, its volatile oils rapidly dissipate, leaving you with only a hint of what might have been. It is therefore preferable to make it yourself from roasted whole seeds, grinding them only minutes before use.

### Flamande

A typical Northern French or Belgian meat **garnish** of braised cabbage, turned carrots, new potatoes and turnips.

### Florentine (à la)

The French culinary term for any dish which is served on a bed of spinach, usually with a cheese sauce. The 'Florentine' in question was Catherine de Medici, who is credited with having introduced many new foods into French cuisine, including spinach.

### Fond

A French culinary term for a well-reduced base stock.

### Food Processor

When they first came out in the '70s, we all thought food processors were magical devices, miraculously blending, chopping and beating. Rather like learning to cook with an Aga, we told ourselves that this was all we needed, one simple machine for everything. Food processors are still remarkably useful pieces of kit, but they do not do everything. They do not chop meat so much as bludgeon and tear it into a woven mass. They do not purée, but brutalize, extracting starch and turning potatoes into wallpaper paste in seconds. They slice onions so violently that excessive water is produced, making frying impossible. They are, however, brilliant for grating, for making mousselines, and will produce a good cake batter and a reasonable instant hollandaise. With practice you can make workable **yeast** doughs, but not as well as using a dough hook in a mixer.

This meant that, until the advent of a new generation of processor systems two years ago, serious cooks needed a liquidizer and a mixer to go alongside their processors, which was expensive and took up a lot of space. Today, while still expensive at around £200, a new generation of combination units offers every function needed in one machine, though the add-ons which attach to the motor and control unit still occupy a large shelf in a cupboard.

We have tested both Braun and Philips systems and been impressed by both, though not by their manuals, which confuse rather than instruct. The Braun has the design edge in that it fits together more easily and has a more solid feel to it, but the Philips system performs brilliantly once you have worked out what bit fits where and why. As a general rule, cooks are not engineers and it is many years since they assembled Airfix kits with poor instructions. The first manufacturer who invests in a well-written user manual – produced by cooks and not engineers masquerading as home economists – will add value to the product, win friends and end up owning the market.

### Forcemeat

The old English word for minced or ground meat, typically pork, often with added chopped aromatic vegetables, herbs and spices, used as a stuffing or in sausages or in a terrine. The equivalent French term is *farce*.

### Fragrant Meat

The Chinese euphemism for dog.

### Free-range Chicken

Precisely what 'free-range' means in Britain is dependent on how commercial chicken producers choose to define it. Indeed, the majority of chickens sold as free-range in our supermarkets are raised in large sheds with very little individual space and without any outdoor access. It is worth going to a reputable butcher and discussing what you can buy that is genuinely free-range, that is fed on grain or corn, without high-dosage prophylactic antibiotics and with the birds enjoying the opportunity to roam and peck on grass.

Various French chickens meeting these criteria are available in wholesale markets here, including *poulet noir*, so called because of their black plumage and legs, usually sold as *label rouge fermier*, a reference to the breeder and 'farm' location. These birds are killed at 14 weeks, have some outdoor access to grass and a final two-week fattening on skimmed milk. The description '*label rouge*' by comparison is a quality statement, but still means **battery-**raised.

The most expensive French chickens are poulet de Bresse, poulet Bourbonnais and poulet Le Mans, all from centres of excellence for free-range birds. Their names on the labels and a breeder's metal identity tag clipped to a wing guarantee the source stated and that the birds have lived outside for four months on a diet of cereal, concluding with two weeks on skimmed milk, oats and field corn before slaughter. See also Battery Farming and Eggs.

### Frittata

An Italian omelette, cooked slowly until set and served at room temperature.

### Friture

This, the French culinary term for a deep pan of oil or fat for deep-frying, has become generalized to denote fried food.

### Fumet

Is a **fond** which has been further concentrated by reduction. It is most usually associated with fish stocks.

### Functional Foods

Functional foods, or so called life-enhancing foods, are already a multi-million-pound business in Japan and the USA, where manufacturers include nutritionally beneficial elements in products generally perceived to be unhealthy. You might, for example, have a chocolate cake which includes cardio-beneficial oils like omega fatty acids and perhaps some fibre included in a way that would not be apparent in its taste and texture. Here is another opportunity for the manufacturer to add value, a description that is often the opposite of what it says.

The concept is hardly new, just the scale of the profit potential. Breakfast cereals were the first foods to be promoted with added vitamins, presumably to compensate for the fact that the majority have little nutritional value. You could argue that if a person has a bad diet based on junk food, adding nutritionally good elements to frozen pizzas or burgers is a positive and responsible thing to do. On the other hand, promoting consumption of an intrinsically unhealthy product on the basis of added health beneficial elements is, at best, nutritionally suspect, at worst manipulative and dishonest.

# G

### Galangal

Until recently you could only buy galangal, also known as galanga or laos, in Asian grocers, but the explosion in Thai restaurants and the attendant public interest in Southeast Asian cooking means it is now much more widely available. Like ginger, galangal is a tuberous rhizome and has a similar appearance, though on close inspection you will note that it has a smoother and more shiny skin, and when you try to cut into it you will find it is much harder – indeed it is almost as hard as wood. The easiest way to deal with it, therefore, is to grate it.

The flavour has a certain similarity to ginger and there is no recipe demanding galangal in which you could not use ginger. However, its taste is discernibly different, though this difference is difficult to describe, having both earthy and resinous overtones. The resin is most obvious to the nose when the galangal is raw, but not so discernible when cooked, as some of the volatile oils are driven off with the application of heat. It is also generally much hotter on the tongue than ginger and is an indispensable element in Thai curries.

### Galantine

A galantine is a classic construction of the French kitchen and is usually made from a veal **forcemeat**, studded with pistachios and flavourings, that is rolled and wrapped in butter muslin to keep its shape and physical integrity during poaching.

### Garam Masala

This aromatic spice mix, added towards the end of cooking in Indian dishes, is typically a mixture of ground **cardamom**, cinnamon, cloves, cumin and black peppercorns. **Coriander**, mace and bay are also often included.

### Garnish

The word is from the professional kitchen and means the visual, edible enhancement of a dish just prior to serving. Typically this means scattering over a chopped herb, but also describes a number of more complex formulae to finish dishes that include **turned** root vegetables, fried garnishes and so forth (see **Duxelles**, **Flamande**, etc.). The word garnish has rather gone out of fashion in food writing, being considered vulgar by some, though garnishing a dish is something most of us do just before serving, whatever we say to the contrary.

### Garon, Garum, see Fish Sauce

### Gelatine

Powdered and leaf gelatine are both made commercially from pig skin, the latter being the more refined and preferred form, which has the benefit of dissolving immediately without leaving any residue. Soak the leaves in cold water for 5 minutes, then squeeze them dry before adding to the hot liquid you want to set. Nine gelatine leaves will set 600 ml / 1 pt of liquid to a firm jelly. When making stock at home, the cooking extracts gelatine from the bones, which is what causes the stock to jelly or set when cold.

### Ghee

Extensively used as a cooking medium in Indian dishes, ghee is currently being blamed by cardiologists for the high incidence of heart disease in the Indian community in Britain. It is basically a type of **clarified butter**, that is butter from which all the milk solids have been removed, so increasing the temperature at which it burns. Ghee differs from plain clarified butter in that the strained product is cooked on at a low steady heat to drive off moisture, concentrate it and develop flavour.

If the thought does not give you palpitations, it is easy to make at home. Put 500 g / 1 lb unsalted butter in a pan over a low heat. As it melts, it will start to throw a scum which you skim off as it rises to the surface. After about 10 minutes, brown particles will form and also rise to be removed (a tea strainer is a good thing with which to do this). Pour the remaining clear liquid through muslin or a clean J-cloth into a bowl. Clarified butter keeps for months in the fridge.

### Giblets

The heart, liver, gizzard and kidneys of poultry. Giblets are rather more difficult to get hold of now that EU regulations forbid the sale of undrawn birds. However, chicken livers are widely available in 500-g tubs, and gizzards may also be bought separately. When you can get giblets with your birds, they (livers excluded) are useful for making quick stocks to use as the bases for rich gravies.

## Gigot

French term for the hind-leg joint, usually of lamb or mutton, still also used in Scotland (pronounced 'jiggutt'), an inheritance from the Auld Alliance.

## Ginger

A smooth-skinned fibrous rhizome with a sharp, aromatic flavour underpinned with a hot spiciness, ginger is an essential element in Chinese and Indian cooking and is also widely used throughout Southeast Asia (see also **Galangal**). The skin is usually first peeled off and the flesh grated or sliced. Special ginger graters are used to separate pulp and liquid from the fibrous base. Ready-ground dried ginger will not give the same result and should be reserved for baking.

## Glace de Viande

This is rich stock reduced down to its strongest expression, the point where if you are not careful people might think you are using Bovril.

## Gram Flour

This flour, made from ground dried chickpeas, is also called *besan* in India and makes very good batter for deep-fried food like onion bhajias.

## Gran Canarian Potatoes

If the number of letters we receive on the subject are anything to go by, it would appear that everybody who goes to the Canary Islands on holiday eats the local salted potatoes and, on their return, wants to know how to make them.

They are simply unpeeled new potatoes put in a pan with only just enough heavily salted water to cover them. The potatoes are boiled hard until the all the water has evaporated and they are then shaken in the hot, dry pan, which sets the salt on the skins in a delicious crisp, frosted coating.

## Grana

Meaning 'grain' this is the general term for a range of Italian hard cheeses, characterized by their granularity due to long ageing, which are usually grated for use in cooking. **Parmigiano-Reggiano**, or Parmesan, is perhaps the best-known.

## Gratin

A dish finished with a crisp crust, typically of buttery breadcrumbs and cheese, either in the oven or under the grill. Wide, shallow heatproof gratin dishes are usually used for the purpose.

## Gratinate

An Anglicized form of the French *gratiner*, not as yet recognized by the OED; it means sprinkling breadcrumbs or cheese over a dish and browning this under a grill or in a very hot oven.

## Gravlax

Meaning 'buried salmon', this Swedish speciality consists of salmon cured with masses of fresh dill. Now widely available internationally, it is served thinly sliced like smoked salmon, usually with a dill mustard sauce.

## Green Peppercorns

Green peppercorns are unripe black peppercorns and can be bought fresh in some supermarkets, from specialist Asian grocers or most commonly brined in jars. These last should be rinsed thoroughly under lots of cold running water before use. Green peppercorns were very chic in restaurant cooking 20 years ago and are currently suffering a well-deserved revival.

## Gremolata or Gremolada

This Italian condiment of finely chopped parsley, garlic and lemon zest is traditionally sprinkled over osso buco (page 118) and other dishes just before serving.

## Grenadine

A syrup made from pomegranate seeds which is used in a number of cocktails and as a soft drink base.

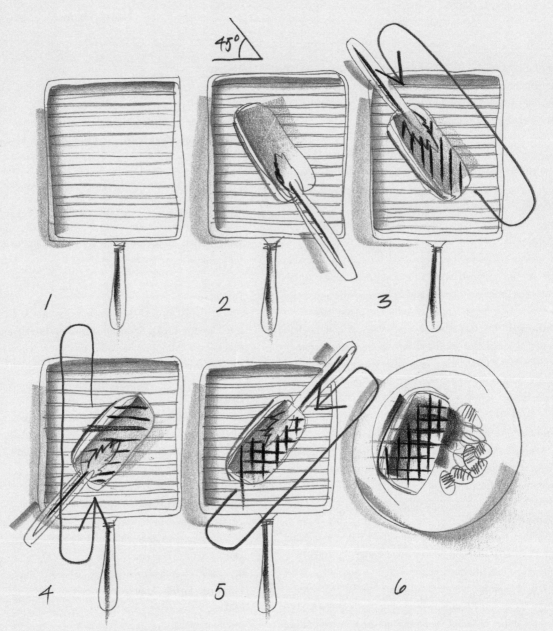

**To get the attractive cross-hatched effect, called quadrillage, on food using a ridged grill pan:**

❶ Get the grill pan smoking hot and brush both sides of the the meat with oil.

❷ Lay the meat on the pan at an angle of 45 degrees to the ridges.

❸ Halfway through the planned cooking time per side, flop the piece of meat over on to the other side, so that it is still lying at an angle of 45 degrees to the raised ridges on the pan.

❹ After a similar interval, turn the meat again, but this time also turn it by 90 degrees so that it is now at an angle of 45 degrees to the ridges the other way.

❺ Finally, after another similar interval, flop it again, keeping it at the same angle to the ridges.

❻ At the end of cooking, both sides of the meat will have the cross-hatched sear marks.

### Grill Pan

The heavy ridged steel grill pan emulates the charcoal grill and is now widely used because it delivers intense sealing heat with the added benefit of searing lines on the outside of the food being cooked, to present an attractive cross-hatched effect called *quadrillage* by chefs.

The grill pan is ideal for things like steak and chops, but only if the ridges stand proud from the base of the pan, otherwise the food will fry rather than grill. The heat of the grill pan can, however, be too fierce for some delicate foods. The overhead grill, for example, is better for cooking whole fish or fillets of, say, Dover sole. In an ideal world you will have both in your kitchen. After that, it's horses for courses; and, of course, when cooking horse a ridged pan is better than an overhead grill.

A good grill pan should be of cast-iron and have pronounced, narrow ridges (there are some very badly made grill pans on the market which are lightweight and have wide ridges and shallow depressions between them). Don't wash the pan with detergent between uses. Before you use it for the first time, simply wipe it with a little neutral cooking oil like sunflower and put it on a low heat for an hour. The first time you use it after this treatment, start it on a low heat, increasing it gradually to maximum. When cooking on it, always lightly oil the food, never the pan. Follow these simple procedures and your food should never stick.

### Groundnut

This is the proper name for the peanut, which accurately describes the way it grows under the soil. Extensively featured in the cooking of Southeast Asia, the nuts are also used to express a neutral cooking oil much favoured in stir- and deep-frying because of its high smoke-point..

### Guacamole

Originally a Mexican sauce or dip and now invariably eaten with deep-fried corn tortilla chips, guacamole consists of mashed ripe avocado with diced onion, chopped coriander leaves and lemon or lime juice.

### Guanabana, see Soursop

### Guinea Fowl

With a flavour somewhere between chicken and pheasant, guinea fowl have a relatively low fat content and are usually served simply roasted. They may be substituted for chicken in most recipes.

### Gumbo

A rich and spicy Louisiana Cajun stew, usually containing large prawns or freshwater crayfish and **okra**. The latter exude their mucilaginous juices during prolonged cooking which, with the addition of **filé** powder, give the dish its characteristic thick texture.

# H

### Haché

Anglicised as hash, *haché* describes a dish based on finely chopped or minced ingredients, usually meat. *Hachis parmentier* is French for cottage pie.

### Haggis

An ancient Scottish dish of sheep's stomach stuffed with chopped sheep offal, including the pluck (that is, the lungs and heart), highly seasoned and mixed with oatmeal and suet, which is then sewn up and poached.

Haggis is traditionally served with 'bashed' or mashed neeps (swede) and potatoes, notably at Burns' Night suppers. The done thing is to pour a little whisky over the haggis on the plate and to drink a great deal more of the same while eating it.

### Haloumi or Halumi

This mild salty Cypriot goats' cheese is always grilled and served hot. When cold it is very tough.

### Haricot

The generic description for a type of small white kidney bean, usually sold dried.

### Harissa

North-African **chilli** sauce which always accompanies couscous. Garlic, cumin, coriander and caraway are among its other principal flavourings.

### Herbes de Provence
Herbes de Provence are distinguished by vigorous flavours and include thyme, rosemary, oregano, bay and basil – and lavender in Provence itself. This is the bouquet to use in a Provençal stew.

### Hoisin Sauce
A Chinese sweet soya-based sauce which includes sugar, salt and vinegar. It is used in cooking and as a dip. This is the sauce spread on pancakes for Peking duck.

### Holy Basil
Also called Thai basil, this leaf imparts a flavour that has an aniseed edge and which is quite different from that of Mediterranean basil. It is one of the unique flavours of the Thai kitchen. The leaves have a purple/mauve tinge and are coarser in texture than Mediterranean basil.

### Homogenization
The process whereby the differently sized fat cells in milk are given a uniform size, so that the cream does not separate out into 'top of the milk'.

### Hominy
Also called grits, hominy is coarsely ground white field corn (maize), cooked like a porridge and similar to **polenta**, which is eaten throughout the southern USA.

### Opposite: The Basic Batterie de Cuisine
*You obviously don't need to have a lavishly equipped kitchen to turn out good food, but below is our checklist of ideal kit, some of which is illustrated opposite:*

- *small vegetable knife • all-purpose knife with a curved blade*
- *boning knife • ham-slicing knife • carving knife • Chinese chopper*
- *strong serrated knife • tomato knife • sharpening stones and steel*
- *potato peeler • wheel pasta cutter • poultry shears*
- *pin-boning tweezers • cherry and olive stoner • apple corer*
- *pastry cutters • scissors • potato ricer • nutmeg grater*
- *mandolin grater • box grater • sprung tongs*
- *metal and bamboo skewers*
- *measuring jug • kitchen spoons • measuring spoons • sugar thermometer*
- *2 whisks, large and small • metal skimming • spoon*
- *fish slice • plastic spatula • wooden spatula • palette knife*
- *heavy rolling pin • at least 3 chopping boards • assorted wooden spoons*
- *cutlet bat • range of heavy steel saucepans with well-fitting lids, from very small to very large*
- *blanching basket • colander • round and conical sieves*
- *tea strainer • heavy roasting tin • casserole dishes in three sizes.*
- *range of ovenproof dishes, rectangular, round and oval*
- *frying pans: two large non-stick frying pans and a large, heavy cast-iron frying pan • ridged grill pan*
- *iron omelette pan • iron pancake pan • 4 small blini pans*
- *flat-based wok • steamer (or Chinese steaming baskets)*
- *2 terrine dishes, one with a lid*
- *4 non-stick Swiss roll tins • spring-form cake tin*
- *2 non-stick loaf tins*
- *metal tart tins with detachable bases, 20-cm / 8-inch and 25-cm / 10-inch, 2 of each*
- *2-3 bun tins • large basin-shaped dish for pasta and tossing salads*
- *mixing bowls of different sizes • many plastic boxes of different sizes*
- *cling-film • zip-lock bags • foil • hand-cranked pasta maker*
- *food processor • electric mixer • coffee grinder for spices*
- *several pudding basins of different sizes • assortment of pastry cutters*
- *pastry brush • potato masher • bulb baster*

*Nice but inessential:*
*espresso machine • ice-cream maker • fish kettle • pizza pans*
- *second oven • microwave oven • hibachi-type barbecue • waffle iron*
- *flat griddle*

## Honey

The taste of honey is determined by the flowers from which the bees have derived their nectar. In order to encourage the bees to collect from one type of flower, their keeper moves the hives to different locations at different times during the summer. This is called migratory bee-keeping and allows the bees to range in an area during the time when a particular blossom holds sway, a practice that carries inevitable costs and accordingly makes single-blossom (monofloral) honeys more expensive.

These single-source honeys, such as thyme, lavender, rosemary and lime, are heavily perfumed, making them ill-suited to most cooking, though they work well enough in ice-cream. The EU regulates honey production and polices claims of organic provenance. Since a bee ranges over several miles, proximity to inorganic fertilization of flowering plants and trees or industrial pollution has to be taken into account when labelling pots and jars.

### Opposite: The Basic Store Cupboard

*The following is a check-list of items we always like to keep in stock to prepare us for most eventualities, some of which are illustrated opposite:*

*extra-virgin olive oil • olive oil*
*• neutral frying oil (corn, groundnut or sunflower) • sesame oil*
*• strong white bread flour • cake flour • self-raising flour • potato flour*
*• baking powder • cornflour • 'easy-blend' yeast • corn meal (polenta)*
*• dried pasta, esp. spaghetti, ready-to-cook lasagne and cannelloni, and favourite shapes • basmati rice • risotto rice • jasmine (glutinous) rice*
*• couscous • bulghur*
*• different varieties of dried beans, especially red kidney beans, cannellini and flageolets • dried chickpeas*
*• muscovado sugar • caster sugar • icing sugar • sultanas • seedless raisins • Californian no-soak prunes and apricots*
*• sherry vinegar • balsamic vinegar • white wine vinegar • red wine vinegar • dry sherry • brandy*
*• Kikkoman soya sauce • Pearl River soy sauce*
*• Colman's mustard powder • Dijon mustard*
*tinned flageolets • anchovy fillets in olive oil • dolphin-friendly tuna in oil • sardines in olive oil • tinned Italian plum tomatoes*
*Lea & Perrin's Worcestershire sauce, • good-quality tomato ketchup*

## Horse Meat

It has never been thought odd to eat horse meat in Belgium and France, where chevaline butchers still ply their trade, while in Italy there is a highly prized and expensive salami made from donkey. André Simon wrote in *A Concise Encyclopaedia of Gastronomy* that older horses and work animals were too tough to be enjoyable, but that the fillet of a three-year-old thoroughbred was a costly luxury, only available when a horse broke its neck at exercise.

A British aversion to the idea of eating horse meat is, in any case, comparatively recent. Plenty of people ate it here in the '40s and early '50s when rationing made us reconsider what was acceptable fare. In 1947 alone, 19,000 horses were slaughtered in Britain for human consumption. London at that time certainly had at least one restaurant, Rose's, which served nothing else.

Bruce Bernard, the art and photographic historian, remembers just after the war, when he was a young and impecunious scene-shifter, a grilled horse steak at Rose's in Soho's Greek Street was considered an expensive treat. The rather Spartan dining room was ruled with an iron hand by the elderly Belgian woman who gave it her name. 'The choice was horse steak and chips for 3/6d – then a not inconsiderable sum – or horse stew and chips, which was slightly cheaper. I thought both dishes rather good,' Bernard recalls.

Horse flesh is very red and close-textured, with yellow fat and a rather sweet taste caused by the high starch content of the muscle tissue. Horse joints include topside, silverside and sirloin cuts, all at a fraction of the price of beef. These can be cooked as you would the equivalent beef cuts, but all benefit from plenty of onions and wine-based sauces, which complement the meat's natural sweetness.

## Hummus

A Middle-eastern purée of chickpeas with sesame, garlic, lemon juice and olive oil, which is served as a sauce or dip.

## Hush Puppies

These slightly sweet deep-fried corn batter puffs served with savoury dishes are a speciality of the southern USA. Typically accompanying fried catfish, they are an acquired taste.

### Hydrogenation

The process whereby vegetable oils are chemically altered so that they are solid at room temperature, for use in products such as margarine. The vaunted health benefits of products resulting from the process are now being called into question because of the possibility that the trans fats produced may be even more seriously implicated in heart disease than natural saturated fats.

# I

### Ikan Bilis

Ikan bilis is another of those preserved fish products so dear to Southeast Asian cooks. They are actually fry, that is baby fish of different varieties, similar to whitebait, which are salted and sun-dried. After frying until crisp, they are sprinkled over rice dishes as a crisp savoury **garnish**.

### Italian Cured Meats and Sausages

Italy is the source of a huge range of delicious cured meats (*salumi*), eaten traditionally as **antipasti**, a cold appetiser before the obligatory pasta course. There are dozens of different salami, including Felino, Napoli, Milano, Toscani and Coppa, the latter made exclusively from the fore-shank of the pig.

Different areas produce different kinds of cured sausages. Bologna, for example, is the home of mortadella, a large, delicately flavoured sausage, its smooth pink cut surface studded with milk-white fat. Pancetta is a national pleasure, a superior unsmoked bacon, essential for so many cooked dishes, that can also be eaten raw like Parma ham.

Regional differences are also found in fresh pork sausages, some spiked with fiery peppers. Cotechino and **zampone** are boiling sausages, all of which make great hot dishes with **lentils**, beans or polenta. Bresaola, originally from Lombardy, is salted, air-dried beef which may also be pressed and makes a delicious **antipasto** alternative to any of the pork products.

Of the pork products, prosciutto – salted, air-dried raw ham – is one of the most elegant, with Parma ham the most famous and most expensive, and produced exclusively in the small area between the Taro and Baganza rivers. The finest prosciutto is created from the upper leg portion of the

hindquarters of pigs fed on by-products of cheese-making; it may also, exotically, be made from wild boar, though this is astronomically expensive.

There is not one prosciutto, but hundreds of types with subtle yet distinguishable flavour and texture differences. For example, the hams of the Chianti region are saltier than those of Parma, which have a distinctively sweet taste. These variations are caused by the breed of pig used, what they have been fed on and whether they have been raised inside or have been allowed to range in a field. The humidity of the air in which the hams dry also makes a difference. The Parma pigs benefit from the local Parmesan production and are fed principally on whey, a by-product of the cheese-making.

Unless you have a proper slicing machine, do not buy a whole ham which would, in any case, cost enough to make your eyes water. Unlike some of the mountain hams of France and Spain, prosciutto should be sliced very thinly; cut thick with a knife it becomes too chewy and loses the delicacy which makes it a symbol of all that is best in Italian produce.

Generally, the Italian pork curing process does not involve smoking, with the exception of speck – cured fat back or belly – which is found only in the most northern regions of Italy and is really more Swiss and German in origin than it is Italian.

# J

### Jaggery

Also called loaf sugar, jaggery comes from India and is made from the dark honey brown sap of the nippah palm. Similar to the **palm sugar** of Southeast Asia, it goes very hard on exposure to the air, so keep it in a zip-lock bag in the fridge. It is not as sweet as cane sugar; if it is not available, muscovado sugar may be substituted.

### Jambalaya

A highly seasoned rice dish typical of the **Cajun** cooking of southern Louisiana. It may include any combination of chicken, beef, pork, smoked sausage (*andouille*), seafood and ham. It is thought the name comes from the French *jambon* for ham, *à la* and *ya*, a West-African word for rice.

*Japanese Pepper, see Sansho and Szechuan Pepper*

### Jerk

Originally meaning 'pork prepared in the Quichua Indian manner', jerk is now a generic description of an aromatic barbecue marinade paste common throughout the Caribbean. While everybody has their own version in varying degrees of complexity, most include **chillies**, onions, lime juice and **allspice**.

The right chilli to use is the Scotch Bonnet, a small round capsicum that looks like a brightly coloured lantern. While it has visual similarities to Mexico's habanero, the Scotch Bonnet is indigenous to the West Indies and its pronounced and distinctive flavour is the result of growing in a tropical climate with extremes of heat, sunshine and high humidity. In common with the habanero, it is fiercely hot and the amount you use is very much a matter of personal choice.

If you can't find any, use Encona West Indian pepper sauce, which is made from Scotch Bonnets and is redolent of their flavour. It is now to be found on every supermarket shelf and is as useful to have in the kitchen as Tabasco, since it can be used as an ingredient as well as a hot sauce at the table.

### Julienne

A classic French cooking term for uniformly cut vegetable sticks about 4 cm / 1½ inches long and 2 mm / $\frac{1}{12}$ inch thick. Nowadays it is used of anything that has been cut in the same way.

### Jus

Technically, this describes the meat juices left in the pan after roasting, but the word now has a wider application and you find some restaurants using it incorrectly to describe a reduced sauce.

## K

### Kaffir Lime

Both the knobbly, coarse-skinned citrus fruit and the leaves of the kaffir lime tree are extensively used in Southeast Asian cooking, where they feature in soups and curries and are an essential flavouring, most notably in Thai food.

An EU plant health directive banned the importation of lime leaves in 1994 because of the supposed risk of whitefly and leaf mosaic coming in with them. Britain's climate precludes commercial citrus growing and, since both diseases already exist in Europe while cooking destroys any disease or infestation, the UK plant health people at the Ministry of Agriculture & Fisheries took the view that this was not really something to worry about and turned a blind eye. Unfortunately the French and Germans complained about our relaxed view and now the total import ban is being rigidly enforced. Yet you can still buy them... Hmm.

### Karhai

Also know as *kodai* or *kadahi*, these are the small woks used in the cooking of the Indian subcontinent, especially in the making of **balti** stir-fried curries. *Karhai* is Urdu for 'bucket'.

### Ketchup

The original ketchup was almost certainly of the soy or Southeast Asian fish variety. The word ketchup comes from a Malay word and *kecap* or *ketjap manis*, a thick Indonesian soy sauce sweetened with palm sugar, is still an essential ingredient in Malay cooking, as is the thinner saltier *kecap masin*.

In eighteenth-century England, the first catchups or catsups were thin, vinegar-based sauces and were typically flavoured with oysters, mushrooms, anchovies or walnuts. The most common thin sauce sold today with the qualities of the early catchups is **Worcestershire sauce**. The thick sweet tomato ketchup which became hugely successful internationally in this century – mostly as an accompaniment to convenience food – is based on an eighteenth-century New England recipe.

*Ketjap or Kecap Manis, see Ketchup and Soy Sauce*

### Kibbeh

Lamb pounded to a paste with **burghul** or **bulgur wheat**, onion and spices, which is traditionally eaten raw or cooked in the Middle East.

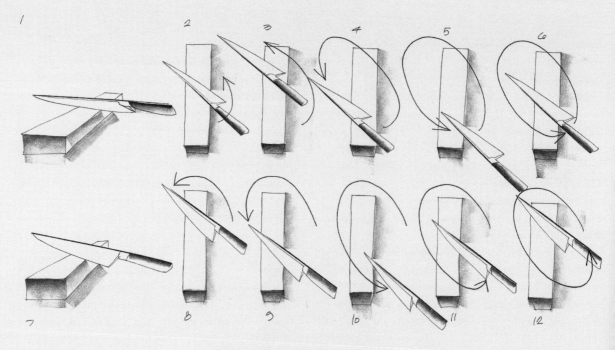

**Sharpening knives on a whetstone**

*To sharpen a knife on a whetstone: holding the knife in your right and with the blade at an angle of 45° to the stone angled away from you, and working in long circular anticlockwise movements, push the blade down and away from you, applying pressure with the fingertips of your left hand as you do so.*

*After five or six circles, reverse the blade and repeat with the edge now angled towards you.*

*Continue, alternating the side of the blade being worked on, until the knife starts to take an edge.*

*At this point, reduce the angle and continue sharpening, continuing to reduce the angle progressively until satisfied with the degree of sharpness.*

### Knives

Blunt knives are worse than useless and indeed can be dangerous. Once blunt, a steel will never bring a knife back to the razor-sharpness that is its ideal state, but should still be applied every time you use a knife as you see butchers doing. In reality nobody does this, but in an ideal world you should. It helps maintain the edge, and the more expensive the steel the better it is likely to be.

The best way to sharpen knives in the kitchen is with whetstones of varying coarseness, which are lubricated prior to use, either with oil or water, depending on the type of stone used. Buy these from a hardware store, take along a knife when you buy one, and have them show you how to use it before you take it home. Alternatively, buy Japanese water stones. These are soaked in water and you then make an abrasive paste on the surface by rubbing with a soft stone called *nagura*.

Many restaurants use the service of knife-grinders and some still ply their itinerant trade, knocking on doors. A word of caution here: while some grinders are professional, others are not. Good knives cost a lot of money and, before handing them to somebody who may damage them irreparably, why not learn to take care of them yourself? Regular use of a whetstone will keep them honed and cost nothing save the initial investment in the stone.

Sharpening steels coated in diamond dust are excellent though inevitably expensive, as are ceramic ones. You have to treat these carefully though; if dropped, they shatter.

### Kofta
Indian or Middle-Eastern spiced meat ball.

### Konbu
Konbu or kombu is a dried Japanese kelp seaweed used in the making of **dashi**.

### Kulfi
This very sweet Indian iced dessert is made from condensed milk, often with almonds and pistachios. It is invariably presented in a truncated pyramid shape, like a larger goats' cheese.

### Kumquat
A Lilliputian orange-coloured citrus fruit, both the flesh and the skin of which are eaten, often after poaching the fruit in syrup.

# L

### Lard
Rendered pig fat in English, but bacon in French, where lard is called **saindoux**. Despite its low profile in this era of healthy eating, for many it is still the favoured cooking medium and shortening for sweet and savoury pastries.

### Larding
Larding is a technique – now largely gone out of fashion – by which, using a special hollow needle, long thin ribbons of pork fat are sewn through very lean pieces of meat, like veal or venison (or, on occasions, tuna), to keep them moist during roasting.

### Lardons
Fat matchstick strips of streaky bacon.

### Lassi
The Hindi name for a cold yoghurt drink, which can be either salty or sweet.

### Lassie
A very intelligent collie dog which, because of its poor flesh-to-bone ratio, is only rarely eaten.

### Laver
Prepared Welsh laver is a variety of seaweed, similar to **nori**. The dense sticky greenish black pulp is usually sold in 225-g tubs. In this cleaned and prepared form it is called laver bread and is traditionally served with roast lamb or bacon and fried oatmeal.

### Lemon Grass
Lemon grass is a stiff, elongated, bulb-like grass made up of tightly rolled, rather tough leaves of which only the bottom 15–17.5 cm / 6–7 inches are used. It has a sweet, aromatic and powerful lemony verbena flavour that features widely in Southeast Asian cooking. It is, for example, one of the fundamental flavourings of the cooking of Thailand, where it is called *ta krai*.

Trim off the hard base and the outer leaf, then cut the softer inner stalk across into the thinnest slices you can achieve. Whole lemon grass stalks may be added to dishes and removed at the end of cooking in the same way as bay or lime leaves. Never use dried lemon grass, which tastes like cheap soap.

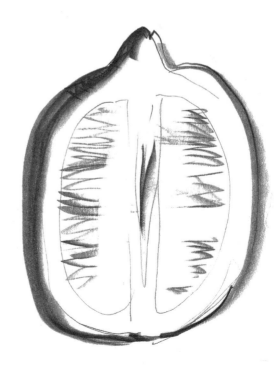

### Lemon Zest

Lemon zest, the thin outermost layer of the rind, is used in many recipes as it contains the precious oils which deliver an inimitable taste. Sadly, most lemons have been subjected to a horrendous and protracted exposure to every weapon in the agricultural chemist's arsenal before being coated in antifungal wax to keep them from going mouldy.

Supermarkets have laid down strict acceptability criteria that define size, colour and shelf-life, and the lemon producers, wanting to stay in business, have danced attendance. The worst are those obscenely oversized lemons which, cut open, reveal a spongy layer of pith concealing an undersized fruit. One suspects they have been soaked in water to achieve their grossness. Happily, you can now buy organic lemons, that come in different sizes and are slightly knobbly. If you can't and are going to use the rind, wash it in warm soapy water, scrubbing gently, then rinse and dry before use.

### Lentil

Lentils are small pulses that come in a variety of types and colours. They may have been the first vegetable ever cultivated, as there were references to them in Mesopotamia 7,000 years ago. Throughout history they have been a staple diet of the poor, the Biblical 'mess of pottage', though they are now widely appreciated.

Certain varieties, like the tiny green French lentille de Puy, are both fashionable and relatively expensive. Lentils feature heavily in the cooking of the Middle East and India, but also play an important part in French, Spanish, Portuguese and Italian regional cooking.

### Levain

A **sourdough** starter for raising bread, levain describes dough which has been colonized by natural airborne yeasts rather than having yeast introduced by the baker. Levain gives bread a slightly sour taste, hence sourdough.

### Liaison

From the French *lier*, to bind, a culinary term for anything used to thicken sauces, including cornflour, potato starch, arrowroot, **beurre manié**, **roux**, blood and egg yolks and cream.

### Liquorice

Liquorice is a woody leguminous plant that grows wild in the Far East, where its root is prized for the sweet and intense flavour it imparts to savoury and sweet dishes. Although hardly used at all in this country except in sweets, the flavour can also be found naturally in **fennel** and **star anise**. This strong and unmistakable taste comes from a natural oil present in all three of these ingredients called anethole, the flavouring element used to give Pastis, Pernod, Arak and Sambuca drinks their distinctive aniseed and liquorice tang.

Liquorice is such an intense and aromatic flavour that you have to be very restrained when using it. A few drops of Pastis, for example, will perfume a fish soup or stew. How you use liquorice root is really up to your imagination. A small piece included in a **bouquet garni** for a fish stew, for example, would permeate the dish. Just remember that a lot of people loathe liquorice (and that it is a natural purgative) before experimenting with it too enthusiastically.

### Litchi see Lychee

### Lobscouse

Scouse – short for lobscouse and an affectionate description of a Liverpudlian as well as of the dish – is a basic sort of meat stew, usually of neck of lamb (scrag end), potatoes, onions and other root vegetables, thickened these days with pearl barley. Originally the stew was based on mutton and thickened with ship's biscuits, the hard plain water biscuits which also crop up in a classic Boston chowder and are typical of any cooking in areas with strong seafaring connections.

The word lob in dialect means boil, though nobody seems to know where scouse comes from. We published a recipe from a chef who hailed from Liverpool which suggested the stew be finished in the oven like a Lancashire hot-pot. Thirty people wrote incensed by this revisionist nonsense. Whatever meat you use, and this is very much dependent on what is available, scouse is cooked on top of the stove. As a matter of interest, if you can't afford the meat you make a vegetable stew in the same way and call it blind scouse.

### Lo Mein
Fresh Chinese noodles equivalent to the Japanese ramen. Oriental markets sell them from the chill cabinet in 500-g and 1-kg bags. They freeze well and may be cooked from frozen.

### Long Pig
Early **Pacific Rim** term for barbecued human.

### Lox
Jewish term for smoked salmon, from *laks*, Yiddish for salmon. It is most famously eaten with cream cheese on a **bagel**.

### Lychee or Litchi
Oriental sweet white stone fruit with brown, papery skin. Usually sold tinned in syrup, they make an excellent sorbet.

# M

### Macadamia Nut
These round nuts look rather like big hazelnuts. Hawaii is now the largest exporter, although most of the macadamias sold here come from New South Wales. They have a similar texture to Brazil nuts (although oilier) and candlenuts, and are used mainly in sweet dishes.

### Mace, see Nutmeg

### Macédoine
A mixture of diced vegetables or diced fruit, really a presentational nicety.

### Macerate, see Marinate

### Maltose
A purplish coloured sugar syrup, rather like glucose, maltose is very sticky but has little flavour. It is sold in small pots in Chinese stores and supermarkets and is used to glaze poultry. It has to be heated gently to liquefy it for use.

### Mandarin Orange
Mandarin oranges, tangerines and satsumas are all members of the mandarin family, small bright-skinned and fragrant oranges that originated in China and were first brought to England in the 18th century.

Tangerines, which are characterized by a loose skin and lots of pips, were not actually called tangerines until the middle of the last century, when somebody with a shrewd commercial sense gave them what he thought was a more exotic and therefore more saleable name. Those of a certain age will always think of tangerines as obligatory Christmas stocking presents in the days when such sweet juicy fruit were a rare treat. Dried tangerine peel is a popular ingredient in Oriental cooking. Originally Japanese, the hardier satsuma is smaller and usually seedless.

Clementines differ in having a very shiny skin (they are thought possibly to be a cross between the mandarin and the orange) and, being juicy and seedless, are definitely the children's favourite. Now, as they are not as expensive as they used to be and are available all year round, you can substitute them for their big cousin the orange in jellies, curd tarts and sorbets.

### Mangetout
Literally 'eat everything', mangetouts are flat edible pea pods containing barely formed peas. They cook in seconds.

### Mango
Until recently rarely seen in Britain in their fresh state, mangoes are now available in supermarkets. They are used both ripe and in their green, unripened state in savoury dishes and in chutneys and pickles, where their high pectin levels help give a good set.

When buying them ripe, the skins should be unblemished and the flesh very sweet and succulent. Allow them to ripen fully for a few days at room temperature, wrapped in paper. They are ready when they give to gentle pressure and smell sweet and perfumed.

### Mangosteen
Mangosteens are enjoying a fashionable popularity, though their availability here is scarcely new. The first mangosteens were brought back from Southeast Asia as long ago as the sixteenth century, the name coming from the Malay. The fruit is round, with a reddish brown skin. Inside is a pink pith containing six segments of white-fleshed fruit, which is what you eat. The flavour is unique, so the only way you are going to find out what it tastes like is to eat one.

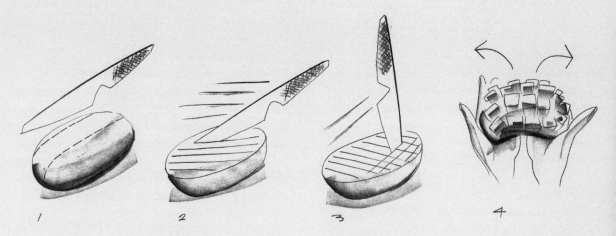

**Removing the flesh from a mango**

*A mango has a thin, centrally positioned oval stone which means the stone is sideways on as the mango sits on a flat surface. The stone is also a real clinger, so ingenious means have had to be found to remove the flesh from it.*

❶ Turn the unpeeled fruit on its side, so the stone is in a vertical plane. With a flexible-bladed knife, cut downwards just to one side of an imaginary median line, following the contour of the stone. Repeat on the other side to detach the other half. The stone will be left surrounded with very little flesh within a thin strip of skin, which is easily trimmed off. Discard the stone.

❷ and ❸ Cut a cross-hatch through the flesh of each cut surface down to the skin.

❹ Turn the skin inside out to open out the cuts made into the flesh, which will then detach as cubes.

### Maple Syrup

Pure maple syrup is nothing more nor less than the sweet sap of the maple tree reduced to a syrup consistency by boiling. It is very expensive, but has an extraordinary taste that is sensational in desserts. It bears no resemblance to commercially produced pancake syrups.

Often sold in tins, once opened the syrup should be transferred to a glass jar and kept, tightly closed, in the fridge, where it will keep forever. It may also be kept in the freezer without detriment. If left too long in the opened original can it will darken but, more importantly, the flavour may be affected. Syrups described as 'maple-flavoured' are poor imitations and are best avoided.

### Marbling

The culinary use of this term describes the veining of intra-muscular fat or flecks of fat in otherwise lean meat. This is a desirable phenomenon from the cook's point of view, since it has both a moisturizing and flavour-intensifying effect. Marbling is the whole point of Japan's famous and fabulously expensive Kobe snow beef, where it is encouraged to develop in prime cuts by giving the pampered animals massages following their daily bottle of stout.

### Marc

This is the rough French distillate of must, that is the skins, pips and stalks left over after the grapes have been pressed to make wine. The flavour depends on the type of grapes used, thus, Marc de Bourgogne, Marc de Champagne etc. In Italy a similar drink is called grappa.

### Margarita

Mexican cocktail of white tequila, orange-flavoured liqueur and lime juice, properly served straight up in a shallow glass with a salt-frosted rim.

### Margherita

The classic and perfect Neapolitan pizza topped with mozzarella, tomatoes and basil.

### Marinade, Marinate

Technically, marinate and macerate mean the same, soaking food in a liquid (the marinade) to flavour it and, sometimes in the case of meat and poultry, to make it more tender – and more moist in the case of dry meats, like venison. The distinction usually made is that maceration describes leaving fruit in a liquid that usually includes liquor and sugar syrup, but you marinate meat and fish in a marinade of wine, oil or citrus juices.

One of the best marinades for lamb, chicken, pork or beef to be barbecued is a mixture of lemon juice, **soy sauce** and **Worcestershire sauce**. Fish needs less aggressive treatment, for a marinade of citrus juices 'cooks' the flesh, changing taste and texture. This is, in fact, ceviche, fish or shellfish deliberately so marinated to be served raw.

### Marmite

An earthenware pot glazed on the inside. The characteristic shape of the jars in which Marmite, the proprietary vegetable extract, is sold reflects the shape of such pots.

### Masa

This heavy ground flour made from starchy white dried corn is a Central American staple. It is used in many dishes and to make corn tortillas.

### Mascarpone

Resembling clotted cream, this soft creamy cheese features in many Italian desserts, perhaps most famously in the ever-popular tiramisu. It may also be eaten on its own, simply sprinkled with sugar.

### Masoor Dal

The Indian name for red **lentils**, hulled pink split peas that turn yellow when cooked.

### Matjesherring

The term for any Dutch pickled herring, though the name infers that the fish in question is young, plump and of good quality. The fillets are often preserved in oil and sold in jars or tins.

### Medlar

This brown-rinded, apple-like fruit used to be called 'openarse' in English and is still called *cul de chien* – 'dog's bum' – in French. You really have to look at a ripe one to understand why. The ripe fruit is seldom eaten fresh and instead they are 'bletted' on beds of sawdust to allow them to ferment slightly and achieve their full aroma. Perhaps their best-known use these days is in making a thick jelly preserve.

### Mee

Thai dried rice vermicelli noodles which only need brief soaking in hot water before incorporation in any of a wide range of dishes.

### Melba Toast

Melba toast is another of the edible things inspired by the Australian soprano Nellie Melba, along with the dish of ice-cream and peaches with a raspberry sauce created for her by Escoffier. The toast was supposedly made for her when she was recuperating at the Ritz in 1897, following a gruelling tour of the USA. Melba was a woman with a *bella figura* and the toast named after her was thought to be slimming, an idea which persists to this day.

Melba toast is easy to make by toasting slices of bread on both sides, then cutting off the crusts and running a knife between the toasted surfaces to produce 2 thin slices. If using a sliced loaf, you will find the untoasted surfaces rather gluey. Scrape this off before returning the bread under the grill on a low setting and toasting. Reposition the toasts frequently to get an even browning. The bread is now very thin and burns quickly.

### Mesclun

Originally a Provençal description of a salad of miscellaneous wild leaves and herbs, then adopted for mixed salad leaves planted together and harvested while very young, this term is now most familiar as a description used for supermarket packs of assorted baby salad leaves of different types, usually including lamb's lettuce (mâche), dandelion leaves, chicory (frisée), radicchio, **fennel**, sorrel and **rocket**.

### Meunière

*À la meunière* means 'in the style of the miller's wife', presumably because the fish is coated in seasoned flour before being fried, a treatment most frequently associated with cooking Dover sole on the bone but equally appropriate for plaice or any skinned flat fish. It is a classic technique of the professional kitchen and demands an initial high heat to fry the fish, as this sets the flour to a crisp coating. The fish is then finished over a lower heat until just cooked through, turning it once.

Purists would argue that the fish should first be fried in **clarified butter** (though sunflower oil works as well or better), then, after it is cooked and transferred to a hot serving plate, the pan is wiped clean, and a big knob of unclarified butter is added and heated briefly until it foams and goes golden brown, when it is known as *beurre meunière*. This is poured over the fish, which is sent to the table accompanied only by a lemon quarter and a little parsley. It must not be allowed to sit in the hot butter for more than a few seconds, but must served at once or it will go greasy as the butter coagulates and the crisped skin goes soggy.

### Mirepoix

A mirepoix is a mixture of coarsely chopped onion, celery and carrots, the essential flavouring trilogy for stews and braises. It is usually first sweated in butter.

### Mirin

Mirin is a very sweet Japanese cooking wine made from glutinous rice which can be bought from most Chinese grocers as well as Japanese food shops. It is used as a tenderizing marinade, as one of the ingredients in a number of dipping sauces and – in conjunction with **soy sauce**, **sake** and aromatics – as a poaching or braising liquid for meat and fish. It imparts sweetness to a dish and, when used as a baste, gives a lacquered glaze. When mirin is not available, mix sake with sugar in the proportion of 1 tablespoon of sake to 1 teaspoon of sugar.

### Mise en Place

The term used in the professional kitchen for the practice of preparing ingredients and some early stages of dishes in advance.

### Miso

A fermented soya bean paste made from malted barley, rice or soya beans, miso features widely in Japanese cooking and is used both to start and to finish dishes. It typically flavours broths, but may also be used as a seasoning ingredient in fried and grilled foods. Overcooking can make it bitter.

### Mizuna or Mizuma

This currently fashionable salad leaf, originally from Japan, is peppery and slightly bitter. Its distinctive red edges make it attractive in presentation.

### Mode (à la)

In Europe this term, meaning 'in the manner of', is generally applied to beef braised with vegetables, which is either served hot in a rich, dark gravy or cold in aspic. In the USA the term is used to denote any dessert served with ice-cream.

### Molasses

This is the thick dark brown sticky liquid which is left after sugar cane has been boiled down and the sugar extracted. It is used to manufacture treacle and in the making of dishes as varied as gingerbread and Boston baked beans.

### Mole

*Mole* is a Nahuatl word for a sauce or mixture containing **chilli** and, sometimes, chocolate. Mole Poblano de Guajalote – turkey with poblano mole sauce – is probably the most celebrated and complex of these, and a rich dish served at Mexican wedding feasts and other grand occasions. The original 17th-century recipe called for more than 100 ingredients and, though the present-day version is more restrained, it is still a far from simple dish, for it includes (three kinds of) chillies, tomatoes, garlic, almonds, peanuts, cloves, cinnamon, aniseed and raisins. Pieces of unsweetened chocolate are beaten into the sauce towards the end of cooking and this has the effect of thickening it while giving a rich flavour and a dark glossy finish.

Chocolate is also used in some French and Spanish game cooking. Sologne, an area between the Loire and Cher rivers famous for its hunting, is known for rich wine-dark stews notably using hare, finished with dark chocolate.

## Monosodium Glutamate

Sometimes sold as 'taste powder', monosodium glutamate (MSG) is essentially glutamic acid, an amino acid found naturally in a number of foods, including kelp, seaweed, soy sauce and wheat, and which is commercially extracted from fermented molasses to make this much used and abused flavour-enhancer on a huge scale.

Yan-Kit So, an authority on Chinese food, says 400,000 tonnes of MSG (*weijing*) are produced worldwide each year. Since it is added to food in powder form in tiny amounts to give a rich, meaty flavour this gives some indication of how widespread its use has become. Though originally a Japanese invention, it is today omnipresent in Chinese restaurant kitchens, where a pinch of MSG is added to a dish as automatically as a pinch of salt.

When used excessively it can cause allergic reactions in a small percentage of people. These reportedly range from skin rashes to palpitations, nausea, diarrhoea and headaches. However, the evidence of MSG making people ill remains anecdotal and clinical research into its potentially toxic effects, including central nervous system damage, has not been conclusive. The Glutamate Council, the body which exists to endorse the use of MSG, insists that there is no evidence it has ever harmed anybody and sends very tetchy letters to those who suggest it might.

## Mooli, see Daikon

## Morel

Also known by their French name *morilles*, these very expensive black spongy-headed wild mushrooms have a distinctive taste and are usually sold dried.

## Mortadella, see Italian Cured Meats and Sausages

## Mouli-légume

The mouli-légume or food-mill was invented in France in the 1930s and is the manually operated precursor to the electric mixer and food processor of today. It utilizes a hand-cranked blade fitted above a perforated base which, when turned, forces cooked foods through the perforations to produce a purée, the consistency of which can be varied by changing the base plate. You can mill things unpeeled with the side benefit of leaving the skins and any pips in the base, as the cooked centres are extruded through the perforations.

You can achieve similar effects by forcing food through different mesh sieves with a wooden spoon, but this is much slower and harder work. Purists will insist that a mouli does some jobs better than a electrically powered machine. It is great for ricing (i.e. dry mashing) potatoes, for example, and because of its gentle action never causes elements like starch to be forced out as happens if you whip cooked potatoes in a food processor.

## Muscovado

Muscovado, from the Portuguese word *muscavado* meaning unrefined, is the dark brown sugar produced as the first stage of refining from boiled sugar cane, giving it a treacly intensity of flavour.

## Mushrooms, see Dried Mushrooms

## Mustard

All mustards are made from the same black and brown seeds, which are usually ground into a powder, though roughly crushed, mild grain varieties are equally valid mustards. Only when the powder is mixed with a liquid are the hot-tasting oils released and with them the heat delivered to the tongue. These oils are literally volatile, that is unstable, and their heat is lost during cooking, so even a lot of Colman's mustard exposed to temperatures in excess of 40°C / 100°F will lose all its ferocity. Mustard should therefore always be added towards the end of cooking. If cooked too long it not only loses its ability to excite but also becomes bitter.

Dijon, both as a style and as a producer, is perhaps the best-known mustard, with any dish described as *à la dijonnaise* containing it. Dijon, the capital city of Burgundy, has been associated with mustard since the 14th century and remains a principal producer to this day. Grey Poupon was established in the city in 1777 and is globally the most famous exponent of the Dijon style, which combines the mustard powder with white wine and **verjuice**, the latter sour by-product of wine-making giving Dijon mustard its distinctive flavour.

Among the French mustards you will find many variations on the aromatic rather than hot theme, with mild coarse-grain mustards described as *moutarde à l'ancienne*, while mustards with added flavourings are called *aromatisées*, or will have specific reference on their labels to the herb or herbs they contain.

## N

### Nam Pla, see Fish Sauce

### Nap

When you nap something, you barely coat it with a sauce.

### Nori

These thin sheets of Japanese dried cultivated seaweed are of the same type as Welsh **laver**, which is found clinging to rocks at low tide, though they are treated differently and have a different flavour. Nori is most often eaten grilled and wrapped around glutinous rice in **sushi**. It is also very good briefly grilled and eaten in pieces as a nibble with drinks.

### Nouvelle Cuisine

A term coined in the '70s in France to describe an initiative promoting a lighter style of cooking. Eventually, style took over from content, as presentation on the plate became more and more important. Despite its most ludicrous expressions, both visually and in terms of minuscule portions served on giant plates, the long-term influence of nouvelle cuisine is undeniable and, in the manner of *1066 and All That*, it may be generally judged a good rather than a bad thing.

### Nuoc Mam, see Fish Sauce

### Nutmeg

Nutmeg is the seed of the fruit of *Myristica fragrans*, the tropical nutmeg tree, which originated in the Moluccas, or Spice Islands, but is today cultivated in many tropical countries, with Grenada the single largest producer. The seed is covered with a red fibrous membrane which separates it from the flesh of the fruit. When dried and flattened this becomes mace. Mace and nutmeg do smell and taste similar and are interchangeable, though mace is stronger in flavour. They both contain a volatile oil called myristicin, apparently hallucinogenic in large quantities. In the 18th century, nutmeg was so fashionable that people had their own silver nutmeg holders and graters that they would take with them when they went out to dine.

Mace and nutmeg should be kept in small quantities in airtight jars, since the oil is given off in time and the flavour lost. This unique flavour enhances both sweet and savoury custards and is particularly good in cheese sauces. It can be used instead of cloves in a bread sauce (see pages 152-3), is often included in béchamel sauces and in dishes like spinach à la Florentine and to replace vanilla in ice-cream.

## O

### Okra

Also called 'ladies' fingers' and *bhindi* in India, these green edible seed pods exude a mucilaginous excretion on prolonged cooking which thickens slow-cooked liquid dishes, most notably the **gumbos** of Louisiana.

### Olive Oil

Unless you have tasted a particular oil before, there is no way of knowing from the label or the price how good it is, though as a general rule those classified as 'extra-virgin' and with a darker green colour will be superior to pale-coloured oils described simply as olive oil. It is not a new dilemma, for the fruit of the olive tree has been eaten since pre-history. The Abyssinians recorded their cultivation of olive trees in 5,000 BC and the culinary importance of the heavy fragrant oil produced from the ripe black fruit has been huge ever since.

Up to six pressings of the olives may take place, first pressings using traditional coir mats and wooden presses being the most highly prized, with latter extractions using factory techniques. The description 'extra-virgin' to describe the best oil was originally an International Olive Oil Council classification. It is now an EU-recognized legal definition of first-pressing oil with an acidity of less than per cent. The acidity level does not affect the flavour but determines the speed at which the oil decomposes and becomes rancid; the lower the acidity, the longer it lasts.

'Olive oil', as a general term, describes a blend of refined and virgin oils and is pressed all over the Mediterranean countries, with Spain the largest producer but Italy the biggest exporter internationally. Italy buys much of this oil from Spain and Greece, blending it with local product, a questionable practice that is not always made clear on the labels. This is not to say that Italian olive oil is intrinsically better than the best Spanish or Greek olive oil. The bias is purely to do with marketing-driven perceptions, though Italian estate-bottled extra-virgin oils – such as Colonna, Badia Coltibuono, Dell'Ugo and Tenuta di Saragano – are amongst the finest in the world. Olives and olive oil are also produced to a lesser extent in the USA, Central and South America, South Africa and Australia.

The very best olive oils are used not for cooking but to dress salads and cooked dishes at the table or to eat with bread instead of butter. They have different characteristics, varying enormously from place to place and producer to producer. The only way to find out which style you like best is to try several. Don't be tempted to buy in bulk to save money, because even the very best oils deteriorate with time. They are best stored in a cool dark place. Oil can be refrigerated without detriment, though the oil's high fat content means it will solidify in the fridge, returning rapidly to its liquid state at room temperature.

### Olla Podrida

Olla podrida, Spanish for 'all mixed together', is not so much a dish as a general description of a one-pot poached meal of meat and vegetables in which the broth and vegetables, often including chickpeas, were eaten first as a thick soup, the meat element being eaten afterwards. This is an ancient tradition you find throughout the Western world, in Italy *bollito misto*, in France the *pot au feu*. A close modern Spanish equivalent is the soup stew *cocida*, a robust affair of sausages and chickpeas. John Ayto points out in his fascinating *The Diner's Dictionary* that olla podrida has been used metaphorically in English for any 'heterogeneous jumble'. Sir Walter Scott even turned it into an adjective, 'My ideas are olla podrida-ish', though the phrase fell out of use around the middle of the last century.

### Ostrich

This strange-looking giant flightless bird, long eaten in South Africa as *biltong* (dried meat), has enjoyed a wider popularity with the introduction of commercial ostrich farming in Europe and the USA. A number of gullible people encouraged to invest in ostrich farms have lost their money, thinking they owned entire birds only to discover a few thousand other people thought the same thing about the same few birds.

The meat is quite strongly flavoured and dark in colour but very low in saturated fat, presumably the reason why it has been heavily promoted. Treat ostrich meat as you would a lean piece of steak, but grill it only briefly as it toughens with overcooking.

### Oxidization

Oxidization causes the browning and discoloration of fruit and vegetables which have been peeled or sliced. It is actually caused not so much by the contact with air as by the action of the plant enzyme polyphenoloxidase on phenolic compounds in the tissue as the result of cell damage caused by the bruising or cutting.

## P

### Pacific Rim

In culinary terms, this phrase describes the contemporary eclectic cooking of California, Australia, Hawaii and New Zealand, with its multicultural influences and emphasis on Oriental – particularly Southeast Asian – flavours, ingredients and techniques.

### Paillard

A paillard is a thinnish slice of beef, veal or lamb. It is also called a schnitzel.

### Palm Sugar

The sap of the palmyra tree, a tropical palm, is simply boiled down, producing a crystallized, brown and sticky sugar that is sold in tins and as cellophane-wrapped cakes. It has a pronounced caramel flavour and is less sweet than cane sugar. When unavailable, **muscovado sugar** may be substituted.

### Palmier

Sugary biscuit made from puff pastry.

### Panada

A stiff mixture of breadcrumbs, rice or flour cooked in milk or water and used commonly to thicken, bind or extend a **forcemeat**.

### Pancetta

This traditionally cured Italian unsmoked **bacon** has become the fashionable choice for restaurants and discerning cooks in recent times, for no better reason than the dire state of our own mass-produced bacon. In Italian production, a 9-kg / 20-lb side will typically be salted for 14 days before being rinsed, dried, boned, rolled and tied, or in some cases, sold as a flat piece. It is then left to rest for another week or two before it can be sold as pancetta.

It is best bought in a piece and will keep unwrapped for a couple of months in the fridge, though it is a good idea to keep the cut end covered. The pancetta will harden with time as it dries, and crystals may appear on the surface, but these are only salt. Look out, however, for any sliminess on the cut surface, as this indicates bacterial contamination. Any pancetta so affected should be cut off and thrown away. The great thing about having bacon in a piece is that you can cut it thickly for lardons to go in stews or in larger pieces to boil or cook as a joint with beans. Cutting thin slices to fry for breakfast is not so easy, particularly as pancetta dries and hardens with keeping. See also **Italian Cured Meats and Sausages**.

### Panchphoran

Panchphoran is an Indian spice mix made up of equal quantities of **fennel** seeds, cumin seeds, **fenugreek** seeds, black **mustard** seeds and kalonji or nigella seeds. It is mostly used to flavour vegetable dishes, such as the Spicy Grilled Aubergines on page 166.

### Pandan Leaf

Widely used in Southeast Asia to flavour sweet dishes such as rice pudding – to which it imparts a flavour reminiscent of coconut – pandan, pandanus or screwpine leaves are bright green and resemble palm leaves.

### Pané

An egg-and-crumb coating for fried food, a pané gives a crisp exterior that also forms a barrier against the excessive absorption of fat during cooking.

### Paneer or Panir

This fresh Indian curd cheese is used in cooked dishes, the best-known of which are probably *matar panir* and *saag panir*, based on curried peas and spinach respectively.

### Panettone

A light sweet **yeast** bread, containing candied peel and sultanas, eaten in Italy at Christmas and Easter.

### Panforte

A Siennese compressed cake of fruit and nuts, candied peel, lemon zest and spices, including cinnamon and mace, made with virtually no flour. The recipe goes back to the 14th century.

### Papaya

Also known as the paw-paw, this large pale-yellow-skinned tropical fruit has sweet bright-orange flesh studded with black seeds. Papain, an enzyme extracted from the unripe fruit, is used to tenderize meat as it accelerates the breakdown of animal protein.

### Papillote

Cooking food *en papillote* means baking it in a paper bag or foil pouch. The technique keeps in almost all the food's flavour and moisture, and is particularly suited to fish and shellfish.

### Pappadum or Poppadum

A thin Indian wafer-like bread made from chickpea flour which, when deep-fried, puffs up into a giant crisp.

### Paratha

Simple unleavened Indian wholemeal bread made light and flaky by careful rolling of the dough interleaved with layers of **ghee** in the same way as butter is layered into puff pastry.

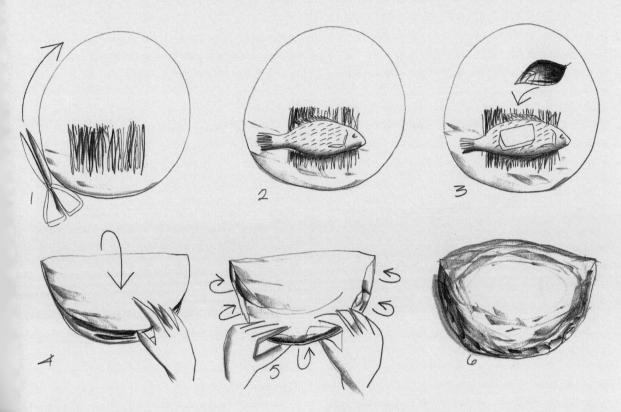

### Cooking food en papillote

❶ Cut out a circle of foil or baking paper large enough to sit the fish, or other item, on one half, while leaving a margin around the circumference to fold over and secure the package.

❷ Put any vegetables and aromatics in an even layer on one half.

❸ Lay the fish, etc., on top, and scatter the remaining aromatics and vegetables on top.

❹ Fold the other clear half over and fold in the margin.

❺ Wrap loosely and crimp all round the edges carefully to seal the package tightly.

❻ When cooked, present the food still sealed in its package so that it may be opened at the table, allowing the delicious aromas to escape.

### Parmentier

Properly, this term describes a finely diced fried potato **garnish**, but more loosely it is used of any dish finished with potatoes, which may be boiled or mashed, for example, *hachis parmentier*, see **Haché**.

### Parmigiano-Reggiano

Parmesan is Italy's most famous full-flavoured hard cheese. The true Parmigiano-Reggiano, pale yellow in colour, flecked with white, is a long-matured cows'-milk cheese made only in that part of the Po Valley which includes Parma, Mantova, Modena, Reggio-Emilia and Bologna. Any similar cheese made anywhere else cannot be described as Parmigiano Reggiano.

Because Parmesan is so hard, it is cut with a special sharp trowel from the huge 34.5-kg / 75-lb wheels in which it is produced. It is the finest of the so-called *grana* cheeses, hard cheeses which are usually grated and cooked, although the best Parmesan is also delicious eaten in a piece after a meal or shaved over salads or carpaccio.

### Pasta Flour

Italian type 00 (*doppio zero*) flour has a high protein content, making it ideal for pasta-making. Your local Italian delicatessen may stock it, or buy a 14-per-cent-protein flour like Marriage's Finest Strong Flour, now available from Waitrose, or Robinski's Andel Brand. Both are made from Canadian wheat. For stockists of the Robinski crupczatka flour, call 0181 896 3360.

Commercially produced dried pasta, like spaghetti, is made from semolina, a coarse hard flour made from durum wheat, which produces the very stiff dough needed for the best manufactured dried pasta. Less than 5 per cent of all wheat produced in the world is durum, the hardest of all wheat grains, that is, its kernel has the highest protein content, making it too hard for bread-making. Durum semolina is not practical for domestic use, being too hard to knead by hand and tough enough to burn out the motor of any domestic food mixer in minutes.

### Pasteurization

Milk is a kind of culture soup for bacteria and other disease-causing organisms and has, in the past, been the vehicle for the spread of vile things like tuberculosis and listeria. Pasteurization is nothing more than heating the milk to a temperature high enough to kill dodgy microbes.

The most frequently used technique is that of heating the milk to 62°C/144°F and keeping it at that temperature for half an hour, then rapidly cooling it. This also extends the milk's life before the fats split and it sours.

The milk used in the making of most cheeses is pasteurized – a contentious issue with most traditional cheese-makers wanting to produce cheeses which will mature through bacterial action, changing taste and texture as they develop.

### Pâté

Originally a pâté was specifically something cooked and enclosed in pastry, the term being applied to fruit and vegetables as well as **forcemeat**. With the passage of time, however, it came to refer more to the pastry's content rather than the container and to imply a savoury dish exclusively.

Thus we find now *pâté en croûte* and *pâté en terrine*, and logically, terrine (the traditional container) to mean not the pot in which the forcemeat was cooked but also the cooked forcemeat itself.

### Paupiette

A thin slice of meat – usually beef or veal, beaten out thin with a **cutlet bat** – which is rolled around a **forcemeat** stuffing and then cooked. The term is also used of fish fillets rolled round a stuffing.

### Pavé

Pavé means 'paving stone' and refers to the original cobbled streets which still challenge the most advanced vehicle suspensions in old French towns. In culinary terms, it is used of a thick-cut steak of Charolais beef, and is today also used for desserts, implying a moulded rectangular presentation, usually of chocolate. However, in the contemporary menu, which seeks novel descriptions, it might well crop up among the first courses.

### Pecorino

The name of this Italian cheese comes from *pecora*, the Italian word for sheep, and it is generally a fresh sheep's-milk cheese, made all over Italy, with minor regional variations. Not many of these uncooked or semi-cooked artisanal cheeses are exported, the majority being sold and eaten locally. Fresh pecorino rarely weighs more than 1 kg and may be formed in balls, cylinders or the distinctive fish shapes. The flavour and character of the cheese varies from farm to farm, depending on pasture and time of year.

### Opposite: Exotic Stores
*For the more adventurous fusion freak*

mirin • maltose • squid ink • Chinese salted blackbeans • dashi-no-moto (Japanese instant dashi stock grains) • coconut milk • coconut cream • dried shrimps • dried wild mushrooms • dark sesame oil • rice vinegar • sake • kecap manis • tamarind • nori • wakame • shrimp paste (belachan) • ikan bilis • Thai or Vietnamese fish sauce • wasabi • rice-paper wrappers • dry rice noodles • beanthread noodles • soba (Japanese buckwheat noodles) • masoor dal • hoisin sauce • oyster sauce

The pecorino you see in delicatessens outside Italy is most often pecorino Romano, a hard cooking cheese and very different from the delicate, fresh cheese the Italians enjoy locally. Shaped in wheels or giant cylinders, it weighs between 7 kg / 16 lb and 18 kg / 40 lb. When sold as pecorino Romano, it can only legally have been made in the Lazio area outside Rome. It is salted and has a much stronger flavour than fresh pecorino. It may be white or pale yellow, and is first eaten at about four months old, but is more often matured to eight months, when it is used for cooking and grating like parmesan or grana padano.

A similar pecorino is produced in Sardinia – pecorino Sardo – often just called Sardo; the finest examples are called fiore Sardo. Sicily also produces the same type of pecorino but containing peppercorns – pecorino pepato.

### Opposite: Herbs and Spices

*These are the magic ingredients that breathe life into your cooking. Below is a list of those that we like to keep handy. Remember, where possible, buy whole spices rather than ready-ground and keep them away from heat, light and damp. Try to buy fresh herbs with their stalks (and roots where possible, especially in the case of coriander) and keep them in a jug of water like cut flowers.*

*freeze-dried oregano • bay leaves • cinnamon sticks • allspice berries • cloves • whole nutmegs • Maldon sea salt • black peppercorns • cumin seeds • coriander seeds • saffron threads • turmeric • fenugreek • vanilla beans and good-quality extract • fresh chillies • dried chilli flakes • asafoetida • sichuan pepper • sansho pepper • sichimi seven-spice powder • five-spice powder • star anise • cardamom pods • kaffir lime leaves • curry leaves • lemon grass • ginger • galangal • pandan leaves (screwpine) • chillies • flat leaf parsley • coriander leaf • curry leaves mustard seeds*

### Persillade

This classic French mixture of finely chopped parsley and garlic – and sometimes breadcrumbs – is typically added to fried potatoes or mushrooms towards the end of cooking. It is also used to coat meat prior to roasting.

### Petit Four

Petits fours are Lilliputian cakes and biscuits served with strong coffee after dinner, providing an opportunity for restaurants to make money by 'adding value' to the coffee.

### Petit Salé

French salted belly pork that is usually boiled and served with **lentils**.

### Phyllo, see Filo

### Pie and Mash

There are not very many eel, pie and mash shops left in London, though they seem to be coming back into fashion, with new ones opening for the first time in many years. The long-established shops still sell the same old favourites to enthusiastic devotees, from rather Spartan and unlicensed premises.

Most offer the same basic fare. The pies have a home-made shortcrust base which is pressed into individual pie tins and these are not baked blind but are filled with minced beef that has been browned and then cooked in a Bisto gravy. The filling is seasoned with salt, no pepper, and topped with puff pastry. This is brushed with milk and baked for about 40 minutes at 190°C/ 375°F/gas 5, then served with a green (parsley) liquor and potatoes mashed with milk, not butter. The liquor is that in which the eels have been cooked and which, left to go cold, jellies. This is not as strange as it sounds, because eel taste more like meat than fish.

### Pine Nut

In Middle-Eastern cooking, pine nuts – the kernels of the Mediterranean stone pine – are used a great deal and often in large amounts. This is all very well in places like Turkey, where pine nuts grow abundantly and are cheap, but a more

49

restrained hand is called for here, where they are very expensive. Don't be tempted to buy them in bulk to save money, however, since when exposed to the air they rapidly go stale and acquire an unpleasant chemical taste. Store them in the freezer in zip-lock bags. Pine nuts, or pine kernels as they are sometimes known, are essential in a number of classic Mediterranean dishes, notably that linchpin of Italian cuisine, pesto sauce.

### Piri-piri

These are very hot small red **chillies** from the former Portuguese colony of Angola. *Molho de piri-piri*, piri-piri sauce and the Portuguese equivalent of Tabasco, is found on every café and kitchen table in Portugal, where it is used liberally on everything from chips to green vegetables.

*Piri-piris* are closely related to the Mexican *chili pequin*, which in Brazil was renamed the *malaguéta*. This was taken by the Portuguese colonials across to Angola, where it acquired its African name, and from there back home to Portugal.

### Plantain

A type of banana which is sold unripe (green) and ripe (black). It must be cooked, usually by baking, grilling or deep-frying, and is central to much of the cooking of Africa and the West Indies.

### Pluck

The generic term for the lungs, heart, liver and connecting tubes and bits of a sheep. These form the principal ingredient of **haggis**.

### Pochouse

Elsewhere in France this Burgundian stew of mixed freshwater fish and eels is called a *matelote*.

### Poêlé

This is another term for the cooking technique of pot-roasting or *soffrito*, by which a relatively tender piece of meat, poultry or game is cooked slowly in a covered heavy pot with very little liquid. The bottom of the pot is first covered with chopped vegetables like onions, carrot, garlic and celery and the seasoned meat placed on top of it. A few spoonfuls of wine or stock are poured over, a lump of butter or some olive oil added, and the covered pot put into a low oven and cooked for a long period, during which the meat is basted at regular intervals.

### Poolish

A natural **yeast** batter used for baking bread, poolish is more liquid than a **levain** but does the same job.

### Poppadum, see Pappadum

### Porcini

Porcini, or ceps, are the most widely used wild mushrooms in Italian cooking and are universally available dried, in which state they acquire a unique depth of flavour, so much so that they are valued more highly than fresh, playing an important and distinctive role in Italian cuisine.

### Pot-au-feu

This is a classic French country dish of beef, chicken and ham poached in the same pot. The broth is served first as a soup, the meats afterwards with boiled root vegetables.

### Pousse-café

A term for a spirit taken as a **digestif** with a strong black coffee after dinner.

### Poussin

The poussin is a baby chicken killed at 4 weeks. Euphemistically called 'spring chickens', virtually all are **battery-farmed** and are fairly tasteless.

### Preserved Lemons

These lemons, pickled in a strong **brine**, feature widely in North-African cooking.

### Printanière

Literally 'of the spring' (*printemps*), printanière is a me **garnish** of turned carrots and baby turnips, peas and fine chopped green beans. It is often served with new seaso lamb.

### Profiterole

This is a small choux pastry bun (see Chocolate Éclairs, page 280), usually filled with pastry cream or whipped cream.

### Prosciutto, see Italian Cured Meats and Sausages

### Prosecco

A dry sparkling wine produced around Trieste in north-east Italy, most famously used with peach nectar in a **Bellini** cocktail.

# Q

### Quadrillage, see Grill Pan

### Quatre-épices

Quatre-épices is the mixture of white pepper, nutmeg, cloves and cinnamon or ginger which is widely used in classic French charcuterie, a word which properly describes prepared and cooked pork products. The spice mix is also used in soups, stews and vegetable dishes. The precise ratio of the spices depends on personal preference, but pepper should always predominate.

Make it yourself by mixing 55 g / 2 oz white peppercorns, 15 g / ½ oz nutmeg, 8 g / ¼ oz cloves and 15 g / ½ oz ground ginger. Put the peppercorns, nutmeg and cloves into a coffee grinder and pulverize to a fine powder. Mix in the ginger and store the mixture in a screw-top jar, giving it a shake. After 3 months it will deteriorate and lose pungency.

### Quenelle

A light **forcemeat** dumpling, usually of fish, eggs and cream. The classic French *quenelle de brochet* is made from pike, the best way to treat this bony, muddy-tasting fish.

### Quinoa

A South American relative of spinach, quinoa originated in the Peruvian Andes. It is eaten both as a high-protein savoury grain, rather like cracked wheat and, when grown on, as a leaf vegetable. Until recently the grain was sold mainly through health-food shops, but is now acquiring a wider and more fashionable popularity. It is generally cooked like rice.

# R

### Ragout

The term for a rich meat stew, but also implying a dish which started its life as a sauté and is finished with a sauce that is often thickened with cream.

### Ragu

An Italian meat or tomato sauce, served with pasta.

### Raising Agents

Bicarbonate of soda and baking powder (which contains bicarbonate of soda) are chemicals that generate carbon dioxide to raise flour batters during baking. They were first used in the last century as raising agents for flour with low gluten levels, which is more suitable for cake-making than strong flour, the high-gluten type used for baking breads. Chemical raising agents only generate gas briefly, which is why they are unsuitable for the extended raising required for a high-gluten dough, gluten being the protein element in wheat that gives a dough its essential plasticity and elasticity, and which makes bread texturally different from cake.

When bicarbonate of soda, an alkali, is mixed with an acid, a chemical reaction occurs and carbon dioxide is generated. Bicarbonate of soda can therefore only be used on its own to lift a dough or batter if a suitable natural acid is present. This may be in the form of lactic acid, contained in yoghurt and buttermilk, or citric acid or vinegar.

Baking powder is a complete raising agent, a mixture of bicarbonate of soda and acid salts with ground dry starch, the last added to absorb moisture from the atmosphere and so prevent premature chemical reactions in the tin in humid conditions. Baking powder is described as 'double-acting' because it contains two different types of water-soluble salt crystals which are activated sequentially. The first, typically cream of tartar or monocalcium phosphate, reacts with water in the batter at room temperature and initiates the chemical reaction with the bicarbonate of soda, immediately giving off little bubbles of carbon dioxide. A second acid salt crystal, usually sodium aluminium sulphate, activates only at high temperature, generating a larger amount of carbon dioxide in the oven. The moist solids cook, dry out and firm around the gas bubbles, before the short-lived gas generation stops, producing a light yet moist texture. Self-raising flour already has baking powder mixed into it. See also Yeast.

### Raita

This is a yoghurt-based relish, often containing mint, served as a cold and refreshing counterpoint to hot curries.

### Ramen, see Lo Mein

### Reduction

This is the process whereby the flavour of a cooking liquid is intensified by boiling it rapidly to concentrate it by driving off water. A reduction is thus, in one sense, a simple sauce or gravy.

### Rennet

Rennet is not only used in junket puddings but also in most cheese-making. It is extracted from the fourth stomach of ruminants, usually calves, by soaking. How man discovered, thousands of years ago, the coagulating properties of this gastric extract is one of those charming mysteries that makes the history of food so fascinating. Goats' milk would have been carried in bags made from the stomachs of slaughtered animals. Residual gastric enzymes in the skin curdled the milk – ergo, primitive cheese.

The substance in rennet which causes milk molecules to hold together, turning them from a liquid to a solid, is the enzyme rennin. Fortunately you do not have to soak the stomach of a goat or cow yourself, but can buy it in powdered form from any supermarket. It is powerful stuff and only a small amount is needed to set quite a large quantity of milk. Just add to blood-warm milk, following the packet instructions, stir in and refrigerate. Junket will result.

### Repère

Some recipes call for a pan or pot with a very tight-fitting lid to prevent loss of moisture. To ensure a complete seal, a stiff flour-and-water mixture, *repère* or luting paste in English, is used to make the join between lid and edge airtight. Make it in a proportion of 125 g / $4\frac{1}{2}$ oz flour to $3\frac{1}{2}$ tablespoons water. It is thrown away after the dish is finished.

### Rice

There are many different kinds of rice. The most common in British shops is American long-grain, a generic description of husked white rice which cooks to a dry, fluffy finish with separate firm grains and is suitable to eat plain boiled with a curry or stew. Basmati rice is also long-grain, but comes from northern India and because it is aged has a finer flavour. Brown rice is unmilled, the brown husk of the grain giving its name.

If bought by weight from Asian grocers, rice needs to be picked over for small stones and washed before use. The easiest way to do this is in a sieve under cold running water. Japanese rice is a round-grained rice that should also be washed in the same way, as should glutinous rice. These both cook to a sticky finish.

Risotto rice from Italy, such as arborio, carnaroli or fresco baldo, is shaped somewhere between long-grain and glutinous and has the unique characteristic of slowly absorbing liquid while retaining discernible grains in the finished dish, a combination of silky smoothness with a residual bite.

Different types of rice demand different cooking techniques. Let's start with long-grain, white unhusked rice, the sort you would expect to eat with an Indian curry. You have a choice. Either cook it in masses of rapidly boiling salted water and start tasting after 8 minutes and thereafter every 30 seconds until done to your liking, before draining immediately and fluffing with a fork, or follow the packet instructions exactly. This usually involves precise measuring and cooking in a pan with a lid on. Other kinds of rice are usually cooked in this way and, if you eat a lot of rice, buying a rice cooker is a sound investment. They cost about £35 and have the added benefit of freeing up a burner on the hob. Cooking risotto is a different technique altogether, demanding specific types of rice, and is described on page 218.

### Rice Vinegars

Important in both Chinese and Japanese cooking, these are mild-flavoured and available in both light-, yellowish- and darker-coloured forms like the much admired Chinkiang Black Vinegar. They are used as flavourings in stir-fries and braises.

### Rice Wine

This features prominently in both Chinese and Japanese cooking and is available in dry and sweet forms, the Japanese wines being **sake** (dry) and **mirin** (sweet). Mirin is used only for cooking. Shaoshing, Chinese rice wine, is used extensively in that country's cooking.

### Rocket, rucola, arugula

Currently enjoying fashionable attention as a salad leaf, rocket is mentioned in Elizabethan gardening and cookery books at a time when all salads were classified as herbs and grown in herb gardens. This historic definition seems to have confused major food outlets who sell rocket in 55-g / 2-oz packs alongside the mint, rosemary and basil. This must astonish French and Italian cooks who understand that a generous hand is called for when using rocket and who, if their shops tried to charge British prices for it, would go on the rampage. If you have a vegetable garden, then grow it yourself. It crops readily and abundantly in four-week cycles, though it is easily damaged by rain as it nears the time when it is ready for picking. Rocket – also called *roquette* in France and *arugula* and *rucola* in Italy – has a lovely, peppery flavour reminiscent of watercress.

### Romaine

The American term for Cos lettuce.

### Roux

Flour and butter cooked together and used as the thickening base for a sauce such as béchamel. Also, one of two famous French chef brothers.

# S

### Saffron

Saffron is the ultimate spice, for it takes up to 300,000 crocus blooms to produce one kilogram of the tiny vermilion-red dried stigma in a process virtually unchanged from that first recorded in Mesopotamia more than 4,000 years ago. The largest producer of saffron in the world today is Northern India, but the best indisputably comes from Spain, where it has been grown since the Arabs first planted the crocus there the 11th century.

Saffron was most highly prized during the Middle Ages, when spices were important enough to motivate global exploration and even war. Saffron was then also produced in England – Saffron Walden in Essex takes its name from the local industry – France, Germany and Italy, but as tastes changed it became less popular and by the 18th century Spain alone in Europe continued to produce saffron on a significant scale.

Spanish production today is smaller than it used to be and takes place exclusively in La Mancha in Southern Castille, where the same families have been repeating the labour-intensive rituals of the autumn crocus harvest without variation for hundreds of years. This takes place in a week-long window that opens briefly as October slips into November. The flowers are picked early in the morning, before the day becomes too hot, their petals removed and the stigmas extracted, before being dried the same day in drum sieves over gas heaters. The harvest concludes with the crocus bulbs being dug up and stored to be replanted the following year in a four-year cycle. After that they are no longer deemed productive, while the fields have to be rested for as long as 10 years before they can be used to grow crocuses again. It is therefore scarcely surprising that the families can sell their saffron for up to £650 a kilo wholesale.

True saffron is uniquely the dried stigma of *Crocus sativus* and its quality is judged by the length of the stigma, the level of red pigment (*crocina*), the intensity of flavour (*picrocrocina*) and the strength of aroma (*safranal*). Once assessed subjectively by eye and nose, today's saffron is analysed scientifically by photospectrometry. Finally, the batches from single producers are graded by the percentage of bright red stigma into Mancha Selecto, the best, Rio and Sierra. Coupé, a premium grade, is made from Mancha Selecto, with any white or yellow strands removed. The high price of saffron means that it has been fraudulently imitated since Roman times, with many substitutes being sold in its name, including marigold, turmeric and sunflower.

Saffron is valued both for its intense aromatic flavour and its ability to colour things a beautiful glowing yellow. Its culinary uses are varied, and risotto Milanese, bouillabaisse and paella could not be made authentically without it.

When buying saffron you have a choice between powdered and thread. More than 70 per cent of all Spanish saffron is exported as powder, which is still regarded as inferior to the more expensive thread, though improved quality control means that a more accurate judgement can be made by reading the guarantees on the packet. If you don't have a spectrometer in your shopping basket, the only way you can be sure that it is genuine saffron is by smell and taste, so when buying a brand with which you are not familiar, initially purchase a small amount. Be suspicious if what you are offered is very cheap.

In the kitchen, saffron should be stored in an airtight and lightproof tin or box, damp and light causing rapid deterioration. Saffron also needs to be treated carefully when it is cooked since high temperatures destroy the full intensity of its smell and flavour, both of which show to best effect against a fairly bland backdrop like rice, potatoes, pasta or yeast doughs. If using threads of saffron, they need first to be soaked in warm liquid, like stock or wine, and left to infuse for 15–20 minutes.

Recipes are usually unhelpful about how much to use, but this is very much dependent on its quality. A risotto for four using 350 g / 12 oz of rice will need about 20 threads, perhaps as many as 30. These should be added during the last 5 minutes of cooking with the soaking liquid. References to a pinch of saffron usually mean 12–15 threads.

### Sake

Japanese **rice wine**, with a complex flavour that is somewhat similar to dry sherry, is traditionally drunk warm, but the current fashion is to serve it chilled like white wine. Sake is also widely used in Japanese cooking, particularly in sauces and marinades.

### Salami, see Italian Cured Meats and Sausages

### Salsa

A salsa – properly salsa Mexicana – is a raw sauce based on chopped ripe tomatoes flavoured with finely chopped onion, **chillies**, garlic and, usually, coriander. Variations on this theme are served on most Mexican tables as a standard accompaniment to tacos and snacks. Sharp-tasting green salsas based on **tomatillos** are also common.

### Salt Cod

Called *baccalà* in Italian, *bacalao* in Spanish, *bacalhau* in Portuguese and *morue* in French, dried salt cod is an ancient culinary institution. The first known written reference to it was in eleventh-century Holland, which suggests it had been around for a long time prior to that. It has been an important ingredient in Mediterranean cooking since the latter part of the fifteenth century, when the Portuguese and Spanish were first fishing on a large scale for cod over Newfoundland's Great Banks, salting it heavily for preservation during the long voyage home.

Once dried in the sun, the fish sets hard as wood and needs lengthy desalination in cold water before it can be eaten, but when adequately soaked it is not remotely salty. Salt cod is employed in numerous recipes in many cuisines, but perhaps the best known internationally is the French purée, *brandade de morue*.

Spain and Portugal have more than 300 ways of cooking salt cod including *bacalao al pil pil*, a Basque treatment which simmers it in lots of olive oil with parsley, and *bacalhau à Gomes de Sa*, stewed with onions and potatoes, Portugal's best-known dish and named after an Oporto restaurateur.

### Saltpetre

Saltpetre is an old name for potassium nitrate, $KNO_3$, one of the ingredients in improvised explosive devices. It has been valued for hundreds of years for its preservative impact. In reality, the colouring element is the closely related nitrite – $KNO_2$ – a fact that was discovered only in this century. It is actually the nitrite which turns meat pink, and it is this rosy colour which understandably affects our perceptions of the food. Would ham be as nice if it was grey? However, nitrite also plays an important role in limiting the growth of the bacteria which cause food poisoning, most notably *clostridium botulinum*, responsible for botulism which, while fortunately rare in these days of refrigeration, can be fatal.

There has been some discussion in recent times about the possibility that nitrate and nitrite are carcinogens, but the tiny concentrations needed to impart colour and flavour rather than preservation are unlikely to be significant increasing the risk of cancer.

If you find it difficult to buy saltpetre, then explain to your chemist that you are not a bomb maker and you are really looking for pure nitrite which he can supply in liquid form. Butchers can buy nitrite in tablet form and will happily sell these on to you, with instructions on how many you need to use.

### Sambal
A fiery Southeast Asian **chilli** relish or any dish cooked with a chilli paste.

### Sansho Pepper
A Japanese seasoning, closely related to **Szechuan pepper** and often also confusingly called Japanese pepper, sansho is not really pepper at all but the ground aromatic husk of the prickly ash seed.

### Sashimi
Japanese raw fish, always served with **wasabi** and a dipping sauce.

### Satsuma, see Mandarin Orange

### Schnitzel, see Paillard

### Screwpine, see Pandan Leaf

### Seal, Set or Sear
All three of these terms mean setting cut meat surfaces in a very hot pan to brown and crisp them. See also **Caramelization**.

### Sechuan Pepper, see Szechuan Pepper

### Sesame Oil
The powerfully flavoured extract of sesame seeds is available in two forms: pale milder-flavoured sesame oil is used in Middle Eastern cooking, while dark full-flavoured Oriental sesame oil is made from toasted seeds and is generally used at the last minute to dress many stir-fried dishes. Use both types of the oil with caution as their potent flavour can swamp a dish.

### Sesame Seeds
Sesame seeds have a nutty flavour and are high in protein and calcium. They are available as unhulled black seeds, unhulled brown seeds and hulled white polished seeds. Their high oil content means they go rancid easily, so store in a screwtop jar in the fridge. They are used in baking and for dressing vegetable dishes or in coatings for fried food.

### Shichimi
This Japanese spice mixture includes ground **chilli** flakes, **sansho pepper**, **sesame seeds**, toasted **nori** and dried orange peel. It is used as an aromatic dressing for grilled foods.

### Shiitake
Also known as Chinese black mushrooms, these meaty cultivated fungi with a dark brown cap are widely available dried, and increasingly fresh may be seen in supermarkets. Both fresh and dried are widely used in Oriental dishes.

### Shoyu, see Soy Sauce

### Sichuan Pepper, see Szechuan Pepper

### Skirt
Generally, a thin cut piece of beef from the diaphragm, also called *onglet*, the so-called butcher's piece. In France this has long been popular briefly grilled and served very rare. Cooked any longer it goes tough and then demands long, slow simmering to deliver a tender result. Skirt also describes a thicker cut from the muscular tissue of the belly.

### Smoked Salmon
In Scotland, salmon have been preserved by salting and smoking since the 13th century, a process known to the native North American Indians of the North Eastern seaboard even earlier. Precisely when the lightly cured and cold-smoked fish that we now call smoked salmon was first produced is not clear, though it was probably as recently as 100 years ago. These would have been fish prepared specially for people who had caught them by rod, a service that some smokers still provide.

The quality and price of what you buy varies enormously, wild smoked salmon being much more expensive than farmed. You can buy both as whole sides to slice yourself or in good delicatessens you can have any amount sliced to order. However, most is bought ready-sliced and vacuum-packed. You can pay anything from £10 a pound to £18 a pound and what value this represents will be as much to do with your personal taste as any objective criteria that may be applied. How long the fish is cured, whether the cure includes ingredients other than salt, like sugar or rum, and the type of wood used to burn for the smoke will all affect the way it tastes.

All salmon smokers now use farmed salmon, the quality of which varies enormously, and you have to look closely at the packs to make sure that what you are buying is the real thing, because there is a lot of imported low-grade Norwegian salmon being passed off as Scotch. To be absolutely sure, only buy packets which have the gold quality mark of the Scottish Salmon Smokers' Association.

### Snail

Making snails edible is not easy. The process begins with the starving of the snails for 7 to 10 days until they have been purged of anything toxic they may have eaten. This is done in a box with holes which give them air and through which water can be poured at intervals to keep them moist. For the final two days the condemned snails eat a hearty meal of flour to plump them up. They are then soaked and tossed in sea salt to draw out any sticky unpleasantness, before their execution in a boiling vat of water flavoured with a sharp white wine or wine vinegar, bay leaves, salt, peppercorns and thyme or rosemary, in which they are left to simmer for two hours. They then have to be drawn from their shells and have their stomach sacs removed.

### Soba

These Japanese buckwheat noodles are sold both fresh and dried.

### Somen

This type of Japanese thin dried wheat noodle is often used in soups or served cold in summer.

### Sourdough

A description of a bread raised with a **levain**, a starter dough colonized by natural airborne yeasts. The lengthy fermentation of the starter dough imparts a distinct sour flavour to the bread baked using it as a raising agent rather than cultured brewer's sugar fungus (see **Yeast**), the standard baker's leavening. The name sourdough was first used by miners during the San Francisco gold rushes, which is why some bakers call sourdough loaves 'San Francisco style'.

### Soursop

A spiny dark-skinned fruit from South America with a delicate and slightly sour flesh, the soursop is also known as the guanabana or prickly custard apple. Available canned, it is mostly used in ice-creams and drinks.

### Soy Sauce

This fermented soy bean product is made throughout Southeast Asia and is available in a huge variety, both dark and light, and varying in thickness, saltiness and sweetness, qualities which can only be judged by tasting. The best Japanese soy sauce is Kikkoman, which includes fermented wheat and is thin, dark and salty; it should be used in all dishes with Japanese antecedents. Pearl River is one of the best Chinese soy sauces; it is an excellent dark, full-flavoured sauce. *Kecap* or *ketjap manis* is a thick Indonesian soy sauce sweetened with palm sugar; A.B.C. is a good brand. *Kecap manis* is different from *kecap masin*, also called black sauce, which is salty and not at all sweet.

### Soya Milk

This thick liquid by-product of soaking, grinding and straining dried soya beans is used in drinks and puddings, particularly in countries that do not eat dairy products. It is now widely available in the West.

### Speck, see Italian Cured Meats and Sausages

### Spices

People imagine that dried spices keep indefinitely. Not true. There is nothing more sinister in a kitchen than one of thos dusty wooden racks with little bottles of colourless flake strapped to the wall, because it screams 'old and stale, and completely missing the point'. Indeed, as spices are best stored away from light and heat, nothing could be worse for them. When you do an audit of your spice store, be particularly ruthless with ground spices as these rapidly lose their potency and the sooner you use them the better, so throw away anything in small opened containers that is more than six months old, and really three months is a better deadline (particularly in the case of ready-ground spices).

Many people on holiday in hot countries buy jars of spices as presents to bring home. These gifts are dubious and should be looked at carefully before use. Reports of insect infestation are common, while that rare present of saffron often turns out to be nothing more special than turmeric.

Freeze-dried spices are better than those dried by basic exposure to heat and air, and many dried spices benefit from being kept in the freezer. Buy only small amounts at a time, choosing whole rather than ground spices and grinding exactly the amount you need fresh for each application. Do this in a coffee grinder or a liquidizer with a grinder attachment (make sure you clean it properly afterwards if you don't want spiced coffee).

Curry spices, including **coriander**, cumin and mustard seeds, benefit from a brief roasting in a dry heavy pan over a low flame before grinding.

### Squab

Since the Middle Ages these grain-fed, ring-necked doves have been kept in dovecotes and have a much better flavour than ordinary pigeons. Unlike wild pigeons, they have a high meat-to-bone ratio and are much more tender and flavourful.

### Squid Ink

The natural black dye found in the ink sacs of squid is now available in small sachets. It is very effective in risotti or pasta, but through processing has lost all flavour, so always use it in sauces in combination with a well-flavoured fish or shellfish stock. It is not as strong a dye as the cuttlefish ink favoured in Italy.

### Star Anise

This intensely scented woody anise-tasting seed pod held in a star-shaped cluster is much used in Chinese cooking and an essential element in **five-spice powder**. It is also currently very fashionable in Western cooking.

### Star Fruit, see Carambola

### Stilton

Stilton is a British cheese tradition, forever linked in the public mind with port and walnuts on the table and, for many, the best moment of a Christmas dinner. It is produced all year round, with manufacture in Leicestershire, Derbyshire and Nottinghamshire centred on Melton Mowbray. Stilton has never been made in Stilton, which is in Huntingdonshire, the connection coming from its early supply to the town's Bell Inn from a cheese-maker at Quemby Hall in Leicestershire.

A good Stilton is a rich unpressed cows'-milk cheese, ivory in colour and marbled with blue veins which are caused by penicillin bacteria. Its rind is brown and slightly wrinkled, and may have white patches (you can also buy white Stilton). When young, the cheese is relatively mild, becoming more forceful with age, a mature, strong-tasting mouthful, complex and tangy on the tongue and fully justifying Stilton's proud claim to be the 'king of English cheeses'.

The production process of the best Stilton is labour-intensive, with much of the work still being done by hand. Chris Morley of the Cropwell Bishop Creamery, one of Stilton's main producers still using traditional methods, says that the time from milk coming into the dairy to completed cheese ready for sale is a minimum of 10 weeks. Cheeses are turned daily for the first week, in what is called a 'hastening room', before being 'rubbed up on the coat with a knife' which helps the crust develop. Penicillin, a mould, is added to the milk at the start of the process and develops the blue veining only after 4–6 weeks, when the cheeses have been transferred to a maturing room and pierced. They continue to be turned 3 times a week. Maturity is assessed by pushing a cheese iron into the cheeses and pulling out a plug, which the expert then judges by texture, smell and sight.

After all this it is hardly surprising to find that Stilton is expensive. A whole cheese, or truckle, weighs 7–8 kg / 16–18 lb and, bought direct from the producer, will set you back some £60, including post and packing. Half-truckles are also standard and Stilton is sold in pieces as small as 225 g / 8 oz and also in stoneware jars of varying sizes. Harrods, for example, prices its 550-g / 1¼-lb pack at £14.95 and sells a 1-kg / 2¼-lb 'whole baby Stilton' for £32. It is probably best to buy the amount you want cut from a whole cheese. Keep it in a cool place, wrapped in slightly moistened cloth – a tea towel will do. It can be kept in the fridge, but allow it to come up to room temperature before serving.

### Succotash

A dish from the southern states of the USA, succotash is a sauté of corn and broad beans (called lima beans locally) and derives its name from a Native American word.

### Sugar Snap Pea

This sweet-tasting vegetable is like a cross between the garden pea and the **mangetout**. Like the latter, the whole thing may be eaten, pod and all. Treat it like the mangetout.

### Sushi

Bite-size rolls of Japanese vinegared rice wrapped in **nori**, which may or may not include raw fish.

### Sweating

The gentle frying of vegetables, like onions, as a preliminary cooking step to soften and develop flavour without browning.

### Sweet Potato

With its distinctive dense and sweet orange flesh, tasting rather like chestnuts, this elongated tuber is unrelated to the potato. Sweet potatoes are, however, cooked in all the same ways, as well as featuring in sweet dishes like pies and tarts. The darker-skinned varieties of sweet potato are often erroneously called **yams**.

### Szechuan, Schezuan or Sichuan Pepper

Also known variously as Chinese, Japanese or anise pepper, or fagara, this highly aromatic spice from Northern China is not related to pepper, but is the berry of a small shrub, *Xanthoxylum pipesitum*. It needs to be dry-roasted before grinding and is also used whole as an aromatic stock ingredient. It is one of the constituents of **five-spice powder**. See also **Sansho**.

# T

### Taco

A description which covers a wide variety of filled corn tortillas, but not necessarily the deep-fried shell of Tex-Mex cooking.

### Tahini

Tahini is a paste of ground **sesame seeds**, and its strong flavour is what gives hummus – chickpea purée – its distinctive nutty taste. Tahini is easy to make in a food processor. The sort of seeds you want are the white hulled ones available in any supermarket. Put 115 g / 4 oz sesame seeds in a dry heavy frying pan over a low-to-medium heat and toast, shaking and stirring. If the heat is too high they will burn and pop, shooting about the kitchen in an alarming manner, so keep it down. As they brown they will give off a discernible aroma. Continue cooking until they are a uniform golden colour, then transfer to a food processor. Blitz to a paste, adding cold water through the feeder tube a tablespoon at a time, until you have a moist spoonable texture. This should take about 100 ml / 3½ fl oz of water. Use immediately or keep in the fridge for 7–10 days in a sterilized screw-top jar. After that time it will start to go rancid.

### Tajine or Tagine
This term describes both the spicy North-African poultry, meat, fish or vegetable stew and the round earthenware dish, with its characteristic tall conical lid, in which it is cooked.

### Tamarind
Although the name comes from the Arabic for 'Indian dates', tamarinds are not dates, but pods. They have a sour taste and are used extensively in Indian and Southeast Asian cooking. You find it in Oriental and Asian grocers, peeled and seeded in packets. Always bend and press the packets to make sure it is pliant; if it has gone hard then it has dried out and you will not be able to extract much pulp. To do so, break 450 g / 1 lb of it off in lumps, put these into a bowl and pour over 1 litre / 1¾ pints of boiling water, then leave to steep overnight. Strain through a sieve, working as much of the pulp through as you can with a wooden spoon. This extract is the tamarind water that is used in cooking, the leftover solids being discarded. Put the liquid pulp into ice-cube trays and freeze, transferring the cubes to a zip-lock bag so you will always have tamarind pulp to hand when you need it. You can now also buy liquid tamarind extract, which is simply thinned with hot water in a ratio of about 10 to 1.

### Tangerine, see Mandarin Orange

### Tapas
Literally Spanish for 'lids', *tapas* describes a vast range of small savoury snacks that are eaten with drinks, particularly sherry or wine. The name comes from the pieces of bread originally put on top of glasses of wine to keep the flies off.

### Tapenade
There is no one recipe for this Provençal speciality, an intensely flavoured and finely chopped paste consisting predominantly of ripe black olives, capers, garlic and – optionally – anchovies and basil. It may also contain lemon

juice or wine vinegar. The name comes from *tapeno*, the old Provençal word for capers. Tapenade may be used to dress grilled fish or eaten with a selection of raw vegetables crudités or with hard-boiled eggs and toast.

### Tempeh
Available from Asian markets, tempeh is an Indonesian variant of **beancurd** (tofu) which is also used in Malaysia and Singapore. It is rich in protein and forms an edible mould on the surface. It is sold fresh in slabs and deteriorates if frozen. Find out which day it is delivered and then buy that day.

### Tempura
A Japanese dish of food, usually vegetables or seafood, deep-fried in a light batter. The cooking method is thought to have been introduced to Japan by the Portuguese in the 17th century.

### Teriyaki
Japanese grilled fish or meat which has first been marinated in a mixture of **soy sauce**, **sake**, sugar and ginger juice. The marinade is reduced by rapid boiling and then poured over the food just prior to serving.

### Terrine, see Pâté

### Thai Basil, see Holy Basil

### Thai Celery, see Ceun Chai

### Thali
The round tray on which Indian food is presented to each diner, the food being served in metal bowls called *katori* which are placed on it.

### Timbale
This term is used to describe both moulded food (usually custards, **forcemeats** or rice) cooked in, for example, a dariole mould or basin, and the mould itself.

### Tofu, see Beancurd

## Tomatillo

At the time of writing, Mexican tomatillos, also called *tomate verde*, are not generally available here, though the speed with which our global larder now responds to demand suggests that this currently fashionable Californian alternative to green tomatoes will soon be brightening our supermarket fruit and vegetable sections.

The tomatillo is a green fruit covered by a brown, papery husk or calyx which is removed and discarded before use. Although it looks like an unripe tomato the tomatillo is, in fact, a relative of the Cape gooseberry and its flavour has a distinct lemon note and a sharp taste. Since the flesh is harder than that of a tomato, the tomatillo is usually cooked before eating, though they are frequently used raw in **salsas** either instead of tomatoes or in combination with them. Substitute green tomatoes when you can't buy the real thing.

## Truffle

All truffles are fungi with similarities to wild mushrooms, that is living plants which, being devoid of chlorophyll, derive nutrients from other organic matter. They are subterranean, growing just beneath the ground, and mostly exist in symbiosis with trees, helping their hosts to assimilate phosphorus while in return taking sugars from the tree roots. There are more than 30 truffle species, of which the most sought after and expensive is *Tuber magnatum*, the white truffle. After a dry summer, like that of 1997, the price can reach £2,000 a kilo. They are principally found in Piedmont, where they usually grow near the bases of willows and poplars and are sniffed out by specially trained dogs. *Bene, Fido!*

The white truffle is not so much white as a pale yellowish grey. It is in season only from the middle of September to the beginning of December. The first time you smell a white truffle when you open the airtight container in which it must be kept, both to reduce flavour loss and to prevent contamination of nearby foods, the experience is extraordinary, beyond anything your olfactory senses have ever experienced. There are no analogous scents that make it possible to describe meaningfully the unique aroma, for it can be offensive and overpowering as well as delightful in the same way a ripe unpasteurized Camembert in the wrong context can give off a smell open to unattractive interpretation. The taste, for the truffle connoisseur, however, is quite sublime.

White truffles are never cooked, but are shaved raw over pasta, polenta, risotti, scrambled eggs or potatoes, all of which provide a suitably delicate backdrop to the truffle's complex delivery. There are special truffle slicers, but you can achieve the same result by using the largest slicer on a box grater or a mandolin.

The black Périgord truffle, *T. melanosporum*, is probably what most people mean when they refer to truffles. It is more widely distributed than the white truffle, being found in south-eastern and south-western France, in the Pyrénées and in Spain and Italy. Although called a Périgord truffle in France, the majority are gathered in Provence, where they are referred to as *rabasses*. Black truffles are in season between the first and last frosts, which means roughly from mid-November to the end of February. Truffles gathered before mid-December are inferior, pale in colour and lacking in flavour.

The French tradition of eating truffles at Christmas means that they are at their most expensive during the holidays, though black truffles will not be at their best until mid-January, a prime condition that lasts about four weeks. From then, deterioration continues until the end of April, which is generally conceded to be the end of the truffle year. Black truffles feature in many classic dishes, especially pâtés, and are usually cooked, but may also be added raw to things like scrambled eggs. They are not as expensive as white truffles but at around £300 a kilo will always be a luxury.

Other truffles include the Burgundy truffle, *T. uncinatum*, less strongly scented than *T. melanosporum*, and the widely distributed summer black truffle, *T. aestivum*, which is occasionally found in Kent and other southern English counties.

## Truffled Olive Oil

Truffled oil is very expensive, at around £16 per 250 ml / 8 fl oz, but a little goes a long way. It is by far and away the most successful flavoured oil, for the taste of white truffle shines through strongly without any sense of this being ersatz. It became very much the thing in the mid-'80s dribbled over **carpaccio** with some **rocket** and shaved Parmesan. Be circumspect when you use it as it is so dominant a heavy hand will soon turn nice into nasty.

### Turned Vegetables

An affectation of the professional kitchen, in which peeled vegetables are shaped into uniformly sized barrels for a formal presentation of a dish.

## U

### Udon

Thick Japanese wheat noodles.

### Ugli Fruit

A hybrid fruit, developed in the West Indies in the 1930s, which combines the sweet juiciness of a **tangerine** with the size of a grapefruit. It has an odd, slightly crumpled appearance, hence – presumably – the name.

### Umeboshi Plum

These dried sour salt-pickled plums are actually eaten by the Japanese with their breakfast, a cultural shock for *geijin* who use them mostly as a condiment.

## V

### Vanilla

Vanilla pods, also called beans, are the fruit of a flowering climbing vine originally found in Central America but now mostly cultivated on islands off the East Coast of Africa. Unripe they have no flavour, but after lengthy exposure to sunshine, followed by slow drying over a period of months, they develop their characteristic taste and aroma. Most of the 1,500 tonnes produced each year goes into commercially manufactured ice-cream, the rest being used by cooks to impart its unique and subtle flavour by exposing them to heated liquid.

For maximum impact you need to cut the pod open so that the tiny seeds it contains are in direct contact with the liquid, for it is the seeds that contain vanillin, the flavour agent, but only at a concentration of 2 per cent. The pod can be dried and stored in sugar after use, and over time it flavours the sugar.

When buying liquid vanilla you can choose between vanilla essence, which is extracted from the seeds in a process using alcohol and water, costing about 90p for ml, or the much cheaper vanilla flavouring that is made from artificially formulated chemical vanillin and costs 32p. Purists will always go for the beans, but it should be pointed out that these are not cheap – vanilla pods are the second most expensive spice after saffron. As Peter Tiwari, technical manager of Rayner & Co – one of Britain's largest producers of culinary essences – says, the cook does not have the same degree of control on the flavour impact as when using drops of essence. 'You will have connoisseurs who can distinguish between the use of pods and essence in a dish, but for most people essence delivers an excellent result for a very reasonable price.' With one vanilla pod costing more than a pound his argument is convincing.

### Variety Meats, see Fancy Meats

### Verjuice

Verjuice, in its original medieval French *vertjus*, literally 'green juice', was first made from sorrel juice and then from unripe plums. From the sixteenth century it has been made from crushed and strained unripe grapes and has been an inexpensive culinary by-product of wine-growing areas ever since. It remains a neat way of using up grapes in cold wet summers, when they do not ripen sufficiently to make good wine; although it can just as well be made from the sediment left over after the young wine is first racked.

Verjuice is used mostly as a mild alternative to vinegar in salad dressings, but makes an interesting alternative cooking medium to wine. It can also be mixed with coarsely ground mustard seed and sugar to make a Meaux-type mustard. At his Sussex vineyard near Hastings, David Carr Taylor is Britain's only verjuice producer. He started bottling and selling it four years ago after reading about its historic place in English cooking, as something first made from the medieval vin gris used as sacramental wine.

His verjuice is not acidic like vinegar, having a sherry-like quality with a relatively high alcohol content of 10.5 per cent. This makes it an effective carrier of flavours like herbs, garlic and lemon juice, and a good marinade for oily fish.

### Vert-pré

A **garnish** of straw potatoes, watercress and steamed baby carrots, usually served with grilled meat dishes.

## W

### Wakami

A dried seaweed that is reconstituted in warm water before being eaten as a salad.

### Wasabi

A Japanese dried powdered hot radish which is dyed green. Its taste is rather like the strongest and hottest horseradish you could imagine. It is traditionally served with **sashimi** and **sushi**.

### Won Ton Wrappers

This term describes both the thin square sheets of Chinese pasta that are filled to make dumplings, and the dumplings themselves, perhaps best known in the form of pork dumplings in broth – won ton soup. Won ton wrappers, or skins, are sold ready-made and fresh from chill cabinets in Chinese markets. They freeze well.

### Worcestershire Sauce

This is one of our oldest commercially produced sauces and a direct descendant of the earliest bottled sauces or **ketchups**. Worcestershire sauce is a thin dark liquid, the composition of which includes vinegar, molasses, sugar, salt, **tamarind**, shallots and garlic. Worcestershire sauce and **soy sauce** may look deceptively similar but they are certainly not interchangeable.

Our British sauce has conquered the world and no self-respecting barman from Hong Kong to Cape Town, from Helsinki to San Francisco, would dream of making a Bloody Mary without it. It also makes a brilliant marinade for any meat. For example, to be instantly converted to its charms try mixing it with equal amounts of lemon juice and marinating pork chops in it overnight.

## Y

### Yam

The edible tubers of the Dioscorea family, yams come in different shapes and sizes and may have either white or yellow flesh. They are cooked in the same way as **sweet potatoes**. In the southern USA, the term yam refers to the sweet potato.

### Yeast

Why yeast causes dough to rise remained a mystery for 6,000 years and was only understood 141 years ago, when its carbon-dioxide-generating effect was discovered by Louis Pasteur. Natural microscopic yeasts are fungi and are all around us in the air. When the type called brewer's sugar fungus or brewer's yeast settle in an appropriate environment, they give off carbon dioxide and cause fermentation, delivering a distinct flavour and – in liquid solutions of grape or grain – alcohol.

Brewer's yeast is the perfect raising agent for strong, high-gluten bread flours, because it generates gas slowly and over hours, or even days. This is trapped as bubbles by the unique elastic and plastic qualities of the gluten, causing the dough to rise and producing leavened (as opposed to unleavened) bread. Putting raised dough in a hot oven makes the gas bubbles expand further and the dough cooks around them, delivering light-textured loaves.

The first leavened breads were almost certainly raised accidentally by the colonization and action of airborne yeasts, until the Egyptians discovered that the froth produced on the top of beer during fermentation, when mixed into dough, caused it to rise. Beer froth, also called must, was still being used by bakers in the first half of the last century. Since then we have used cultured yeast and reconstituted dried yeast to do the job, although sourdough loaves are still proved using a starter dough or **levain** colonized by airborne yeasts. Levain gives bread a slightly sour taste from the lengthy fermentation, hence the name, sour dough. See also **Raising Agents**.

## Z

### Zabaglione

An Italian custard of egg yolks, sugar and Marsala whisked to a froth.

### Zampone

An Italian speciality consisting of a pig's trotter stuffed with a rich, fatty pork sausage mixture. It originates from Modena and is traditionally served poached and sliced with **lentils**.

See also **Italian Cured Meats and Sausages**.

# HOT AND COLD SOUPS

**M**any readers ask for recipes for specific soups which they have enjoyed at a restaurant and are often surprised by how easy it is to achieve delicious results. Once people realize how quick and simple the process is, they never look back, unless it is with astonishment at the fact they ever relied on tins or packets.

A good stock makes all the difference to the quality of a soup. A light chicken stock makes a good base for almost any soups and there is no strong argument for using a meat-based stock in any vegetable soup, with one or two honourable exceptions, like French onion soup.

Our soup subjects range from polished and elegant consommés to filling one-dish meals. One of the most frequently requested recipes is for Brown Windsor Soup, neither simple nor fashionable, but complex, robust and quaintly old-fashioned. Researching its origins was a lengthy business, for it is not included in any cookbook in print that we could find.

## CHILLED TOMATO AND BASIL SOUP

SERVES 6

1.15 kg / 2½ lb plum tomatoes
oil
1 tsp sugar
salt and pepper
150 ml / ¼ pt chicken or vegetable stock
150 ml / ¼ pt double cream
2 tbsp tomato ketchup
4 slices of white bread
2 garlic cloves
4 tbsp olive oil
20 basil leaves
extra-virgin olive oil, to serve

Allow the tomatoes to ripen for 4–5 days uncovered in a single layer on a tray in a warm room.

Then put them in a bowl, pour boil-ing water over them and leave for 3⟨ seconds. Refresh in cold water and skir⟨

Preheat the oven to 200°C/400°F gas 6. Cut 450 g / 1 lb of the tomatoe⟨ in half and put on an oiled bakir⟨ sheet. Sprinkle with the sugar and 1 te⟨ spoon of salt and bake for 30 minute⟨

*Opposite (clockwise from the top): Bors⟨ (page 67), Asparagus Soup (page 66), Car⟨ and Coriander Soup (page 68)*

Put the baked tomatoes in a blender or food processor with the remaining tomatoes and the stock. Blitz to a purée and push through a sieve into a bowl.

Stir in the cream and ketchup, then taste and season. Cling-wrap the bowl and refrigerate overnight.

Just before serving, cut the slices of white bread into 2-cm / ³⁄₄-inch cubes. Peel, smash and chop the garlic cloves and put them into a bowl with the olive oil and a little salt and pepper. Turn the bread cubes in this, then sauté in a hot non-stick frying pan until crisp.

Shred the basil leaves and stir half into the soup. Ladle it into bowls, scatter a few croutons on top of each with the remaining basil. Finish by drizzling some extra-virgin olive oil on the top.

## CHILLED CUCUMBER SOUP

SERVES 6–8

1 onion, diced
60 g / 2 oz butter
550 g / 1¼ lb cucumber, diced
1.75 litres / 3 pints light chicken
or vegetable stock
salt and pepper
handful of flat-leaved parsley,
chopped
juice of ½ lemon
600 ml / 1 pt single cream
handful of chives

In a heavy-based pan, sweat the onion in the butter until soft and translucent, then add the cucumber and continue to cook gently for 5 minutes.

Opposite (top to bottom): Caldo Verde (page 75), Mussel Soup with Saffron and Cream (page 73)

Pour in the stock, bring to the boil, lower the heat, season with salt and pepper and simmer for 5 minutes.

Add a handful of chopped flat-leaved parsley and the juice of half a lemon and continue to cook for a final 5 minutes.

Transfer to a blender or food processor and blitz to a purée, then pour into a bowl and, when cool, refrigerate. This can be done the day before.

To finish the soup, whisk in the single cream. Taste and adjust the seasoning. Serve with chives snipped over the top.

## GAZPACHO

Gazpacho benefits from being made the day before and refrigerated overnight to allow the flavours to develop. It should be served ice-cold and sometimes has ice put into it just before it is brought to the table. This is not really a good idea, however, since the melting ice melts thins the soup and makes it watery.

SERVES 4–6

2 slices of white bread, crusts
removed and torn into pieces
850 ml / 1½ pt tomato juice
6 ripe plum tomatoes
1 red onion
1 red pepper, roasted and
peeled
1 small cucumber
3 garlic cloves
1 tsp Tabasco sauce
1 tbsp sherry vinegar
salt and pepper
extra-virgin olive oil, to finish
torn basil leaves, to garnish

for the croutons:
3 tbsp olive oil
2 slices of white bread, crusts
removed and cut into 1-cm /
½-inch cubes

Put the bread in a large bowl and cover with the tomato juice.

Plunge the plum tomatoes in boiling water for 20–30 seconds, refresh in cold water and skin. Cut them in quarters, strip out and discard the pips and the pulp. Cut the tomatoes into 1-cm / ½-inch dice.

Cut the red onion across into 5-mm / ¼-inch slices. Dice the roasted red pepper flesh. Peel the skin from the cucumber in strips and cut these strips lengthwise into 1-cm / ½-inch slices, then cut these into strips and finally cut those strips into dice. Dice the flesh. Peel and chop the garlic cloves as finely as you can.

Stir all these together with the tomatoes into the contents of the bowl. Add the Tabasco sauce and sherry vinegar. Season with salt and pepper (generously, as it is to be chilled). Cling-wrap the top and refrigerate for 6 hours or overnight.

To make the croutons: season the olive oil and toss the cubes of bread in it, then fry them gently in a non-stick pan until they are nicely crisp and a good golden brown.

Ladle the chilled gazpacho into 4–6 soup bowls and zig-zag the tops with some extra-virgin olive oil. Scatter over the croutons and some torn basil leaves to garnish.

## ASPARAGUS SOUP

Now that jumbo jets whiz it in from all over the world, fresh asparagus is available all year round. Our own English asparagus is in season from April to June and for the rest of the year it comes to us from the USA, Mexico, Spain, Peru and Thailand. Quality and type vary, and the cost of long-distance sourcing is reflected in its price, which can soar to nearly the £7 mark around Christmas, a strong argument for eating only our domestic asparagus during its season.

Although you can buy special tall, narrow asparagus pans with baskets in them which leave the heads to steam while the thicker part of the stalks are submerged in boiling water, this is an unnecessary refinement since the woody base flesh is never eaten. Depending on the thickness of the stalks, asparagus will take from 3–5 minutes to cook.

It may be served hot with melted butter or a hollandaise sauce, or dressed simply with extra-virgin olive oil and salt. Cold asparagus is usually eaten with a light vinaigrette or mayonnaise. Older or woodier asparagus and asparagus trimmings make excellent soup, which is equally good hot or cold.

### SERVES 4

**60 g / 2 oz butter**
**500 g / 1 lb 2 oz asparagus stalks, cut into thirds**
**225 g / 8 oz diced onion**
**2 garlic cloves, chopped**
**225 g / 8 oz potato, diced**
**salt and pepper**
**300 ml / ½ pt single cream**

Melt the butter in a large heavy-based pan, then add the chopped asparagus stalks, reserving the tips, together with the diced onion, chopped garlic and diced potato. Sweat over a low heat for 5 minutes, being careful not to brown the onion.

The soup is actually nicer without stock confusing its fresh flavour, so pour in 1.75 litres / 3 pints of water (preferably filtered). Bring to the boil, then simmer for 20 minutes.

Purée in a blender or food processor and return to the pan. Season to taste with salt and pepper.

In another pan of boiling salted water, blanch the asparagus tips for 3 minutes, refresh in cold water and reserve. The soup can be held at this stage for several hours or overnight in the fridge.

About 10 minutes before serving, gently heat the soup until very hot but not boiling. Add the asparagus tips and simmer them for a minute, then stir in the cream, taste and season again if necessary.

Serve hot in large warmed bowls. If serving the soup cold, stir in the cream at the last minute before bringing to the table. Adjust the seasoning when you do so. The addition of the cream changes the flavour balance and may demand a little more salt and pepper.

## CREAM OF JERUSALEM ARTICHOKE SOUP

This soup can be made a day ahead. How much artichoke you have to work with after peeling will depend on how knobbly they are to start with. The smoother they are, the less waste.

### SERVES 6

**900 g / 2 lb Jerusalem artichokes**
**225 g / 8 oz onion, diced**
**1 garlic clove, peeled, smashed and chopped**
**60 g / 2 oz unsalted butter**
**225 g / 8 oz potato, peeled and diced**
**2 litres / 3½ pints light chicken or vegetable stock**
**salt and pepper**
**100 ml / 3½ fl oz double cream**
**chopped flat-leaved parsley, to garnish**

Trim off any black bits from the Jerusalem artichokes, then peel them and chop them into roughly 2.5-cm / 1-inch pieces.

Put these into a pan with the diced onion, chopped garlic and butter, and sweat the vegetables over a low heat until soft.

Add the diced potato and pour over the chicken or vegetable stock. Season with salt and pepper and bring to the boil. Lower the heat to a gentle simmer and cook for 20 minutes.

Liquidize the mixture in a blender or food processor and pass it through a sieve into a clean saucepan.

About 20 minutes before you want to serve the soup, reheat it gently, then stir in the double cream and adjust the seasoning to taste.

Serve the soup in warmed soup bowls, scattered with chopped flat-leaved parsley.

## AVGOLEMONO SOUP

Greek chicken soup with egg and lemon is properly called *kotopoulo soupa avgolemono*. *Avgolemono* is actually the name of the sauce made from eggs (*avgo*) and lemons (*lemono*), which is added to soups and stews to thicken them and add a sharp lemony taste. It is never added to dishes that are made with garlic or tomatoes, but may otherwise be added to any poached savoury dish. Skilled Greek hands frequently use whole eggs, but the rest of us are probably safer using only the yolks.

**SERVES 6**

**1 chicken, about 1.35 kg / 3 lb**
**about 3 litres / 5¼ pints water**
**or chicken stock**
**2 onions**
**1 carrot**
**1 celery stalk**
**1 bay leaf**
**2 tsp salt**
**12 black peppercorns**

**for the avgolemono sauce:**
**3 egg yolks**
**juice of 3 lemons**

Cover the chicken with cold water or, better still, good chicken stock, and bring to the boil. Lower the heat and skim, then add the onions, carrot, celery, bay leaf, salt and peppercorns. Simmer for 50 minutes, or until a leg will pull away easily.

Transfer the chicken to a chopping board, drain the broth into another saucepan and discard the vegetables.

Make the avgolemono sauce: in a mixing bowl, first whisk the egg yolks with a tablespoon of water, then beat in the lemon juice. Whisk a few spoonfuls of the hot (but not boiling — if the liquid is too hot, the eggs will cook in visible strings) cooking liquid into this mixture and then add the contents of the bowl back to the pan off the heat. Stir gently over a low heat and adjust the seasoning.

Normally the soup would be served like this or with the addition of a little cooked long-grain rice. Though the chicken would usually be served separately, it can be shredded and served with the broth poured over.

## BORSCHT

Anybody who has splashed their clothes with beetroot juice has empirical knowledge of its efficacy as a vivid food dye, and Borscht — Russian or Polish beetroot soup — would be unremarkable if it were not for its startling appearance which needs no further enhancement.

**SERVES 6**

**1 kg / 2 lb 3 oz large raw beetroot**
**1 litre / 1 pt chicken or beef or vegetable stock**
**225 g / 8 oz onion, diced**
**225 g / 8 oz leeks, sliced**
**2 celery stalks, chopped**
**60 g / 2 oz butter**
**1 bay leaf**
**freshly grated nutmeg**
**salt and pepper**
**150 ml / ¼ pint sour cream,**
**plus a little more to serve**
**grated horseradish, to serve**
**(optional)**

Boil the beetroot whole in salted water for 15 minutes. Drain and refresh in cold water. Peel and cut into 2.5-cm / 1-inch chunks.

Gently sauté the onion, leek and celery in the butter until softened. Add the beetroot, the stock and bay leaf. Bring to the boil, skim, lower the heat and simmer for 45 minutes.

Remove the bay leaf and liquidize. Return to a clean pan, season with grated nutmeg, salt and pepper and bring back to a simmer. Then, off the heat, stir in the sour cream.

Serve with a little more sour cream dribbled over. Grated horseradish is a nice final addition for those who like it hot.

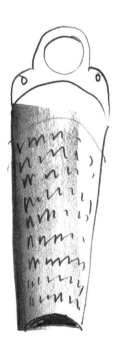

## CARROT AND CORIANDER SOUP

This also makes a nice cold soup, in which case do not add the whipping cream but instead mix a few tablespoons of thick plain yoghurt into the chilled soup.

**SERVES 6**
170 g / 6 oz onion, diced
60 g / 2 oz butter
500 g / 1 lb 2 oz carrots, sliced
1 garlic clove, finely chopped
large handful of coriander, with roots
1.1 litres / 2 pints chicken or vegetable stock
salt and pepper
1 tsp caster sugar
150 ml / ¼ pt whipping cream

Sweat the diced onion in the butter until soft and translucent.

Add the sliced carrots to the pan and cook, stirring from time to time, for a further 5 minutes.

Add the garlic and the washed and chopped stems of the coriander. Pour over the chicken stock, season with salt and pepper and the sugar, and bring to the boil. Lower the heat and simmer for 30 minutes.

Put the contents of the pan into a food processor or blender with most of the coriander leaves and blitz to a smoothish purée.

Pour back into a clean pan and add the whipping cream. Taste and adjust the seasoning, then heat the soup through gently, stirring.

Scatter over the reserved coriander leaves before serving.

## CREAM OF CAULIFLOWER SOUP

The soup is thickened with egg yolks and cream, and also given an interesting texture by puréeing half the cauliflower and leaving the remaining florets whole.

**SERVES 4–6**
1 medium-sized cauliflower
600 ml / 1 pt chicken or vegetable stock
600 ml / 1 pt single cream
3 egg yolks
salt and pepper
freshly grated nutmeg
handful of chives, to garnish

Cut the stem from the base of the cauliflower and separate the head into florets, discarding the green outer leaves. Blanch the florets in rapidly boiling salted water for 3 minutes, drain and purée half of them.

Put the chicken or vegetable stock in a pan with the single cream. Heat slowly to simmering. In a small bowl, whisk the egg yolks, then whisk a ladleful of the hot liquid into them and pour this mixture back into the pan, whisking all the time.

Add the cauliflower purée and season to taste with salt, pepper and some freshly grated nutmeg. Continue to cook, stirring, until the soup starts to thicken, then add the reserved whole florets. Cook, stirring, for another minute or so to warm them through.

Serve the soup in warmed bowls with chives snipped over. If a smooth soup is preferred, simply purée all the florets.

## CURRIED PARSNIP SOUP

Curry spices work well with parsnips, balancing their rather sweet flavour.

**SERVES 6**
about 550 g / 1¼lb parsnips
3 tsp cumin seeds
3 tsp coriander seeds
2 tsp mustard seeds
1 tsp cardamom seeds
225 g / 8 oz onion, thinly sliced
4 tbsp olive oil
225 g / 8 oz white parts of leeks, thinly sliced
2 celery stalks, thinly sliced
salt and pepper
150 ml / ¼ pt double cream
whole flat-leaved parsley and coriander leaves, to garnish

**for the stock:**
225 g / 8 oz onion, chopped
225 g / 8 oz leek greens, chopped
1 bulb of fennel, chopped
4 celery stalks, diced
2 carrots, diced
5-cm / 2-inch piece of ginger, sliced
handful of parsley stalks
2 bay leaves
1 tsp salt
16 black peppercorns

Quarter the parsnips and cut out the woody cores. Coarsely chop the flesh and reserve. Put peelings and cores into a large pot with the remaining stock ingredients. Add 2.25 litres / 2 quarts cold water. Bring to the boil, lower the heat and simmer for 25 minutes. Pass through a fine sieve and reserve.

In a dry pan over a low heat, toast the cumin, coriander, mustard and cardamom seeds. Grind to a fine powder.

Fry the onion gently in the olive oil until golden. Stir in the spice powder and continue to cook, stirring, for 2 minutes. Add the stock, parsnips, white parts of leeks, celery stalks and salt and pepper. Bring to the boil, lower the heat and simmer for 20 minutes.

Blitz to a smooth purée in a blender or food processor and return to the pan.

Just before serving, stir in the double cream and adjust the seasoning. Heat through gently. Garnish with whole leaves of flat-leaved parsley and coriander.

## CORIANDER AND COURGETTE SOUP

Strongly flavoured herbs like coriander can be used to advantage in soup and sauces, where small amounts have a big impact. This recipe is from Mexico.

**SERVES 6**
500 g / 1 lb 2 oz courgettes
large bunch of coriander, with roots
3 tbsp olive oil
1.5 litres / 2¾ pints light chicken or vegetable stock
225 g / 8 oz onion, diced
2 small hot chillies, deseeded and sliced into rings
6 tbsp dry mashed potato
60 g / 2 oz chopped coriander leaves
125 ml / 4 fl oz crème fraîche
salt and pepper
little milk (optional)
crisp fried tortilla chips (optional)

Cut the courgettes into quarters, then across into batons. Cook with 60–85 g / 2–3 oz chopped coriander roots, 2 tablespoons water and 1 tbsp of olive oil for 4 minutes in a covered pan over a medium to high heat, shaking from time to time.

Transfer to a blender or food processor, add the stock and whiz until smooth. Reserve.

Sweat the onion in the remaining olive oil until soft and translucent. Add the chillies, mashed potato and the courgette purée. Simmer, stirring occasionally, for 10 minutes.

Stir in the chopped coriander leaves and the crème fraîche. Season and simmer for a final 2 minutes. If too thick, thin with a little milk and serve garnished with tortilla chips if you like.

## MINESTRONE

There is no absolute recipe for minestrone, but it should always contain beans and a soup pasta like ditalini. Many Italians insist that it is cooked with a Parma ham bone for the flavour, but there is no reason why minestrone should not be entirely vegetarian.

**SERVES 8**
250 g / 8 oz dried borlotti beans, soaked overnight
250 g / 8 oz soup pasta
6 tbsp olive oil
about 1.35 kg / 3 lb assorted vegetables, for example equal amounts of courgettes, French beans, broccoli, leeks, potatoes, peas, carrots and onions
3 celery stalks
3 garlic cloves, thinly sliced
piece of ham bone (optional)
salt and pepper
8 tbsp Pesto sauce (see page 293), to serve

Drain the soaked beans, cover with fresh water and bring to the boil. Boil vigorously for 10 minutes, then drain. Cover with fresh water, bring back to the boil and simmer for about 1½ hours. Do not salt the water as this will toughen the skins of the beans.

Cook the soup pasta in plenty of rapidly boiling salted water until half done. Drain and reserve. Add 1 tablespoon of the olive oil and turn to coat.

Prepare the vegetables: trim them, then cut them into 5-mm / ¼-inch chunks or rounds as appropriate. Separate the florets from the broccoli stalks, cutting the stalks into small dice.

Put the remaining olive oil in a large saucepan and sweat the onion, garlic, carrots and celery for 5 minutes, stirring from time to time. Add a ham bone if liked and the remaining vegetables, except the broccoli and French beans. Cover with cold water. Bring to a boil, turn down the heat and simmer until the vegetables are just cooked.

Add the drained borlotti beans, taste then season with salt and pepper and cook for a further 5 minutes. Ideally, remove from the heat, leave to cool and then refrigerate overnight to allow the flavours to develop and amalgamate.

To serve: reheat the soup gently, stirring in the half-cooked pasta, French beans and broccoli florets. Simmer for a final 5 minutes. Serve in large warmed bowls, stirring a tablespoon of pesto into each bowl at the table.

### CELERY AND STILTON SOUP

A lot of people who do not like the taste of raw celery are converted when they try it cooked. If you don't have Stilton, any strong blue cheese will do.

**SERVES 4**

450 g / 1 lb onions, chopped
60 g / 2 oz unsalted butter
1 large head of celery, thinly sliced
1 tbsp flour
600 ml / 1 pt chicken or vegetable stock
salt and pepper
85–115 g / 3–4 oz Stilton or other blue cheese (quantity depending on how dominant you want the flavour to be)
few leaves of flat-leaved parsley, to garnish

In a large heavy-based saucepan, sweat the onions in the butter over a low heat, stirring until softened but not coloured.

Add the celery to the onions, continuing to sweat gently until the vegetables have softened but taking care not to brown.

Scatter the flour over and stir in for a minute, then add 600 ml / 1 pt of water and the stock. Season lightly with salt and pepper, bring to the boil, then lower the heat and simmer for 30–40 minutes, until the celery is soft.

Put into a blender or food processor, add the blue cheese and blitz until you have a smooth soup. Taste and adjust the seasoning if needed.

Serve at once, garnished with flat-leaved parsley leaves. If reheating, be careful not to boil.

### POTAGE SAINT-GERMAIN

Any recipe with the words 'Saint-Germain' or 'Clamart' in the title means the dish contains peas, since both areas of Paris were once famous for growing them. This is a very simple soup, made principally of dried split peas, though both the flavour and the colour are improved if you include some fresh petits pois, turning a determinedly khaki presentation into something more appealingly green. The technique here is contemporary, though the recipe is generally traditional.

**SERVES 6**

275 g / 10 oz green split peas
1 bay leaf
salt and pepper
170 g / 6 oz frozen peas
225 g / 8 oz onions, thinly sliced
60 g / 2 oz butter
1 garlic clove, finely chopped
300 ml / ½ pt single cream
croutons fried crisp in unsalted butter (see page 65) or shredded mint leaves, to serve

Rinse the split peas under cold running water, then put them in a pan with 1.75 litres / 3 pints cold water and bring to the boil. Lower the heat, add the bay leaf, season with pepper only and simmer until cooked, which will take between 45 minutes and 1 hour.

Blanch the frozen peas for 1 minute in rapidly boiling water. Drain and reserve. Sweat the onions in the butter until soft and translucent, adding the garlic for the last minute or so. Transfer to a blender or food processor and add the split peas with their cooking water and the blanched frozen peas. Add a little salt and blitz, pouring the cream through the feeder tube as it processes to a smooth purée.

Return to the pan, taste and adjust the seasoning. Heat through gently, being careful not to boil. Serve with croutons fried crisp in unsalted butter or with some shredded mint leaves scattered on top.

### GARLIC SOUP

This rich soup from the Languedoc in South-Western France uses goose or duck fat, but you can substitute a mixture of butter and olive oil if you have to. Though the recipe calls for 20 cloves of garlic, they cook to a mellow and gentle taste and the result is not at all harsh.

**SERVES 4**

4 slices of baguette
2 tbsp olive oil
60 g / 2 oz fat (see above)
900 g / 2 lb onions, sliced
20 garlic cloves, chopped
2 tbsp flour
2 tsp turmeric
salt and pepper
3 egg yolks
1 tbsp white wine vinegar
snipped chives, to garnish

Preheat the oven to 180°C/350°F, gas 4.

Brush the slices of baguette with olive oil, spread on a baking tray and cook in the oven until golden brown, about 10 minutes. Check every few minutes as they burn easily.

Heat the fat in a heavy pan and fry the onions over a low heat until golden but not brown. Add the garlic and continue to fry, stirring, for 2 or 3 minutes.

Sprinkle over flour and turmeric, stir in and cook for a minute, then add 1.75 litres / 3 pints of water. Season and bring to the boil over a high heat. Lower heat and simmer for 20 minutes.

Liquidize in a blender or food processor, return to the saucepan and bring back to a simmer.

In a small bowl, beat the egg yolks with the vinegar. Continuing to beat, add about half a ladleful of the broth in a thin stream and, when well combined, pour this liaison back into the soup, stirring vigorously. Remove immediately from the heat. Taste and adjust seasoning if necessary. The soup must not boil or the eggs will separate from the liquid.

Put a croûte in each bowl, ladle over the soup and snip over some chives.

## RASAM

Rasam is the fiercely hot vegetarian soup of Southern India and Sri Lanka. The leftover dal not used in the soup can be stir-fried with onions and garlic.

### SERVES 4–6
450 g / 1 lb can of plum tomatoes
2 tamarind cubes (see page 59)
7 garlic cloves, sliced
2 tsp turmeric
16 curry leaves
6 hot red chillies
2 tsp ground coriander seeds
large handful of coriander
2 tsp salt
5 tbsp sunflower oil

3 garlic cloves, sliced
2 tsp mustard seeds
2 tsp cumin seeds
about 8 curry leaves

for the dal:
115 g / 4 oz dal (red lentils)
2 tsp turmeric
3-cm / 1¼-inch piece of ginger, peeled and cut into thin strips

First cook the dal: put in a pan with 1.1 litres / 2 pints of water, the turmeric and ginger. Bring to the boil, cover, lower the heat and simmer for 45 minutes. Check regularly to ensure the pan doesn't dry out, stirring in a little more water if it does. Remove from the heat.

Put the contents of the can of tomatoes in another pan with 850 ml / 1½ pints water, the tamarind, 4 of the garlic cloves, the turmeric, half the curry leaves, the chillies, ground coriander, chopped coriander stems and roots, and salt. Bring to the boil, cover, lower the heat and simmer for 1 hour.

Skim out 300 ml / ½ pt of the liquid from the top of the dal and add to the tomato pan with 4 tablespoons of the dal. Sieve into a clean pan, pushing through the solids with a spoon.

In a frying pan, heat the sunflower oil until hot but not smoking. Toss the remaining garlic cloves in the oil with the mustard seeds, cumin seeds and remaining curry leaves. As the garlic browns and the seeds start to pop, pour and scrape into the soup.

Chop a handful of coriander leaves and stir in. Leave off the heat for 5 minutes with the lid on to allow the flavours to mix and develop before serving.

## SWEETCORN SOUP

Corn kernels make a great soup base and their sweet, gentle flavour allows you to dress this dish up in lots of ways. You can be very New England and serve it chowder-style with crisp bacon, or for an elegant dinner party offer guests a chilled purée enriched with pieces of lobster, crab or prawns.

Fresh corn is best, but frozen works perfectly well. Remember, though, that it is already part-cooked and needs little further cooking — certainly never as much as the packet says. You can also chill the soup, in which case don't add the cream until just before you serve it.

### SERVES 4
225 g / 8 oz onion, diced
225 g / 8 oz potato, diced
60 g / 2 oz butter
salt and pepper
575 g / 1¼ lb corn kernels
150 ml / ¼ pt single cream
freshly grated nutmeg
coriander leaves, to garnish

In a large heavy pan, sweat the onion and potatoes in the butter until soft.

Pour in 1.1 litres / 2 pints of water. Season, stir and bring to the boil, then simmer until the potato is just tender.

Add 450 g / 1 lb corn kernels and simmer for 3 minutes. Purée in a blender or food processor, return to the pan with the remaining whole corn kernels and simmer for a further 3 minutes.

Add the cream, grate in nutmeg to taste and heat through gently, taking care not to boil. Taste, adding more seasoning if needed and serve scattered with whole coriander leaves.

## ROCKET, RUCOLA, ARUGULA SOUP

Rocket was a popular salad ingredient in Britain in the sixteenth century, then it disappeared from public awareness in this country until just a few years ago, when it was rediscovered with its more exotic Italian names – also used in the USA – rucola and arugula.

**SERVES 4**
**60 g / 2 oz unsalted butter**
**450 g / 1 lb potatoes, diced**
**1 leek, thinly sliced**
**225 g / 8 oz onion, diced**
**salt and pepper**
**little milk (optional)**
**60–85 g / 2–3 oz rocket leaves, finely chopped**

Melt the butter in a heavy saucepan over a moderate heat and sweat the potatoes, leek and onion for 2–3 minutes, stirring constantly with a wooden spoon and taking care not to brown the vegetables.

Barely cover with about 1.1 litres / 2 pints of cold water and bring to the boil. Lower to a bare simmer, season with salt and pepper and cook until the potatoes are just done.

Purée in a blender or food processor and return to the pan. You can hold at this point for several hours before reheating gently until hot. If the soup is too thick at this point, thin it with a little milk until you have the consistency of single cream.

Just before serving, stir in the chopped rocket leaves. Remove from the heat, taste, adjust for seasoning and serve at once.

## FRENCH ONION SOUP

The most important element in this soup is caramelizing the onions properly, to give depth of flavour and a good colour. Make this Lyonnaise soup only when you have a good beef stock, the other essential ingredient. Stock cubes just don't give the same full-bodied taste.

**SERVES 4 HUNGRY PEOPLE**
**675 g / 1½ lb onions, thinly sliced**
**60 g / 2 oz unsalted butter or goose fat**
**60 g / 2 oz flour**
**1.25 litres / 2¼ pints well-flavoured beef stock**
**salt and pepper**
**12–16 thin slices of baguette**
**350 g / 12 oz of Gruyère cheese**
**butter**
**4 tbsp brandy**
**1 egg yolk**
**1 glass of red wine**

Preheat the oven to 220°/425°C/gas 7.

Fry the onions gently in the butter or goose fat for 20 minutes, stirring frequently, until well browned.

Sprinkle over the flour and stir in. Cook for a further 2 minutes.

Pour in the stock. Season and bring to the boil. Lower the heat and simmer gently for 30 minutes.

Toast the baguette slices. Grate half the Gruyère and slice the rest very thinly on a mandoline grater.

Rub an ovenproof tureen with butter, sprinkle in enough grated cheese to coat the bottom and sides, then pack the toasts into it, layering them with the sliced Gruyère and finishing with more cheese on the top. Ladle over enough soup to soak the toasts, then put the tureen into the oven for 5 minutes, or until all the stock has been absorbed.

Add the rest of the soup and the brandy, sprinkle the top with the remaining grated cheese and return to the oven for a final 10 minutes.

Beat the egg yolk with the red wine and, when you take the soup bubbling from the oven, stir this mixture into the top just before serving.

## TOM YAM GUNG

Probably the best known Thai soup, tom yam gung is a delicious clear broth fragrant with lemon grass and kaffir lime, hot spiced with chilli and filled with just-cooked tiger prawns.

**SERVES 4 GENEROUSLY**
**20 Tiger prawns**
**salt**
**3–4 tbsp peanut or sunflower oil**
**1 onion, diced**
**2 stalks of lemon grass, thinly sliced**
**3 garlic cloves, peeled, smashed and chopped**
**2 hot green chillies, sliced with their seeds**
**1.75 litres / 3 pints chicken or vegetable stock**
**4 lime leaves**
**juice of 2 limes, reserving the skins**
**2 tbsp nam pla fish sauce**
**1 hot red chilli, thinly sliced**
**4 spring onions, thinly sliced**
**coriander leaves, to garnish**

Peel the tiger prawns, cutting down through their back and removing the intestinal tracts and reserving the shells and heads. Put the peeled prawns in a bowl of iced salted water and rub them gently between your fingers. Drain.

In a saucepan, heat the oil and fry the onion until translucent. Add the lemon grass, garlic, green chillies and the prawn shells. Stir until the shells blush pink, then pour over the stock. Bring to the boil and skim.

Add the lime leaves, the peel of 1 of the limes and 2 teaspoons of salt. Lower the heat and simmer for 20 minutes.

Strain into a clean pan through a muslin-lined sieve and return to a simmer with just the odd bubble breaking the surface. Add the prawns and poach for 2–3 minutes until barely cooked.

Remove the pan from the heat and stir in the fish sauce and lime juice. Ladle into warmed bowls, allocating 5 prawns to each. Scatter the red chilli and spring onions on the surface, together with some whole coriander leaves. Serve steaming hot.

## MUSSEL SOUP WITH SAFFRON AND CREAM

Mussels do look pretty in their shells, but an easy variation is to serve them shelled and in a broth thickened with cream and flavoured with saffron.

**SERVES 4**

**1 kg / 2¼ lb mussels**
**1 leek, thinly sliced**
**60 g / 2 oz butter**
**1 bottle of cheap dry white wine or dry cider**
**salt and pepper**

**20 saffron threads**
**about 300 ml / ½ pint single cream**
**large handful of flat-leaved parsley, to garnish**

Debeard and scrub mussels. Discard any that don't shut when tapped.

In a saucepan large enough to hold the mussels comfortably and which has a lid, sweat the leek in the butter until just soft. Pour over the wine or cider, bring to the boil, lower the heat and simmer for 5 minutes.

Turn up the heat and sprinkle the contents of the pan with pepper. Add the mussels, cover with the lid and boil vigorously for a couple of minutes. Strain through a fine sieve into another saucepan. Return this broth to the boil and reduce it by one-third.

Shell the mussels, discarding any that have stayed firmly shut. Lower the heat under the broth and add about 20 saffron threads, then stir in the cream. Carefully adjust the seasoning (the mussels will have imparted quite a lot of salt). Add the shelled mussels and heat through gently for a minute.

Ladle into warmed soup bowls and garnish with plenty of chopped flat-leaved parsley.

## PARTAN BREE

Partan Bree is a Scottish crab soup thickened with cream and a little rice.

**SERVES 4 GENEROUSLY**

**about 225 g / 8 oz crab meat (what you should get from a 675 g / 1½ lb crab with some careful picking, or use frozen)**

**60 g / 2 oz pudding rice**
**600 ml / 1 pt milk**
**1 bay leaf**
**115 g / 4 oz onions, finely diced**
**60 g / 2 oz butter**
**4 anchovy fillets, drained and chopped**
**450 ml / ¾ pt fish, shellfish or light chicken stock**
**300 ml / ½ pt double cream**
**salt and pepper**
**little finely chopped parsley, for garnish**

If picking a fresh crab, reserve the claw meat to add just before serving.

Put the rice in a pan with the milk and bay leaf. Bring to the boil, lower the heat and simmer until the rice is soft, about 20 minutes.

While it is cooking, sweat the onion in the butter until soft and translucent. Reserve.

Remove the milk from the heat, stir in the crab meat (except for the claw pieces if you have them) and put into a food processor or liquidizer together with the onion and chopped anchovies. Blitz to a purée. With the machine still running, pour the stock through the feeder tube.

Use a wooden spoon to push this mixture through a sieve into a clean pan and bring to a simmer over a low heat. Add the remaining crab meat and stir in the double cream. Season to taste with salt and pepper, and heat through but do not allow to boil. Add any reserved claw meat.

Serve in warmed soup bowls with a little finely chopped parsley sprinkled on top.

### COCK-A-LEEKIE

This is one of our most ancient dishes, similar in many respects to Hindle Wakes (page 146) but served hot and with the broth playing an important part, more a substantial stew than a soup. The name is Scottish, though the dish has similarities with *pot au feu* and a New England boiled dinner. All would once have been made with a tough old farmyard cock or a boiling fowl, but a free-range chicken will cook in a fraction of the time and deliver an excellent result. Although the dish can be cooked in water, a better result is achieved using chicken stock.

**S E R V E S  4**

**1 boiling fowl or free-range chicken (see above), about 1.5 kg / 3½ lb**
**about 2.75 litres / 5 pints chicken stock**
**1 bay leaf**
**1 onion, whole and unpeeled**
**450 g / 1 lb stoned prunes**
**salt and pepper**
**550 g / 1¼ lb leeks, cut into 2.5-cm / 1-inch pieces**

In a large pot, cover the bird with chicken stock and bring to the boil. Skim, add a bay leaf and the whole onion and lower the heat to simmer.

After 30 minutes, add the stoned prunes and season with salt and pepper. The bird should be cooked after 50–55 minutes. Remove from the broth, but keep the broth warm.

When cool enough to handle, carve off the legs, separating each of them into drumstick and thigh. Remove the breasts whole and carve these into 2 across the grain.

Turn up the heat under the pan and add the leeks. Cook until just tender, about 5 minutes. Lower the heat and return the chicken pieces to the pan just to warm through.

Discard the onion and bay leaf. Adjust the seasoning and serve in warmed soup bowls, dividing the chicken, prunes and leeks equally and with the broth ladled over.

### BROWN WINDSOR SOUP

This thick meat soup was first concocted in Victorian times, but as a nation we seem to have fallen out of love with it as, with the passage of time, its original robust dimensions were watered down and adulterated until the very name became synonymous with British food as a poor joke, conjuring up the ghost of Hancock saying of his mother's gravy that 'at least it moved'.

Perhaps this substantial recipe may help restore its good name. The amounts are for 8, as it hardly seems worth going to all this considerable trouble for 4 and it will, in any case, freeze.

**S E R V E S  8**

**225 g / 8 oz shin of beef, cut into 2.5-cm / 1-inch cubes**
**225 g / 8 oz lamb fillet, cut into 2.5-cm / 1-inch cubes**
**60 g / 2 oz dripping or butter**
**1 large onion, thinly sliced**
**2 carrots, cut into small dice**
**60 g / 2 oz flour**
**1 marrow bone, sawn into 5-cm / 2-inch pieces**
**2.25 litres / 2 quarts beef or chicken stock**
**bouquet garni of celery, bay leaf and thyme tied with string**
**salt and pepper**
**1 tsp cayenne pepper**
**sherry glass of sweet sherry or Madeira**
**chopped chives, to garnish (optional)**

In a heavy casserole, brown the meat in the dripping or butter.

Add the sliced onion and carrots to the casserole, lower the heat and fry them gently until they wilt. Sprinkle over the flour, turn up the heat and brown, stirring.

Add the marrow bone pieces, pour over the stock and bring to the boil. Skim carefully, then lower the heat to a simmer. Add the bouquet garni and season with salt and pepper. Simmer for 2 hours, topping up with water as required. Remove the bones and the bouquet garni.

The Victorians would have had a scullery girl to grind the mixture, then work it through a tammy cloth, but you can blitz it to a smooth purée in seconds in a blender or food processor, then push it through a sieve with a wooden spoon.

Return the soup to a clean pan, adjust the seasoning and add the cayenne pepper and sweet sherry or Madeira. If the soup is too thick, add some water.

Heat through gently before serving. If you find the brown expanse too depressing, sprinkle in some chopped chives.

## OXTAIL CONSOMMÉ

Oxtail is an ideal base from which to make a clear soup with a terrific flavour. Drink a glass of fino with it, and call it *consommé de queue de boeuf* to win a gold star.

### SERVES 6
1 oxtail, cut into pieces
2 onions, topped and tailed but not peeled
2 carrots, split into 4
3 celery stalks
2 bay leaves
150 ml / ¼ pt dry white wine
salt and pepper
sherry glass of dry sherry
handful of chives

Preheat the oven to 250°C/475°F/gas 9. Begin by trimming off all the fat you can from the joints of oxtail. Put them with the unpeeled onions in a roasting tray and brown in the oven for 20 minutes.

Put the browned meat and onions in a pan with the carrots, celery and bay leaves. Cover with 2.25 litres / 2 quarts of cold water and the wine. Bring to the boil, skim and lower the heat to a bare simmer. Cook gently for 4 hours, adding more water from time to time as necessary.

Pass through a sieve, allow to cool and refrigerate overnight. Refrigerate the meat also.

Next day, carefully lift off any fat that has set on the surface of what will now be a bowl of glossy meat jelly. Return this to a pan and bring to a simmer. Taste and season. The broth should be as clear and bright as a jewel.

Cut a few very thin slices of meat from the tail and lay them in the bottoms of warmed soup bowls. Ladle the broth into the bowls. Add a tablespoon of dry sherry to each bowl and snip over a few chives.

## CALDO VERDE

Caldo verde, which means 'green broth', is arguably the national dish of Portugal. This simple but delicious soup of diced potatoes and finely shredded cabbage is enriched with olive oil and the addition of slices of *chouriço*, a strong-flavoured, salty pork-and-garlic sausage that is called *chorizo* in Spain.

The soup is actually quite delicious without the addition of the sausage, in which case a little chopped garlic is added to the potatoes to deepen the flavour.

Use a strong-flavoured long-leaved brassica like curly kale or spring greens rather than a hard round cabbage, and slice the leaves as finely as grass. The Portuguese themselves traditionally use kale, or a good Savoy cabbage does just as well.

In Portugal the bread served with the soup would be of maize, *broa de Milho*, and dishes of tasty small black olives would be put on the table to go with it.

### SERVES 4 GENEROUSLY
450 g / 1 lb of greens (see above), shredded
450 g / 1 lb floury potatoes, diced
salt
2 garlic cloves, chopped (optional)
4 tbsp extra-virgin olive oil, plus more to serve
eight 2-cm / ¾-inch slices of chouriço
few whole leaves of flat-leaved parsley
coarse black pepper
sourdough bread, to serve (optional)

In Portugal, you can actually buy a special piece of kit for shredding the greens, but an ordinary kitchen knife does the job perfectly well. Cut out the stem from each leaf and roll the leaves together like a cigar, then cut these across again into the thinnest strips you can manage.

Lightly salt 1 litre / 1¾ pints of water and boil the potatoes in this until they are soft. If serving the soup without the sausage, add the chopped garlic to the potatoes at the beginning of cooking.

Add the 4 tablespoons of extra-virgin olive oil to the pan of potatoes and cooking liquid, and mash the potatoes into the liquid to produce a smooth purée.

Add the shredded cabbage and slices of chouriço. Return the soup to the boil, lower the heat and simmer gently for a few minutes barely to cook the cabbage and just heat the slices of sausage through.

Serve the soup in warmed soup bowls, scattered with a few whole leaves of flat-leaved parsley and grind over some coarse black pepper. Offer more olive oil at the table and serve a nice sourdough bread to accompany this simple feast.

## SUPPE MIT SCHINKENKLOESSCHEN

This is not as heavy as some of the other soup and dumpling combinations that are so typical of old-fashioned German cooking. The actual soup is traditionally a beef consommé, but is just as nice with a well-flavoured chicken stock.

**SERVES 6**
1.5 litres / 2¾ pints well-flavoured chicken stock
snipped chives, to garnish

for the dumplings:
60 g / 2 oz butter
60 g / 2 oz flour
30 g / 1 oz fresh white bread-crumbs
115 g / 4 oz ham, minced
1 tbsp chopped parsley
salt and pepper
freshly grated nutmeg
2 eggs

Melt the butter in a pan, add the flour and cook to a roux for 2–3 minutes. Add the breadcrumbs, minced ham and parsley. Season with salt, pepper and grated nutmeg, then continue to cook over the lowest heat, stirring, for 3–4 minutes. Remove from the heat and beat in first one of the eggs, then the second. Leave to cool.

Take a spoonful of the mixture at a time, roll it into small balls on a floured surface. These can be cling-wrapped and kept in the fridge for up to 4 hours.

Put the stock in a pan and heat to a simmer. Put a large pan of salted water to heat for the dumplings. When the water is boiling, drop in the dumplings,

lower heat and simmer for 15 minutes. Put into soup bowls, ladle the broth over and garnish with snipped chives.

---

### POACHING LOTS OF DUMPLINGS, RAVIOLI OR GNOCCHI

*Poaching dumplings or stuffed pasta does not require a great depth of water. The surface area is more significant, particularly when cooking large quantities. A ready solution is to use a roasting pan rather than a saucepan and place it over two burners. This way all the individual items can expand on the surface without overcrowding.*

---

## PORK WON-TON SOUP

Won-ton are Chinese soup dumplings, which are usually filled with minced pork and served in a clear broth made from duck and pork. Buy them from Chinese markets where they are cheap. They will freeze for up to 6 weeks, when they become increasingly brittle and unworkable. Won-ton in most Chinese restaurants tend to be pretty basic dumplings and you will be able to make superior ones at home.

You can make all sorts of different fillings, including duck, fish and shell-fish, but the ingredients must be raw – if you fill won-ton with cooked meat or fish, they disintegrate.

Always cook won-ton in simmering lightly salted water, ladling clear broth over them just before serving. If more convenient you can freeze won-ton on a

floured tray, then bag for storage and cook in simmering water from frozen; in which case allow 5–7 minutes.

**SERVES 4**
1.25 litres / 2 pints well-flavoured chicken stock
chopped chives, to garnish

for the won-tons:
30 won-ton wrappers
450 g / 1 lb minced pork
1 garlic clove, finely chopped
2 spring onions, thinly sliced
2.5-cm / 1-inch piece of peeled ginger, finely chopped
1 tbsp chopped coriander leaves, plus more whole leaves for garnish
2 tbsp Chinese soy sauce
2 tsp sesame oil
1 tbsp dry sherry
salt and pepper
flour, for dusting

Put the pork into a bowl, then add the garlic, spring onions, ginger, chopped coriander leaves, soy sauce, sesame oil dry sherry, salt and black pepper to taste. Mash all together with a fork.

Put a heaped teaspoon of mixture on each wrapper. Brush edges with a little water, then pinch 2 opposite corners together. Draw up the 2 remaining corners one at a time and nip shut at the top and along edges. This takes a little time to perfect, but you get quicker and neater as you go. Put on a floured tray.

Poach in boiling salted water for about 3–4 minutes. Drain and divide between 4 bowls. Ladle stock over and scatter with coriander and chives.

# FISH AND SHELLFISH

In five years we have seen a food revolution taking place here in this country and nowhere has this been more apparent than when dealing with fish and seafood, as more and more people stop eating meat completely or, more commonly, exclude beef, lamb and pork from their diets. When our column began in 1992, the difficulty in finding really fresh fish around the country was nothing short of a national disgrace. The quality of what some supermarkets offered then – and, in some cases it has to be said, to this day – defied description, other than in terms that might have been deemed actionable. One of the most encouraging aspects of our changing food perceptions has been an outcrop of new fishmongers opening on high streets, totally against the national trend of widespread closure of specialist food shops – a direct result of supermarkets' failure to supply really fresh fish.

It is both sad and ironic that, as more people learn to love fish, availability is increasingly governed by stock depletion, for over-fishing threatens extinction to many popular species.

## WARM LOBSTER WITH ORANGE AND DILL SALAD

Lobster remains a treat for most people, and one that they rarely consider cooking at home, probably because of the need to handle the live crustacean. This is not difficult and the cooking could not be easier, since it simply means poaching in a lot of heavily salted water.

The water should be as salty as the sea, a salinity achieved by adding about 140 g / 5 oz salt to every 5 litres / 1 gallon of water. A lobster weighing 550 g / 1¼ lb will take 13 minutes, a 675 g / 1½ lb lobster 15 minutes and one up to 1.125kg / 2½ lb, 20 minutes. If you are lucky enough to be working over that weight, allow an extra 5 minutes per

450 g / 1 lb. A very large lobster is however, a very old lobster, and is nei ther as sweet nor as tender as th smaller ones.

For many people, the cooking of live lobster is a moral and ethic dilemma, as the post bag demonstrat whenever such a procedure is su gested. If you are concerned abo

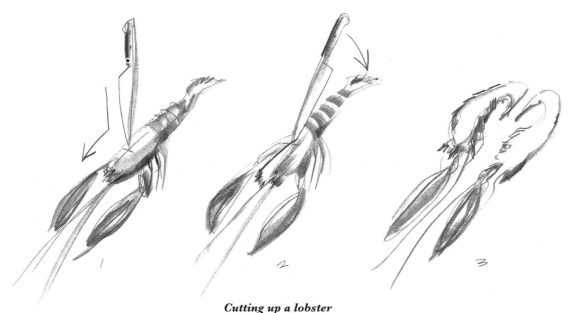

### Cutting up a lobster

*The best way to cut open a lobster, dead or alive is to position a heavy knife centrally at the point where the head meets the body and drive downwards with commitment, splitting the head first. Reverse the lobster and complete the cut through the tail section. When dealing with a live lobster, this is possibly the swiftest and most humane of terminations.*

putting a living creature into boiling water, first chill it in a freezer or an ice slurry for 30 minutes before putting it in the pot. According to the RSPCA, the exposure to extreme cold causes it to become unconscious.

**SERVES 2**
**675 g / 1½ lb lobster**
**140 g / 5 oz salt**

**for the Orange and Dill Salad:**
**2 little gem lettuces**
**3 tbsp olive oil**
**3 tsp lime juice**
**salt and pepper**
**2 oranges**
**300 ml / ½ pt thick plain yoghurt**
**2 tsp chopped fresh dill**

ok the lobster: put 5 litres / 1 gallon water and the salt in a large pot and bring to a rapid boil. Add the lobster, allow the water to return to the boil, then lower the heat to a simmer for 15 minutes. Remove and leave to cool.

Cutting a lobster in half demands a firm hand. If you are right-handed, put the lobster on its belly and with the head pointing to the right. Using a heavy, pointed and sharp-bladed knife, insert the point where the carapace joins the tail section, then drive down and cut through the head, slamming down with the flat of your hand on the knife to cut cleanly through the shell. Turn the lobster, reinsert the knife in the same central line and cut through to the tail. Crack the claws and remove the flesh. Pull out the tail section in one piece and cut across into rounds. Everything is edible apart from the gravel sac and intestinal tract behind the mouth. The green tomalley in the carapace is delicious.

Make the salad: cut off the base of the lettuces and separate the leaves. Make a basic dressing with the olive oil, lime juice and salt and pepper, then toss the leaves in this to coat and arrange on 2 plates. Cut off the peel of the oranges and all pith, then cut the flesh into segments and discard all the pips. Toss the orange segments in the yoghurt with the dill and a little pepper. Spoon these over the leaves.

Share the lobster meat between the 2 plates, arranging it on top of the salad. Garnish with a sprig of dill.

*Never throw away the shells from your cooked crab or lobster. Use them to make stock, which can be reduced and frozen, or use them to flavour cooking oil.*

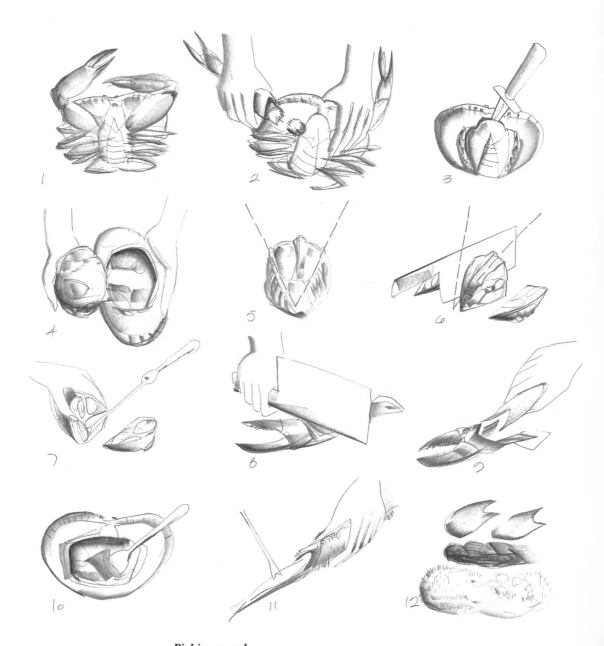

### *Picking a crab*

*1 Set cooled cooked crab on its back. 2 Twist off claws and legs. 3 Lever up flap. Discard gills and stomach. 4 Remove bony central section. 5 Identify 'V' to guide cuts. 6 Cut down and through twice along lines of imaginary 'V', producing three pieces and six accessible planes. 7 Use skewer or lobster pick to remove flesh from little channels revealed by cuts. 8–9 Crack claws and knuckles with back of heavy knife or cleaver, pulling out meat. 10 Use spoon to remove dark meat and liver from under sides of shell. 11 Crack legs and extract meat. 12 You now have the prime white meat and claw and knuckle meat, the ivory shell meat and brown liver.*

*Opposite (top to bottom): C[...] Fried Tigers (page 82), Gri[...] Mussels (page 85)*

## DÉLICES DE CRABE

These make a fine starter or good party food. You can get reasonable results with canned crab, though boiling one fresh yourself will pay dividends in taste and texture.

You can make délices de fromage in exactly the same way, substituting the same weight of grated Cheddar or a mixture of Cheddar and Gruyère for the crab.

**MAKES 24**
**1 bay leaf**
**strip of lemon peel**
**freshly grated nutmeg**
**150 ml / ¼ pt milk**
**30 g / 1 oz unsalted butter**
**30 g / 1 oz flour**
**3 tbsp double cream**
**1 tbsp brandy**
**2 tsp Worcestershire sauce**
**¼ tsp cayenne pepper**
**salt and pepper**
**about 225 g / 8 oz picked white crab meat**
**flour, for dusting**
**3 eggs, beaten**
**85–115 g / 3–4 oz fine breadcrumbs**
**sunflower oil, for deep-frying**

Put the bay leaf, lemon peel and nutmeg to taste in the milk and bring slowly to the boil. Remove from the heat, cover with a lid and leave to infuse for 15 minutes.

In a heavy-based saucepan, melt the butter over a low heat and add the flour. Cook gently to make a roux. Pour the milk through a sieve into the roux, whisking, and cook over a low heat until it forms a very thick white sauce.

Beat in the cream, brandy, Worcestershire sauce, cayenne pepper and salt and pepper to taste. Cook over a low heat for 2–3 minutes, stirring vigorously. The mixture will be very thick. Remove from the heat and stir in the crab meat.

Spoon on to a plate, spread out into a 15-cm / 6-inch circle and leave to cool, then refrigerate for 2 hours or overnight.

Divide the chilled mixture into 24 and roll into balls, with lightly floured hands. Roll one at a time in beaten egg, then roll in fine breadcrumbs. Repeat to give a double crust, then refrigerate until needed.

Preheat a deep-fryer or a large pan half filled with sunflower oil to 190°C/375°F. Fry the délices in batches for about 3 minutes each time, until crisp and golden brown.

## POTTED SHRIMPS

Traditionally made from Morecambe Bay shrimps, the tiny ones the French call *crevettes grises*, the first problem is the dwindling supply and, when you can find them, the attendant high cost. Peeling them is a pretty hellish task, but if you are lucky you may find the fresh Dutch ready-peeled ones which your fishmonger should be able to obtain. A word of warning: they cost around £25 per kilo wholesale, so how this converts at retail is anybody's guess.

Potted shrimps are one of our finest English starters, but their apparent simplicity is deceptive. The clarified butter in which they are turned and then packed must not be too hot or it will toughen them and it must be flavoured only with nutmeg and/or mace and a little cayenne.

It is important when packing the shrimps into pots for chilling that not too much butter is used. The set butter should not be more than 5 mm / ¼ inch thick. A generous serving would be 75g / 3 oz, though in the few restaurants which still serve them you would be lucky to get 60 g / 2 oz.

**SERVES 6 AS A FIRST COURSE**
**300 g / 10½ oz unsalted butter**
**¼ small nutmeg**
**1 tsp cayenne pepper**
**550 g / 1¼ lb peeled shrimps**
**melba toast, to serve**
**quarters of lemon cut lengthwise, to serve**

Melt the butter in a pan over the lowest heat. The milk solids will separate. Pour the clarified butter carefully through a muslin-lined sieve into a bowl, leaving the solids in the pan.

Grate the nutmeg into the butter and season with cayenne pepper. Add the shrimps and turn to coat evenly.

Leave in the hot butter for 2 minutes, then pack into ramekins in 75 g / 3 oz portions. Press down gently to ensure the surfaces of the shrimp are covered with butter.

Chill before serving with melba toast and lemon quarters.

❶ Cut just behind the head to remove it.

❷ Cut through the back and peel off the shell.

❸ Cut down through the length of the back.

❹ Prise out and discard the dark vein of intestinal thread. Continue the cut almost all the way through, but not quite.

❺ Butterfly the prawn by pressing down gently to open and flatten.

❻ To achieve a flat presentation when cooked, slide a skewer lengthwise through the prawn to hold it neatly in place.

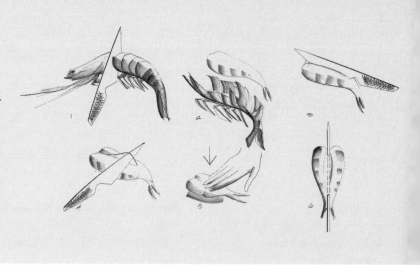

## GARLIC PRAWNS

This is amongst the simplest of dishes to cook and one that never fails to please. You can use scampi, crayfish or tiger prawns. Since you will be eating them with your fingers, a nice touch is to cut through the back of the shellfish, removing the intestinal tract (see above) and flattening them slightly before they go in the pan. This makes it much easier to get at the flesh and both speeds and assists even cooking.

How many you allow per person will depend on your generosity and the greed factor of your guests. Finger bowls filled with hot water and lemon will be appreciated.

**5 tbsp olive oil**
**4 garlic cloves, smashed and chopped**
**16–20 scampi, crayfish or tiger prawns**
**3 tbsp dry white wine**
**pepper**
**handful of flat-leaved parsley, chopped**
**1 lemon, quartered lengthwise, to serve**
**good bread, to serve**

Put the olive oil in a large heavy frying pan and place it over a moderate heat. Add the garlic to the hot oil and stir a couple of times. Add the shellfish and white wine and sauté, tossing, turning and shaking the pan fairly continuously. They will cook very quickly and are done when the flesh has become firm and white.

Immediately transfer the contents of the pan to a warmed serving dish, season generously with black pepper and scatter over the chopped flat-leaved parsley. Serve the dish with lemon quarters and some chunks of good rustic bread to mop up the delicious garlicky juices.

## CRISP FRIED TIGERS

You can buy reconstituted dried bean-curd sheets to make this dish authentically Thai, but ordinary won-ton wrappers – which you can buy in packets from any Oriental market – are the easiest to use and work well. These come in different shapes and sizes. The ones you want for this job are rectangles about 7.5 cm / 3 inches long. You can buy frozen tiger prawns in 500 g and 1 kg packs at the same markets more cheaply than you can at most fishmongers. Allow 4 or 5 per person.

**16–20 frozen tiger prawns**
**1 tbsp cornflour**
**16–20 won-ton wrappers**
**vegetable oil for deep-frying**

**for the Sweet-and-sour Chilli Tomato Sauce:**
**100 g / 3½ oz sultanas**
**3 garlic cloves, chopped**

4 hot red chillies, deseeded and
chopped

2 tbsp white wine vinegar

225 g / 8 oz canned chopped
tomatoes, drained

3 tbsp sunflower oil

4 tbsp tomato ketchup

1 tsp salt

1 tsp pepper

Tabasco or other chilli sauce
(optional)

First make the Sweet-and-sour Chilli
Tomato Sauce: put the sultanas, garlic,
chillies, vinegar and chopped tomatoes
in a pan with the oil. Bring to the boil,
lower the heat and simmer gently for 15
minutes. Add the ketchup, simmer for
another 5 minutes, then transfer to a
blender or food processor. Season with
salt and pepper and whiz to a purée.
Taste and adjust the seasoning. If the
sauce is not fiery enough, add some
Tabasco or other chilli sauce. Leave to
cool before serving. If you like this
sauce, make it in larger amounts and
keep it in jars in the fridge.

Let the prawns defrost fully, then
peel off the shells. Leave the tail fans on
and remove intestinal threads as
described opposite. Wipe with paper
towels, then sweeten as described above.

Make a paste with the cornflour and
a little water. Lay a won-ton wrapper in
front of you with a corner towards you.
Brush the edges with the paste, then lay
a prawn on it with the tail fan sticking
out to the right of the corner nearest to
you. Fold the left-hand side over the
head end of the body and roll the package away from you to wrap tightly.
Repeat until they are all ready to cook.

Deep-fry as soon as possible in 2
batches at 190°C/375°F for 1 minute on
each side, turning with a slotted spoon.
Cook them for any longer and the wrappers will burn and the prawns overcook,
which is when they go rubbery. Drain
on paper towels and serve with Sweet-
and-sour Chilli Tomato Sauce.

### SWEETENING FROZEN PRAWNS

*Whenever you are preparing
frozen prawns, once they are
defrosted put them in a bowl of
ice-cold heavily salted water.
Leave them for 10 minutes,
swirling them with your fingers
from time to time. Then rinse
under cold running water and
pat dry. This brief salting
process both sweetens and
intensifies the flavour in a
rather magical fashion.*

## MILD PRAWN CURRY

SERVES 4

85 g / 3 oz unsweetened
desiccated coconut

300 ml / ½ pt boiling milk

2 eggs

1 onion, finely chopped

3 tbsp sunflower oil

2.5-cm / 1-inch piece of ginger,
peeled and chopped

2 tbsp fish sauce

1 kg / 2¼ lb raw tiger prawns

350 g / 12 oz basmati rice

60 g / 2 oz chopped coriander
leaves

for the masala (spice mix):

½ tbsp cumin seeds

½ tbsp coriander seeds

seeds from 6 cardamom pods

½ tsp black peppercorns

1 tsp chilli flakes

½ tsp turmeric

First make a masala (spice mix) by
toasting the cumin, coriander and cardamom seeds, black peppercorns, chilli
flakes and turmeric in a dry frying pan
over a low heat for 2–3 minutes. Grind
to a powder in a coffee grinder.

Put the coconut in a bowl and pour
the boiling milk over it. Let steep for 20
minutes. Boil the eggs for 8 minutes,
refresh in cold water and refrigerate.

Sweat the onion in the oil until
translucent. Add the masala, stir in and
fry gently for 2–3 minutes. Add the ginger and strain in the coconut milk
through a sieve. Simmer for 10–15 minutes, then add the fish sauce. The dish
can be refrigerated at this point and
held for up to 24 hours.

Peel and devein the prawns (see
opposite) and sweeten in salted cold
water (see above left).

Cook the rice in masses of rapidly
boiling lightly salted water, tasting after
8 minutes. It may need 10 minutes, but
be careful not to overcook. Drain and
fork over a very low heat to dry.

While the rice is cooking, reheat the
sauce to a simmer. Drain and rinse the
prawns and add them to the sauce with
the chopped coriander leaves. Cook for
2 minutes, when they will have curled
into tight circles and gone pink. Do not
cook past this point or they will
toughen. Serve the curry with the rice.

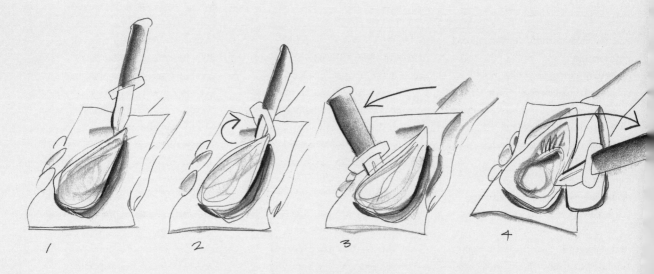

AN EASY WAY TO OPEN OYSTERS AND CLAMS

*Put the molluscs on a tray and place it in the freezer for 15–20 minutes. The shells will open a tiny crack, just enough to allow you to slip in a knife with which to lever them open fully.*

## PO' BOY OYSTER SANDWICH

It has been some time since the word 'poor' could be applied to oysters in this country, but they are still cheap and cheerful fare in Louisiana, where po' boy sandwiches are as popular as hot-dogs or hamburgers are in other American cities. These sandwiches became synonymous with wild nights out in the last century on and around Bourbon Street in the French Quarter of New Orleans, in the same way that onion soup is still eaten as a pick-me-up in the early hours of the morning in Les Halles in Paris.

The kind of bread you use makes all the difference. A ficelle or small baguette is perfect. Allow 6 large Pacific (rock) oysters each. This recipe stems from the 18th century. These days the oysters are either crumbed or battered and deep-fried. A po' modern variation on the original.

SERVES 4

**4 ficelles or small baguettes**
**45 g / 1½ oz melted butter**
**24 large Pacific (rock) oysters**
**1 tsp Tabasco sauce**
**3 tbsp double cream**
**pepper**
**3 tbsp crème fraîche**

Preheat the oven to 200°C/400°F/gas 6. Split the lengths of bread, brush them inside and out with one-third of the melted butter and put in the oven for 5 minutes to crisp.

Shell the oysters, reserving their juices. Sauté the shelled oysters briefly in the remaining butter, removing them from the pan as soon as they become opaque. Add the oyster juices to the pan with the Tabasco sauce and the double cream, a turn or two of pepper and the crème fraîche. Turn up the heat and boil, whisking the liquid mixture to a thick sauce.

Return the oysters to the pan, toss to coat, then put them into the bread, spooning the sauce over. Shut your eyes and hear that jazz.

## COOKING CLAMS

The tiniest clams, *vongole* in Italian, are classically cooked in a rich tomato sauce and served in their shells with spaghetti. This looks pretty, but extracting the flesh is a bit of a bore. On the Eastern seaboard of the USA, clam chowder is the most famous treatment, a milky broth thickened with crumbled crackers and enriched with lardons of fat bacon. The simplest treatment is the one to choose for a start point. You need about 200 g / 7 oz per person.

Palourdes, currently very fashionable, are put into a pan over a high heat with a squirt of extra-virgin olive oil and a little garlic. Put the lid on, shake a couple of times and cook for about 6 seconds. Take a peek. If all the shells are open then they are done. Add a handful of chopped parsley and toss to coat. During cooking the clams exude a delightful salty liquid which combines with the olive oil, parsley and garlic to make all the sauce you need. Add a piece of decent bread to mop up the sauce and a glass of dry white wine to drink and you have a perfect dish.

Variations on this spring to mind:

• Put a glass of dry white wine and shallots in a pan and boil briefly before adding your clams and you have a different take on *moules marinière*.

• Add spices like cumin and coriander with the olive oil and suddenly your clams taste Middle-Eastern.

• Skin, peel, deseed and dice ripe tomatoes and add them with torn basil to the clams and you have a delightful sauce for grilled cod.

All you have to keep in mind is that clams are delicate so don't overcook and don't spice too heavily. Otherwise, the world is your bivalve.

## GRILLED MUSSELS

SERVES 4 AS A FIRST
COURSE OR 2 AS A MAIN
**1 kg /2¼ lb mussels**
**5 tbsp white wine**
**30 g/ 1 oz Parmesan, grated**
**60 g / 2 oz breadcrumbs**

**for the herbed butter:**
**2 garlic cloves, smashed and chopped**
**2 tbsp flat-leaved parsley**
**125 g / 4 oz unsalted butter**
**pepper**

### CLEANING CLAMS OR MUSSELS OF GRIT

*These days shellfish tend to be put through cleaning tanks before they are sold. If, however, you have gathered them yourself (from an area you know is not polluted), to rid them of grit and sand, soak them in water at a sea level salinity for 1 hour. You can achieve this by adding 115 g / 4 oz sea salt to every 1 litre / 1 ¾ pints of water. Add a couple of trays of ice.*

Make a herbed butter by forking the chopped garlic and parsley with the softened butter together in a bowl. Season with pepper. Roll into a cylinder in cling-film or foil and refrigerate. Preheat a hot grill.

Scrape the mussels to remove beards, discarding any that don't close when tapped, then open them by putting them with a little white wine in a saucepan, covering them with a lid and shaking them over a high heat for 2–3 minutes.

Take the mussels off the heat as soon as they open and, when cool enough to handle, detach and discard the top half of the shells. Arrange the mussels in their half shells on a tray, dot each one with half a teaspoon of the herbed butter, scatter on a little grated Parmesan cheese and a few breadcrumbs. Put them under the preheated grill for a few minutes until they are well browned and bubbling hot. Serve at once.

## SEARED SCALLOPS

The mistake most people make with scallops is overcooking, which – as with squid and lobster – makes the flesh tough and rubbery. When absolutely fresh, scallops can be eaten raw, simply marinated in lemon juice and olive oil. Add a little chopped onion and chilli to the marinade and you have *ceviche*.

Always buy scallops fresh from the fishmonger, where you can see the shells opened and have them cleaned for you.

SERVES 4 AS A FIRST
COURSE
**8–12 large scallops, cleaned and shelled**
**oil**
**salt and pepper**
**flat-leaved parsley or coriander leaves, to garnish**
**a little melted butter or extra-virgin oil, to dress**

Heat a heavy frying pan until smoking-hot (don't use a non-stick pan, it will destroy it). Cut any corals away from the scallops and reserve for another dish. (If you want to eat the corals at the same time, they take a little more cooking than the scallops themselves for most tastes.) Brush the scallops lightly with oil and season with pepper, but not salt at this stage as this will toughen them.

Turn up the heat and lay them in the pan for 60 seconds. Turn and cook for a further 45 seconds.

Season with a little salt, cut across into 2 or 3 slices depending on size and serve at once, scattered with parsley or coriander leaves and with a little melted butter or extra-virgin oil dribbled over.

## SCALLOPS À LA BORDELAISE

*Coquilles St Jacques à la Bordelaise* is a speciality of South-Western France, a classic simple sauté, involving butter, sliced shallots and chopped parsley. The dish is not particularly fashionable these days, when scallops tend to be briefly seared rather than fried, but it is delicious – as long as care is taken not to overcook the scallops to turn them into expensive rubber.

The simple addition of a couple of chopped garlic cloves turns this dish into *coquilles St Jacques à la provençale.*

**SERVES 4 AS A FIRST COURSE**

**12 large scallops**

**flour, for dusting**

**salt and pepper**

**6 shallots, thinly sliced**

**150 g / 5 oz butter**

**good handful of chopped parsley**

**1 or 2 baguettes, to serve**

Cut the scallops horizontally through the middle and separate any corals. Fashion foolishly dictates that the corals are not served in the same dish, but this is nonsense. Toss the scallop slices in well seasoned flour.

Fry the shallots gently in 30 g / 1 oz of the butter and reserve.

Heat a large heavy frying pan until very hot. Throw in 60 g / 2 oz butter, immediately add the scallops and sauté for 2 minutes, allowing them to take a good colour. Stir in the shallots and parsley, lower the heat and continue cooking for 1 minute. Remove from the heat and swirl in the remaining butter.

Serve at once with some baguette to mop up the juices.

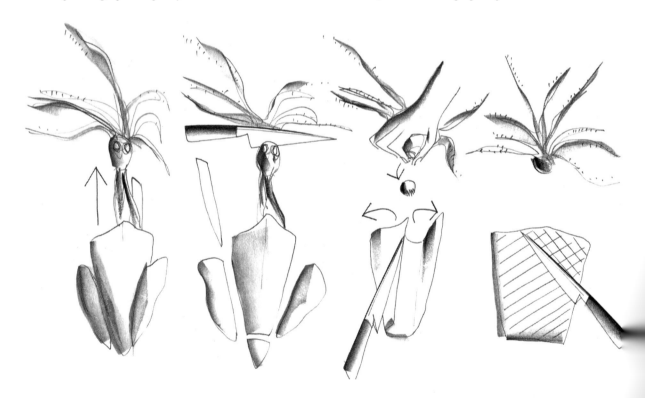

***Cleaning squid*** *is easy enough: pull firmly but gently by the head and the insides will slither out. Cut through just behind the eyes and discard the guts. Remove the hard knob from behind tentacles – this pops out when squeezed – and remove transparent quill from inside body sac. Try to leave the ink sacs intact and freeze for use in a future risotto nero or black fish sauce. (The ink, as well as being an efficient dye, has a strong flavour.) Pull off the fins – these are edible. Larger squid need their lacy outer skin removed. Slit the body open down one side and trim to a rough rectangle. Incise a shallow 1-cm / ½-inch diamond cross-hatch on the inside only, taking care not to cut all the way through. This causes the squid to roll up when cooked. Rinse*

## SEARED SQUID WITH SHALLOTS AND DEEP-FRIED TENTACLES

Cleaning squid can be unpleasant, with surprising revelations about their last meal – sometimes you find fish inside that completely fill the body and you can only marvel at how they were swallowed.

One of the nice things about this dish is the contrast between the texture of the meaty bodies and that of the crisp fried tentacles. If you can't get shallots, just use onions in the same way.

**SERVES 4**

**1 kg / 2¼ lb small squid**
**450 g / 1 lb shallots, thinly sliced**
**3 tbsp corn or groundnut oil**
**1 garlic clove, finely chopped**
**2 hot red chillies, diced**
**oil for deep-frying**
**salt and pepper**
**flour, for dusting**
**15 g / ½ oz whole coriander leaves**

Prepare the squid as described opposite.

Sweat the shallots in the corn or groundnut oil until soft, turn up the heat and fry, stirring, until browned and starting to crisp.

Stir in the garlic and half the diced chillies. Cook for 30 seconds, stir and leave in the pan to keep warm.

Heat the oil for deep-frying to 190°C/375°F.

Slice the squid flesh into strips. Heat a heavy frying pan until smoking hot. Season the squid strips with salt and pepper, toss into the pan and sauté.

They will start to become opaque and curl. After about 30–45 seconds, the strips will have curled up and be cooked. As soon as this happens, transfer them to a warmed plate – cook any longer and they will toughen up and go rubbery. Scatter over the crisp shallots.

Toss the squid tentacles in the seasoned flour (if any are large, first cut them in half or into four lengthwise), then deep-fry for 60 seconds only. Drain well and distribute between the plates.

Finish by scattering over the remaining chilli and whole coriander leaves.

## COD OR HADDOCK FISH CAKES

Binding the flaked fish, mashed potato and parsley with some very thick white sauce produces deliciously moist fish cakes. Because they are so creamy inside they need no further embellishment, but are particularly nice when served with a rocket salad dressed with lemon juice and olive oil.

**MAKES 8 CAKES**

**550 g / 1¼ lb potatoes, peeled**
**600 ml / 1 pt milk**
**450 g / 1 lb boneless cod or haddock**
**30 g / 1 oz unsalted butter**
**30 g / 1 oz flour**
**salt and pepper**
**freshly grated nutmeg**
**2 tbsp chopped flat-leaved parsley**
**2–3 eggs, beaten**
**85 g / 3 oz fine breadcrumbs**
**sunflower oil, for frying**

Boil the potatoes in lightly salted water until tender. Drain, mash dry and reserve.

While the potatoes are cooking, put the milk in a pan. Skin the cod and put it, with the skin, in the milk and bring to the boil. Turn off the heat and leave to stand for 5 minutes. Take the fish out of the milk and leave to cool, reserving the cooking liquid.

Flake the fish, leaving about three-quarters of it in the form of large flakes and finely chopping the rest of it. Reserve.

Make a roux: melt the butter in a heavy-based pan over a low heat, stir in the flour and cook gently for about 1 minute, stirring continuously. Whisk in 300 ml / ½ pt of the reserved cooking liquid and cook gently over a low heat, whisking at regular intervals, until the sauce is very thick. Taste and season with salt, pepper and freshly grated nutmeg. Stir in the chopped flat-leaved parsley.

Mix together the reserved mashed potato and this white sauce, then fold in all the fish – both the large flakes and the chopped fish. Spread the mixture out on a Swiss roll tin and leave it until it is quite cold.

Divide the cooled mixture into 8 and form into balls. Coat with beaten egg, roll in breadcrumbs and flatten into cakes.

Shallow-fry the fish cakes in the oil on both sides over a low heat until they are golden brown, turning them only when they are nicely crisped on the bottom.

Serve the fish cakes as soon as all of them are cooked.

*In the age of efficient refrigeration, bacteria, moulds and other micro-organisms are what mostly cause meat to go off.*

*Unless frozen, meat and fish will suffer from oxidation in necrotic tissue. Meat is from hot-blooded animals, so muscle enzyme activity takes place most prolifically at live body temperature – even after death. When chilled to between 1 and 4°C / 34 and 40°F this decomposing enzyme effect is significantly slowed, becoming the gradual tenderizing and flavour-enhancing process know to the meat trade as ageing. This is why the best beef is hung in cold storage for up to 3 weeks, an expensive process which explains why properly aged beef costs more.*

*Fish, being cold-blooded creatures, have protein-consuming enzymes in their systems which continue to work* post mortem *at the temperature of the water from which they came. Unless frozen immediately after they are caught, however, this means that their decomposition is inevitable and very rapid.*

## EASY THAI FISH CAKES

Any white fish will do for these spicy fish cakes but, as you are using very strong flavouring ingredients, take this opportunity to use something cheap and cheerful like coley.

To serve the fish cakes as a dinner-party first course, sprinkle them with a scattering of crisply fried julienne of shallots or leeks.

MAKES 10–12

550 g / 1¼ lb white fish fillets (see above)
1 lemon grass stalk
handful of coriander
2 hot green chillies
1 tbsp fish sauce
1 egg
flour, for dusting
sunflower oil, for frying

Skin the fish fillets, cut them into pieces and put them in a blender or food processor.

Peel off the thick outer leaf of the lemon grass stalk, top and tail it and cut across into the thinnest rings you can manage. Finely chop the coriander and chillies. Add all of these to the fish, together with the fish sauce and the egg. Blitz the mixture to a smooth purée, scrape this into a bowl, cling-wrap the top and refrigerate for at least 2 hours or overnight.

Using a tablespoon to give the right amount, form the mixture into balls and then flatten these into cakes. Dredge the fish cakes with flour and shallow-fry them in the oil for about 3–4 minutes on both sides until they are golden brown.

## DEEP-FRIED WHITEBAIT

Whitebait, while usually baby herrings or sprats, can be the fry of any fish, including sand eels, smelts and small gudgeon. A traditional accompaniment is deep-fried curly parsley, but lots of whole flat-leaved parsley leaves scattered over is a fresher alternative and a pleasantly astringent taste to balance the richness of the fish.

SERVES 6 AS A FIRST COURSE

1 kg / 2¼ lb whitebait
115 g / 4 oz flour
salt and pepper
vegetable oil for deep-frying
a little cayenne pepper
whole flat-leaved parsley leaves, to garnish
lemon quarters to serve

Preheat the oven to 130°C/275°F/gas 1 and the oil for deep-frying to 190°C/375°F.

Season the flour well and put it in a plastic bag. Add the fish, a handful at a time, and shake to coat. Transfer to a sieve and toss gently to remove excess flour (returning this to the plastic bag as you go).

Fry the whitebait in batches, which will take about 2 minutes each time. Lift them out with a wire scoop and put them on a pile of heaped kitchen towels to drain, keeping them warm in the oven with the door ajar.

To serve, shake a little cayenne pepper over the whitebait, scatter them with lots of whole flat-leaved parsley and add a lemon quarter for each person.

## SMOKED SALMON TARTARE

Salmon either raw, seared and raw in the middle or lightly smoked all show the fish at its best, and it is possible to combine raw with smoked to good effect. When raw or smoked, salmon is very rich, so one does not need a large amount for a first course.

Few would dispute that the best smoked salmon comes from Scotland and, while wild salmon is the ultimate choice, we now have very good organically farmed salmon which is raised in pens that are not overcrowded and are situated in strong currents that make the fish swim. You can always tell by the price: if the salmon is very cheap it will be nasty, flabby and rank-tasting. Buy fillet from the tail end, which will be cheaper than a middle cut.

If you can get them, salt-packed capers are preferable to the ones sold in brine. Rinse them and the fish before use.

SERVES 4 AS A FIRST
COURSE
**450 g / 1 lb fillet of salmon**
**115 g / 4 oz smoked salmon, diced**
**2 tsp freshly made English mustard**
**juice of 1 lemon**
**1 tbsp capers, rinsed and drained**
**2 shallots, finely chopped**
**small bunch of chives, chopped, plus a few more whole stalks for garnish**
**salt and pepper**
**150 ml / ¼ pint double cream**
**4 slices of white bread, to serve**

Run your finger along the pin bone line of the salmon fillet to ensure that all the bones have been removed, then skin and cut the flesh into small dice. Put into a bowl with the smoked salmon.

Add the mustard, lemon juice, capers, shallots and chives. Season with a little salt and lots of pepper and refrigerate for 2–4 hours.

Whip the cream to soft peaks in a bowl, being careful not to take it too far, and fold the tartare into it.

Toast the slices of bread, cut off the crusts and put on cold serving plates. Pile the mixture neatly on top and garnish with 2 chives cut in half on each.

## HERRINGS IN OATMEAL

Herrings coated in oatmeal used traditionally to be cooked in bacon fat, which gave them a lovely smoky flavour. They are also just as good cooked in a mixture of sunflower oil and butter or in olive oil.

SERVES 4
**4 whole herrings**
**1 egg**
**salt and pepper**
**85–115 g / 3–4 oz coarse ground oatmeal**
**4 tbsp oil**
**30 g / 1 oz butter**
**lemon wedges, to serve**

Cut off the heads of the fish and gut them, cutting them open from head to tail. Run your thumbs down the back to detach the spines, then ease these away from the skin and flesh. Use tweezers to pull out as many of the remaining bones as possible.

Beat the egg with some salt and pepper, brush this on both sides of the flattened fish, then lay them in the oatmeal, pressing it in with your fingers.

Heat the oil and butter in a large frying pan and fry the fish over a moderate heat for 4 minutes each side.

Serve the fried herring with lemon wedges.

## HERRING ROES

Herring roes are lovely when simply grilled or fried in butter, but the latter treatment makes them very rich indeed. Instead, try dusting them lightly with flour, dipping them in some beaten egg, then coating them with raspings (fine breadcrumbs, see page 303).

Fry the egged-and-crumbed roes in 5 mm / ¼ inch of sunflower oil over a low-to-moderate heat, turning them once and only after the base crumb has gone a crisp golden-brown.

On turning you may need to add some more oil to the pan. Resist the temptation to push the roes around while they cook, as this will only break the crust, which takes about 5 minutes to form. They are so moist you do not need to worry about overcooking if you find it takes longer. It is important not to cook over too high a heat or the crumb will burn.

Drain the cooked roes on a pile of kitchen paper before serving on warmed plates with a wedge of lemon and a little bunch of watercress, or simply sprinkled liberally with chopped flat-leaved parsley.

## ROLLMOPS

Rollmops or vinegar-soused herring is a very Northern European treatment, but gross depletion of this undervalued fish from brutal over-netting off our coasts and EU quota systems means that the herring you buy to make the dish will probably be imported from Norway. While traditionally baked in malt vinegar, white wine vinegar or cider vinegar gives a more delicate result.

They can be cooked the day before and refrigerated.

SERVES **8** AS A FIRST
COURSE
**8 fresh herrings**
**1 onion, sliced**
**salt and pepper**
**1 tbsp pickling spice**
**4 bay leaves**
**300 ml / ½ pint vinegar (see above)**
**brown bread and butter, to serve**

Preheat oven to 180°C/350°F/gas 4.

Wash and scale the herrings, cut off their heads, slice open the underside and gut them. Rinse the cavity well.

Remove the backbones by first pressing down through the skin to detach it from the surrounding flesh. Turn the fish on their backs and pull out the backbones, using a small knife to detach them with the tail, then flatten the filleted fish with the heel of your hand. Remove any obvious bones with tweezers or small pliers. Put the herring skin side down.

Place a slice of onion on each herring. Season with salt and pepper and, starting at the tail, roll each up neatly, securing it with a toothpick.

Sprinkle the pickling spice in the bottom of a gratin dish just big enough to hold the rollmops in a single layer and pack them into it. Stick the bay leaves between the fish and pour over the vinegar and an equal volume of water to come about halfway up the fish. If you need more liquid, add equal parts of vinegar and water until it does.

Bake for 30 minutes. Remove and let cool, then chill for at least an hour.

Serve with brown bread and butter.

---

### NO-COOK KIPPERS
*Kippers should not be cooked at all, but soaked briefly in very hot water, when they emerge plump and succulent. Stand them, tails upwards, in a jug and pour in boiling water from a kettle. Leave to steep for 2–3 minutes, remove, drain and serve on warmed plates with a small knob of butter on top.*

---

## SOUSED HERRINGS

When making the Scottish soused herring you can use malt vinegar and water in equal parts, which is authentic but tends to make the dish very forceful, or substitute a mixture of dry white wine and white wine vinegar.

Alternatively you can use equal parts dry cider and cider vinegar. This is not classically Scottish, but makes an excellent marinade just the same. Unless you feel up to the task, have your fishmonger fillet the herrings for you

SERVES **6**
**6 herring, filleted**
**1 carrot, thinly sliced**
**1 onion, sliced into thin rings**
**chopped flat-leaved parsley, to garnish**
**for the marinade:**
**300 ml / ½ pt white wine vinegar (see above)**
**300 ml / ½ pt dry white wine**
**225 g / 8 oz onion, cut into thin rings**
**1 carrot, sliced**
**8 parsley stalks**
**4 cloves**
**3 bay leaves**
**sprig of tarragon**
**½ tbsp salt**
**12 black peppercorns**

First make the marinade: put the vinegar and the wine in a pan with all the other ingredients. Bring to the boil, lower the heat and simmer gently for 20–30 minutes. Remove from the heat and leave to cool completely.

Arrange the herring fillets skin-side down in a flameproof roasting pan, pour over the marinade and slowly bring it to the boil on the hob. Immediately remove from the heat and leave to cool.

To finish the dish, blanch the carrot sliced in boiling salted water for 2–3 minutes, then refresh them in cold water and drain.

Arrange the cooled fish fillets on a serving plate and spoon over some of the marinade. Scatter the carrot slice over the fish and arrange the rings of onion on top. Garnish with some flat leaved parsley.

## MACKEREL WITH VERJUICE

SERVES 4 AS A FIRST
COURSE
**2 whole mackerel**
**4 bay leaves**
**125 ml / 4 fl oz verjuice (page
61)**
**1 tbsp whole coriander seeds**
**1–2 tbsp olive oil**
**salt and pepper**
**5 tbsp extra-virgin olive oil**

Have your fishmonger fillet the
mackerel and remove the pin bones, or
do this yourself with small pliers or
strong tweezers (see below).

Put the fillets skin side down on top
of the bay leaves in an earthenware
dish and spoon over the verjuice.
Scatter over the coriander seeds, cling-
wrap the top and refrigerate overnight.

The next day, remove the fillets and
pat dry, brushing the skin with olive oil
and seasoning with salt and pepper. Put
a dry heavy frying pan over a medium
heat and heat the overhead grill until
both are very hot. Lay the fillets skin
side down in the pan for 30–45 seconds,
then transfer the pan to under the grill
and continue to cook for 2–3 minutes
or until just done.

Transfer the fillets to warmed plates
and return the pan to the hob over a
high heat. Add the marinade and the
extra-virgin olive oil, bring to the boil
and bubble vigorously to reduce by
one-quarter. Spoon over the fillets and
serve immediately with boiled Jersey
Royal potatoes.

## BAKED SALMON

SERVES 4
**4 salmon steaks, about 200 g /
7 oz**
**2 tbsp olive oil**
**salt and pepper**
**4 fresh lime leaves or sprigs of
fennel**
**4 tbsp dry white wine**
**juice of ½ lemon**

Preheat the oven to 200°C/400°F/gas
6. Lay a sheet of foil on a Swiss roll tin.

Brush your salmon steaks with olive
oil and season both sides with salt and
pepper. Arrange them on one side of the
sheet of foil. Put a lime leaf or sprig of
fennel on top of each steak. Pour a
spoonful of dry white wine and a
squeeze of lemon juice on each. Lift over
the other half of the foil and wrap
loosely to make a large parcel, then
crimp the edges together tightly to seal
the parcel well.

Bake for 20 minutes, remove from
the oven and leave to cool in the foil.

When cool, open the package and
lift the skin away from the side of the
steaks with a knife. They should be
moist, pink and well-flavoured.

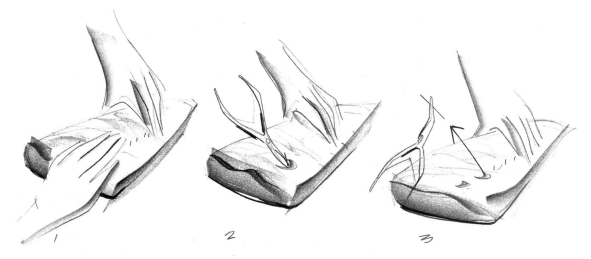

***Pin-boning a fish fillet***
*The pin-bones are located in the first quarter of the thick, head end of the fillet. Feel for them, running your finger tips along the bone line towards the
tail end. Pull them out with fish tweezers or small pliers. Run your fingers along the fish again to check you have not missed any.*

## POACHED SALMON

A whole wild salmon, poached and served cold, is one of the finest British dishes. People who have never cooked a whole fish before think it is going to be difficult but it is, in fact, so simple it sounds too easy to be true. You will need a fish kettle, which is a long narrow pan large enough to hold the fish lying on its side. This is very expensive to buy but many fishmongers lend or rent kettles.

Serve the poached salmon accompanied by freshly made mayonnaise, new potatoes and a lightly dressed leaf salad. Leave garnishing horrors like fake scales made from cucumber to the kind of caterer you have sensibly avoided.

SERVES 8–10
1 whole salmon (preferably wild), about 2.25–2.75 kg / 5–6 lb, cleaned
1 bottle of cheap dry white wine
2 bay leaves
2 onions, sliced
1 celery stalk
4 tbsp white wine vinegar
2 carrots
1 tbsp salt
12 black peppercorns

Put the cleaned salmon into the kettle on the rack which comes with it. Pour over the wine, topping up with cold water until the fish is completely submerged. You now have the correct amount of liquid in the kettle.

Remove the fish and put in the remaining ingredients. Bring to the boil using two burners, lower the heat and simmer for 20–30 minutes. Remove from the heat and leave until cold. This liquid is now called a court-bouillon.

Put the fish into the court-bouillon and bring to the boil. As soon as the poaching liquid bubbles, turn off the heat, put on the lid and leave until cold. The salmon will be perfectly cooked all the way through, but still remain moist and succulent.

Remove the fish from the court-bouillon, scrape off the skin and place the fish on a large flat dish. To serve, cut and gently lever off portion-sized pieces of salmon.

## POTTED SALMON

This is easily made from leftover poached salmon. Use roughly one part butter to four of fish. Don't worry about being too precise, make your decisions by tasting regularly as you incorporate butter and seasonings into the mixture.

It is easiest made in a processor, but before such gadgets existed it was made just as well with a pestle and mortar.

SERVES 4 AS A FIRST COURSE
225 g / 8 oz boneless, skinless salmon
4 anchovy fillets, finely chopped
¼ nutmeg, grated
½ tsp salt
½ tsp pepper
60 g / 2 oz butter

Flake the fish and remove all bones. Put in the processor bowl or a mortar. Add the anchovy, nutmeg, salt and pepper.

Melt the butter in a pan over a low heat. If using a processor, pour this in through the feeder tube while working at full speed. Otherwise, pound it into the mixture gradually in a mortar with the pestle. Taste and adjust the seasoning.

Pack the salmon mixture into ramekins or small jars you have sterilized in boiling water and pour on more melted butter to seal. Chill.

Store in the fridge for up to a week or freeze for up to 3 months.

## BLACKENED REDFISH

Blackened redfish was one of the Louisiana dishes which found international favour in the mid-'80s, when Cajun food was briefly all the rage. You could use red snapper or pompano if no redfish is to hand.

The original Paul Prudhomme recipe uses a lot of butter and his seasoning mix includes onion and garlic powder. This version retains all the right flavours but is much lighter.

SERVES 4
4 skinned redfish fillets, each about 225 g / 8 oz
1 tbsp paprika
1 tsp salt
1 tsp cayenne pepper
1 tsp ground white pepper
1 tsp ground black pepper
½ tsp dried thyme
½ tsp dried oregano
60 g / 2 oz unsalted butter
3 garlic cloves, sliced
2 spring onions, thinly sliced
1–2 tbsp olive oil
1 lemon, quartered lengthwise to serve

Remove any remaining pin bones from the fish (see page 91).

In a bowl, mix together the paprika, salt, cayenne, white pepper, black pepper, thyme and oregano. Set aside.

In a small pan, melt the butter. Add the garlic and spring onions, and leave to infuse over the lowest heat for about 10 minutes. Then strain through a muslin-lined sieve into another bowl, discarding the garlic and onion.

Brush the fillets on both sides with olive oil. Scatter half the mixed seasonings in a tray, then lay the fillets on top and press down gently. Scatter the remaining mixture over the fish, press in and turn to give an even coating.

Heat a large heavy dry frying pan until it is red hot – at least 5 minutes at maximum. (Don't do this to a non-stick pan or you will ruin it!) Lay the redfish fillets in the hot pan and dribble a teaspoonful of the flavoured butter on top of each. (Switch on the extractor or open the kitchen door as acrid black smoke will billow from the pan.) Give the fillets 2 minutes and then turn them over and cook for another 2 minutes.

Serve the fish on warmed plates with lemon quarters, spooning over the remaining flavoured butter.

## JAPANESE GRILLED EEL

In Japan you find restaurants which specialize in cooking only one thing, such as noodles, tofu, grilled chicken or even eel. To grill eel in the Japanese manner you will need sake, mirin and soy sauce, which in combination together form a teriyaki basting mix. The eel is also seasoned with aromatic sansho pepper.

Unless feeling very bullish about doing the job yourself, have your fishmonger kill, skin and fillet the eels, but ask him to leave the fillets whole. This should give you enough for 4 portions as eel flesh is very rich. You want to cook them as soon as possible after you get them home.

Serve the eel with steamed glutinous rice and, for authenticity, drink some warm sake or cold Japanese beer to accompany it.

SERVES 4
**2 large eels, filleted**
**5 tbsp Kikkoman soy sauce**
**4 tbsp mirin**
**2 tbsp sake or dry sherry**
**1 tsp caster sugar**
**sansho pepper**

First, cut the eel fillets into 10-cm / 4-inch lengths, lay them flat on a work surface and thread each piece on 2 water-soaked bamboo skewers, pushing these through the fillets from one side.

Put the skewers into a steamer, cover and steam the eel fillets for about 10 minutes.

While they are steaming, make a basting liquid by mixing the soy sauce with the mirin, sake or sherry and caster sugar.

Preheat an overhead grill or flat grilling plate and grill the eel for 2 minutes on each side. Brush with the basting liquid and cook for a further 6 minutes, turning and brushing every minute.

Season with sansho pepper just before bringing to the table.

## RED SNAPPER EN PAPILLOTE

An ideal fish for roasting or baking, red snapper has long been popular in the USA, the West Indies and South America and is now widely available.

SERVES 4
**4 red snapper, each weighing 200–225 g / 7–8 oz**
**4 small leeks, thinly sliced**
**85 g / 3 oz unsalted butter**
**salt and pepper**
**4 bay leaves, halved**
**flat-leaved parsley, to garnish**

Preheat the oven to 200°C/400°F/gas 6. Cut out 4 foil circles large enough to fold in half and wrap each fish loosely inside one, crimping the edges to seal them well.

Sweat the leeks in the butter for a few minutes until soft. This eliminates some of the water from the vegetable.

Pile the leek equally on the four foil circles, lay the fish on top, spoon over the butter, season with salt and pepper and place a piece of bay leaf on top of each. Fold the foil over and crimp the edges to make a moisture-resistant seal.

Place the four papillotes in an ovenproof dish in which they will just fit and cook in the oven for 20 minutes. Open one papillote and test the fish by pushing the tip of a sharp knife in at the backbone and lifting gently. If the flesh comes away easily it is done. If not, reseal and cook for 5 minutes more.

Serve with plain boiled basmati rice or small boiled potatoes. For those who prefer, substitute olive oil for the butter. Flat-leaved parsley is an appropriate garnish.

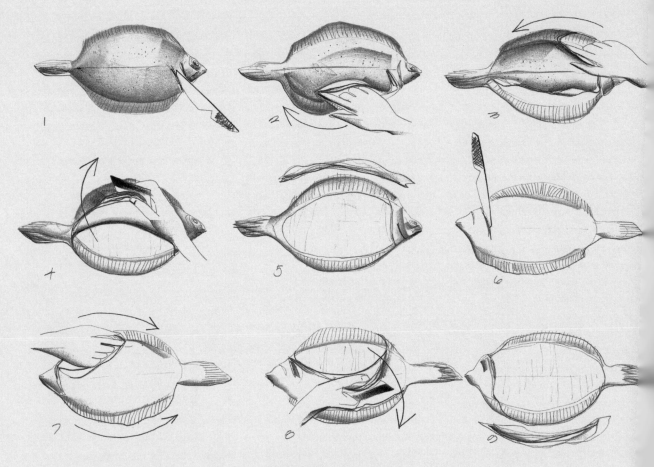

## SKINNING A FLAT FISH

*The technique is the same for any flat fish. Put the fish on a flat surface, dark side upwards. Just in front of the head, make a shallow incision. Use the tip of the knife to wiggle under the skin until you have a flap you can get hold of. Grip the tail firmly in one hand (a cloth will help prevent it slipping) and with the other pull the skin flap in a smooth continuous motion towards the tail. Trim off the edges all around the fish. Sometimes with Dover sole the white skin on the other side is also removed in the same way but this is an unnecessary refinement. It is only the dark skin which is unpalatable.*

### SOLE MURAT

Why this dish – which is basically *sole meuniére* with vegetables – should be called *sole Murat* is one of those little mysteries that makes the terminology of the French professional kitchen: (a) endearing, (b) insufferably pretentious.

Murat was for a time Napoleon's favourite general. A small man, he was famous for going into battle armed with a whip with which he used to flog the retreating foot soldiers from his superior position on horseback. Perhaps he celebrated his victories with fried soles, noisette butter and a garnish of diced artichoke bottoms and diced potatoes.

SERVES 2

**2 large globe artichokes**
**170 g / 6 oz potatoes**
**115 g / 4 oz unsalted butter**
**4 tbsp olive oil**
**2 soles, black skin removed**
**flour**
**about 100 ml / 3½ fl oz**

sunflower oil
1 large tomato, cut into 4 slices
lemon juice
1 tbsp coarsely chopped flat-
leaved parsley

Strip the leaves from the artichokes, cut away the choke hairs and any stalk. Cut the bottoms into dice and reserve. Peel and dice the potatoes.

Put 30 g / 1 oz of the butter and half the olive oil in a frying pan over a moderate heat and immediately add the potato dice, stirring and turning to coat. Turn down the heat and fry, tossing from time to time until the potato dice begin to brown. Transfer to a dish and keep warm. Fry the artichoke dice in the same amount of butter and oil until just cooked. Add to the potatoes.

Put 2 frying pans over a medium heat. Season the soles and dust them with flour. Put 3 tablespoons of the sunflower oil in each pan and fry the soles, turning once. Depending on size, they should take between 6 and 8 minutes. When done, transfer the fish to a hot serving dish, spooning the vegetable dice around them.

Dust the tomato slices with flour, season them well and fry them in a little more oil over a high heat until browned on both sides. Place 2 tomato slices on each fish.

Wipe out the pan with kitchen paper. Put in the remaining butter, place over a moderate heat and, as it just begins to go brown, pour it over the fish. To finish, squeeze over some lemon juice and scatter the chopped parsley over the dish.

## FILETS OF SOLE NORMANDE

Of all the fish dishes for which the Northern coast of France is justifiably famous, *filets de sole Normande* is arguably the most archetypal since it brings together Dover sole, mussels and tiny shrimp – three of the region's finest seafoods – with a velouté sauce that includes dry cider, shallots and crème fraîche, all equally fine Norman ingredients.

Have your fishmonger fillet the sole for you, but remember to ask for the heads and bones and use these to make a fish stock.

.

SERVES 4

4 small Dover sole (or slip
soles)
about 1.25 litres / 2 pints fish
stock (see above)
900 g / 2 lb mussels
5 tbsp dry cider or dry white
wine
4 shallots, chopped
225 g / 8 oz of mushrooms,
thinly sliced
salt and pepper
45 g / 1½ oz butter, plus more
for the dish
30 g / 1 oz flour
4 tbsp crème fraîche
250 g / 8 oz peeled shrimps
finely chopped parsley, for
garnish

Use the sole trimmings to make a fish stock, of which you will need about 1.25 litres / 2 pints.

Beard and scrub the mussels well, discarding any open ones that do not close when tapped. Put them in a pan which has a tight-fitting lid with the cider or wine, cover tightly and cook over a high heat, shaking occasionally, for about 6 minutes or until they are all open. Drain the mussels through a colander, reserving the cooking liquid. Shell the mussels.

Preheat the oven to 190°C/375°F/ gas 5 and a hot grill. Butter a baking dish and scatter the chopped shallots and mushrooms over the bottom. Roll up the fillets, skin side inwards, and arrange on top. Season with a little salt and pepper. Pour the fish stock over, dot with one-third of the butter and cover with foil.

Bring to a boil on the hob, then transfer the dish to the oven and bake for 6 minutes.

Carefully lift out the fillets with a slotted spoon (reserving the cooking liquid) and put on a warmed serving plate. Keep warm while you make the sauce: make a roux with the remaining butter and the flour, beating in 450 ml / ¾ pint of the reserved cooking liquid along with the shallots and mushrooms. Bring to the boil, whisking. When thickened, beat in the crème fraîche. Stir in the mussels and shrimps. Taste, adjust the seasoning and pour and spoon over the sole.

Put the fish under the hot grill briefly to bubble and brown the surface, and serve at once, garnished with a little finely chopped parsley.

## STEAMED SOLE

Steaming is a very Chinese approach to fish cooking and is a great technique as long as the fish are cooked whole and on the bone. The fish does not have to be expensive; lemon sole is excellent cooked this way and so is whiting. If you want to go up-market, try steaming a sea bass or a Dover sole.

You may have a dedicated piece of kit to do the job, but others can improvise. A large wok with a lid and a rack is ideal. You steam the fish on the plate on which you serve it, allowing 450 g / 1 lb weight per person on the bone, so make sure it is large enough for the fish to sit flat on the base.

If serving the fish as part of a Chinese meal, a 900-g / 2-lb fish will be enough for 4. The Cantonese tend to scatter the fish with lots of flavouring ingredients, like dried shrimp and bits of ham, but this is not essential. Set up the steamer with water in the bottom and put to boil. Make sure the fish is scrupulously clean. If there is any blood in the body cavity, rub with salt and rinse under cold running water.

**SERVES 2**

**1 whole sole, weighing about 675 g / 1½ lb**

**1 carrot**

**3 spring onions**

**5-cm / 2-inch piece of ginger**

**1 garlic clove**

**1 hot red chilli**

**2 tbsp sesame oil**

**2 tsp sunflower oil**

**3 tbsp soy sauce**

**whole coriander leaves, for garnish**

> ### FREEZING FISH
>
> *Take a tip from the sea-fishermen's practice of gutting and icing fish the instant it comes on board. A cold-bag is the best alternative and is an essential piece of kit on a warm summer's day. One hour at 30°C/80°F, for example, will do more damage than four days in the fridge.*
>
> *The next on-site precaution is to gut the fish as soon as possible after they are caught, because their guts contain powerful enzymes which, after death, speed decomposition (see page 88). Fish should be rinsed of any visible blood when they are gutted and cleaned, and before freezing, to avoid discoloration of the flesh.*
>
> *When freezing small fish, do so whole. Larger fish should be filleted or cut into steaks to aid rapid freezing. The larger the amount to be frozen, the longer time it takes and the bigger the resulting ice crystals and the poorer the quality of the flesh texture and flavour once thawed. Always freeze on the day the fish is caught and remember that the efficiency of your freezer will affect the end-product. The lower the temperature the better, and the less time in the freezer the better. When freezing, use zip-lock bags to ensure an airtight seal and to prevent freezer burn.*
>
> *Shellfish are not really for domestic freezing. Indeed, even the very rapid industrial freezing of things like scallops does them no favours. Mussels and clams can be frozen, but this is best done after cooking, taken out of their shells and in their cooking liquid.*

Cut the carrot, spring onions and ginger into julienne strips, putting them immediately into a bowl of iced water and tossing to mix the strands. Cut the garlic clove into paper-thin slices and the chilli into thin rings.

Put the sesame and sunflower oils in a small pan with the garlic and chilli and heat gently.

Pour 1 tablespoons of soy sauce on the base of the plate for the steamer and then lay the fish on top, skin uppermost. Pour the remaining soy sauce over and put to steam. The size of the fish does not affect the cooking time, which will be between 12 and 15 minutes, as much as it does with other cooking methods.

Test that it is done after 10 minutes by sliding the tip of a knife into the back at the centre and pulling upwards. The flesh should detach easily. You do not want it undercooked because it will not come off the bone. Conversely, it is difficult to overcook because steaming is a gentle, forgiving technique and you would probably have to leave the fish for about 20 minutes before it was actually ruined.

*Opposite (left to right): Cod or Haddock Fish Cakes (page 87), Easy Thai Fish Cakes (page 88)*

Remove the fish and plate from the steamer and wipe round the edge of the plate for a neat presentation. Drain the vegetable julienne and heap on top of the fish. Pour the now hot and aromatic oil on top to wilt the vegetables and complete the dish by scattering whole coriander leaves over.

Eat immediately – if the oil is allowed to cool it will make the dish greasy.

## KEDGEREE

Kedgeree should properly be made from smoked haddock and include hard-boiled eggs. It has its roots in the early days of the Raj, an example of Anglicizing an Indian dish – probably *khicharhi*, boiled rice and lentils tossed in ghee with spices – first referred to in 1845 by Eliza Acton. Her version included boiled rice and flaked boiled fish, bound and cooked with raw eggs. By 1861 Mrs Beeton's recipe takes for granted that the fish is smoked haddock and the eggs hard-boiled and chopped finely. In a Victorian context, when big breakfasts were commonplace, it must have seemed a wholly appropriate way to start the day, though now it is more likely to be eaten for lunch or supper.

Kedgeree is a *réchauffée*, that is an assembly of cooked ingredients which are gently reheated, either in a pan on the hob or in a low oven. The amount of cream used is a matter of personal preference, with the richer variations coming close to a pilaf in texture.

*Red Snapper en Papillote (page 93)*

**SERVES 4**

**275 g / 10 oz cooked basmati rice**

**275 g / 10 oz cooked smoked haddock, picked over and all bones removed**

**3 hard-boiled eggs, shelled and halved**

**1 tsp cayenne**

**freshly grated nutmeg**

**salt and pepper**

**150 ml / ¼ pt double cream**

**60 g / 2 oz butter**

**chopped chives, for garnish**

**1 lemon, quartered, to serve**

Preheat the oven to 160°C/325°F/gas 3 and butter a large ovenproof dish. Push the egg yolks through a sieve and chop the whites.

In a bowl, mix together the rice, fish and the chopped egg whites. Season with cayenne, nutmeg, pepper and a little salt. Stir in the cream, put into the dish and dot the top with the butter.

Heat through in the oven for about 20 minutes.

To serve: mound the kedgeree in the centre of 4 warmed plates. Garnish with the sieved egg yolk and chopped chives. Put a lemon quarter on each plate and serve.

## BROILED PIKE-PERCH

Pike-perch, also called sandre, made the news recently when it was cast in the role of villainous European interloper, a vicious fish that was killing and bullying its way to dominance in our canals. It has always been very popular in France and Switzerland (where it is called zander) and is a firm, white-

fleshed freshwater fish which can indeed be cooked in any number of different ways. Anything you can do with cod, you can do with pike-perch, so start by treating it in the most simple way possible and broiling it.

Serve the fish on a bed of spinach blanched in rapidly boiling water for no more than a minute, then drained and dressed with a little butter and seasoned with pepper.

**SERVES 4**

**4 pike-perch steaks, each weighing about 200 g / 7 oz**

**olive oil**

**salt and pepper**

Check the fish steaks for any pin bones and remove them with small pliers or strong tweezers. Brush the steaks all over with olive oil and season with salt and pepper.

Preheat the grill and heat a heavy frying pan until very hot, then lay the fish in it, skin-side down. Cook for 2–3 minutes without touching or pushing the fish or you will cause the skin to stick and break. You want the skin to crisp and take a good, dark colour.

Transfer to under the grill and finish cooking for a further 2–3 minutes, no more. The flesh should only just be opaque, but be cooked all the way through.

## MATELOTE

While a French sailor is a *matelot*, *matelote* is not a Wren-type person, but usually a stew of freshwater fish. Matelotes can be made from individual fish, like trout, pike, perch and carp, or may be a combination of all or any of them. The consistency of the dish is important in that identifiable pieces of fish should be served with a thickened sauce – it is not a soup. The fish should never be so overcooked it falls to pieces.

You find variations all over France, with regional recipes stressing local produce. In Alsace a matelote is cooked in Riesling and cream, in Burgundy red wine, and in Normandy dry cider. Onions, mushrooms and bacon are also typical ingredients. Norman matelote is also unique in being made with sea fish.

The Loire version given here is made of eels, the meaty flesh of which is particularly appropriate for a matelote. Even if you can't face the killing and skinning eels yourself, this dish is well worth cooking at home.

**S E R V E S  6**
**1 kg / 2 lb eels**
**20 button onions, peeled**
**30 g / 1 oz unsalted butter**
**5 tbsp olive oil**
**20 button mushrooms**
**2 onions, diced**
**2 garlic cloves, chopped**
**1 bottle of Muscadet or other**
**very dry white wine**
**bouquet garni of celery,**
**parsley, bay leaf and thyme**
**salt and pepper**
**fried croutons (page 65) and**
**chopped parsley, for garnish**

Find a fishmonger who will kill and skin the eels for you and then chop them into 5-cm / 2-inch pieces.

Sauté the button onions in the butter and 2 tablespoons of the olive oil until soft.. Add the button mushrooms and toss until just cooked; reserve.

Heat the remaining oil in a large heavy-based pan and fry the onions until soft. Add the garlic, turn up the heat and add the eel. Stir and toss, then add the wine and bouquet garni. Season, bring to the boil, then lower the heat and simmer gently for 10–12 minutes, until the flesh just starts pulling easily from the bones.

Drain through a colander into another saucepan, reserving the eel and onion, and reduce the liquor by half at a rapid boil. Discard the bouquet garni.

Put the eel, onions, button onions and mushrooms into the sauce and heat through gently. Serve garnished with fried croutons and chopped parsley.

## FISH PIE

Readers regularly complain of poor results with their fish pies, usually – we guess – because they over-cook the fish before putting it into the pie. The preliminary poaching of the fish in milk should be only very brief, for this is only to cook it enough to facilitate removal of the skin and bones and to rid it of excess water.

People also wonder why their potato topping so often melts into the sauce and this is almost certianly because they have mashed their potatoes with too much added butter or cream. The potatoes for the toping should be mashed almost dry.

**S E R V E S  6**
**1 kg / 1¼ lb skinless cod or**
**haddock fillets**
**850 ml / 1½ pints milk**
**1 bay leaf**
**85 g / 3 oz butter, plus more for**
**the dish**
**60 g / 2 oz flour**
**1 kg / 2¼ lb potatoes**
**6 eggs**
**2 tbsp chopped flat-leaved**
**parsley**
**salt and pepper**
**freshly grated nutmeg**
**beaten egg**
**little milk**

Poach the fish in the milk with the bay leaf for 3 minutes. Strain through a colander, reserving the liquid.

In a large heavy pan, make a roux by melting two-thirds of the butter over a low heat, stirring in the flour and cooking gently, stirring, for about 1 minute. Whisk in the strained milk, bring to a simmer and cook over a low heat, stirring occasionally for 20 minutes.

Boil the potatoes in salted water until tender, drain and mash with the remaining butter only. Preheat the oven to 200°C/400°F/gas 6.

Boil the eggs for 7–8 minutes, refresh in cold water, shell and chop. Put into a buttered pie dish.

Flake the fish into large pieces, discarding all skin and bones. Discard the bay leaf from the sauce, then stir the chopped parsley into the sauce and season it with salt, pepper and freshly grated nutmeg. Continue to simmer for 2–3 minutes. Taste and adjust the seasoning.

Off the heat, mix the fish and sauce together, then pour and spoon the mixture into the pie dish. Spoon the potato on top, spreading it into an even layer with a fork. Brush the top of the potato with beaten egg mixed with a little milk.

Bake the pie for about 20 minutes, until the top is a good uniform golden colour. (Alternatively, make the fish pie the day before you want to serve it and refrigerate until you need to put in the oven next day.)

## BACCALÀ

SERVES 4 AS A FIRST COURSE

**450 g / 1 lb piece salt cod, soaked and desalinated**
**300 ml / ½ pt milk**
**1 bay leaf**
**2 garlic cloves, finely chopped**
**½ tsp black pepper**
**about 250 ml / 8 fl oz extra-virgin oil**
**squeeze of lemon juice**
**a little freshly grated nutmeg (optional)**
**fried triangles of bread or toast, to serve**

Drain the soaked and desalinated fish, break it into pieces and put in a saucepan with the milk and bay leaf. Bring to the boil, lower the heat and simmer gently for 10–12 minutes. Drain, reserving the milk but discarding the bay leaf.

Remove the skin and bones from the fish and put the flesh into a food processor. Add the garlic and pepper,

then blitz, pouring in the oil in a thin stream through the feeder tube. Add a few tablespoons of the milk, a tablespoon at a time. The purée should be very smooth, but stiff enough to hold its shape when spooned on to a plate.

Finish with a squeeze of lemon juice and a little grated nutmeg, if you like. Serve the baccalà with fried triangles of bread or toast.

## TATAKI OF TUNA

The Japanese, for whom the freshest fish is central to their diet, often eat tuna raw as *sashimi*. Getting hold of tuna fresh enough to be eaten uncooked is difficult in Britain, while for those who have not tried it, the idea of raw fish often seems quite alien and unpleasant. Absolute freshness is of paramount importance, of course, as tuna deteriorates rapidly once it is butchered.

When you buy it, take it home in a cool-bag and, as soon as you can, trim the fillet of any bloody bits and generally tidy it up with a very sharp knife before brushing with a neutral oil, cling-wrapping and refrigerating. The flesh discolours rapidly when exposed to the air, so this air-resistant seal is a good idea. Even so, try to eat the tuna the day you buy it.

Another brilliant Japanese way of dealing with tuna is tataki, searing the outside but leaving it raw in the middle. This is also an excellent way of cooking salmon and even fillet of beef. It is better if you are able to cook the flesh in a piece rather than as individual steaks. Since tuna is so rich you need no more than 115 g / 4 oz per person.

SERVES 4

**4 tuna fillets, each about 115 g / 4 oz**
**2 tbsp oil**
**salt and pepper**

**to serve:**
**soy sauce**
**wasabi (Japanese green horseradish)**
**English mustard**

Start by heating a ridged grill pan or heavy frying pan dry over a moderate heat until smoking-hot.

Brush the tuna fillets with a little oil and season all over generously with salt and pepper. Sear for 30–45 seconds on each side, turning with tongs.

Plunge into ice-cold water to stop the cooking process and immediately pat dry with kitchen paper.

Cut into 2-cm / ¾-inch thick slices and serve with soy sauce, wasabi and English mustard in separate small dishes for each person. This is a good opportunity to practise chopstick skills.

## TEMPURA

Though it is now considered uniquely Japanese, *tempura* – deep-fried large prawns and vegetables – was actually introduced to Japan in the second half of the sixteenth century by the Portuguese. It was probably rather leaden fare compared to the sophisticated and feather-light crisp batter of today's tempura.

If you want to eat the very best, go to specialist restaurants where you sit at a bar and the chef fries the food in front of you, putting it into individual bamboo baskets lined with absorbent paper the instant it is done. The batter is so delicate it does not stay crisp for long, so this is what you should try to emulate at home, deep-frying and serving your tempura in batches in the kitchen.

There are a number of essential requirements to ensure good results, starting with the quality of the ingredients. Tiger prawns of about 20–25 to the kilo (10–12 to the pound) are perfect for the job and must be very fresh. They are expensive, but you only have three each. You could also fry white fish fillets, for example 1-cm / ¹/₂-inch strips of sole, cod or haddock taken off the skin. Whitebait, too, or squid are delicious in tempura batter. For the vegetables, green beans, mushroom caps, sweet peppers and spring onions would be an appropriate selection.

Tempura is traditionally served with a light dipping sauce and grated white radish and is followed by steamed rice and pickles. The *dashi-no-moto* – that is, instant Japanese soup stock of bonito and konbu seaweed – required for the sauce is now available from better supermarkets. Once you have your pristine ingredients to hand all you need is clean oil and, most importantly, the right batter, which is made only minutes before it is used, so first prepare the food for frying.

### SERVES 4

**12 large raw prawns, shelled and deveined, heads removed but leaving the tails on**
**¹/₂ green pepper, deseeded**
**¹/₂ red pepper, deseeded**
**16 French beans**
**8 button mushrooms**
**8 spring onions**
**115 g / 4 oz daikon (mooli)**
**sunflower oil for deep-frying**

**for the dipping sauce:**
**1 sachet of dashi-no-moto**
**200 ml / 7 fl oz hot chicken stock**
**1 tsp caster sugar**
**2 tbsp Kikkoman soy sauce**
**2–3 tbsp sake (rice wine) or dry sherry**

**for the batter:**
**1 small egg**
**250 ml / 8 fl oz ice-cold water**
**250 ml / 8 fl oz (measured in a measuring jug) plain flour, sifted**

Put the prawns on kitchen paper to ensure they are completely dry. Slice the green and red peppers lengthwise into 1-cm / ¹/₂-inch strips. Top and tail the French beans and remove the caps from the mushrooms. Top and tail the spring onions and cut them in half lengthwise.

Make the dipping sauce by dissolving the contents of the sachet of dashi in the hot chicken stock. Stir in the sugar, soy sauce, sake or sherry. Divide between 4 bowls.

Grate 115 g / 4 oz daikon (mooli) and put this in 4 neat piles on small plates or saucers.

Heat a deep-fryer or wok half filled with some clean sunflower oil to 190°C/375°F.

Make the batter: in a bowl, beat the egg with the ice-cold water. When completely mixed, dump the flour into it in one go and stir quickly with chopsticks to combine. The finished batter should have lumps and still have discernible traces of flour. (If you mix until smooth, your cooked batter will be more like that for English-style fish and chips.)

Put the vegetables in a bowl with some flour and toss to coat. Dip the individual pieces in the batter and fry for 2 minutes, turning once. Cook one vegetable at a time and do not overcrowd the pan or the temperature will drop, causing the batter to absorb oil and become greasy. In between batches, skim out any pieces of batter left behind and discard. Left in the oil for too long they will burn and taint it.

Remove the cooked pieces and drain on kitchen paper, serving immediately for your guests to eat with chopsticks. Fry the prawns last. People add grated daikon to their dipping sauce as individual preference dictates.

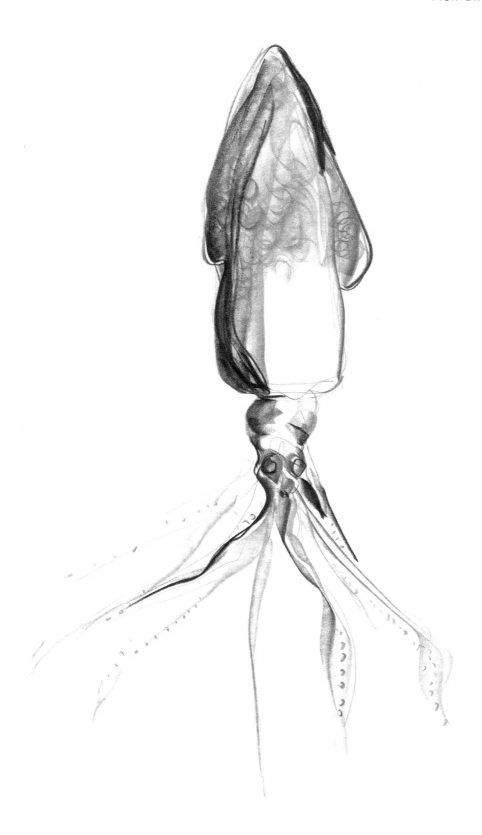

# MEAT AND OFFAL

**S**ix years ago, when the column on which this book is based began, meat was — for the majority of non-vegetarian cooks — just another ingredient. The crisis provoked by BSE, and an increasingly vocal and negative medical lobby, have made us all look at meat in terms that have nothing to do with whether or not, cooked in an appropriate way, it may be delicious. We have been made to think about the potential negative aspects of eating meat, for example its role in a contemporary Western diet which increasingly eschews saturated fat, and have been asked to consider its consumption in a moral context.

Perhaps the most encouraging thing to emerge from all this is a new-found interest in the provenance of the meat we eat. The word 'organic', once applied exclusively to fruit and vegetables, can now be applied meaningfully to meat. More people understand what a cyclo-herd is and think about the implication of retail charges in terms of their humanitarian cost. They now know that there is no such thing as compassion in the production of cheap animal protein. They also understand that animals raised in a decent way generally taste better than those reared intensively. There is consequently a discernible movement away from meat, which most often manifests itself in its selective consumption.

Supermarkets report a swing away from beef, lamb and pork towards chicken and turkey, which is ironic given the conditions in which fowl are generally raised. Good may yet come from all this. If people eat less meat but of a better quality, then this must be a positive trend

## Beef Cuts

### Blade Bone

Usually sold off the bone as blade or chuck steak, its marbling of fat and connective tissue, makes it an ideal stewing cut.

### Brisket

Fatty cut from the shoulder, usually sold boned and rolled and best for braising or pot-roasting.

### Porterhouse

Large steak cut from the thick end of the sirloin and including a piece of the fillet.

### Rib of Beef

The fore-rib is a lean and tender joint for roasting either on or off the bone. Wing rib is the best rib cut of all for roasting.

### Shin of Beef

Beef foreleg, called gravy beef in the USA because of the unctuous sauce delivered by its gelatinous content.

### Silverside

Lean and tough outer thigh muscle. Best salted and boiled as corned beef.

### Sirloin

Roasting joint from the back or loin of beef. The fillet or eye running through it is often cut out and sold separately as rib-eye steak.

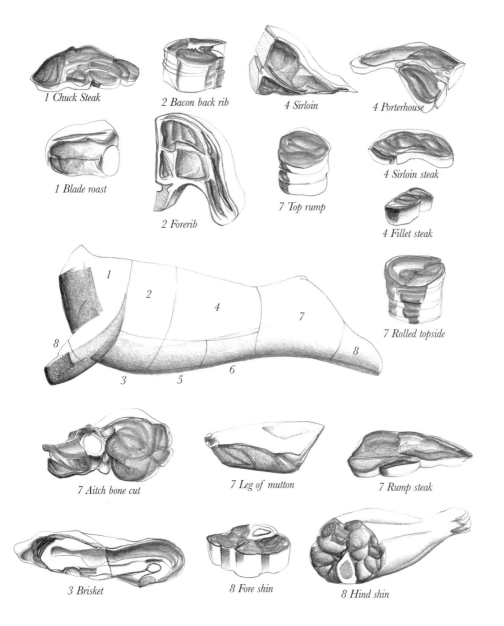

1 Chuck Steak

2 Bacon back rib

4 Sirloin

4 Porterhouse

1 Blade roast

2 Forerib

7 Top rump

4 Sirloin steak

4 Fillet steak

7 Rolled topside

7 Aitch bone cut

7 Leg of mutton

7 Rump steak

3 Brisket

8 Fore shin

8 Hind shin

## ROAST BEEF AND YORKSHIRE PUDDING

Good roast beef begins with the quality of the piece of meat you buy. This should have been aged by the butcher for at least two weeks and perhaps for as long as three. The colour will by then have deepened towards brown, while the meat will have shrunk because of evaporation of internal moisture. Yellowish fat suggests that the animal ate mostly grass, for grain feeding produces whiter fat. If the meat is bright red then it has not been hung for long enough on the carcass to mature.

Restaurants tend to cook meats at a very high temperature and these days flame rotisseries are again all the rage. In some ways this is ironic, since they mimic the earliest roasting in which meat was cooked on a spit in front of an open fire, the domestic oven being a Victorian invention. In the method described below, the meat is roasted by initially applying high temperatures, then reducing these to fairly hot.

Roast beef enthusiasts tend to favour a particular cut and arguably the finest to cook and eat at home is a joint of 5 or 6 wing ribs on the bone. This may, however, weigh as much as 4.5–5 kg / 10–11 lb and will be a correspondingly fierce price, the sort of thing you might cook once a year at Christmas and in itself a problem because most of us are not so well organized that we document precisely what we did a year ago.

A rib joint also cooks unevenly and is difficult to carve, so when cooking for others use precisely the same boned cut at a constant weight, thereby achieving consistent results for every serving. For best results the joint should not weigh less than 1.75 kg / 4 lb. Choose either a joint cut from the eye of the middle ribs or a rolled and boned sirloin – both lean cuts. In either case, the joint should be barded, that is wrapped with beef back fat by the butcher before it is tied. If you like a spicy hot and crunchy exterior, brush it all over with Dijon mustard then roll it in cracked black pepper.

The following recipe was tested in a domestic electric oven without convection. If using fan assistance, adjust cooking times according to the manufacturer's instructions. This method delivers an excellent, uniformly medium-rare finish, but only if you allow the meat to rest for 20–25 minutes in a warm place before carving it across into 2 cm / ³/₄ inch thick slices – each just right for a single portion.

The importance of resting meats after roasting is absolute and perhaps the least understood part of the cooking process. The resting process allows the partial reversing of the protein coagulation that has taken place during roasting, and lets the muscle fibres – which had tightened up in the tense heat – relax, recover their fluids and change from tough to tender, giving a more moist and succulent result. Serving roast meat very hot is not as important as this, but compensate by making sure that plates and vegetables are very hot when they come to the table.

Serve with a simple gravy made from the pan juices and reduced stock, horseradish sauce, Yorkshire pudding and crisp roast potatoes. Those who prefer their meat less rare should extend the cooking time by 10–15 minutes.

No single subject excited so much interest or debate from our readers as the Yorkshire pudding, one of the classic accompaniments to roast beef or, traditionally, served as a first course with gravy before the meat and vegetables. Although properly made from plain flour, it really makes little difference if you use self-raising since the most significant activators are the number of eggs you use, how liquid your batter is and how hot the fat is in to which you pour it.

The pudding batter given here is heavy on the eggs by Yorkshire standards but will meet the most exacting criteria of lightness and crispness. You can cook a Yorkshire successfully in oil, but good beef dripping is essential if you are to have the right flavour.

SERVES 6–8
**1.8 kg / 4 lb joint of beef (as above)**
**salt and pepper**
**splash of red wine**
**300 ml / ½ pt reduced chicken stock**

**for the Yorkshire Pudding:**
**170 g / 6 oz plain flour**
**1 tsp salt**
**300 ml / ½ pt cold milk**
**3 eggs, beaten**

First prepare the Yorkshire pudding batter: sift the flour into a mixing bowl with the salt. In another large bowl, mix together the milk with 150 ml / ¼ p cold water and whisk with the beaten eggs. Add this to the flour in a thin stream, whisking to a smooth batter. Leave to stand for 60 minutes at room temperature.

Allow the joint to come to room temperature. Season heavily with salt and pepper, rubbing it in all over. Preheat the oven to 250°C/475°F/gas 9.

Sit the joint on a rack in a roasting pan and put to roast for 25 minutes, then lower the temperature to 200°C/400°F/gas 6 and continue cooking for a further 25 minutes. It is important not to open the oven door for more than a few seconds at any time from start to finish.

Remove the meat from the oven and allow to rest on its rack for about 30 minutes in a warm place, covered with foil. Increase the oven setting to 230°C/450°F/gas 8.

While the meat is resting, cook the Yorkshire pudding: put 5 tablespoons of beef dripping into a metal pan at least 6.5 cm / 2½ inches deep and place in the oven until smoking hot. Give the batter a final whisk and pour into the fat. Bake for 25–30 minutes, when the pudding will be well risen with a crisp golden crust. You could also use this batter to make individual popovers in a bun tin.

Make a gravy by pouring off the fat from the roasting pan. Put the pan over a high heat and deglaze it with a splash of red wine. Add the stock and boil fiercely, scraping and rubbing the stuck-on sediment with the back of a wooden spoon. Taste and adjust the seasoning if necessary.

> **IMPROVING SHOP-BOUGHT HORSERADISH SAUCE**
> *Wasabi, super-hot Japanese powdered radish, can be used to boost the insipid flavour of shop-bought horseradish cream. Just mix a teaspoon of wasabi powder to a paste with cold water and mix with the bottled horseradish or use it to spike mayonnaise and other sauces.*

### RAGU BOLOGNESE

No two Italian cooks use an identical recipe or can agree on precise ingredients for a Bolognese sauce. Bologna is the home of a number of meat dishes, like *arrosto di maiale al latte* (poached pork loin), which use milk rather than stock as the cooking liquid, and several knowledgeable writers, including Marcella Hazan, promote the use of milk in a *ragu Bolognese*. Some cooks would say a *ragu* must have chicken livers, others find they make the result too rich with a bitter aftertaste. Opinions differ as to the appropriateness of including tomato.

Whatever, the key to success is long, slow cooking for at least 3 hours – or even longer. The finished *ragu* should be meltingly tender and quite intense, moist but not too runny. This is not, therefore, the definitive recipe, but one that has never failed to please. When serving with spaghetti remember that the idea is to coat the pasta, not smother it, and always offer freshly grated Parmesan at the table.

**SERVES 4**

115 g / 4 oz pancetta or
unsmoked streaky bacon
3 tbsp olive oil
450 g / 1 lb minced beef
1 onion, diced
2 garlic cloves, chopped
1 carrot, diced
1 glass of dry white wine
600 ml / 1 pt full-fat milk
600 ml / 1 pt chicken or beef
stock
1 celery stalk
300 ml / ½ pt passata
1 bay leaf
freshly grated nutmeg
3 tsp dried oregano
salt and pepper

Cut the pancetta or bacon into matchstick strips and fry in a spoonful of oil until nearly crisp. Using a slotted spoon, transfer to a heavy-based saucepan.

Brown the beef in the oil and fat remaining in the frying pan and transfer to the saucepan. Add the remaining olive oil and sweat the onion, garlic and carrot until soft. Put into the saucepan.

Deglaze the pan with the dry white wine and pour over the meat and vegetables. Add the milk, stock, celery, passata, bay leaf, nutmeg to taste and oregano. Stir, season and bring to the boil. Lower the heat and simmer gently, uncovered, for about 3 hours. Check from time to time, adding water to keep the meat just covered.

After 3 hours, reduce over a moderate heat until you have a thick, moist sauce. Taste and add more salt if needed. Remove and discard the bay leaf and celery.

## COTTAGE PIE AND SHEPHERD'S PIE

Until only fairly recently, cottage pie, made from minced beef, and shepherd's pie, made from minced lamb, used to appear with monotonous regularity during the early part of the week as easy ways of using up the leftovers from the Sunday joint. The following recipe delivers a rather special cottage pie.

SERVES 4

115 g / 4 oz pancetta or unsmoked streaky bacon, cut into matchstick strips
450 g / 1 lb lean beef mince
2 tbsp olive oil
225 g / 8 oz onion, diced
175 g / 6 oz carrot, diced
2 garlic cloves, chopped
1 glass of red wine

300 ml / ½ pint reduced beef or chicken stock or water
450 g / 1 lb canned chopped tomatoes
1 bay leaf
2 tsp dried oregano
2 tbsp Worcestershire sauce
3 tbsp tomato ketchup
salt and pepper
creamy mashed potatoes (page 195), to serve

### THICKENING SAUCES AND GRAVIES

*Whether your sauces have depth and vigour depends very much on the strength of flavour in the base medium. Chicken stock, for example, must be reduced considerably before it takes on the strength of flavour you want. This is achieved after straining the stock of bones, meat and vegetables by rapidly boiling to reduce the volume. Boil without straining first and you will produce a cloudy and nasty bone-tasting broth. You then have a number of options.*

*· Reducing stock and stirring in cream at the last moment is one.*

*· Potato flour is an excellent thickening agent which does not have the pasty stickiness of cornflour and is, with colouring and salt, the main ingredient of most commercial gravy mixes.*

*· A restaurant technique simply swirls and incorporates knobs of unsalted butter into a reduction of the pan juices left after frying fish or meat. One fashionable sauce, beurre blanc, is made by whisking a lot of butter into an intensely flavoured vinegar-and-wine base in precisely this way.*

*· When using an agent like cornflour or potato flour, always mix to a smooth paste with cold water before adding to the very hot liquid you want to thicken or you will get lumps. If this happens then your last resort is to put your sauce through a sieve.*

*· Another method uses beurre manié, equal amounts of flour and butter worked to a paste and whisked into a sauce to thicken it. This confounds the accepted practice when making a béchamel (white sauce) or velouté (stock sauce) in which the flour and butter are cooked initially together (to a roux) before milk or stock is added and slowly cooked for at least 20 minutes to cook out the raw flour taste. For some reason the beurre manié behaves differently. Only if cooked for more than 2–3 minutes will it taste of flour. There are stranger things in heaven and earth than are dreamt of in your philosophy, Horatio.*

Fry the pancetta or bacon in a hot frying pan until they are almost crisp, then transfer to a saucepan. Brown the beef mince in the first pan and add them to the saucepan. Add the olive oil to the bacon fat and fry the onion, carrot and garlic in it until soft but not brown, adding them to the saucepan when done.

Deglaze the frying pan with the red wine and add this also, topping up to cover with beef or chicken stock or water. Add the canned tomatoes with their liquid, bay leaf, oregano, Worcestershire sauce and tomato ketchup. Stir, bring to the boil and simmer uncovered over a very low heat for 3 hours, topping up with water if it gets too dry and seasoning to taste halfway through.

Preheat the oven to 220°C/425°F/gas 7. Put the contents of the pan into a deep rectangular ovenproof dish, cover it with a topping of the creamy mashed potatoes and brown in the oven, about 20 minutes.

You now have a main course which could sit happily on any decent table in France, where it would be called *hachi parmentier.*

## SHOOTING STEW WITH PARSLEY DUMPLINGS

A shooting stew is something you would serve a shooting party for lunch – if you move in country circles where large numbers of people need to be fed after a long morning spent blasting birds out of the sky, an activity which will leave them cold, tired and famished. It is safe to assume that those so preoccupied enjoy eating as well as killing their prey, so your typical shooters' stew should contain game birds as well as beef.

Other hungry people will enjoy this combination after any form of exercise on a cold day, with or without guns. The amounts, which are generous, may be halved to serve 6 people with hearty appetites, or 8 who have been indoors watching TV.

SERVES 8–12

2 oven-ready pheasants
about 2 litres / 3½ pints chicken stock
450 g / 1 lb piece of smoked fat bacon, cut into lardons
4 tbsp sunflower oil
2.7 kg / 6 lb shin of beef, cut into 225 g / 8 oz portions
flour, for dusting
1.35 kg / 3 lb onions, sliced
450 g / 1 lb carrots, sliced lengthwise
4 celery stalks, cut across into thin slices
4 garlic cloves, chopped
2 tbsp flour
2 bay leaves
4 tbsp Worcestershire sauce
1 bottle of red wine
salt and pepper

for the dumplings:
450 g / 1 lb self-raising flour
170 g / 6 oz butter, diced
2 eggs
30 g / 1 oz flat-leaved parsley leaves

Poach the pheasants in simmering chicken stock for 45 minutes. This is a good way of dealing with badly shot birds or last year's from the freezer. Allow to cool in the stock and, when cool enough to handle, strip off all the meat and reserve, returning the carcass to the stock and continuing to simmer for 1 hour. Strain and reserve the stock.

Fry the lardons gently until the fat runs and they start to brown. Transfer with a slotted spoon to a big pot.

Add some sunflower oil to the frying pan and turn up the heat. Dust the beef shin portions in seasoned flour and sear them a few at a time, adding them to the pot.

Put some more oil in the pan and sweat the onions until soft but not brown, then scatter them over the meat.

Fry the carrot strips slowly until caramelized. Add the celery, garlic and 2 tablespoons of flour. Stir and fry all together for a minute or two, then add to the pot with the bay leaves and Worcestershire sauce.

Pour over the bottle of red wine and top up with pheasant stock to cover. Bring to the boil, skim, lower the heat and season with a little salt and lots of pepper. Simmer uncovered for 2 hours. Check to see if the meat is done, then adjust the seasoning if needed. If not quite done, continue cooking, checking every 15 minutes until it is. It is much better to do this than overcook, as this results in dry, flaky meat. The stew can be held until the next day and reheated.

To make the dumplings, put the flour in a food processor with the diced butter, salt and pepper. Blitz briefly to a crumb. Add the eggs and parsley leaves. Pulse-chop and then dribble a spoonful or two of cold water through the feeder tube until it starts to hold as a coherent mass. Remove and transfer to a lightly floured surface. Divide into 2 pieces and roll each into a cylinder. Cut each cylinder into 12 and roll the slices gently into 24 balls.

Poach the dumplings in simmering salted water for 20 minutes or, for the best result of all, steam them. They take about the same time but emerge firm, light and dry. They are always better cooked separately from a stew and using butter rather than suet gives a nicer taste.

About 10 minutes before you are ready to serve, stir the pheasant meat into the stew and serve with the dumplings.

## BAECKENOFFE

As its name might suggest, baeckenoffe, meaning literally 'the baker's oven', is a speciality of Alsace-Lorraine, that northern part of France which abuts Germany.

Originally this stew was taken in a sealed pot to the baker's on a Sunday to be cooked in his oven after the bread was baked. This meant a hot meal would be provided on Monday, when women were apparently occupied in pre-emancipation days with the weekly wash. It is suitably serious fare and just the thing to keep waistbands snug and the cold at bay.

This will feed 6 trenchermen or 8 normal eaters. Apart from the browning of the meat, which improves flavour and appearance, the recipe is fairly orthodox.

SERVES 6–8

450 g / 1 lb shin of beef, cut into large chunks

450 g / 1 lb lamb neck fillet , cut into large chunks

450 g / 1 lb pork loin, cut into large chunks

1 bottle of dry white wine

30 g / 1 oz beef dripping

60 g / 2 oz lard

450 g / 1 lb onions, sliced

4 garlic cloves, chopped

450 g / 1 lb carrots, sliced

1.5 kg / 3.5 lb potatoes, peeled and sliced

tied bouquet garni of celery, bay leaf and thyme

salt and pepper

flat-leaved parsley, to garnish

Marinate the beef, lamb and pork in the wine overnight.

Next day, when ready to cook, pre-heat the oven to 160°C/325°F/gas 3. Remove the meat from the marinade. Heat the beef dripping in a heavy frying pan and brown the meat in it.

Heat the lard in a flameproof casserole and fry the onions, garlic and carrots until they start to brown. Arrange the potato slices overlapping on top of the onions. Lay the bouquet garni on that and arrange the meats on top. Season generously with salt and pepper and pour over the marinade.

Bring to the boil on the hob, cover with a tight-fitting lid (use foil if it isn't) and put into the oven for 2½ hours.

Serve in large soup bowls, scattered with flat-leaved parsley.

## BROWNING MEAT

*Browning meat fulfils both flavour-enhancing and aesthetic functions, literally changing its taste and colour. For a long time people thought that searing the outside of meat kept juices in by creating an impermeable barrier that prevented loss of moisture. We now know this is just wishful thinking, but to get that inimitable and robust depth of flavour into, for example, a Burgundian beef stew, then the meat, the vegetables and the flour which thickens the sauce all need to be browned at a high temperature, for liquid alone cannot caramelize the exterior. There are, of course, many wonderful dishes that do not require preliminary browning, of which* pot au feu *and* bollito misto *are primary examples, though you should remember that meat like beef and lamb is intrinsically high in saturated fat whatever you do or don't do to it. Dishes poached without the benefit of a preliminary browning are much more subtle and delicate in effect and in one analysis – and given current medical thinking – healthier. This can be argued about, but the fattening implication is absolute: frying adds calories that would not otherwise be there.*

## HUNGARIAN GOULASH

An authentic goulash is more a soup than a stew, and its preparation traditionally begins with the beef or veal being fried in lard, though you may prefer to use olive oil or a mixture of sunflower oil and butter.

SERVES 4

about 85g / 3 oz lard or oil (see above)
salt and pepper
flour
900 g / 2 lb of shin or chuck steak, cut into 115-g / 4-oz pieces
400 g / 14 oz onions, cut into chunks
2 garlic cloves, smashed and chopped
1 tbsp paprika
450 g / 1 lb canned chopped tomatoes
1 litre / 1¾ pints beef or chicken stock
1 bay leaf

for the horseradish dumplings:
170 g / 6 oz self-raising flour, plus more for dusting
60 g / 2 oz white breadcrumbs
4 tsp grated horseradish
1 tbsp chopped parsley
1 tsp salt
85 g / 3 oz unsalted butter
white of 1 egg

Heat the lard or oil in a frying pan. Season and flour the shin or chuck steak pieces and brown vigorously all over, transferring them to a heavy casserole dish as they are done.

Fry the onions in the pan until brown, adding a little more lard or your chosen fat if needed. As it browns, stir in the garlic and paprika. Cook, stirring for 2 minutes, then spoon over the meat.

Season with salt and pepper and pour in the canned tomatoes and stock. Add the bay leaf and bring to the boil. Skim off any scum that rises to the surface, lower the heat, cover and simmer for about 1½ hours, stirring occasionally. You can cook on the hob or in an oven preheated to 160°C/325°F/gas 3. Don't take the meat too far; it should be tender but coherent. Overcooking will deliver a dry finish.

The goulash may be eaten immediately, but improves by being left until the next day, when it should be reheated very gently, adding water if necessary to give a soupy consistency.

To make the dumplings, put the flour, breadcrumbs, grated horseradish, chopped parsley, salt and butter in a food processor. Blitz to a crumb texture, then, with the machine still running, add the egg white through the feeder tube. Add a little cold water until the dough balls. With floured hands and on a floured surface, shape the dough into ping-pong-sized balls. Poach in simmering salted water for about 20 minutes, when they should be well risen and light.

Serve the dumplings with the goulash.

BRAISING AND STEWING
*The difference between braising and stewing is, essentially, the amount of liquid used and whether or not the dish is cooked with the lid on or off. Both stewing and braising are done in a pot, which may either be heated on the hob or in the oven. Braising uses less liquid in a pot with the lid on and is therefore closer to steaming, while stewing covers the meat being cooked with liquid and is usually done without a lid. A braise often means pot-roasting a single large piece of meat. A stew usually has the meat cut into portion-sized or bite-sized pieces.*

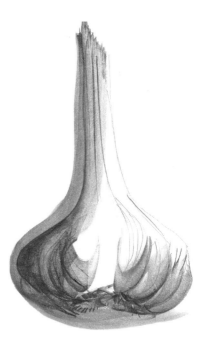

## RED FLANNEL HASH

Red flannel hash, a New England speciality, is coloured by beetroot. Before you can make it you need to have some leftover corned beef, that is, proper salted brisket. Here is how to pickle some American deli-style corned beef. The quantities given make beef for 10 sandwiches and enough left over to make hash for 4.

**for the corned beef:**
**300 ml / ½ pt red wine vinegar**
**8 garlic cloves, smashed**
**500 g / 1 lb 2 oz sea salt**
**115 g / 4 oz brown sugar**
**30 g / 1 oz sodium nitrite (4 tablets)**
**3 tbsp pickling spice**
**5 bay leaves**
**6 cloves**
**20 juniper berries**
**20 black peppercorns**
**2.3-2.5 kg / 5-5½ lb piece of brisket**
**2 onions, quartered**
**handful of celery leaves**
**rye bread and mustard and dill pickles, to serve**

**for the red flannel hash:**
**115 g / 4 oz streaky bacon, diced**
**225 g / 8 oz onion, diced**
**450 g / 1 lb boiled potatoes, diced**
**225 g / 8 oz cooked beetroot (not vinegared), diced**
**2 tbsp chopped flat-leaved parsley, plus more to serve**
**3 tbsp sunflower oil**
**30 g / 1 oz butter**
**4 poached or fried eggs**

First pickle the corned beef: put 4.5 litres/ 8 pints water in a large saucepan with the red wine vinegar, garlic cloves, sea salt, brown sugar, sodium nitrite, pickling spice, bay leaves, cloves, juniper berries and peppercorns. Bring to the boil, lower the heat and simmer for 20 minutes, then leave to cool.

Wash a lidded plastic bucket, then rinse it with Milton's fluid to sterilize it. Put the brisket in it and pour the brine over through a sieve. Weight the meat with a heavy sterilized plate to keep it submerged. Put the lid on the bucket and leave in a cool place for 10–12 days. (The pickle can be reboiled and used again but add another 225 g / 8 oz salt and resterilize the bucket first.)

Rinse the beef and place in a large pan. Cover with cold water and bring to the boil. Throw this water away and replace with fresh, rinsing the beef again under running water. Bring back to the boil, adding the quartered onions and celery leaves. Lower the heat and simmer for about 1¼ hours. The brisket should be tender enough to be pierced easily with a carving fork.

Make the sandwiches while the beef is still hot, piling thick slices between rye bread and serving with mustard and dill pickles.

A couple of days later, you should be ready to reacquaint yourself with the beef – this time in the red flannel hash. Fry the streaky bacon gently until crisp. Transfer to a large bowl with a slotted spoon. Add the diced onion and sweat until soft, then put with the bacon. Dice about 450 g / 1 lb of the corned beef then mix this, together with the potatoes, beetroot and parsley, evenly with the bacon and onion.

Add the sunflower oil to the pan and heat until shimmering hot. Put in the hash, pressing down gently to make an even cake, and lower the heat as far as you can. Cook for about 30 minutes, turning the pan to ensure an even crisp crust.

Preheat a hot grill. Dot the top of the hash with the butter and finish under the grill for a few minutes to brown the top.

Cut into wedges and serve with a poached or fried egg on top and a little more parsley scattered over.

## REUBEN SANDWICHES

Nobody knows why these corned beef, sauerkraut and Gruyère sandwiches on rye bread with caraway seeds are called Reuben, or where they first originated, though it might be reasonable to guess that the inventor had that name and he probably lived in New York, the historic centre of all deli sandwiches, around the turn of the century.

Corned beef is not the stuff you buy in cans, a uniquely British product, but boiled salted silverside, called 'corned' because when the meat come out of the pickle and dries, salt crystals form on the surface in small seeds looking like tiny corn kernels.

Americans build their sandwiches so big you can get lockjaw trying to fit one in your mouth.

SERVES 2
**4 slices of caraway seed rye bread (or plain rye if this proves difficult to find)**
**Dijon mustard**

2 slices of Gruyère cheese
225 g / 8 oz corned beef (see
above), thinly sliced
2 tbsp well-drained sauerkraut
60 g / 2 oz melted butter
potato crisps and dill pickles,
to serve

for the Russian dressing:
1 tsp Tabasco
2 tsp Worcestershire sauce
1 tsp lemon juice
2 tbsp tomato ketchup
3 tsp grated horseradish
5 tbsp mayonnaise

First make the Russian dressing: whisk the Tabasco, Worcestershire sauce, lemon juice, tomato ketchup and grated horseradish into the mayonnaise.

Preheat a heavy frying pan dry over a low heat. Lay out your 4 pieces of bread and spread 2 of them with Russian dressing and the other 2 with mustard. Put a slice of cheese on the bread spread with dressing, trimming it to fit neatly. Arrange half the corned beef on top of each mustard-spread slice. Top with the sauerkraut and invert the cheese bread slice on top to complete the sandwiches.

Brush one side of each sandwich with half the melted butter and place in the pan, butter side down. Increase the heat slightly and cook for 3 minutes. Brush the top with the remaining melted butter, turn and give it another 3 minutes.

Remove the sandwiches from the pan and cut in half diagonally before serving with potato chips and dill pickles on the side.

## CORNISH PASTY

The pasty was the world's first portable lunch. There are as many questions about exactly what goes into a Cornish pasty as there are recipes. First let it be said that the pasty may not have actually originated in Cornwall, though it certainly became uniquely associated with that county a long time ago. The word 'pasty' was used in medieval times to mean a pie containing venison and to distinguish it from a pie which had several different ingredients.

In the past, Cornish pasties were made from whatever was available and were food associated very much with poverty. Thus rabbit, bacon scraps and vegetables would have been the authentic fillings of hard times.

The true Cornish pasty of today is half-moon-shaped and usually made with chuck steak, potatoes and onion, though it may also contain diced turnip, the proportions varying depending on individual preference.

The amount of filling given below is only a rough guide. You could increase the percentage of potato, for example. Chuck, cut from the bladebone of the top forequarter, is considered the ideal beef for this treatment, as it is lean but marbled throughout with connective tissue.

MAKES 4
for the pastry:
675 g / 1½ lb plain flour,
sifted
175 g / 6 oz lard
175 g / 6 oz butter
1½ tsp salt
a little iced water

for the filling:
450 g / 1 lb chuck steak
225 g / ½ lb potatoes
225 g / 8 oz onion
salt and pepper
beaten egg (optional)

First make a short pastry with the flour, lard, butter and salt as described on page 287, bound with a little iced water. Cling-wrap the dough and chill for 30 minutes.

Preheat the oven to 200°C/400°F/ gas 6 and grease a baking tray. Cut the chuck steak into pieces the size of your little fingernail. Chop the potatoes and onion into small dice. (Some purists would say the potatoes should be sliced thinly, then cut into strips.)

Roll the pastry out to a thickness of about 5 ml / ¼ inch and, using a plate as a guide, cut out 4 circles with a diameter of 15 cm / 6 inches. Distribute the filling ingredients equally between them, putting a layer of potato first, then meat, then onion, seasoning generously with salt and pepper. Brush the edge of one half of the pastry with water, bring the other half over and press together firmly to seal. Crimp the edge together in a tight seal and brush with beaten egg (a fancy and possibly heretical suggestion).

Bake on the greased tray in the oven for 20 minutes. Turn down the oven to 160°C/325°F/gas 3 and continue to cook for a further 40 minutes. Serve warm or cold. Pasties may be reheated in a 180°C/350°F/gas 4 oven for 10–15 minutes.

## FRIKADELLER

Meatballs are universal throughout Scandinavia and really in any part of the world where meat production was limited, since they are a way of making the best of not-very-good meat.

**SERVES 4**

225 g / 8 oz minced beef

115 g / 4 oz minced pork

2 tbsp fresh breadcrumbs

2 eggs

2 tbsp chopped parsley

salt and pepper

1 tsp caster sugar

1 onion, chopped

15 g / ½ oz butter

2 tbsp lager (optional)

**clarified butter or a mixture of olive oil and butter, for frying**

Put the minced beef and pork in a large bowl together with the breadcrumbs, eggs, chopped parsley, salt, pepper and sugar.

Fry the onion gently in the butter until soft. Add to the other ingredients in the bowl and mix well, adding a little lager if the mixture is too dry (if, for example, you overdid it with the breadcrumbs). Roll into walnut-sized balls.

Fry the meatballs for about 5 minutes in the clarified butter or olive oil and butter, turning, until brown all over.

## DAPHINA

This is a stew traditionally cooked overnight on Friday for eating on the Jewish Sabbath. In a goyish (non-kosher) variation, a pig's trotter will thicken and enrich just as well as the calf's foot. The overnight cooking is an authentic touch, but you may prefer instead to cook at 130°C/275°F/gas 1 for 4 hours or on top of the stove at a bare simmer for 1½–2 hours.

**SERVES 6**

225g / 8 oz chickpeas

1 kg / 2¼ lb shin of beef

**flour, for dusting**

3 tbsp light olive oil

salt and pepper

4 large carrots, cut lengthwise into strips

350 g / 12 oz onion, diced

3 garlic cloves, thinly sliced

1 split calf's foot or pig's trotter

1 bay leaf

sprig of rosemary

about 2 litres / 3½ pints beef or chicken stock or water

4 potatoes, peeled

4 raw eggs in their shells

Starting 2 days ahead, soak the chickpeas overnight in cold water.

Next day, drain and cover with fresh water. Bring to the boil and boil hard for 10 minutes. Drain and reserve.

---

### CASSEROLE COOKING

*The cheaper cuts of meat can be transformed into the most tender and delicious by slow cooking in liquid. Ideally choose gelatinous cuts with an even distribution of fat, that is marbling, like shin of beef or lamb neck fillet, for low-fat meat just does not work in a slow-cooked stew and will always emerge dry and chewy. Do not let the butcher cut the pieces too small. Ask for pieces large enough to make individual servings or, better still, buy the meat in a piece and cut it up yourself. Preliminary marinating in some wine, beer or a couple of tablespoons of wine vinegar will improve the flavour. Pat dry, then flour the meat and brown it in a little oil in a very hot pan. Slowly fry the onions, carrots, celery and garlic separately, then mix them with the meat in a heavy pot and cover with the reserved marinade and stock. Chicken stock will work with any casserole or stew. Cook it slowly with a bay leaf and some suitable bundle of herbs with just the occasional bubble breaking the surface – what the French call* frémir *or* tremble. *Taste after about 1½ hours, when it may well be done. If not, then taste again every 10 minutes until it is.*

*We are encouraged to think that the best stews are cooked for hours and hours. This is generally untrue, though ox cheek, a currently fashionable restaurant cut for daubes – and the muscle which has never stopped working the beast's jaws – can very easily take 4 hours.*

---

*Roast Beef with Yorkshire Pudding (page 10⸱*

Preheat the oven to 120°C/250°F/ gas ½. Cut the beef into 6 thick post-card-sized slices. Roll in seasoned flour and brown in the oil over a high heat, transferring to a casserole when done.

Fry the carrot strips in the same pan over a low heat until caramelized, then add them to the beef. Sweat the onion until translucent, then stir in the garlic cloves and cook for 2–3 minutes more.

Add the contents of the pan to the casserole with the chickpeas, calf's foot or trotter, bay leaf and rosemary. Season. Pour over enough beef or chicken stock or water to cover and lay the potatoes and eggs in their shells on top. Bring to the boil on top of the stove and skim. Put on a lid, transfer to the preheated oven and cook overnight.

Next day, remove the eggs and allow them to cool in cold water. Shell and mash them, then stir into the stew before serving.

## SHABU-SHABU

Shabu-shabu is simplicity itself. A well-flavoured pot of simmering broth is put over a flame at the table for guests to cook their chosen ingredients as they like. This involves the skilful use of chopsticks, but is great fun – a Japanese variant on the fondue party. The ingredients to be cooked in the broth may be as your fancy and pocket dictate, but consider strips of chicken breast, peeled raw prawns, shiitake mushrooms, beansprouts, tofu, strips of beef fillet and spinach.

*ted Flannel Hash and Reuben Sandwiches*
*page 110)*

SERVES 4

**2 skinless chicken breast fillets, cut into strips**
**8 large peeled raw prawns**
**4 shiitake mushrooms**
**about 115 g / 4 oz beansprouts**
**about 225 g / 8 oz tofu**
**225 g / 8 oz beef fillet, cut into strips**
**115 g / 4 oz spinach**
**steamed rice, to serve**

**for the broth:**
**1.75 litres / 3 pints chicken stock**
**3 tbsp Mitsukan rice vinegar**
**4 tbsp Kikkoman soy sauce**
**1 sachet of instant dashi powder**
**4 small carrots**
**5-cm / 2-inch piece of ginger**
**8 spring onions, cut into 2.5 cm / 1-inch pieces**

Put the stock in a saucepan, add the rice vinegar, soy sauce and dashi powder.

Peel the carrots and cut lengthwise into wafer-thin slices (a potato peeler makes this easy). Cut the ginger into similar slices. Add these and the spring onions to the pan. Bring to the boil, lower the heat and simmer for 10 minutes.

Pour the flavoured broth into the serving pot which will go on the table. After cooking and eating the solid ingredients you drink the broth. Serve steamed rice as well.

## HAMBURGER

A proper hamburger is made only from minced beef seasoned with salt and pepper. Any additions are those added to in the bun, like raw onion, pickles, ketchup and mustard. It is important to use good-quality mince, but this should have about a 15 per cent fat content or the burger will split and taste dry and chewy. The best way to get this correct proportion of lean to fat is to have your butcher mince a selected piece of meat for you. Blade bone – also called chuck – or flank steak are perfect.

An overcooked hamburger is an abomination, but some people will want to cook them all the way through because of fears about salmonella and E-coli. These bacteria tend to be found on the surface of the meat and, if present, mincing therefore distributes them throughout the patty.

MAKES 6

**900 g / 2 lb minced beef**
**salt and pepper**

Spread out the beef, season with flake sea salt and black pepper and divide into 6 portions. Form these into balls, squeezing gently between your hands to compact the meat. The dilemma is how hard to squeeze. If you pack too loosely they will fall apart, but squeeze too tight and they will cook tough and dry.

Cook the hamburgers is in a dry heavy, non-stick frying pan, preheated over a low heat, and then turned up to moderate a minute before you start cooking. Turn once, giving both sides an equal time. This size of hamburger will cook to medium-rare in 5 minutes.

## COOKING STEAKS

The most expensive cut is fillet, that is the meat found under the blade bone of the loin and a piece of muscle which weighs between 2.3 kg / 5 lb and 3.2 kg / 7 lb in a carcass weighing between 225 kg / 500 lb and 325 kg / 600 lb – which goes some way towards explaining its price. It is also used to describe the extension of that same muscle which is part of the unboned whole rump, correctly termed the undercut.

The fillet produces at least 4 different steaks:

(1) Châteaubriand is large and thick, weighing at least 450 g / 1 lb and usually 550 g / 1¼ lb. This is cooked whole and only to rare and, after resting, is carved at the table for two people, usually accompanied with a béarnaise sauce and *pommes frites*. It is named after François René, the Vicomte de Châteaubriand, who was French ambassador to London in the 1820s. Apparently it was during his time here that his chef invented béarnaise.

(2) Tournedos are small round steaks cut from the thinner end of the middle part of a fillet of beef. They should be carefully trimmed of all external fat and membrane and are also sometimes surrounded with back fat and tied with string. Tournedos are what you would preferably use for a dish like *steak au poivre*. They should be 3–4 cm / 1–1½ inches thick and weigh about 100–125 g / 4–4½ oz. Filet mignon is just a superior tournedos and should always be served rare, having been cooked no more than 2 minutes each side on a very hot ridged grill pan or heavy dry frying pan.

(3) Noisettes are tournedos poor relation, being cut thinner and having an oval shape.

(4) A T-bone steak is cut on the bone from the sirloin, giving what amounts to 2 steaks, on one side a loin steak and on the other part of the fillet. An entrecôte is a loin steak, that is a sirloin steak without the undercut and off the bone.

When cooking steaks, make sure the meat is at room temperature and your ridged grill pan smoking-hot. Just before grilling the meat, brush it all over with olive oil and season well with salt and pepper. It really is impossible to be absolute about how long to grill because there are so many determining factors but, as a rough guide, for a steak weighing 350 g / 12 oz a total of 4 minutes on each side will deliver a rare finish and the meat should be allowed to rest in a warm place for 5 minutes before serving.

## STEAK DIANE

Steak Diane is one of those preparations from a largely bygone restaurant era where waiters used to cook simple dishes by the table, with much stylish flambé work.

**SERVES 1**

**1 rump steak, about 250 g / 8 oz**
**salt and pepper**
**45 g / 1½ oz butter**
**2 tbsp brandy**
**2 tbsp Worcestershire sauce**

Take the rump steak and batter it out with a cutlet bat or rolling pin to a uniform thickness of about 5 mm / ¼ inch. Season well.

Heat a heavy frying pan until it is smoking hot. Throw in 30 g / 1 oz of the butter and swirl it quickly round the pan. Lay the steak in the pan and give it just a minute on one side, then turn and repeat for a minute on the other side. The meat must not be allowed to overcook.

Add the brandy, shake the pan and keep your eyebrows out of the way as it ignites. When the pyrotechnics have died down, transfer the steak to a warmed plate while you finish the sauce.

Add the remaining butter and the Worcestershire sauce to the pan. Bubble the mixture down, stirring vigorously with the back of a spoon until you have a coating consistency – about a minute, no more. Pour over the steak and serve at once.

## LOW-CAL STEAK IN BROTH WITH NOODLES

Diets are grim, but low-calorie food can be delicious. The trick appears to be to eat the minimum of fat and lots of carbohydrates, so you feel full.

Ideally, have a dish that others who are not on a diet can enjoy eating with you. There is nothing more depressing than serving yourself a boxed MeanCuisine meal while all those about you are tucking into fish and chips.

Steak is normally completely banned from the meals of those on a diet because even lean meat is fairly full of saturated fat. Since this recipe only calls for 85 g / 3 oz per serving it is not too sinful, for a little goes a long way with this treatment.

SERVES 2

**175 g / 6 oz strip sirloin steak**

**1 tbsp Kikkoman soy sauce**

**1 tbsp lemon juice**

**115 g / 4 oz instant thread noodles**

**about 600 ml / 1 pint chicken stock**

**2 spring onions, chopped**

**3-cm / 1¼-inch piece of root ginger, peeled and cut into julienne strips**

**handful of coriander leaves**

Trim off excess fat from the steak and then put it in the freezer for 15 minutes to chill and stiffen. This will make it easier to shave the beef into wafer-thin slices with a razor-sharp knife.

Marinate the beef slices at room temperature in the soy sauce and lemon juice for 30 minutes.

Soak the noodles briefly in boiling water, then drain.

Poach the beef in the boiling chicken stock for 10 seconds. Serve in the chicken broth, with the noodles, a splash more of soy sauce and sprinkled with the chopped spring onions and julienne of ginger. Scatter over the coriander leaves to serve.

## SEA PIE

Why a beef pie should have been called a 'sea' pie is not clear unless its simplicity meant a ship's cook could produce one even in rough weather. This recipe daringly includes beer and a bay leaf. Use bitter or stout, not lager, but if you want to be basic just use water. Just-cooked Savoy cabbage makes a nice accompaniment.

SERVES 4–6

**900 g / 2 lb shin of beef, cut into 8 roughly equal pieces and trimmed of any large bits of fat**

**flour for dusting**

**60 g / 2 oz lard or beef dripping**

**225 g / 8 oz onion, sliced**

**225 g / 8 oz carrots, thinly sliced**

**1 bay leaf**

**2 tsp chopped thyme or ½ tsp dried**

**salt and pepper**

**about 2 litres / 3½ pints beer to cover**

**for the suet crust:**

**225 g / 8 oz self-raising flour**

**115 g / 4 oz suet**

**1 tsp salt**

**125 ml / 4 fl oz ice-cold water**

Dredge the pieces of beef in flour and brown them in the lard or beef dripping in a medium-hot pan. Transfer to a shallow saucepan. Fry the onion and carrots in the remaining fat. When softened put them with the meat.

Add the bay leaf and thyme, season with salt and pepper, and push down with a slotted spoon or potato masher to compress, then pour over just enough beer to cover. Bring to the boil, lower the temperature and simmer gently for 40 minutes, topping up with the rest of the beer and/or water as required to keep the meat just covered.

While the meat is cooking, make the suet crust: put the flour in a bowl with the suet, salt and ice-cold water. Stir and work the mixture with a fork until it balls. Alternatively, use a food processor briefly (flour, suet and salt in first, adding water through the feeder tube to bind), but avoid using your hands. The less you handle suet pastry the lighter it will be.

Roll this out on a floured surface and cut out a round just smaller than the diameter of a pudding basin. Carefully sit the suet crust on top of the meat, put the pastry lid on top and continue cooking for 50–60 minutes. Test that the meat is done by pushing a skewer through the crust and into the meat.

When it gives to your satisfaction, cut the crust into 4, lift it out, a piece at a time, and place on individual plates, then divide the meat, vegetables and gravy.

## RED-COOKED SHIN OF BEEF WITH STEAMED CHILLI AND CORIANDER DUMPLINGS

The description 'red-cooked' does not necessarily imply a literal colour, but is rather a Chinese description of stewing with soy sauce, in the same way that 'white cooking' describes poaching in a clear liquid. It can also be applied to roasting meats, but here maltose and red rice vinegar or hoisin sauce may also contribute to the colour.

This recipe for red-cooked shin of beef is rich and aromatic, almost French in character. The meat, however, is not browned first as it would be in a daube.

SERVES 4

6 garlic cloves, cut into wafer-thin slices
16 whole peeled shallots
4 spring onions
4 tbsp sunflower or groundnut oil
900 g / 2 lb piece of shin of beef, trimmed of any excess fat and cut into 5-cm / 2-inch pieces
5-cm / 2-inch piece of root ginger, peeled and thinly sliced
1 large strip of dried orange peel
150 ml / ¼ pt Chinese dark soy sauce
150 ml / ¼ pt Shaoxing (Chinese rice wine) or dry sherry
30 g / 1 oz brown sugar
2 heads of star anise
1 cinnamon stick
1.1 litres / 2 pints chicken stock

for the Chilli and Coriander Dumplings:

140 g / 5 oz self-raising flour
30 g / 1 oz butter
1 egg
1 tsp chilli flakes
salt and pepper
1 tbsp chopped coriander leaves

Put the garlic in a heavy casserole dish with the shallots and spring onions. Add the oil and cook gently over the lowest heat, stirring from time to time, for 10 minutes, taking care not to let the garlic get too dark or it will become bitter.

Add the beef to the casserole with the ginger, orange peel, soy sauce, rice wine or sherry, brown sugar, star anise and cinnamon. Pour over the stock, stir to combine and bring to the boil. Lower the heat, put on a lid and simmer for about 2 hours, when the meat should be very tender.

To make the chilli and coriander dumplings: put the flour in a food processor with the butter. Work briefly to a crumb, then add the egg, chilli flakes and salt and pepper. Whiz again to combine. Add the chopped coriander leaves and, with the machine at full speed, dribble spoonfuls of cold water through the feeder tube until the dough balls. Do not overwork or the dumplings will be heavy. Turn out on a lightly floured surface and roll gently into a cylinder, then cut into 8 pieces.

Put the dumplings on a plate and steam for 20–25 minutes, when they will be well risen and have an almost bread-like quality. Serve with the stew.

## VEAL MARSALA

Veal escalopes are thin slices of veal cut for you by the butcher from the calf's thigh. Place them between sheets of greaseproof paper and pound them with something wooden and heavy to make them even thinner – about the thickness of a pound coin.

SERVES 2

2 veal escalopes (as above)
salt and pepper
8 field mushroom caps, thinly sliced
30 g / 1 oz butter
2 tbsp sunflower oil
½ wine glass of a not-too-sweet Marsala

Season the escalopes with salt and pepper. Sauté the mushrooms in some butter until cooked and reserve.

Put a couple of tablespoons of sunflower oil and a knob of butter in a heavy frying pan over a moderate heat and fry the escalopes for a couple of minutes on each side. Transfer to warm plates to rest while you finish the sauce.

Pour the wine into the pan and boil it down, scraping up any bits stuck to the pan. Add the sliced mushrooms and toss. Pour over the escalopes and serve immediately.

## CÔTES DE VEAU DIJONNAISE

This is a classic mustard-flavoured dish.

**SERVES 4**

**4 veal chops**
**4 tbsp olive oil**
**salt and pepper**
**30 g / 1 oz flour**
**150 ml / ¼ pt white wine**
**150 ml / ¼ pt chicken stock**
**1 bay leaf**
**3½ tbsp crème fraîche**
**3 tbsp Dijon mustard**

**to serve:**
**buttered boiled potatoes**
**flat-leaved parsley**

Brush the veal chops with olive oil and season both sides with salt and pepper. Brown them in a pan over a moderate heat, turn this down to low and continue cooking, turning from time to time until just done, which will take (depending on thickness) between 15 and 20 minutes. Transfer to a warmed plate and keep warm.

At the same time, put 3 tablespoons of olive oil into a pan and stir in the flour, then add the wine and chicken stock. Increase the heat to boil, season with salt and pepper and add a bay leaf. Lower the heat until bubbles just break the surface and simmer.

When the chops are done, remove the bay leaf from the sauce and whisk in the crème fraîche into the sauce. Bring to the boil, stirring. Remove from the heat and whisk in the mustard.

Spoon the sauce over and round the chops and serve with buttered boiled potatoes scattered with parsley.

## SALTIMBOCCA

Saltimbocca, Italian for 'jump into the mouth', is one of the great dishes of the world, a thin veal escalope flavoured with sage and wrapped in Parma ham before being briefly pan-fried. Serve with boiled new potatoes. Use a potato peeler to shave off a few curls of Parmesan and scatter them over the potatoes together with a few snipped chives.

**SERVES 4**

**8 veal escalopes, each about 45 g / 1½ oz**
**pepper**
**8 sage leaves**
**8 thin sheets of Parma ham**
**4 tbsp olive oil**
**1 garlic clove, finely chopped**
**100 ml / 4 fl oz red wine**
**15 g / ½ oz unsalted butter**

Beat the escalopes out gently to a uniform thickness of 3 mm / ⅛ inch, using a cutlet bat, rolling pin or child's wooden hammer. Season with pepper, put a sage leaf on top then wrap a thin sheet of Parma ham round, roll up and beat softly so it adheres to the veal.

Put the olive oil in a small pan, add the garlic and stew it over a low heat for 10 minutes. Pass half through a sieve into a frying pan, discarding the garlic.

Over a high heat, fry 4 of the saltimbocca for 1 minute on each side, then transfer them to a warmed plate. Add the remaining garlic-infused oil and fry the second batch in the same way.

Deglaze the pan with the red wine, swirling in the butter and bubbling down to a syrupy residue. Spoon this over the saltimbocca and serve.

## OSSO BUCO

Osso buco is cut from the shank of a veal calf, with its bone and marrow, and the dish is a classic of the Italian kitchen, where it is most frequently served with a saffron risotto but is also very good with mashed or boiled potatoes.

Osso buco is also often served with gremolata, a piquant dressing of parsley, garlic and lemon zest.

**SERVES 4**
4 ossi buchi
flour for dusting
salt and pepper
2 tbsp olive oil
225 g / 8 oz onion, finely chopped
4 inner celery stalks, finely chopped
1 carrot, finely chopped
300 ml / ½ pt tomato passata
850 ml / 1½ pt dry white wine
1 bay leaf

for the gremolata:
1 small garlic clove
handful of flat-leaved parsley
zest of 1 lemon

One at a time, shake the ossi buchi in a bag of seasoned flour. Then brown them lightly in the olive oil in a hot frying pan, doing 2 at a time. When they are brown all over, transfer to a tray and reserve.

Fry the onion, celery and carrot over a low heat until translucent.

Transfer to a casserole dish in which the meat will just fit in one layer, sit the ossi buchi on top and season. Pour over the tomato passata and just enough dry white wine to cover, topping up with water if needed. Bring to the boil, skim and lower the heat to a bare simmer. Add the bay leaf and cook gently until the bone starts to loosen from the meat. This will take about 90 minutes. The stew can be allowed to cool and held at this point to be reheated gently.

Make the gremolata by finely chopping together the garlic with the parsley and lemon zest.

Serve the osso buchi in 4 large warmed soup plates with some risotto Milanese (flavoured with saffron) or boiled new potatoes and the gremolata sprinkled sparingly over the top.

## CALVES' LIVER WITH ONIONS AND DEEP-FRIED SAGE

Calves' liver is the finest and most expensive offal. Much of what is sold, however, comes from box-reared, liquid-fed veal calves from Holland. You may want to speak to your butcher about obtaining liver from animals raised in less ghastly circumstances. Expect to pay a premium.

**SERVES 4**
900 g / 2 lb onions
85 g / 3 oz butter
oil for deep-frying
500 g / 1 lb 2 oz calves' liver, cut into 4 slices
flour, for dusting
salt and pepper
3 tbsp olive oil
2 tbsp dry sherry
2–3 tbsp jellied chicken stock
8–12 sage leaves

Slice the onions into thin rings. Melt 60 g / 2 oz of the butter in a large heavy pan or casserole over a low heat, add the onions and stir. Sweat the onions slowly for about 20 minutes. You want to get as much moisture out of them while taking them to the point where they are soft and translucent.

Turn up the heat to moderate and fry the onions until nicely brown, but do not take them too far or they will burn and go bitter.

Preheat the oil for deep-frying to 190°C/375°F. Carefully remove any tubes or threads from the liver, then coat the slices lightly in seasoned flour, shaking off any excess.

Heat a large sauté pan over a moderate heat. When smoking hot, add the oil, then 30 g / ½ oz of the butter and immediately lay in the slices of liver. Cook for 2 minutes then turn and cook for 60 seconds more. Remove the liver and sit the slices atop a mound of fried onions on a warmed serving plate.

Turn up the heat and deglaze the pan with the sherry, scraping and stirring. Add the jellied chicken stock and bubble through, then swirl in the remaining butter. Pour over the liver.

Plunge the sage leaves in the hot oil for 60 seconds until crisp. Drain on paper towels, scatter over the liver and serve at once.

*Pork Cuts*

### Belly

*Also called flank, this is one of the most useful of pork cuts, with about equal proportions of meat to fat. It is used for streaky bacon, pancetta and petit salé. The ribs attached are the spare ribs.*

*Chops*

*The loin chops are cut from the fore loin, thicker chump chops from the hind loin.*

### Fore loin

*The bony rib end, when boned, is stuffed and rolled.*

### Hind loin

*Roasting cut which includes the tenderloin fillet — a prime lean cut sold separately — and the kidneys.*

*Leg*

*Big roasting cut weighing about 5 kg / 10 lb. Often divided into knuckle and half-leg fillet.*

### Shoulder

*Forequarter divided into three joints, bladebone, shoulder and knuckle.*

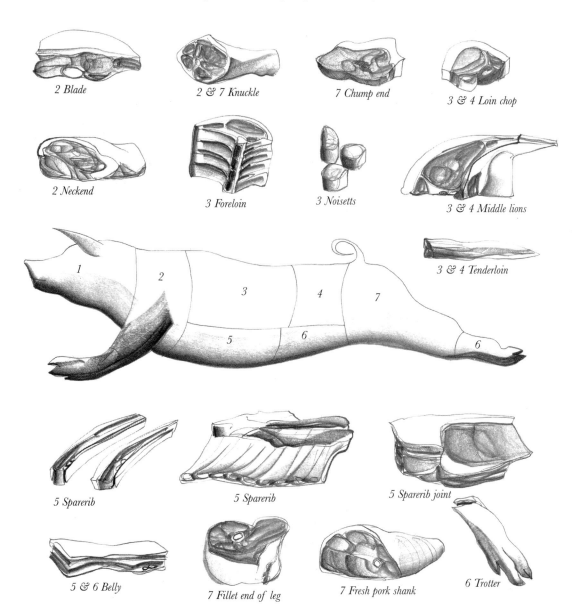

*2 Blade*

*2 & 7 Knuckle*

*7 Chump end*

*3 & 4 Loin chop*

*2 Neckend*

*3 Foreloin*

*3 Noisetts*

*3 & 4 Middle lions*

*3 & 4 Tenderloin*

*5 Sparerib*

*5 Sparerib*

*5 Sparerib joint*

*5 & 6 Belly*

*7 Fillet end of leg*

*7 Fresh pork shank*

*6 Trotter*

## ROAST LOIN OF PORK

Roast pork was a celebratory dish served at Christmas and other feasts centuries before turkeys came on the scene. Within the last century, it has been served traditionally with sage and onion stuffing, crisp roast potatoes, apple sauce, just-cooked small Brussels sprouts and rich thick gravy, a fine British dinner.

Choose a 2.75 kg / 6 lb cut from the rib end, with at least half an inch of fat between skin and meat. Have your butcher chine the joint by removing all the bones except the ribs. Ask for these bones for a stock, but say you want to score the skin yourself, which you will do carefully the day before you cook it, incising a neat 2.5-cm / 1-inch diamond pattern with a small, razor-sharp knife.

### SERVES 10–12

2.75 kg / 6 lb pork cut from
the rib (see above)
Maldon sea salt
1 tbsp chopped rosemary

for the gravy:
1 bottle of dry white wine
1.1 litres / 2 pints well-
flavoured chicken stock
2 tbsp Worcestershire
sauce
1 celery stalk
1 onion, topped and tailed but
skin left on
1 carrot, chopped
1 bay leaf
a few rosemary leaves
butter
flour

for the Apple Sauce:
900 g / 2 lb unpeeled and
uncored Bramleys
strip of orange rind
30 g / 1 oz caster sugar
black pepper
60 g / 2 oz butter

for the Sage and Onion
Stuffing:
900 g / 2 lb onions, thinly sliced
115 g / 4 oz butter, plus more
for the dish
12 sage leaves
handful of parsley leaves
170 g / 6 oz fresh white
breadcrumbs
450 g / 1 lb pork sausage meat

for the roast potatoes:
about 2 kg / 4½ lb potatoes, cut
into 3.5-cm / 1½-inch chunks
oil for the pan

for the Brussels sprouts:
about 1 kg / 2¼ lb Brussels
sprouts
60 g / 2 oz butter

Rub the joint all over with Maldon salt. Sit it on the rosemary leaves and put to cure in the fridge overnight, removing for an hour to bring to room temperature before cooking.

Make a base for the gravy by bringing the bones to the boil in the wine and stock. Lower heat slightly and skim, then lower heat again to a simmer. Add the Worcestershire sauce, celery stalk, onion, carrot and bay leaf. Simmer for 2–3 hours, skimming from time to time. Allow to cool, then sieve and chill.

Make the apple sauce by chopping the Bramleys coarsely and putting them in a pan with 150 ml / ¼ pint of water, the orange rind and the caster sugar. Bring to the boil, lower the heat and simmer until the apples are soft. Push through a sieve and return this purée to the saucepan, then continue to cook over a moderate heat until you have a coherent sauce that is not too sloppy. This can be refrigerated until needed.

Preheat the oven to 250°C/475°F/ gas 9. About 2½ hours before you plan to serve, put the pork, skin side down, in a lightly oiled pan and put to roast for 20 minutes. Take out of the oven, turn the meat over to sit on the ribs and use a bulb baster to remove excess melted fat to a bowl. Keep all this excellent lard for roasting the potatoes and return the joint to the oven, lowering it to 180°C/350°F/gas 4. Cook for a further 1½ hours, basting regularly, when it will be firm to the touch, the joint having shrunk noticeably while the flesh will have pulled away from the bones.

About 1 hour before the pork will be ready, make the sage and onion stuffing: sweat the onions in the butter until translucent. Chop the chopped sage leaves and a handful of parsley leaves and stir into the onions. Cook for 2 minutes. Stir in the breadcrumbs, remove from the heat and allow to cool. Mix with the sausage meat and pack into a buttered pie dish or terrine to a depth of 3.5 cm / 1½ inches. Cook in the oven for 40 minutes.

Prepare the vegetables: try this different method for the Brussels sprouts. First parboil them for 3 minutes, refresh in cold water and refrigerate unti needed. Parboil the potatoes for 10 minutes, drain and put to roast, cut side down in an oiled pan with fat from the joint half an hour before the pork is due to come out of the oven.

Remove the cooked pork from the oven and transfer to a tray. Put to rest somewhere warm for 15–20 minutes. Turn the potatoes, sprinkle with salt and a little pepper and continue to cook, increasing the oven temperature to 220°C/425°F/gas 7, until they are crisp and brown – which should coincide with when you carve the joint.

While the pork is resting, finish the sprouts: put the butter for them in a frying pan large enough to hold them in a single layer. Season with salt and pepper and put the sprouts on top, cut side upwards. Put over a low heat and stew gently for 20 minutes. Do not turn or shake.

While the sprouts are cooking, finish the gravy: bring the stock to a boil with a few rosemary leaves in it, then lower the heat to a simmer. Thicken it by whisking in little pieces of beurre manié – a paste made from equal amounts of butter and flour. Do not cook for more than 5 minutes once thickened.

Brush the surface of the sage and onion stuffing with the finished gravy and return to the oven to keep warm until ready to serve. Reheat the apple sauce gently, grinding over some black pepper and stirring in the butter just before serving.

Serve the pork carved into thick slices, pouring any juices into the gravy. Serve the sprouts brown side upwards, with the gravy and any crispy bits from the pan.

## ROAST PORK TENDERLOIN WITH CRISP CRACKLING

Getting pork to crackle is a tricky thing and one where people pursuing the perfect crunchy skin often lose sight of the meat it covers. The result – great crackling over inedibly overcooked, fibrous meat. Another problem is the current trend towards leaner pork, where less fat makes achieving that crunch more difficult. If the amount of fat is not a concern, then one approach is to cook two joints: a piece of inexpensive pork belly for the crackling, keeping the meat to eat cold or incorporate in a Chinese dish; and either a whole hind loin, which includes the fillet and kidney, or just the fillet (which is also called the tenderloin). Since the latter is very lean, it benefits from being wrapped in caul fat (page 17) before roasting. The average tenderloin weighs about 400 g / 14 oz, so you will need one for every two people. The great advantage of combining tenderloin and belly pork in your roast pork with crackling is that you can cook it for just two people if you want.

SERVES 6-8

**1.35-1.8 kg / 3–4 lb piece of belly pork on the bone**
**Maldon salt**
**a little olive oil**
**pepper**
**2 pork tenderloins**
**½ tsp dried oregano**
**2 sheets of caul fat**

Buy a piece of belly pork on the bone, a cheap and much undervalued cut. Don't allow the butcher to score the skin. Most slash a few random cuts that are too deep and do not have the desired effect of making it easy to separate the finished crackling into bite-sized pieces. Do that yourself neatly and carefully, using a craft knife or scalpel to incise a 2.5-cm / 1-inch diamond crosshatch, being careful not to cut too deep. Rub the joint all over with Maldon salt and chill for 2–4 hours.

At the end of this time, rinse the salt off the belly pork and pat dry. Brush the scored skin with a little olive oil and rub in a little more salt and plenty of pepper. Allow to come to room temperature. Preheat the oven to 220°C/425°F/gas 7 and roast the belly pork for 20 minutes per 500 g / 1 pound. Remove from the oven and cut off the skin in one piece with 1–2 cm / ½–¾ inch of subcutaneous fat attached. Put this on a rack, fat down, and either return to the oven until beautifully crisp or achieve the same effect under a grill. Have the latter at a low setting or the skin will burn before it crisps.

The tenderloins do not take a lot of cooking and can go into the oven when you first remove the belly pork. Season with salt, pepper and oregano before wrapping in a double layer of caul. Roast for 15 minutes. Remove and allow to rest in a warm place for 10-12 minutes before carving the moist and succulent meat across in thick slices.

Tart eating apples like Granny Smiths make a nice accompaniment, sliced and fried briefly in butter and olive oil. Serve with crunchy roast potatoes (previous page). The need for gravy really is a matter of personal preference, since there is nothing remotely dry about any of the components.

121

> ROASTING
>
> *Oven-roasting, which we take for granted today, is only about 150 years old. Roasting was originally the technique of turning joints of meat and birds on spits, or spit-jacks, before an open fire. A pan set under the meat caught the fat and juices as they ran down and these were then constantly ladled back over the meat to limit evaporation and to give an inimitable crunchy exterior.*
>
> *The problem with basting in the oven is that you must either remove the meat and close the oven door, which may be difficult and dangerous if the joint is heavy, or baste with the door open. In a restaurant kitchen, where the ovens run very hot and doors are opened and shut constantly, this does not matter. The temperature of domestic ovens drops dramatically within seconds of the door being left open and if you baste at regular intervals it means you have a fluctuating temperature which will extend the overall cooking time.*
>
> *Basting is done often from habit rather than necessity. Meat can be barded, that is, wrapped in back fat so that fat is generated to flow over the surface, while chicken or pork have natural basting material in the skin.*

## CHINESE SPARE RIBS

The flavour that is most distinctively Chinese is star anise, which is the dominant ingredient in aromatic five-spice powder. You could serve the ribs on their own as a first course, or with steamed rice as a main dish.

SERVES 4

1 kg / 2 lb 2 oz pork spare ribs
150 ml / ¼ pt Chinese dark soy sauce (for example, Pearl River)
2.5-cm/ 1-inch piece of root ginger, peeled and grated
3 tsp five-spice powder
¼ tsp chilli flakes
4 garlic cloves, crushed and finely chopped
100 ml / 3½ fl oz sunflower oil
3½ tbsp liquid honey

The day before: chop the spare ribs with a cleaver into 5-cm / 2-inch pieces. In a large bowl, mix together the soy sauce, ginger, five-spice powder, chilli flakes, garlic and 3½ tablespoons of the sunflower oil. Add the rib pieces and toss to coat. Cling-wrap the top and refrigerate for 24 hours, shaking occasionally to ensure even marination.

Next day: drain the pork through a colander into a saucepan. Put a heavy frying pan with the remaining sunflower oil over a moderate heat. When very hot, add the ribs a few at a time and sear, transferring to the saucepan with the marinade when browned.

Bring the contents of the saucepan to the boil, lower the heat and cover with a lid. Simmer gently for 30–45 minutes, when the meat should be meltingly tender.

Remove the lid and stir in the honey. Increase the heat and reduce, tossing and stirring, until the water content has evaporated and the ribs are covered with a rich glaze. Do not leave the pan while reducing the marinade because it will burn easily.

Serve on a warmed serving plate for people to help themselves.

## WHITE-COOKED PORK

White cooking is an elegant Chinese euphemism for poaching in water. Although we have a great tradition of boiled meats in this country, most people go no further than gammon or a piece of salt beef. For a delicious new angle on an ancient theme, try this cold summer dish of white-cooked pork with spicy Sichuan dressing.

SERVES 6

1.35-kg / 3-lb piece of pork loin, cut from the best end
1 tbsp salt
3 heads of star anise
3 kaffir lime leaves

for the dressing:
2 garlic cloves, smashed and chopped
4 spring onions, sliced into thin rounds
1 hot red chilli, deseeded and sliced into thin strips
1 tbsp chilli oil
3 tbsp Pearl River or other good dark Chinese soy sauce
3 tsp white wine vinegar
1 tbsp sesame oil
1 tbsp sunflower oil
handful of chopped coriander

The day before: cover the piece of pork with cold water, add the salt and bring to the boil. Skim, add the star anise and kaffir lime leaves, reduce the heat to a bare simmer and cook for 1 hour. Remove from the heat but leave the pork in the liquid while it cools.

Meanwhile, make the dressing: put the garlic, spring onions and chilli into a bowl with the chilli oil, soy sauce, vinegar, sesame oil and sunflower oil, then stir. Refrigerate the pork and the dressing separately overnight.

About 30 minutes before you are ready to eat, remove both meat and dressing from the fridge. Slice the loin as thinly as you can, arranging the slices slightly overlapping on a serving dish. Stir a handful of chopped coriander leaves into the dressing and splash one-third of this over the meat, passing the remainder in a sauce boat for people to add more if they wish.

## CHAR SIU PORK

**SERVES 4**
**1 kg / 2¼ lb shoulder of pork**
**salt and pepper**
**2 tbsp sunflower oil, plus more**
**for greasing**
**1 tbsp soy sauce**
**2 tbsp dry rice wine**
**115 g / 4 oz shallots, finely**
**chopped**
**3 garlic cloves, finely chopped**
**5 tbsp hoisin sauce**
**2 tbsp honey**

The day before you want to cook: cut the pork into strips 5–6 cm / 2–2½ wide and put them into a dish into which they will just fit in a single layer. Season lightly with salt and pepper, then dribble over the oil, soy sauce and rice wine. Sprinkle over the shallots and garlic. Spoon over the hoisin sauce, cling-wrap and refrigerate overnight.

The next day, remove the pork from the fridge about 1 hour before you start cooking to allow it to come to room temperature. Preheat the oven to 180°C/350°F/gas 4.

Brush a roasting tin with oil. Lay the pork in it and dribble over half the honey.

Put to roast, turning the pork over after 20 minutes. Turn again after 10 more minutes, baste with the remaining honey and cook for 10 minutes more. By this time the exterior should be slightly charred and the meat just cooked. If not, turn the pork over again and give it a final 5 minutes, turning the temperature up to 200°C/ 400°F/gas 6.

Remove the pork to a board, chop into bite-size pieces and serve at once.

---

### FIVE-SPICE POWDER
*You can make your own five-spice powder, superior to that you can buy, from fennel seed, cassia bark – similar to cinnamon – cloves, star anise and Sichuan pepper, the last being an aromatic mixture in its own right. Toast equal amounts of the spices in a dry pan over a low heat, then grind to a powder. Keep in a small jar with an airtight lid.*

## SALT PORK

As long as you take some simple hygiene precautions, home-salted pork is easy to pickle and cook. A plastic bucket with a lid is the best thing to use for the brine, and it needs to be scrupulously cleaned and then wiped out with Milton's fluid, the stuff used for sterilizing baby's bottles. Also wipe a clean plate with the solution. The inclusion of sodium nitrite is cosmetic as it gives the meat a pink colour. You can buy sodium nitrite tablets through your butcher.

SERVES 8

450 g / 1 lb sea salt
375 g / 13 oz muscovado sugar
2 sodium nitrite tablets
(optional)
3 bay leaves
20 juniper berries, crushed
20 black peppercorns, crushed
1 head of star anise
½ nutmeg, grated
2.25 kg / 5 lb piece of belly pork

Put 3.3 litres / 6 pints water to boil with the sea salt, sugar, sodium nitrite tablets (if using), bay leaves, juniper berries, black peppercorns, star anise and nutmeg. Boil briskly for a minute, skim and leave to cool.

Put the piece of belly pork in the sterilized bucket (see above) and pour in enough of the cold brine through a sieve to cover the meat. Put the sterile plate (see above) on top to keep the meat submerged and put the lid on the bucket. Leave for 5 days.

Before cooking, either soak the meat overnight in cold water or bring to the boil in the water and throw away the water, replacing with fresh. Return to the boil, skim, lower the heat and simmer for 2 hours.

Serve cut in thick slices, with lentils or a purée of haricot beans and garlic. Mustard is always nice with boiled salted meats, as are mostarda di Cremona, Italian sweet mustard pickles.

## PORK PIE

Hot-water crust pastry gives essential strength to raised pies, that is pies which stand alone without the benefit of a container and which are normally eaten at room temperature.

SERVES 4

for the hot-water crust:
800 g / 1¾ lb plain flour
250 g / 9 oz lard, diced
2 tsp salt
oil for the bowl
melted butter

for the filling:
900 g / 2 lb chopped shoulder of pork
140 g / 5 oz onion, chopped
salt and pepper
freshly grated nutmeg
150 ml / ¼ pint dry white wine
1 egg, beaten
about 150 ml / ¼ pint firmly jellied chicken or pork stock, warmed to a liquid

First make the crust: sift the flour into a food processor. In a saucepan, bring 300 ml / ½ pint of water with the diced lard and salt to a rapid boil. With the processor at full speed, carefully pour this boiling mixture in a thin stream down the feeder tube, which will produce a smooth elastic dough.

When the dough is cool enough to handle, transfer it to an oiled bowl, cover with a cloth and leave to stand in a warm place for 20 minutes. Brush a large glass jar with melted butter. Press out about four-fifths of the dough into a round on a non-stick surface. Stand the jar in the middle and shape and pull the dough up round it to a uniform thickness of about 1.5 cm / ½ inch. It's a bit like working with putty. Recruit help and wrap round with greaseproof paper, tying it in place with string. Put in the fridge to set firm.

Preheat the oven to 180°C/350°F/gas 4. To remove the jar, soak a tea towel in very hot water, squeeze it out and push it into the jar. After a minute or two the heat will have melted the butter and you should be able to lift the jar out.

To make the filling: in a bowl, mix the chopped pork by hand with the chopped onion. Season with salt, pepper and nutmeg and moisten with the wine. Pile this into the raised crust.

Roll out the remaining pastry to make a lid and crimp it on top. Push a hole through the centre, brush the top with beaten egg and bake in its paper for 45 minutes in the oven.

Remove from the oven, carefully cut the strings and take off the paper. Return to the oven for a further 20 minutes, raising the temperature to 190°C/375°F/gas 5.

Remove from the oven, allow to cool and refrigerate. Using a funnel, pour in the warmed jellied stock through the hole to fill and chill to set.

## STUFFED PIGS' TROTTERS

Ironically, these days the cheap and tasty pig's foot is not a very popular cut outside our Michelin three-star restaurants, where Pierre Koffmann of La Tante Claire first made them gourmet fare by stuffing them with truffles and foie gras.

Jellied trotters are less exotic but very easy to make – if labour-intensive – and their high natural gelatine content means the cooking liquid sets to a splendid jelly. For this reason a split trotter is a good thing to include in any stew, where it gives both textural and flavour benefits.

The whole process set out below takes several days, so plan well ahead.

**SERVES 4**

**4 pig's trotters**

**salt**

**300 ml / ½ pint dry white wine**

**175 ml / 6 fl oz white wine vinegar**

**2 onions, quartered**

**2 carrots, sliced**

**2 celery stalks**

**handful of parsley**

**2 bay leaves**

**20 black peppercorns**

**6 cloves**

**3 shallots, thinly sliced**

**2 tbsp chopped capers**

Have the butcher split the trotters lengthwise for you. When you get them home, singe off any hairs with your blow torch or children's cigarette lighter, then give them a good scrub, paying particular attention to the pedicure.

Put them in a pan with plenty of water and bring to the boil. Throw this away and rinse and scrub the trotters again under cold running water.

Being very rich, the trotters benefit from an initial salting. Scatter salt on a tray, lay the split trotters on it, cut side down, and scatter more salt on top. Cling-wrap and refrigerate. After 24 hours, turn them and give them another 24 hours.

Rinse, bring to the boil in plenty of water, boil for 5 minutes and throw away the water. Rinse out the pan and rinse the trotters under cold running water, then put them back in the pan with the wine and all but 2 tablespoons of the white wine vinegar. Cover with cold water, bring to the boil and skim carefully.

Add the onions, carrots, celery, a handful of parsley stalks, the bay leaves, peppercorns and cloves. Simmer for 5–6 hours. Leave them to cool in the liquid, which may already be close to a set. If so, turn on the heat until it liquefies before you remove the trotters, otherwise they will come out with lots of sticky jelly on them and be more difficult to handle.

Pull out all the bones with your fingers, before cutting up the flesh and skin into bite-sized pieces and putting them in a bowl. Pour 850 ml / 1½ pints of the liquid through a sieve into another pan and boil to reduce it by half. Test for set by putting a spoonful on a cold plate.

To the trotter meat, add the remaining white wine vinegar, the thinly sliced shallots, chopped capers and chopped parsley leaves. Toss together with a spoon and pack loosely into a shallow rectangular dish. Pour over the reduced liquid to cover and refrigerate to set.

Cut the set jelly into rectangles and serve with an astringent orange, red onion and olive salad and plenty of dry toast.

## GLAZED HAM

Nothing looks more splendid than a glazed ham studded with cloves and it is, fortunately, not difficult to achieve. A ham weighing 2.25–2.75 kg / 5–6 lb off the bone will serve 10, with some left over for sandwiches. All it needs are some boiled and buttered new potatoes and some blanched green beans to go with it.

**SERVES 10**
**900 g / 2 lb dried apricots**
**½ bottle of cooking brandy**
**1 ham, weighing 2.25–2.75 kg /**
**5–6 lb**
**3 tbsp clear honey**
**2 tbsp mustard powder**
**about 12 cloves**
**1 cinnamon stick**
**2 tbsp caster sugar**

Several days before you want to serve the ham, put the dried apricots to soak in the brandy.

In a large pan, cover the ham with water, bring to the boil and throw away the water. Replace with fresh water, bring to the boil, lower the heat and simmer for 50 minutes and drain.

Preheat the oven to 190°C/375°F/ gas 5. Leave the ham to cool until you can handle it while wearing rubber gloves, then cut the skin off but take care to remove as little fat as possible. Cut a diamond pattern into the fat and put the ham into a roasting pan. Mix the honey with the mustard powder and coat the ham with it. Push cloves into the corners of the diamond shapes and roast for 45 minutes. Remove from the oven and allow to cool completely.

Put the drained apricots in a saucepan with 600 ml / 1 pt water, the cinnamon stick and caster sugar. Bring to the boil, lower the heat and simmer gently until the apricots have plumped and the liquid evaporated. They are now ready to serve as a sweet relish with the sliced ham.

## JAMBON PERSILLÉ

Ham cooked in white wine and served in a parsleyed aspic is a classic Burgundian dish.

**SERVES 8**
**1-kg / 2¼-lb piece of uncooked**
**ham or unsmoked mild**
**gammon**
**1 bottle of dry white wine**
**1 pig's trotter, split, blanched**
**and rinsed**
**2 bay leaves**
**4 garlic cloves**
**4 onions**
**8 cloves**
**2 carrots, sliced**
**large handful of flat-leaved**
**parsley**
**4 celery stalks**
**15 g / ½ oz leaf gelatine**
**2 tbsp white wine vinegar**
**salt and pepper**

The day before you want to serve the dish, soak the ham or gammon in water overnight.

Next day, bring to the boil in fresh water, lower the heat and simmer for 15 minutes. Throw this water away and pour over the dry white wine, topping up with water to cover. Add the pig's trotter, bay leaves, garlic, onions (one studded with the cloves), carrots, a handful of parsley stalks and the celery stalks. Bring to the boil, skim, lower the heat and simmer for 1¼ hours.

Strain the cooking liquid through a muslin-lined sieve into a bowl. Add the leaf gelatine and white wine vinegar and stir well until the gelatine is dissolved. When the ham is cool enough to handle, remove the skin and fat and discard, then cut the meat into dice. Put into a bowl with a handful of chopped flat-leaved parsley. Taste the reserved liquid, adding salt and pepper as needed. Pour over the ham and refrigerate to set. You should have a transparent aspic jelly with the meat and parsley suspended in it.

When well set, turn out of the bowl and serve cut in wedges.

## SAUSAGES

The best kit to use for making sausages is an electric mixer with a special attachment. If you have a mixer, you can buy this nozzle-like add-on for a few pounds. If not, there are hand-pumped sausage-makers which look like giant cake-decorating syringes and these are an inexpensive way to start. Failing that, your butcher may be willing to fill skins with your mixture, though he may insist on making a minimum of 3 kg or so.

We are seeing a renewed interest in quality sausages after years of Britain producing some of the nastiest objects ever to bear the name and made from truly horrible centrifuged animal slurry. For purists who believe a sausage should be made primarily from good-quality pork or beef, this resurgence has had its downside, with the introduction of frankly bizarre ingredients for the sake of novelty and, in marketing parlance, 'to add value'. Things like fruit, for example, feature widely, and you either like that sort of thing or hate it. Commercially produced sausages also tend to have a lot of cereal filler, which you can happily leave out when you make them at home.

Sausages must have a fat content of at least one-third to one-quarter of the total weight if they are to be succulent and tasty. Apologies to the cardiologist who wrote in saying that our recipes lacked fibre and had too much fat, but a sausage without fat and which is not well salted is inedible. Much better not to eat them at all than make a travesty.

The lean-meat-to-fat ratio in sausages is very important for if too lean they will be dry and crumbly. You want

about 3 parts lean to 1 part fat, and back fat will give the best flavour, though you will also get good results from belly pork. The inclusion of bread as a filler is very English, but is not really necessary. Sausages must be well seasoned if they are to taste of anything. This recipe makes an excellent French-style sausage.

Start by preparing the sausage casings. Your butcher will sell you natural hog and sheep casings dried and salted in packets. If he is uncooperative, they can be obtained by mail order from the Natural Casing Company, 01252 850454, who also sell various pieces of sausage-making equipment and books about sausage-making. Cut off about 1 metre of 4 cm / 1½ thick hog casing, wash under running water and leave to soak for 1 hour or overnight. Rinse in running water again.

**MAKES ABOUT 10**
750 g / 1½ lb lean pork
225 g / ½ lb pork back fat
1 garlic clove, crushed and
finely chopped
1½ tsp salt
1½ tsp quatre épices
2 tbsp dry sherry
about 2 sausage casings
olive oil, for brushing

Three or four days before you want to cook and eat the sausages, put both the lean pork and back fat through the coarse plate of a mincer. In a bowl, mix them with the garlic, salt, quatre épices and the dry sherry. Cling-wrap the top and refrigerate the mixture for 24 hours. Soak the sausage casings in cold

water overnight.

Check the seasoning by making a small patty, frying it and eating it, then adjust as you like. Wash the sausage casings under cold running water. Tie one end of a casing, gathering the open end over the feeder tube of the mixer. Fill the casing through the feeder tube, trying not to overfill or your finished sausages will burst. Tie the open end, then tie off at intervals as 10-12 individual sausages. Refrigerate for 2-3 days.

To cook the sausages: preheat the oven to 220°C/425°F/gas 7, brush the sausages with olive oil and cook them in the oven for about 20 minutes.

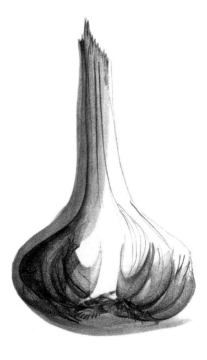

## FRANKFURTERS

The frankfurters you buy are generally very poor in quality and some canned franks are mostly fat, water and salt. To obtain the correct texture you will need to put the meat through the finest blade of the mincer three times.

Since all sausages benefit from two to three days maturation in the fridge, hygiene is particularly important. After careful washing, soak all the equipment you will be using in Milton's sterilizing fluid.

225 g / 8 oz onion, diced
2 garlic cloves, chopped
2 tsp ground coriander
1 tsp dried marjoram
freshly grated nutmeg
2 tsp Colman's mustard powder
2 tsp paprika
1 tsp caster sugar
2 tsp salt
1 tsp ground black pepper
white of 1 egg
150 ml / ¼ pt milk
450 g / 1 lb lean pork fillet
350 g / 12 oz lean beef
225 g / 8 oz pork back fat

Put the onion, garlic, coriander, marjoram, nutmeg, mustard powder, paprika, caster sugar, salt and pepper in a food processor and blitz to a purée. While continuing to run the machine at full speed, add the egg white and milk through the feeder tube.

Now cut the pork fillet, beef and back fat into large dice and mince, using the finest blade and putting them through separately. Mix together and mince a second time. Put in a large bowl

with the purée from the processor and mix thoroughly with a fork, then with your hands. It is a very sticky mixture, so wet your hands with cold water first. Cover with cling-film and refrigerate for 1 hour.

Remove from the fridge and put through the mincer a third time. Gather the casing on the feeder tube and stuff, twisting into individual, 15-cm / 6-inch sausages.

Leaving them joined together, poach in simmering water for 15 minutes. Remove and immediately immerse in a bowl of iced water. When cold, remove and pat dry. Then serve or refrigerate for up to a week. They also freeze well.

### HOT DOGS

*You have made your frankfurters... Well, perhaps not, but you have bought some decent examples from a delicatessen. Now you wish to create the perfect hot dog.*

*The first problem is finding a roll. Most rolls sold for hot dogs are synthetic to a degree that defeats the exercise even prior to construction — weak, spongy, chewy and sugared. Much time must be put into tracking an appropriate roll. It is not enough that it is the right size or shape. Talk to a real baker, should you have such a thing in the neighbourhood.*

*You have your perfect sausage. You have found the right roll for it to nestle in, so it is time to address the onions which must accompany it. Peel and thinly slice them and sweat them over the lowest heat in a little unsalted butter until soft and translucent. They must not brown. Put on a ridged grill pan over a low to medium heat. When hot, brush the sausages with melted butter and lay them in between the grill ridges. Turn them every few seconds with tongs. They should acquire a little charring from the ridges.*

*To toast or not to toast the bun? All but the finest buns should be split and lightly grilled on the cut side only.*

*Finally, the assembly. Lay a frank in the toasted bun. Stripe it with Dijon mustard. Slather it in moist sweet onions. If serving on a plate and not in a paper napkin, put a mound of coleslaw on the side. Those who put ketchup anywhere near a hot dog should be shot.*

*Opposite (clockwise from the top left): Chinese Spare Ribs (page 122), White-cooked Pork (page 122), Char Siu Pork (page 123)*

## BARBECUED LEG OF LAMB

The larger the piece of meat, the more difficult to barbecue, particularly without a spit. One cannot be absolute in giving instructions because the temperature on one barbecue will be different from another, depending on the type of wood or charcoal used and the distance of the grill from the fire. The answer in any case is to cook it very slowly.

**SERVES 6**

**1.8 kg / 4 lb leg of lamb**
**sunflower oil, for brushing**
**salt and pepper**
**juice of 2 lemons**
**4 garlic cloves, smashed**
**2 tbsp olive oil**
**2 tbsp chopped rosemary**

Brush the leg of lamb with sunflower oil and season all over with salt and pepper.

On a very hot barbecue, sear it quickly on all sides, then remove and put it on a big double layer of foil. Squeeze lemon juice on it, rub it with the smashed garlic and dribble over the olive oil. Sprinkle on the rosemary leaves and wrap loosely in the foil, crimping it closed. It must not be tightly wrapped but have plenty of air around the meat.

Move the grill 20 cm / 8 inches away from the fire and put the package on it. Cook, turning from time to time. Add more wood or coals after 1 hour and again after another hour, cooking for a total of 3 hours, when the meat should still be pink but done all the way through and will be very tender.

## KLEFTIKO

As one of the most ubiquitous Greek dishes, it is surprising that very few cookbooks give a recipe for it. Basically a braised lamb shank, kleftiko is simple in the extreme and is therefore open to many interpretations. Expatriates and Greek restaurateurs will doubtless state their case in due course, when they take exception to this version, but for the time being assume that it is as authentic as any version not cooked on an island in the Aegean. The shank is the bottom portion of the leg, which when trimmed, presents nicely as an individual if substantial joint. Serve it with plain boiled rice or mashed potatoes. Play Zorba's Dance as you frisk the plates to the table.

**SERVES 4**

**4 lamb shanks**
**salt and pepper**
**5 tbsp olive oil**
**450 g / 1 lb onions, thinly sliced**
**4 garlic cloves, smashed and chopped**
**300 ml / ½ pt dry white wine**
**450 g / 1 lb can of chopped plum tomatoes**
**1 bay leaf**
**1 tsp dried oregano**
**coarsely chopped flat-leaved parsley, to dress**

Rub the shanks generously with salt and pepper, then brown them vigorously all over in a frying pan in 3 tablespoons of the olive oil. Put into a casserole with a tight-fitting lid.

Add some more olive oil to the frying pan and, over a low heat, sweat the onions until soft and translucent. Add the garlic and fry for 2 minutes, then transfer to the casserole, distributing around the shanks.

Over a high heat, deglaze the pan with the wine, stirring and scraping, then pour over the lamb. Add the can of chopped plum tomatoes with its liquid, the bay leaf and oregano. Bring to the boil, put on the lid and lower the heat to a bare simmer. Check from time to time that it is not drying out, adding a little water if it does. Test the meat is done after 90 minutes. Depending on the size of the shanks, it may be; if not, continue cooking until the meat is tender enough to pull easily from the bone.

Taste and season about 5 minutes before you judge the meat will be cooked. Remove the shanks and keep warm on serving plates. Discard the bay leaf and transfer the tomato and onion mixture to a food processor. Blitz briefly and pass through a sieve. Spoon this sauce around the shanks and dress with lots of coarsely chopped flat-leaved parsley.

### Lamb Cuts

#### Best End of Neck

A rack of 6-7 small neck chops from middle of neck to loin. The trimmed eye is a neck fillet.

#### Breast

Fatty fore-part of belly, usually boned and stuffed.

#### Chops and Cutlets

Thick chump chops are cut from the loin, while the thinner cutlets are cut from the best end of neck.

#### Leg

A whole leg is a substantial roasting cut, weighing from 1.75 kg / 4 lb in first spring lambs to 3.25 kg / 7 lb in older animals. Often cut across into leg chops or steaks.

#### Noisettes

Neat rounds cut from a boned eye of loin, often surrounded with a protective layer of back fat.

#### Saddle

A cross-section cut through the back, including both loins and kidneys. A saddle from the youngest lamb weighs about 2.75 kg / 6 lb.

#### Shoulder

This large fatty joint is succulent but a beast to carve. Any butcher will bone it out for you.

#### Scrag End

The neck and bony end of the forequarter.

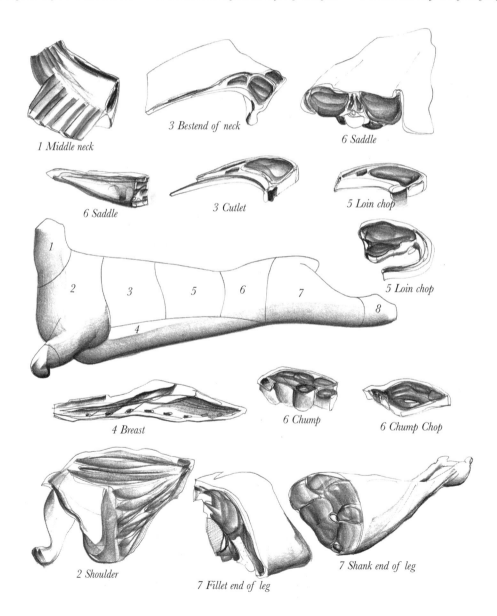

1 Middle neck

3 Bestend of neck

6 Saddle

6 Saddle

3 Cutlet

5 Loin chop

5 Loin chop

4 Breast

6 Chump

6 Chump Chop

2 Shoulder

7 Fillet end of leg

7 Shank end of leg

## GUARD OF HONOUR

A guard of honour is no more than two French-trimmed racks of lamb cooked together standing upright, with the cutlet bones interleaved and presented after carving with a herb and mushroom stuffing. The bones should be scraped bare and any excess fat removed if the covering over the meat is too thick. Cut a neat diamond pattern into the fat and season generously with salt and pepper, pressing it in with your fingers. Serve the lamb with French beans or mashed potatoes.

SERVES 4 (3 CUTLETS EACH)

2 racks of lamb, trimmed (as above)
2 slices of white bread, crusts removed and cut into cubes
a little milk
60 g / 2 oz pancetta or streaky bacon, cut into strips
30 g / 1 oz butter
1 onion, finely diced
225 g / 8 oz flat-cap mushrooms, cut into small pieces
grated zest of ½ lemon
salt and pepper
¼ tsp chilli flakes
1 glass of red wine
300 ml / ½ pt strong chicken stock (or lamb stock if available)
2 tbsp chopped parsley
1 tbsp chopped chives

Preheat the oven to 250°C/475°F/ gas 9. Push the racks together by crossing the bones and stand them upright in a roasting pan.

In a small bowl, moisten the cubes of bread with a little milk and then squeeze them dry. Reserve.

Fry the pancetta or bacon gently until the fat runs. Sweat the butter and the onion in it for 15 minutes over a low heat, until soft and translucent. Add the mushrooms and continue to cook for a further 5–10 minutes. Add the grated lemon zest, stir in the bread, season with salt and pepper and the chilli flakes, then remove from the heat.

Roast the lamb for 15–20 minutes, depending on how pink you like your lamb. Remove from the pan and leave to rest for 15 minutes, covered, in a warm place. Pour off excess fat from the roasting pan, put the pan over a high heat and add the red wine. Reduce, scraping up any caramelized bits to incorporate. Add the stock and boil to reduce by half. Taste and season.

About 5 minutes before serving, return the stuffing to a low heat to warm through, stirring in the chopped parsley and chives. Carve the racks across into individual cutlets, putting 3 on each of 4 warmed plates with the stuffing beside them and the gravy poured around.

## BOBOTIE

The South-African dish bobotie is a rather more exotic version of shepherd's pie, lightly flavoured with curry spices and covered with savoury custard.

SERVES 4

1 slice of white bread
300 ml / ½ pt milk
170 g / 6 oz onion, diced
30 g / 1 oz butter, plus more for the dish
1 sharp dessert apple, peeled, cored and diced
1 tbsp medium-hot curry powder
450 g / 1 lb minced lamb
1 tbsp mango chutney
30 g / 1 oz flaked almonds
30 g / 1 oz sultanas
juice of ½ lemon
salt and pepper
3 eggs
1 tsp mustard powder
2 lime or fresh bay leaves

Preheat the oven to 180°C/350°F/ gas 4. Tear the slice of bread up into a small bowl and cover it with the milk.

Over a low heat, sweat the diced onion in the butter until soft and translucent. Add the apple and curry powder and continue to cook, stirring, for 2 minutes.

In a bowl and using a fork, mix this spiced onion and apple mixture with the lamb, mango chutney, flaked almonds, sultanas, lemon juice and salt and pepper. Squeeze the bread dry, reserving the milk, and mix this through the meat mixture. Then spoon it into a buttered, ovenproof dish. This should be large enough to give you 2.5 cm / 1 inch between the surface of the meat and the rim of the dish. Put to bake for 15 minutes.

Whisk the eggs with the reserved milk and the mustard powder, salt and pepper. Pour over the meat, sit the lime or bay leaves on top and continue cooking for 25–30 minutes, or until the custard is just set.

## MUTTON WITH CAPER SAUCE

Lamb used to be the exclusive product of spring, starting with the winter-born lambs of southern England, followed by Welsh and Scottish lambing as weather permitted. Now imports mean it is available all year round. Lamb technically remains lamb up to a year old, when it becomes mutton, though connoisseurs insist that mutton is from an animal aged six to ten years. Less than 5 per cent of lambs are allowed to live past one year, which explains why mutton is so difficult to find.

Stuart Baker, who still produces mutton sheep on his Exmoor farm, offers a mail order service of haunch, leg and loin cuts. (Lingcomb Farm, Chagford, Newton Abbot, TQ13 HEF, 01647 433300). He maintains that mutton comes only from ewes that have fulfilled every other useful purpose and would not countenance mutton from a ram.

### SERVES 10
1 leg of mutton, about 4 kg / 9 lb (see above)
4 celery stalks, chopped
4 carrots, chopped
2 onions, chopped
20 black peppercorns
salt and pepper
about 2 kg / 4½ lb potatoes, peeled and cut into chunks

for the caper sauce:
30 g / 1 oz butter
20 g / ¾ oz flour
1 heaped tsp Colman's mustard powder
3 tbsp drained capers
3 tbsp double cream

Having tracked down your leg of mutton, the day before you want to eat it put it in a very large pan, cover it with cold water and bring to the boil. Skim, lower the heat to a bare simmer and add the celery, 2 of the carrots, the onions and black peppercorns. Poach for 2 hours and remove from the heat, then leave overnight in the poaching liquid.

Next day, skim any fat from the surface of the poaching liquid, remove the vegetables and discard. Return to the boil and skim again. Add a little salt, then lower the heat again to simmer and cook for a further 1 hour. Add the potatoes and remaining carrots to cook with the mutton for the last 25–30 minutes.

To make the caper sauce, mix the butter with the flour and mustard powder to make a firm paste (a beurre manié). Ladle 250 ml / 8 fl oz of the mutton stock into a pan and bring to the boil. Whisk in the flour paste in small knobs, which will instantly thicken it. Season with salt and plenty of pepper and simmer for 2 minutes. Stir in the drained capers and double cream, and take to the table in a sauceboat.

## LAMB TAGINE WITH APRICOTS

Tagines are the meat dishes which sit closest to the heart of Morocco, rich and aromatic without being fancy or contrived. It is also the name for the earthenware casseroles with conical lids like witches' hats in which the meat is simmered. Tagines are everyday food in the same sense as Lancashire hot-pot, or a shin of beef stew. Tagines are most often of lamb, but they can just as easily be made with beef. Fruit is not a constant, but its inclusion is typical.

### SERVES 6
225 g / 8 oz dried apricots
1.25 kg / 2½ lb lamb neck fillet
5 tbsp olive oil
salt and pepper
450 g / 1 lb onion, sliced into rings
5-cm / 2-inch piece of ginger, peeled and cut into julienne strips
1 tsp chilli flakes (more if you like it hot)
1 tbsp paprika
4 tsp cumin
1 cinnamon stick
2 lime or bay leaves
1.75 litres / 3 pints chicken or lamb stock
couscous or rice, to serve
handful of flat parsley leaves, to garnish

Pour boiling water over the dried apricots and leave to soak for 2 hours or overnight.

Preheat a dry pan until very hot. Butterfly the lamb neck fillet and cut it into rectangles about the size of a postcard. Brush with some of the oil, season with salt and pepper and sear on both sides. Reserve.

Heat the remaining olive oil in a heavy-based casserole and fry the onion until translucent. Add the ginger, chilli flakes, paprika and cumin, fry for 2 minutes, then add the lamb and drained apricots. Put in the cinnamon stick and lime or bay leaves. Season with salt and pepper. Pour over the stock and bring to the boil. Lower the heat to a bare simmer, cover with a lid and cook for 1 hour.

Remove the lid and check to see that the lamb is tender. Remove the cinnamon stick and lime leaves and discard. Taste and adjust the seasoning. Serve in warmed soup plates or in large bowls with a mound of couscous or rice and parsley leaves scattered over.

## SEARED VENISON STEAKS WITH MUSHROOMS AND GIN SAUCE

Venison is lean, well-flavoured and tender if it has been properly hung. Ask the butcher for the bones with the loin.

SERVES 4

**675 g / 1½ lb venison loin**
**about 6 tbsp olive oil**
**225 g / 8 oz carrots**
**225 g / 8 oz onion**
**handful of parsley**
**3 tbsp red wine vinegar**
**300 ml / ½ pt red wine**
**12 juniper berries**
**zest of 1 lemon**
**2 tsp sugar**
**2 tbsp gin**
**225 g / 8 oz flat-cap mushrooms**
**2 garlic cloves**
**60 g / 2 oz butter**
**2 tbsp chopped parsley**
**salt and pepper**

Preheat the oven to 250°C/475°F/gas 9. Cut the meat into 12 small steaks, brush them with olive oil and reserve.

Chop the carrots, onion and parsley roughly and put in a roasting pan with the bones and the remaining olive oil. Brown in the oven for 20 minutes.

Transfer to the hob over a moderate heat. Add the red wine vinegar, then the red wine and 300 ml / ½ pt of water. Bring to the boil, skim then lower the heat. Add the juniper berries, the lemon zest and the sugar, and simmer for 60 minutes. Pass through a fine sieve into a saucepan, add the gin and reduce to 150 ml / ¼ pint. Reserve.

Cut the mushrooms into 1-cm / ½-inch slices and the garlic cloves into paper-thin slices. Put the garlic and the butter in a frying pan over a low heat for 5 minutes to allow the flavour to infuse. Turn up the heat, add the mushrooms and sauté them for 2–3 minutes until wilted. Season, add the chopped parsley and toss. Turn off the heat and leave in the pan to keep warm.

Heat a dry frying pan until smoking hot. Season the steaks with salt and pepper and sear in the pan for 2 minutes on one side, 1 minute on the other.

Arrange 3 of the steaks on each of 4 warmed plates with mushrooms in between and pour the sauce round.

## THAI-STYLE RABBIT

SERVES 4

**1 rabbit**
**1 glass of dry white wine**
**350 g / 12 oz brown onion, diced**
**4 garlic cloves, chopped**
**3 tbsp sesame oil**
**3 tbsp fish sauce**
**two 2.5-cm / 1-inch pieces of galangal, grated**
**2 hot red chillies, thinly sliced**
**1 small carrot, diced**
**sunflower oil for frying**
**2 celery stalks, thinly sliced**
**300 ml / ½ pt chicken stock**
**salt and pepper**
**1 whole lemon grass stalk**
**2 kaffir lime leaves**
**Thai fragrant rice, to serve**
**6 spring onions, sliced thinly, to garnish**

Get the butcher to lose the head and joint the carcass by cutting off the front legs, severing back legs and cutting the body in half along the spine, separating rib cage from saddle and chopping off bony rib extremities. Ask him to cut the loin and rib pieces laterally into three.

In a large bowl, mix the wine, 225 g / 8 oz of the onion, half the garlic, the sesame oil, fish sauce, half the galangal and the chillies. Put in the rabbit pieces and turn to coat. Cling-wrap and marinate in the refrigerator overnight.

Just before cooking, sear the pieces of rabbit in a little sunflower oil in a heavy frying pan and transfer to a plate. They should still be raw in the middle.

Add a couple more tablespoons of oil to the pan and fry the remaining onion and garlic, and the celery until softened, then add the remaining galangal and stir before returning the rabbit to the pan. Pour over the chicken stock and the remaining marinade. Season with salt and pepper. Add the lemon grass and lime leaves. Cover the pan and simmer for 10–15 minutes. Check the largest piece of rabbit to make sure it is done.

Remove the lemon grass before serving the rabbit with Thai fragrant rice, scattered with pieces of spring onion. This would have been a revelation for Mr McGregor.

## HARE STEW

Hare is a big muscular animal, with very little fat, which makes roasting or grilling tricky. A slow simmer is therefore your most forgiving approach and the hare's strong flavour cries out for a sauce, so stewing is definitely your best bet.

Classically the sauce for hare is always thickened with its own blood and if this idea appeals, make sure the butcher keeps it for you. If you feel this is getting closer to reality than you like, then thicken with a beurre manié, a paste made from equal parts flour and butter which you whisk in a little at a time at the end of cooking and which thickens almost instantly.

SERVES 6

**1 hare, weighing 2–2.3 kg / 4–5 lb, cut into 12 pieces**
**225 g / 8 oz fat smoked bacon, cut into lardon strips**
**6 tbsp olive oil**
**225 g / 8 oz onions, sliced**
**2 garlic cloves, chopped**
**salt and pepper**
**flour, for dusting**
**600 ml / 1 pt robust red wine**
**600 ml / 1 pt chicken stock**
**bouquet garni of celery, thyme and bay leaf tied together with string**
**24 pickling onions**
**30 g / 1 oz butter**
**225 g / 8 oz button mushrooms**
**about 60 g / 2 oz beurre manié (optional)**
**2 tbsp chopped flat-leaved parsley**
**croûtes of fried bread, to serve**

Cut the hare into 12 pieces and the bacon into lardon strips.

Fry the bacon strips slowly in 2 tablespoons of the olive oil until almost crisp, transferring to a casserole with a slotted spoon. Fry the onions in this fat until soft and translucent. Add the garlic and cook for 2 minutes, then add to the pot.

Season and flour the pieces of hare. Add some more of the oil to the pan then, increasing the heat to moderate and brown the hare on all sides. Transfer to the pot. Mound the onions and bacon on top of it.

Turn up the heat under the frying pan, add the wine and deglaze, scraping up any bits sticking to the pan. Pour over the hare with the stock. Put in the bouquet garni and season with salt and pepper. Bring to the boil, skim, then lower the heat, cover and simmer for about 1 hour.

About 15 minutes before the end of cooking time, fry the pickling onions in the butter and remaining olive oil. Season lightly with salt and pepper and sauté for 5–10 minutes until golden brown. Transfer to a dish and keep warm while you fry the button mushrooms. Add these to the onions.

Transfer the hare to a warmed serving dish and strain the sauce through a sieve, discarding the sliced onions and bouquet garni but scattering the lardons over the hare.

If using blood, put in a bowl. Bring sauce to the boil, turn off the heat and whisk it in a thin stream into the blood. Return to the pot over a low heat, stirring until thickened. Alternatively, whisk in the beurre manié.

When the sauce is thickened by either method, stir in the baby onions and mushrooms before ladling it over the hare.

Scatter over the chopped parsley and serve the dish with croûtes of fried bread.

## SNAILS

You can buy prepared snails in a can, with a bag of nice clean shells which you can wash and reuse *ad infinitum*.

Here, with a herb and garlic butter, is the classic *escargots a la Bourguignonne*. Serve them with good bread to mop up the tasty butter.

**SERVES 4**
**48 canned snails**

**for the herb and garlic butter:**
**4 tbsp chopped parsley**
**115 g / 4 oz butter**
**4 garlic cloves, smashed and chopped**
**1 tbsp lemon juice**
**salt and pepper**

First make the herb and garlic butter: blanch the chopped parsley briefly in boiling water, then drain, pat dry and finely chop. Cream the butter in a food processor, add the parsley and garlic, and beat into the butter. Then, with the machine still running, drip in the lemon juice and season with salt and pepper. Put to chill.

Preheat the oven to 200°C/400°F/gas 6. Drain the snails and put one in each shell. Pack the herb butter into the shells, then arrange in an ovenproof dish to sit, opening upwards, so the butter does not run out. (There are special metal snail dishes which can go in the oven and be brought sizzling to the table).

Heat the snails in the oven just until they are very hot (the snails are already cooked).

## LAMB'S KIDNEYS WITH MUSTARD SAUCE

Kidneys oozing blood are a little too rare for the British taste, but veal or lambs' kidneys should only be rapidly but lightly cooked, brown outside and a rosy pink within. Cook them too long and they will be tough and dry. The exception to this rule is ox kidney, which is the preferred one for use with steak in a pie or pudding, when long slow cooking is needed to produce a succulent texture.

**SERVES 4**
**675 g / 1½ lb lambs' kidneys**
**flour**
**salt and pepper**
**about 3 tbsp sunflower oil**
**about 30 g / 2 oz unsalted butter**
**115 g / 4 oz shallots**
**3 tbsp brandy (optional)**
**250 ml / 8 fl oz red wine**
**125 ml / 4 fl oz chicken stock**
**125 ml / 4 fl oz double cream**
**1 tbsp Dijon mustard**
**4 tbsp flat-leaf parsley**

**for the olive oil toasts:**
**4 slices of white bread, crusts removed**
**2–3 tbsp oli**

First make the olive oil toasts: preheat the oven to 200°C/400°F/gas 6. Brush the bread with olive oil, put on a baking tray and bake until golden brown, about 8–10 minutes. Reserve.

While they are in the oven, skin the kidneys and cut them in half lengthwise. With sharp scissors, snip out their cores and primary tubes, then toss them in heavily peppered seasoned flour to coat lightly, shaking off any excess.

Melt the butter with the oil in a heavy frying pan over a moderate heat and fry the kidneys, stirring and tossing, for 2–3 minutes, then transfer to a colander to drain.

Add some more oil and butter to the pan if needed and fry the chopped shallots over a moderate heat until just softened and translucent. If you like, you can add some brandy, shake and ignite carefully.

Add the wine and stock and reduce by half at a rapid boil. Stir in the cream and the mustard. Return the kidneys and stir all together to heat through very gently for 2 minutes. Do not allow it to boil again or the kidneys will toughen and the mustard become bitter.

Serve at once on the olive oil toasts, scattered with lots of chopped parsley.

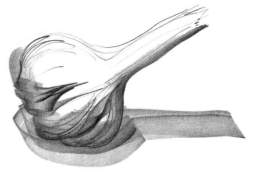

## MARROW BONES WITH TOAST

Marrow was served in its bones at Victorian dinner parties, wrapped in heavy linen napkins and eaten with long-handled silver spoons. It is incredibly rich and a little goes a long way. An accompanying parsley or rocket salad will offset the richness. Your butcher will either give you beef marrow bones or make only a nominal charge. Ask him to saw the bones into 10-cm / 4-inch pieces.

SERVES 4

**4 beef marrow bones, cut into 10-cm / 4-inch pieces (see above)**

**to serve:**
**dry toast**
**sea salt and pepper**

Scrape and scrub the pieces of marrow bone. Wrap the ends in foil to prevent the marrow slipping out of the bottom during poaching and tie the bones together with string so they will stand upright. Put them into a saucepan, pour round boiling water to come halfway up the bones, put on a lid and simmer for 90 minutes.

Remove the foil and serve while still very hot with dry toast, sea salt and pepper.

## STIR-FRIED AROMATIC CROCODILE

Following on from buffalo and ostrich, crocodile and alligator are the latest low-fat animal proteins to be touted in the high street. Alligator and crocodile are very similar in taste and texture, the meat in both taken from the tail and usually pre-packed in trimmed fillets.

Enthusiasts describe the flavour as being like lobster with the texture of lean chicken. Ernest Matthew Mickler says of Florida alligator in his book *White Trash Cooking*: 'If you haven't eaten 'gator tail before, you're in for a surprise. It's gonna taste a little bit like pork, a little bit like chicken, and a little bit like fish. It's so good you'll wanna lay down and scream.'

In Southern Florida they cook farmed alligator like a pork chop – 'salt, pepper and flour each piece of tail and then fry in hot grease until golden brown.' Perhaps, at £10 a pound, this is rather a brutal treatment. Instead, stir-fry with some aromatic ingredients and serve with boiled basmati rice. If no crocodile is to hand, substitute chicken, lobster tail or peeled tiger prawns.

SERVES 4

**115 g / 4 oz crocodile fillet**
**1 stalk of lemon grass**
**4 spring onions**
**1 garlic clove**
**1 hot red chilli or ¼ tsp chilli flakes**
**2 tbsp sunflower oil**
**1 tbsp soy sauce**
**1 tbsp fish sauce**
**handful of coarsely chopped coriander leaves**

Cut the crocodile fillet into 4 strips. Top and tail the lemon grass stalk, remove the coarse outer leaf and cut the stalk across into thin rounds. Slice the spring onions across at an angle into 2.5-cm / 1-inch pieces. Smash and chop the garlic clove. Deseed the chilli if using.

Put the sunflower oil in a wok or large frying pan and place over a high heat. Add the lemon grass, onions and chilli and stir-fry for 1 minutes.

Add the crocodile fillet and fry for a further 2 minutes, tossing to ensure even cooking.

Add the soy sauce and fish sauce. Stir for 15 seconds, throw in the chopped coriander leaves and serve immediately.

## TRIPE À LA MODE DE CAEN

Tripe, being the lining of the first three stomachs of a ruminant, starts its life as a foul-smelling material that is popular in this green state only with undiscerning canines. Anybody who has cooked green tripe for a pet will know why it must be scraped, bleached and pre-cooked before going into the kitchen. However, the majority of tripe now sold here has been so zealously cleaned and boiled it has no flavour at all.

You can try talking to your butcher, because there is excellent French tripe on sale in the wholesale markets. You could also try a Chinese or Asian market and Halal butchers are another possible source of supply. When you do get your hands on the real thing, try cooking it *à la mode de Caen*, one of Normandy's great dishes. Drink dry cider with the meal, Calvados after.

SERVES 4

1 kg / 2¼ lb honeycomb tripe
1 pig's trotter
4 tbsp olive oil
450 g / 1 lb onions, thinly sliced
275 g / 10 oz carrots, sliced
2 garlic cloves, smashed and chopped
1 bay leaf
sprig of thyme
salt and pepper
1 litre / 1¾ pints dry cider
100 ml / 3½ fl oz Calvados
flat-leaved parsley, to garnish
some good bread, to serve

Preheat the oven to 160°C/325°F/gas 3. Cut the tripe into 5-cm / 2-inch squares and reserve. Give the pig's trotter a thorough pedicure and blanch it in boiling water for 5 minutes. Throw this water away and give the trotter a rinse under cold running water.

Heat the oil in a casserole over a moderate heat and fry the onions and carrots until soft but not browned. Add the tripe, the trotter, garlic, bay leaf, thyme and salt and pepper. Pour over the cider and add water to cover. Bring the casserole to the boil on the hob, skimming off any scum that comes to the surface. Put on a lid, put into the oven and cook for 4 hours. If necessary, this can now be held until the next day. Remove the trotter and discard.

Bring the tripe to the boil on the hob, lower the heat and simmer for 10–15 minutes uncovered. Just before serving, stir in the Calvados. Serve scattered with lots of flat-leaved parsley and with some good bread to mop up the juices.

## FAGGOTS

Faggots from pork butchers often contain pig's lungs and hearts so, unless feeling determinedly authentic, use belly pork instead.

MAKES 6 FAGGOTS

450 g / 1 lb pigs' liver, cut into bite-sized pieces
about 300 ml / ½ pint milk
450 g / 1 lb minced fat pork
225 g / 8 oz onion, diced
2 garlic cloves, smashed and chopped
3 sage leaves, chopped
1 tsp dried mixed herbs
salt and pepper
115 g / 4 oz white breadcrumbs
2 eggs
¼ nutmeg, grated
2 sheets of caul fat (see page 17)
150 ml / ½ pint beer

First soak pigs' liver pieces in the milk overnight in the fridge.

Next day, drain and discard the milk. Put the liver in a pan with the minced fat pork, diced onion, garlic, sage and dried mixed herbs. Season with salt and pepper and cook over a low heat for 30 minutes, stirring from time to time. Drain through a colander, reserving the cooking juices.

Preheat the oven to 190°C/375°F/gas 5. Put the meats into a bowl and add the breadcrumbs, eggs and nutmeg. Mix together with a fork. Cut the sheets of caul fat into six 25-cm / 10-inch squares. Divide the mixture between them and wrap in neat balls (see page 17). Arrange them, not touching, in a gratin dish and pour round the beer. Bake for 30 minutes.

Pour off the beer and cooking juices into a pan with the juices reserved from the first cooking procedure. Bring to the boil and skim, then simmer. Taste and adjust the seasoning if necessary. Return the faggots to the oven for a further 20 minutes.

Serve them with the reduced stock poured round and a purée of split peas or buttery mashed potatoes.

# POULTRY AND GAME BIRDS

**A** genuine free-range chicken is a marvellous thing, full of flavour and capable of so many culinary expressions. Finding such a chicken is not always easy. The majority of birds so described by supermarkets are patently not free-range – having, in reality, been raised intensively in giant sheds without access to the outdoors, to the sunshine, grass, earth, worms and insects which give the words 'free-range' significance. The French produce genuine free-range chickens and they are sold here, though mostly to restaurants. A halfway decent butcher will get you French chickens if you ask him or they may know somebody who raises real free-range birds locally.

### ROAST CHICKEN

It always used to be said that the sign of a good cook was his or her ability to roast a chicken perfectly. It remains a valid gauge of competence today, for people stubbornly tend to over-cook while still ending up with a flabby skin. Perhaps one reason for over-cooking is that people have become paranoid about salmonella. To be absolutely safe, no trace of pink should be found, even around the bone. Thus the challenge is to produce a roast chicken which is golden and crisp-skinned without, yet meltingly moist and tender within.

If you are cooking a larger bird, then consider cutting it up into a breast joint for roasting, and using the legs and thighs in a sauté for another meal. Chickens are very easy to dismember: simply run a small sharp knife down each side of the body, following the contour of the ribcage to remove the legs in one piece, cutting carefully through the ball-and-socket joint. You can see where to cut through the backbone and cartilage, to leave a neat joint that looks like a smaller version of the turkey breast joints sold in supermarkets. Leave the wings on to provide a stable base for the joint to sit upright, then pull the skin carefully away from the breast meat and slide thin slices of fat bacon, pancetta or Parma ham between the skin and the meat. Roast in the same way as a whole bird, but test to see if it is done after 30 minutes.

SERVES 4

**1 free-range chicken, cleaned and trussed, about 1.35 kg / 3 lb**
**1 tbsp olive oil**
**salt and pepper**
**knob of butter**

Preheat the oven to its hottest setting say 250°C/475°F/gas 9. Brush the bird all over with olive oil and season generously. Put the knob of butter inside the bird and put it to roast, breast side down on a rack, in the preheated oven

Cook for 15 minutes, then turn it breast side up and continue cooking with the oven lowered to 200°C/ 400°F/gas 6 for 35–40 minutes. Push a skewer into the thigh at the thickest point. If the juices run clear, it is done; if not, give it another 5 minutes.

Put the cooked bird to stand in a warm place for 15 minutes before carving. This standing time is vital. The bird finishes cooking while the juices are recovered and are absorbed back into the meat, making every slice moist.

Remove the legs, cutting through at the joint into thighs and drumsticks. Remove the breasts whole, cutting them across at an angle into thick slices. Pull out the oysters under the bird. Use the carcass for stock.

> ### RESTING A ROAST CHICKEN
> *Never leave a chicken more than 20 minutes before carving if eating it hot. It will lose its freshness and start to taste 'reheated'. It is, surprisingly, better to let it cool to room temperature, when its true flavour will return.*

## POTTED CHICKEN

Originally seen as a way of being creative with leftovers when the Sunday joint had to do service for several meals, potted meats were later reproduced commercially as bland pastes for sandwich fillings. You can make a fine potted meat today to serve as a first course with toast and, thanks to the food processor, do so in seconds.

SERVES 4 AS A FIRST
COURSE
**170 g / 6 oz cold roast chicken**
**85 g / 3 oz of cold ham**
**115 g / 4 oz unsalted butter**
**freshly grated nutmeg**
**½ tsp ground black pepper**

Dice the chicken and the ham. Put them in a blender or food processor with 85 g / 3 oz of the butter, and nutmeg and pepper to taste. Blitz to a smooth purée, stopping the machine and scraping down the sides 2 or 3 times.

Spoon into sterilized ramekins, pressing down flat to eliminate any air pockets and smoothing the surface flat. Melt the remaining butter and use it to film the surface. Refrigerate for up to a week.

## UMBRIAN LEMON POUSSIN

SERVES 2
**2 whole poussin**
**juice of 2 lemons**
**4 tbsp olive oil**
**black pepper**

Cut down on either side of the backbone of each bird and flatten it by slamming down hard on the breastbone with the heel of your hand.

Make a marinade by mixing the lemon juice and oil. Put the birds into zip-lock bags with half the marinade each and marinate at room temperature for 2 hours, turning and shaking the bags occasionally.

Cook on a charcoal grill preheated to moderate or under a preheated over-head grill. Arrange the birds on a rack and grind over a lot of black pepper. Start grilling cut side up at least 15 cm / 6 inches away from the heat. Turn frequently, basting with the marinade, until done, which takes about 20–25 minutes.

## CHICKEN BREASTS WITH CORIANDER AND LEMON

Lemon-based marinades like this one are particularly effective with chicken.

SERVES 4
**juice of 2 lemons**
**2 tbsp chopped coriander**
**leaves**
**3 tbsp sunflower oil**
**½ tsp pepper**
**4 chicken breast fillets**
**flour, for dusting**
**salt**
**a little olive oil**

In a bowl, mix the lemon juice, chopped coriander, sunflower oil and pepper. Put the chicken into a large zip-lock bag, add the marinade and refrigerate overnight or for up to 24 hours.

Remove the bag from the fridge well ahead to bring the chicken to room temperature before cooking. Pat the breasts dry, flour lightly and season them with salt.

Cook in a little olive oil over a low heat, turning frequently, for about 15 minutes, until the skin is crisp and the flesh just done.

Remove from the pan and allow to rest in a warm place for about 5 minutes before serving.

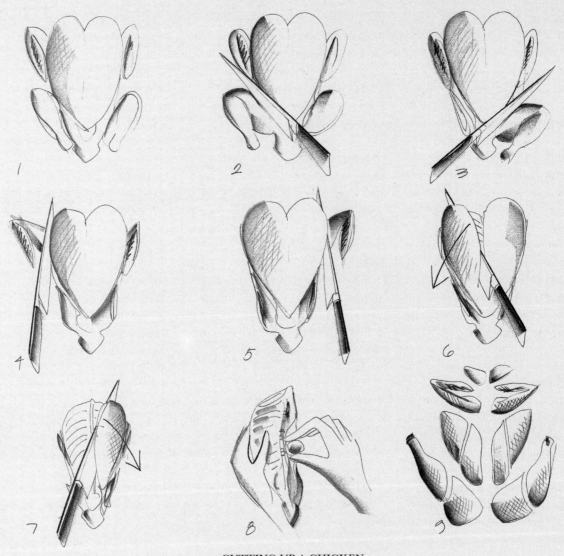

## CUTTING UP A CHICKEN

❶ Position the bird with the legs pointing towards you.

❷ Pull the leg away from the body and slice down between it and the carcass, cutting through the ball and socket joint at the base.

❸ Repeat on the other side.

❹ Remove a wing in the same way.

❺ Repeat on the other side.

❻ Carve off a breast whole in one piece, slicing down flat against the backbone.

❼ Repeat on the other side.

❽ Detach the fleshy oysters from the undersides with your fingers.

❾ Cut through the legs to separate them into drumsticks and thighs. Cut off and discard the wing tips. Carve the breasts across at an angle. This gives 10 pieces plus the oysters.

## CHICKEN SAUTÉ WITH GARLIC

*Poulet à l'ail* is the kind of simple food that is more often cooked at home in France than served in restaurants. It is traditionally made in a deep iron pan in a seamless process, but one which actually benefits from some elements of separation. A 1.8-kg / 4-lb chicken will feed 4 hungry people, but a 1.35-kg / 3-lb bird will satisfy most appetites.

**SERVES 4**

**1 chicken, about 1.35 kg / 3 lb**
**salt and pepper**
**flour, for dusting**
**4 tbsp olive oil**
**30 g / 1 oz unsalted butter**
**41 large garlic cloves, unpeeled**
**300 ml / ½ pt dry white wine**
**8 slices of baguette**
**2 tbsp brandy**
**handful of coarsely chopped flat-leaved parsley**

Joint the bird, removing the legs first before cutting through the joint to separate drumsticks from thighs and then taking off the breasts with the wings attached, before cutting through the breasts diagonally into two. This will give you 8 pieces in total (see opposite). You can always ask your butcher to do this for you but, if you do, retain the carcass for stock. (Alternatively the dish can be made using only leg or thigh joints.)

Season the chicken pieces with salt and pepper, coat them lightly with flour and put them skin side down in a non-stick pan over a low heat until the skin exudes fat and crisps to a golden brown.

Increase the heat, turn the pieces and briefly brown the other side before removing and reserving.

In a heavy casserole in which the chicken will fit in a single layer, put the olive oil and butter over a moderate heat. Add all but one of the garlic cloves (this may sound a lot, but after cooking they will not be too ferocious – indeed, some recipes call for 60 cloves!) and fry, stirring, until the skins start to colour. Lay the chicken on top, skin upwards, and pour in the wine. Bring to the boil, lower the heat and simmer gently for 30–40 minutes.

Toast the slices of baguette, rub the slices of toast with the remaining garlic clove, peeled, and put them on a warmed serving plate. Check the chicken is cooked through to the bone (the juices run clear – rather than pink – when the thickest part of the flesh is pierced with a skewer or the tip of a sharp knife) before arranging it on top of the toasts. Remove the garlic with a slotted spoon and add to the chicken.

Turn up the heat and bubble down the sauce to a few syrupy spoonfuls. Add the brandy, light and flame carefully, shaking the pan. When the flames have died down, pour this on top of the chicken and finish the dish with a handful of coarsely chopped flat-leaved parsley.

## CHINESE-STYLE STEAMED CHICKEN

The Chinese use steamers a great deal, partly because the majority do not use ovens in the domestic kitchen in the Western way. Steaming in the British consciousness is still synonymous with invalid food, implying blandness. The Chinese imbue flavour in steamed food with aromatics and never overcook, which leads to dryness. Chicken cooked this way is usually served with steamed rice but it is also very good with a bowl of noodles and some chicken broth ladled over.

**SERVES 4**

**4 skinless chicken breast fillets**
**4 tbsp soy sauce**
**8 spring onions, chopped**
**1 star anise**
**1 hot chilli, finely chopped**
**salt and pepper**
**3-cm / 1¼-inch piece of ginger, peeled and cut into wafer-thin slices**
**steamed glutinous rice, to serve**
**coarsely chopped coriander leaves, to finish**

Brush the chicken all over with half the soy sauce and leave to marinate for about 30 minutes.

On a plate which will just fit in the steamer, put the chopped spring onion and the star anise and sit the chicken on top. Sprinkle on the chilli and season with salt and pepper. Cover the top with the ginger and pour over the remaining soy sauce. Steam for 8–12 minutes, remove and leave to stand for 3 minutes.

To serve, slice the chicken and serve it with steamed glutinous rice, with the juices and vegetables from the plate on top, but discarding the star anise.

For a fresh finish, scatter over some coarsely chopped coriander leaves.

## CHICKEN TIKKA

*Tikka* means 'boned and cut into cubes'. The best meat to use is chicken thighs, which are inexpensive in large packets.

SERVES 4

5-cm / 2-inch piece of ginger, peeled and chopped

4 garlic cloves, peeled and chopped

600 ml / 1 pt plain yoghurt

30 g / 1 oz plain flour

¼ nutmeg, grated

2 tsp ground cumin

2 tsp ground pepper

2 tsp chilli powder

2 tsp turmeric

1 tsp cardamom seeds

1 tsp salt

6 tbsp sunflower oil

juice of 2 lemons

1 chicken, about 1.5 kg / 3¼ lb

a little melted butter

The day before, put the ginger into a food processor with the garlic and 4 tablespoons of the yoghurt. Blitz this to a paste and put into a bowl with the remaining yoghurt, the flour, nutmeg, cumin, pepper, chilli powder, turmeric, cardamom, salt, sunflower oil and lemon juice. Mix all together.

Skin and bone the chicken, cut the meat into equal-sized pieces and put into the marinade, turning with a spoon to coat evenly. Refrigerate overnight.

Next day, preheat a barbecue, grill or grill pan. Brush off most of the marinade, thread the chicken on 8 skewers and grill for 6–8 minutes, turning frequently and basting with a little melted butter

## CHICKEN KIEV

Chicken Kiev is a skinned suprême, that is, the breast attached to the scraped wing bone after the pinion bone has been removed. The fillet is removed from the middle of the breast and the remaining flesh is then beaten into an escalope. The small fillet is opened and stuffed with a piece of chilled *maitre d'hôtel* butter, essentially herb butter, though many people like to incorporate garlic into the amalgamation. The escalope is wrapped around it, the whole is coated in egg and breadcrumbs and then deep-fried. This is all much more difficult to describe than it is to do.

MAKES 4

4 chicken suprêmes

2–3 eggs, beaten

about 115 g / 4 oz fine dry breadcrumbs

oil for deep-frying

1 lemon, quartered lengthwise

mashed potatoes or thin-cut chips, to serve

for the maitre d'hôtel butter

2 garlic cloves, finely chopped

3 tbsp finely chopped flat-leaved parsley

1 tbsp finely chopped tarragon

115 g / 4 oz softened unsalted butter, diced

salt and pepper

1 tbsp lemon juice

Start by making the butter: put the garlic, parsley and tarragon in a bowl with the butter. Season with salt and pepper and the lemon juice. Using a wooden spoon, beat to a smooth paste. A food processor may be used but, if so, pulse-chop briefly to avoid amalgamating the herbs and butter into a pale-green mass, It should be yellow-flecked with discernible pieces of parsley. Roll the butter in foil or cling-film and refrigerate. You can do this up to a week ahead, or it may be frozen for a month.

Remove the skin from the first suprême, laying it skinned side down. Detach the small fillet from the underside of the main fillet and cut this small fillet along its length and almost all the way through, folding open, and flatten by beating gently with a cutlet bat or rolling pin. Put a walnut-sized piece of the chilled butter in the middle and wrap the meat round it. Repeat with the 3 other small fillets, returning all 4 to the fridge.

Cut open the larger fillets in the same way, place between plastic sheets and gently beat out. Lay the small buttered fillet in the middle and wrap the escalope around it. Dip in beaten egg and then in breadcrumbs. Repeat to give a double coating. Refrigerate for at least 1 hour before cooking.

Heat oil for deep-frying to 180°C/ 350°F and cook the Kievs in two batches for 7–8 minutes each. When the crisp golden-brown shell is cut open the melted butter gushes out, giving off a lovely garlicky aroma.

Serve with lemon quarters and mashed potatoes or thinly cut chips.

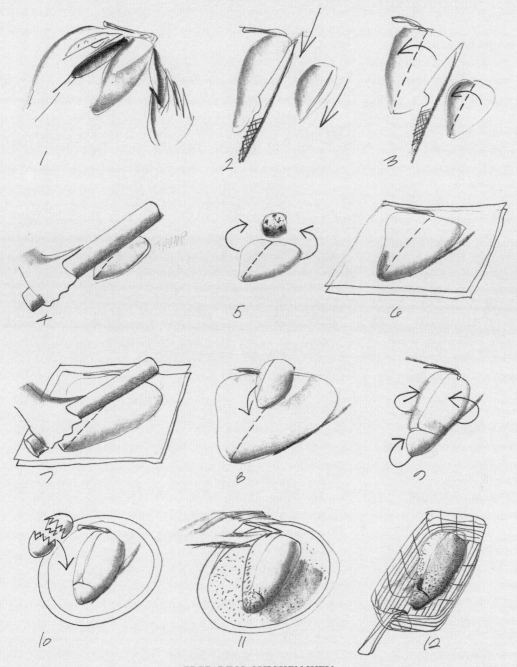

## PREPARING CHICKEN KIEV

*1 Remove and discard the skin from the breast and detach the small fillet on its underside. 2–3 Cut both fillets almost all the way through from the side, and open them out. 4 Beat the small fillet out flat. 5 Put a piece of herb butter in the middle of the small fillet and wrap it up. Refrigerate. 6 Put the larger fillet between plastic sheets. 7 Beat it out flat. 8 Lay the butter-stuffed fillet on this escalope. 9 Wrap the meat around it. 10 Dip in an egg wash. 11 Coat with fine breadcrumbs, then repeat the egging-and-crumbing process. 12 Deep-fry in hot oil as described opposite.*

## FRIED CHICKEN IN BATTER

Battered deep-fried chicken is a great favourite with children, who are never happier than when fed from a high-street fast-food outlet. The late Colonel Sanders' batter recipe is a trade secret, just like the formula for Coke or Heinz baked beans. However, this recipe for deep-fried chicken in a herbed batter should please the most discerning young palate, especially when served in striped boxes to be eaten with their fingers. Battered chicken is Michael Jackson's favourite food, which he always demands when he stays at the Lanesborough Hotel on Hyde Park Corner, so a parent entering into the spirit of things could add to the sense of occasion by providing the children with black surgical masks to don afterwards.

SERVES 4

8 chicken thighs
2 garlic cloves, finely chopped
juice of 2 lemons
oil, for deep-frying
lemon wedges or tomato
ketchup, to serve

for the batter:
115 g / 4 oz plain flour
2 eggs
200 ml / 7 fl oz light ale or lager
2 tbsp olive oil
1 tsp salt
2 tsp dried oregano
½ tsp chilli flakes (optional)
½ tsp black pepper

The day before, remove the skin from the chicken thighs and cut out the bones (see Kentish Pudding, page 146). Put the boned thighs in a dish, add the garlic, pour over the lemon juice and toss to coat. Cling-wrap and refrigerate overnight.

Next day, remove the chicken from the fridge well ahead to allow it to come to room temperature before cooking.

Make the batter: in a bowl, mix the flour, eggs, light ale or lager, olive oil, salt oregano, chilli flakes if you like, and black pepper. Whisk until smooth and leave to stand for 1 hour at room temperature.

Heat oil for deep-frying to 190°C/ 375°F and stir the batter. Wipe the marinade from the chicken and pat dry with kitchen paper, then coat in the batter. Fry the chicken in 2 batches, for about 8 minutes each, turning once. Keep the first batch warm while you cook the second lot. Remove and transfer each batch to kitchen paper to drain, returning the first batch for a minute to recrisp after you have cooked the second.

Serve with lemon wedges. Oh, all right then, tomato ketchup.

### DEEP-FRYING

*Deep-frying is a technique which is dependent on precise temperatures and clean oil to deliver consistent good results. Whatever heating system you use, you must be able to achieve a temperature of 190°C/375°F to seal food and remember that putting in too many pieces at a time will dramatically lower the temperature. Then, if a fast and efficient seal has not been made by the initial plunge into the oil, the food will absorb an excess of fat during cooking.*

*Domestic electric deep-fryers have two potential problems: the manufacturers may be using cheap bought-in thermostats which do not give accurate temperature control or the size of the frying container is too small, leading to overloading. The only way to monitor this is to check the temperature with a thermometer and to experiment with the amounts you cook at one time.*

*Alternatively, you can simply use a large flat-bottomed wok or a big heavy-based saucepan, gauging the temperature with a thermometer. Never fill the pan more than half full and be very careful. Pans of boiling oil on top of the stove are very dangerous.*

*Opposite: Umbrian Lemon Poussin (page 139)*

## ITALIAN POACHED CAPON SALAD

Technically a capon is a hand-castrated cock, and while exotic and expensive, your butcher will be able to track one down in the wholesale market. Capon was greatly favoured in the Middle Ages, great big chickens that they were, and still are, weighing anything from 2.7 kg / 6 lb upwards.

A suitably Renaissance treatment is to serve it as the Italians would in Mantua. The combination of succulent chicken with the tangy marinade is both unusual and delicious. Where most meat dishes are marinated before cooking, this is one instance where the bird is first poached and then marinated, the marinade being served as a sauce.

You can cook an ordinary chicken in the same way. A 1.35-kg / 3-lb bird will take 45 minutes from the point at which the cooking liquid has boiled.

**SERVES 6–8**

**1 capon, about 2.7-kg / 6-lb (see above)**
**about 3 litres / 5¼ pints cold water or chicken stock**
**2 celery stalks, plus a handful of celery leaves if available**
**1 onion**
**6 cloves**
**3 tsp salt**
**85 g / 3 oz pine nuts**
**200 ml / 7 fl oz red wine vinegar**
**2 bay leaves**
**zest of 1 orange**

*Opposite: Hindle Wakes (page 146)*

**zest of 1 lemon**
**about 1 tbsp caster**
**½ tsp salt**
**1 tsp ground pepper**
**115 g / 4 oz sultanas**
**extra-virgin olive oil, to dress**
**sliced ripe plum tomatoes and torn basil leaves, to serve**

Poach the bird well ahead, ideally 2 days before you want to serve: put the capon in a large pan and cover it with cold water or chicken stock. Add the celery stalks and leaves if available, with the onion studded with the cloves and the salt. Bring to the boil, skim, lower the heat and simmer for 1½ hours. Leave to cool in the broth.

Put the pine nuts in a dry pan and toast lightly over a low heat, stirring, for 2–3 minutes. Set aside.

Heat the red wine vinegar in a pan to a simmer. Add the bay leaves, orange and lemon zest, caster sugar, salt and pepper, and simmer for 15 minutes. Taste for sweetness: if too sour, add a little more sugar. Add the sultanas and toasted pine nuts and set aside.

Take the bird out of the poaching water, pull off and discard any fat and skin. Remove the flesh from the bones and shred with your fingers. Put in a serving bowl and pour over the warm dressing, mixing thoroughly. Leave to macerate at room temperature for 2–3 hours, then refrigerate overnight.

Next day, remove the bowl from the fridge and allow to come to room temperature. Just before bringing it to the table, dress with extra-virgin olive oil. Serve with sliced ripe plum tomatoes and torn basil leaves.

## CRISP GRILLED CHICKEN WINGS

Chicken wings are cheap and their high fat content makes them ideal for grilling. Children aged 3 to 80 adore them, while your stockpot will love the bones. Experiment with other marinades – for example, replace the chilli oil, Worcestershire sauce and cumin with Tabasco, soy sauce and paprika.

**SERVES 4**
**16 chicken wings**

**for the marinade:**
**juice of 2 lemons**
**1 tbsp chilli oil**
**2 tbsp Worcestershire sauce**
**1 tbsp ground cumin**

Put the chicken wings into a large zip-lock bag. Mix the marinade ingredients, pour into the bag and shake well to coat. Refrigerate overnight or for up to 24 hours. The bag is not essential, but is an effective way of using a relatively small amount of marinade to best advantage.

Preheat a barbecue, grill or grill pan. The wings will take between 20 and 30 minutes to grill. Start off at least 15 cm / 6 inches away from the grill, cooking the wings on a rack. Turn frequently, brushing with leftover marinade until it is all used up. They will be golden brown and crisp-skinned, with the flesh succulent.

## HINDLE WAKES

Wakes were originally feasts held the night before the dedication of a church, the date being celebrated annually with a parish fair. By the 17th century these had become riotous affairs held in the church yards with 'indecent and scandalous behaviour', as an 18th-century historian noted, and were for a time banned by Cromwell. Over the years, wakes expanded from occasions for eating, drinking and behaving badly to big fairs like that held each year on All Saints Night in Wakefield in Yorkshire and Wakes Week is still a popular holiday week in the north of England.

Hindle Wakes is a very ancient dish indeed, consisting of cold poached chicken stuffed with prunes and flavoured with vinegar, sugar, mace and cinnamon. It would originally have been made with a boiling fowl, which would have been poached for 4–5 hours, but is just as nice with a free-range bird simmered for about an hour.

**SERVES 4**

about 18 pitted no-need-to-soak Californian prunes
100 g / 3½ oz breadcrumbs
30 g / 1 oz suet
1 tsp ground cinnamon
½ tsp freshly grated nutmeg
2 tbsp chopped parsley
6 sage leaves, chopped, or 1 tsp dried mixed herbs
salt and pepper
juice of 2 lemons and zest of 1
1 free-range chicken, about 1.5 kg / 3¼ lb
3 celery stalks, roughly chopped
1 onion, halved
2 carrots, quartered
2 bay leaves
2 tsp salt
150 ml / ¼ pt wine vinegar
30 g / 1 oz muscovado sugar
lemon wedges, to serve
more chopped parsley, to garnish

The day before: reserving 12 whole prunes for garnish, coarsely chop the rest and mix in a bowl with the breadcrumbs and suet. Season with cinnamon, nutmeg, parsley, sage or dried mixed herbs, salt and pepper and mix together with the juice of 1 of the lemons.

Stuff the chicken with this mixture and sew up tightly. Put it in a saucepan with the celery, onion, carrots and bay leaves. Cover with cold water and add the salt, wine vinegar and muscovado sugar. Bring to the boil, skim, lower the heat and simmer gently for 1 hour. Turn off the heat, cover and leave to cool overnight in the broth.

Remove the chicken from the broth, skin and cut it into neat serving pieces, returning the bones to the broth and reserving the stuffing. Return the stock to the boil, lower the heat and simmer for 2 hours.

Pass the stock through a sieve into a clean pan, discarding the bones and aromatics and reduce the poaching liquid at a rapid boil to about 300 ml / ½ pint. Add the juice of the second lemon.

Spoon the stuffing along the centre of a serving dish and arrange the chicken around it. As the reduced broth starts to set, spoon it over the chicken.

Grate over the zest of the lemon and put in the fridge for the stock to set to a jelly.

Just before serving, garnish the dish with the reserved prunes, cut in half, and the lemon quarters, and sprinkle over some chopped parsley.

## KENTISH PUDDING

Originally, a jointed and boned boiling fowl would have been used for this dish, but you can make an excellent Kentish pudding today using a packet of chicken thighs.

**SERVES 6**

6 chicken thighs
600 ml / 1 pt chicken stock
85 g / 3 oz smoked streaky bacon, cut into thick matchstick strips
150 g / 5 oz large mushrooms, coarsely chopped
15 g / ½ oz butter, plus more for the basin
115 g / 4 oz onion, diced
3 tbsp chopped parsley
salt and pepper
1 sherry glass of dry sherry (optional)

for the suet crust:
275 g / 10 oz self-raising flour, plus more for dusting
140 g / 5 oz suet
½ tsp salt
¼ tsp pepper

Start by boning the chicken thighs, using a small sharp knife, cut the flesh away from the bone. Slide the knife underneath the bone and cut along its length, detaching it by slicing through next to the cartilaginous ball joint. Pull off the skin and discard.

Add the bones and skin to the chicken stock and simmer until reduced by half. Reserve.

Make the suet crust: mixing the flour and suet in a bowl with the salt and pepper. With a fork, stir in just enough cold water to bind, then turn the soft and slightly sticky dough out on a heavily floured surface and roll into a ball. Cover with a cloth and leave to rest for 15–30 minutes. Divide the rested pastry into 2 pieces, 1 being one-third of the whole.

Fry the bacon gently until just cooked but not crisp. Remove with a slotted spoon and transfer to a bowl. Fry the mushrooms in the bacon fat with the butter until softened and put with the bacon. Stir in the onion and chopped parsley.

Roll out the larger piece of dough and use to line a buttered 1.5-litre / 2³⁄₄-pint pudding basin, rolling the smaller piece into a disc for the lid.

Cut the chicken thighs into 2 and roll them in flour. Mix thoroughly with the bacon, mushrooms, onion and parsley, season with salt and pepper and fill the basin with the mixture. Strain the stock through a sieve and use to fill the pudding almost to the top, adding the sherry if you like. Brush the rim with cold water and put on the lid, pinching the edges together to seal.

Tie a pleated round of foil on the top – the pleat will allow for expansion – and make a string handle to facilitate lifting the pudding. Sit the pudding on a trivet or upside-down saucer in a large

pan and pour boiling water in to come halfway up the basin. Put on a lid and boil for 3–3¹⁄₂ hours, topping up with more boiling water to compensate for evaporation.

Lift out, remove the foil and serve straight from the basin.

> ## WHEN RED WINE MARINADES ARE A MISTAKE...
>
> *A red wine marinade is unsuitable for chicken breasts unless the marination is very short. If left overnight you will end up with a very strong-tasting flesh. Even coq au vin, where all the chicken is used and not just the breasts, is not marinated for more than 6 hours at room temperature. Better stick to citrus juice, soy sauce and oil.*

## CHICKEN TERIYAKI

Teriyaki is a lovely Japanese grilling glaze, but it is sticky because of the sake and mirin – dry and sweet rice wines – and burns easily. It is therefore important to start grilling the meat with nothing on it but salt and pepper, before brushing with the glaze. Both sake and mirin can be bought from Oriental markets. One of the nicest things to grill teriyaki-style is chicken.

### SERVES 4

**675 g / 1¹⁄₂ lb mixed skinless and boneless chicken thigh and breast meat**

**juice of 1 lemon**
**5 tbsp Kikkoman soy sauce**
**4 tbsp sake**
**4 tbsp mirin**
**3-cm / 1¹⁄₄-inch piece of ginger, peeled, chopped and cut into tiny dice**
**8 spring onions, cut across into quarters**
**sunflower oil for brushing**
**salt and pepper**

The day before, start by boning out the thighs, then cut the thigh and breast meat into rectangles about 3 x 2 cm / 1¹⁄₄ x ³⁄₄ inch in size. Put into a zip-lock bag with the lemon juice, soy sauce, sake and mirin. Shake well to coat and refrigerate overnight.

Next day, pour the marinade into a pan. Add the ginger and bring to the boil. Immediately remove from the heat and allow to cool. When cool, strain through a sieve to remove the ginger.

Wipe the chicken with a damp cloth and thread on 8 wooden satay skewers which have been soaked in water (to prevent burning), putting a quarter of a spring onion between each piece.

Preheat a grill or barbecue. Brush the chicken with a little sunflower oil and season with salt and pepper. Put to cook 15 cm / 6 inches away from the heat. Brush on the marinade after 2 minutes and turn. Brush the other side and turn back after a further 2 minutes. Repeat, giving them a total of 6 minutes each side. They should be a burnished mahogany colour outside and cooked all the way through, but still moist and tender within.

Serve with steamed fragrant rice.

## BUFFALO CHICKEN WINGS WITH BLUE CHEESE DIP

The combination of crisp deep-fried chicken wings and a dip of blue cheese mayonnaise is said to have originated in Buffalo, in upstate New York, hence the name.

**SERVES 4**

16 chicken wings
3 tbsp Worcestershire sauce
3 tbsp olive oil
2 tbsp Tabasco sauce
melted butter, to serve
(optional)

for the blue cheese dip:
300 ml / ½ pt mayonnaise
1 celery stalk, chopped
115 g / 4 oz blue cheese, crumbled
¼ onion, diced
1 tsp Tabasco
2 tsp Worcestershire sauce

Cut each chicken wing into 3 through the joints, reserving the tips for stock.

Put the Worcestershire sauce, olive oil and Tabasco in a bowl and add the wing segments. Turn to coat and leave to marinate for 4 hours at room temperature, turning from time to time, or refrigerate overnight and remove 2 hours before cooking in the oven rather than deep-frying, the US preference.

Preheat the oven to 220°C/425°F/gas 7. Arrange the wings on a rack in a roasting pan and cook for 30 minutes, turning frequently until crisp-skinned. If your oven contains an internal grill, then switch this on for the last 10 minutes. The cooking time is not precise, just keep turning them until the skin is really crunchy. The wings are mostly fat and you really want to cook as much of this out as possible.

While the chicken is cooking, make the blue cheese dip in a food processor by blitzing all the ingredients together.

Serve the wings as soon as they are cooked, with the dip in small cocottes on the side of the plate. In Buffalo they would dribble melted butter over the wings before sending them to the table, but this is not essential.

## CHICKEN LAKSA

This soupy Malaysian dish has distinct regional variations. In Penang or Assam, a *laksa* – named after the indigenous mint leaves which play an important role in its flavouring – is cooked with fish in a tamarind broth bulked with noodles and fresh pineapple, quite a sweet-and-sour presentation. In Malacca, laksa also includes chicken, coconut milk, prawns, beancurd and fish balls, but leaves out the tamarind and pineapple. The most important part is not the precise mix of ingredients but the distinctively aromatic Malaysian curry paste that gives it heat and complexity. This would traditionally be made with a pestle and mortar, which gives the best texture, but a food processor does the job effectively, effortlessly and very quickly.

**SERVES 4 GENEROUSLY**

1 chicken, preferably free-range
2 tsp cumin seeds
1 tsp coriander seeds
20 Asian mint leaves (laksa)
8 shallots
7.5-cm / 3-inch piece of galangal, grated
3 garlic cloves
2 stalks of lemon grass, outer leaves removed and cut across into thin rings
2 tsp chilli flakes (use less if you don't like very spicy food)
1 tbsp belacan (dried shrimp paste)
2 tsp turmeric
400 g / 14 oz dried rice noodles (vermicelli type)
2–3 tbsp sunflower or groundnut oil
1 tsp sugar
500 ml / 16 fl oz coconut milk
12 raw peeled tiger prawns
225 g / 8 oz firm tofu (beancurd), cut into 2.5-cm / 1-inch cubes
8 fish balls (optional)
2 tbsp fish sauce
coriander leaves, to finish

The day before, poach the chicken gently in simmering water for 50 minutes. Remove and, when cool, take off the breasts whole and cut into bite-sized pieces, then refrigerate (keep the rest of the meat for another dish). Return the carcass and bones to the poaching liquid and simmer for 2–3 hours. Strain and boil to reduce to 1.5 litres / 2½ pints.

Next day, toast the cumin seeds and coriander seeds in a dry pan over a low heat until aromatic. Grind and reserve.

Put the mint leaves in a processor with the shallots, galangal, garlic, lemon grass, chilli flakes, belacan, turmeric and the ground toasted cumin and coriander. Blitz to a paste and reserve.

Cook the noodles in rapidly boiling water for 4 minutes, or as directed on the packet. Refresh in cold water and drain.

Put the oil in a wok and, when hot, add the curry paste and fry, stirring, for 3–4 minutes over a moderate heat. Pour in the chicken stock, add the sugar and bring to the boil. Lower the heat to a simmer and add the coconut milk. When hot, add the cooked chicken, prawns and tofu cubes. If you are able to get them from the chill cabinet of an Asian market, add the fish balls. When the prawns turn pink, it is ready.

Finish by stirring in the fish sauce and serve in deep bowls, scattered with coriander leaves.

## CHICKEN FAJITAS

Fajitas are a very popular Southern Californian – rather than Mexican – dish and are made from wheat-flour tortillas stuffed with a spicy filling, usually strips of chicken sautéed with red peppers, onion, a little hot chilli, coriander and garlic. The filling can also contain beans, salsa and sour cream. The tortillas are easy to make and the dough can be made the day before and kept, cling-wrapped, in the fridge.

**MAKES 12**

**for the tortillas:**
**450 g / 1 lb strong white bread**
**flour, plus more for dusting**
**3 tbsp lard**
**3 tbsp sunflower oil**
**1 tsp salt**
**300 ml / ½ pint warm water**

**for the filling:**
**2 red peppers, cut into strips,**
**discarding the seeds and pith**
**1 habanero chilli, finely**
**chopped**
**2 brown onions, thinly sliced**
**3 tbsp sunflower oil**
**3 tsp cumin seeds**
**3 tsp coriander seeds**
**½ tsp salt**
**1 tsp pepper**
**4 skinless chicken breast fillets,**
**cut into thin strips**
**coriander leaves**

**to serve:**
**guacamole (page 31)**
**sour cream**
**refried beans (page 203)**
**tomato and red onion salad**

First make the tortillas: put the flour, lard, oil and salt into a food processor and whiz to combine. Continue to process, pouring the warm water through the feeder tube in a thin stream until the dough balls. This may not take all the water or it may take a little more. Process until you have a smooth elastic dough. Turn out on a floured surface and divide into 12 pieces. Roll these into balls, put them on a plate, cling-wrap and leave to rest for 30 minutes.

Heat a heavy frying pan over a moderate heat, but don't oil it. On a floured surface, roll out a ball of dough, rotating, rolling and turning until you have a 17.5-cm / 7-inch circle. Dust with flour if it sticks. Place the tortillas one at a time on the hot metal. The top will start to bubble with hot air. Turn when the underside blisters. Cook for another 30 seconds, remove and wrap in a cloth to keep warm and moist. Do not overcook or the tortilla will go crisp.

Make the filling: sweat the peppers, chilli and onions over a low heat in the sunflower oil for 5 minutes, or until soft. While they are softening, put the cumin seeds, coriander seeds, salt and pepper into a dry heavy iron pan over a very low heat and toast them for 2–3 minutes, stirring. Grind to a powder. Sprinkle the frying vegetables with this, then turn up the heat and add the chicken to the pan, tossing and turning to cook. This takes very little time, no more than 3 or 4 minutes.

Scatter over coriander leaves over before bringing to the table. Serve with the tortillas, guacamole, sour cream, refried beans and a tomato and red onion salad.

## CHICKEN SATAY WITH PEANUT SAUCE

*Satay*, small pieces or strips of marinated meat grilled on bamboo skewers, is truly a Malay dish, but these days it is so popular in Thai restaurants people would be forgiven for thinking that it is a Thai dish. You can use beef, pork or chicken. The day before you cook your satay, put a packet of bamboo skewers to soak in cold water. This will help stop them burning. Serve the satay with some plain boiled rice.

SERVES 4

**8 chicken thighs**
**2–3 garlic cloves, smashed and chopped**
**1 onion, diced**
**juice of 2 limes**
**2 tbsp nam pla fish sauce**
**1 tbsp palm sugar or muscovado**
**2 tbsp tamarind pulp (optional)**

**for the peanut sauce:**
**225 g / 8 oz raw peanuts**
**3 tbsp groundnut or sunflower oil**
**1 onion, diced**
**2 garlic cloves, smashed and chopped**
**1 tsp chilli flakes**
**2.5-cm / 1-inch piece of ginger, peeled and finely chopped**
**1 stalk of lemon grass, thinly sliced**
**juice of 1 lemon**
**1 tbsp brown sugar**
**2 tbsp nam pla fish sauce**
**1 tbsp dark soy sauce**
**375 ml / 12 fl oz hot water**

Bone the chicken thighs (see Kentish Pudding, page 146), using the bones for stock. Strip off the skin and discard. Cut the meat into strips about 5 cm / 2 inches long by 1–2 cm / $^{1}/_{2}$–$^{3}/_{4}$ inch wide and put into a bowl.

In a food processor, put the garlic, onion, lime juice, fish sauce, sugar and tamarind, if you have some. Blitz to a smooth paste and pour over the meat, turning with a fork to coat, and leave to marinate for 2 hours at room temperature or overnight in the fridge.

Make the satay sauce: shell the raw peanuts and fry them over a low heat in the oil, stirring continuously until browned. Transfer to a food processor and add the onion, garlic, chilli flakes, ginger, lemon grass, lemon juice, sugar, fish sauce and soy sauce. Work to a smooth paste, pouring the hot water through the feeder tube as you process. Pour into a saucepan, bring to the boil, lower the heat and simmer for 1 minute. Remove and leave to cool.

Preheat an overhead grill and thread the marinated meat on the skewers. Grill the chicken fiercely, close to the flame, until just done – about 4 minutes on each side.

> DEALING WITH HARD PALM
> SUGAR OR JAGGERY
> *When exposed to air, palm sugar and jaggery – also called loaf sugar because of its tendency to form into a solid block – are most easily dealt with by grating.*

## CHOPPED LIVER

Chopped chicken livers are used to make one of the most traditional and popular Jewish first courses, and every Jewish family has its own variations. It can be very basic, and kosher food preparation insists that the livers be completely cooked so that no trace of pink from blood can be seen. This means that moistening agents are needed to avoid the mixture being too dry. Proper chopped liver is made using *schmaltz* – chicken fat, though you could substitute goose fat or olive oil.

SERVES 6

**450 g / 1 lb chicken livers**
**225 g / 8 oz onion**
**3 tbsp schmaltz, goose fat or olive oil**
**4 eggs**
**3 tbsp jellied chicken broth**
**85 g / 3 oz red onion**
**salt and pepper**

Pick over the livers, cutting off and discarding any green parts, tubes or stringy bits. For a kosher procedure, sear the livers dry under a hot grill.

Dice the ordinary onion and sweat in the fat or oil until soft. Turn up the heat, add the livers and fry, stirring continuously, until the onions start to brown and the livers are cooked through, about 5 minutes. When they are done they will be firm to the touch. Leave to cool.

Hard-boil the eggs and cool in cold water. Put the liver, chicken jelly, cooked onions and raw red onion through the coarse blade of a food-mill or pulse chop in a food processor. If the latter cut the raw red onion into tiny dice by hand and add to the minced liver as the processor will not deliver uniform pieces of onion and will tear them.

Shell and chop the eggs, then stir them in, seasoning with salt and pepper to taste.

## ROAST GUINEA FOWL

Guinea fowl has a pronounced and delicious flavour that is reminiscent of game without being at all strong tasting. It is probably closest to pheasant and partridge and, in common with them, virtually fat-free, so it needs finely timed cooking if it is not to be too dry.

The best way to achieve this is to seal the bird in a pan before it goes into the oven – a restaurant technique used to save time that works well in the domestic context, where oven temperatures tend not to be as hot. After sealing, 20–25 minutes in an oven preheated to 250°C/475°F/gas 9 will be enough time for a 900 g / 2 lb bird. A 10–15 minute rest after coming out of the oven and before carving will ensure juicier meat and give a tender and moist result.

One guinea fowl will serve 2 people generously, three at a pinch. Take the bird out of the fridge at least an hour before you plan to cook it and preheat the oven well in advance to bring it up to the highest temperature. Serve with roast potatoes (page 120).

SERVES 2–3
**1 guinea fowl, about 900 g / 2 lb**
**olive oil**
**salt and pepper**
**15 g / ½ oz butter**

**for the gravy:**
**splash of red wine**
**300 ml / ½ pt strongly flavoured chicken stock**

Preheat the oven to 250°C/475°F/ gas 9. Brush the bird all over with olive oil. Heat a dry heavy frying pan until smoking hot and lay the bird in it, one breast downwards, and seal. Turn and repeat on the other breast, then on the legs and back until all the surfaces are golden brown. Season generously with salt and pepper, push a knob of butter into the cavity and smear the rest over the breast and legs.

Transfer to a rack, breast upwards over a roasting tray, then roast for 20–25 minutes. Remove and allow to rest for at least 10 minutes before carving off the legs, thighs and breasts.

Serve with a gravy made with the drippings from the roasting pan deglazed with a splash of red wine and bubbled with the chicken stock.

## ROAST SQUAB

Squab – really doves that have been bred for the table – have always been honoured in France and, to a lesser extent, in Italy. Our climate seems to be a bit too damp for squab, so they are mostly imported from France, where they are called *pigeonneaux* as opposed to *palombes*, wood pigeon, and are very expensive, with a 450 g /1 lb cleaned bird selling wholesale at around £5. Slightly cheaper Italian birds are starting to make an appearance.

Squab are stunning fare and very different in flavour and texture from their wild, wood pigeon cousins. Where the wood pigeon is tough and lean, the squab is plump and succulent. Birds range in dressed weight from 350 g / 12 oz to 500 g / 1 lb 2 oz and one bird makes a generous single serving.

The best way to cook squab is straightforward high-temperature roasting. The restaurant standard technique is to brown the bird in olive oil in a pan on the hob over a very high heat then put it into the oven for between 5–10 minutes, which delivers a medium-rare finish after being rested for 5 minutes. Since restaurant ovens are probably operating at 300°C/600°F and the British taste leans towards a rather less bloody dish, dispense with the initial browning.

SERVES 4
**4 squab (see above)**
**olive oil**
**salt and pepper**

**for the gravy:**
**splash of white wine**
**about 5 tbsp reduced chicken stock (optional)**

Preheat the oven to 250°C/475°F/ gas 9. Brush the birds all over with olive oil and season well with salt and pepper.

Put them on a rack, breast side down, for 15 minutes, then turn them breast up for a further 5 minutes.

Remove from the oven and allow to rest in a warm place for 10 minutes.

Make the gravy by deglazing the pan with a splash of wine and the reduced chicken stock.

Serve the squab with the gravy and a few roast or some mashed potatoes.

## ROAST TURKEY, MEAT LOAF STUFFING, GIBLET GRAVY AND BREAD SAUCE

Every Christmas, letters pour in seeking guidance on roasting a large turkey, suggesting that the last time our correspondents thought about cooking a turkey was a year past. If it did work out well then they have forgotten exactly what it was they did right and if it was an over-cooked disaster then the memory has been mercifully shuffled away with the enduring hope that next time things can only get better.

People the world over look upon these turkey-centred celebrations with mixed feelings. Invariably the first hurdle is the size of the bird, which most people tend to buy much larger than they need. This produces another hardy perennial post-bag demanding what to do with the left-over cold turkey.

Planning ahead and keeping everything simple remains the best advice to ensure that the cook enjoys dinner along with everybody else. The best strategy is to limit what actually has to be done on the day to the minimum, applying the restaurant approach of mise-en-place, which means most things can be prepared in advance.

It is a good idea not to stuff the cavity of the bird, but to make the meat stuffing separately in a loaf tin like a terrine. This makes it easier to judge the cooking time of the bird, because the empty cavity is filled with hot air. Filling it with stuffing turns the turkey into a solid mass which means that the meat on the outside will be ruined by the time heat has penetrated and cooked the forcemeat at the centre.

The first thing to do is to buy the smallest possible turkey to feed the number of people it needs to feed. A 4.5 kg / 10 lb bird will easily feed 10–12 people. Don't forget the chipolatas, bacon rolls, stuffings, roast potatoes, bread sauce, gravy and sprouts which in themselves make a substantial lunch.

SERVES 10–12

1 oven-ready turkey, weighing about 4.5 kg / 10 lb
500 g / 1 lb 4 oz streaky unsmoked bacon
about 115 g/ 4 oz unsalted butter, melted
flat-leaf parsley, to garnish

for the meat loaf stuffing:
170 g / 6 oz smoked streaky bacon in a piece
2 tbsp lard or goose or duck fat
285 g / 10 oz onions
3 garlic cloves
1 tbsp chopped tarragon
3 tsp dried oregano
½ nutmeg
2 tbsp Worcestershire sauce
3 tbsp brandy
3 eggs
400 g / 14 oz minced pork belly
500 g / 1 lb 4 oz lb premium pork sausagemeat
1½ tsp salt
1 tsp pepper
170 g / 6 oz chicken livers
the turkey's liver from the giblets, cut into 4
3 bay leaves
115 g / 4 oz thinly sliced Parma ham

for the bread sauce:
1.25 litres / 2¼ pints milk
55 g / 2 oz butter
8 shallots, peeled
¼ nutmeg
1 garlic clove
1 bay leaf
8–10 slices fresh white bread, crusts removed

for the giblet gravy:
575 ml / 1 pt chicken stock
about 150 ml / ¼ pint double cream

Make the stuffing 2 days before you want to cook it (this is both convenient and gives time for the flavours to develop): cut the bacon into 5-mm / ¼-in dice and fry gently in the lard or goose fat until the bacon starts to brown. Cut the onions into similarly sized dice and add to the pan. Continue to cook until soft and translucent. Add the chopped garlic and stir for a minute, then remove from the heat.

Put the tarragon, oregano, nutmeg, Worcestershire sauce, brandy and eggs into a mixing bowl. Beat together, then add the minced belly pork, sausagemeat, onions, salt and pepper. Mix everything together thoroughly with a fork. Take a spoonful and fry it. Eat this to assess the seasoning, adding more salt and pepper to the forcemeat at this point if needed.

Pick over the livers, cutting off and discarding any tubes, fat or green bits. Heat a dry frying pan until smoking hot, season the livers and the turkey liver and sauté vigorously in 2 tablespoons of oil for 1 minute. Set aside.

Position the bay leaves down the middle of the base of a rectangular terrine or large non-stick loaf tin. Line this with the Parma ham, leaving some overhanging the sides which can be folded back to cover the top. Fill with half the forcemeat, packing down with a fork. Arrange the livers down the centre and cover with the remaining forcemeat. Smooth the surface level and bring the ham overhangs up over the top. Clingwrap and refrigerate.

The bread sauce can be made several days ahead and refrigerated. Its flavour also benefits from this chilled maturation. The mistakes people most frequently make with bread sauce are failing to include sufficient aromatic flavourings, using stale breadcrumbs and just not making enough. Unusually in this version, shallots and garlic are included and puréed into the sauce.

Put the milk, butter, shallots, grated nutmeg, chopped garlic, bay leaf and salt and pepper in a pan over a low heat for 30 minutes. Remove and discard the bay leaf. Put everything else in a food processor. Dice the bread and add it. Blitz until smooth, then taste and adjust the seasoning as you like. If too thin, add more bread, if too thick, thin with a little more milk. The sauce should be pourable, not stodgy-spoonable.

On the day, make the gravy: don't rely solely on the turkey giblets to make a stock but base your gravy on a well-flavoured chicken stock, adding the chopped turkey neck and gizzard to it, but not the liver which would make the gravy bitter and which you are in any case using to better effect in the stuffing. For the best flavour, brown the giblets before simmering them in the stock.

Work your fingers between the skin of the turkey and the breasts to detach and pull away the skin from the breast meat, being careful not to tear holes in the skin. Push and spread slices of streaky unsmoked bacon flat under the skin to make a layer between the meat and the skin. This will act as a baste, keeping the breast moist during roasting. Brush all over with melted butter and return to the fridge or larder or leave in the garden if it is cold enough (inside a secure box unless you want the neighbourhood cats to beat you to it).

Calculate the cooking time for the turkey, which will be cooked using a combination of roasting at high heat followed by low heat. The bigger the bird, the fewer minutes per 450 g / 1 lb:

A 3.5–5.5 kg / 8–12 lb bird will need 45 minutes at 220°C/425°F/gas 7, followed by 1½–2 hours at 170°C/325°F/gas 3.

A 5.5–6.8 kg / 12–15 lb bird needs 45 minutes at the high heat followed by 2–2½ hours at the lower. If you have not read this until after you bought an ostrich-style turkey of between 6.8–9 kg / 15–20 lb, the same 45 minutes at the high heat then 2½–3 hours at the lower temperature applies.

Work back from your estimated serving time to calculate when the bird should go in the oven, allowing 20–30 minutes for the first course and approximately the required resting time for the cooked turkey before it is carved. It is a good idea to write these down as an *aide-memoire* and as part of a general time-plan. There is a lot going on and it is easy to get distracted or plain forget.

The cooking sequence:

1 Make sure the turkey and the stuffing have come up to room temperature before they go in the oven.

2 Brush the turkey all over generously with melted butter and season.

3 Cover it loosely with foil and put on a rack in the roasting tin and position as high up the oven as space will allow, but with at least 2.5 cm / 1 in clearance to allow circulation of air.

4 If cooking a 4.5-kg / 10-lb bird, preheat the oven to 220°C/425°F/gas 7 and roast for 45–50 minutes. Remove the foil, baste and lower heat to 160°C/325°F/gas 4. Baste occasionally.

5 Put the forcemeat into the oven below the turkey about 1 hour before the bird is due to come out of the oven.

6 Add some of the roasting juices to your prepared reduced chicken and giblet stock and put in a pan to reduce over a moderate heat.

7 By the time you are ready to carve the bird, the stuffing should be done. You can tell when this is by inserting a skewer into the middle of the loaf and leaving it for 5 seconds before pulling it out. When cooked in the middle, it will come out clean and feel warm to the tongue. Turn out the forcemeat and leave for 10 minutes before slicing.

8 Whisk a little cream into the gravy, taste and adjust the seasoning.

9 It is much easier to put the turkey and stuffing on plates in the kitchen, offering the vegetables in serving dishes at the table. Just make sure your plates are hot. If oven space has made this difficult, put them in the sink and pour boiling water over them. Pass the bread sauce and gravy separately.

## NO-HASSLE CHRISTMAS TURKEY

A turkey breast joint is the answer to those who are few in numbers but still like the idea of eating roast turkey on Christmas Day. Supermarkets sell them all year round or ask your butcher to bone and tie a breast joint weighing about 1 kg / 2¼ lb and ask for the breast bone, which will contribute to the flavour of the roasting pan juices.

You can still have all the traditional accompaniments – bread sauce, bacon rolls and chipolata sausages are always great with turkey and are even more welcome should an unexpected guest turn up at the last moment.

Should you want to serve sprouts, ring the changes by parboiling them for 2 minutes then stir-frying them in olive oil with grated ginger, garlic and cooked peeled chestnuts (you can buy these vacuum-packed – the Merchant Gourmet label from France are very good).

Should time considerations put you off roast potatoes, why not serve chips, and if feeling very lazy, frozen chips are fine. With such a full main course, starter and dessert can be very simple. Perhaps slices of smoked cod's roe with lemon quarters and sourdough toast to begin, and cheeses and fruit at the end.

SERVES 4

1 kg / 2¼ lb turkey breast joint
olive oil
salt and pepper
60 g / 2 oz butter
4 slices of unsmoked streaky bacon
a big sprig of rosemary
300 ml / ½ pt dry white wine

Preheat the oven to 190°C/375°F/gas 5. Brush the joint with olive oil and season all over with salt and pepper. Spread the butter on top, then lay the bacon over it to cover. Sit the joint on top of the breast bone and a good big sprig of rosemary, then pour over the white wine.

Roast for about 40 minutes, or until firm when pressed. Turn and baste from time to time. If the pan dries out add more wine.

Transfer to a cutting board and allow to rest for 15 minutes, covered, then carve across in thick slices. Discard the bone and rosemary and serve the whisked pan juices as a gravy.

## TURKEY PIE

Every Christmas brings several bags of letters bewailing the remains of the turkey and asking for good new ideas about how to treat it. How moist your cold turkey is will determine the best way to treat it. If it is on the dry side, make a pie with the meat bathed in a rich and creamy velouté sauce infused with saffron.

There is no need to make a pastry case, instead just bake individual pieces of frozen puff pastry. Serve with mashed potatoes and some blanched winter greens.

SERVES 6

900 g / 2 lb leftover turkey meat, cut into bite-sized chunks
about 500 g / 1 lb 2 oz frozen puff pastry, defrosted
1 egg yolk
1 tbsp milk or cream

for the turkey stock:
1 onion
2 carrots
1 bay leaf

for the saffron velouté:
60 g / 2 oz butter
60 g / 2 oz flour
salt and pepper
about 20 threads of saffron
2 tbsp chopped parsley

After cutting off all the meat from the bird, make a turkey stock by simmering the carcass gently in lots of water with the onion, carrots and bay leaf for 4–6 hours. Strain into a clean pan and reduce at a fast boil to about 1.1 litres / 2 pints, which will make the right amount of sauce for the 900 g / 2 lb of meat.

Towards the end of the cooking of the stock, preheat the oven to 200°C/400°F/gas 6. Incise a neat crosshatch on the top of each piece of puff pastry and brush with the egg yolk beaten with the milk or cream. Bake the pieces of frozen puff pastry for 20 minutes until risen and golden.

When the stock is sufficiently reduced, make the saffron velouté: make a roux with the butter and flour, whisk in the stock and cook gently, stirring at regular intervals, for 20 minutes. Season with salt and pepper, add the saffron and continue cooking for 5 minutes, then stir in the turkey chunks and chopped parsley and warm through for 5 minutes before serving topped with a piece of pastry.

## DEVIL OF TURKEY

Another option with leftover turkey is to make a devil, a very spicy Victorian treatment. This is good with plain boiled rice. Cooked turkey can also be curried, of course, though as here add the meat to the sauce only for a few minutes towards the end of cooking to warm it through or it will go tough.

**SERVES 4**

**900 g / 2 lb leftover turkey meat, cut into bite-sized chunks**
**300 ml / ½ pt turkey or chicken stock**
**300 ml / ½ pt double cream**
**1 tbsp Dijon mustard**
**1 tsp cayenne pepper**
**½ tsp ground black pepper**
**1 tbsp Worcestershire sauce**

Put the turkey pieces in a pan with the stock and heat through gently over a low heat. Transfer to a warmed ovenproof serving dish and keep warm.

Preheat a hot grill. Whip the cream to soft peaks, then fold in the mustard, cayenne pepper, black pepper and Worcestershire sauce. Spoon this over the turkey and put under the hot grill until the surface bubbles and browns.

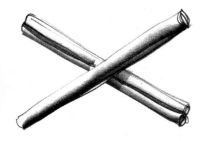

## CANTONESE ROAST DUCK

Getting the skin of a roast duck to crisp and gloss the way Chinese restaurants do demands special techniques. One of the most important is to inflate the skin away from the subcutaneous fat and, in order to do so, you need a duck with its neck on because otherwise making an airtight seal is impossible. The skin is separated from the flesh using a bicycle pump fitted with a football inflater.

**SERVES 6**

**1 duck, about 2.25 kg / 5 lb**
**1 tsp Sichuan pepper**
**1 tsp five-spice powder**
**200 ml / 7 fl oz maltose**
**250 ml / 9 fl oz dark soy sauce**
**200 ml / 7 fl oz chicken stock**
**4 heads of star anise**
**1 cinnamon stick**
**steamed rice, to serve**

Start by pulling out any lumps of fat from the cavity, then give the duck a thorough massage, concentrating on the breasts and legs and kneading and pummelling like a masseur for 5 minutes. This will start to loosen the skin away from the flesh. Make an incision about halfway down the neck. Now the fiddly part: gently insert a sharpening steel into this cut and carefully push it between the skin and the neck all the way down to the breast and legs, levering the skin outwards. The tricky bit is not puncturing the skin because, if you do, a John Bull repair patch won't fix it. Tie a piece of string tightly near the top of the neck, leaving a loop to hang it up by. Loop a second piece of string just beyond the cut in a loose granny knot.

Rub the inside of the duck with the Sichuan pepper and five-spice powder. Push the football inflator into the incision and under the second string and pump it up like a ball, then have somebody pull the granny knot tight as you pull out the pump.

Put the maltose in a pan (maltose is a strange thick purplish substance that looks like hair gel and sets hard when cold – it is the secret of that burnished glaze you see on Cantonese roast ducks and is sold in Chinese markets in plastic pots). It needs to be warmed by standing it in hot water to make it pourable. Add 5 litres / 8 pints of water and 200 ml / 7 fl oz of the soy sauce. Bring to the boil and simmer for 5 minutes.

Holding the duck by the string, lay it breast side down in the liquid for 20–30 seconds, no more. Pull it up and baste with a ladle until the skin tightens, then hang it up in a dry airy place overnight.

Bring the chicken stock, star anise, cinnamon stick and remaining soy sauce to the boil, lower the heat and simmer until reduced by half. Leave to cool while you preheat the oven to 200°C/ 400°F/gas 6.

Hold the duck neck downwards, and have somebody pour the stock mixture into the cavity, then sew it up. Place on a rack, breast upwards, and roast for 50–60 minutes.

Remove from the oven and allow to rest for at least 15 minutes before carving off the breasts and legs. Chop into pieces with a cleaver and serve with steamed rice, pouring over the aromatic liquid from inside the duck as a sauce.

## CONFIT OF DUCK

Confit – lightly salted goose or duck poached slowly in fat – is one of the most delicious food traditions of South-Western French farmhouse cooking and very easy to make. If you are scrupulously careful about cleanliness of hands and dishes during preparation, confit will keep for months stored in the fridge, in the fat in which it was cooked. You are unlikely to want to do so, but leave it for a couple of weeks for the flavour to develop.

The classic accompaniment to duck confit is thinly sliced potatoes cooked in a heavy frying pan with a few tablespoons of the fat and some garlic, and plenty of chopped flat-leaved parsley stirred in just before you bring it to the table.

**MAKES 4 PORTIONS**

6 tbsp sea salt

4 duck legs

1 garlic clove, chopped

1 bay leaf

2 tsp chopped thyme

about 450 g / 1 lb goose fat or lard

Scatter half the salt in a dish, then lay the duck portions on top. Scatter the garlic evenly over the duck. Crumble the bay leaf over and sprinkle over the thyme, followed by the remaining salt on top. Put in the fridge for 24 hours, then turn the duck and return to the fridge for a further 24 hours. The salt will have partially liquefied.

Preheat the oven to 130°C/275°F/gas 1. Rinse the duck in cold water and pat dry. On the hob, gently melt the fat in a casserole or ovenproof dish in which the duck pieces will just fit and, when hot, add the duck which must be covered. If not, top up with lard. When just simmering, put the dish in the oven and cook for 1½ hours, when the meat will be golden brown, the fat translucent and you should be able to slide a skewer easily through the meat. At this point remove from the oven and transfer the confit to the container in which you will store it, ladling the fat through a fine sieve to cover. Be careful not to ladle in any of the meat juices which will have been generated and will sit on the bottom of the cooking dish, as these will eventually go bad. (They are, however, delicious added to a gravy or to boost the flavour of a stock.) When cold, refrigerate the confit until needed.

To serve, remove the duck from the fat, scraping off as much as you can, then place on a baking tray for an hour to come to room temperature. Preheat the oven to 200°C/400°F/gas 6. Pour off any melted fat from the tray and roast the confit, skin side down, for 20 minutes.

Serve with garlic and parsley potatoes (see above).

Melt the stored fat from which you took the confit and let it bubble before straining back into a bowl to keep in the fridge for the next time.

## DUCK RILLETTES

Rillettes are shredded potted meat that come originally from the South-west of France. They may be made from pork, duck, goose, rabbit or even hare, though pork is probably the most common. A combination of duck and pork is very good, and if you had a goose for Christmas and are wondering what to do with the bowl of fat you have winking at you in the fridge, this is your opportunity to put it to good use. Alternatively, you can use lard or a can of duck fat.

**SERVES 4**

4 duck leg and thigh joints, cut into 2 through the joint

450 g / 1 lb shoulder of pork, cut into cubes

glass of white wine

sprig or rosemary

sprig of tarragon

2 tsp mixed dried herbs

2 bay leaves

3 tsp sea salt

1 tsp black pepper

about 450 g / 1 lb fat (see above), melted

toasted sourdough bread and cornichons (the little cucumber pickles), to serve

Preheat the oven to 160°C/325°F/gas 3. Put the pieces of duck and the pork cubes into a heavy casserole. Add the wine, rosemary, tarragon, dried mixed herbs, bay leaves, salt and pepper. Spoon over fat to cover. It will probably take about 450 g / 1 lb. Bring to the boil, skim, put on a lid and immediately transfer to the oven and cook for 3–4 hours. From time to time, move the pieces of meat around.

Remove from the oven. The fat should now be completely clear, and pass through a sieve into a bowl. When cool enough to handle, pull the duck off the bones and use 2 forks to shred the duck and pork. Taste the meat and season with a little more salt and pepper if you think it needs it, taking into account that cold things need more seasoning.

Now put the meat into another bowl, add 5–6 tablespoons of the fat and mix in gently. Pack this mixture into sterilized Kilner jars, pouring a little more fat on top. (Pour the remaining fat into a bowl and refrigerate to use for roasting potatoes or for making confit or more rillettes.) Refrigerate for 3 days before eating. The rillettes will keep for a month unopened and improve in flavour during that time.

Ideally serve the rillettes with toasted sourdough bread and cornichons.

## ITALIAN ROAST QUAIL WITH RAISINS

Quail are migratory game birds that winter in Africa and which are still shot in Italy, Spain and France. In the past an expensive delicacy, large quantities were netted in Egypt for fattening in this country in the 18th century and were also to be found wild in southern England. They were more expensive then, with a dressed bird fetching two shillings and two pence at Smithfield in 1752. Today reared on a large scale in heated barns, like Lilliputian chickens, they retail for about £1 each. They are small, so you will need 2 for a main course, 1 for a first course.

The largest producer of quail and quails' eggs in the UK is Fayre Game, who can produce up to 45,000 birds and 115,000 eggs a week at their Lancashire nursery near Lytham. The quail are reared in what the company describes as warmed barns on deep litter and are fed on a diet of mixed wheat, maize and soya. No hormones or growth-promoters are used, the birds are killed at 6 weeks and are plucked and gutted before being sold oven-ready, or boned and stuffed, or smoked. They are best simply roasted, here with the addition of some raisins plumped in brandy or grappa, a very Italian treatment, *quaglie con uvetta*.

SERVES 4

115 g / 4 oz butter

8 cleaned quail

olive oil, for brushing

salt and pepper

about 350 g / 12 oz soft instant polenta

115 g / 4 oz mascarpone

for the raisin sauce:

60 g / 2 oz raisins

100 ml / 3½ fl oz brandy

30 g / 1 oz unsalted butter

splash of white wine

The night before, put the raisins for the sauce to soak in the brandy.

Next day, when ready to cook, preheat the oven to 250°C/475°F/gas 9. Put a knob of butter inside each of the quail, then brush the skin with olive oil and season liberally with salt and pepper. Roast the birds for 10 minutes, remove and allow to rest for 10 minutes.

While the birds are cooking, make the polenta following the packet instructions and keep warm.

While the birds are resting, make the sauce by adding to the roasting pan the raisins, butter and a splash of white wine, bubbling and stirring over a high heat to reduce to a syrupy residue.

Just before serving, finish the polenta by beating in the mascarpone. Serve the quail on a bed of the polenta. Pour the sauce over and around the quail.

## ROAST GOOSE WITH STUFFING

Goose is a lovely bird for a winter dinner, but there is always that daunting feeling when cooking something expensive for the first time. It has a high bone-and-fat ratio to meat, so you need to allow at least 450–675 g / 1–1½ lb per person uncooked weight and, even then, people are not going to get seconds. However, the meat is very rich so you do not need very much. The crisp skin is one of the most delicious aspects of the bird and the large quantity of fat produced during roasting is not waste but a bonus to be stored in the fridge for weeks to be used when roasting and frying potatoes.

Avoid buying too big a bird. A bird of about 4.5–5 kg / 10–11 lb is best. You can get whoppers up to 9 kg / 20 lb, but they are much more difficult to cook and have an inferior flavour. Make your goose go further by cooking a forcemeat separately in a non-stick loaf pan. Do not stuff the body cavity of the goose as this will slow the roasting process and make judging cooking time more difficult.

**SERVES 6**

**1 goose, about 4.5 kg / 10 lb**
**salt and pepper**
**fried apple slices, black**
**pudding (optional), potatoes**
**roasted in goose fat and a**
**green vegetable, to serve**

**for the stuffing:**
**1 kg / 2¼ lb good-quality**
**sausagemeat**
**1 onion, chopped**
**1 garlic clove, smashed**
**1 egg, beaten**
**freshly grated nutmeg**
**2 tbsp brandy**

**for the gravy:**
**about 600 ml / 1 pint chicken**
**stock**

Remove the giblets from the bird. (The liver can be lightly fried in butter and eaten on toast as a treat, while you can use the neck, gizzard and heart in stock or a gravy.) Prick the bird all over with a needle, rub generously with salt and pepper then roast on a rack over a deep tin, starting it loosely covered with foil at 220°C/425°F/gas 7 for the first 15 minutes, then turning the temperature down to 190°C/375°F/gas 5. Continue to cook for 15 minutes per 450 g / pound. From time to time, remove fat from the roasting pan and reserve (this is easiest done with a bulb baster). Remove the foil 30 minutes before your calculated completion time to allow the skin to brown and crisp.

While the bird is roasting, make the gravy: chop up the neck, gizzard and heart, and simmer in the stock for about 2 hours, topping up with more stock or water as necessary. Season.

About 1 hour before the bird is due to come out of the oven, make the forcemeat stuffing: in a large bowl, mix all the ingredients together well and then spoon the mixture into a non-stick loaf pan. Put in the oven with the bird and leave it in there when you take the bird out.

Put the goose to stand for 20 minutes before attempting to carve it, the most difficult part of the operation. Transfer to a large chopping board and first sever the legs. Cut off one breast in a single piece, then the other, reversing the bird to point the other way to make this easier. Cut through the legs at the ball-and-socket joint to separate them into drumsticks and thighs. Lay the breast pieces skin side down and cut into slices across and down at a 45 degree angle. Arrange the slices on a warmed ovenproof dish. Cut slices off the legs and arrange them, skin side up, around the breast meat. Detach the wings and cut them in half across the middle joint, slicing off what meat you can. Pick over the carcass, removing any meat that is left. Just before serving you can flash this carved meat under the grill briefly. If the skin is flaccid, this will crisp it. Turn the forcemeat stuffing out and slice it like a meat loaf.

Serve accompanied by slices of the forcemeat or black pudding, fried apple slices, potatoes roasted in goose fat, and a green vegetable. Pass the gravy separately. The carcass and bones will make lovely stock while the fat can be used for roasting or frying potatoes and for making confit of duck (see page 156).

## ROAST PHEASANT

Pheasant is a very lean bird, which makes it difficult to roast. Often if the legs are done to perfection then the breast is overcooked, while if the breast is moist and slightly pink the legs are inedibly bloody. The first thing you need to address is the time for which the bird or birds have been hung before being plucked and drawn. A pheasant eaten on the day it is shot will be tough and tasteless. On the other hand, the unseasonably mild weather we often seem to have in autumn these days means that hanging for more than two days will produce a very gamy tasting pheasant, a quality that has mercifully become as unfashionable as it is unpalatable. Ideally you will know when the bird was shot and for how long it has been hung, but most of us are in the hands of butchers and supermarkets, so ask. You may not get a sensible answer but ask anyway.

Assuming you are happy with its provenance, the next thing to consider is how to keep the bird as moist as possible during roasting. Game dealers traditionally bard game birds by tying a piece of pork back fat over the breast, but fat streaky bacon is in many ways a better option. As the fat melts it imparts some of its smoky, salty flavour to the breast meat and is a nice accompaniment to the finished dish. An old English trick for reducing dryness was to put a 225 g / 8 oz piece of rump steak in the body cavity. This was not eaten with the pheasant, but used later cold in sandwiches.

What you serve with roast pheasant will also change your perception of its moistness. Traditional accompaniments like a butter-rich bread sauce, thin gravy made from the pan juices and some chicken stock, and roast potatoes are hard to beat, though you might like to ring the changes with little sausage cakes and creamy mashed potatoes, the carved meat presented with a round of herbed butter (page 291) on top.

**SERVES 4**

**brace of oven-ready pheasant**
**olive oil**
**salt and pepper**
**8 slices of streaky bacon**
**flour, for dusting**

Preheat the oven to 250°C/475°F/ gas 9. Brush the pheasant all over with olive oil and season generously with salt and pepper.

Start the bird roasting breast side down for 10 minutes. Remove, turn it breast side up and cover this with the slices of streaky bacon. Return it to the oven for 15 minutes. Remove the bacon, shake a little flour over the breast and baste before returning to the oven for a final 10 minutes.

Remove and allow to rest in a warm place for 12–15 minutes before carving off the breasts, legs and thighs. Cut the breasts across at an angle into 4 thick slices. This is a better way of doing it than cutting the meat into thin slices off the carcass.

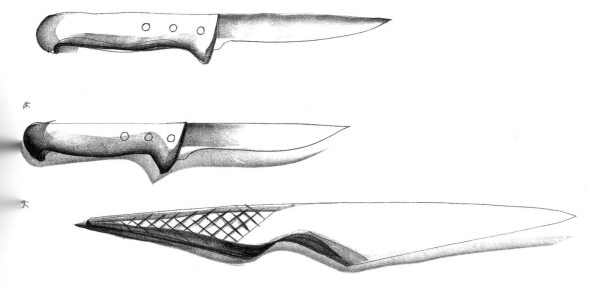

## SALMIS OF PHEASANT

Pheasants, being virtually fat-free, are difficult birds to roast. If badly shot or in plentiful supply, a salmis – which combines roasting with brief stewing – will deliver a moist result.

**SERVES 4**

**115 g / 4 oz butter**
**2 oven-ready pheasants**
**3 tbsp olive oil**
**salt and pepper**
**1 onion, diced**
**2 garlic cloves, chopped**
**1 glass of red wine**
**600 ml / 1 pt strong chicken**
**stock**
**1 bay leaf**
**sprig of fresh thyme or 2 tsp**
**dried oregano**

**whole flat-leaved parsley or**
**young celery leaves, to garnish**

**to serve:**
**pieces of bread fried in oil and**
**butter**
**sautéed sliced mushrooms**

Preheat the oven to 220°C/425°F/ gas 7. Put half the butter inside each pheasant, brush the outside with a little olive oil and season with salt and pepper. Roast the birds, breast side down, for 20–25 minutes.

Remove from the oven, pour the buttery roasting juices into a pan and allow the birds to cool until you can handle them.

While they are resting, add the remaining olive oil to the pan and fry the onion and garlic until soft and translucent. Add the wine, stock, bay leaf and thyme or oregano. Bring to the boil and bubble vigorously until reduced by half, then lower the heat to a bare simmer.

Joint the birds, cutting the breasts off whole before slicing them in half. Scrape the blood and juices into the sauce and keep the carcasses for stock. Add the breast meat, legs and thighs to the sauce and reheat gently.

Serve on pieces of fried bread with sautéed sliced mushrooms and garnish with whole leaves of flat-leaved parsley or young celery leaves.

*Opposite: the Meat Loaf Stuffing served with Roast Turkey, Giblet Gravy and Bread Sauce (page 152)*

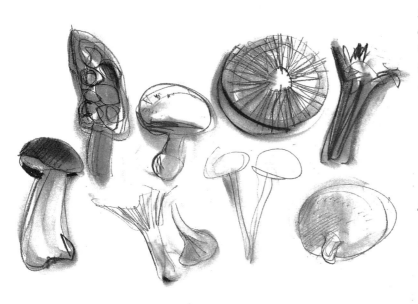

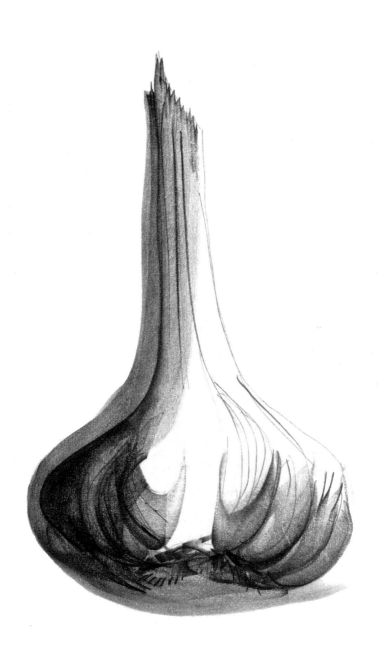

# VEGETABLES, SALADS, PULSES AND FUNGI

**P**eople in Britain today care more about vegetables than they did even ten years ago, and more private cooks now understand about cooking them. The range and quality of fruit and vegetables from around the world available in our supermarkets is extraordinary, and has stimulated great interest in cooking vegetables as primary ingredients.

The role played by vegetables in our diet has changed dramatically. The number of those choosing to stop eating animal protein altogether is growing apace, with a current annual increase judged to be around 20 per cent. Leaving any moral, ethical or health issues aside, it is interesting to note the comparative costs of producing vegetable protein and animal protein. A chicken must eat three kilos of grain to produce one kilo of meat, a bullock 16 kilos. An acre of land growing soya beans produces 10 times the amount of edible protein – bean-curd – as the same amount of land growing cattle feed converts to edible animal protein.

Arguments of this sort in any case tend to obscure the culinary benefits that have come from a greater appreciation of vegetables. In most parts of the world meat does not play a central role in the diet. The popularity of Mediterranean-style cooking – the eating of more fish and less meat, the use of olive oil rather than butter, and an appreciation of fruit and vegetables as primary rather than secondary ingredients – has been a key factor in our change. Eating more fruit and vegetables is now considered to be the basis of a healthy diet, but for the keen cook this is only a bonus. The joy of eating fresh vegetables is the real cause for celebration.

*Preparing Globe Artichokes*

❶ Prior to cooking: break off the stems carefully to leave just a flat stub, without damaging the globe itself, then pull off and discard the coarser outer leaves.

❷ Slice right across the globe to cut off the top half.

❸ After cooking: scrape out the inner choke hairs.

❹ If you want, trim back to make a neat 'fond,' base or cup.

## GLOBE ARTICHOKES

Artichokes are edible thistles, a harsh description for one of the most delicious and intriguingly flavoured of vegetables. Only asparagus shares such a fine and complex quality, something reflected in the price of both, though artichokes are actually much easier to cultivate than asparagus.

To prepare globe artichokes, break off the stems and put the heads to soak upside down in iced salted water for 45–60 minutes. The close-packed leaves sometimes have dirt or insects between them and this is therefore a sensible preliminary.

When trimming artichokes always rub any cut surfaces with a lemon and, while waiting to cook, keep them away from the air in a bowl of acidulated cold water. The acid can come from either lemon juice or vinegar, so since vinegar is less expensive than lemons, put them in a solution of three tablespoons of vinegar to every litre / 2 pints of water

and always cook them in a solution of the same strength.

It has become common practice to trim the outer leaves but it is not essential. Indeed, Jane Grigson railed against the practice: 'There is no point in deforming such a beautiful object. I have never done this, and no one has pricked their finger and fallen asleep for 100 years at our table.'

As far as sauces are concerned, nothing can better a fine vinaigrette using a good wine vinegar or balsamic vinegar. Into one part of vinegar whisk sea salt and pepper, followed by four parts of the best extra-virgin oil you can lay your hands on. (Always put the salt in before adding the oil as it dissolves more readily.) It is that simple, but cannot be bettered. Vinaigrette is also excellent with hot vegetables like fine French beans or asparagus.

If you always serve your artichokes cold, try eating them hot for a change, served with a rich buttery hollandaise or

an easy sauce made by cooking chopped garlic, anchovies and olive oil in a saucepan over a low heat. Essentially the *bagna cauda* dipping sauce of Northern Italy (see page 185), this tasty mixture is also great with crudités to nibble with drinks.

---

### ACIDULATED WATER

*A level tablespoon of lemon juice for every litre / 2 pints of cold water is about right. Some cooks add salt as well – say 3 teaspoons for every litre.*

*You can substitute ordinary malt vinegar for lemon juice in most cases, though this is not advisable when the vegetables are to be included in a very delicately flavoured dish.*

## ASPARAGUS WITH PARMESAN AND BALSAMIC VINEGAR

English asparagus is the finest in the world and the first sweet, green spears of May are a seasonal joy, to be cooked simply and eaten with the minimum of saucing. All they need is a little melted butter or olive oil to shine. There is nothing better than local produce when it is in season and at its most delicious.

Select medium-sized, even bunches of asparagus with closed tips and a good green colour. After you have eaten your first few bunches plain boiled and buttered, you might like to try this Italian treatment. Only a few drops of balsamic vinegar are needed and this is the ideal moment to use that very special bottle of liquid gold from Modena, the very best barrel-aged vinegar your budget allows.

**SERVES 4**
**salt and pepper**
**1 kg / 2¼ lb fresh green**
**asparagus**
**85 g / 3 oz Reggiano**
**Parmigiano in a piece**
**1 tbsp balsamic vinegar**
**3½ tbsp extra-virgin olive oil**

Bring a large pan of salted water to the boil.

Undo the bunches of asparagus and lay them out on a chopping board, with their tips touching the same imaginary straight line. Trim off the woody bases to give an equal length of about 12.5 cm / 5 inches.

Drop the asparagus into the pan of boiling water, bring it back to the boil and cook for 2-4 minutes, tasting after 2 minutes. Precisely how long you give them depends on how thick the spears are and how al dente you like them.

Drain and serve immediately or refresh in cold water. You can then keep them refrigerated for up to 24 hours. If so, plunge into boiling water for 30 seconds to reheat before serving.

Shave wafer-thin slices of the Parmesan with a potato peeler.

Divide the hot asparagus between 4 warmed plates, laying them in a single neat layer. Dress with balsamic vinegar and olive oil, then lay the shaved Parmesan on top. Finish with some black pepper and serve with a basket of sliced baguette.

## ROAST ASPARAGUS WITH HOLLANDAISE

Hollandaise, a rich butter sauce, is a classic accompaniment to boiled asparagus. The first thin green stems do cook well on a raised grill pan or may be roasted. Grilling is very brief, turning the asparagus with tongs until they wilt and acquire the distinctive dark striping from the red hot grill ridges.

**SERVES 4**
**1 kg / 2¼ lb asparagus**
**about 6 tablespoons olive oil**
**salt and pepper**

**for the hollandaise sauce:**
**3 egg yolks**
**2 shallots, finely diced**
**1 tbsp white wine vinegar**
**juice of ½ lemon**
**1 teaspoon pepper**
**225 g / 8 oz unsalted butter**
**salt**

Preheat the oven to 250°C/475°F/gas 9. Select a roasting tray which will just hold the asparagus in a single layer. Trim the asparagus.

Start making the hollandaise: bring a pan of water to a simmer. Have ready a bowl which can sit over the water.

Melt the butter in a small pan over a low heat. Put the shallots in another saucepan with the pepper, lemon juice and vinegar. Boil down to about 2 teaspoons of liquid.

To cook the asparagus, put 4 tablespoons of the olive oil in the roasting tray, then arrange the asparagus on it. Season evenly with salt and pepper and dress the asparagus with a little more oil. Roast for about 8–10 minutes until wilted and starting to show traces of brown.

Towards the end of the asparagus cooking time, finish the hollandaise sauce: strain the shallot reduction through a fine sieve into the food processor. Add the egg yolks and process for a few seconds to combine. Season with salt and pepper then, with the motor at full speed, pour the butter in through the feeder tube in a thin stream.

Pour into the bowl set over hot water and whisk until it thickens. Taste and adjust the seasoning if necessary.

Serve the roast asparagus on warmed plates, offering the hollandaise in a sauceboat at the table.

## SAUTÉ OF JERUSALEM ARTICHOKES WITH WALNUTS

The flavour of Jerusalem artichokes is wonderful and thinking of it only in terms of soup severely limits its potential. Boiled artichokes mashed with equal parts of potatoes are brilliant, but leave a few pieces in the purée to emphasize that you are eating a very superior mash. Here they are fried with walnuts to give a fabulous dish which goes well with any game bird or even chicken or turkey. When you have vegetarian guests, it stands up well as a dish in its own right, but double the amounts.

SERVES **4** AS A SIDE DISH

800 g / 1¾ lb Jerusalem artichokes

salt

5 tbsp olive oil (or 4 tbsp, plus 1 tbsp walnut oil)

1 tsp caster sugar

pepper

85 g / 3 oz shelled walnuts, cut into quarters

Peel the artichokes (a tedious chore best given to somebody else – this sounds like a lot of artichokes but you lose a lot in the peeling) and cut each into 2 or 3 pieces, depending on size. Blanch them in boiling salted water for 3–4 minutes, then drain.

Heat the oil(s) in a frying pan over a medium heat. Add the artichoke pieces and sauté for 6–8 minutes. Scatter over the sugar, season with salt and pepper, then add the walnut quarters. Continue cooking for a further 3–5 minutes, until the artichokes are tender to a fork and golden brown.

Taste and add more salt and pepper if needed.

## SPICED GRILLED AUBERGINES

SERVES **4**

about 6 tbsp sunflower oil

1 tbsp Panchphoran (see page 45)

1 large onion, sliced

3 garlic cloves, sliced

675 g / 1½ lb aubergines

salt and pepper

to dress:

4–6 tbsp thick plain yoghurt

2 tbsp coarsely chopped flat-leaved parsley

small handful of snipped chives

Put 3 tablespoons of the oil in a pan over a high heat and throw in the panchphoran mixture. Fry for 10 seconds and, as the seeds start to pop and jump, add the onions and garlic. Lower the heat and cook gently for 10 minutes.

Preheat a ridged grill pan until very hot. Top and tail the aubergines, then cut them lengthwise into 1 cm / ½ inch thick slices. Brush them with more sunflower oil, season with salt and pepper and grill on the very hot ridged grill pan, in batches if necessary, turning the slices twice to mark them with grill lines (see page 30).

Arrange the slices on warmed plates, spoon on the spiced onion mixture and top with a spoonful of thick plain yoghurt and some flat-leaved parsley and chives.

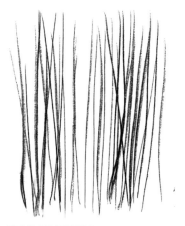

## IMAM BAYILDI

'The Imam [or priest] fainted' is the literal translation of the name for this Turkish dish of cold tomato-stuffed aubergine. It is odd how many cultures have dishes called things to do with clerics and their fondness for the table. The Italians, for example, have a dish of spinach and ricotta dumplings called 'priest-throttlers'.

In the case of this dish the Imam was so taken with how delicious the aubergine tasted he swooned, presumably after eating rather too many of them.

SERVES 4 AS A FIRST
COURSE

**6 small purple-black smooth-
skinned and plump aubergines**
**450 g / 1 lb onions, thinly sliced**
**4 garlic cloves, smashed and
chopped**
**6 tbsp olive oil**
**6 ripe plum tomatoes, peeled
and chopped**
**salt and pepper**
**1 tsp sugar**
**4 tablespoons chopped flat-
leaved parsley**
**juice of 1 lemon**

Cut off both ends of the aubergines.
Forget about all this salting nonsense: if
the aubergines are old and bitter, no
amount of salting is going to change
them for the better. Peel off 1-cm /
$^{1}/_{2}$-inch wide strips lengthwise to produce a striped effect. Cut down through
one side the length of each aubergine,
being careful not to cut all the way
through.

Fry the onions and garlic gently in 4
tablespoons of the olive oil until soft and
translucent. Add the chopped tomatoes,
season with salt, pepper and the sugar
and continue to cook, stirring, until the
water in the tomatoes has evaporated.
Stir in the parsley, add the lemon juice
and leave to cool.

Put the remaining oil in another pan
and fry the aubergines over a moderate
heat to seal them, turning to brown
lightly all over. Remove and drain.

Preheat the oven to 200°C/400°F/
gas 6. When the aubergines are cool
enough to handle, carefully open each
aubergine along the cut and spoon in as

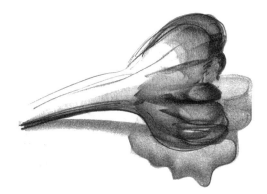

much stuffing as you can. Then arrange
them, cut side up, in an ovenproof dish
just large enough for them to sit snugly
in a single layer without falling over.
Spread any remaining stuffing over the
top, pour over 300 ml / $^{1}/_{2}$ pint of cold
water and cover loosely with foil.

Bake for about 45 minutes, when
they should be tender but not collaps-
ing. Check from time to time that they
have not dried out, adding a little more
water if needed. Take out and leave to
cool, serving at room temperature as a
first course.

## BABA GHANOUSH
## (AUBERGINE PURÉE)

Originally thought to be Lebanese in
origin, this sesame-and-garlic-flavoured
purée crops up in similar forms
throughout the Middle East, Turkey
and Greece. Use small sweet purple
aubergines with a good shiny and tight
skin.

SERVES 4

**675 g / 1½ lb aubergines**
**about 6 tbsp olive oil**
**salt and pepper**
**2 garlic cloves, smashed and
finely chopped**
**juice of 1 lemon**

**2 tbsp chopped flat-leaved
parsley**
**1 tbsp sesame oil**
**1 tsp toasted ground cumin
seeds**
**handful of flat-leaved parsley,
to garnish**
**hot pitta breads, to serve**

Preheat the oven to 250°C/475°F/gas
9. Cut the aubergines in half lengthwise
and brush the cut surfaces with some of
the olive oil, then season with salt and
pepper. Bake for 20 minutes, cut side
down, when they will brown and collapse.

Scoop out the aubergine flesh with a
metal spoon and put in a food processor. Add the garlic with the lemon juice,
chopped flat-leaved parsley, sesame oil
and cumin. Season generously with salt
and pepper and blitz to a purée.

With the machine still running, pour
in the remaining olive oil through the
feeder tube. You want a scoopable consistency, so add more oil if you think it
needs it. Taste, adding more lemon
juice and more salt and pepper if
desired. Whiz briefly to combine.

Spoon into a bowl and chill. Scatter
over a handful of flat parsley leaves and
serve with hot pitta.

## BABY BEETS IN PARMESAN AND ONION SAUCE

This dish is particularly good with boiled gammon.

**SERVES 4**

**675 g / 1½ lb baby beets**
**3 spring onions, finely chopped**
**30 g / 1 oz butter**
**30 g / 1 oz flour**
**600 ml / 1 pt milk**
**300 ml /½ pt chicken stock**
**salt and pepper**
**freshly grated nutmeg**
**juice of 1 lemon**
**60 g / 2 oz freshly grated Parmesan cheese**
**chopped chives, for garnish**

Baby beets are usually sold ready-cooked. If raw, trim off the leaves, leaving about 2 cm / ¾ inch of the stalks protruding and cut off the straggly root tip. Boil for about 30 minutes in lots of lightly salted water, but always check that they are cooked because even young beets are very woody. Refresh in cold water and peel while still warm.

Sweat the spring onions in the butter until soft. Stir in the flour and cook, stirring, over a low heat for 2 minutes. Turn up the heat and whisk in the milk, followed by the chicken stock. Season with salt and pepper and add nutmeg to taste. Simmer for 30 minutes, stirring from time to time with a wooden spoon and making sure you push the spoon right into the base edge where there is a tendency for the sauce to catch and burn. You should end up with about 600 ml / 1 pt of sauce.

Preheat the oven to 180°C/350°F/ gas 4. Whisk the lemon juice and grated Parmesan into the sauce. Add the beets and stir to coat, then transfer to a gratin dish. Heat through in the oven until very hot. Garnish with chopped chives before serving.

## BROAD BEANS

Broad beans are indisputably at their best when they are only just fully formed and the skin is a bright green colour. The pod will, at this stage, be of a regular shape and about 15 cm / 6 inches long. They may be briefly blanched in boiling salted water – say 30 seconds – but this is the only time they can be eaten raw, dressed with a little lemon juice and extra-virgin olive oil and seasoned lightly with sea salt and pepper. Both the Italians and the French prize them at this stage and it really is the only time they should be eaten with their skins on. It is the tough skin, that develops as the beans mature, which has put so many people off broad beans over the years.

The next stage is when the beans will be about 1 cm / ½ inch long. The pod will have grown longer and its appearance will have changed from a neat cylindrical form to an elongated and flattened shape, bulging around where the beans have formed. Where before the skin had a pleasant and barely discernible bitterness, it is now downright nasty and should be removed before cooking, though the flesh of the bean will be delicious and tender. They need only a couple of minutes' boiling and can be served dressed with olive oil and lemon juice,

like a warm salad, or tossed in butter with some chopped flat-leaved parsley.

The next change occurs when the beans have reached a size of 2½ cm / 1 inch. Their character now is very different, paler in colour, the flesh now firming towards hard. They must be peeled and will take 7–8 minutes to cook. They are now nicest puréed. If the beans are left unpicked they will lose all their green colour, going an unpalatable dun yellow. At this point, feed them to livestock.

## BROCCOLI

Broccoli means 'tiny shoots' in Italian. The purple flowering type used to be the most common, with its dark-coloured clusters of tight-packed florets, but calabrese – a green variant with fewer leaves – is now also widely available and has rather taken over.

However you intend to finish broccoli, cooking invariably begins with brief blanching in rapidly boiling salted water. It may then be refreshed in cold water and held before being stir-fried in olive oil with chilli and garlic for a pasta sauce or roasted, as for example when used to stuff pasta shells (*conchiglie*) with anchovies and garlic, flavours which go particularly well with the vegetable.

Broccoli is such a fine vegetable it can be enjoyed as a dish in its own right, like asparagus. If so, serve it with melted butter, or extra-virgin olive oil and lemon juice, or with a warm anchovy-and-garlic dip – bagna cauda (see page 185) – or, most impressively, with hollandaise.

## BRUSSELS SPROUTS

Why are Brussels sprouts so called? Because, presumably, it was around the city that they were first grown.

Effectively tiny cabbages, Brussels sprouts need very little cooking as those over the age of 40 will testify, having suffered them boiled to perdition, developing in some cases a life-long aversion. This recipe may win such sufferers round.

**SERVES 4**

**1 kg / 2¼ lb small Brussels sprouts**
**salt**
**1 tbsp sunflower oil**
**1 tbsp dark (Oriental) sesame oil**
**3.5-cm / 1-inch piece of ginger, peeled and cut into matchstick strips**
**2 garlic cloves, finely chopped**
**1 tbsp oyster sauce**
**pepper**

Trim off the outer leaves of the sprouts and parboil the sprouts for 3 minutes in lots of rapidly boiling salted water. Refresh in ice-cold water and refrigerate until needed. You can do this the night before if you are feeling very pressed.

Put the sunflower oil and sesame oils in a wok or big frying pan over a high heat. Throw in the ginger strips and the chopped garlic, stir, add the sprouts and toss to coat them well in the aromatics for a minute or so.

Add the oyster sauce, toss the contents of the pan one last time and transfer to a warmed dish. Grind some black pepper over the sprouts and serve them immediately.

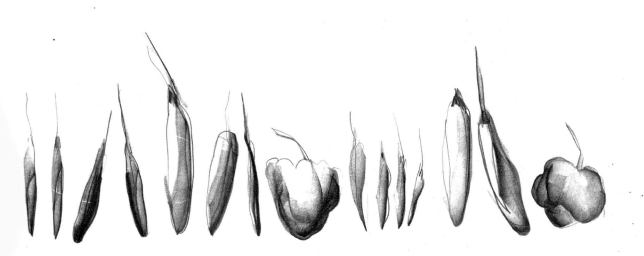

### CABBAGE

Dark green cabbage treated sympathetically can be one of our finest vegetables. The only time cabbage smells unpleasant is when it is overcooked, a smell incidentally that is a dilute version of mustard gas.

The smell of long-boiled greens and repulsively overcooked cauliflower has haunted many a childhood and still permeates British institutions today, for it seems that old habits die hard.

As a nation we are also prone to cooking those hard, compacted white cabbages which are ill-suited to boiling and should be reserved for eating raw in salads, like coleslaw, or for pickling and cooking as sauerkraut.

Trim and discard the outer leaves and base stalk of the cabbage, cut it into quarters and then blanch these for 4 minutes in lots of rapidly boiling salted water, before plunging them quickly into very cold water to stop the cooking. Drain.

Now you can either reheat the cabbage by plunging it briefly in more boiling water before serving, simply dressed with a knob of butter, or you can roast it, bake it or shred it and stir-fry it.

> KEEPING RED CABBAGE RED
> *Never boil red cabbage hard or it will lose colour, turning an unappealing greyish mauve. Cook it gently, ideally by braising. Adding a little red wine vinegar also helps keep the colour.,*

### BRAISED SAVOY CABBAGE

SERVES 4

**2 tbsp sunflower oil**
**1 Savoy cabbage, blanched and refreshed as above**
**225 g / ½ lb unsmoked streaky bacon in a piece, cut into 5-mm ¼-inch strips**
**1 onion, diced small**
**1 leek, trimmed and thinly sliced**
**1 celery stalk, strings removed and sliced**
**1 carrot, diced**
**salt and pepper**

Put the oil in a roasting tin or ovenproof dish just large enough to hold the quartered cabbage and fry the lardons of bacon over a moderate heat for 2 minutes.

Add the onion, leek, celery and carrot, and continue to cook, stirring occasionally, for 5–6 minutes, or until they have just started to colour.

Cut the stalk from the cabbage quarters and squeeze out any excess moisture. Add to the pan and stir, continuing to cook for a few minutes until the cabbage starts to brown.

Season and serve at once.

### COLESLAW

Commercially produced coleslaw tends to be rather bland. If you want to put your family off coleslaw, organize a trip to a large-scale producer and watch half a ton of it being spewed into a trough from a machine.

The recipe below makes something vastly superior to the glop for which you pay silly prices.

SERVES 8

**2 tbsp Dijon mustard**
**2 tsp sugar**
**1 tbsp wine vinegar**
**1 tsp salt**
**2 garlic cloves, smashed and chopped**
**600 ml / 1 pt homemade mayonnaise (page 294)**
**1.35 kg / 3 lb round hard cabbage**
**3 carrots**
**1 red pepper**
**1 green pepper**
**1 onion**
**2 celery stalks**
**2 tbsp chopped flat-leaved parsley**

First beat the mustard, sugar, vinegar, salt and garlic into the mayonnaise.

Shred the cabbage and carrots. Deseed and slice the peppers and cut them into strips, then cut these across into dice. Dice the onion. Destring and slice the celery thinly.

Mix all the ingredients together in a bowl. Every element should have a thin coating of the mayonnaise. If not, add a few more spoonfuls and toss to coat evenly.

## RED CABBAGE

Red cabbage, unlike Savoy cabbage or spring greens which are cooked as little as possible in lots of water, is slow-cooked for a long time in a closed pan using its own high water content. You can ring the changes by adding some sultanas or sliced apples for the last 30 minutes of covered cooking. Alternatively, at the start, fry 115 g / 4 oz lardons of smoked streaky bacon with a diced onion in the butter before adding the cabbage.

> **1 red cabbage**
> **60 g / 2 oz butter**
> **salt and pepper**
> **a little freshly grated nutmeg**
> **3 tbsp red wine vinegar**
> **1 tbsp caster sugar**

Start by cutting the stalk off the cabbage and cutting the cabbage into quarters, then slice these across into 1-cm / ½-inch slices. Toss the slices in cold water. The water left clinging to the leaves should be all you need for the cooking.

Put the butter in a casserole dish, pile on the cabbage slices, season with salt, pepper and a little grated nutmeg and put on the lid. Cook over the lowest heat for 1½–2 hours. Check from time to time that it is generating sufficient liquid and give it a stir.

Remove the lid, add the red wine vinegar and sprinkle the caster sugar over. Turn up the heat and boil, stirring to evaporate the liquid.

This can be served immediately, or left to cool and then reheated gently. It can also be frozen without detriment.

## CARROTS VICHY

The French have a profound relationship with their livers and still believe in the efficacy of mineral water in keeping this all-important organ healthy under a daily onslaught of good food and wine. Vichy water is bottled natural spring water that contains a lot of minerals and salts and is an acquired taste. The saltiness makes it a good boiling medium for carrots.

> **SERVES 4**
> **450 g / 1 lb carrots**
> **about 600 ml / 1 pint Vichy water**
> **30 g / 1 oz butter**
> **2 tsp caster sugar**
> **1 tbsp chopped flat-leaved parsley**

Peel the carrots and cut them into neat batons. Put these in a pan and cover with Vichy water. Bring to the boil and cook for 6–8 minutes until tender. Drain.

Return to the pan with the butter and sugar, and cook over a low heat until the surfaces of the carrot sticks are lightly caramelized. Scatter over the parsley and you have carrots Vichy.

### GLAZING ROOT VEGETABLES

*Onions and carrots contain natural sugars which are released during frying to give a characteristic sweet taste and brown finish. Glazing just involves helping nature along with a bit more sugar. While not essential, it is also a good idea to parboil the vegetables so they are partially cooked before they go into the frying pan.*

*As a garnish to finish a stew, peel pickling onions and carrots. Cut the carrots lengthwise into ½-cm / ¼-inch slices, then into sticks and finally across into neat batons about 4 cm / 1½ inches long. Using separate frying pans, gently fry the onions and carrots in equal parts of butter and olive oil, turning the carrots frequently. Shake the pan with the onions. Push them around and they will fall apart. After 10 minutes, sprinkle both of them with a few teaspoons of caster sugar and continue to cook over a low heat until they are nicely browned and coated with the sugar glaze.*

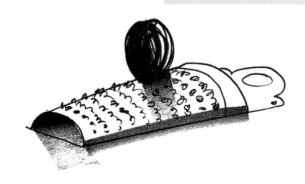

## CAULIFLOWER

There are a number of ways of cooking a cauliflower but, as with asparagus, you are dealing with a vegetable which has two edible elements where one needs less cooking than the other. This is always problematic.

If you want to cook a cauliflower whole, start by stripping away the outer leaves, then cut out the centre of the stem at the base and place the cauliflower in a saucepan into which it will just fit in about 3.5 cm / 1.5 inches of rapidly boiling salted water and cover with a lid. The tougher stem area is now covered by boiling water, while the more tender florets will steam gently. It is impossible to give a precise cooking time because cauliflowers come in different sizes, but about 7–8 minutes should suffice. You want to cook it to the point when the stem just gives to the tip of a knife or skewer.

If cooking the florets only, blanch them briefly – say 3 minutes – in lots of rapidly boiling salted water. They should be slightly resistant to the bite and are delicious with hollandaise or tossed, while still warm, in a light vinaigrette or simply dressed with olive oil and a little sea salt. Cauliflower is also good eaten raw with an anchovy and garlic dip.

## CAULIFLOWER CHEESE

That much-maligned nursery concoction of overcooked smelly vegetable in a floury and lumpen sauce has caused tears before bedtime in too many childhoods. It can, however, make a sensational and elegant dish for grownups when treated sympathetically.

While a whole cauliflower presents well at the table, it is really more sensible to use florets.

**SERVES 4**
450 g / 1 lb cauliflower florets
2 tbsp fresh breadcrumbs
15 g / ½ oz butter

for the cheese sauce:
45 g / 1½ oz butter
45 g / 1½ oz flour
850 ml / 1½ pt milk
sherry glass of dry sherry
85 g / 3 oz freshly grated farmhouse Cheddar cheese
30 g / 1 oz grated Parmesan cheese
4 tsp freshly made English mustard
freshly grated nutmeg
salt and pepper

Blanch the cauliflower florets as above. Drain and refresh in ice-cold water, drain again and reserve. Preheat the oven to 200°C/400°F/gas 6.

Make the cheese sauce starting with a roux made by melting the butter over a low heat and stirring in the flour. Cook briefly, stirring. Beat in the milk and sherry and cook over a low heat, stirring from time to time, for 20 minutes. Add the grated Cheddar and Parmesan, the mustard and nutmeg to taste, and stir until amalgamated. Season to taste with salt and pepper.

Put the cauliflower florets into a gratin dish and pour over the sauce. Scatter the fresh breadcrumbs on top, dot with butter and bake for 20 minutes for a memorable cauliflower au gratin.

## CHOUFLEUR À LA GRECQUE (PICKLED CAULIFLOWER)

**SERVES 4**
about 450 g / 1 lb cauliflower
salt and pepper
300 ml / ½ pt dry white wine
1 bay leaf
sprig of thyme
handful of celery leaves
1 tsp black peppercorns
1 tsp cumin seeds, lightly crushed (do this in a zip-lock bag with a rolling pin)
juice of 2 lemons
about 125 ml / 4 fl oz extra-virgin olive oil
whole coriander leaves, to garnish

Cut off the stem from the cauliflower and trim the head into florets. Blanch these in rapidly boiling salted water for 2 minutes, refresh in cold water and reserve.

Put the wine in a pan with the bay leaf, thyme, celery leaves, black peppercorns and cumin seeds. Bring to the boil and reduce at a fast boil by two-thirds.

Pass through a sieve into a frying pan. Add the lemon juice and extra-virgin olive oil. Bring to the boil, add the florets and cook, tossing and shaking, for 2 minutes. Remove the florets and transfer to a warmed serving dish.

Continue to boil the pan liquid, stirring, until you have a syrupy residue. Spoon this over the cauliflower, and season with salt and pepper. Add a drizzle more olive oil, scatter over some whole coriander leaves and serve warm or at room temperature.

## CHAYOTE

Chayote, a vine-grown gourd related to the squash, is now available in Britain. It is called mirliton in Louisiana, choko in Australia and vegetable pear and pear squash elsewhere. It comes in dark green spiny varieties and, more commonly, in a paler smooth-skinned form. They are usually peeled, halved and deseeded before cooking, which may be boiling, frying, or stuffing and baking. Boiling is the least successful approach, leaving them watery. In the following recipe, which goes well with any pieces of grilled fish, you could substitute courgettes if your local supermarket tells you that chayote exists only in the holiday imagination of your dreams.

675 g / 1½ lb chayote
5 garlic cloves
3 tbsp olive oil
30 g / 1 oz butter
juice of 1 lime
salt and pepper
handful of chopped flat-leaved
parsley

Peel, deseed and slice the chayote and thinly slice the garlic cloves.

Put the oil and butter in a large frying pan and melt the butter over a low heat. Add the garlic and cook, stirring for 3 minutes, but do not allow to brown except slightly round the edges. Remove with a slotted spoon and reserve.

Add the chayote to the pan, turn up the heat to moderate and sauté for 4–5 minutes. Stir in the lime juice and the reserved garlic. Season lightly with salt and pepper. Add a handful of chopped flat-leaved parsley, toss and serve.

## WILTED COURGETTES

While all vegetables have a high water content, courgettes have an even higher percentage than most and will therefore collapse if cooked too long, becoming slithery and unpleasant. The best method is to use their internal water to good effect, as here. This is a good way of cooking many similar vegetables, including mangetout or sugarsnap peas – and spinach.

SERVES 4
675 g / 1½ lb courgettes
salt and pepper
2 tbsp olive oil
1 garlic clove, chopped

Unless the courgettes are very small, in which case cook them whole, top and tail them, then cut them in half lengthwise. Finish by cutting across again to give you pieces about 3 cm / 1¼ inches long and season with salt and pepper.

Put the olive oil in a pan with a tight-fitting lid and put over a moderate heat. Add the garlic to the hot oil, stir in and immediately add the courgettes. Put on the lid, shake and cook for 1½–2 minutes. Remove from the heat and take off the lid or they will go on cooking.

## STUFFED BAKED COURGETTES

The courgettes are hollowed out, stuffed with a mixture of onion, garlic, breadcrumbs, Parmesan and thyme, then baked.

SERVES 4
8 courgettes
1 onion
2 garlic cloves
sprig of thyme
30 g / 1 oz Parmesan cheese
about 3 tbsp olive oil
85 g / 3 oz fresh breadcrumbs

Preheat the oven to 200°C/400°F/gas 6.

Halve the courgettes lengthwise and scoop out the flesh with a teaspoon to make little 'canoe' shapes, what Cajun chefs call *pirogues*. Reserve the pulp.

Finely chop the onion and garlic. Strip the leaves from the sprig of thyme and chop them. Grate the Parmesan.

Sweat the onion, garlic and courgette flesh in 1 tablespoon of the oil in a frying pan, until the onion is soft and translucent.

Put this mixture with the breadcrumbs and Parmesan into a food processor and blitz until you have a smooth purée. Add the thyme leaves and 1 tablespoon of the olive oil and work briefly to mix together.

Fill the pirogues with the mixture and arrange in a baking dish so they are all sitting up. Dribble a little more olive oil over and bake for about 30 minutes, when they will have wilted slightly and browned round the edges.

Serve warm rather than hot.

### DEEP-FRIED COURGETTE FLOWERS

Deep-frying is a very difficult thing to get right at home, particularly when using a domestic electric fryer. These are much better than they used to be, but are still very small and the first thing people get wrong is overloading them. This causes the temperature to drop significantly, with a resultant absorption of oil. The other problem is getting them hot enough. You want a temperature of 190°C/375°F to seal the crust or set the batter, otherwise excessive oil absorption will take place.

The batter used is obviously significant, and for this dish use one which borrows from Japanese tempura, to give a light and very crisp finish. Even when you do get it right, remember that you need to serve the flowers the instant they come from the fryer and after only a brief draining on absorbent paper. Left to sit, steam generated by the super-hot filling will soften the crispest of batter envelopes.

**SERVES 4 AS A FIRST COURSE**

**12 courgette flowers**
**oil for deep-frying**
**lemon quarters, cut lengthwise, to serve**

**for the stuffing:**
**85 g / 3 oz buffalo mozzarella, drained and diced**
**8 anchovy fillets, drained and chopped**
**8 basil leaves, chopped**
**pepper**

**for the tempura batter:**
**115 g / 4 oz plain flour**
**60 g / 2 oz cornflour**
**½ tsp baking powder**
**200 ml / 7 fl oz iced water**

First make the stuffing: put the mozzarella into a bowl with the chopped anchovy fillets and basil. Season with pepper and mix together with a fork. Using a teaspoon, stuff the courgette flowers with the mixture, twisting the ends of the flowers to keep the filling in.

Preheat oil for deep-frying to 190°C/375°F. Make the batter: sift the flour into a bowl with the cornflour and baking powder. Put the iced water in another large bowl. Dump the flour mixture into the iced water in one go and quickly mix with a fork. There should still be lumps. (Do not overmix to a smooth batter or the end result will be chewy rather than crisp.)

Coat the flower parcels in the batter and fry in two batches if your fryer is small, serving in stages after draining on paper. Serve with lemon quarters.

### CHICORY OR ENDIVE

Chicory and endive are the same thing, a slightly bitter-tasting, tight-leafed vegetable that looks a bit like a smaller version of a Chinese cabbage. The more common white-leaved variety is produced by being forced in darkness, a technique first used in Belgium in the 1840s, and where it is called *witloof*. There are Italian red-leaf varieties too, like rossa di Treviso, which taste very like the white. Chicory can be blanched like cabbage, but we think it is nicest braised in butter in the oven.

Allow one head per person and wash carefully in plenty of cold water, because they are grown in sand. Cut a wedge out of the stalk end of each to help even cooking and arrange in a buttered ovenproof dish which will just hold them packed tightly, dot the top with butter, squeeze over the juice of 2 lemons, and season. Some recipes specify the use of sugar, but the lemon actually cuts the bitterness very effectively. Cover loosely with foil and bake at 160°C/325°F/gas 3 for about 1 hour, until golden brown.

These are also very good in a béchamel sauce, with or without strips of ham, and finished under a grill with a cheese-and-crumb gratin.

### STABILIZING YOGHURT FOR COOKING

*Yoghurt needs to have a stabilizing agent cooked into it before it is added to a boiling or simmering agent or it will separate. The easiest way to do this is to put 600 ml / 1 pt thick natural yoghurt in a food processor with 1 level tablespoon of cornflour mixed to a paste with cold water and 1 teaspoon of salt (if using for a savoury dish). Work until smooth. Put into a pan and bring to the boil over a low heat then simmer, stirring at regular intervals, for 10–15 minutes, until thick and creamy. You can now pour it into your curry or stew with impunity.*

## CORN FRITTERS

More like pancakes, these fritters are good for breakfast with bacon, but are also nice with a grilled pork chop.

**MAKES 16–18**
**600 ml / 1 pt yoghurt**
**30 g / 1 oz cornflour**
**4 ears of sweetcorn (enough to make 225 g / 8 oz kernels; defrosted frozen corn will do if you can't get any fresh)**
**2 eggs, separated**
**170 g / 6 oz self-raising flour**
**150 g / 5 oz instant polenta**
**a pinch of chilli flakes**
**salt and pepper**
**sunflower oil**

Stabilize the yoghurt by bringing it slowly to the boil and stirring in the cornflour which has first been mixed to a paste with cold water. Turn down the heat and simmer gently for 10 minutes. Leave to cool.

Strip off the husks and silky threads from the corn and slice off the kernels.

Whisk the egg yolks in a bowl, then beat the yoghurt into them. Whisk in the self-raising flour and the instant polenta, with a pinch of chilli flakes and salt and pepper. Leave the mixture to stand for about 30 minutes at room temperature.

Heat a heavy frying pan or non-stick pan or griddle over a low to moderate heat. Stir the corn into the batter. Whisk the egg whites until stiff and fold these gently into the mixture.

Film the pan with sunflower oil and put 4 kitchen spoonfuls of batter in. These will spread to form 4 pancakes about 11 cm / 4½ inches across. Cook until bubbles come to the surface and then turn, to cook the other side for the same length of time.

When they are done, transfer them to a tray and keep warm in a low oven while you cook the rest. Wipe the pan between batches with oiled kitchen paper.

## MUSTARD GREENS

Mustard greens have a strong, slightly bitter flavour and can be blanched in rapidly boiling salted water like any other leaf vegetable, but a brief sauté with some olive oil is probably better. Cooked this way they go well with any grilled fish.

**SERVES 4**
**675 g / 1½ lb mustard greens**
**3 tbsp olive oil**
**salt and pepper**
**knob of butter (optional)**

Wash the mustard greens and spin dry. Discard any dodgy leaves and cut out thick stalks.

Heat a wok or large frying pan until very hot. Add the olive oil and swirl to coat the base. As soon as the oil starts to smoke, throw in the greens and toss, turning with tongs until uniformly wilted, which will take about 2 minutes, depending on the size of your pan and its temperature.

Just before you judge them to be done, season with salt and pepper. Drain in a colander for a minute before transferring to a warmed serving bowl or straight on to serving plates. Dress with a knob of butter or with a little more oil.

## SPRING OR WINTER GREENS

Greens used to be considered rather poor fare and eating them was more of a duty than a pleasure. Some of us are old enough to remember the grim edict: 'Eat your greens or you'll grow up spotty,' or worse, 'You'll sit there 'til they're all gone.' Greens are characterized by rather coarse leaves, strong ribs and a slightly bitter taste which you either love or loathe. Spring greens usually refers to cabbages which have not formed a massed centre of closely packed leaves, the heart.

Start by throwing away the outer leaves, then cut off the basal stalks of the remainder and wash them. Bring a big pan of salted water to the boil and blanch the leaves in it for 3 minutes. Remove them and plunge them immediately into very cold water to arrest the cooking.

You can now finish the leaves in a pan with butter, grating over a little nutmeg before bringing them to the table, or try a very different approach and dress the warm leaves with a mixture of Dijon mustard, Kikkoman soy sauce, lemon juice and a little olive oil. This has a Japanese feel to it and sets off the strongly flavoured leaves to perfection. Flavoured this way they go well with grilled fish or chicken.

## SPRING GREENS WITH BONITO

Bonito flakes are made from grated dried fish by the Japanese (see page 13).

**SERVES 4**
1 kg / 2¼ lb spring greens
salt
3 tbsp olive oil
juice of ½ lemon
3-cm / 1¼-inch piece of root ginger, grated
1 tbsp Dijon mustard
2 tbsp bonito flakes

Discard the rough outer leaves of the spring greens, wash the remainder thoroughly and trim away the stalks. Blanch in plenty of rapidly boiling salted water and drain in a colander.

Transfer to a serving bowl which has a close-fitting lid. Dress the greens with the olive oil, lemon juice, ginger and mustard. Toss to coat evenly. Scatter over the bonito flakes and put on the lid.

Remove the lid after 30 seconds and take to the table at once to alarm your guests with the sight of the bonito waving like something live and alien (the heat and moisture cause the light little flakes to 'dance').

## GREEN GARLIC

Green garlic is very young garlic that is pulled from the ground before the full cloves have developed. Fully developed garlic is an annual crop, but green garlic can be cropped three or four times in a growing season.

If you have a garden you can grow it yourself by planting garlic cloves bought from the market in good, well-drained soil and keeping it well watered.

The cloves only start to develop as a separate entity from the stem after about six weeks. Up until then they are like tiny leeks or spring onions and don't look dissimilar.

Green garlic has a very delicate flavour and is currently hot food fashion in California and Australia. The young shoots do not contain the powerful aromatic flavouring oils allin and allinase that give mature garlic its characteristic pungency and can, therefore, be used with impunity in salads or very lightly cooked. Eat all of it except the upper dark green leaves and the roots.

## KOHLRABI

Originally grown in this country in the last century for cattle feed, kohlrabi is a strange-looking vegetable, like a purple- and green-tinted turnip with stalks growing out of it at random. It is, in fact, related more closely to a brassica. You want to buy them small, because the larger they grow the woodier they get. Kohlrabi makes an excellent gratin.

**SERVES 4–6**
1 tbsp olive oil
300 ml / ½ pint single cream
2 garlic cloves, finely chopped
½ tsp salt
¼ tsp pepper
60 g / 2 oz freshly grated Parmesan cheese
about 1 kg / 2 lb 2 oz kohlrabi, peeled

Preheat the oven to 200°C/400°F/gas 6. Choose an ovenproof dish 25.5 x 15 x 5 cm / 10 x 6 x 2 inches deep and brush it all over with the olive oil.

Put the cream in a bowl with the garlic and season with the salt and pepper. Stir in half the grated Parmesan.

Cut the kohlrabi in half and, with the flat surface downwards, cut it into slices. Put half the slices into the cream and turn them to coat. Remove them one at a time, allowing excess cream to drip off, and lay them in the dish overlapping in layers. Repeat with the second half. Pour any remaining cream mixture over the top and scatter over the remaining grated cheese.

Bake for about 1 hour, when the surface will have glazed to a golden colour while the kohlrabi will have cooked all the way through to a creamy finish.

## MUNG BEANSPROUTS

Within three days you can sprout mung beans with 115 g / 4 oz of beans producing 450 g / 1 lb of succulent white shoots for cooking or to eat in a salad.

Pick over the beans and discard any that look decrepit. Rinse, put in a bowl, pour over 1.1 litres / 2 pints of tepid water and leave 8 hours or overnight.

Punch a plastic bag full of holes, drain the beans, rinse again with warm water and put them in it. Don't tie the bag shut, but wrap it loosely in a damp drying-up cloth, put in a colander and put it in a warm cupboard (not an airing cupboard which is usually too hot).

After 4 hours, remove and rinse the whole package with warm water again and put it back to drip quietly to itself. Do this every 4 hours until you go to bed, when you say something rude to it and

*Opposite: Deep-fried Courgette Flower (page 174)*

leave it until the morning. After 3 days of this nonsense you should have a big bag of mung sprouts.

Put the sprouts in the sink and cover with lots of cold water. Rub through your fingers to remove skins from the residual bean. Discard the skins, drain and use the crunchy, sweet-tasting sprouts. They are particularly good stir-fried with spring onions, chilli and garlic.

## SHALLOTS AND ONIONS

What is the difference between shallots and onions and can they be substituted for one another? Shallots and onions are both members of the lily family – along with leeks, chives and garlic – but are not the same thing at all.

Shallots are much smaller than onions, but are distinct from baby onions and have a more subtle flavour. The best are almost purple in colour and form the basis for a number of classic dishes and preparations like beurre blanc. Shallot vinegar is also a fine accompaniment with oysters.

While some dishes, like a carbonnade or onion soup, call for onions to be fried until brown, shallots are never overcooked in this way, but used either raw or lightly sautéed. If browned, they will become bitter and unpalatable.

Shallots are now available in good supermarkets all year round, but are more expensive than onions. A recipe which calls for shallots means what it says: they have a different flavour. You could substitute onions for shallots in any recipe but the taste would be different.

*Opposite (clockwise from the left): Onion Confit, Caramelized Onions, Roasted Onions (overleaf)*

---

### PEELING SMALL ONIONS OR SHALLOTS

*This tedious and time-consuming task is made easier if you first pour boiling water over them and leave them for 20 seconds. Refresh in cold water and proceed as usual, using a small sharp knife.*

## CARAMELIZED ONIONS

A frequent cause of complaint is onions disintegrating during slow cooking. The trick is to cook them slowly and to shake them rather than stir them during the latter stages because, once softened, aggressive stirring will cause them to disintegrate.

SERVES 4
675 g / 1½ lb smallish onions
60 g / 2 oz unsalted butter
½ tsp salt
1 tbsp sugar
2 tbsp chicken stock

Peel the onions. Melt the butter in a shallow, wide saucepan, add the onions, season with the salt and stir gently with a wooden spoon to coat. Cook over a low heat for about 20 minutes, shaking at regular intervals to prevent them sticking.

Scatter over the sugar and, when this dissolves into the butter and the colour begins to turn to golden brown, add the chicken stock and swirl the pan around until the onions are nicely glazed.

## ONION CONFIT

This recipe sounds like it uses a lot of onions but, after long slow cooking, they go down to a small intensely flavoured residue. Anyway you cannot cook a small amount in this way and get the right result. As well as serving onion confit as a vegetable, you could also try it tossed with pasta or on crostini. The addition of cassis, the blackcurrant liqueur used with dry white wine to make kir, is a suggestion from Alice Waters, the celebrated Californian restaurateur and food writer.

1.35 kg / 3 lb onions, thinly
sliced
60 g / 2 oz butter
salt and pepper
1 tbsp caster sugar
500 ml / 16 fl oz red wine
250 ml / 8 fl oz red wine
vinegar
1 tbsp thyme leaves
1 tbsp cassis (optional)

Put the onions in a heavy saucepan with the butter. Season and fry over a medium heat, stirring, for 5 minutes. Sprinkle with the sugar and stir in. Lower the heat, cover and cook for 5 minutes more, when the onions will have softened.

Add the red wine and red wine vinegar, with the thyme leaves and, if you have some to hand, the cassis. Lower the heat, stir and simmer gently for about 1½ hours, or until all the liquid has evaporated and you are left with a dark-coloured syrupy mass.

Serve immediately or keep in the fridge for up to a week.

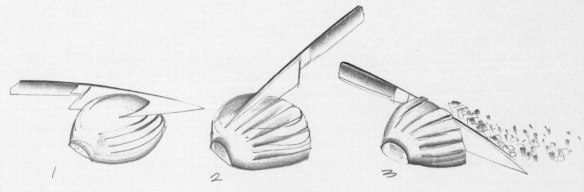

*Dicing an Onion*

❶ To cut an onion into neat dice quickly, cut it in half through the root end, then place each half cut side down. Make a series of parallel lateral cuts through each half almost to the root end, but not cutting all the way through.

❷ Make a series of vertical cuts at right angles to these lateral cuts, going all the way through down to the cutting board.

❸ Slice across, again at right angles to the vertical cuts, from the loose end. The onion will fall into small uniform dice.

## BHAJA

*Bhaja*, a Bengali dish which in this country has become synonymous with spiced onion in batter, can be any deep-fried vegetable or mixture of vegetables and not always coated in batter. Try vegetables like courgettes, turnips, swedes, potatoes and sweet potatoes.

---

TEAR-FREE ONIONS

*Some onions are fiercer than others. You can sometimes find imported Vidalia sweet onions from the USA, and red or purple onions are also milder-flavoured. With any raw onions, if you peel and slice them, then put the rings in a bowl covered with cold water in the fridge overnight it will help calm them down. Drain them and put to dry on heaped kitchen paper. The onions will be much milder, but still crisp.*

---

SERVES 4

60 g / 2 oz besan flour
75 g / 2½ oz rice flour
½ tsp bicarbonate of soda
1 tsp hot chilli powder
1 tsp black pepper
1 tsp turmeric
1 tsp salt
oil for deep-frying
1 tbsp poppy or mustard seeds
450 g / 1 lb onions, sliced across into rings
plain flour, for dredging

Make the batter by mixing the flours in a bowl. Add the bicarbonate of soda, chilli powder, pepper, turmeric and salt. Whisk in 250 ml / 8 fl oz cold water and leave to stand for 30–45 minutes.

Preheat oil for deep-frying to 190°C/375°F. Stir the poppy or mustard seeds into the batter. Dredge a handful of onion rings in plain flour, then dip them in batter and deep-fry for 5 minutes, turning once. Drain on paper towels and serve immediately.

## TINNED PETITS POIS

The tinned peas described as *petits pois à la Francaise* can be very good. Made properly, they are garden peas fresh from the pod but since the peas here are stewed for up to 20 minutes the tinned variety make rather a good substitute.

4 slices of unsmoked streaky bacon
85 g / 3 oz butter
8 spring onions, cut into 2-cm / ¾-inch pieces
leaves of 3 Little Gem lettuces
450 g / 1 lb tin of petits pois, drained and rinsed
2 tsp sugar
black pepper

Cut the bacon into matchsticks, then small dice and sweat the 60 g / 2 oz of the butter until the fat has run out and the bacon starts to brown.

Add the spring onions and lettuce leaves. Turn to coat well, add the petits pois, sugar, some black pepper and put on the lid. Simmer gently for 10 minutes, or until the lettuce is cooked.

Stir in the remaining butter and serve.

## PUMPKIN GNOCCHI

Pumpkin gnocchi are best made from small butternut squash, not those huge great gourds which look desperately for edible exits but usually end up as lanterns at Hallowe'en.

Before the flesh is usable for gnocchi or ravioli you will need to get rid of excess water. Cut the orange flesh into lumps and roast it in a hot oven to throw the first lot of moisture, then put it through a sieve to lose the seeds. Finally simmer it in a pan, stirring with a wooden spoon, until you achieve a dry dense mass.

**450 g / 1 lb prepared dried squash as above (you will need to start with about 1.25 kg / 2½ lb of squash)**
**2 tbsp flour**
**1 egg**
**150 g / 5 oz freshly grated Parmesan cheese**
**1 tsp salt**
**1 tsp pepper**
**flour, for dusting**
**15 g / ½ oz butter**

In a large bowl, mix together the prepared dried squash, flour, egg, 115 g / 4 oz of the grated Parmesan cheese and some salt and pepper. Beat until the mixture holds the spoon, then turn it out on a floured surface, roll it into a sausage shape and cut this into bite-sized pieces. If you want to be presentation-smart, roll these on a fork to make them into a shell shape. If not, just cylinders will do.

Preheat the grill. Poach the gnocchi for a few minutes in lots of boiling salted water. They are done when they bob to the surface, but leave them for about another minute to make sure. Put them in a hot dish, dot with pieces of the butter, strew over the remaining Parmesan and flash under the hot grill. That's it.

## COOKING SALSIFY

Salsify produces a long white tap root rather like a carrot and is closely related to scorzonera, with which it is almost interchangeable. Its flavour is difficult to describe, perhaps a little like a parsnip but not at all sweet. It is not a very widely known or eaten vegetable, but ask any decent greengrocer and he will get you some when it is available, from October.

Top and tail the roots and peel off the tough brown skin. Cut the root into pieces about 5–8 cm / 2–3 inches long then slice these into neat batons. If you are not cooking them immediately then leave them in some cold water acidulated with 1 tablespoon of vinegar per 600 ml / 1 pt to prevent them from discolouring.

Boil them as you would potatoes in salted water for about 20 minutes or until softened. The older and larger the salsify, the more woody and consequently the longer the cooking time needed. Drain them, return them to the pan and shake over a low heat to dry them off, then add a knob of butter and some pepper and toss with chopped parsley.

Alternatively, mash the salsify with a little butter and cream and season with some freshly grated nutmeg. You can also make salsify soup (see overleaf) or a gratin, and salsify crisps or chips, slicing the peeled roots on a mandolin or as appropriate.

## SALSIFY SOUP

SERVES 4–6

225 g / 8 oz onion, diced

30 g / 1 oz butter

1 garlic clove, finely chopped

675 g / 1½ lb salsify, peeled and
cut into chunks

1.1 litres / 2 pt chicken stock

salt and pepper

freshly grated nutmeg

3 tbsp chopped flat-leaved
parsley

150 ml / ¼ pt double cream

Sweat the diced onion in the butter until
soft and translucent. Add the garlic and
continue to fry gently for a minute, then
add the salsify chunks and stock. Season
with salt, pepper and nutmeg to taste.
Bring to the boil and immediately lower
the heat and simmer for about 30 minutes.

Transfer to a blender or food processor and blitz to a purée. Return to a
clean pan over a low heat, stir in 2 tablespoons of the chopped flat-leaved
parsley and then the cream. Taste,
adding more salt and pepper as needed
and heat through without boiling.
Scatter the remaining parsley on top
when you serve.

## SPINACH IN FILO

Cook the spinach only briefly and
ensure that all excess water is squeezed
out.

SERVES 6 AS A STARTER

10–20 strands of spaghetti

450 g / 1 lb spinach

60 g / 2 oz butter, plus more for
the baking sheet

2 tbsp pine nuts

1 tbsp sultanas, plumped
overnight in a few spoonfuls of
some suitable liquor, such as
brandy

freshly grated nutmeg

1 tsp black pepper

2 tsp red wine vinegar

about 8 sheets of filo pastry

Start by bringing a big pot of salted
water to a fast boil. Put in the spaghetti
and cook until just softened, about 2
minutes. Remove from the water with a
slotted spoon and reserve.

Pick over the spinach, discarding
large stalks and any dodgy leaves.
Plunge it into the boiling water and as
soon as it wilts – about 30 seconds –
drain in a colander, squeezing gently to
remove as much water as you can.

Melt the butter in a pan over a low
heat and add the pine nuts. Increase the
heat slightly and fry the nuts until they
just start to colour, stirring. Turn your
back for an instant and they will burn
and go bitter. Add the sultanas, nutmeg
to taste, black pepper and red wine
vinegar. Add the spinach off the heat
and toss to coat. Reserve.

Preheat the oven to 190°C/375°F/
gas 5. Working with 1 sheet of filo

pastry at a time, cut out six 15-cm /
6-inch circles using a plate or baking tin
as a guide. Put one-sixth of the spinach
mixture in the centre of each and draw
up the edges to the middle. Tie shut
with a piece of spaghetti as you would a
shoelace.

Put on a lightly greased Swiss roll tin
and bake for 10–15 minutes, when the
filo should be crisp and golden.

## SPINACH POLPETTINE

Polpettine are little shallow-fried balls
that can be made from vegetables or
minced meat. Just-blanched spinach is
very good cooked this way.

SERVES 4–6

about 450 g / 1 lb picked
spinach

3 eggs, beaten

60 g / 2 oz freshly grated
Parmesan cheese

60 g / 2 oz breadcrumbs

salt and pepper

¼ tsp chilli flakes

freshly grated nutmeg

a little sunflower oil

a little olive oil

small knob of butter

Plunge the spinach into lots of rapidly boiling salted water for 30 seconds to 1 minute, then refresh in cold water to stop it cooking. Drain and squeeze gently to extract as much moisture as possible. Chop roughly.

Beat the eggs in a large bowl. Whisk into them the grated Parmesan and the breadcrumbs. Season with salt, pepper, chilli flakes and nutmeg to taste. Add the chopped spinach and work all together with a fork. Form into walnut-sized balls.

Film a large frying pan with equal parts sunflower oil, olive oil and butter to give a depth of 3–5 mm / $\frac{1}{8}$–$\frac{1}{4}$ inch. Put over a moderate heat and, when shimmering-hot but not smoking, add the polpettine. Fry in 2 batches, rolling them round to brown them evenly, transferring the finished polpettine to kitchen paper to drain and keeping them warm in a low oven while you fry the second batch.

## SPINACH POLONAISE

In French cooking, a garnish of chopped hard-boiled eggs, capers and butter-fried breadcrumbs is called polonaise and is classically served with cauliflower, but is also very good with lightly blanched spinach, asparagus or broccoli.

SERVES 4

**4 eggs**
**2 tbsp fresh breadcrumbs**
**85 g / 3 oz unsalted butter**
**500 g / 1 lb 2 oz young spinach leaves**
**salt and pepper**
**2 tbsp capers, rinsed and well dried**
**2 tbsp finely chopped flat-leaved parsley**

Hard-boil the eggs (cook for 7–8 minutes), refresh in cold water and shell. Cut the eggs in halves, push the yolks through a sieve with a spoon and chop the whites.

Fry the breadcrumbs in 60 g / 2 oz of the butter gently over a low heat, stirring until they are nice and brown and crisp.

Blanch the spinach leaves in rapidly boiling salted water and drain, then squeeze out excess water. Put in a warmed serving bowl, teasing out the leaves with tongs. Scatter over the fried breadcrumbs, the egg yolk and the chopped egg whites.

Put the remaining butter in the frying pan and quickly sauté the capers. Scatter these and the parsley on top of everything, season with pepper and serve at once.

## SAAG PANEER

Paneer is an Indian fresh curd cheese (see page 46) traditionally served with spinach or peas, though it may also be paired with spring greens or Swiss chard.

SERVES 4

**about 450 g / 1 lb spinach, spring greens or Swiss chard leaves**
**salt**
**4-cm / 1½-inch piece of root ginger**
**8 garlic cloves, chopped**
**2 hot green chillies, chopped**
**about 350 g / 12 oz paneer**
**5 tbsp sunflower oil**
**1 tsp ground cumin**
**1 tsp cayenne pepper**
**3 tbsp single cream**

Blanch the leaves in rapidly boiling salted water for 1 minute, refresh in cold water and drain in a colander.

Peel and chop the ginger and put into a food processor with half the garlic, the chillies and 3½ tablespoons of water. Blitz to a purée.

Cut the paneer into bite-sized pieces, brush with a little sunflower oil and scatter with the cumin and cayenne pepper, then sauté in a hot, non-stick frying pan to brown on both sides. Remove and reserve.

Put the remaining oil in the pan. Stir in the remaining garlic, then add the blanched leaves and the ginger purée. Put on a lid, lower the temperature and simmer gently for 10 minutes.

Stir in the paneer and cream and continue to cook for 5 minutes, uncovered.

## SWEET POTATO, BACON AND LEEK PIE

Any method for an ordinary floury potato can be used to cook sweet potatoes, though their flavour would make them unsuitable for some recipes. Thus boiled and mashed, deep-fried as chips or crisps, or parboiled and sautéed all work.

SERVES 6–8

115 g / 4 oz pancetta or smoked streaky bacon, cut into strips
4 tbsp olive oil
675 g / 1½ lb sweet potatoes, peeled and cut into thick chips
225 g / 8 oz carrots, peeled and cut into thick chips
4 leeks, trimmed and cut into strips
2 garlic cloves, chopped
60 g / 2 oz fresh breadcrumbs
15 g / ½ oz butter

for the thick béchamel sauce:
30 g / 1 oz butter
30 g / 1 oz flour
600 ml / 1 pt milk
freshly grated nutmeg
salt and pepper

Preheat the oven to 200°C/400°F/gas 6. Gently fry the pancetta or bacon in 2 tablespoons of the olive oil until the fat has run and the bacon is browned but not crisp. Remove with a slotted spoon and reserve.

Put the sweet potatoes and carrots into a gratin dish, sprinkle over the remaining olive oil and put to roast for 30 minutes.

Meanwhile, make a thick béchamel: melt the butter in a heavy-based pan over a gentle heat, stir in the flour and cook gently, stirring, for a minute. Stir in the milk and bring to a simmer. Cook stirring, until thick and smooth. Season with grated nutmeg and salt and pepper. While the sauce is cooking, sweat the leeks and garlic in the pan with the bacon fat until soft, then stir the contents of the pan into the sauce with the bacon.

Remove the gratin dish from the oven, pour over the sauce and scatter the breadcrumbs on the top. Dot with butter and return to the oven for 15 minutes.

## LE POUNTI

Nobody is sure why chard, which is a form of beet – where we eat the leaves rather than the root – should be described as Swiss. It is common throughout northern Europe and is greatly honoured in France, where it is called *blette*.

The green leaves have similarities to spinach and need very little cooking, which is why it is best to cook them separately from the stalks. Simply blanched in salted water, drained then dressed with a little butter, the leaves make an excellent green vegetable. Le Pounti is a dish from the mountainous Auvergne region in central France.

225 g / 8 oz cooked ham, diced
150 g / 5 oz Swiss chard leaves
1 onion, chopped
2 garlic cloves, chopped
big bunch of flat-leaved parsley, chopped
85 g / 3 oz flour
600 ml / 1 pt milk
5 eggs
salt and pepper
freshly grated nutmeg
butter, for greasing

Preheat the oven to 180°C/350°F/ gas 4. Mix together the ham, torn Swiss chard leaves, onion, garlic and parsley.

Make a thin batter with the flour and milk, then beat in the eggs. Season with pepper and a little salt and nutmeg. Fold in the ham and vegetable mixture. Pour and spoon into a buttered dish and bake for 45 minutes or until just set.

Serve hot with any cold meat or at room temperature as a first course.

## HOME-DRIED TOMATOES

Whenever plum tomatoes are cheap or if you are lucky enough to have a greenhouse and a glut of tomatoes to deal with, dry some in the oven and make the rest into a roast tomato sauce (page 293).

To dry tomatoes, cut them in half, scoop out the pulp and seeds, and sit the halves, cut side up, in baking trays. Sprinkle with a little salt and caster sugar, then drizzle with olive oil and roast in an oven preheated to 150°C/300°F/gas 2 until most of the moisture has evaporated from them. Depending on how many you are drying at a time, this can take anything from an hour upwards. All domestic ovens have hot spots, so reposition the tomatoes to avoid burning any of them.

Remove and, when cool, pack tightly in jars, covered with olive oil. They are fabulous in salads, as a relish with cold meats or cheese or on pizzas or open tarts.

## HOME-DRIED TOMATO TART

The temperature and length of time you take to dry tomatoes obviously makes a difference to their texture. For this tart you want them still quite moist.

**SERVES 8**

**1 kg / 2¼ lb ripe plum tomatoes**
**oil for the tin**
**1 tsp sugar**
**1 tsp salt**
**4 eggs**
**300 ml / ½ pint single cream**
**85 g / 3 oz grated Parmesan cheese**
**pepper**
**freshly grated nutmeg**

**for the pastry:**
**200 g / 7 oz flour**
**100 g / 3½ oz unsalted butter, diced**
**pinch of salt**
**1 egg**
**about 1 tbsp iced water**

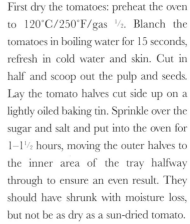

First dry the tomatoes: preheat the oven to 120°C/250°F/gas ½. Blanch the tomatoes in boiling water for 15 seconds, refresh in cold water and skin. Cut in half and scoop out the pulp and seeds. Lay the tomato halves cut side up on a lightly oiled baking tin. Sprinkle over the sugar and salt and put into the oven for 1–1½ hours, moving the outer halves to the inner area of the tray halfway through to ensure an even result. They should have shrunk with moisture loss, but not be as dry as a sun-dried tomato.

Make the pastry: put the flour, butter and a pinch of salt in a food processor and blitz to a crumb. While continuing to work, add an egg through the feeder tube, then add the iced water, a tablespoon at a time, until the pastry balls. Remove, cling-wrap, form into a ball then press into a 2 cm / ¾ inch thick disc and refrigerate for an hour.

Roll the chilled pastry out thinly and use to line a 25-cm / 10-inch tart pan. Return to the fridge to rest for at least an hour or overnight before baking.

When ready to make the tart: preheat the oven to 180°C/350°F/gas 4. Line the pastry shell with foil, then weight the top with beans or ceramic baking weights and bake blind for 15 minutes. Remove the weights and foil and continue baking until golden brown in the centre, about 10 minutes more.

Arrange the dried tomato halves to cover the base. In a large bowl, whisk the eggs then stir the cream followed by the Parmesan and season with salt, pepper and grated nutmeg to taste. Pour over the tomatoes and return to the oven, immediately lowering the temperature to 150°C/300°F/gas 2, and bake for 25–30 minutes or until just set.

## COOKING TURNIPS

The larger and older a turnip, the woodier and less flavourful it becomes. For those who have eaten only the geriatric variety, whole baby turnips – what the French call *petits navets* – are a revelation.

For about 6 people, wash and trim – but do not peel – about 1 kg / 2 lb of small turnips. Put in a single layer in a heavy saucepan or casserole dish and barely cover with chicken stock or water, season with salt and pepper and bring to the boil. Cook briskly until only a few spoonfuls of liquid remain, about 15–20 minutes, then add 60 g / 2 oz of unsalted butter, 3 tablespoons of olive oil, 1 tablespoon of caster sugar and a grating of nutmeg. Turn down the heat, shake the pan to coat the turnips and continue to cook, shaking from time to time, until they are caramelized to a golden brown. These go particularly well with a rich bird like duck, but are also nice with roast lamb.

Either of the following treatments could also result in conversion – if not turnip addiction.

## SAUTÉED TURNIPS WITH HERBS

**SERVES 4**

450 g / 1 lb small white turnips, cut across into 1-cm / ½-inch slices, then into uniform dice
3 tbsp olive oil
30 g / 1 oz butter
1 garlic clove, peeled, smashed and chopped
salt and pepper
2 tbsp chopped flat-leaved parsley
2 tbsp chopped chives

Blanch the turnip dice in rapidly boiling salted water for 3 minutes and drain.

Put the olive oil and butter in a frying pan and sauté the turnip dice with the garlic, tossing and shaking the pan until the turnips are a pale golden colour and cooked through but not a mush. Season with salt and pepper.

Stir in the herbs.

## SUGAR-ROAST TURNIPS

**SERVES 4**

450 g / 1 lb small white turnips, peeled and into neat batons about 7.5 cm / 3 inches by 2 cm / ¾ inch
2 tbsp olive oil
2 tsp caster sugar
salt and pepper

Preheat the oven to 220°C/425°F/gas 7.

Brush the turnip batons with olive oil, sprinkle with the sugar, season with salt and pepper and roast for 45 minutes, turning after 15 minutes and again 15 minutes after that.

## TURKISH BRAISED VEGETABLES

This can be served hot or at room temperature as a salad.

**SERVES 6**

450 g / 1 lb turnip
225 g / 8 oz potatoes
115 g / 8 oz onions
115 g / 4 oz celeriac
115 g / 4 oz carrots
3 garlic cloves
about 150 ml / ½ pint olive oil
2 leeks, cut across into thin slices
juice of 3–4 lemons
2 tbsp chopped dill

Cut the turnip, potato, onion, celeriac and carrot into uniform cubes about 2.5 cm / 1 inch across. Cut the garlic cloves into paper-thin slices. Keep the component elements separate.

Put a large, heavy pan over a low heat and pour in all the oil. Sweat the carrot and onion in this for 10 minutes, stirring occasionally, then add the rest of the vegetables except the leeks. Stew together, stirring from time to time, for another 15 minutes, then add the leeks for a final 5 minutes. The vegetables should not colour. Check to see that everything is just cooked, with all the elements retaining a residual bite.

Season generously and add the juice of 3 lemons. Taste, adding the juice of the fourth if you think it needs it. Transfer to a bowl and leave to cool. It benefits from resting overnight in the fridge before serving.

Return to a pan to warm through gently or allow to return to room temperature. Just before bringing to the table, stir in the chopped dill.

## VEGETABLE CRUDITÉS WITH BAGNA CAUDA

You could add other raw vegetables as you like, for example, fennel or endive for a slightly bitter emphasis, while mangetout peas and baby sweetcorn make contrastingly sweet additions.

**S E R V E S  6**
**2 red peppers**
**1 yellow pepper**
**6 carrots**
**1 head of celery**
**florets from 1 small**
**cauliflower**

**for the bagna cauda sauce:**
**12 garlic cloves, peeled**
**about 100 ml / 3½ fl oz milk**
**two 60 g / 2 oz tins of**
**anchovies, chopped**
**6 tbsp crème fraîche**
**pepper**

Deseed the peppers and cut the flesh into strips. Cut the carrots and celery into similarly sized strips.

Make the sauce: put the garlic in a pan and just cover with milk. Bring to the boil, lower the heat and simmer for 15 minutes. (If you don't cook the garlic before incorporating into the sauce it will be very pungent and indigestible. This preliminary poaching gentles it without taking away all its vigour.)

Add the anchovies to the milk and garlic. Traditionally butter is now added, but crème fraîche is nicer. Whisk together until smooth with a uniform distribution of the garlic and anchovies. Season with pepper, stir in and transfer to the bagna cauda over the night-light or candle.

Sit the bagna cauda on a large serving dish and arrange the vegetables round it for people to help themselves. Open a bottle of Barolo to let it breathe before you start making the dish.

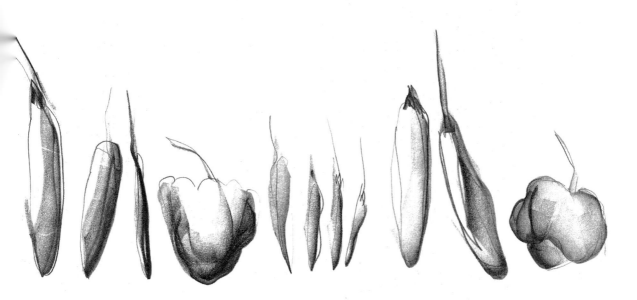

## VEGETABLE CURRY THALI

Here are three vegetable curries – a spicy potato curry, a spinach stir-fry and a lentil dish – that, when served with some plain boiled rice, combine well to make a complete vegetarian meal for 4 people.

All the dishes reheat successfully and you can always add further variety by serving an onion and tomato salad with some minted garlic yoghurt on the side and, if the fancy takes, a couple of crunchy pappadums that you buy in a packet and briefly deep-fry.

**SERVES 4**

**for the spiced lentils:**
225 g / 8 oz red lentils
2 bay leaves
1 cinnamon stick
1 onion, chopped
3 tbsp sunflower oil
2 green chillies, chopped
3 garlic cloves, chopped
2 tsp ground black pepper
2 tsp mustard seeds
2 tsp asafoetida
salt

**for the spicy potato curry:**
3 tbsp oil
450 g / 1 lb potatoes, cut into
2-cm / ¾-inch dice
1 large onion, sliced
2 garlic cloves, peeled, smashed
and chopped
4 tsp coriander seeds
3 tsp cumin seeds
1 tsp fennel seeds
½ tsp cardamom seeds
2 tsp turmeric
1 tsp salt

**for the spinach stir-fry:**
3 tbsp oil
3-cm / 1¼-inch piece of peeled
root ginger, cut into strips
3 garlic cloves, thinly sliced
2 tsp ground fenugreek
450 g / 1 lb spinach
fresh coriander leaves, to serve

Start by making the spiced lentils: put the red lentils in a pan with the bay leaves and cinnamon stick. Cover by 3 cm / 1¼ inches with cold water, then bring to the boil. Reduce the heat and simmer for 20–30 minutes, until the lentils turn yellow and start to mush.

Meanwhile, fry the chopped onion in the sunflower oil until soft and translucent. Add the chopped chillies, garlic, pepper, mustard seeds and asafoetida. Fry briskly until the seeds start to pop and jump, then scrape into the lentils. Stir in, taste, season with salt and keep warm.

Make the spicy potato curry: heat the oil in a large frying pan over a moderate heat. Put the potatoes and onions in the pan to fry, tossing and stirring until done, then add the garlic.

Meanwhile, in another dry frying pan, toast the coriander, cumin, fennel and cardamom seeds in a dry pan over a low heat.

Grind to a powder and add, with the turmeric and salt, to the potato mixture. Keep warm.

Make the spinach stir-fry: put the oil into a pan and, when smoking-hot, add the ginger, garlic and fenugreek. Immediately add the spinach and stir and toss until it wilts.

Serve all three dishes together, as soon as the spinach is ready, with some fresh coriander leaves.

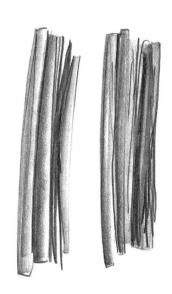

## COOKING POTATOES

Potatoes are woven so hard into the tapestry of our eating that it is difficult to imagine a diet without them. The odd thing is that, despite the fact that most of us eat potatoes in one form or another every day of our lives, we still tend to think of them as the bland vegetable which accompanies the main ingredient.

As many of the recipes that follow demonstrate, however, the humble potato can often play a starring role.

## ALIGOT

*Aligot* is one of those very basic foods which arouses great passion and disagreement over its precise composition. Richard Olney describes such dishes as '...rustic cooking which necessarily embodies complicated aspects, one of its roles being essentially alchemical – the magical transformation of poor or vulgar elements into something transcendental'. Quite.

Basically *aligot* is mashed potatoes beaten over a low heat with first butter, then crème fraîche and finally grated Cantal, a hard cheese from the centre of France that has similarities to Cheddar – which can happily substitute for it. The dish is characterized by its ribbon-like consistency.

**SERVES 4**
**1 kg / 2¼ lb floury potatoes, chopped into chunks**
**salt and pepper**
**60 g / 2 oz butter**
**300 ml / ½ pt crème fraîche**
**350 g / 12 oz Cantal or farmhouse Cheddar, grated**

Cook the potatoes in boiling salted water for 15–20 minutes, or until done in the middle. Drain. Return to the hot pan and mash.

Add the butter and beat this in thoroughly over a low heat with a wooden spoon. Then add the crème fraîche, continuing to beat and turn, until smoothly amalgamated.

Finally, add the grated cheese, beating until the mixture forms ribbons. Season generously with pepper, only adding salt to taste, and serve immediately.

## CLAPSHOT

Clapshot is a very Scottish combination of mashed potatoes and swede, and is traditionally served with haggis. Just to confuse Sassenachs, the Scots call swedes 'turnips', or 'baigie' or 'neeps'.

**SERVES 4**
**550 g / 1¼ lb potatoes, cut into large chunks**
**350 g / 12 oz swede, cut into large chunks**
**60 g / 2 oz butter**
**salt and pepper**
**a little grated nutmeg (optional)**

Cook the potatoes and swede in separate pans of boiling salted water until just done. Drain and return to their respective pans.

Mash the potatoes dry until very smooth, but mash the swede to leave small pieces. Beat these into the potato with the butter and season with salt and pepper. A little grated nutmeg is also nice, if a somewhat effete touch at a Burns Supper.

## LATKES

Latkes are traditionally fried in *schmaltz* – the Jewish term for rendered chicken fat. This might not be what you would be served in an orthodox Jewish home but, if anybody gets difficult about their authenticity, just call them potato cakes. They are great with smoked salmon and scrambled eggs, or simply with a fried egg. You will find matzo meal in the kosher section of any supermarket.

**MAKES 8 SMALL CAKES**
**2 eggs**
**125 ml / 4 fl oz milk**
**4 heaped tbsp matzo meal**
**115 g / 4 oz onion, finely diced**
**salt and pepper**
**550 g / 1¼ lb potatoes**
**4 tbsp sunflower oil**

Either use 2 pans or cook in batches, keeping the first warm in the oven.

In a mixing bowl, whisk the eggs with the milk. Whisk in the matzo meal and stir in the diced onion. Season.

Remove any eyes or dirt patches from the potatoes, but don't peel them. Grate them in a food processor using the finer of the two grating discs. Put into a drying-up cloth and squeeze dry. Stir into the contents of the bowl.

Heat 1 or 2 large non-stick pan(s) over a low heat. When hot, turn up the heat and add half the oil. Spoon the mixture into the pan(s) to make 8 cakes with a diameter of about 5 cm / 2 inches. Turn down the heat and cook slowly for 6–8 minutes, when the underside will be crisp and golden. Add the remaining oil, turn the cakes and cook for 3–4 minutes on the other side.

187

## PAN HAGGERTY

Pan haggerty sits somewhere between a French gratin and a Welsh onion cake, being a layered dish of potatoes, cheese and onion, cooked on the hob in a frying pan. It is properly made with beef dripping, but can also be made with butter, lard or goose fat – or, for a distinctly Mediterranean slant, with olive oil, in which case call it something else to avoid recriminations from purists.

SERVES 4

550 g / 1¼ lb potatoes
60 g / 2 oz fat of choice (see above)
285 g / 10 oz onions, sliced
140 g / 5 oz Cheddar cheese, grated
salt and pepper

Peel the potatoes and slice them as thinly as you can, ideally on a mandolin grater. Soak in cold water for 10 minutes, drain and dry with a cloth. (This is not, strictly speaking, essential but will help prevent exuded starch from causing the potatoes to stick to the pan.)

Put a 23-cm / 9-inch frying pan over a low heat and melt your chosen fat. Remove the pan from the heat and cover the base with a layer of overlapping potato slices. Season with salt and pepper, then put on a layer of onion, then one of cheese, repeating the layers until all the ingredients are used up and finishing with a layer of potatoes. Brush this top layer with melted fat.

Return to a low heat for 20–25 minutes, turning the pan at regular intervals to ensure an even heat distribution.

Transfer the pan to under a grill, also set to a low temperature, for about 10 minutes. Turn the grill to maximum briefly and, as soon as the potatoes are a uniform golden brown, transfer back to the hob over a high heat for a minute.

Slide the haggerty out on a cutting board and slice into wedges like a tart. Serve while still very hot.

## POTATO AND GARLIC WON-TON RAVIOLI

If you do not have a pasta machine, or find yourself pressed for time, some Italian delis sell sheets of pasta. You can, however, make very good ravioli by substituting Chinese won-ton wrappers. The fillings do not have to be remotely Oriental, as in this recipe adapted from Deborah Madison's *The Savory Way*, one of three vegetarian cookbooks based on the food served at Green's restaurant in San Francisco. These won-ton ravioli are stuffed with a potato-and-garlic purée and are served with a béchamel sauce.

SERVES 4

450 g / 1 lb potatoes, peeled
6 garlic cloves, coarsely chopped
3 tbsp chopped parsley
30 g / 1 oz unsalted butter
32 won-ton wrappers, 7.5 cm / 3 inch square

flour, for dusting
a little freshly grated
Parmesan cheese
chives or basil leaves, to
garnish

for the béchamel sauce:
30 g / 1 oz butter
30 g / 1 oz flour
freshly grated nutmeg
salt and pepper
850 ml / 1½ pt milk

Make a béchamel sauce: melt the butter in a heavy pan over a gentle heat, stir in the flour and cook gently, stirring, for a minute. Stir in the milk, bring to a simmer and cook, stirring until thick and smooth. Simmer gently.

Meanwhile, cook the potatoes in boiling salted water for 10 minutes, then add the chopped garlic and continue cooking until the potatoes are done. Drain and return to the hot pan to dry off.

Mash dry until smooth, then add the chopped parsley and butter, beating it to a smooth purée. Keep warm.

Season the béchamel sauce with nutmeg, salt and pepper and leave over the lowest heat, stirring from time to time, while you make the ravioli.

Put a big pan of salted water to come to the boil. While it heats, put 2–3 teaspoons of the potato purée in the middle of 16 of the won-ton wrappers. Brush the edges lightly with water, then place a second wrapper on top. Press the edges together with your fingers, then use a crimping wheel to seal. If you do not have one, use the back of a teaspoon, working your way all around

and pushing down hard. Put the ravioli on a lightly floured tray as you go along.

Poach the finished ravioli in the simmering water. They are done when they float to the surface, about 3–5 minutes. Remove with a slotted spoon and drop them into the béchamel sauce, turning them gently to coat.

Put 4 ravioli in each of 4 warmed bowls, dust with freshly grated Parmesan and either snip some chives over or tear a couple of basil leaves to scatter over the top.

---

### DEEP-FRIED WON-TON WRAPPERS
*These make an unusual alternative to potato crisps. Simply deep-fry a few at a time and drain on kitchen paper as soon as they puff up. Sprinkle with salt and paprika or a little grated Parmesan and chilli flakes.*

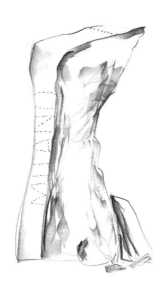

## SAVOYARDE POTATOES

Savoyarde is a variation on the gratin theme, in which thinly sliced potatoes are baked in cream. Savoyarde is distinguished by being cooked with chicken or veal stock, flavoured with garlic and enriched with Gruyère.

This dish can be the main feature of a single-course lunch or supper, served with some cold ham, bacon or fried eggs.

SERVES 4
900 g / 2 lb potatoes
salt and pepper
1 tsp freshly grated nutmeg
3 garlic cloves, smashed, peeled and finely chopped
115 g / 4 oz Gruyère cheese, grated
butter, for greasing and dotting
about 450 ml / ¼ pt chicken or veal stock

Preheat the oven to 190°C/375°F/ gas 5 and generously butter a shallow gratin dish. Peel the potatoes and cut them across into 5-mm / ¼-inch slices. Put them in a bowl and season with salt, pepper and nutmeg. Stir the garlic into the potatoes, add the grated Gruyére and toss to coat.

Pack the sliced potatoes into the buttered gratin dish and pour over just enough of the stock to cover the surface. Dot the top with butter and bake for 45 minutes, when all the ingredients will have amalgamated into a glorious, golden bubbling gratin. Take it to the table for people to help themselves.

## LYONNAISE POTATOES

*Pommes de terre Lyonnaise* is a classic French treatment of sautéed sliced potatoes and onions. People often make the mistake of cooking it at too high a temperature, resulting in the outside being excessively browned before the centre is properly cooked; they also fry the potatoes and onions together, when they should be done separately and only combined just before serving.

You can use olive oil, duck or goose fat or lard as a cooking medium; or if you prefer, you could even use equal parts olive oil and sunflower oil – it really depends on the depth and style of flavour you want to achieve. These potatoes are good with any grilled meat or with bacon and eggs or an omelette.

**SERVES 4**

**450 g / 1 lb onions**
**about 85 g / 3 oz fat of choice**
**(see above)**
**675 g / 1½ lb floury potatoes**
**chopped parsley, to garnish**

Slice the onions into thin rings and fry gently over a low heat in your chosen fat. Stir from time to time, until golden brown but not crisp. Reserve.

While the onions are cooking, put a pan of salted water to boil. Peel the potatoes and cut them across into 2-cm / ³⁄₄-inch slices. Blanch these for 3–4 minutes, then drain.

Fry the potatoes in your chosen fat, again very slowly over a low heat. You want just to film the base of the pan, or pans, and do not touch the potatoes for at least 10 minutes, when they will have formed a crisp base. Move them too soon and the surface will break. When you turn them, add more fat as needed. They will take up to 30 minutes over a low heat and for this amount you will probably need to use 2 frying pans, because the potatoes should not be touching.

When the potatoes are crisp and golden on both sides, stir in the cooked onions, turn up the heat and sauté for 2 minutes to heat the onions through.

Serve immediately, scattered with chopped parsley.

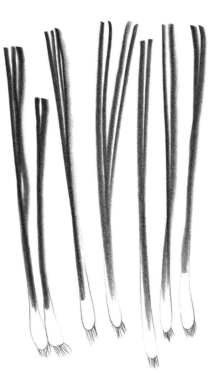

## POMMES SOUFFLÉS

These are essentially thick-cut crisps, where the outer layer separates from the inner core to give a puffed effect. Even the most skilled and practised cook will experience a high failure rate with these, but then the freshly made thick crisps are delicious anyway, so it does not matter too much. Use large, floury potatoes – Maris Piper are widely available and as good as any for the job.

**SERVES 4**

**about 675 g / 1½ lb floury**
**potatoes**
**vegetable oil, for deep-frying**
**salt**

Slice the potatoes on a mandolin to a thickness of slight less than 5 mm / ¹⁄₄ inch. Trim the slices into ovals and immerse them in very cold water. Drain and rinse under cold running water, then dry thoroughly in a towel.

Heat oil for deep-frying to 160°C/ 325°F. Cook the potatoes in batches until soft, but don't allow them to colour.

Increase the temperature to 180°C/ 350°F and give them a second frying, until they just begin to brown.

Increase the temperature to 190°C/ 375°F. Return the potatoes to the oil, a few at a time, and, with a bit of luck, they will puff up into crisp pillows.

Drain on kitchen paper, season with salt and serve immediately.

## RÖSTI

Despite indications to the contrary on Loyd Grossman's Sunday Morster-Bate, rösti is a potato dish... period... and the secret of this delicious but calorific Swiss treatment for potatoes is lots of clarified butter, that is butter which has been heated to extract the residual milk solids.

**SERVES 6**

**1 kg / 2 lb 2 oz floury potatoes**
**170 g / 6 oz clarified butter**
**salt and pepper**

Preheat the oven to 220°C/425°F/gas 7. Boil the potatoes in their skins for 15 minutes. Run them under cold water until they are cool enough to handle and then peel them.

Grate the potatoes coarsely into a bowl and pour over the clarified butter. Season with salt and pepper, then turn with a spoon to coat.

Pack the potato mixture into a 23-cm / 9-inch metal-handled frying pan or shallow ovenproof dish with curved sides. Bake until crisp and brown on top, about 25–30 minutes.

Remove from the oven, run a palette knife round the edge to loosen, invert a plate on top and turn upside down to turn out on the plate to serve.

## OATMEAL POTATOES

Oatmeal fries well and makes a nice crunchy counterpoint to plain boiled potatoes. Serve these potatoes with any grilled or pan-fried fish.

**SERVES 6**

**900 g / 2 lb even-sized medium**
**potatoes**
**about 60 g / 2 oz butter**
**about 60 g / 2 oz oatmeal**
**1 tsp salt**
**½ tsp pepper**

Peel the potatoes. There is no need to turn them, restaurant-style, but trim them to a roughly uniform shape, then cook in lots of rapidly boiling unsalted water.

When they are nearly done, which will take about 20 minutes, melt the butter over a low heat and fry the oatmeal in it with the salt and pepper, stirring, for about 5 minutes or until golden brown.

Drain the potatoes, return them to the pan and shake over a low heat until all residual water has evaporated. Add the buttery oatmeal and shake and toss gently to coat. Serve at once.

## SAUTÉ POTATOES

**SERVES 6**

**900 g / 2 lb floury baking-type**
**potatoes, peeled and cut across**
**into slices 1 cm / ½ inch thick**
**salt**
**about 3 tbsp of olive oil**
**about 3 tbsp sunflower oil**
**flat-leaved parsley, to garnish**

Parboil the potatoes for 5 minutes in rapidly boiling salted water, then drain through a colander.

Over a low heat and in a heavy frying pan large enough to hold the potato slices in a single layer, put the olive oil and sunflower oil. It is important to cook the potatoes slowly so that when the outside is golden-brown and crisp, the inside will be floury and cooked all the way through. Too high a heat will lead to burning the outside while the middle is still raw. Once the oil is hot but not smoking, carefully lay your potatoes in with a little space between each. If they touch too closely there is a risk of steam playing an unwanted part. Leave them for at least 10 minutes before turning them for the first time. This allows a crust to form. Many people make the mistake of pushing the slices around before this has happened, causing the surface to break and the potatoes to stick.

Turn the potato slices over. If all the oil has been absorbed when you turn them, add a little more. The base of the pan should be filmed at all times but not swimming in fat. After another 10 minutes turn again and finally give them 5 minutes on each side. Depending on the temperature and the extent of parboiling, the total cooking time in the pan will be between 20 and 30 minutes.

Turn out to drain on kitchen paper, sprinkle with a little sea salt and flat-leaved parsley to serve. Bon appetit!

## POTATO CAKE CHEZ L'AMI LOUIS

The late Antoine Magnin became identified with this potato cake, served daily at L'Ami Louis, his Paris restaurant. It owes its flavour to goose or duck fat, in which sliced potatoes are first fried then baked until crusty on the outside and moist and succulent within. As a cooking medium you can use goose fat, beef dripping, or a mixture of dripping and olive oil, or good-quality lard and olive oil in equal proportions. Serve the potato cake with any roast meat.

**SERVES 6**

**900g / 2 lb potatoes, peeled and sliced**
**fat of choice (see above), for frying**
**4–6 tbsp melted butter**
**salt and pepper**
**2 garlic cloves, chopped**
**handful of flat-leaved parsley**

Preheat the oven to 200°C/400°F/ gas 6. Fry the potatoes in a heavy pan with the fat of choice over a medium heat, tossing and shaking until they are just starting to brown. This takes about 20 minutes.

Brush a 23-cm / 9-inch pan with butter, then season the partially cooked potatoes with salt and pepper and transfer them to the pan, pressing down gently with a spatula. Brush the top with more melted butter and put to bake in the preheated oven for 20–30 minutes, until the surface is golden brown.

Mix the garlic and parsley. Unmould the cake by placing a plate upside down on top of the pan then inverting them together. Strew the garlic and parsley mixture over the top and serve piping hot.

## POMMES PARISIENNES (PARISIAN POTATOES)

For this you need one of those metal vegetable scoop things that people used to use for making melon balls. Peel the potatoes and cut out as many balls as you think appropriate.

**SERVES 6**

**900 g / 2 lb waxy potatoes**
**salt and pepper**
**85 g / 3 oz butter**

Cut the potatoes into balls as described above. Blanch these balls in rapidly boiling salted water for 4–5 minutes, then drain through a colander.

Melt the butter in a big frying pan and fry the potato balls in this over a low to moderate heat, tossing and turning them constantly until they are brown all over.

Season with salt and pepper and serve immediately.

*Opposite: Home-dried Tomato Tart with some Home-dried Tomatoes (page 183)*

## STOVIES

Stovies, short for 'stoved potatoes' in Scotland and the North East, were – and probably still are – a way of making the most of leftovers. Stoved potatoes can be as basic as potatoes stewed with some of the gravy and dripping left over from the Sunday roast, or a grander affair with pieces of beef and onions, bringing it closer to a cottage pie. Stoving is also a good technique for new potatoes.

There are many variations on this theme: peeled large potatoes can be cooked with beef dripping or lard and garlic. Diced leftover meat can be added, or lardons of bacon, ham or salt pork. Scattering on lots of parsley as you serve it might not be traditional, but will give it a nice fresh touch.

S E R V E S  4
**900 g / 2 lb new potatoes**
**1 onion, sliced**
**3 tbsp chicken or beef stock**
**60 g / 2 oz butter**
**salt and pepper**

If the potatoes have formed a skin, peel them. Put the potatoes into a large shallow pan in which they will sit in a single layer. Scatter the onion on top. Add the stock and butter, then season. Put on a lid, which must be tight-fitting so steam does not escape and the liquid evaporate – if this happens they will burn.

Cook over the lowest possible heat for 30–40 minutes, resisting the temptation to remove the lid to check on progress.

*Opposite (clockwise from the left): Colcannon (page 196), Stovies, Rösti (page191)*

## HASH BROWNS

A lot of American recipes for this classic use diced potatoes, but grated are better. The type of potato does not really matter. An American diner would almost certainly cook hash browns in bacon fat, which gives them their distinctive flavour; however, butter or an oil-and-butter mixture work well.

S E R V E S  4
**675 g / 1½ lb potatoes**
**60 g / 2 oz butter**
**2 tbsp sunflower oil**
**salt and pepper**

Peel the potatoes and coarsely grate them into a bowl of cold water to remove excess starch, then spin them dry in a salad spinner or press in a colander to squeeze out as much liquid as you can before spreading on a cloth. The drier you can get them, the better.

Melt the butter with the oil in a heavy frying pan. Distribute the grated potato in an even layer and press down hard with a metal spatula to compress it into a cake. Season with salt and pepper and cover. Lower the heat and cook gently for 15 minutes.

Remove the lid, raise the heat to medium and fry for a further 5 minutes.

Slide the spatula under the potato mass making sure it has not stuck. If you feel bullish about the whole thing, flip the cake over and cook the top for 5 minutes to crisp and brown. If a more wimpish mood holds sway, put a warmed plate upside down on the top and turn out the cake on it, browned base upwards.

Cut into wedges to serve.

## BUBBLE AND SQUEAK

While bubble and squeak is usually made from leftovers, it is much nicer if you cook both potatoes and cabbage fresh. Use a Savoy-type cabbage, not a hard round one, and don't overcook it. Frying in beef dripping gives a better flavour – and goose fat is best of all.

S E R V E S  4
**800 g / 1¾ lb potato**
**400 g / 14 oz cabbage**
**salt and pepper**
**freshly grated nutmeg**
**about 5 tbsp oil or fat of choice**
**(see above)**

Cook the potatoes in rapidly boiling salted water until tender. Drain well.

At the same time, cut out the big stalks from the cabbage, shred the leaves and blanch for 2–3 minutes in rapidly boiling salted water. Refresh in cold water and drain thoroughly, squeezing out all the moisture you can.

Mash the potatoes dry and mix the cabbage in while the mash is still warm, seasoning with salt and pepper. Grated nutmeg, if unorthodox, makes an improving addition.

Heat 4 tablespoons of the oil or fat in a frying pan over a low to moderate heat. Put in the mixture and flatten to a cake. Cook over a low heat until a crust forms on the bottom, about 10 minutes.

Break it up with a spatula, mix and press down again. Cook for another 10 minutes. Preheat a hot grill.

Brush the surface with a little more fat or oil and put under the grill to brown the top. Slide out on to a board and cut into wedges to serve.

## DAUPHINOISE POTATOES

*Gratin Dauphinois* – layered sliced potatoes baked in cream – needs neither
flour nor cheese in its composition.

**SERVES 6**
**butter, for greasing**
**600 ml / 1 pt double cream**
**150 ml / ¼ pt milk**
**1 garlic clove, finely chopped**
**900 g / 2 lb potatoes, peeled and**
**sliced**
**salt and pepper**
**freshly grated nutmeg**

Preheat the oven to 150°C/300°F/
gas 2 and butter a 3.5–5-cm /1½–2-
inch deep gratin dish.

In a saucepan, gently heat the cream
and milk with the garlic.

Put the potatoes in a bowl, season
with salt, pepper and nutmeg, pour over
the cream mixture and turn with a
spoon to coat evenly.

Transfer to the gratin dish, pack
down with the spoon and bake for
about 1 hour.

If the surface is not golden brown
after this time, remove from the oven
and finish under a preheated hot grill.

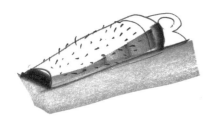

## ROAST POTATOES

A roast potato is a simple thing, but
being simple and getting something
perfect is not necessarily easy. 'Simple'
does not mean taking shortcuts or being
tricky. A half-and-half mix of goose fat
and sunflower oil is lovely as a cooking
medium; or try olive oil and sunflower
oil, or beef dripping and sunflower oil;
or just beef dripping. Roast potatoes are
forgiving: you can do them at a higher
temperature for less time, or lower the
temperature for a longer period then
raise it for a final crisping. The thing is
to keep turning them. The effort will be
worthwhile.

**SERVES 4**
**salt**
**about 900 g / 2 lb large baking**
**potatoes, cut into roughly**
**5-cm / 2-inch cubes**
**about 5 tbsp fat of choice (see**
**above)**
**salt and pepper**

Put lots of salted water to boil and preheat the oven to 220°C/425°F/ gas 7.
Parboil the potatoes in the rapidly boiling water for 6–8 minutes and then
drain in a colander.

While they are boiling, put a roasting tin into the oven to heat with
enough fat in it to give you a depth of
1 cm / ½ inch. When the fat is shimmering hot, tip in the drained potatoes
and turn to coat.

Put in the oven and roast for 15 minutes, remove and turn the potatoes,
then put them back with the oven setting reduced to 200°C/400°F/gas 6 for
another 15 minutes.

Remove and turn again, season with
salt and pepper and give them another
15 minutes. Repeat this process twice
more, giving a total cooking time of
about 1¼ hours.

## POTATO PANCAKES

Potato pancakes are very good with
smoked salmon and scrambled eggs, or
with bacon and a fried egg. There are
lots of different ways of making them,
with richer versions containing cream
as well as eggs. The amount of eggs
varies too.

The best thing to cook them in is a
blini pan, because this will give you a
perfect round thick cake, but you can
get excellent results with an omelette or
crêpe pan, particularly if you use plenty
of egg whites in the mix as these will
cause the pancakes to rise well.

If you have leftover mashed potatoes
then they will form the basis of
perfectly good parmentier batter.

**MAKES 4 SUBSTANTIAL**
**PANCAKES**
**450 g / 1 lb potatoes**
**60 g / 2 oz flour**
**125 ml / 4 fl oz milk**
**2 eggs, plus whites of 3 extra**
**eggs**
**salt and pepper**
**freshly grated nutmeg**
**sunflower oil, for frying**

Preheat the oven to 150°C/300°F/
gas 2. Cook the potatoes in boiling
salted water, drain and then mash them
dry. Beat in the flour.

In a bowl, whisk the milk with the
eggs and extra whites. Beat this into the

potato to form a thick smooth batter. Season with salt, pepper and nutmeg, then leave the batter to stand for about 10 minutes.

Heat your pan to smoking-hot, then film the base with sunflower oil, wiping out any excess with a paper towel. Pour in one-quarter of the batter and turn down the heat slightly. Cook for about 3 minutes, lifting gently with a spatula to check that it is nicely browned underneath before turning and cooking the other side.

Transfer them to to a warmed plate in the low oven while you cook the rest of the pancakes, wiping the pan with oiled paper for each.

## POTATO PURÉE OR PERFECT MASH

People wonder what the difference is between a potato purée and mashed potatoes. They are, in fact, the same thing, though the quality of the end-result will depend on the type of potatoes used, the method of mashing and the exact amount of butter incorporated.

Never use a food processor, as the blade whizzing at such high speed extracts the starch from the potato molecules, delivering something you could possibly use to hang wallpaper but nothing you would ever likely want to eat.

An electric whisk delivers good results, or you can put the potatoes through a potato ricer or push them through a sieve before adding the emollient elements of butter, olive oil or cream to finish the purée. An old-style potato masher still does the job best.

Potatoes which are good for baking are equally good for mashing and how light a purée you achieve will depend in part on the kind of potatoes you use. Perversely, potatoes described as 'for baking' will often be the most floury and deliver the best results when boiled and mashed. At last, more varieties are available in supermarkets, so experiment and find the type which works best for you. Maris Piper and Golden Wonder are both good and are available all year round.

SERVES 6
1 kg / 2¼ lb floury potatoes
about 100 ml / 3½ fl oz full-fat milk
85–115 g / 3–4 oz butter
salt and pepper
2 tbsp coarsely chopped flat-leaved parsley (optional)

Peel the potatoes and cut them into uniform chunks, then boil in lots of lightly salted water until just done, about 20 minutes. Drain through a colander and return to the pan, shaking over a low heat to evaporate all moisture.

Mash the potatoes dry, then add the milk, beating it in with a wooden spoon. Next add the butter and beat it in. The amount used really depends on how creamy you like your mash. Taste and season with salt and pepper.

Optionally, stir in some chopped flat-leaved parsley before serving.

## GARLIC MASHED POTATOES

You can either boil your potatoes while the garlic is in the oven, or bake them at the same time. Baked potatoes make beautifully floury mashed potatoes and you also then have the added bonus of the skins, which children love to eat deep-fried with sour cream or blue cheese dressing. (Adults who are not counting calories like eating them the same way too).

SERVES 4 GENEROUSLY
1 kg / 2¼ lb potatoes
1 whole head of garlic
salt and pepper
60 g / 2 oz butter

Preheat the oven to 200°C/400°F/gas 6. Bake the potatoes for about 1 hour until cooked.

While the potatoes are in the oven, saw the top off the whole head of garlic, then wrap the garlic head in a double thickness of foil and bake the parcel in the oven with the potatoes for the last 30 minutes.

When the potatoes are cool enough to handle, cut them in half, scoop out the flesh and push it through a potato ricer into a bowl or mash the flesh dry with a potato masher, seasoning it with salt and pepper to taste.

When the mashed potatoes are smooth, open the foil packet at the top and squeeze out the garlic, which will have puréed during cooking. Beat this purée and the butter into the mashed potatoes.

The result is quite good enough to eat on its own, but it also make a great accompaniment to roast meat

## POTATO GNOCCHI

SERVES 6
1 kg / 2¼ lb floury potatoes
salt and pepper
200 g / 7 oz self-raising flour,
plus more for dusting
white of 1 egg
freshly grated nutmeg
large knob of butter
30 g / 1 oz freshly grated
Parmesan cheese

Peel the potatoes and cut them into uniform chunks, then boil them in lots of lightly salted water until just done, about 20 minutes. Drain through a colander and return to the pan, shaking over a low heat to drive off all moisture. Be careful not to burn them. Mash thoroughly. Taste and add more salt if necessary.

Put on a large pan of salted water to boil for the gnocchi. Beat the self-raising flour and egg white into the mashed potato, then season with freshly grated nutmeg and pepper. You should have an elastic, malleable dough. Turn it t out on a floured surface and divide it into 4, rolling each into a long sausage shape with a diameter of about 2 cm / ³/₄ inch. Cut off pieces of dough about the same length and if you are feeling authentic, run them down the tines of a large fork to produce ribbed shapes.

Preheat the grill. Cook the gnocchi immediately in the rapidly boiling salted water. They deteriorate quickly when left sitting around and will discolour with oxidization. They float to the surface when done, but to be sure to leave them on the surface for about 20–30 seconds before scooping them out, draining them well and transferring them to a warmed flameproof dish.

Dot with butter and scatter with freshly grated Parmesan and flash under the grill for a minute or so until nicely browned, or serve with a tomato sauce or pesto.

## COLCANNON

Colcannon, while made from mashed potato and blanched greens, is not – as many on this side of the water believe – the same thing as bubble and squeak, since it is not fried. In Ireland it is traditionally a Friday fast day dish.

For an authentic Irish treatment, mash some peeled boiled potatoes until smooth with a little milk, seasoning with salt and pepper. Beat in an equal amount of chopped, just-cooked greens (some say it should properly be made with curly kale, not cabbage) and mound the mixture on a plate. Push down with a spoon to create a depression in the middle and fill this with melted butter.

Four people who wrote to us on the subject insisted it contains raw diced onion, while three others said that parsley is vital. Two different correspondents said colcannon should be turned out on a serving plate in the middle of the table and melted butter poured into a well in the centre. People eat from the outside in, dipping their forkfuls into the butter. What happens as diners cross forks over who gets the buttery centre piece is not recorded.

## STRAW POTATO CAKE

For whatever reason, Lyons has more culinary specialities associated with it than any other French city. These include charcuterie, Lyonnaise potatoes, which are shallow-fried and mixed with fried onions, and the potato dish called *pommes paillasson* – straw potato cake.

SERVES 4–6
900 g / 2 lb baking potatoes
60 g / 2 oz unsalted butter
salt and pepper
115 g / 4 oz butter

Peel the potatoes and put them through a rotary food-mill fitted with a shredding disc or use the designated disc on your food processor to produce the longest strings you can. Rinse them in cold water, drain through a colander, roll up in a tea towel and squeeze gently to get them as dry and starch-free as possible.

In a large, and preferably shallow, frying pan set over a low heat, melt 60 g / 2 oz of the unsalted butter, brushing to coat the sides. Season generously with salt and pepper, then pack the potato strings into the pan, pressing them down with a spatula to form a coherent mass, ideally domed in the middle because as it cooks down and moisture evaporates, this is where it will sink and you want to finish with as flat a top as possible. Season lightly.

Dice 30 g / 1 oz of the remaining butter and dot it evenly round the edge. As it melts and trickles down this help prevent burning. Put on a lid and cool for 20–25 minutes, keeping the heat low and turning the pan to ensure the base cooks to a uniform crunchy brown finish. Every 5 minutes remove the lid and wipe out condensation. Shake the pan only after 20 minutes. If it has stuck, gently work a spatula round the sides, pushing it under the cake at different points until it slides easily.

Turn the potato cake out by putting a large flat plate on top of the pan and turning it and the pan upside down together.

Melt the remaining butter in the pan and slide the cake back in on the other side for another 10–15 minutes. Alternatively, dot the top with the butter and finish under a grill on a low setting.

When done, slide the potato cake on to a warmed plate and serve it cut into wedges.

## TIROLER GRÖSTL

This is a filling hash of sausage, bacon and potato, famously cooked at the Gasthaus Bodenalpe at Lech in the Tyrol.

**SERVES 4**

**500 g / 1 lb 2 oz baking potatoes**
**1 onion**
**4 tbsp sunflower oil**
**115 g / 4 oz speck (smoked fatback), cut into lardons**
**115 g / 4 oz smoked bratwurst, cut into thin slices**
**1 garlic clove, peeled and chopped**
**1 tbsp chopped fresh marjoram leaves**
**salt and pepper**
**4 tbsp chopped flat-leaved parsley**

Peel the potatoes and onion and cut both into identical thin slices.

Put the sunflower oil into a heavy frying pan and heat until hot but not smoking. Fry the speck lardons until fat begins to run, then add the potato and onion slices and the bratwurst. Sauté for 10–15 minutes, until the potatoes are nicely browned.

Add the garlic and marjoram, and season with salt and pepper. Toss and cook for a further minute. Remove from the heat and stir in the parsley. Serve at once.

## CROQUETTE POTATOES

**SERVES 6**

**1 kg / 2¼ lb potatoes, peeled**
**salt and pepper**
**freshly grated nutmeg, to taste**
**85 g / 3 oz unsalted butter**
**2 eggs, beaten, plus 4 egg yolks**
**flour for dusting**
**115 g / 4 oz fine breadcrumbs**
**oil for deep-frying**

Boil the potatoes in salted water until tender. Drain, return to the pan over a low heat and mash dry with a potato masher. Season with salt pepper and grated nutmeg to taste, then beat in the butter. Remove from the heat and beat in the egg yolks.

When the mixture is cool enough to handle, form it into 60 g / 2 oz pieces and roll these gently into cylinders on a lightly floured surface.

With the beaten eggs in one bowl and the breadcrumbs in another, coat them in egg then roll them in the crumbs. Repeat to give a double coating.

Preheat oil for deep-frying to 190°C/375°F. Deep-fry the croquettes until golden brown. drain on kitchen paper and serve immediately.

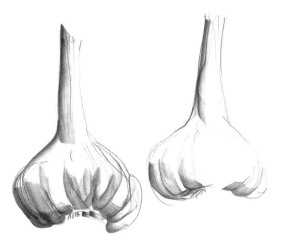

## PREPARING SALADS

The idea of a salad as a dish in its own right was first given prominence in the USA in the 1920s. Caesar salad, created by Caesar Cardini in his Tijuana hotel Is a fine example – stylish, elegant and delicious, with its contrast of sweet Cos lettuce and crunchy garlic croutons, the vinaigrette underpinned with a hint of anchovy and enriched with egg and Parmesan.

By comparison, for most of this century the British salad was a miserable affair – acid-sharp, vinegared beetroot, limp lettuce and tasteless, unripe tomatoes for too long being the order of the day. No limpid olive oil for dressing or wine vinegar for taste, our salads were grim travesties of the real thing. The wind of change was heralded by Elizabeth David in 1950 in *Mediterranean Food*, a wake-up call to the dormant sybarite to reach out and grasp the flavours of the sun.

Today our global larder offers us pristine fresh ingredients which allow us to enjoy salads all year round. A growing concern with a healthier diet has helped stimulate the popularity of salads in restaurants. Salads are no longer the dreary summer fall-back of the unthinking cook, but an opportunity to experiment and explore and to enjoy uncooked fresh ingredients at their best.

---

### TOSSING SALAD

*It seems a very obvious point, but it is much easier to coat a salad with a dressing if you toss it in a large shallow bowl.*

---

## CUCUMBER AND YOGHURT SALAD

Called *cacik* or *tsatzike*, depending what part of the Eastern Mediterranean you are in, this lovely salad can also be thinned with iced water and served as a cold soup.

**SERVES 6**

1 large cucumber
6 mint leaves, chopped, plus more whole leaves for garnish
1 large garlic clove, peeled and finely chopped
salt and pepper
600 ml / 1 pt thick plain yoghurt
paprika, to garnish

Cut the cucumber lengthwise into 1-cm / ½-inch slices, then cut these into strips and finally into dice.

Put the cucumber dice in a bowl with the chopped mint leaves and garlic. Season with salt and pepper and stir in the yoghurt. Cling-wrap and refrigerate overnight.

Just before serving, thin the mixture with a little iced water. Dust the surface with a little paprika and garnish with a few whole mint leaves.

## PURSLANE SALAD

Purslane is called *pourpier* in France and is a popular vegetable in the Middle East. Jane Grigson noted that in Malawi the local name for purslane means 'buttocks of the wife of a chief', something to bear in mind when you ask your greengrocer to stock it. With that description on the label it would walk off the shelves.

As a salad, no special treatment is needed other than a well-seasoned vinaigrette, or it can be treated as a brassica, briefly cooked in boiling salted water and eaten as a delicate alternative to spinach or Swiss chard.

## SALADE DE PISSENLITS

*Salade de pissenlits au lard* is a warm salad from Champagne in Northern France. With its strong and bitter flavours, however, it is definitely not a dish with which you would drink that most gastronomic of fine wines, champagne.

**SERVES 4**

140 g / 5 oz dandelion leaves
200 g / 7 oz new potatoes
115 g / 4 oz unsmoked streaky bacon, cut into lardon strips
3 tbsp red wine vinegar
2 tbsp Marc de Champagne
pepper

Wash the dandelion leaves and spin them dry. Boil the new potatoes until just tender. Drain, refresh in cold water and cut across into 5-mm / ¼-inch slices. Put in a salad bowl.

Fry the bacon in the olive oil until cooked but not to the point of being crisp. Put the dandelion leaves over the potatoes and strew with the lardons.

Put the red wine vinegar into the hot bacon fat and boil, stirring and reducing by half. For a final authentic touch you can add some Marc de Champagne, the rough local brandy, and bubble for 30 seconds before pouring the mixture over the salad.

Toss to coat and serve while still warm, seasoned with black pepper.

## MUSHROOM SALAD

SERVES 4

450 g / 1 lb flat-cap field
mushrooms
150 ml / ¼ pint olive oil
4 garlic cloves, finely chopped
juice and zest of 1 lemon
10 black peppercorns
1 bay leaf
sprig of thyme
3 tbsp chopped flat-leaved
parsley

Preheat a hot grill. Wipe the mushrooms clean with a damp cloth. Remove their stems and peel the caps. (Use the stalks and peelings in a stock or soup.)

Grill the mushrooms, tops down, until water exudes from the surface and fills the depression where the stalk joined the cap. Turn over and grill for a further minute. Remove, pat dry with kitchen paper and put in a glass or china serving dish.

Put the olive oil in a saucepan with 3 of the garlic cloves, the lemon juice and zest, the peppercorns, bay leaf and thyme, and heat gently for 5 minutes at a bare simmer. While still very hot, strain through a fine sieve over the mushrooms. Leave to cool. When cool, refrigerate overnight.

Just before serving, turn the mushrooms in the marinade, and scatter over the remaining garlic and the parsley. Voilà, *les champignons aux aromates*! If you do not wish to serve them the next day, these will keep in the fridge for up to 4 days, but will then start to become rather slippery.

## JAPANESE CUCUMBER SALAD

This Japanese salad is delicious in its own right, but even better with poached prawns or dressed crab. Rice vinegar and sansho, Japanese aromatic pepper, are now sold in good supermarkets.

SERVES 4

2 tbsp sesame seeds
1 cucumber
2.5-cm / 1-inch piece of ginger
3 tbsp Mitsukan or other good
rice vinegar
1 tsp dark sesame oil
4 spring onions, thinly sliced
½ tsp sugar
1 tsp salt
½ tsp sansho pepper

Put the sesame seeds in a dry frying pan and toast over a low heat, stirring until golden and aromatic. Reserve.

Cut the cucumber in half lengthwise and scrape out the seeds with a spoon. Cut each half in half through the middle and shave into long, wafer-thin strips on a mandolin, piling them into a bowl.

Peel the ginger and grate it into the bowl. Add the sesame seeds, vinegar, sesame oil, spring onions, sugar, salt and sansho pepper. Toss to coat well and chill for 30 minutes before serving.

> ### SALTING DRESSINGS
> *Salt dissolves more quickly in vinegar alone. When making a vinaigrette or other oily dressing, add salt to the vinegar or lemon juice and stir to dissolve before adding the oil.*

## RADISHES AND SALATIT FIJL

Radishes go best of all with, well, radishes. Throughout history they have been eaten in glorious isolation, usually with nothing more than a little sea salt, and are delicious as a nibble with an aperitif. Being naturally peppery, they don't need anything else to enhance their flavour. The French eat them with unsalted butter, salt and baguette, and they are equally good with thin toasted slices of sourdough bread.

In Morocco, they are successfully paired with oranges, the radishes cut into thin slices and the oranges into small segments, which are then tossed with lemon juice and a little salt.

The Lebanese *salatit fijl* is properly made from the giant white winter radish and raw diced onion but is nicer, we think, with an English radish like White Icicle mixed with spring onions.

SERVES 4

2 bunches of radishes
8 spring onions
1 tbsp lemon juice
1 tsp salt
1 garlic clove, finely chopped
4 tbsp olive oil
handful of coriander leaves

Thinly slice the radishes and cut the spring onions at an angle into pieces about 2 cm / ¾ inch long.

Put the lemon juice and salt in a salad bowl, and stir to dissolve the salt. Then add the garlic clove and stir in the olive oil. Add the radish slices and spring onions and toss to coat.

Scatter over a handful of coriander leaves and serve immediately.

## SALADE NIÇOISE

While usually included, cooked green beans would be a seasonal variation in Nice – the city from which the salad originates – as would new potatoes.

The absolutes are that this is a first course which must include lettuce, tomatoes, hard-boiled eggs, black olives and anchovies, the last two being ubiquitous in Provence. Little Gem lettuces are also not authentic, but the original recipes call for the crisp hearts of lettuce, something Little Gem duplicates nicely all year round.

You can really give the salad an upscale twist by substituting briefly grilled slices of fresh tuna loin for the canned.

In common with many other famous dishes, the quality of the ingredients used and a sense of balance in its execution will determine whether you create something memorable or a dish about which people will ask 'why all the fuss?'

SERVES 4

225 g / 8 oz of angel-hair French beans (optional)
4 eggs
4 Little Gem lettuces
350 g / 12 oz best tinned tuna in olive oil
4 ripe plum tomatoes
one 60-g / 2-oz tin of anchovy fillets, rinsed and drained
16 stoned black olives
whole flat-leaved parsley leaves
good crusty bread, to serve

for the vinaigrette:
1 tbsp red wine vinegar
4 tbsp of extra-virgin olive oil, plus more for drizzling
salt and pepper

If you are using beans, cut off the stems and blanch the beans in rapidly boiling water for 3–4 minutes, or until done to your liking. Refresh briefly in cold water.

Boil the eggs for 6 minutes and then refresh them in cold water for 3–4 minutes. Shell them and cut them into quarters.

Trim the lettuces and cut them in halves lengthwise.

Reserving the tuna, eggs and tomatoes, put all the other main ingredients except the parsley into a large bowl.

Make the vinaigrette by mixing all the ingredients, pour it over the salad and toss.

Heap the salad in equal amounts on 4 plates, then divide the tuna on top. Quarter the tomatoes and then arrange around the outside with the quartered eggs.

Drizzle over a little more olive oil, scatter over some whole flat-leaved parsley leaves and serve the salad with good crusty bread.

A decent, dry rosé is the appropriate accompaniment.

## COOKING PULSES

Pulses are the seeds of leguminous plants which develop in pods, so they include peas, beans and lentils. The word usually refers to them in their dried form. Another common characteristic is that they consist of two identical parts held together by a tough outer skin. Lose or remove this and you have, for example, split peas. The outer skin may be a different colour from the inner, split elements. Once the skin is removed, the pulse cooks more quickly, but tends to collapse to a purée. Older pulses take longer to cook and do not taste as nice.

Toxins are present in some pulses, most notably red kidney beans, but these are destroyed by rapid boiling. As a general rule, always boil them hard for the first 10 minutes, throwing away this water and replacing with fresh. This procedure is also anti-flatulent.

Britain has only recently started to wake up to the wider culinary opportunities provided by dried beans and lentils, even though our food traditions have always included pulses. Northern fish and chips would not be complete without mushy peas, and split pea soup has always been a splendid way of making the most of a piece of bacon or a ham bone. Today supermarkets offer us a huge choice, from green haricots to red and white kidney beans, sweet black beans and butter beans.

Dried beans play a more central role in other food cultures, for example that of Spain. There it is even widely understood that pulses are at their best some two to three months after the initial drying process and people are happy to pay a premium for them in the spring. French farmhouse cooking honours dried beans, perhaps most famously in the cassoulets of the South West, while Mexican food would be unthinkable without its ubiquitous *frijoles*. The brown butter bean of Egypt's *ful medames* is that country's national dish. Black-eyed beans with spinach, garlic and olive oil are a delicious way to start a Greek meal. Bean purées fragrant with garlic and parsley and dressed generously with good olive oil are delicious with lamb or as a first course in their own right served with warm pocket breads.

Lentils, too, are greatly favoured. The French *lentilles de Puy*, for example, have a beautiful green colour and a pronounced, slightly nutty flavour, while Indian cooking without lentils would be unthinkable.

## ITALIAN BEAN SALAD

About 450 g / 1 lb of dried beans, when rehydrated, will make 6 servings. Start by putting them to soak overnight in lots of cold water – at least 3 times the volume of water to beans. In the morning, drain and rinse them, then put them in a pan and cover with fresh water. Bring to the boil, skim then lower the heat and simmer, adding any flavouring ingredients, and cook until just done.

How long this takes will depend on how old the beans are, but in most cases it will take between 50 minutes and 1½ hours. Taste at 50 minutes, then every 10 minutes thereafter, until they are fully tender but not disintegrating. If overcooked, the best thing to do is to

purée them. Small black beans cook much more quickly and will take no more than 20 minutes.

Whatever kind of beans, when done remove them from the heat and leave to cool in their cooking liquor if you do not want to serve them immediately.

450 g / 1 lb dried beans
4 whole garlic cloves
1 hot chilli, split lengthwise
2 bay leaves

for the gremolata:
60 g / 2 oz flat-leaved parsley
1 garlic clove
grated zest and juice from 2 lemons
salt and pepper
extra-virgin olive oil, to dress

Soak and cook the beans as described above, adding the garlic, chilli and bay leaves as flavourings. Drain, discarding the flavouring ingredients.

Make the gremolata: chop the parsley and garlic, and mix with the grated lemon zest. Stir the gremolata into the beans, squeeze over the lemon juice, then season with salt and pepper.

Finally dress liberally with extra-virgin olive oil. The dish has fresh flavours, looks lovely and has a nice texture. It can also be served cold as a salad.

## BEAN PURÉE

If time is very pressing, use canned flageolets, but rinse them thoroughly in a sieve under cold running water before heating gently in a little water with a couple of crushed garlic cloves. Then purée as below.

SERVES 6
450 g / 1 lb white haricot beans
1 onion
1 tsp chilli flakes
5 garlic cloves
salt and pepper
2 spring onions, chopped
3–5 tbsp olive oil
3 tbsp chopped parsley or coriander leaves
chopped chives, to garnish
warm pitta breads, to serve

Put the beans to soak overnight in cold water.

Next day, bring them to the boil in fresh water. Boil briskly for 10 minutes and throw this water away, too, unless you want to introduce a flatulent note into the proceedings.

Cover with fresh water, add the onion, chilli flakes and 4 peeled whole cloves of garlic. Bring back to the boil, lower the heat and simmer until done, when the beans will crush easily. Season towards the end of the cooking and throw away the onion and garlic but retain the cooking liquid.

Put the cooked beans in a food processor with the remaining raw garlic clove, chopped, and the spring onions. Blitz to a purée. Add spoonfuls of the cooking water to achieve this and finish with 3–5 tablespoons of the olive oil and the chopped parsley or coriander leaves, adding both through the feeder tube while processing. Taste and add more salt and pepper if needed.

Serve the purée warm, sprinkled with some chopped chives and with warm pitta breads in a basket on the table.

## HUMMUS
## (CHICKPEA PURÉE)

Hummus, like its relative taramasalata, is one of the world's most abused dishes. Quite what supermarkets do to convert this simple and pure dish of chickpeas, garlic, sesame and olive oil into an offensive chemical glop is difficult to fathom. Hummus is so easy to make that a perverse and malign force must be at work, interceding to turn something innately good into something thoroughly bad.

The secret of success, as in all absolutely simple dishes, is in the ability of the cook to taste and define, for precise measurement will never deliver the goods. A little squeeze of lemon juice, then taste... now a touch more oil... this, in turn, demands some salt to balance it. Two people will start with the same ingredients and follow the same recipe, but end up with very different results.

Tahini paste (page 57), for example, can vary in its strength. If it is not to hand, you can substitute cold-pressed sesame oil; if you do, however, beware the strength of its flavour.

This recipe is, therefore, only a guide. The consistency should not be too smooth, with discernible nutty pieces of chickpeas giving texture. Properly, the olive oil is not included in the hummus, but is instead poured on the top just before the dish is taken to the table.

SERVES 6 GENEROUSLY

**450 g / 1 lb chickpeas**
**2 bay leaves**
**3 hot red chillies**
**juice of 3 lemons**
**150 ml / ¼ pt tahini paste (page 57)**
**1 tsp salt**
**1 tsp cayenne pepper**
**4 large garlic cloves, chopped**
**extra-virgin olive oil, to dress**
**little paprika, to garnish**
**chopped flat-leaved parsley, to garnish**
**warm pitta bread, to serve**

Soak the chickpeas overnight in plenty of water. Discard the water, cover with cold water and bring to the boil. Lower the heat and simmer for between 1 and 1½ hours with the bay leaves and chillies. Drain, reserving some of the water and a few whole chickpeas for garnish. Discard the bay leaves and chillies.

Put the remaining chickpeas in a food processor with the lemon juice, tahina paste, 150 ml / ¼ pt of the reserved cooking water, 1 teaspoon of salt and the cayenne pepper. Add the garlic and then blitz the mixture to a coarse purée. Add more of the cooking water if the mixture is too dry. Taste and start playing with the flavourings and seasonings as described above.

When satisfied, spread the hummus on individual plates, making circular movements to ridge the surface. Pour over a little extra-virgin olive oil. Arrange a few chickpeas on top, dust with a little paprika and garnish with chopped flat-leaved parsley. Serve with warm pitta bread.

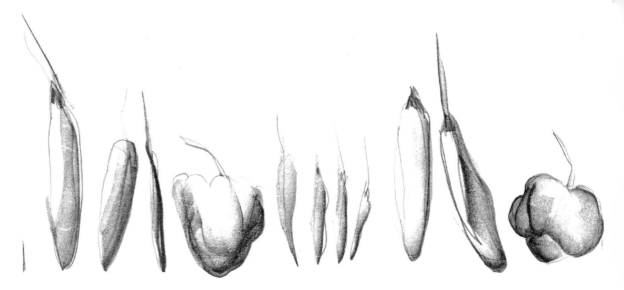

## PEASE PUDDING

Pease pudding is made from yellow or green dried split peas, onion and bacon. Dating from the Middle Ages and invariably served with salt pork. It is one of our oldest dishes and was a popular street food in the eighteenth century, when it was sold from barrows with the cry, 'Pease pudding hot, pease pudding cold, pease pudding in the pot, nine days old.' It would originally have been boiled in a cloth, but it is easier to steam it. A variation includes diced bacon in the pudding. Leftover pudding can be turned into soup by adding stock or water and a few herbs.

**SERVES 4**

**450 g / 1 lb split peas**
**bouquet garni of parsley, bay**
**leaf, mint and thyme**
**1 onion, diced**
**60 g / 2 oz of butter, plus more**
**for the pudding basin**
**salt and pepper**

Rinse the split peas in cold water, then put them in a pan with the bouquet garni and onion. Cover with water and bring to the boil. Lower the heat and simmer until the split peas are soft, about 60 minutes. Drain off the bulk of the water, if any (you need some of the cooking water for the purée).

Discard the bouquet garni, put the peas into a food processor with the butter and season with salt and pepper. Blitz to a purée or put through a mouli.

Spoon into a buttered pudding basin, pressing down. Cover with foil and steam for 1 hour.

To unmould, run a knife round edge and turn out carefully (it is quite soft).

## REFRIED BEANS

Refried beans are not really fried at all but – after cooking in water – mashed in a pan with lard. This sounds odd – not to say distinctly unhealthy – to contemporary Western ears, but a small amount of good homemade lard (page 273) delivers a wonderful flavour. In this recipe the typical Mexican amount of lard is halved, then used with an equal amount of olive oil.

**SERVES 6**

**375 g / 12 oz black or pinto**
**beans**
**2 Spanish onions**
**3 whole hot red chillies**
**2 bay leaves**
**salt and pepper**
**60 g / 2 oz lard**
**3 tbsp extra-virgin olive oil**
**crumbled feta, to serve**
**(optional)**
**corn chips, to serve (optional)**

Soak the beans in cold water overnight or for at least 4 hours. Discard any beans that float to the top.

Bring the beans to the boil in fresh water and boil hard for 5 minutes. Drain in a colander, rinse under cold running water and return to the pan.

Cover with cold water by 2.5 cm / 1 inch and bring back to the boil. Lower the heat to a gentle simmer. Add one of the onions, diced, the chillies and bay leaves. Cook for 1–2 hours until tender. The precise time will depend on how old and dry the beans were and exactly how long you soaked them.

Discard the bay leaves and chillies, then season to taste. Turn off the heat and leave in the cooking liquid for 20–30 minutes before refrying.

Over a moderate heat, melt the lard in a frying pan. Add the remaining onion, cut into thin strips, and fry, stirring, for about 5 minutes or until golden brown. Traditionally these are discarded, but don't do so; when cooked more they will go crisp and make a terrific addition to the dish, so transfer them to another pan with a slotted spoon and continue frying over a low heat, stirring from time to time.

Add the olive oil to the lard remaining in the pan, then two 300 ml / ½ pt cups of the beans with their liquid and mash with a potato masher. Gradually add another 2 cups of beans and more liquid, continuing to mash until you have a coarse moist purée. Stir over a moderate heat until this starts to dry, then transfer to a warmed serving dish.

Scatter over the crisped onions. If liked, crumble over some feta. Serve with corn chips as a dip or as a side dish.

203

## FUL MEDAMES

*Ful medames*, slow-cooked brown beans served with long-simmered *hamine* eggs, is often described as Egypt's national dish and, while today offered at both lunch and dinner, it was originally eaten for breakfast. An ancient food recorded from the time of the pharaohs, it is traditionally cooked overnight in the *damassa*, a broad-bellied clay pot, surrounded by the hot ashes of the dying charcoal or wood fires still used in many Arab kitchens.

Once the staple diet of the poor, *ful medames* has now been elevated into the realm of fashion and you will find it in Cairo's grandest hotels and restaurants, accompanied by a range of pickles, herbs and spices, the field beans providing a simple backdrop to the more pungent flavours. You should be able to find brown beans in Cypriot delis or, if in London, you can buy them from Lebanese markets in Kensington and Earls Court.

SERVES 4

500 g / 1 lb 2 oz **brown beans**
4–8 **eggs**
3 **garlic cloves, crushed and**
**finely chopped**
1 tsp **salt**
**juice of 1 lemon**
100 ml / 3½ fl oz **olive oil**
4 tbsp **coarsely chopped flat-**
**leaved parsley**

**to serve:**
**warm pitta bread**
**more olive oil**
**lemon quarters**
**pepper**

Soak the beans in plenty of water overnight.

The hard-boiled eggs need to be dealt with first, as they should be simmered for a minimum of 6 hours. Put them in a large pan of cold water with as many onion skins as you have to hand. Bring to the boil, lower the heat and simmer for 6–8 hours. A lid partially covering the top will reduce evaporation, but keep an eye on them and top up with water as needed. The interesting result of this treatment is that the eggs will emerge from their shells with the whites tinted pale brown from the natural dye of the onion skins, while the yolks will be pale yellow, the texture not hard as you would expect, but creamy.

Rinse the soaked beans, cover by 2.5 cm / 1 inch with cold water and bring to the boil. Boil hard for 5 minutes, then turn down the heat and simmer for 1–2 hours. The precise cooking time will depend on how old they are but, as you don't want to overcook them to a mush, start tasting after 1 hour.

Drain the beans and stir in the garlic and salt. Dress generously with lemon juice and olive oil and scatter the coarsely chopped flat-leaved parsley on top.

Serve in soup bowls with a peeled egg, or eggs, on top and offer warm pitta bread and more olive oil, lemon quarters, salt and pepper at the table.

> QUICK BEANS
> *Although dried beans are usually rehydrated by soaking them in cold water for 6–8 hours, you can achieve the same result more quickly. Cover the beans by 2.5 cm / 1 inch with cold water, bring to the boil and boil for 5 minutes. Turn off the heat and leave to stand for 1 hour. Drain, rinse and cover with fresh cold water. They are now ready for cooking.*

## RICE AND PEAS

Rice and peas is the ubiquitous dish of Jamaica, a national food like our fish and chips, yet its title is something of a misnomer, since the peas are actually dried red kidney beans. In Jamaica it may be eaten at any time of the day, including breakfast. For lunch or dinner, it accompanies everything from curried goat to salt fish.

SERVES 4

225 g / 8 oz **red kidney beans**
3 tbsp **sunflower or**
**groundnut oil**
3 **garlic cloves, sliced wafer-**
**thin**
2 **hot red chillies, finely**
**diced**
350 g / 12 oz **long-grain rice**
600 ml / 1 pt **coconut milk**
1 tsp **chopped fresh thyme or**
¼ tsp **dried**
**salt and pepper**
**shredded spring onion, to**
**garnish**

Soak the beans in cold water overnight.

Next day, bring to the boil and boil hard for 10 minutes, then drain, rinse and cover with fresh water by 2.5 cm / 1 inch. This is a necessary preliminary to rid red beans of the toxins they contain. Bring to the boil again, lower the heat and simmer until tender, which will take 1 to 1½ hours.

Put the oil in a large frying pan over a moderate heat. Add the garlic and chillies, and stir-fry for 1 minute. Add the rice and stir to coat for another minute.

Add to the beans with the coconut milk, thyme and salt and pepper. Stir thoroughly and bring to the boil. Put on a lid, turn down to the lowest heat and simmer gently for 20 minutes, when all the liquid should have been absorbed. If not, turn up the heat a little and evaporate any excess, stirring continuously or the rice will stick and burn.

Transfer to a warmed serving dish and garnish with shredded spring onion.

## MASOOR DAL

Red lentils, *masoor* in India, are actually pink in colour and turn yellow when cooked. Many kinds of split peas and beans are used to make dal, which can be served with lots of liquid to give a soupy consistency or have the liquid reduced to deliver a drier finish. In this version two flavouring stages are used. Fresh ginger, garlic and a bay leaf are boiled with the lentils, while the spices and onions are cooked separately and added to the dal only prior to serving.

**SERVES 4**

**170 g / 6 oz lentils**

**3 garlic cloves, smashed and chopped**

**2.5-cm / 1-inch piece of ginger, peeled and cut into fine strips**

**1 bay leaf**

**salt**

**3 tbsp sunflower oil**

**1 large onion, thinly sliced**

**2 tsp ground coriander**

**2 tsp ground cumin**

**1 tsp black mustard seeds**

**lots of fresh coriander leaves, to finish**

Start by washing the lentils in a sieve under running cold water. Put them in a pan and cover with 1.1 litres / 2 pints of cold water. Add the garlic, ginger and bay leaf. Bring to the boil, skim, lower the heat and simmer, stirring from time to time until the lentils purée. Depending on the age of the lentils, this will take from 40 to 60 minutes. At all times keep the surface covered with water, topping up if the lentils start to dry out. When you deem them to be nearly done, add some salt to taste.

Put the sunflower oil in a pan and fry the sliced onion over a moderate heat until golden brown. Add the ground coriander, ground cumin and black mustard seeds. Stir in and fry for 2 minutes.

Stir into the dal, remove the pan from the heat and put a lid on it. Leave to stand for 4 minutes, before serving with lots of fresh coriander leaves sprinkled over.

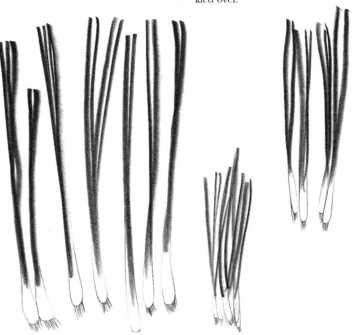

## WARM LENTIL SALAD WITH POACHED EGGS

The best lentils to use for a salad are the nutty-flavoured dark-green French *lentilles de Puy*, which are now widely available. When cooked they do not turn into a porridge. With all pulses you can calculate that 450 g / 1 lb dried, when rehydrated and cooked, will give you 6–8 portions for a first course and about 4–6 for a main course. There is never a problem having some left over. They reheat well and are as nice cold as hot and, of course, all pulses can be puréed.

SERVES 4

285 g / 10 oz green lentils
115 g / 4 oz smoked streaky bacon
4 tbsp olive oil
170 g / 6 oz onions
2 celery stalks, with their leaves
115 g / 4 oz carrot
3 tbsp red wine vinegar
1 tsp sugar
1 bay leaf
1 garlic clove
1 tbsp vinegar
4 very fresh large eggs
handful of flat-leaf parsley

for the vinaigrette:
5 tbsp extra-virgin olive oil
1 tbsp red wine vinegar
1 tbsp Dijon mustard
salt and pepper

Rinse the lentils in a sieve under cold running water and reserve.

Cut the bacon into fat matchsticks and fry gently in the olive oil until the bacon starts to brown.

Cut the onion, celery and carrot into

5 mm / ¼ in dice and stir into the pan. Sweat the vegetables until soft and translucent, stirring from time to time.

Add the lentils, stirring to coat, for 2 minutes. Turn up the heat and add the vinegar, sugar, bay leaf and finely chopped garlic. Pour over enough cold water to cover the lentils and bring back to the boil. Turn down the heat and simmer gently for 15–20 minutes.

About 10 minutes before the lentils are done, put on a wide shallow saucepan of lightly salted water to boil. Add the vinegar. You want the water just bubbling. Break the eggs on to saucers and slide them into the water, one at a time. The white will start to set at once and the eggs will be done in 90 seconds to 2 minutes. Remove carefully with a slotted spoon and put a warm plate. Trim to a neat shape with scissors.

While the water is heating, make the vinaigrette by mixing all the ingredients in a large bowl and reserve.

When cooked, turn off the heat under the lentils and remove the bay leaf. Chop half the parsley and stir into the lentils. Drain through a sieve, put into the bowl with the vinaigrette and toss. Adjust the seasoning.

Mound the lentils on 4 warmed plates. Put an egg on top of each and scatter on a few whole leaves of parsley to finish.

## GRILLED TOFU

Grilling imparts a smoky flavour to tofu, while changing the surface texture. You buy it in packs, usually of 500 g.

### SERVES 6

**about 1 kg / 2¼ lb firm tofu**
**15 g / ½ oz dried wild mushrooms**
**300 ml / ½ pt boiling water**
**300 ml / ½ pt red wine**
**150 ml / ¼ pt soy sauce**
**2 garlic cloves, chopped**
**12 black peppercorns**
**1 head of star anise**
**2 cloves**
**½ tsp salt**
**6 shiitake mushrooms, halved lengthwise**
**2 aubergines, cut into large chunks**
**3 tbsp oil**

Cut the tofu into 2.5-cm / 1-inch slices and lay these on a cake rack. Put a tray on top, weight it with 3 or 4 tins and leave for 30–45 minutes to get rid of excess water.

Put the dried wild mushrooms in a bowl, pour the boiling water over them and leave for 20 minutes to plump up.

Drain the mushrooms through a muslin-lined sieve into a pan, then rinse the mushrooms.

Add these back to the soaking liquid, together with the red wine, soy sauce, garlic, peppercorns, star anise, cloves and salt. Bring to the boil, lower the heat and simmer gently for about 15 minutes.

Arrange the tofu in a single layer in a plastic container and pour the marinade over it through a muslin-lined sieve. When cool, put on a lid and refrigerate for a minimum of about 24 hours, though it will benefit from 3–4 days.

Drain the tofu, passing the marinade through a muslin-lined sieve again. Once reboiled and strained a second time the marinade will keep in the fridge for a week and can be used again.

Thread the tofu pieces on water-soaked wooden skewers (to prevent scorching) interspersed with shiitake mushrooms and pieces of lightly oiled aubergine.

Grill on a metal plate or over a barbecue, turning frequently for about 8 minutes. The tofu will be meaty and full of flavour.

## COOKING MUSHROOMS

There is nothing in nature so reminiscent of meat as the mushroom, some types being meatier than others. Perhaps this stems from their being fungi which, having no chlorophyll to conduct photosynthesis, derive nutrients directly from organic matter.

The majority of mushrooms eaten are cultivated, and the range of types available has expanded rapidly in recent times, with supermarkets now offering oyster and shiitake mushrooms, as well as the most common flat-capped mushrooms which are sold as buttons, and flats or open mushrooms, the largest and the best flavoured. The most common wild mushrooms are *Agaricus campestris*, 'field mushrooms', which look like their cultivated cousins but have a superior flavour.

The most widely available dried wild mushrooms are called *porcini* in Italian, *cèpes* in French and ceps in English. Of these you are most likely to find *porcini* in the supermarket. They have an intense flavour, and a little goes a long way. Dried wild mushrooms available all year round include yellow chanterelle and *trompettes-des-morts*, the extravagantly shaped black 'trumpets of death', known more prosaically in English as horns of plenty.

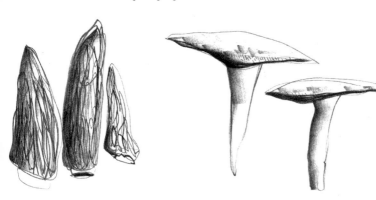

Cultivated mushrooms, particularly buttons, are not intensely flavoured. The first thing to do is to cook out some of the water and, while this can be achieved by grilling, sautéing in olive oil will give a better flavour. If the mushrooms are large, then first cut them into thick slices, but don't peel the caps – the skin has the strongest flavour.

You can enhance this further by adding a few dried wild mushrooms which you have first reconstituted in warm water for 20–30 minutes. Always put these through a sieve and rinse them carefully before use to rid them of dirt and twigs. The soaking liquid should not be thrown away, but passed through muslin and added to stocks, soups or stews.

Alternatively, towards the end of cooking stir in some chopped garlic and parsley. They are natural partners for any mushroom and will impart flavour to the most tasteless examples of the breed. Another way is to stir a little truffled olive oil into the cooked mushrooms just before serving.

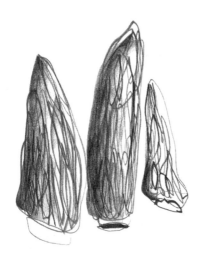

## MUSHROOM TART WITH BÉCHAMEL

Mushroom tarts are most often cooked with an egg and cream custard. A béchamel lightly flavoured with Parmesan and cooked with egg yolks to set is another appropriate setting for any mushrooms – and equally delicious.

This recipe makes the most of ordinary cultivated mushrooms, but if you use a mixture of wild mushrooms, it becomes a spectacular feast.

SERVES 6–8

**1 recipe-quantity of shortcrust pastry (p 00)**
**285 g / 10 oz mushrooms (see above)**
**30 g / 1 oz butter**
**2 garlic cloves, chopped**
**1 tbsp olive oil**

**for the béchamel sauce:**
**30 g / 1 oz butter**
**30 g / 1 oz flour**
**700 ml / 1¼ pt milk**
**2 tbsp dry sherry**
**1 bay leaf**
**salt and pepper**
**¼ nutmeg, grated**
**60 g / 2 oz Parmesan, grated**
**1 egg yolk**

Preheat the oven to 190°C/375°F/gas 5. Roll out the pastry on a floured surface and use to line a 24-cm / 9½-inch tart tin with a detachable base.

Cover with foil, weight with beans and bake blind for 10 minutes. Remove the weighted foil and continue cooking for about 5 minutes or until the pastry base starts to brown. Remove.

Make the béchamel sauce: make a roux by melting the butter in a heavy pan and stirring in the flour. Cook gently, stirring, for a minute or so. Pour over the milk, whisking, then add the sherry and bay leaf. Season with salt, pepper and nutmeg, and cook over a low heat for 20–25 minutes, stirring regularly.

Remove the bay leaf and discard. Whisk in the Parmesan.

In a bowl, whisk the egg yolk, then whisk 2 to 3 tablespoons of the sauce into them. Remove the sauce from the heat and whisk in this mixture.

While the sauce is cooking, sauté the mushrooms in the butter and oil for about 10 minutes. Add the garlic and sauté for another minute, stirring, then stir this into the sauce. Mix thoroughly and pour and spoon into the tart shell.

Put into the oven and immediately lower it to 180°C/ 350°F/gas 4 and bake for 20–25 minutes. Take out of the oven and leave to cool for 5 minutes before removing from the tin.

*Opposite (from the top): Salatit Fij (page 199), Salade Niçoise (page 200), Japanese Cucumber Salad (page 199)*

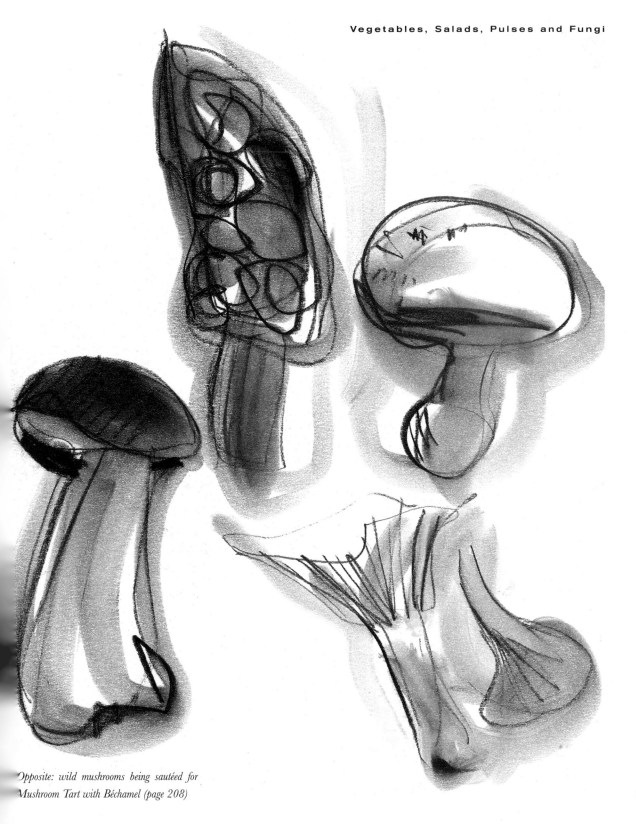

*Opposite: wild mushrooms being sautéed for*
*Mushroom Tart with Béchamel (page 208)*

# PASTA, RICE AND GRAINS

**T**ogether with pulses, pasta, rice and grains are the essentials of the dry store cupboard. They provide us with substance cheaply, their role in diet being partly one of bulk, and at the same time the textural and taste counterpoints to the fresh ingredients which often need a supporting player before they can really shine. These are ancient and modern parts of our stores. Dried foods were once essential to support people through the winter or in times of famine. Today we can make the most of them, and be grateful that they can play as many roles as our imagination permits.

More than any other ingredient of the last 30 years, pasta has become naturalized in the British diet. Once we had the choice of spaghetti – inevitably over-sauced with a bastard bolognese – and macaroni, always masked with an insipid cheese sauce. Now we have dozens of dried pastas from which to choose and a range of fresh pastas in every chill cabinet.

There is also a better understanding of how pasta should be cooked and the description al dente has entered our kitchen language. Many people have been encouraged to make pasta and have discovered that a hand-cranked machine brings it within every cook's grasp. If one misconception remains then it is that fresh pasta is somehow superior to dried. It is not, simply having a different textural quality that is more appropriate for some sauces than others. The very best dried pastas are made from durum wheat which is too hard for home pasta-making. Some pastas – for example, spaghetti and cannelloni – are only sold dried.

## MAKING BASIC PASTA DOUGH

(Also see the step-by-step sequence overleaf.) Once you get the knack of feeding the dough through the rollers you will be cranking out fresh pasta with the best of them. Seek out Italian imported double zero (00) flour or use a high-protein bread flour for best results. The basic dough given here is made very quickly in a food processor, is cheap and suitable for a wide range of uses. As it is easy to handle and dries quickly, it is particularly suitable for ravioli.

**SERVES 4**
500 g / 1 lb 2 oz flour (see above), plus more for dusting
5 eggs

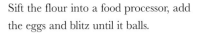

Sift the flour into a food processor, add the eggs and blitz until it balls.

Transfer to a floured surface and knead for 5 minutes, until smooth, elastic and shiny, shaking on more flour if it sticks. Cling-wrap the dough and refrigerate for 1 hour before use. You can leave it for up to 3 hours but no longer, or it will become too solid to work with (see more overleaf).

## PASTA NERO
## (BLACK PASTA)

Black pasta is made black by cuttlefish ink, a most efficient dye which works as well on clothes and teeth as it does on dough. The real thing comes from the ink sacs of the cephalopod of the genus *sepia*. Its ink was originally used to produce monochrome water-colours and gave its name to them. Seppia are the small Venetian cuttlefish used in the city's famous black risotto. Cuttlefish ink is starting to be sold in small plastic sachets; it is good as a food dye but has little flavour and is not as good as fresh cuttlefish ink. When using it to colour a risotto you need to do so in conjunction with a well-flavoured fish stock or your rice wont taste of anything.

## PASTA CON I BROCCOLI ARIMINATI

This recipe comes from Sicily, which has many Arab references in its cooking, here pine nuts and currants. Traditionally this dish is made with perciatelli, hollow dried noodles, but pretty much any dried pasta will do, including spaghetti.

**SERVES 4**
675 g / 1½ lb broccoli
1 onion, diced
3 tbsp olive oil
4 tinned anchovy fillets, chopped
125 ml / 4 fl oz tomato passata
1 glass of dry white wine
3 tbsp pine nuts
3 tbsp currants
salt and pepper
350 g / 12 oz pasta (see above)

Trim the broccoli and separate it into florets, then blanch these for 2 minutes (in a blanching basket if you have one) in rapidly boiling salted water. Refresh them briefly in cold water and reserve, keeping the cooking water to cook the pasta.

Fry the onion in the oil until golden. Stir in the anchovy, tomato passata and wine, turning up the heat and bubbling hard for 3 minutes. Add the broccoli florets, pine nuts and currants. Season with salt and pepper, lower the heat and simmer for 2–3 minutes. Keep warm.

Cook the pasta until just cooked. If using spaghetti, taste after 8 minutes. It should still have some bite, that is, al dente. Drain, return to the pan and toss with the sauce before serving.

## SPAGHETTI AGLIO OLIO CON PEPERONCINO

This is one of the simplest and purest of pasta dishes – originally a poor man's meal, for the ingredients are literally spaghetti, olive oil, garlic and chilli. Like all brilliant flavour and texture combinations, however, it is now enjoying popularity in a market where cost is not the most significant thing. How spicy-hot you make it is entirely up to you and the chillies you use.

**SERVES 4 AMPLY**
**4–6 garlic cloves**
**4 small dried red chillies**
**6 tbsp olive oil**
**handful of flat-leaved parsley**
**400 g / 14 oz spaghetti**
**salt and pepper**

Soak the dried chillies for 30 minutes in warm water. Put a large pan of salted water to boil.

Slice open the chillies, scrape out the seeds and cut the chillies across into thin strips. Cut the garlic into paper-thin slices and heat with the chillies in the oil over a low flame. You want to infuse the flavours into the oil, but not brown the garlic too much or you will get a bitter result. Finely chop the parsley and reserve.

When the water reaches a fast boil, cook the pasta for 8–10 minutes until just al dente, that is, retaining a residual bite. Drain in a colander, reserving some of the cooking water, and return immediately to the hot pan. Never, in any case, drain pasta until all the water has evaporated – it should go back into the pan still with a coating of water to contribute to the sauce.

Immediately pour over the hot oil, garlic and chillies and toss to mix and coat the spaghetti. If too dry, add a few spoonfuls of the reserved cooking water. Season with salt and pepper, toss again and serve heaped in hot bowls. This dish is so good it is addictive.

## FETTUCCINE ALLA PUTTANESCA

*Puttanesca* means 'in the style of the whores', supposedly because it was much favoured by working girls as a late night pick-me-up. Using a food processor, this sauce takes only seconds to make, and is thus pretty neat for all kinds of workers.

**SERVES 4**
**12 stoned black olives**
**3 garlic cloves, chopped**
**6 anchovy fillets**
**2 tbsp capers, rinsed**
**8 basil leaves**
**2 shallots, chopped**
**1 tsp ground black pepper**
**150 ml / ¼ pt extra-virgin olive oil**
**350 g / 12 oz pasta noodles**
**4 ripe plum tomatoes**
**flat-leaved parsley, to garnish**
**freshly grated Parmesan cheese, to serve**

The day before or at least 6 hours before you want to eat, put the olives in a food processor with the garlic, anchovies, capers, basil, shallots, pepper and olive oil. Pulse-chop briefly to a coarse purée, scraping down the sides in between chopping. Transfer to a bowl, cover and refrigerate.

Cook the noodles in lots of rapidly boiling salted water, checking they are done after 8 minutes, then at 30-second intervals, until cooked al dente.

While the pasta is cooking, scald the tomatoes in boiling water, refresh in cold water and skin. Cut the tomatoes into quarters, strip out the pulp and cut the flesh into small dice.

Put the chilled puttanesca mixture into a large frying pan and heat through over a moderate heat.

Drain the pasta quickly, returning it to the pan while it still has a little water adhering to it. Add the puttanesca sauce and diced tomatoes and toss together.

Serve immediately in large warmed bowls, garnished with plenty of flat-leaved parsley and with freshly grated Parmesan.

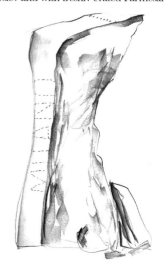

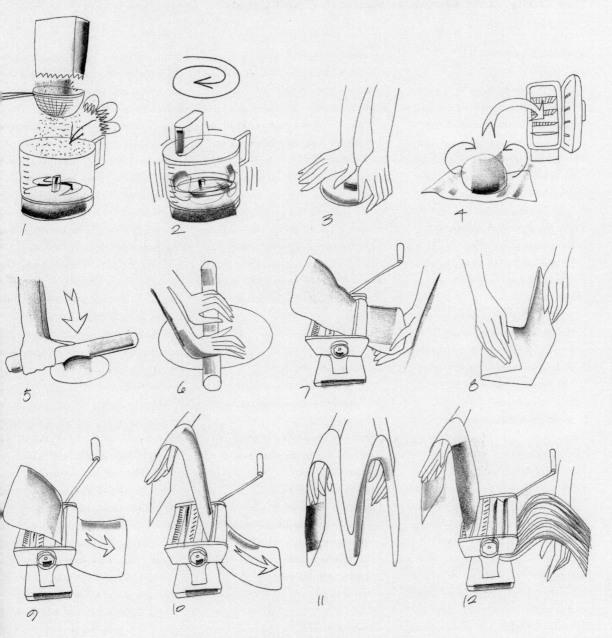

## Making Pasta

❶ Sift the flour into a food processor and add the eggs.

❷ Blitz until the dough balls.

❸ Remove to a floured surface, knead and form into a ball.

❹ Cling-wrap and chill.

❺ Knock down the chilled dough with a rolling pin.

❻ Roll out and divide into manageable pieces.

❼ Feed through the pasta machine on the thickest setting.

❽ Fold in three like a letter.

❾ Feed through the machine again.

❿ Repeat on progressively narrower settings.

⓫ Gather up a finished sheet.

⓬ Feed through with the cutter set to desired width to make noodles.

## PORCINI LASAGNA

SERVES 4–6
85 g / 3 oz dried mushrooms
225 g / 8 oz fresh mushrooms,
wiped and sliced
30 g / 1 oz butter
2 garlic cloves, peeled,
smashed and chopped
3 tbsp chopped flat-leaved
parsley
olive oil, for greasing
12 sheets of oven-ready lasagne
2 tbsp freshly grated Parmesan
cheese

for the béchamel sauce:
60 g / 2 oz butter
60 g / 2 oz flour
1.25 litre / 2 pint milk
salt and pepper
freshly grated nutmeg

Pour hot water over the dried mushrooms in a small bowl and leave to rehydrate.

Make a béchamel sauce: melt the butter in a heavy pan and stir in the flour. Cook gently, stirring, for about 1 minute, then add the milk and cook, stirring, until thick and smooth. Season with salt, pepper and nutmeg. Cook gently for 20 minutes, stirring regularly.

Rinse the plumped dried mushrooms, then chop them coarsely. Sauté them with the fresh mushrooms in the butter over a high heat. When done, add the garlic, stir in and cook for 2 minutes. Stir in the parsley and season with salt and pepper.

Brush the sides and base of a rectangular 25 x 20-cm / 10 x 8-inch ovenproof dish with olive oil. Spoon in a layer of sauce, lay 4 sheets of the pasta on top and cover with a layer of mushrooms with their liquid from the pan. Lay another 4 sheets of pasta on top. Cover with sauce and grated Parmesan. Add another layer of mushrooms, a final layer of lasagne and finish with a surface coating of béchamel sauce. The pie can be left to stand for an hour or so before cooking, or can be refrigerated overnight.

Bake in an oven preheated to 190°C/375°F/gas 5 for 45 minutes or as instructed on the pasta packet.

## SPINACH LASAGNA

SERVES 4–6
450 g / 1 lb of spinach
12 sheets of oven-ready lasagne

for the cheese sauce:
60 g / 2 oz butter, plus more for
greasing
60 g / 2 oz flour
1.25 litres / 2 pints milk
115 g / 4 oz Cheddar cheese (or
equal parts Cheddar and
Parmesan), grated
freshly grated nutmeg
salt and pepper

Pick over and destalk the spinach, then blanch in rapidly boiling salted water for 60 seconds. Refresh in cold water, drain and squeeze out all the moisture you can.

Make a béchamel sauce: melt the butter in a heavy pan and stir in the flour. Cook gently, stirring, for about 1 minute, then add the milk and cook, stirring, until thick and smooth. Cook gently for 20 minutes, stirring regularly. Stir the grated cheese into the sauce and cook for a further minute or two. Season with grated nutmeg, salt and pepper and remove from the heat.

Butter a suitably sized ovenproof dish and coat the base with a few spoonfuls of the cheese sauce. Cover this with a single layer of oven-ready lasagne. Cover this with spinach and a few spoonfuls of sauce. Repeat with another layer of lasagne and the rest of the spinach and finally a layer of lasagne topped with the rest of the cheese sauce.

Bake at 180°C/350°F/gas 4 for 30 minutes, or as the pasta packet instructs, when the top should be golden and bubbling hot.

### DRAINING SOAKED DRIED MUSHROOMS
*The grit which floats
free from dried wild
mushrooms can contain
particles which are too large to
pass through a fine sieve. It is a
good idea, therefore, to drain
them through a fine sieve to
capture the soaking liquid, then
rinse the mushrooms briefly in
a colander.
It also helps to give
the dried mushrooms a brief
but thorough rinse under fast-
running cold water before
soaking, as this gets rid
of the worst of the grit
at the outset.*

## SINGAPORE NOODLES

This dish is based on fried curried rice stick noodles, the word Singapore in any such recipe denoting the inclusion of Indian curry spices, but not necessarily implying a Singapore origin. Once you have gathered the elements together and soaked the noodles, its preparation takes less than five minutes. Rather than use a commercial curry powder, make your own from freshly roasted whole spices, thereby lifting a very good dish to a much higher plane.

**SERVES 6**

225 g / 8 oz rice stick noodles
4 eggs
1 tbsp dark sesame oil
½ tsp salt
3 tbsp sunflower oil, plus more for greasing
115 g / 4 oz skinned chicken breast, cut into 6-mm / ¼-inch slices, then into matchsticks
1 tbsp fish sauce
225 g / 8 oz peeled Tiger prawns
1 hot red chilli, deseeded
1 red pepper, deseeded
2 garlic cloves, sliced paper-thin

2.5-cm / 1-inch piece of root ginger, peeled and cut into tiny matchsticks
5 tbsp chicken stock
8 spring onions, shredded
115 g / 4 oz beansprouts
1–2 tbsp soy sauce
whole coriander leaves, to finish
pepper

**for the curry powder:**
1 tsp coriander seeds
½ tsp cumin seeds
½ tsp black peppercorns
½ tsp black mustard seeds
½ tsp fennel seeds
½ tsp fenugreek powder
½ tsp turmeric

First make the curry powder: put all the ingredients in a heavy dry pan over a low heat and toast, stirring for 3–4 minutes. Grind to a powder and reserve.

Pour boiling water over the noodles and leave to stand for 3 minutes. Drain in a colander and leave for 45 minutes before using.

Put a 25-cm / 10-inch frying pan over a medium heat. In a bowl, whisk the eggs with the dark sesame oil, 1 teaspoon of the curry powder and ½ teaspoon of salt. Brush the pan with sunflower oil, pour in the eggs and, with the back of a fork, quickly turn them with a circular movement in the middle before tilting the pan to spread the eggs and make a flat omelette that coheres but is still moist. Transfer to a cutting board and reserve.

Cut the chicken breast into 6-mm / ¼-inch slices, then cut these across into matchsticks. Put a tablespoon of the sunflower oil in the same pan as the one in which the omelette was cooked and stir-fry the chicken strips until just done, which will take only 60–90 seconds. Transfer to a bowl, toss with the fish sauce and reserve.

Butterfly the prawns (see page 80), put another tablespoon of oil in the pan and stir-fry the prawns quickly. Add to the chicken, toss and reserve.

Put the remaining oil in a large wok over a medium heat. When smoking-hot, add the chilli, red pepper, garlic and ginger, and stir-fry. As the vegetables start to soften, add the remaining curry powder and toss and stir in, cooking for about 60 seconds.

Add the chicken stock and bubble until it has evaporated, then add the shredded spring onions, the noodles and the beansprouts, tossing. Add the prawns and chicken, and toss until hot. Add soy sauce to taste and serve immediately in deep warmed bowls.

Slice the omelette into 2.5-cm / 1-inch strips and arrange on top, finishing with some whole coriander leaves and a turn or two of the pepper mill.

## FRIED NOODLES

Japanese noodle restaurants are all the rage, yet it is very easy to be just as fashionable at home, where you can make your own variations on the noodle theme in minutes. You can dress the dish up with luxurious ingredients like scampi, but you could as easily use stir-fried strips of chicken breast, where a little goes a long way cheaply.

**SERVES 4**
450 g / 1 lb 'instant' Oriental-style noodles
2 tbsp sunflower oil
3 skinless chicken breasts, cut into strips
6 spring onions, cut into 1-cm / ½-inch pieces
2.5-cm / 1-inch piece of root ginger, peeled and cut into fine julienne strips
2 garlic cloves, smashed and chopped
2 tbsp dark sesame oil
small bunch of fresh coriander leaves, to dress
Kikkoman soy sauce, to serve

Blanch the noodles according to the packet instructions and drain.

Put the sunflower oil in a heavy frying pan and stir-fry the chicken over a moderate heat for about 3 minutes. Add the spring onions, ginger and garlic, and continue to stir-fry for 1 minute.

Add the sesame oil, dump in the noodles and toss to mix. When the noodles are hot, tip into bowls, scatter with coriander leaves and serve with soy sauce to individual taste. Very street-credible indeed.

## STEAMING RICE

Wash the rice to rid it of excess starch before cooking and measure the amounts of rice and water precisely. At no time – and not even for a second – remove the lid from the pan until you are ready to serve the rice.

**SERVES 4**
300 g / 10½ oz Oriental rice

Put the rice in a sieve and run cold water through it until the water runs clear. Put the sieve over a bowl and leave to dry for 20–30 minutes.

Transfer to a saucepan with 200 ml / 7 fl oz water. Put on the lid and bring to the boil. As soon as it boils, lower the heat to the lowest setting and cook for 15 minutes.

Turn off the heat and leave with the lid on for a further 15 minutes. Do not be tempted to peek, leaving the lid firmly in place until you spoon the rice into your guests' bowls.

## RICE PILAF

As steamed rice is central to the cooking of Southeast Asia and the Far East, so pilaf is the ubiquitous rice dish of the Middle East. It is closest to a risotto in execution, the rice being fried with onion and spices to flavour it prior to being cooked in water or stock. The rice is, however, long-grain, and the finish much drier than a risotto. A pilaf may be enriched with butter and coloured with saffron, and it frequently includes dried fruit and nuts.

**SERVES 4**
115 g / 4 oz onion, diced
3 tbsp olive oil
1 tbsp pine nuts
275 g / 10 oz long-grain rice
¼ tsp ground black pepper
¼ tsp ground allspice
6 whole cardamom pods
500 ml / 18 fl oz chicken stock
1 cinnamon stick
2 tbsp raisins
1 bay leaf
salt
30 g / 1 oz butter, diced

Sweat the onion in the oil over a low heat until soft and translucent.

Turn up the heat, add the pine nuts and sti-fry, until just starting to brown.

Add the rice and the ground spices, and stir to mix and coat. Pour over the stock and add the cinnamon, raisins, bay leaf and ½ teaspoon of salt. Bring to the boil, lower the heat to simmer , cover and cook for 15–18 minutes.

Just before serving, discard the bay leaf and cinnamon and stir in the butter. Serve hot or at room temperature.

## DIRTY RICE

Dirty rice is a Cajun dish, Cajuns being the Acadian French who moved to the bayous of Louisiana from Nova Scotia in the 1750s. Cajun cooking is characteristically spicy, uniquely uses sassafras powder (filé) and emphasizes long-cooked roux for flavouring as well as thickening stews. When Robichoux isn't shooting bad guys he's boiling crawfish or fixing gumbo, and is indeed partial to a mess of dirty rice. Paul Prudhomme, a big Cajun chef in every sense, says the 'dirty' is from the dark appearance that comes from the inclusion of chicken livers and gizzards.

**SERVES 6**

**3 tbsp chicken fat or sunflower oil**
**225 g / 8 oz chicken gizzards, chopped**
**115 g / 4 oz minced pork**
**2 bay leaves**
**1 onion, diced**
**3 celery stalks, thinly sliced**
**1 green pepper, deseeded and diced**
**2 garlic cloves, peeled, smashed and chopped**
**60 g / 2 oz unsalted butter**
**225 g / 8 oz long-grain rice**
**600 ml / 1 pt chicken stock**
**115 g / 4 oz chicken livers**

**for the cajun spice mix:**
**2 tbsp paprika**
**1 tbsp ground white pepper**
**1 tbsp hot chilli powder**
**2 tsp garlic powder**
**2 tsp onion powder**
**2 tsp dried thyme**
**2 tsp dried oregano**

Start by mixing the Cajun spice mix: ingredients and put to one side.

Put two-thirds of the chicken fat or sunflower oil in a pan and, over a high heat, brown the chopped gizzards and minced pork.

Add the spice mix and bay leaves. Reduce the heat to moderate and cook, stirring, for 60 seconds. Add the onion, celery, green pepper and garlic with the butter and cook for 8 minutes, stirring.

Stir in the rice and pour on the chicken stock. Bring to the boil, lower the heat and cover. Cook for 5 minutes.

Heat the remaining oil in a frying pan and sear the livers quickly. Add to the rice, put on the lid again and give it a further 2 minutes. Remove from the heat and leave to stand for 8 minutes.

Stir and serve alone or as a side dish.

## MUSHROOM RISOTTO

Truffled olive oil is used as a final addition to this risotto, where its earthy vigour enhances the mild flavours of farmed mushrooms. It is essential to use Arborio or similar risotto rice like Vialone. Any other type of rice will not work.

**SERVES 4**
1.75 litres / 3 pints chicken stock
1 onion, diced
85 g / 3 oz butter
2 tbsp olive oil
2 garlic cloves, chopped
350 g / 12 oz Arborio rice
450 g / 1 lb field mushroom caps, sliced
60 g / 2 oz grated Parmesan cheese
1 tbsp truffle oil

Put the chicken stock on to heat to a simmer. Keep it at this temperature.

In a heavy saucepan, fry the onion in 60 g / 2 oz of the butter and the olive oil. As it becomes translucent, add the garlic, then the rice. Stir for 2 minutes until every grain is shiny with its individual coating of oil and butter.

Add the stock, a ladleful at a time, stirring in and not adding the next ladleful until it is all absorbed. After 10 minutes, season and add the sliced mushrooms. Continue adding the stock and stirring. Taste after 20 minutes. The rice should still have a discernible bite and the texture should be thick and porridge-like. If you find you have used up all the stock but the rice is not quite done, finish with ladlefuls of boiling water.

Remove from the heat and leave to stand, covered, for 3 minutes then stir in the remaining butter and grated Parmesan. Finally stir in the truffle oil and serve immediately.

## STIR-FRIED RICE WITH OMELETTE AND PRAWNS

The dish for which leftover long-grain rice was intended, fried rice can be as simple as a mixture of onion and rice or a rather grand concoction including shellfish and pretty much any ingredient except oily fish. A big wok is the best thing to stir-fry in but, if so, sweat the onions initially in an ordinary frying pan.

**SERVES 4**
400 g / 14 oz cooked shell-on Atlantic prawns
160 g / 6 oz onion, thinly sliced
5 tbsp groundnut or sunflower oil
3 eggs
salt and pepper
1 hot red chilli, shredded
1 garlic clove
500 g / 1 lb 2 oz cooked long-grain rice
1 tbsp soy sauce
coarsely chopped coriander leaves, to garnish

Peel the prawns and reserve.

Sweat the onions in 2 tablespoons of the oil over a low heat, stirring frequently, until soft and translucent. Reserve.

Put 1 tablespoon of the oil in a frying pan over a medium heat. Whisk the eggs with 2 teaspoons of water in a bowl. Season with salt and pepper and pour into the pan, swirling and tilting to make an even layer. Cook without touching, until just set. Slide out on to a cutting board and reserve.

Put a large wok over a moderate to

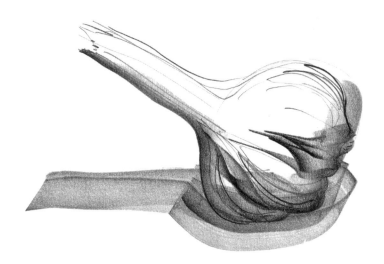

high heat. When smoking hot, swirl in the remaining oil. Add the onion, chilli and garlic, and stir-fry for a minute, then add the rice. Toss and stir-fry for 2–3 minutes. Remove from the heat and stir in the prawns.

Mound the contents of the wok in warmed deep bowls. Cut the omelette into strips and arrange on top. Zig-zag a little soy sauce on each and scatter over some coarsely chopped coriander.

## COUSCOUS

Couscous, steamed yellow semolina grains, is Morocco's national dish. There it may be served with a spicy vegetable, fish or lamb stew. It is made from hard – that is high-protein – wheat, which is formed into tiny pellets which are then coated in flour and traditionally cooked in a *couscoussière*, a double saucepan in which the upper portion is perforated with small holes like a colander. The liquid in the pan may just be boiling water but, typically, is the stew or sauce which will accompany the couscous.

You can now buy 'instant couscous' which needs only to be covered with boiling water, stirred and left to soak before eating and it really is very good. Old-style couscous must be soaked, then steamed for about 30 minutes. Look on the packet to see which type you are buying. With both, the key to a lump-free result is frequent stirring with a fork. If you do not have a *couscoussière*, line a colander with muslin and sit it on top of a pan into which it will just fit.

SERVES 4
**350 g / 12 oz dry couscous**
**1 large onion, sliced**
**3 tbsp olive oil**
**2 tbsp sultanas**
**salt and pepper**

If using instant couscous, follow the packet instructions; if traditional couscous, put it into a bowl, cover with lots of cold water and leave to soak for 15 minutes.

While it is soaking, fry the onion in the oil until golden-brown.

Drain the couscous well, then stir in the onion and sultanas. Season with salt and pepper, put this mixture into a muslin-lined colander and steam over boiling water, uncovered, for 30 minutes, occasionally stirring and turning with a fork.

## MIELE PAP

*Miele pap* is the Afrikaans corn porridge made from ground white field corn or maize meal, similar to the soft grits you find throughout the southern USA. It is usually served with a chunky tomato-and-onion sauce and as an accompaniment to meat dishes. Peter Goffe-Wood, a South African chef, gives this family recipe which he frequently includes on his menu at the Phoenix restaurant in Putney, London.

'Another version is *krummel pap*, a much thicker and stiffer porridge made with only one-third of the amount of water. A classic country way of serving pap is with *kaiings*, which is made from fatty lamb cuts rendered down by slow cooking rather like *rillettes*. The *kaiings* are then shredded with forks and mixed through the pap.'

SERVES 4–6 GENEROUSLY
**salt**
**500 g / 1 lb 2 oz white maize meal**
**125 g / 4½ oz butter**

Bring 3 litres / 5 pints of salted water to a rolling boil, then stir in the maize meal. Turn down the heat to its lowest setting and cook for 45 minutes, stirring occasionally.

'Traditionally you stir it precisely seven times during cooking, then remove it from the heat before beating in the butter,' Peter explained.

## POLENTA BUBBLE AND SQUEAK

Polenta is corn meal porridge and was, for hundreds of years, the food of the poorest people in northern Italy. It has very little nutritional value and no vitamin or mineral content, an inauspicious health base for its current popularity. It does, though, make a splendid foil for richer flavours and, while some people find it unpalatable as a basic gruel, the addition of butter and grated Parmesan elevate it and make it a delicious alternative to mashed potatoes.

There is no need to use traditional polenta flour, which does take 40 minutes to cook and must be stirred constantly if it is not to stick and form lumps. Purists insist traditional polenta is much nicer than the instant, Valsugana-type, polenta available in most supermarkets, but it takes only boiling water and about five minutes to produce.

For an interestingly different side dish, try making this polenta bubble and squeak, which is excellent served with slices of hot gammon, with crisp bacon and fried eggs, with a hamburger or even makes as a nice accompaniment for a beef stew.

SERVES 4

225 g / 8 oz spring greens
salt and pepper
about 175 g / 6 oz instant polenta
60 g / 2 oz butter
60 g / 2 oz grated Parmesan cheese
olive oil, for greasing and frying

Shred the spring greens and blanch them in rapidly boiling salted water for 3–4 minutes. Refresh in cold water and drain.

Make up the polenta following the packet instructions.

Beat in the butter, grated Parmesan, salt and pepper, and then stir in the greens. Pour into an oiled dish and leave to set.

When cold, cut the polenta into squares or use a pastry cutter to make rounds, then shallow-fry the pieces in olive oil until the outsides are brown and crusty.

## TABBOULEH

Tabbouleh is a refreshing salad of cracked wheat, called burghul, bulgar or bulghur depending on where you are. It was originally Lebanese and is characterized by its green colour, the result of using lots of herbs.

Serve with the inner leaves of a Cos lettuce for scooping.

SERVES 4

115 g / 4 oz burghul
½ cucumber
salt
8 spring onions, cut across into thin slices
bunch of flat-leaved parsley, finely chopped
bunch of coriander, finely chopped
bunch of mint, finely chopped
about 100 ml / 3½ fl oz extra-virgin olive oil
juice and zest of at least 1 lemon
salt and pepper

Rinse the burghul in a sieve under cold running water until the water runs clear. Put it into a large bowl and leave it to soak in fresh water for about 1 hour.

Cut the cucumber into small dice and put it in a colander. Sprinkle with salt and leave it to drain. Cover with cold water and leave for 30 minutes to drain.

Transfer the burghul to a sieve and press to extract as much moisture as you can, squeezing it with your hands. Return to the bowl and add the spring onions.

Put the cucumber into a clean cloth and squeeze to extract as much water as possible, then stir it into the burghul.

Add the chopped parsley, coriander and mint, the extra-virgin olive oil and the lemon juice and zest. Season well with salt and pepper, then stir everything together with a fork. Taste. It really needs quite a lot of salt and pepper, and may benefit from a little more lemon juice and, perhaps, even some more oil.

Serve as a salad or to accompany grilled meat or poultry.

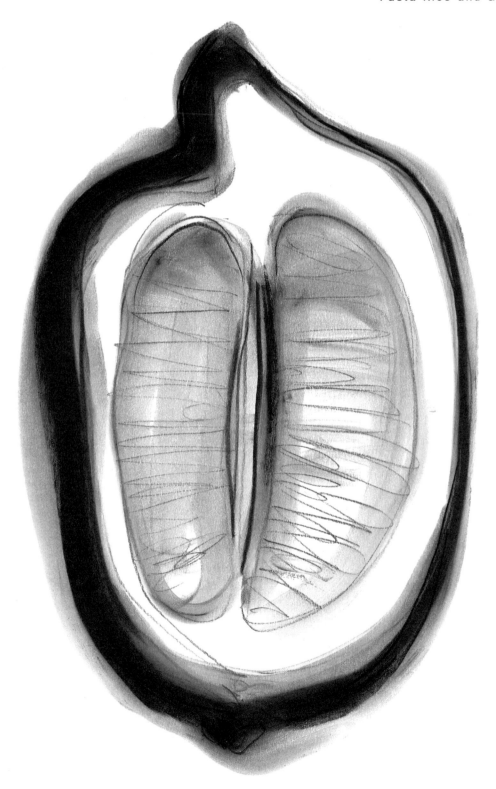

# FRUIT AND NUTS

Fruit at the moment of perfect ripeness is always going to be a joy. It does not have to be exotic to be special. Think of all the different apples we can now buy seasonally. The benefit of a global larder is that we can have many kinds of fruit in peak condition for more of the year, though nothing compares with locally grown fruit.

English strawberries, raspberries and cherries, picked at their best and eaten as soon afterwards as possible, will always be better than the same soft fruits flown in from the other side of the world, not to mention cheaper.

Some fruits have always been imported. Citrus, for example, bananas, pineapples, mangoes, guavas, lychees and other tropical fruits, will never be home-grown commercially, a fact of climate and topography.

Cooked fruit features in many desserts and in savoury dishes too. Dried fruits, important in so many dishes, are not to be compared with fresh. Once dried for the practical need of winter storage, they now play a different role in the kitchen.

We take the huge range of delicious fruits from around the world for granted. We should not. They remain a precious gift.

## APPLE AND SULTANA RELISH

MAKES ABOUT 450 G / 1 LB
85 g / 3 oz sultanas
30 g / 1 oz mint leaves, chopped

1 large Granny Smith or other tart eating apple, peeled, cored and diced
1 orange, peeled, pith and pips removed and cut into segments

2 red shallots, thinly sliced
1 hot chilli, deseeded and shredded
juice of 1 lime
salt and pepper

Put the sultanas in a bowl and pour hot water over them to cover generously. Leave to rehydrate for about 1 hour.

Drain and put in another bowl with the mint leaves, apple, orange, shallots and chilli. Pour over the lime juice and season lightly. Toss well.

Leave for 30 minutes at room temperature before serving.

## CORN AND APPLE RELISH

Dean Fearing, the guitar-playing chef of The Mansion on Turtle Creek in Dallas, makes this sweetcorn apple relish to partner grilled chicken breasts.

MAKES ABOUT 450 G / 1 LB
**3 corn cobs or 225 g / 8 oz
frozen sweetcorn kernels
30 g / 1 oz bacon fat or butter
2 tbsp white wine vinegar
115 g / 4 oz onion, diced
½ red pepper, deseeded and
diced
¼ green pepper, deseeded and
diced
2 Granny Smith apples
juice of 1 lemon**

If using fresh corn, remove the kernels from the cobs with a sharp knife then scrape off the mush that is left behind with the back of the knife and reserve.

In a frying pan over a moderate heat, melt the bacon fat or butter and sauté the corn kernels for 3 minutes if fresh and 1 minute if frozen, stirring constantly. They must not brown.

Add the vinegar, onion, peppers and corn pulp if you have it, then simmer for 4 minutes, or until the liquid has evaporated.

Remove from the heat. Peel, core and dice the apples and stir in with the lemon juice. Season with salt and pepper to taste.

## GREEN MANGO CHUTNEY

If you can get hold of green mangoes readily, then making this chutney involves no special skills.

MAKES ABOUT 2 KG /
4½ LB
**1.5 kg / 3 lb green mangoes
salt
115-g / 4-oz piece of root ginger
3 hot green chillies
4 garlic cloves
450 ml / ¾ pint malt vinegar
about 900 g / 2 lb caster sugar
450 g / 1 lb stoned, peeled
plums**

Cut up the mangoes and remove and dice the flesh (see page 40). Put the dice into a colander, sprinkle with salt and leave for an hour.

Peel the ginger. Split and deseed the chillies. Cut these and the garlic into thin slices and purée to a smooth paste in a processor with one-third of the malt vinegar.

Put the mango with an equivalent weight of sugar in a heavy saucepan, bring to a bubble and cook for 45 minutes, or until you have a thick jam.

Add the ginger paste and plums and simmer, stirring, for 10 minutes. Add 300 ml / ½ pt of the remaining malt vinegar and 1 tablespoon of salt and continue to simmer, stirring from time to time, for 15 minutes, when the consistency should be – well, chutney-like!

Allow to cool until cold enough to taste and add more salt if you think it needs it. When cold, bottle in scrupulously clean, airtight jars.

STERILIZING JARS
*To ensure completely sterile jars, first wash them in detergent then rinse in very hot water. Put into a large saucepan, cover with water and bring to the boil, put a lid on the pan and bubble for 10 minutes, timing from boiling point. Then add the lids and continue to boil for a further 5 minutes. Turn off the heat and leave to stand, covered, until you can just handle them while wearing rubber gloves. When ready to fill, remove them and stand them inverted on kitchen towels. Always fill jars while they are still hot.*

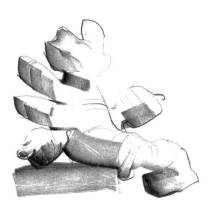

### GOOSEBERRY CHUTNEY

To make this amount of chutney you need quite a lot of mustard seeds – 115 g / ¼ lb of white or brown mustard seeds (white give a hotter finish than brown). These are best bought from an Asian grocer or market.

**MAKES FIVE 450 G / 1 LB JARS**
**115 g / ¼ lb white or brown mustard seeds**
**450 g / 1 lb muscovado sugar**
**1.25 litres / 2 pints malt vinegar**
**450 g / 1 lb onions, chopped**
**4 garlic cloves, chopped**
**550 g / 1¼ lb sultanas**
**15 g / ½ oz ground allspice**
**60 g / 2 oz sea salt**
**1.8 kg / 4 lb gooseberries**

Put the mustard seeds into a zip-lock bag and bruise by crushing gently with a rolling pin.

Put the sugar in a pan with half the malt vinegar, bring to the boil, lower the heat and cook to a syrup.

Add the chopped onions, garlic, sultanas and allspice with the mustard seeds and sea salt. Stir together and continue to simmer.

Meanwhile, in another pan, cook the gooseberries with the remaining vinegar until soft, then add to the first pan and continue to simmer until thick.

Put into sterilized jars and keep for at least a month before eating, refrigerating the jars once they are opened.

### ROWAN AND APPLE JELLY

This jelly is very good with lamb and makes a refreshing change from the ubiquitous mint.

**MAKES ABOUT 2 KG / 4½ LB**
**900 g / 2 lb tart eating apples, peeled, quartered and cored**
**900 g / 2 lb rowan berries**
**1 cinnamon stick**
**juice, rind and pips of 1 lemon**
**450 g / 1 lb caster sugar**

Put the apple quarters in a pan with the rowan berries, cinnamon stick, lemon juice, rind and pips, and 1.1 litres / 2 pints of cold water. Bring to the boil, lower the heat and simmer gently for 30 minutes.

Pour into a jelly bag over a bowl, or line a colander with several layers of muslin, and leave to drip through overnight.

Press gently with a wooden spoon to extract any remaining liquid then pour the results into a measuring jug. You should have about 600 ml / 1 pt; if not, make it up with water. Return this to a saucepan with the caster sugar and heat slowly to boiling point, then boil for 5 minutes. Turn off the heat and check for setting by dripping a teaspoonful on a cool plate. Leave to cool for 5 minutes, then push it gently with your finger; if it wrinkles, it is fine. If not, return the liquid to the boil and boil for a further 3 minutes, then repeat the setting test. When it passes the wrinkle check, put the mixture into sterilized jars and cap them.

### RHUBARB RELISH

This is very good with cheese.

**MAKES ABOUT 2 KG / 4½ LB**
**1.5 kg / 3¼ lb rhubarb, stringed**
**900 g / 2 lb onions, cut into 2-cm / ¾-inch chunks**
**500 ml / 16 fl oz white wine vinegar**
**1 cinnamon stick**
**2 tsp salt**
**2 tsp ground black pepper**
**1 tsp ground allspice**
**½ tsp ground cloves**

Chop the rhubarb into 2-cm / ¾-inch lengths. Stew in a closed pan with a little water for about 45 minutes until softened. Drain well.

Put the rhubarb into a pan with the onions, vinegar, cinnamon, salt, pepper, allspice and cloves. Bring to the boil, lower the heat and simmer, uncovered, stirring occasionally for 45 minutes when you should have a thick purée.

Remove the cinnamon and put the mixture in sterilized jars. Keep for 2 weeks before eating.

*Opposite (clockwise from the top): Spaghetti Aglio Olio con Peperoncino (page 212), Pasta con i Broccoli Ariminati (page 211), Fettuccine alla Puttanesca (page 212)*

## PICKLED PEACHES

Pickled peaches are an American invention and go well with duck or pork.

MAKES ABOUT TWO
450 G / 1 LB JARS
350 g / 12 oz caster sugar
300 ml / ½ pt white vinegar
1 cinnamon stick
6 cloves
10 not-too-ripe peaches, skinned

In a large wide pan, mix the caster sugar with the vinegar. Add the cinnamon and cloves, then bring to the boil.

Lower the temperature, add the skinned peaches to this sweet-and-sour syrup and turn to coat with a spoon. Put on a lid and simmer for 15 minutes. Remove and allow to cool.

They can be eaten immediately or kept in sterilized, sealed jars.

*Opposite (clockwise from left): Apple Charlotte (page 228), Blackberry and Apple Crumble (page 229), Summer Pudding (page 253)*

## DRIED APRICOT JAM

Dried fruit makes very acceptable jam and has the advantage of being available all year round. With the inclusion of almonds, this is a Provençal speciality, *confiture d'abricots secs*. Some people have difficulty getting it to set. A little pectin can be added if you wish, but if you ensure that the sugar is slowly and completely dissolved before the final boiling, this problem should be overcome.

MAKES 2 KG / 5 LB
750 g / 1½ lb dried apricots
750 g / 1½ lb caster sugar
zest and juice of 2 lemons
3 tbsp brandy

Put the dried apricots to soak overnight in cold water.

Next day, drain them and put them in a pan with 1.5 litres / 1¾ pints cold water and bring to the boil. Turn down the heat and simmer for 1¼ hours.

Add the sugar, lemon juice and brandy. Stir continuously over the lowest heat until the sugar has completely dissolved.

Turn up the heat, add the lemon zest and bring to the boil. Boil hard for about 10 minutes. Turn off the heat and spoon a little of the liquid on to a cold plate. Leave for 3–4 minutes then push with a finger: if the jam wrinkles, it will set; if not, bring back to the boil for another 2–3 minutes and check again. Repeat until it passes the wrinkle test.

Leave to cool until just warm, before putting in sterilized jars, and then sealing when completely cold to prevent condensation on the lid (which will otherwise encourage mould).

## DUKKAH

*Dukkah* is apparently Egyptian in origin, a mixture of dry roasted crushed nuts and spice seeds which makes a pleasant change from the average packet of peanuts or bowl of crisps with your aperitif.

There is no absolute recipe, so you could vary the mixture using different nuts and seeds as you like. The texture however is important. The nuts should be coarsely chopped, rather than ground, or too much oil will be exuded and the end-result will be greasy.

Rather than roasting or grilling the ingredients, where it is very easy to burn them, dry-fry the constituent elements separately in a heavy pan over a medium heat, stirring constantly with a wooden spoon.

SERVES 6
115 g / 4 oz walnuts
115 g / 4 oz hazelnuts
60 g / 2 oz coriander seeds
30 g / 1 oz sesame seeds
15 g / ½ oz cumin seeds
salt and pepper
pinch of ground cinnamon

Carefully dry-fry the walnuts and hazelnuts in a dry frying pan over a moderate heat, transferring them to a food processor when nicely toasted.

Next dry-fry the coriander seeds, followed by the sesame and cumin seeds. Add these to the nuts in the processor and pulse-chop briefly.

Put in a bowl and scatter over salt, pepper and a pinch of cinnamon. They make a great nibble and are good for inducing thirst.

225

## CHESTNUT STUFFING

The best chestnuts are the ones imported from France, where commercial production is centred on Privas in the Ardèche, in northern Languedoc. There the nuts are cultivated, with most of them being canned or sold as sweetened and unsweetened purées. The best nuts are used for the toothachingly sweet marrons glacés. These days the best way to buy chestnuts is vacuum-packed. These are fresh, have been peeled and are in every way superior to the tinned variety. This stuffing can be cooked inside a bird if desired.

SERVES 6–8

450 g / 1 lb peeled chestnuts
600 ml / 1 pt chicken stock
2 celery stalks
1 bay leaf
1 tsp salt
½ tsp sugar
30 g / 1 oz butter, plus more for greasing
170 g / 6 oz onion, diced
450 g / 1 lb minced pork
2 tbsp chopped flat-leaved parsley
2 tbsp brandy or rum
½ tsp ground allspice
salt and pepper

Preheat the oven to 180°C/350°F/gas 4. Put the peeled chestnuts in a pan with the stock, celery, bay leaf, salt and sugar. Bring to the boil, lower the heat and simmer for 20 minutes. Top up with water if they become uncovered.

Melt the butter in a frying pan over a low heat. Add the diced onion, stir and sweat until soft.

In a bowl, mix together thoroughly with a fork the onions, chestnuts, minced pork, parsley, brandy or rum, allspice and salt and pepper. Take a spoonful, mould into a patty and fry. Taste this and adjust the seasoning of the raw mixture accordingly.

Pack into a 900-g / 2-lb non-stick loaf tin. Cover the top with a buttered paper. Cook standing in a bain-marie in the oven for 1 hour 20 minutes, when it will be firm to the touch.

Leave for 10 minutes before turning out and slicing.

## PENNSYLVANIAN APPLE BUTTER

This version of apple butter is probably Dutch in origin, since many Dutch people went to America in the eighteenth century and settled in Pennsylvania. Despite the name, it doesn't contain butter at all, just lots of stewed apples cooked with sweet cider, sugar and spices to a thick purée, which is usually spread on toast. The main texture determinant is the amount of sugar used: the more sugar, the stiffer it is.

MAKES ENOUGH TO FILL FOUR 450 G / 1 LB JARS

1.5 litres / 2¾ pints sweet cider
1 cinnamon stick
3 cloves
2 kg / 4½ lb apples, peeled, cored and chopped
450 g / 1 lb caster sugar
1 tsp ground allspice

Put the cider in a pan with the cinnamon stick and cloves, and boil rapidly to reduce to about 600 ml / 1 pt.

Stir the apples into the cider. Return to the boil, then lower the heat and simmer gently for 30 minutes, stirring every couple of minutes and making sure you push the spoon right to the edges where it is most likely to burn. Remove and discard the cinnamon stick and cloves.

Transfer to a food processor and blitz briefly before pushing through a sieve back into the pan. Add the caster sugar and allspice and continue to cook over the lowest heat for 40–45 minutes, stirring frequently and thoroughly.

Allow to cool, put into sterilized jars and seal with lids. This apple butter can be eaten immediately, but will keep for about 6 months. Once opened, keep it in the fridge.

## CRYSTALLIZING FRUIT

Crystallizing is a process which gradually exposes partly poached fruit to a stronger and stronger syrup so that the water content diffuses out and is replaced by sugar. The reason candied fruits are expensive is not related to difficulty of production but is down to the fact they can only be made using tedious and painstaking procedures repeated every day for 12 days. Be warned that there are no short-cuts, which is why most people leave this kind of specialized artisanal food craft to small family businesses in the south of France.

The fruit used should be quite firm and it is peeled, then poached for about 8 minutes in simmering water. Different fruits at different stages of ripeness will take varying cooking times. If you do not have somebody to demonstrate this, then it is going to be very much a case of trial and error: too long and the fruit will collapse, not long enough and it will darken quite unattractively during the crystallizing process.

For every 450 g / 1 lb of fruit, make a syrup from 300 ml / ½ pint of the water in which the fruit was poached and 170 g / 6 oz caster sugar. Bring to the boil and pour over the drained fruit to cover. Leave for 24 hours.

Pour the syrup back into a saucepan, adding another 115 g / 4 oz sugar to every 600 ml / 1 pint of syrup, bring to the boil again then pour it back over the fruit.

Leave for another 24 hours, then repeat the procedure on a daily basis for three days, making the syrup stronger by adding 115 g / 4 oz sugar to each

600 ml / 1 pint of syrup each time.

On the sixth day, add 170 g / 6 oz sugar to each 600 ml / 1 pint of syrup and bring it to the boil with the fruit in it, then simmer for 4 minutes. Leave for 48 hours.

On the eighth day, add another 170 g / 6 oz sugar to each 600 ml / 1 pint of syrup and again bring to the boil with the fruit in it. When it cools, the syrup should be as thick as clear honey. Leave for 4 days.

You have come this far, so stiffen the sinews for the end is thankfully nigh and, if you are cursing ever starting, this is the moment when you can take a break because the fruit will sit happily in its syrup for up to 3 weeks before the final

drying. Do not throw the syrup away: it will keep in a jar in the fridge forever and can be used for sorbets or in fruit salads.

Remove the fruit from the syrup and put the pieces on a wire rack to drain, before drying it in the oven at its lowest possible temperature, say 110°C/230°F/gas ¼, with the door ajar, for between 3 and 6 hours, turning the pieces at regular intervals.

Pack the fruit in those waxed ruched sweet wrappers you can buy and arrange them in a pretty box. Resist the temptation of telling the recipient that each mouthful cost more time and effort than you would like to consider. If they say they hate candied fruit, hit them with the box.

### *Cutting up a Pineapple*

*When unripe, a pineapple's skin is tinged green and the surface is hard and unyielding; when ripe, the skin turns a golden colour and will give to the pressure of your fingers at its extremities. It now smells sweetly and strongly, as a pineapple should.*

● Following the direction of the ridges and at an angle, cut off the skin in strips. Cut off the end.

● Either cut out the bristles individually with the tip of a knife or, making v-shaped incisions, cut out several at a time.

● Cut the pineapple across in slices.

● Cut out the discs of woody central core, using the knife tip.

## APPLE CHARLOTTE

This is one of our best apple puddings when made with Bramleys.

> 900 g / 2 lb cooking apples
> 115 g / 4 oz caster sugar
> 150 g / 5 oz unsalted butter
> juice of 1 lemon
> 3 tbsp sieved apricot jam
> 8 slices of white bread
> clotted cream, whipped cream
> or vanilla ice-cream, to serve

Preheat the oven to 180°C/350°F/gas 4. Peel, core and slice the apples and put them in a pan with the caster sugar and 30 g / 1 oz of the unsalted butter. Add 3 tablespoons of water, cover the pan and stew gently over a low heat for 10 minutes. Then remove the lid, stir and turn up the heat, continuing to cook until you have a thick purée. Stir in the lemon juice and apricot jam, and reserve.

Melt the remaining butter and cut the crusts off the slices of white bread. Cut them into fingers, brush with the butter and use them to line a 20-cm / 8-inch mould or soufflé dish. Pour and spoon in the purée and cover the top neatly with more butter-soaked bread.

Bake on a baking sheet in the oven for 35 minutes, when the top will be crisp and golden-brown. Remove and leave to cool for 10 minutes, before sliding a palette knife round the edge and turning out on a serving dish.

Cut into wedges and serve with clotted cream, whipped cream or vanilla ice-cream. Do not serve immediately it comes from the oven as the apple filling will be incandescent.

## CARAMELIZED APPLE TARTS

The combination of hot caramelized apples, crisp pastry and cold cinnamon ice-cream is texturally as interesting as it is good to eat.

> SERVES 4
> about 15 g / ½ oz icing sugar
> 500 g / 1 lb 2 oz bought puff
> pastry
> 4 Granny Smith apples
> 2 tbsp brown sugar
>
> for the cinnamon ice-cream:
> 700 ml / 1¼ pt milk
> 4 cinnamon sticks
> 7 egg yolks
> 115 g / 4 oz caster sugar
> 450 ml / ¾ pint double cream

Bring water to a simmer in a saucepan over which you can place a bowl to cook the custard for the ice-cream.

Put the milk and cinnamon sticks in another pan and bring to the boil slowly over a low heat.

Whisk 6 of the egg yolks and the sugar together in a metal or glass bowl, until the mixture is pale and ribboned. Pour the scalded milk through a sieve on to this mixture, whisking to incorporate.

Put the bowl over the simmering water and cook, stirring, until the custard coats the back of the spoon. Remove from the heat and, when cooled to warm, whisk in the double cream.

Put in an ice-cream-maker and churn until set, about 15–20 minutes. Transfer to a plastic box with a lid and freeze.

Ideally, eat within 24 hours, removing from the freezer 10–15 minutes before serving.

Preheat the oven to 200°C/400°F/gas 6. Scatter the icing sugar on a work surface and roll out the puff pastry to a thickness of about 6 mm / ¼ inch, scattering on more icing sugar as you roll to stop it sticking. Cut out four 15-cm / 6-inch circles.

Incise a circle 3 mm / ⅛ inch deep about 1 cm / ½ inch in from the edge and place on a baking sheet.

Peel, quarter and core the apples and slice them thinly on a mandolin. Arrange the slices overlapping to cover the inner circle. Brush the pastry rim with a little beaten yolk and bake for 15–20 minutes.

Remove from the oven, scatter the brown sugar over the apple slices and caramelize with a blow torch or under the grill.

Serve the tarts with a scoop of cinnamon ice-cream to the side or on top of each.

## APPLE AND MINCEMEAT STRUDEL

This strudel combines mincemeat with tart apple slices to cut the sweetness. Bramleys are perfect in it.

> SERVES 6
> 2 large apples
> juice of ½ lemon
> 2 tbsp caster sugar
> 85 g / 3 oz butter
> 4 sheets of filo pastry
> 450 g / 1 lb mincemeat
> crème anglaise (page 297), to
> serve

Preheat the oven to 180°C/350°F/gas 4. Core, peel and slice the apples and turn them in a bowl with the lemon juice and caster sugar.

Melt the butter and brush this on the sheets of filo. Arrange them on a Swiss roll tin, overlapping to cover it.

Mix the mincemeat with the apple slices and spoon in a central mound over the pastry. Roll up and wrap the pastry sheets to make a neat roll and tuck the ends under. Brush with the remaining butter and bake for 25 minutes. Serve with crème anglaise.

## BLACKBERRY AND APPLE CRUMBLE

Blackberry and apple crumble is still a great British dish, with the automatic proviso that it can be awful if treated with a leaden hand. Try this version in which the crumble is made buttery to the point of caramelization, the apples used are tart eating apples and the filling, spiked with brandy, is encased in a crisp almond and lemon crust. It all adds up to a blackberry and apple experience far removed from the giant metal tins of schooldays, their cement-like topping cracking to allow the lava-like substance beneath to ooze unattractively through the surface, dark-streaked and malevolent.

**SERVES 8–10**

**for the tart shell:**
125 g / 4½ oz caster sugar
60 g / 2 oz almonds
125 g / 4½ oz flour, plus more for dusting
100 g / 3½ oz butter, cut into small cubes

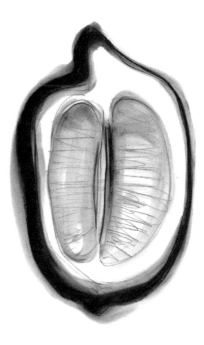

1 medium egg, plus 1 extra yolk
zest of 1 lemon
pinch of salt

**for the filling:**
170 g / 6 oz blackberries
900 g / 2 lb crisp, tart eating apples like Jonathan, Braeburn or Granny Smith, peeled and cored and cut into 2.5-cm / 1-inch chunks
60 g / 2 oz butter
60 g / 2 oz caster sugar
2–3 tbsp brandy

**for the crumble topping:**
6 tbsp plain flour
6 tbsp brown sugar
6 tbsp ground almonds
85 g / 3 oz unsalted butter, softened

Make the tart shell pastry by putting the sugar, almonds and flour into a processor and turning it on at full speed for a few seconds. Add the butter and work until just crumbed. Add the egg and extra yolk, lemon zest, salt and 2 teaspoons of water and work again until the pastry balls. Scrape out on a sheet of cling-film and form into a cylinder about 5 cm / 2 inches in diameter. Chill for at least 2 hours or overnight.

Flour a work surface heavily and roll out the pastry. If it refuses to be rolled, cut the cylinder across in slices and press these into a 25-cm /10-inch loose-bottomed tart tin with your fingers, making a double thickness round the edges and pushing right up to the top as it shrinks as it bakes. Freeze until needed.

Make the filling: if using frozen berries defrost enough in a sieve to give 170 g /6 oz drained. Sauté the apples in the butter. As they start to brown and soften, scatter over the sugar and continue to cook until lightly caramelized. Add the brandy and shake to evaporate.

Make the crumble topping by sifting the flour into a processor with the brown sugar, ground almonds and butter. Pulse briefly to crumb and reserve.

Preheat the oven to 190°C/375°F/gas 5. Prick the base of the tart shell, line with baking paper or foil and weight with beans. Bake blind for 10 minutes, remove beans and lining, and bake uncovered for another 5 minutes.

Fill with the apple mixture, but leave space for the crumble. Scatter the blackberries over the top, followed by the crumble, pressing down and smoothing level. Bake for 30–40 minutes, when the crumble should be biscuity and golden.

229

## PEAR AND RICOTTA TART

Ricotta is a relatively low-fat whey cheese, made as a second phase of extraction after the full-fat milk has been skimmed. Originally a goats'-milk cheese, these days ricotta is mostly made from cows' milk. It is used primarily in cooking, as in this tart, in which the sweetened cheese is flavoured with lemon and vanilla.

SERVES 6-8

6 large just-ripe pears
250 g / 8½ oz ricotta
2 eggs
150 ml / ¼ pt double cream
115 g / 4 oz caster sugar
30 g / 1 oz plain flour
2 tsp vanilla extract
zest of 1 lemon

for the poaching syrup:
225 g / 8 oz caster sugar
1 cinnamon stick
juice and zest of 1 lemon

In a 25-cm / 10-inch tart tin with a detachable base, bake a sweet shortcrust shell blind (see page 232).

Make the poaching syrup: put the caster sugar in a pan with the stick of cinnamon and the lemon juice and zest. Add 1 litre / 1¾ pints of water and bring to a simmer.

Peel, quarter and core the pears. Put them into the syrup and poach for 10–12 minutes. Using a slotted spoon, transfer them to a colander to drain, being careful not to break the pears which, when cooked, are very fragile.

Preheat the oven to 180°C/350°F/ gas 4. Put the ricotta in a bowl. Beat the eggs with the cream and whisk into the ricotta, with the caster sugar, flour, vanilla extract and lemon zest.

Put the tart shell on a baking sheet, arrange the pear quarters in it, radiating outwards with the thicker end towards the rim, and carefully pour the ricotta custard around. Bake for about 40 minutes, when the custard should be just set. Serve warm.

## LEMON CHEESECAKE

Cheesecakes can be awfully solid. This one has a very light topping and the strong lemon flavour cuts the richness of the cream cheese.

SERVES 6

225 g / 8 oz dark chocolate
digestive biscuits
60 g / 2 oz butter
3 lemons
340 g / 12 oz cream cheese
140 g / 5 oz, plus 2 tbsp caster
sugar
2 tbsp sultanas
3 eggs, separated
2 tbsp plain flour

Put the biscuits in a food processor with the butter and whiz to a crumb. Put this into a 23-cm / 9-inch non-stick cake tin and press down into an even layer.

Grate the zest from 2 lemons and reserve. Juice all three.

Preheat oven to 160°C/325°F/ gas 3.

Beat the cheese with an electric whisk until smooth, then beat in the 140 g / 5 oz caster sugar. Continue to beat until fluffy. Fold in the sultanas. (If you happen to have some ready plumped up in brandy, all the better). Beat the egg yolks into the cheese, along with the flour, lemon zest and juice.

With a clean whisk, beat the egg whites until peaks start to form. Add the remaining 2 tablespoons of sugar and continue to whisk until stiff. Fold into the cheese and spoon over the biscuit base.

Stand the tin in a water bath and bake for 60 minutes, when the cheese should be set and golden. Remove, allow to cool and refrigerate for at least 4 hours or, better still, overnight.

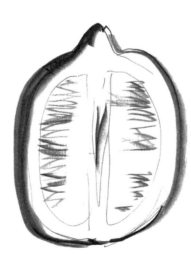

## TARTE TATIN, TARTE RENVERSÉE

The most difficult thing about making a tarte Tatin – an apple tart cooked with the pastry on top, which is then reversed when cooked – is believing that it will turn out when you up-end your pan. When you have gained confidence you can cook it in an ordinary saucepan, but until then an ovenproof non-stick 30-cm / 12-inch frying pan is your best bet.

The French would use Le Golden Delicious, but you will sensibly use a crisp, sharp-tasting English eating apple instead. Use bought frozen puff pastry for the base. It will be soaked with sugary juices, so there is nothing to be gained from making your own.

SERVES 6–8

**1 kg / 2¼ lb frozen puff pastry**
**140 g / 5 oz chilled unsalted butter**
**225 g / 8 oz caster sugar**
**2.3 kg / 5 lb apples (see above)**
**crème fraîche, to serve**

Defrost the pastry and roll it out to a thickness of about 1.5 cm / ½ inch. Cut to a circle just larger than the circumference of the pan you are using (see above) and refrigerate until needed.

Preheat oven to 220°C/425°F/ gas 7. Cut the butter into thin slices and cover the base of the pan with these. Scatter over the sugar. Peel, halve and core the apples and pack them tightly into the pan, cut side upwards. Wedge quarters of apple between them to fill any gaps.

Put the pan over a low heat and cook for 15 minutes, turning the heat up to medium for another 5 minutes to produce a dark caramel.

Take off the heat and lay the pastry on top, tucking it in round the top, then bake for 15 minutes. Lower the oven setting to 180°C/350°F/gas 4 and cook for a further 10 minutes.

Remove from the oven, place a board or dish slightly larger than the pan upside down on top of it then, holding it tight to the pan, turn it upside down. Slide the board on to the table and lift the pan away. If any bits have stayed glued, spoon them off and squidge them back where they have pulled away. Serve warm, with a dollop of crème fraîche.

***Making Tarte Tatin***

❶ Dot the base of a pan with butter and scatter over sugar. Pack in halved, cored apples to fill, cut side up, and set over a low heat until the sugar and butter melt and caramelize.

❷ Roll out a round of puff pastry slightly larger than the circumference of the pan and drape it over the top of the pan.

❸ Tuck it in down around the apples all around the edges.

❹ Remove from the oven and put a serving plate on top.

❺ Invert both tart and plate to turn the tart out, pastry downwards.

## LEMON MERINGUE PIE

Letters on the subject of lemon meringue pie suggest that people have problems with both the pastry and the meringue. The first thing to do, therefore, is to make sure the pastry shell is baked blind until it is really crisp. This can take longer than some recipes suggest.

MAKES A 24-CM / 9 ½-INCH PIE

**for the pastry:**
**140 g / 5 oz unsalted butter straight from the fridge, cut into small dice**
**250 g / 8½ oz flour**
**60 g / 2 oz sugar**
**1 egg**
**1 tsp grated lemon zest**

**for the filling:**
**4 egg yolks**
**225 g / 8 oz caster sugar**
**40 g / 1½ oz cornflour**
**¼ tsp salt**
**450 ml / ¾ pt milk**
**3 tsp grated lemon zest and 150 ml / ¼ pt juice (about 6 lemons)**
**30 g / 1 oz unsalted butter**

**for the meringue:**
**whites of 4 eggs**
**pinch of cream of tartar**
**115 g / 4 oz caster sugar**

First make the pastry shell: leave the butter dice on a plate to soften. Sift the flour and sugar into a mixing bowl, then rub the butter in with your fingers to achieve a crumb consistency. Whisk the egg and add, working in gently with the lemon zest, to form a ball of dough. Cling-wrap and chill for at least 30 minutes.

After removing from the fridge, leave the dough at room temperature for 5–10 minutes before rolling out and using to line a 24-cm / 9½-inch flan tin.

Preheat the oven to 180°C/350°F/gas 4. Line the pastry case with grease-proof paper and weight this with dry beans or invest in those ceramic weights which have the advantage of never needing replacing and not filling the house with an unpleasant smell which the dried beans give off after a few goes in the oven. Bake for 10–12 minutes, then remove the beans and paper, and return to the oven for a further 10–12 minutes, when the centre should be golden brown. Remove and allow to cool in the tin on a rack. Keep the oven on at the same setting.

Make the filling: whisk the egg yolks in a bowl and reserve. In a pan, whisk the caster sugar, cornflour and salt into the milk. Bring to the boil over a moderate heat, whisking. As it thickens, remove it from the heat and whisk a few spoonfuls into the yolks, then whisk this amalgamation back into the pan. Lower the heat to a minimum and return the pan to it, whisking, for 4 minutes. Off the heat, whisk in the lemon zest and juice, and the butter. When the butter has melted and is fully incorporated, cover the surface with cling-film and reserve.

Make the meringue (it should have a crisp surface but a soft interior, so it needs to be cooked quite quickly): in a glass or metal bowl, whisk the egg whites with the cream of tartar to soft peaks. Whisk in the caster sugar, adding it in a steady stream, and continue to whisk until it holds in stiff peaks.

Pour and scrape the filling into the tart shell, then cover with the meringue, making sure it goes right to the rim of the pastry. Bake for 15–20 minutes, when the surface of the meringue will be crisp and nicely coloured. Transfer to a rack and leave to cool completely before cutting.

## POACHED PEARS

Getting pears at the right stage of ripeness for cooking is quite difficult, since they are only perfectly ripe for a brief period before going bad. Many restaurants get round this by using tinned pears when baking tarts. The best way of dealing with pears which are not fully ripe is to poach them in red wine.

Comice pears, which originated in Angers, are the finest and, when cooked this way, turn an entrancing pink colour. This dish can be made the day before it is needed.

SERVES 6
**6 pears**
**1 bottle of cheap red wine**
**175 g / 6 oz sugar**
**1 cinnamon stick**
**juice and rind of 1 lemon**

Use a saucepan into which the pears will all just fit standing upright and in it put the wine with the sugar, cinnamon and lemon juice and rind. Boil for 5 minutes, then reduce to a simmer.

Peel the pears, leaving the stalks on, and cut the bottoms flat so they will stand upright. You can core them carefully from the bottom, though this is not strictly necessary.

Put them into the wine syrup, topping up with water to cover if there is insufficient liquid, cover and simmer for about 30 minutes, testing after 20 minutes, when they may already be done. The precise time will depend on the degree of ripeness.

Turn off the heat and leave until the syrup is just lukewarm before removing the pears and transferring them to a serving dish.

Strain the syrup through a fine-mesh sieve into a clean saucepan and put over a high heat until reduced to the point where it will just coat a spoon, but not to the point where it caramelizes. When cool, taste, adding more sugar or lemon juice as you like, then spoon over the pears. Refrigerate until very cold.

## PEACH MELBA

Tinned fruit generally is fine for cooking or making ice-cream or sorbets, and since this dish demands poached peaches, tinned are a reasonable substitute for fresh. Peach Melba was created in honour of the diva Dame Nellie Melba, and used peaches poached in syrup which were peeled, halved, stoned and presented on a silver dish piled around a mound of the finest vanilla ice-cream, with a rich iced raspberry syrup poured over. This dish was brought to the table on a larger salver covered in crushed ice.

You can produce a very acceptable Peach Melba by first making a coulis, puréeing 450 g / 1 lb frozen raspberries with 115 g / 4 oz caster sugar and then pushing it through a sieve to remove the seeds before putting it in a jug in the fridge to chill. You have already made a sumptuous ice-cream using vanilla pods, double cream, egg yolks and caster sugar (see page 249) or have taken out from the freezer a large tub of a decent commercial brand like the post-coital Häagen-Dazs to soften.

Open your large can of cling peach halves with a theatrical flourish. Mound your ice-cream on a chilled silver platter, or failing that a plate, arranging the peaches as artistically as you can up against the ice-cream, and pour over the raspberry coulis. Prance to the table singing a suitable aria. That's it.

## BAVAROIS

Bavarois is a simple light custard, usually set with gelatine, which makes an ideal summer dessert, served with fruit or a fruit compote. The recipe specifies using limes, but lemons also work well.

SERVES 6 GENEROUSLY
   3 egg yolks
   60 g / 2 oz caster sugar
   grated zest of 2 limes
   350 ml / 12 fl oz milk
   8 g / ¼ oz powdered gelatine
   3 drops of vanilla essence
   250 ml / 8 fl oz double cream

Bring a saucepan of water to a simmer. In a glass bowl, whisk the egg yolks with the caster sugar until white and ribbon-thick.

Put the lime zest in a pan with the milk and bring almost to a boil. Pour into the egg yolk mixture, whisking. Transfer the bowl over the simmering water and cook, stirring with a wooden spoon, until you have a custard which is thick enough to coat the back of the spoon.

Mix the gelatine with 2 tablespoons of warm water until dissolved and stir into the custard with the vanilla essence. Allow the custard to cool, speeding the process by standing the bowl in iced water.

When it has almost set, whisk the double cream until it just starts to thicken, then fold it into the custard.

Refrigerate for 4 hours or overnight. If you prefer you can spoon the bavarois into individual dariole moulds for a neater presentation.

## LEMON SYLLABUB

SERVES 6
   100 g / 4 oz caster sugar
   juice and zest of 2 lemons
   2–3 tbsp brandy
   600 ml / 1 pt double cream
   ratafia biscuits or brandy
   snaps, to serve

Whisk together the caster sugar, lemon juice and zest, and the brandy.

In another bowl, whisk the double cream until thick, then slowly whisk in the lemon mixture. Pour into wine glasses and refrigerate overnight.

Serve with ratafia biscuits or brandy snaps.

## CHERRY BRANDY

*Cherry brandy is as easy to make as sloe gin, though the brandy needs to be of reasonable quality. Cooking brandy will not do. As a rule of thumb, if you would not drink it on its own then it is not worth the effort or the time involved to convert it to cherry brandy. Pick over 500 g / 1 lb 2 oz morello cherries, removing the stalks, and prick all over with a pin. Put them in one big sterilized jar or distribute them evenly in smaller jars and divide 115 g / 4 oz caster sugar between them. Pour over a bottle of brandy, taking care to cover them completely, put on the lids and shake. Store in a dark place, removing weekly to give them a good shake. After 6 months, pour through a funnel and re-bottle. The brandy is now suitably cherrified, while the cherries make interesting eating.*

### TANGERINE JELLY

**SERVES 6**
**about 1 kg / 2¼ lb tangerines**
**85 g / 3 oz caster sugar**
**45 g / 1½ oz gelatine**
**juice of 2 lemons**

First squeeze enough fruit to make 600 ml / 1 pt of juice and reserve. Grate the zest from the skins of 8 tangerines.

Put 600 ml / 1 pt water in a pan with the sugar, gelatine and zest. Bring to the boil, put on a lid and turn off the heat. Leave to infuse for 10 minutes.

Stir in the tangerine juice and the lemon juice, then pour through a sieve into a wet mould and leave to set.

### RHUBARB AND BANANA CREAM FOOL

**SERVES 6**
**450 g / 1 lb stewed rhubarb (see first step of Rhubarb Relish, page 224)**
**sugar to taste**
**6 ripe bananas**
**300 ml / ½ pt double cream, plus more to serve**

Put the stewed rhubarb into a food processor. Blitz to a purée. Using a wooden spoon, push this through a fine sieve into a bowl. Sweeten to taste.

Mash the peeled bananas and stir into the rhubarb with the cream. Chill.

Serve with a good dollop of whipped cream.

### ORANGE GRANITA

Granita is an Italian granular sorbet which specifically is not made in a churn because it is supposed to have discernible chunks of ice in it. The amount of sugar syrup you use will depend on how tart the oranges are. It is usual, anyway, to add some lemon juice to cut the sugar. Beware those oranges like footballs that have a thick, spongy rind and an excessively pithy flesh. When blood oranges are available use them for their stunning colour and depth of flavour.

**SERVES 6**
**12 medium-sized juicy oranges**
**170 g / 6 oz caster sugar**
**juice of 1 lemon**

Wash the oranges thoroughly, dry and reserve.

Make a syrup by putting the caster sugar in a heavy-based saucepan and adding the lemon juice and 100 ml / 3½ fl oz water. Dissolve the sugar over a low heat, then increase the heat to moderate and bring to the boil. Boil for 3 minutes, then leave to cool.

Grate the zest off the oranges and add to the syrup. Squeeze the oranges and add their juice to the syrup mixture with 125 ml / 4 fl oz cold water. Stir all together and pour into a dish which will go into the freezer.

Freeze, removing every 10 minutes to stir, turning the mixture thoroughly as its starts to freeze, until it is too stiff to turn, about 2 hours. You will have a nice, granular texture.

Remove from the freezer about 10 minutes before scooping out portions to bring to the table. This mixture will obviously freeze as a sorbet if you have a churn.

## LEMON CURD ICE-CREAM

You will really need an ice-cream maker to achieve a smooth result. As always with home-made ice-cream, ideally eat it within 24 hours of freezing.

**SERVES 6**

**6 eggs**
**115 g / 4 oz unsalted butter**
**115 g / 4 oz caster sugar**
**juice and grated zest of 4 lemons**
**700 ml / 1¼ pt thick plain yoghurt**

Start by making the lemon curd: put the eggs, butter, caster sugar and the lemon juice and zest in a heavy-based pan and cook gently over a low heat, stirring, until the mixture coats the back of the spoon.

Leave to cool until hand-hot, then whisk in the thick plain yoghurt. Put into the ice-cream maker and churn until set.

Transfer to a plastic container with a lid and freeze, transferring to the fridge 15–20 minutes before serving.

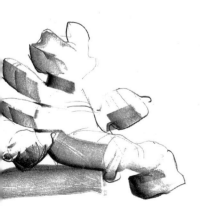

## MELON AND GINGER SORBET

Most dessert recipes use ground ginger automatically, but using ginger juice from freshly squeezed grated ginger gives an altogether more subtle and interesting flavour.

The ginger in this recipe does not make the sorbet hot, just gives it a beautifully exotic flavour which complements any spicy food that has preceded it.

**SERVES 6**

**115 g / 4 oz caster sugar**
**1 kg / 2¼ lb honeydew or 2 cantaloupe melons**
**3-cm / 2¼-inch piece of root ginger**
**juice of 1 lemon**
**white of 1 egg**

Start by making a sugar syrup by putting the caster sugar in a pan with 125 ml / 4 fl oz of cold water. Bring to the boil, then reduce the heat until occasional bubbles just break the surface, and simmer for 10 minutes. Leave to cool.

Now deseed the melon(s) and remove the rind. Peel the ginger and grate it on to a piece of butter muslin. Roll the cloth around the ginger and tighten it to squeeze out as much juice as possible.

Put all the ingredients, together with the lemon juice, into a food processor or blender and purée.

If you have an ice-cream maker, churn this mixture until it freezes. Otherwise scoop it into a suitable shallow container, cling-wrap, put into the freezer and freeze to a slush. Scrape this back into the blender, add the egg white and purée again for 1 minute. Cling-wrap and freeze again until quite firm.

## STRAWBERRY FROZEN YOGHURT

Britain has yet to embrace frozen yoghurt enthusiastically, but it is bound to happen as people slowly become more health-conscious and start to look askance at the fat levels in traditional ice-cream.

When making strawberry frozen yoghurt it helps have a food processor and an ice-cream maker, but it is possible to make it in a tray in the freezer. This is one dish where tinned strawberries actually work better than fresh.

**MAKES 6 GOOD-SIZED SCOOPS**

**400 g / 14 oz tinned strawberries with their syrup**
**500 ml / 16 fl oz plain Greek-style yoghurt**
**125 ml / 4 fl oz single cream**

Whiz the strawberries with their syrup in a food processor or liquidizer to a smooth purée. Add the Greek-style yoghurt and single cream and continue to process until a uniform colour is achieved.

Scrape into an ice-cream maker and churn until set. If you do not have a machine to do the job, pour into trays, cling-wrap and freeze until set. After 30 minutes remove and stir with a fork, and repeat 60 minutes later. It will take between 3 and 6 hours to complete the process.

# DAIRY PRODUCTS AND EGGS

**M**ilk and butter and cream and cheese – for most of us a fridge without all four is effectively empty, since the produce of the dairy is essential in a vast range of dishes. For a cook trained in a Western tradition, cooking without dairy products is a prospect of limited opportunity, but it is interesting to think that there are large parts of the world, like Southeast Asia, where dairy is unknown.

Eggs too are central to our cooking. Perhaps of all foods a truly fresh egg is a thing of enduring beauty and perfection. It may literally rise to culinary heights in a soufflé, but we need do no more than briefly boil one to be reminded when eating it that absolute simplicity illuminates quality more brilliantly than any complex sauce.

Are the eggs you buy free-range or from a battery? What exactly do the words 'free-range' mean anyway, and can they ever imply salmonella-free? Is the cholesterol in eggs bad for us all, or only for those with raised blood cholesterol levels? With the latest research suggesting that the type of cholesterol in eggs is not as bad for those in middle age and later life as saturated fat or dairy cholesterol, the issue remains controversial.

Letters every week express concern over salmonella in eggs and the vexing question of whether it is safe to eat them raw, as in mayonnaise, is raised again and again. All we can say is that we have not stopped using fresh raw eggs where appropriate in the home, though of course it is no longer legal to do so in restaurants. People must decide for themselves but it is wise not to serve dishes using raw eggs to invalids, children or pregnant women.

## MAKING BUTTERMILK

MAKES ABOUT 600 ML / 1 PT

**600 ml / 1 pt full-fat milk**
**6 g / ¼ oz sachet of easy-blend yeast**
**1 tsp caster sugar**

Bring the milk almost to the boil, remove from the heat and leave to cool to the point where you put a finger in and it feels warm. Too hot and it will kill the yeast.

Transfer to a bowl or jar and stir in the yeast and sugar. Wrap the jar in a washed J-cloth (keep washing until it is 'fragrance'-free) and leave at room temperature for 3 days, by which time the fermentation will have soured and thickened the milk slightly.

Use at once or keep in the fridge for a week or so. To make the next batch, take 4 tablespoons of this buttermilk and add it to another pint of scalded, cooled-to-warm milk in exactly the same way and so on *ad infinitum*.

## MAKING CRÈME FRAÎCHE

All mass-produced cream is pasteurized … crème fraîche is pasteurized cream which has had lactic acid and other natural fermentation agents that have been killed by pasteurization put back. Initially the crème fraîche is the consistency of double cream but, as it ages, it thickens and stiffens, while acquiring a sharp, almost cheesy, taste.

You can make it yourself by putting 500 ml / 1¼ pt double cream into a jar or plastic container and stirring in 1 tablespoon of cultured buttermilk. Put this somewhere warm in the kitchen and leave it partially uncovered for 36 hours, when the cream should have thickened discernibly.

At this point, use it or put the lid on fully and transfer to the fridge, where it will keep for 2–3 weeks, continuing to develop slowly. After 3–4 weeks you will have a pleasant sweet cream cheese.

### WHY BUTTER SIZZLES IN THE PAN…

*Butter has a high water content which, when it reaches boiling point as the fat holding it melts, then arrives on the hot metal of the base as liquid droplets. These turn instantly to steam, causing bubbles to ripple rapidly through the fat – hence the sizzle.*
*The milk proteins and salts in the butter are what burn, not the actual fat. This is why butter for frying is often first clarified by melting, which causes the milk solids and salts to separate out.*
*When they are removed you are left with pure butter fat, an oil-like golden liquid (when melted) that is most widely used in Indian cooking, where it is called* ghee. *This makes it excellent for frying because it now has a higher burning point, while retaining all the delicious butter flavour.*

## FRESH CURD CHEESE

Fresh curd cheese can be made from ordinary milk at home.

MAKES ABOUT 350 G / 12 OZ

**1.1 litres / 2 pints full-fat milk**
**3 tbsp lemon juice**

Bring the milk to the boil, stir in the lemon juice and remove from the heat. This will cause it to curdle. Leave for 15–20 minutes to cool.

When cool, strain it through a sieve lined with a double layer of butter muslin or a washed-out J-cloth. You will now have the curds separated from the watery whey. Ball the cloth round the curds, tie the top with string and hang up overnight for further whey to drain.

Next day, put the package on a plate or tray, undo it and press it into an even round cake, which will be about 10 cm / 4 inches in diameter. Fold the cloth over the top and weight it with a heavy saucepan for 4 hours to press more moisture out.

It is now ready to be cooked.

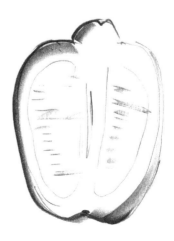

## MARINATED CHÈVRE

*Chèvre* – goats' cheese – is produced all over France, although more than a quarter of that country's large annual production comes from the south-west. The most superior *chèvre* is said to come from Poitou and the Vendée, where goats are kept for their milk rather than their meat. Goats are to be found everywhere in France, however, where they are called *les vaches des pauvres* – poor men's cows – though they produce only 4 litres of milk a day, at best, for goats are notoriously temperamental. (The word capricious comes from the Latin for goat.)

*Chèvre* is always made from unpasteurized milk, which is why the character of the cheese changes so quickly. When newly made, a goats' cheese is mild, but as each day goes by and the bacteria work, it grows more forceful, and the longer it is kept the more pungent it becomes. Day-old goats' cheese is a pudding in Provence, when dredged with sugar and sprinkled with rose water. Such a sweet *chèvre* could also be served with a sharp raspberry coulis.

*Chèvre* comes in many guises: round young cheeses, cylindrical and conical cheeses, cheeses wrapped in vine, chestnut or savory leaves, cheeses bound with straw or rolled in charcoal. *Chèvre* also reflects the seasons, being fragrant in the spring when the goats eat young grass and herbs, and more acidic as autumn approaches and the grazing coarsens. Niolo, a powerful goats' cheese to partner full-bodied red wines, is a speciality of Corsica, but is only produced from May to October.

SERVES 4

**4 young, firm round goats' cheeses, each weighing about 75 g / 2¾ oz**
**2 bay leaves**
**sprig of thyme**
**4 small dried hot red chillies**
**12 black peppercorns**
**about 150 ml / ¼ pint olive oil**
**salad of sharp leaves, such as rocket or dandelion**
**vinaigrette (page 296)**
**1 baguette, sliced into rounds**

Put the cheeses on a cake rack over a bowl. Cover and leave in the fridge overnight to allow excess moisture to drain off.

Next day, put them in a jar with the bay leaves, thyme, chillies and peppercorns. Cover with olive oil and put on a lid. Leave for a week in the fridge before eating, but do not keep for more than six weeks. After that they will disintegrate.

Preheat a hot grill. Make a salad of sharp leaves such as rocket or dandelion and toss with the vinaigrette to dress them.

Toast the baguette slices on one side only. Place half a drained marinated cheese on the untoasted side of each baguette slice and grill until the cheese starts to melt.

Pile the dressed rocket or dandelion leaves on individual plates, lay 2 cheese toasts on top and serve while they are still piping hot. The oil in which the cheeses have been kept makes a nice salad dressing with a squeeze of lemon juice.

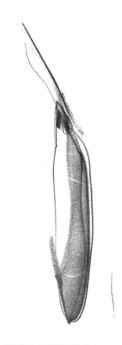

## CHEESE FRITTERS

This is a very old English recipe, dating back to the early eighteenth century.

SERVES 4

**60 g / 2 oz flour**
**200 ml / 7 fl oz double cream**
**4 eggs**
**115 g / 4 oz farmhouse Cheddar cheese, grated**
**60 g / 2 oz butter**
**freshly grated nutmeg**
**1 tsp salt**
**1 tsp cayenne pepper**
**oil for deep-frying**

Whisk the flour into the cream and bring slowly to the boil, whisking from time to time. Remove from the heat and leave to cool slightly.

Whisk the eggs vigorously. Beat these into the cooled cream. Add the grated Cheddar, butter, nutmeg to taste, salt nd cayenne pepper and beat in thoroughly with a wooden spoon.

Heat oil for deep-frying to 190°C/375°F. Drop in 1 tablespoon of batter at a time and cook the fritters for about 1 minute each side, or until golden brown and puffed.

Drain on kitchen paper and eat while still very hot.

## IGRETTES

*igrettes au parmesan* are deep-fried pieces f a thick, set cheese panada (page 45). Usually they are fried without the benefit of a crumb coating, but this is tricky.

MAKES 12–16
60 g / 2 oz butter
115 g / 4 oz flour
300 ml / ½ pt milk
salt and pepper
freshly grated nutmeg
115 g / 4 oz grated Parmesan
cheese (or Cheddar, or equal
quantities of both)
3 eggs
about 115 g / 4 oz fine
breadcrumbs

'ut the butter in a pan over a low heat nd, when melted, add the flour. Mix to thick roux and cook, stirring, for 2 iinutes, then beat in the milk. Continue to cook, stirring hard, until ie mixture comes away from the sides f the pan in a coherent mass.

Remove from the heat and season ith salt, pepper and nutmeg to taste. Iix in the grated cheese, then beat in ie yolks of 2 of the eggs until glossy nd smooth. Whisk the whites of these eggs to soft peaks and stir into the mixture. Turn out and scrape into a baking tin and leave to cool and firm. It will not set hard.

Use a dessertspoon to scoop out bite-size pieces, roll these in the last egg, beaten, and toss to coat in the breadcrumbs, repeating to give a double layer. They are soft and slippery and this makes the task quite fiddly.

When crumbed, roll them into small logs. Aigrettes can be prepared up to this point the day before and kept refrigerated overnight. Heat oil for deep-frying to 190°C/375°F and fry them for 3–4 minutes, until golden. Drain on kitchen paper.

Serve while still hot, but not immediately or people will burn their mouths. The texture is almost that of a moist doughnut inside a crisp shell.

## TIGANITES TIROPITES

These little deep-fried cheese pastries, traditionally a Lenten dish, are cooked all over Greece. They are usually made with a simple olive oil pastry and are filled with a mixture of kefalotyri and feta cheeses, with eggs and mint.

You can use filo pastry but, if so, the pies are better baked rather than deep-fried. Preheat the oven to 180°C/350°F/gas 4. Cut each filo sheet into 3, remembering to keep the remaining sheets covered with a damp cloth while you work to stop them drying out. Brush the strips with more oil, then put a heaped teaspoon of cheese mixture at one end and in the corner nearest to you. Fold across on the diagonal, then back in the opposite direction, repeating until the pastry is incorporated into one triangular package. Brush with oil and place them on a non-stick sheet and bake for 20–25 minutes, when they will be crisp and golden brown.

FOR 12
**for the dough:**
**450 g / 1 lb plain flour**
**1 tsp salt**
**3 tbsp olive oil**
**1 egg**

**for the filling:**
**4 eggs**
**170 g / 6 oz kefalotyri or**
**pecorino cheese, grated**
**170 g / 6 oz feta, crumbled**
**2 tbsp chopped mint leaves**
**1 tsp ground black pepper**
**sunflower oil for deep-frying**

Make the dough by putting the flour into a food processor with the salt. Blitz at full speed, adding the oil through the feeder tube. As it crumbs, add the egg, followed by tablespoons of warm water until it balls. Scrape out on to clingfilm, roll into a ball and chill for 1 hour.

Make the filling: in a bowl, beat the eggs and add the cheeses, together with the chopped mint and black pepper. Mash to a uniform paste with a fork.

Divide the pastry into 12 pieces, roll them into balls then roll these out into circles. Put a heaped tablespoon of the filling in the middle of one side, leaving a 2-cm / ³/₄-inch border. Brush this border with a little water, fold over and press together to make little pasties.

Heat oil for deep-frying to 190°C/375°F and fry the pastries for 2–3 minutes on each side, turning once. Drain on kitchen paper and serve still warm.

239

## CHEESE FONDUE

Cheese fondue is a smooth amalgamation of melted Gruyère and white wine. Fondue parties were all the rage in the 'seventies, with special fondue sets to serve it in. It is best made on the hob in the kitchen, then served in heated individual dishes or in a *bagna cauda*, the Italian terracotta tower – with its glazed bowl kept hot by a night-light – which is traditionally used to present a hot anchovy-and-garlic dip to have with crudités. Raw vegetables also go well with the fondue, along with bite-sized pieces of baguette, the usual accompaniment. Your fondue set would have come with a set of long-handled, two-pronged forks. Ordinary forks work equally well.

**SERVES 6**

300 ml / ½ pt dry white wine
1 bay leaf
2 garlic cloves, crushed
2 juniper berries, crushed
675 g / 1½ lb Gruyère, grated
150 ml / ¼ pt crème fraîche (optional)
3 tbsp Kirsch or eau-de-vie de poire or framboise (optional)
bread, to serve

Put the wine in a saucepan with the bay leaf, garlic and juniper berries. Bring to the boil, turn down the heat and simmer for 5 minutes then pass through a sieve into another pan.

Add the grated Gruyère and melt slowly over the lowest heat. If you like, whisk in the crème fraîche and liquor before serving.

Serve with bread and long forks to dip it in the fondue.

## EGGS

There are a number of ways of assessing the freshness of an egg. When you break a really fresh egg on to a plate, the yolk will stand out in a clearly defined curve when viewed from the side, the white discernibly raised from the surface and made up of two roughly circular layers holding close to the yolk, the inner circle being more gelatinous. A less than fresh egg will spread all over the plate, the two elements of the white intermingled, the yolk no longer standing proud, but flattened.

If you want to assess the freshness of eggs without breaking them: very fresh eggs put into cold water will lie on the bottom on their side; the staler the egg, the more gases will have been produced inside the shell, so it will first rise to sit on its end and then, the more gases there are inside it, it will sit higher in the water – an egg which floats is stale. The hotter the ambient temperature the more rapid the deterioration process.

The important thing is always to use eggs within days of purchase. Freshness is most important for poached eggs. After as little as 3 days they will fly apart on exposure to simmering water. Storing eggs pointed-side down apparently restricts the size of the air pocket inside, therefore slowing deterioration.

Eggs will stay edible for up to six weeks, but should ideally be used within a week of purchase. If you keep them in the fridge, be careful about what you store alongside them. The shells are semi-permeable membranes and allow the absorption of other flavours, something that can be used to advantage if you have a white truffle. When kept in a jar with a truffle, eggs acquire its magical aroma and carry its flavour with them when scrambled or made into an omelette.

Eggs will, of course, keep longer in the fridge, but then you have the irritation of having to bring them to room temperature before use in most applications. Cold eggs are difficult to whisk and the yolk breaks. Conclusion?. Keep them at room temperature and use within 5 days.

When beating egg whites, they must not be tainted with even the tiniest speck of yolk or fat, or they will not take on volume. Plastic bowls do not help either, so always whisk in glass or metal for best results. Work with your eggs at room temperature and never over-beat, as this results in water being exuded from the albumen, causing the mass to break into lumps, with an overall loss of volume. The perfect moment is reached when the egg foam holds in peaks but before it stiffens too much. Continue past that point and you get a diminishing return. A pinch of cream of tartar in the whites helps hold the foam.

When making meringues, only add sugar towards the end of beating. With savoury dishes, never add salt to whites after they have been beaten and before mixing them with other ingredients, as when making a soufflé. It will only make them liquefy and collapse.

*Opposite: Soufflé au Bleu d'Auvergne (page 248)*

## POACHED EGGS

Poached eggs, like pancakes, get better the more you make, so this is another case of practice makes perfect. First of all, the eggs must be as fresh as possible – this means a few days, no older, or the whites will fly apart. The water should not be boiling rapidly and there is no need to create a whirlpool effect before adding the eggs.

Acidulating the water with lemon juice or vinegar helps coagulation of the albumen, but do not use more than a tablespoon or it will impart a flavour to the egg which may not be desirable.

The most difficult part is getting the eggs to hold a nice compact shape without the white going rubbery from overcooking.

Put the water into a wide, shallow pan and bring to a point just off the boil, otherwise bubbling water will encourage the white to break up. Break the eggs into a small cup, one at a time, only just before you slide them into the water. Leaving them to stand exposed to the air will cause rapid deterioration.

They are done as soon as the white has set and become opaque, about 3 minutes. Immediately remove them with a slotted spoon. If using the eggs in a sauced dish like Benedict or Florentine, put in cold water to stop the cooking and then refrigerate until needed.

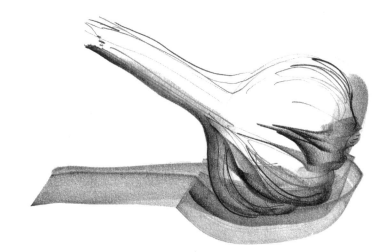

### POACHED EGGS WITH YOGHURT

This is based on a Turkish dish called *yumurta çilbir*, substituting flavoured olive oil for the traditional melted butter.

SERVES 4

**salt and pepper**
**1 garlic clove, finely chopped**
**15 g / ½ oz chopped coriander**
**300 ml / ½ pt thick yoghurt**
**2 tsp balsamic vinegar**
**4 eggs**
**3 tbsp olive oil**
**1 medium-hot green chilli, deseeded and finely shredded**
**4 tsp paprika**
**2.5-cm / 1-inch piece of root ginger, peeled and grated**

Put a wide shallow pan of lightly salted water on to heat to the boil.

Mix the garlic and coriander into the yoghurt with the vinegar and season with salt and pepper. Put into 4 bowls.

Break the eggs, one at a time, into a saucer and slide them into the simmering water. Poach for 2 minutes and remove carefully with a slotted spoon. Transfer to the bowls.

In a small pan over a medium heat, warm the oil with the chilli and paprika. Spoon over the eggs, sprinkle over the grated ginger and serve.

### FRIED EGGS

A perfect fried egg begins with an absolutely fresh egg and a heavy well-seasoned or non-stick frying pan, and cooking the egg over a fairly low heat. Excellent results are obtained using clarified butter or olive oil, or a mixture of butter and oil. If using plain butter, fry at a very low temperature or it will burn.

Put the pan on a low heat. When hot, add your chosen fat – but not too much, a tablespoon will be sufficient. If cooking one egg, use an omelette pan. If cooking several eggs, use just enough fat to film the whole pan thinly. Break them into a cup, one at a time, and pour them carefully into different parts of the pan. They should not splutter or curl up at the edges – this means the pan is far too hot. Cook until the white is just set but the yolk still liquid. Season and serve.

*Opposite: Treacle Tart (page 258)*

241

### SCRAMBLED EGGS

Not so long ago a cook was fired when her food did not meet favour with her employers. One of the issues raised in court was her apparently heinous sin of adding milk to the scrambled eggs. It was not made clear in the transcripts how this was done but, if it was added towards the end of cooking and the eggs were overcooked, then the result would have been horrid. However, there is nothing wrong with including a small amount of milk at the outset, but this should never be more than 1 tablespoon for every 2 eggs.

There are advocates of double-boilers for scrambling eggs but, while ensuring you don't get hard curds, they extend the cooking time interminably. Much better to learn to make them properly in a standard saucepan.

**SERVES 2**

**4 eggs**
**2 tbsp milk**
**salt and pepper**
**30 g / 1 oz butter**
**1–2 tbsp double cream**
**(optional)**

Beat the eggs thoroughly with the milk and season with salt and pepper.

Melt the butter in a heavy-bottomed or non-stick pan, add the eggs and cook, stirring continuously, over a low heat. Be patient and stir constantly. Failure to do so will cause the formation of overcooked curds in the mixture, which should be a uniform creamy texture.

The trick when scrambling eggs is to remove them from the heat before they have quite reached the desired consistency and to continue stirring. At this point, the residual heat of the eggs will finish the cooking off the hob. A tablespoon or two of double cream may be added at this stage, which will enrich the mixture and stop the cooking process.

Scrambled eggs should always be served immediately and never left to sit. Conversely, cold scrambled eggs make excellent sandwiches.

### FRENCH OMELETTE

La Mère Poulard had a restaurant in Mont St-Michel in Normandy and was famous for her omelettes and roast chickens. When asked what was the secret of her omelettes she replied that she beat the eggs well, used a well-seasoned pan and a good-sized lump of the best unsalted Normandy butter, which scarcely reveals any trade secrets. The important thing, though, is not to overcook, so that the centre of the omelette remains *baveuse*, dribbling moist.

**SERVES 1**

**3 fresh free-range eggs**
**salt and pepper**
**30 g / 1 oz butter**

Put a dry 21-cm / 9-inch omelette pan over a moderate heat. Whisk the eggs in a bowl with salt and pepper until frothy.

Throw the butter into the pan, tilting and swirling it, and immediately add the eggs before the butter burns.

With the flat of a fork, stir the centre vigorously for 5 seconds, tilting the pan to move uncooked egg to the edges. Work round the omelette, pulling the eggs gently towards the centre.

The eggs are going to continue cooking after they come out of the pan, so remove them from the heat while the middle is still moist and creamy.

To serve the omelette, tilt the pan and then give the handle a firm tap to turn the furthest edge over, tipping on to a plate with a rolling movement to give a cylindrical shape. This is as hard to do as it is to describe, but practice will make perfect. Omelettes are like pancakes, they get better as you go along.

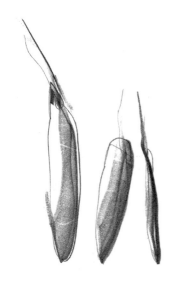

## TORTILLA OR FRITTATA?

Leaving aside the Mexican flat bread which is also called *tortilla*, both names describe large omelettes that are cooked all the way through and allowed to cool to room temperature before being cut into wedges. The only difference is that one is Spanish and the other Italian, and for some reason *frittata* is now a more fashionable name.

This version is flavoured with basil, grated Parmesan cheese and spring onions, and differs in execution by being cooked in two stages. The inclusion of Parmesan and basil push it firmly into the frittata camp. Cooking the eggs in two separate stages has the effect of holding the filling in the middle. New potatoes are preferred, but old potatoes – peeled, boiled and diced – are also fine.

SERVES 4
450 g / 1 lb potatoes
8 eggs
salt and pepper
2 tbsp grated Parmesan cheese

8 large basil leaves, torn into strips
2 tbsp olive oil
6 spring onions, thinly sliced

First cook the potatoes in boiling salted water until just tender. Refresh in cold water and, if they have a full skin, peel and reserve. If using large potatoes, dice them into 1-cm / ½-inch cubes and, if new, cut in half lengthwise.

Beat 3 of the eggs in one bowl and 5 in another. Season both with salt and pepper and add the grated Parmesan and basil to the latter, stirring in.

Put a heavy frying pan over a moderate heat and preheat a hot grill. When the pan is hot, add the olive oil. Pour in the 3-egg mixture and swirl to cover the base of the pan.

When just set, cover with potatoes and spring onions, then pour over the remaining eggs. Lower the heat and cook for 4 minutes, then transfer the pan to under the grill and continue to cook until done. The omelette should be cooked all the way through, but only just.

Slide on to a board and leave to cool. Do not refrigerate and serve at room temperature as a first course.

## PICKLED EGGS

This recipe is rather more sophisticated than your absolutely basic pickle and comes from an English expatriate who introduced pickled eggs to California in the Whale & Ale Pub Restaurant in San Pedro. An unlikely initiative, admittedly, but he says the locals lap them up and they stimulate thirst and, therefore, increased beer consumption.

MAKES 12
12 large eggs
4 garlic cloves, chopped
1 tbsp chilli flakes
2 tsp mustard seeds
1 tsp celery seeds
600 ml / 1 pt champagne vinegar
300 ml / ½ pt malt vinegar
2 tsp caster sugar
2 tsp salt

Hard-boil the eggs by cooking them for 8 minutes and cool in ice-cold water, then shell.

Pack into a sterilized 1.75-litre / 3-pint jar. Sprinkle over the chopped garlic, chilli flakes, mustard seeds and celery seeds.

Put the champagne vinegar and malt vinegar in a pan with the caster sugar and salt. Add 450 ml / ¾ pt of water and bring to the boil. Immediately pour over the eggs.

When cool, put on the lid and refrigerate for at least a week before eating.

## ANGLESEY EGGS

Anglesey eggs – *wnau ynys mon* – can be served as a first course *en cocotte* or as a large dish for a one-course lunch or supper. If serving *en cocotte* as a first course, use only one egg per person, put a layer of leek and potato in the bottom, put the eggs on top and fill the individual dishes with the sauce, again finishing with a layer of the the cheese and crumbs.

**SERVES 4**

550 g / 1¼ lb potatoes
450 g / 1 lb leeks, split and cut into thin slices
70 g / 2½ oz butter
8 eggs
30 g / 1 oz flour
600 ml / 1 pt milk
1 bay leaf
freshly grated nutmeg
salt and pepper
85 g / 3 oz Cheddar cheese, grated
60 g / 2 oz breadcrumbs

Cook the potatoes in boiling salted water, drain and mash dry.

At the same time, in a pan covered with a lid and over the lowest heat, stew the leeks gently in 45 g / 1½ oz of the butter for 15–20 minutes, stirring from time to time.

Hard-boil the eggs, shell them and cut in halves. Preheat the oven to 200°C/400°F/gas 6.

Make a roux by melting the remaining butter in a heavy-based pan and stirring in the flour. Cook gently, stirring, for about 1 minute. Whisk in the milk. Add the bay leaf and nutmeg, salt and pepper to taste. Cook over a low heat,

stirring regularly, for 20–30 minutes. Then stir in the grated Cheddar.

Beat the leeks into the potatoes and spoon them round the outside edge of an ovenproof dish. Arrange the egg halves in the middle and pour the sauce over them, scattering a little more cheese and a few breadcrumbs on top.

Bake in the preheated oven for 20 minutes, when the dish will be bubbling hot with a golden brown gratin finish.

## BRIKS

These deep-fried triangles of paper-thin pastry are called *briks* in both Morocco and Tunisia and, in addition to a raw egg, usually include minced lamb or fish. The tricky part is folding the pastry around the raw egg without breaking the yolk. The pastry traditionally used for briks is called *wharka* and is made over a charcoal grill, but filo makes an acceptable and easy substitute.

**MAKES 4**

115 g / 4 oz minced lamb
2 tsp ground cumin
1 tsp chilli flakes
½ tsp salt
handful of coriander leaves
8 sheets of filo pastry
4 eggs
oil, for deep-frying

In a bowl, mix the lamb with the ground cumin, chilli flakes and salt. Chop the coriander leaves and stir into the mince with a fork.

Working with 2 sheets of filo at a time, cut out four 22.5-cm / 9-inch circles. Keep the other sheets under a damp cloth to prevent them drying out.

Lay the double thickness of filo on a plate and put one-quarter of the meat mixture on one-quarter of the circle, flattening it and making a depression in the centre. Into this break an egg. Brush the edge of the pastry with a little water and bring one half over to meet the other edge. Pinch the edges together to make a half moon. Carefully fold in half again to form a cone and pinch the end edges together. Make three more.

Heat oil for deep-frying to 190°C/ 375°F and deep-fry the briks for 2–3 minutes, turning once. Drain briefly on kitchen paper and serve while piping hot. When you cut into the briks, the yolk should still be liquid, forming a sauce for the meat.

## CHASSE

*Chasse* is a substantial breakfast dish in which the eggs are baked on a bed of cooked ham and potatoes with the addition of diced tomatoes and grated cheese. Rather a daunting way to start the day, you might prefer it for lunch.

**SERVES 4**

550 g / 1¼ lb potatoes, peeled
about 30 g / 1 oz butter, plus more for greasing
4 tomatoes, blanched, skinned, deseeded and diced
4 slices of cooked ham
4 eggs
60 g / 2 oz Cheddar cheese, grated
salt and pepper

Preheat the oven to 200°C/400°F/gas 6. Parboil the potatoes for 2 minutes, drain and put in a buttered ovenproof dish. Scatter over the tomatoes, dot with butter and bake for 20 minutes.

Stir to redistribute and return to the oven until the surface starts to brown, about another 10 minutes.

Remove from the oven and make 4 holes to expose the base of the dish. Lay a slice of cooked ham in the bottom of each, then break the eggs on top of the ham. Sprinkle the grated cheese over all and season. Return to the oven for 5–6 minutes or until the whites of the eggs have just set and the cheese melted.

Serve while still very hot.

## OEUFS SUR LE PLAT MIRABEAU

This is a sophisticated form of baked eggs, thought to have been invented by the great chef Escoffier. Each egg is cooked and served in its own dish.

**SERVES 4**
**15 g / ½ oz drained canned**
**anchovies, plus 4 little strips of**
**anchovy fillet**
**60 g / 2 oz softened unsalted**
**butter**
**4 large black olives**
**4 eggs**
**a few blanched tarragon leaves**
**(optional)**

Preheat the oven to 190°C/375°F/gas 5. Blitz the 15 g / ½ oz of the anchovies in a food processor with the softened unsalted butter. Push this paste through a fine sieve with a wooden spoon.

Cut 4 large black olives in half and remove the stones, then fill the cavities with the anchovy butter.

Smear the remaining anchovy butter on the bases of 4 individual ovenproof gratin dishes. Break an egg into each and bake for about 8 minutes, when the whites should just be set but the yolks soft.

Garnish each with 2 filled olive halves and 4 little strips of anchovy fillet, criss-crossed. The classic version is further garnished with a few blanched tarragon leaves arranged in the centre of the anchovy crosses.

## PIPÉRADE

Pipérade is most usually a purée of tomatoes and red peppers bound with scrambled eggs, a dish that comes from the Basque country in southern France. It may also be presented as a filled omelette or as a flat omelette like a frittata.

People who report problems in its execution are almost certainly not cooking enough water out of the vegetables before adding the eggs. One way of ensuring a perfect result is to scramble the eggs separately, only amalgamating them with the well-reduced purée just before serving.

**SERVES 4**
**1 onion, diced**
**5 tbsp olive oil**
**3 red peppers, deseeded**
**1–2 tsp chilli flakes**
**4 ripe plum tomatoes, blanched**
**and skinned, then quartered**
**salt and pepper**
**8 eggs**

Fry the diced onion in 3 tablespoons of the olive oil until soft and translucent.

Cut the red peppers into strips, then cut these across into 2-cm / ³/₄-inch dice and add to the onions with chilli flakes to taste. Continue to fry over a low heat, stirring frequently, until soft, 5–8 minutes.

Strip out and discard the seeds and pulp from the tomato quarters and them to the pan, season and continue cooking until thick. Keep warm.

Scramble the eggs to soft curds in the remaining oil, seasoning to taste. Fold the pepper purée into the eggs and serve.

## SCOTTISH FARMHOUSE EGGS

This high-cholesterol treat is an easy concoction of eggs, cheese and breadcrumbs, baked in cream.

**SERVES 4 AS A FIRST COURSE OR SNACK**

30 g / 1 oz butter, plus more for greasing
about 60 g / 2 oz breadcrumbs
4 eggs
salt and pepper
85 g / 3 oz Cheddar cheese, grated
300 ml / ½ pt double cream

Preheat the oven to 190°C/375°F/gas 5 and butter an ovenproof dish, then scatter a single layer of breadcrumbs over to coat the base.

Break the eggs into the dish, then scatter more breadcrumbs to coat. Dot with butter and season to taste with salt and pepper, then strew with the grated Cheddar cheese and a few more crumbs. Pour over the double cream and bake for 15-20 minutes, until lightly coloured and bubbling. The yolks should still be runny.

## SPANISH STUFFED EGGS

This is rather a neat trick, which removes the yolks from hard-boiled eggs and replaces them with a thick béchamel sauce flavoured, usually, with diced tuna, though you could just as well include cooked chopped ham or chicken. The eggs are reformed around the filling, coated in beaten egg and crumbs, then deep-fried.

They make excellent nibbles to go with drinks.

**SERVES 4 AS A FIRST COURSE**

8 eggs
115 g / 4 oz leftover cooked meat or fish
about 115 g / 4 oz breadcrumbs
oil, for deep-frying

for the thick béchamel sauce:
30 g / 1 oz butter
30 g / 1 oz flour, plus more for dusting
sherry glass of dry sherry
125 ml / 4 fl oz milk
freshly grated nutmeg
salt and pepper

Hard-boil 6 of the eggs, cool them in cold water and shell. Halve, scoop out the yolks and reserve.

Make a thick béchamel by melting the butter in a heavy-based pan and stirring in the flour. Cook, stirring, over a gentle heat for about 1 minute, then stir in the dry sherry followed by the milk. Season with nutmeg, salt and pepper and cook, beating with a wooden spoon to a thick paste. Lower the heat to minimum and continue cooking, stirring frequently, for 10 minutes.

Stir in the egg yolks pushed through a sieve and the leftover meat or fish.

Pour and spoon on to a Swiss roll tin and leave to set. Fill the eggs with the mixture and press the halves back together.

Beat the remaining eggs in a bowl and put some breadcrumbs in another bowl. Roll the eggs first in flour, then coat them with beaten egg, then toss in the crumbs. Repeat the coating process again.

Heat oil for deep-frying to 180°C/350°F and deep-fry the eggs for about 4 minutes, when the coating will be crisp and golden brown. Drain on kitchen paper.

Leave to cool to warm, before cutting in half again to serve.

## CHEESE AND CRAB SOUFFLÉS

Successful soufflés stem from the confidence which comes from practice, for a soufflé is one of the easiest dishes to make yet one that never fails to impress. The amounts in the following recipe are for a 1.5-litre / 3-pint soufflé dish. Before trying with crab, which is expensive, make a basic cheese soufflé as your training exercise.

For a crab soufflé, follow the same basic steps precisely but, instead of cheese, stir 175 g / 6½ oz flaked cooked fresh white crab meat into the sauce.

SERVES 4

**45 g / 1½ oz butter, plus more
for greasing
about 30 g / 1 oz fresh
breadcrumbs
45 g / 1½ oz flour
400 ml /14 fl oz milk
115 g / 4 oz Cheddar or any
other hard cheese, grated
freshly grated nutmeg
salt and pepper
6 eggs**

Preheat the oven to 180°C/350°F/gas 4. Butter the soufflé dish carefully, taking care to grease the rim, and dust lightly with breadcrumbs. Tip out any excess.

Make a thick béchamel by melting 45 g / 1½ oz butter and stirring in 45 g / 1½ oz flour to make a roux, then whisk in the milk and cook, stirring from time to time, for 20 minutes over a very low heat to eliminate the raw flour taste, by which time the sauce will be thick and reduced to about 300 ml / ½ pt.

Beat in the cheese until melted and incorporated, then season to taste with grated nutmeg, salt and pepper and pour and scrape into a mixing bowl.

Separate the eggs and, one at a time, beat 4 of the yolks into the sauce. (Use the remaining 2 for mayonnaise or freeze).

In a clean glass or copper bowl, whisk the whites of all 6 eggs until they form soft peaks. Stir a tablespoon of the whites into the sauce to lighten it and then fold in the rest, scooping and turning to achieve a light mass, but not stirring as this would break down the foam which will lift your soufflé as it cooks. Pour and spoon into the prepared soufflé dish.

Bake for 15 minutes, when it should be risen proud above the rim of the dish. The centre should be moist, the surface golden brown and resilient to the touch. If too wet and undercooked in the middle, give it 2 minutes more. If you find the soufflé too dry, next time cook for 3 minutes less or you could try turning the oven down to 10°C/ 25°F degrees cooler. After you have made 3 or 4 you will know precisely how thick your béchamel should be and how stiff your whites, which is why it is cheaper to practise with a basic cheese soufflé before going to work with more exotic ingredients.

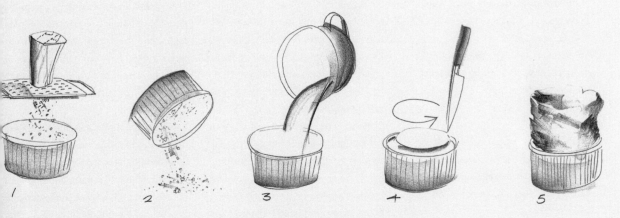

*1*  *2*  *3*  *4*  *5*

### Preparing a Soufflé

❶ Brush the inside of the soufflé dish with melted butter. Add some finely grated Parmesan cheese or breadcrumbs for a savoury soufflé, caster sugar for a sweet one.

❷ Rotate the dish carefully to ensure an even coating, then upend it to get rid of any excess.

❸ Immediately after incorporating the whisked egg whites into the mixture, pour and scrape it into the prepared dish, filling almost to the top.

❹ To give a traditional centrally elevated finish, incise a shallow circular groove into the surface round the rim of the dish (use the tip of a knife or your thumb) just before it goes into the oven on a preheated baking sheet.

## SOUFFLÉ AU BLEU D'AUVERGNE

Bleu d'Auvergne is a strong-flavoured blue-veined cheese from that central, mountainous part of France, the Massif Central. This is a lovely dish that combines soufflé and crisp tart shell, and is delicious served either hot or at room temperature.

> **3 celery stalks, strings**
> **removed and chopped**
> **30 g / 1 oz butter**
> **5 eggs**
> **600 ml / 1 pt warm béchamel**
> **sauce (page 208)**
> **350 g / 12 oz bleu d'Auvergne**
> **cheese, crumbled**
> **salt and pepper**
> **freshly grated nutmeg**
> **25-cm / 10-inch shortcrust**
> **pastry shell, baked blind (see**
> **page 287)**

Preheat the oven to 180°C/350°F/ gas 4. Fry the celery in the butter until soft and reserve.

Separate the eggs and whisk the whites until stiff.

Stir the yolks one at a time into the béchamel sauce , which should be just warm. Stir in the cheese. Season to taste with salt, pepper and nutmeg. Stir in the celery.

Stir in a big spoonful of whites, then fold the rest in gently. Pour into the pastry case and bake for 20–25 minutes, when the top will be nicely risen and golden brown.

## SCOTCH EGGS

Scotch eggs are hard-boiled eggs which are shelled, coated in sausage meat then egged and crumbed, and deep-fried. They used to be something that pubs sometimes had as a racy alternative to ham sandwiches, pickled eggs and crisps. Today, when pubs can't make their minds up about whether – as family restaurants – they should really be serving drink at all, Scotch eggs have largely disappeared in favour of delicacies like soup-in-the-basket and microwaved lasagne. People should rediscover the joy of first-rate Scotch eggs by making them at home.

First, do not boil the eggs too long. The yolk should only just be set, because the deep-frying will cook them further – not much, because the sausage makes an effective insulation against the heat, but enough to make the centre too dry if the egg has been hard-boiled. There is no need to flour the shelled egg before wrapping it in the sausage meat. Instead, flour the coating before rolling in beaten egg and then in fresh crumbs. To be quite certain the coating will hold, repeat the whole process a second time.

Deep-fry in oil preheated to 180°C/ 350°F for 8–10 minutes, turning with a slotted spoon to ensure even cooking. Don't overcrowd the pan or the heat will drop too far and excessive oil absorption will occur. Precise cooking time will depend on the thickness of the sausage-meat coating. Drain on kitchen paper and serve while still hot.

Try making them with quails' eggs for a smaller and more delicate variation on the theme. These make great party food, the ultimate British *mezze*.

## VANILLA ICE-CREAM

It is possible to make ice-cream without an ice-cream maker, but it is not recommended as it is time-consuming and the result will not be as smooth nor the volume as great. This judgement does not apply to ice-cream parfait, which uses a different technique.

You really need an ice-cream maker which, used in conjunction with a food processor or blender, makes it possible to produce a range of perfect ices and sorbets effortlessly. An ice-cream maker is an expensive piece of kit and several of the larger ones need to sit untouched for 24 hours before use because of complex balancing mechanisms. This means that you need space in the kitchen to keep them on a work surface permanently.

We are learning to eat ice-cream all year round, as Americans have always done, but if space is a problem this may be a case for bringing the machine out only for the summer and making home-made ice-cream and sorbets a seasonal treat, when local fruits are cheap and at their best.

Every ice-cream starts with a base which is rich in eggs and cream. People who used to wonder why home-made ice-cream tasted so good compared to the commercial varieties needed to look no further than the ingredients. The arrival of ice-creams like Häagen-Dazs from the USA has helped change our perception of the commercial product because they are made properly with cream and eggs, but they still cannot compare with freshly made ice-cream, which should ideally be eaten within 24 hours of going into the freezer.

Ice-cream deteriorates over time, losing some of the intensity of flavour.

There are two methods for making traditional ice-creams based on eggs. The first is the classic French style, using a custard of egg yolks, sugar and cream – a *crème anglaise* (page 297). This custard is cooked to thicken in a double-boiler before having the flavourings added prior to churning. A lighter custard using fewer eggs and part milk is only a variation on this theme. The second is an ice-cream parfait. Here, a higher proportion of eggs is used, often egg whites are incorporated and a sugar syrup plays a part.

Health concerns over cholesterol and calories have given rise to frozen desserts made without eggs or cream, for example, frozen yoghurt. This can be delicious but is technically not ice-cream.

## BASIC VANILLA ICE-CREAM

The inclusion of a few grains of salt may seem odd, but helps balance the flavours.

MAKES ABOUT 850 ML / 1½ PINTS
**2 vanilla pods**
**600 ml / 1 pint single cream**
**6 egg yolks**
**100 g / 3½ oz caster sugar**
**pinch of salt**

Put a pan of water to heat to the boil. Split the vanilla pods and put them with their seeds in another pan and pour over the cream. Bring slowly to boiling point over a low heat.

While it is heating, whisk the egg yolks, sugar and salt in a bowl to a ribbon point (that is, the mixture is light, thick and smooth and the beaters leave a ripple on the surface).

Pour the hot cream through a sieve on to the mixture, whisking in, then put the bowl over the hot water which should be barely simmering – it must not boil! Stir continuously with a wooden spoon until you have a custard which coats the back of the spoon.

Leave to cool until warm, then pour and scrape into the churn of the ice-cream maker. Most machines take about 20 minutes to produce the ice-cream.

The ice-cream should then be put in a lidded plastic box and transferred to the freezer. Leave for at least 1 hour and ideally eat within 24 hours.

## BASIC MERINGUES

To get a crisp, individual meringue, heavily sugared and stiffly beaten egg whites are cooked very slowly in the coolest oven. They are really dried out rather than cooked. Avoid cementing them to a baking sheet, use silicone paper. Meringues that are to be used to top sweet tarts are cooked for a short time at a higher temperature, giving a crisp browned surface and a light, soft-textured interior mass. The meringues given below may be sandwiched with lemon- or vanilla-flavoured whipped cream or dipped in chocolate and served as a tea-time treat.

MAKES 12–14 MERINGUES
**whites of 4 eggs**
**pinch of salt**
**225 g / 8 oz caster sugar**

Set the oven to its coolest setting – usually 110°C/230°F/gas ¼ – and line a baking sheet with silicone paper.

Using an electric whisk, whisk the egg whites with the salt until they form stiff shiny peaks. Continuing to whisk, add half the sugar, scattering it over the surface in 2 or 3 goes. When fully incorporated, set the speed down a notch and whisk in the rest in the same way.

Use a dessertspoon to scoop out the meringue, dropping it in equal-sized blobs on the silicone paper and leaving room between them to allow for expansion.

Put in the cool oven for 2 hours, or leave the door propped open an inch and leave for about 6 hours or overnight.

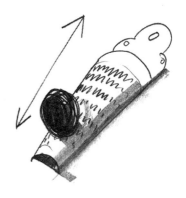

# DESSERTS AND PUDDINGS

**D**esserts — with the exception of steamed puddings, which we can claim to be British — are truly the international section of any menu. Here you will find many old favourites, because often these are the ones for which readers have difficulty finding recipes, as well as lighter desserts reflecting a growing desire for a finale that does not leave people feeling too full when they leave the table. It is worth reminding ourselves that a plate of fruit that has been selected for its ripe perfection and that has been prepared so that all your guests have to do is eat it remains a perfect conclusion to any meal, no matter how simple or complex, and one that will always be appreciated.

## ZABAGLIONE

SERVES 6
6 egg yolks
115 g / 4 oz caster sugar
150 ml / ¼ pint Marsala or
sweet sherry
crisp sweet biscuits, to serve

Put a bowl over a pan of simmering water. Put the egg yolks in it with the caster sugar and whisk vigorously.

Continuing to whisk, slowly incorporate the Marsala or sherry until you have a frothy mixture which has thickened to the point where it leaves viscous trails.

Pour into wine glasses and serve immediately with crisp sweet biscuits.

## CRANACHAN

Mark Barker, chef at St Andrews Old Course Hotel, says the secret of this delicious and very Scottish dish is the whisky.

SERVES 8
85 g / 3 oz pinhead oatmeal
3 tbsp whisky
600 ml / 1 pt double cream
75 g / 2½ oz caster sugar
450 g / 1 lb raspberries

Put the oatmeal on a baking tray and toast briefly under the grill, taking care not to burn it. Remove and, while still warm, sprinkle over the whisky and leave to stand for 10 minutes.

While the oatmeal is absorbing the whisky, whip the double cream, adding the caster sugar as it starts to hold, and continue to whisk until it forms soft peaks. Be careful not to take it too far, or the cream will separate.

Fold the oatmeal into the cream and spoon the mixture into large wine glasses. Divide the raspberries between the glasses, sitting them on top of the cream and chill for 30 minutes to firm up before serving.

## SABAYON

This version of sabayon, the light egg custard is a very old recipe from Eliza Acton, mysteriously called 'German sauce'.

SERVES 4–6

300 ml /½ pint sweet sherry

6 egg yolks

115 g / 4 oz caster sugar

juice of 1 lemon

langues-de-chat or other
biscuits, to serve

Warm the sherry gently until hot, taking care not to let it boil.

In a bowl, whisk the egg yolks with the sugar until pale. Add the lemon juice, then whisk in the hot liquor, pouring it in slowly.

Return this mixture to the pan and continue to whisk over a low heat until the custard thickens. (You may prefer to do this in a double saucepan or in a bowl set over boiling water.) The custard will be light and frothy. Serve with langues-de-chat or other biscuits.

## TIRAMISU

Tiramisu – literally, 'pick-me-up' – is one of the finest puddings ever to have emerged from Italy, a champion dessert and very simple to make. As with all essentially simple dishes, how delicious it is will depend on the quality of the ingredients. The coffee used should be espresso made fresh from high-roasted beans. If this is not possible, then use very strong coffee made in a cafetière. The Savoiardi sponge biscuits which form the base are very sweet, while the mascarpone cheese is so sweet and buttery you need very little additional sugar.

SERVES 4–6

300 ml / ½ pt very strong coffee

60 g / 2 oz sugar

2 eggs, separated

1 tsp vanilla extract

225 g / 8 oz mascarpone

4 tbsp Tia Maria or Kahlùa

about 12 Savoiardi sponge
biscuits

1–2 tbsp cocoa powder

Sweeten the coffee with half the sugar and reserve.

Cream the egg yolks with the remaining sugar until pale and light, then gradually whisk in the vanilla extract and the mascarpone.

Whisk the egg whites to stiff peaks, throw a spoonful into the mascarpone mixture and stir in to lighten, then fold in the rest with a scooping motion while turning the bowl.

Pour the cold sweetened coffee and the Tia Maria or Kahlùa into a shallow dish and, one at a time, briefly turn the biscuits in it. You do not want them too soggy. Arrange these like the spokes of a wheel in a 25-cm / 10-inch round springform cake tin.

Spoon on one-third of the mascarpone cream into the tin, then a second layer of moistened biscuits. Repeat with a second layer of mascarpone and a third layer of biscuits, by which time you will have used 12 sponges, maybe more, and finish with the remaining cream on top. Chill for at least 8 hours.

Remove from the fridge and dust with the cocoa powder before serving.

## CHOCOLATE MOUSSE

Describing this pudding as rich is an understatement. It is smooth, elegant, sophisticated – an intense chocolate experience – with the benefit for the cook that it is easy to make. The recipe includes raw eggs, so you have to calculate salmonella risk for yourself before proceeding. We prefer Grand Marnier for its strong orange taste, a flavour that always works with chocolate, but you could use Drambuie, dark rum, whisky or brandy just as well.

SERVES 8

250 g / 8½ oz best-quality dark
eating chocolate, broken into
small pieces

4 tbsp Grand Marnier

1 tsp good-quality vanilla
extract

8 large eggs, separated

115 g / 4 oz caster sugar

Put the chocolate, Grand Marnier and vanilla extract in a bowl set over a pan of simmering water and stir until the chocolate melts and amalgamates.

In another bowl, beat the yolks of all 8 eggs with the caster sugar until pale and fluffy. Beat the warm chocolate mixture into this and reserve.

Whip the whites of 6 of the eggs until they hold in discernible peaks (you can use the remaining egg whites for meringues or a soufflé). Put about one-third of them in with the chocolate and stir hard to incorporate. This is an initial lightening process. Now carefully fold in the rest of the whites. You want them equally distributed so you do not see any flecks of white. Fold them in with a scooping-and-turning motion to get as much air in as possible.

Pour and spoon the mixture into 8 individual ramekins or one serving dish and refrigerate overnight, or for 6–8 hours.

251

## MOULDING CHOCOLATE

Metal moulds are inherently more difficult to work with. The best sort are those made in Germany from Plexiglas. Whatever material you use, however, a few basic rules need to be applied.

Jane Suthering, whose book, *Wicked Chocolate* (Conran Octopus) is an inspirational source of information on all aspects of chocolate cooking, says that moulding chocolate is inherently difficult and highly skilled, but that this should not prevent somebody from making a reasonable attempt at home.

The first determinant is the quality of the chocolate itself. 'Get hold of the best you can that is high in cocoa solids and, if possible, use a Plexiglas mould which should be absolutely clean. Make sure by washing and drying carefully, then polish with cotton wool just prior to use. You must work in a cool environment.

I know a chocolatier who actually stands on the doorstep in cold weather to swirl the melted chocolate into the mould. When the chocolate is just set but still soft, trim the edges down with a knife and wipe the rim clean which will make it easier to turn out. Leave until it hardens before you attempt to do so, then rap the bottom gently. Don't put it into the fridge while cooling as this causes condensation problems.'

## NORMANDY CHOCOLATE TRUFFLES

MAKES 20

7 oz / 200 g best-quality plain or milk chocolate, broken into pieces, plus more grated chocolate for finishing

3 tbsp sour cream or crème fraîche

2 tbsp granulated sugar

2 tbsp Calvados or brandy

Put the chocolate in a bowl set over barely simmering water and stir until melted.

Bring the sour cream or crème fraîche to the boil over a medium heat with the granulated sugar, then stir this into the chocolate until smooth. Finally, stir in the Calvados or brandy.

Chill this mixture for about 30 minutes until you can take spoonfuls and work them between the fingers into small cylinders. Roll in grated chocolate and chill until required.

## NÈGRE EN CHEMISE

This combination of rice pudding, chocolate topping and whipped cream was seemingly a great favourite before the last war and deserves to be popular again.

SERVES 6

85 g / 3 oz pudding rice

300 ml / ½ pt milk

60 g / 2 oz caster sugar, plus 1 tbsp

3 egg yolks

300 ml / ½ pt double cream

85 g / 3 oz dark chocolate

60 g / 2 oz butter

1 tbsp brandy

300 ml / ½ pt whipping cream, whipped until stiff

Boil the rice in unsalted water for 15 minutes, then drain.

Put this rice into the milk with the

60 g / 2 oz caster sugar, bring to the boil and simmer for a further 10 minutes.

Remove from the heat and spoon a couple of tablespoons of the mixture into a bowl with the 3 egg yolks. Stir and return to the pan. Add the double cream, stir all together, turn into a serving dish and chill for at least 1 hour.

In a bowl set over boiling water, melt the dark chocolate with the butter, extra tablespoon of caster sugar and the brandy. Pour the mixture over the chilled rice pudding.

Finish by piling whipped cream on top.

## MACARONI PUDDING

When instructions on how to cook nursery favourites proves elusive, a good starting point is an older edition of *Mrs Beeton's Cookery and Household Management*. And who can resist a cook book the index of which, under E, lists both 'earache' and 'earwigs' before 'Eastertide biscuits'?

SERVES 6

115 g / 4 oz macaroni

salt

850 ml / 1½ pt full-fat milk

60 g / 2 oz caster sugar

juice and zest of 1 lemon

60 g / 2 oz unsalted butter, plus more for greasing

4 eggs

Cook the macaroni in rapidly boiling salted water until just tender, following the packet instructions for timing.

Preheat the oven to 180°C/350°F/ gas 4. Drain the macaroni and transfer to another saucepan. Pour over the milk, bring to the boil, lower the heat and simmer gently for another 10 minutes, or until quite soft.

Stir in the sugar, lemon juice and zest and the butter, and remove from the heat.

Separate the eggs, beat the yolks in a bowl and add a few tablespoons of the hot milk from the pan, whisking it in. Pour back into the pan, stirring.

Whisk the egg whites to stiff peaks and fold them in.

Butter a suitable ovenproof dish, pour and spoon in the mixture and bake for 20–30 minutes, when the custard will have set and the top will be brown.

Serve warm rather than hot.

## SUMMER PUDDING

One of our finest puddings and unusual in that it is so seasonal because of the berries used.

SERVES 6–8

**225 g / 8 oz each redcurrants, blackcurrants and white currants**
**225 g / 8 oz caster sugar**
**225 g / 8 oz each blackberries and raspberries**
**4–6 large slices of day-old white bread, crusts removed**
**clotted cream, whipped cream or crème fraîche, to serve**

Put the redcurrants, blackcurrants and white currants in a pan with the caster sugar. Bring to a simmer over a low heat and cook for 10 minutes. Stir in the blackberries and raspberries, remove from the heat and leave to cool. The mix will be very liquid.

You can make individual puddings in dariole moulds, but this is really just a piece of presentational nicety. Line a pudding basin with the bread slices, using triangles for the base and half slices for the sides. Spoon in the fruit right to the top. If you run out, fill with more raspberries. Cover the top with more bread triangles.

Stand the bowl in a dish or Swiss roll tin, put a board on top, weight it with 1.8 kg / 4 lb of cans and refrigerate for 24 hours.

To unmould, slide a palette knife carefully between the pudding and the basin. Put a flat serving plate upside down on top of the basin and invert, holding the two firmly together. Rap the bottom of the basin sharply before lifting away to reveal your summer pudding, standing proud and as brightly coloured as a jewel.

Serve in slices with some dollops of clotted cream, whipped cream or crème fraîche.

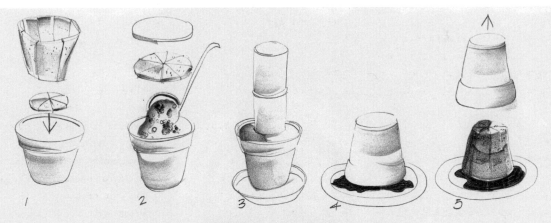

*Making Summer Pudding*

❶ Remove the crusts from slices of white bread. Cut enough triangles to form a base. Cut the rest into rectangles and use to line the sides.

❷ Ladle in the fruit to the top, adding liquid from the pan to cover completely. Put on more bread triangles to form a lid, then place a plate or saucer on top.

❸ Weight and chill overnight.

❹ and ❺ Remove the plate, replacing with an inverted larger flat-based plate. Upend, tap the base of the pudding and turn it out.

## PAVLOVA

Australia's most famous dessert is now popular in restaurants around the world. The keys to success with a 'pav' are extended whisking and the addition of tiny amounts of boiling water and white wine vinegar to the egg whites. An electric whisk, while not essential, is advisable, unless you have a Schwarzenegger wrist and bicep.

MAKES 4 INDIVIDUAL
PAVLOVAS
 whites of 6 eggs
 200 g / 7 oz caster sugar
 1 tsp white wine or champagne
 vinegar
 2 tsp boiling water
 1 tsp vanilla extract
 assorted summer fruit, to
 decorate

Preheat the oven to 130°C/275°F/gas 1 and line a baking sheet with greaseproof paper. In a bowl, whisk the egg whites with the sugar for 1 minute. Then, continuing to whisk, add the vinegar, boiling water and vanilla extract. Whisk hard for 10 minutes.

With a large spoon, spread the mixture in 4 mounded circles on the prepared baking sheet. The sides of the mounds should be higher than the middle to accommodate the filling. Bake for 45–60 minutes. The pavlovas should be crisp, but only lightly tinted on the outside and marshmallow-soft in the centre. It is impossible to be precise about the cooking time, since ovens are variable in their performance at low temperatures and here you have a number of other determinants, like the exact size of the eggs, the stiffness of the mixture and the size and shape of the pavlovas.

Decorate with summer fruit to serve.

## QUEEN'S PUDDING

Queen's pudding or queen of puddings is a sweet lemon egg custard given substance by brioche or sponge crumbs, topped with raspberry jam and finished with a layer of meringue.

SERVES 6
 600 ml / 1 pt milk
 grated zest of 1 lemon
 30 g / 1 oz unsalted butter, plus
 more for greasing
 115 g / 4 oz brioche or sponge
 cake crumbs
 85 g / 3 oz caster sugar
 4 eggs, separated
 115 g / 4 oz raspberry jam
 double cream, to serve
 (optional)

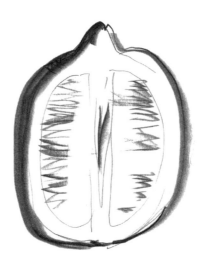

In a pan, bring the milk with the lemon zest and butter to a simmer, then stir in the breadcrumbs or cake crumbs. Remove from the heat and leave to stand for 20 minutes.

Preheat the oven to 180°C/350°F/ gas 4 and butter a suitable ovenproof dish with a capacity of about 2 litres / 3½ pints.

Beat 60 g / 2 oz of the caster sugar and 3 of the egg yolks into the milk mixture.

Stand the dish in a bain-marie of hot water and bake for 35–45 minutes, or until just set. Cover with a layer of raspberry jam.

Whisk the whites of all 4 eggs until they start to cohere and expand, then add the remaining sugar and continue to whisk until stiff. Spread this meringue over the pudding and return it to the oven for a further 15–20 minutes, when the surface should be a pale brown.

Serve warm and, if liked, with some double cream poured around.

## TREACLE PUDDING

Steamed puddings have an honourable place in our food heritage, with dozens of variations that include honey, marmalade, chocolate, ginger, lemon and, of course, *pouding aux raisins de Smyrne*, better known to us all as spotted dick.

Despite their renewed popularity on restaurant menus, they rarely feature in today's private entertaining. This is a pity because they are simple to prepare, can be made well in advance and give great pleasure.

A treacle pudding is actually made from golden syrup, not treacle.

SERVES 6

60 g / 2 oz unsalted butter

115 g / 4 oz caster sugar

2 eggs

170 g / 6 oz flour

2 tsp baking powder

pinch of salt

1–2 tbsp milk

butter, for greasing

4 tbsp golden syrup

Crème Anglaise (page 297), to serve

Cream the butter and sugar in a bowl, then beat in the eggs, one at a time.

Sift the flour, baking powder and salt together and fold into the mixture, adding just enough milk to give a dropping consistency.

Butter a 1.1-litre/ 2-pint pudding basin, then pour the syrup into the base. Spoon the batter in to fill the basin. Cover the top with a round of buttered, greaseproof paper, then crimp foil on to cover.

Stand in a pan of simmering water with a lid on and steam for 1½ hours, topping up with more boiling water as necessary.

Unmould, cut into slices and serve in warmed bowls with crème anglaise.

## GENTLEMAN'S PUDDING

Gentleman's pudding is the lightest of all steamed puddings, containing neither suet nor bread. That being said, the sponge does have butter in it, but less than 30 g / 1 oz per serving. Arabella Boxer suggests this brilliant sauce to go with it. With this accompaniment, it might usefully be considered as a less daunting end to the Christmas meal than a traditional plum pudding.

SERVES 6

140 g / 5 oz butter, plus more for greasing

85 g / 3 oz caster sugar

150 g / 5 oz self-raising flour

3 large eggs, whisked

4 tbsp sieved raspberry or strawberry jam

for the sauce:

2 egg yolks

1 tbsp caster sugar

5 tbsp dry sherry

2 tbsp sieved raspberry jam

Beat the butter with the sugar to a pale cream. Sift in half the flour, then add one of the eggs, and incorporate. Sift in the remaining flour and beat in, concluding with the remaining eggs, beating in to achieve a smooth batter. Add the sieved jam and stir in.

Pour and scrape into a buttered 1-litre / 1-pint pudding basin. Cover with a cloth or cling-wrap and steam for 90 minutes.

Make the sauce: in a bowl set over hot water, whisk the egg yolks with the sugar. As they thicken, add the sherry and sieved jam and cook in briefly, stirring. Serve hot from a sauceboat with the pudding.

## STICKY TOFFEE PUDDING

An old nursery favourite, sticky pudding is now a popular dessert in the grandest restaurants.

SERVES 4

115 g / 4 oz unsalted butter, plus more for greasing

60 g / 2 oz caster sugar

5 tbsp double cream

115 g / 4 oz muscovado sugar

4 eggs, separated

140 g / 5 oz plain flour

1½ tsp baking powder

warm Crème Anglaise (page 297), to serve

Preheat the oven to 180°C/350°F/gas 4 and butter four 300-ml / ½-pint dariole moulds.

In a pan, dissolve the caster sugar in a couple of tablespoons of water over a low heat. Warm the double cream in another pan. When the sugar has all dissolved, turn up the heat under that pan to moderate and boil until golden brown. Remove from the heat and add the hot cream, stirring. Pour equally into the 4 moulds to line the base.

With an electric whisk, cream the unsalted butter and muscovado sugar until off-white, and then whisk in the egg yolks, one at a time.

In a metal or glass bowl, whisk the egg whites to a soft peak and reserve.

Sift the plain flour and baking powder into another bowl, and whisk into the butter cream. Then fold the egg whites into the mixture.

Spoon into the moulds and cover the tops with buttered rounds of greaseproof paper, then with pleated foil to allow for expansion. Put into a roasting tin and pour hot water from the kettle to come halfway up the moulds.

Bake for 40–50 minutes, until a skewer pushed into the middle of one of the puddings comes out warm and clean.

Serve with warm crème anglaise poured around.

255

## BAKED CUSTARD

Egg custards go wrong when the raw mixture does not include enough egg whites, which provide the set, or when cooked at too high a temperature, as this causes partial separation of the custard and a watery result.

**SERVES 6**

**1.1 litres / 2 pints full-fat milk**
**1 vanilla pod, split lengthwise**
**200 g / 7 oz caster sugar**
**8 eggs**

Preheat the oven to 170°C/325°F/gas 3. Put the milk in a pan with the split vanilla pod over a low heat and bring very slowly to the boil.

While it is heating, whisk the caster sugar in a bowl with the eggs until pale and frothy. Pour over the scalded milk through a sieve, continuing to whisk.

Pour into 6 dariole moulds or one shallow dish and sit in a deep roasting tin. Pour in water from the kettle, just off the boil, to come two-thirds of the way up the moulds or dish and bake for 50 minutes to 1 hour. Test the custard is done by inserting a knife. If it comes out clean it is cooked.

Leave to cool, refrigerate for 2 hours or overnight, then run a palette knife round the edge(s) to turn out.

### SHAPING QUENELLES
*The meringue for the floating islands looks best when shaped into a large egg shape known in cuisine-speak as a quenelle, after the similarly shaped poached fish and chicken dumplings. It is achieved by moulding the mixture between two large metal spoons and then scooping this off one spoon with the other. It is also a very attractive way of presenting cream on a dessert plate*

## FLOATING ISLANDS

A classic French dessert, also called *oeufs à la neige*, this pretty pudding of poached meringues set in a sea of egg custard looks a more impressive and difficult construction than it really is.

**SERVES 4**

**600 ml / 1 pint full-fat milk**
**1 vanilla pod, split lengthwise**
**5 eggs, separated**
**150 g / 5 oz caster sugar**
**pinch of salt**

Start by making the custard: put the milk with the split vanilla pod over a low heat and bring to just below boiling.

While it is heating, whisk the egg yolks with 115 g / 4 oz of the caster sugar, beating until you have a pale amalgam which will fall in ribbons from the whisk.

Off the heat, slowly whisk in the milk, then return to a clean saucepan over a low heat. Cook gently, stirring with a wooden spoon, until it forms a custard thick enough to coat the back of a spoon. This will take about 10–12 minutes. Pass through a sieve into a bowl and leave to cool then cling-wrap and refrigerate. This can be done the day before.

Rinse the vanilla pod and put it in a wide, low-sided saucepan with water and bring to boil. Lower the heat to a bare simmer.

Whisk the egg whites with a pinch of salt until they form soft peaks. Sprinkle over the remaining caster sugar and continue to whisk until you have firm peaks.

Dip a metal serving spoon into the hot water, then scoop out an oval of meringue and slide it into the water. Repeat to make 7 more or, if preferred, make 4 large meringues. Poach for 2 minutes then turn over with a slotted spoon and poach for a further 2–3 minutes. Remove to a clean cloth to drain and allow to cool.

To serve, ladle the custard into 4 bowls and float the meringue islands on top.

*Opposite: an assortment of breads from the basic recipe (pages 262-3)*

*Finishing Crème Brûlée*

❶ Just before serving, sprinkle over an even layer of sugar.

❷ Invert the ramekin to get rid of excess sugar.

❸ Heat the sugar layer with a blowtorch, salamander or hot grill until the topping is a good golden brown.

❹ Leave to cool slightly so the sugar layer can crisp up.

## CRÈME BRÛLÉE

The traditional way of cooking crème brûlée is in a water bath at a low temperature in the oven, which should not be more than 150°C/300°F/gas 2, but we find you usually get better and more consistent results from cooking the custard on the hob.

**SERVES 6**

**2 vanilla pods**

**85g / 3 oz caster sugar**

**6 egg yolks**

**500 ml / 16 fl oz double cream**

**1–2 tsp demerara sugar**

Split the vanilla pods and scrape the seeds into a bowl with the sugar. Add the egg yolks and beat with a whisk until stiff.

Scald the cream by bringing it slowly to the boil with the vanilla pods in it, then pour on to the egg mixture, whisking vigorously.

Return to a clean saucepan and cook over a low heat, whisking all the time. As it starts to thicken, change to a wooden spoon and stir, taking particular care that you scrape round the edges of the pan, where it tends to stick and burn.

As it comes to the boil, remove from the heat, stir briskly and pour through a fine sieve into individual ramekins, filling right to the brim as the custard will sink a little when it sets. (Rinse the vanilla pods, dry and keep in a jar of sugar to make vanilla sugar or to use again.) Allow to cool and then chill for at least 1 hour.

Just before serving, caramelize the tops: sprinkle a teaspoon or two of demerara sugar in an even layer on the surface and pat it down, removing any excess by inverting the ramekins. (If you got the custard wrong this is where you find out in a dramatic fashion.) A small blowtorch is the best way to apply heat to the sugar, a relatively inexpensive tool and indispensable for the burnt custard aficionado. Otherwise, flash under a very hot grill until golden brown. If black spots appear, remove immediately. To avoid burning fingers, leave for a few minutes to cool before testing for crispness.

*Opposite: making Girdle Scones (page 276)*

257

## FRANGIPANE TART

Frangipane is the pretty French word for almond paste, familiar to generations of Britons in Bakewell tart, of which this is a variation. The filling and the pastry are quick and easy to make if you have a food processor.

**SERVES 10**

for the pastry:
125 g / 4½ oz caster sugar
60 g / 2 oz ground almonds
125 g / 4½ oz plain flour
100 g / 3½ oz butter, cut into small dice
1 large egg, plus 1 extra yolk
grated zest of 1 small lemon
pinch of salt

for the filling:
60 g / 2 oz butter
60 g / 2 oz caster sugar
60 g / 2 oz ground almonds
60 g / 2 oz fresh white breadcrumbs
1 large egg
3 drops of almond essence
4 tbsp raspberry jam

First make the pastry: put the sugar, almonds and flour into a food processor and turn on at full speed for a few seconds. Add the butter dice and work again until just blended in. The mixture will resemble fine breadcrumbs.

Add the egg and extra yolk, the lemon zest, 2 teaspoons of water and a tiny pinch of salt. Work again until the pastry balls. Cling-wrap and refrigerate for 2 hours.

Preheat the oven to 190°C/375°F/gas 5. Roll the chilled pastry out and use to line a 20-cm / 8-inch loose-bottomed tart tin. If it breaks it can be repaired by pressing with your fingers. Make the shell as even as possible, with a double thickness round the edges and pushed right up to the top as it will shrink as it bakes. Be careful to press into the bottom edges to eliminate air between the tin and the pastry.

Make the filling: put the butter, sugar, ground almonds and breadcrumbs into the processor and work briefly to mix. With the machine running on full speed, add the egg and almond essence until combined to a smooth paste.

Put the shell on a baking tray, prick the base with a fork and line with foil. Fill with beans and bake blind for 10 minutes.

Remove the foil and beans and leave to cool slightly, then fill the base with a layer of raspberry jam. Cover this with the almond paste. Scrape the surface smooth and level.

Return to the oven and bake for 25–30 minutes, until risen and lightly browned.

## TREACLE TART

Sticky, of course, sweet, indubitably, and set off to perfection by an elegant crisp pastry, this great British pudding is made even more special by a large spoonful of the best clotted cream on the side. Almonds are not usually included in a treacle tart, but they give the mixture a lovely crunch. You use more golden syrup than treacle, the latter being kept to a minimum but still playing an important part in balancing the different flavours.

**SERVES 6**

one 23-cm / 9-inch sweet shortcrust pastry case, baked blind (see left)
400 g / 14 oz golden syrup
2 tbsp treacle
150 g / 5½ oz slivered almonds
125 g / 4½ oz fresh breadcrumbs
2 eggs
zest of ½ lemon
clotted cream or double cream, to serve

Preheat the oven to 120°C/250°F/gas ½ and put the pastry shell on a baking sheet.

In a bowl, mix together the golden syrup, treacle, slivered almonds, breadcrumbs, eggs and lemon zest. Spoon into the case and bake for about 1 hour.

Serve warm with clotted cream or offer double cream in a jug at the table.

## SHERRY TRIFLE

Even though it is so easy to make, trifle remains one of our finest desserts. The secret is real custard and plenty of alcohol in the sponge base.

**SERVES 8**

1 Victoria sponge, split in half
3 tbsp raspberry jam
3 tbsp apricot jam
150 ml / ¼ pt brandy
150 ml / ¼ pt sweet sherry
600 ml / 1 pt double cream
handful of flaked almonds

for the custard:
600 ml / 1 pt milk
5 egg yolks
85 g / 3 oz caster sugar
3 drops of vanilla extract

Spread one half of the Victoria sponge with raspberry jam and the other with apricot jam. Cut each into 4 and put into a dish in which they will just fit, alternating raspberry with apricot. Pour over the brandy and sweet sherry, and leave to macerate for 2 hours.

Make a custard by bringing the milk to the boil and pouring it over the egg yolks beaten with the caster sugar, whisking. Put the bowl over simmering water and whisk until thick. Stir in the vanilla extract and pour over the sponge. Refrigerate overnight.

Whip the cream until stiff and spoon over the top, then scatter over some flaked almonds.

## COINTREAU SEMIFREDDO

Sweet, sticky liqueurs are ideal in puddings and in this semifreddo — meaning literally 'semi-frozen' in Italian — dessert it intensifies the orange flavour. When obtainable, use blood oranges to give a nice colour. You can also churn the semifreddo to an ice-cream but, if you do, double the quantity of cream.

**SERVES 4**
**1 orange**
**6 egg yolks**
**115 g / 4 oz caster sugar**
**350 ml / 12 fl oz double cream**
**5 tbsp Cointreau**
**1 tsp good-quality vanilla extract**

**for the syrup:**
**juice and grated zest of 2 oranges**
**30 g / 1 oz caster sugar**
**4 tbsp Cointreau**

Wash the orange thoroughly, grate the zest from it, squeeze the juice and reserve both separately.

In a bowl, whisk the egg yolks with the caster sugar until pale. Put the bowl over a pan of simmering water, with the base just touching the surface, and whisk in 3 tablespoons of the double cream, the Cointreau, the juice of the zested orange and the vanilla extract. Continue whisking until you have a pourable custard consistency. Stir in the grated zest, remove the bowl and leave to cool.

Whip the remaining cream to soft peaks and fold this in. Pour into a plastic container, put on a lid and freeze until firm. How long this takes will depend on the efficiency of your freezer, but probably about 1½ hours.

Remove from the freezer about 10 minutes before serving in scoops. While it is softening, make a syrup by putting the juice and grated zest of the scrubbed oranges in a pan with the caster sugar and Cointreau. Bring to the boil, lower the heat and simmer for 2–3 minutes until thick. Spoon this over the semifreddo while still hot.

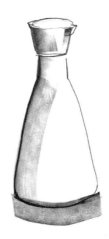

## CARAMEL PARFAIT

You must use a sugar thermometer for this parfait. An electric mixer for the final stage is also desirable, since the caramel should be continuously whisked until it has cooled significantly, prior to the inclusion of the cream.

**SERVES 4**
**225 g / 8 oz caster sugar**
**4 egg yolks**
**575 ml / 1 pt double cream**

Put the sugar and 6 tablespoons of cold water in a pan and bring it slowly to 180°C/350°F, when you will have a dark caramel. Remove from the heat and gradually add 125 ml / 4 fl oz more cold water, stirring in. Do this slowly and VERY carefully because the water coming in contact with the red-hot sugar causes it to bubble and spit and sugar burns really are to be avoided at all costs.

When you have added all the water, return to the heat and bring back to the boil. Remove from the heat and reserve. Allow to cool for 5 minutes, while you whisk the egg yolks to a light froth. Continuing to whisk, pour in the caramel syrup in a thin stream until fully incorporated and continue whisking until cool.

Lightly whip the double cream to soft peaks, then fold this into the caramel custard and mix thoroughly to a uniform brown with no streaks of cream showing.

Pour into a plastic container, put on a lid and freeze for 8 hours or overnight, removing to the fridge to soften for 5 minutes before serving.

## BAKED ALASKA

Baked Alaska is a neat ice-cream dessert that is surrounded with meringue, the meringue acting as an insulation between the frozen ice-cream and the hot oven so that, if you have been careful not to leave any holes, the ice-cream emerges as cold as when it went in. You can make a baked Alaska with a shop-bought sponge and manufactured ice-cream or make them both yourself.

**SERVES 6**

**1-litre / 1¾-pint round tub of vanilla ice-cream**
**20-cm / 8-inch round of Victoria sponge**
**whites of 4 eggs**
**85 g / 3 oz caster sugar**
**4 tablespoons raspberry jam**

Freeze the ice-cream in the coldest section of the freezer and freeze the sponge on a baking sheet overnight.

Preheat the oven to 230°C/450°F/gas 8. Make the meringue. With an electric mixer set at medium speed, whisk the egg whites to soft peaks, then increase the speed to maximum and gradually add the sugar until the peaks are firm, but taking care not to take it too far or the meringue will separate.

Spread the sponge with the jam. Turn out the ice-cream to sit on top of the jam. Smooth the meringue all over it with a palette knife, taking it right down to the edge to seal the ice-cream in entirely.

Bake for 4–5 minutes, until the meringue is just beginning to colour. Remove and serve immediately.

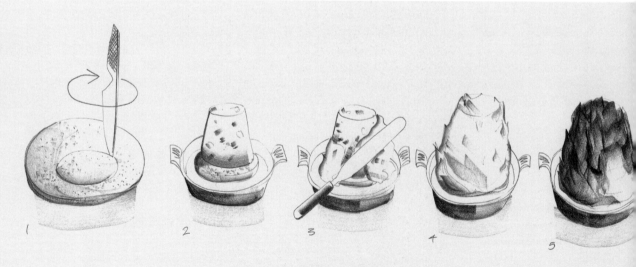

### *Making Baked Alaska*

❶ Cut a round of sponge to match the top of the tub of ice-cream you are using and freeze it and the ice-cream overnight.
❷ Place the sponge in a heatproof dish and turn the ice-cream out on top of it.
❸ Spread the meringue mixture all around the ice-cream to form a protective shell, going all the way down to the edges of the sponge. There must be no gaps for hot air to get to the ice-cream.
❹ Bake until the meringue is just taking a colour, and serve immediately.

# BREADS AND BAKING

**F**ew aspects of cooking are as satisfying as making bread. Once the news that your host baked bread was not something to raise the spirits, since it implied heavy-weight brown loaves with all the sex appeal of a household brick. Small sachets of easy-blend yeast granules have given us a standardized and user-friendly leavening agent that has changed all that. Now more of us have electric mixers and good strong white bread flour is widely available, we can produce excellent breads with very different characteristics and with very little effort. Baking bread is fun, a pleasure for the cook and for those with whom you share your bread. Once you have the basic dough working well, the opportunities really open up. Currently fashionable focaccia and ciabatta are within any cook's grasp, as are brioche, doughnuts and dumplings as light as air.

## BREAD

The easiest and most flexible dough uses a strong white wheat flour and the packet 'instant' easy-blend yeast you can buy in any supermarket in boxes of foil-wrapped sachets. This does not need to be activated separately in warm water, but is simply mixed in with the dough.

Good bread begins with a high-gluten wheat flour, ideally with a 14 per cent protein content. Waitrose are at last selling Canadian wheat flour, the higher-than-average gluten content of which traps more carbon dioxide from the yeast, so producing a lighter loaf with a terrific crust.

A traditional baker uses a wooden peel, a long-handled paddle, to transfer the risen dough into the oven and the finished bread out of it. Pizzas and many breads benefit from being baked in direct contact with heated stone, which is what gives them their crisp base crust. You can buy baking stones to go into domestic ovens but, if you do, you will then have to work out a technique for sliding the dough on to them, as the baker does with a peel. While the loaf will never be quite as good as the bread baked in direct contact with hot stone, heavy baking trays will give good results.

The incredibly versatile dough given below will make loaves, rolls or pizza. Leave the dough in a zip-lock bag and it will make very good focaccia after being knocked down and left to rise a second time at room temperature. Press in slivered garlic and dress with more oil for a garlic bread or roll out as pancakes to make wheat flour tortillas in a hot dry pan on the hob. It also makes brilliant pittas. That which you don't use the first day will keep happily in a zip-lock bag in the fridge for three days.

MAKES ONE LARGE LOAF
OR AS ABOVE

**600 ml / 1 pt hand-warm water
one 7-g / ¼-oz sachet of easy-blend yeast
1 tsp caster sugar
1 tsp salt
1 tbsp olive oil, plus more for greasing
900 g / 2 lb strong white bread flour, sifted, plus more for dusting**

Put the warm water in the bowl of a mixer fitted with a dough hook, and add the yeast, sugar, salt and olive oil. Turn on at the lowest speed, pour in the flour and work for 10 minutes. Increase the speed to maximum and finish for 1 minute.

Turn the sticky dough out on a floured surface and knead for a minute or two. Form into a ball and put to rise at room temperature in a lightly oiled bowl covered with cling-wrap for 2 hours, when it should have more than doubled in size.

Alternatively, use a food processor though you will not get such a good result. Put all the dry ingredients in the bowl and, using the metal blade, process to a crumb texture. In a thin stream, pour in approximately three-quarters of the warm water, adding the liquid more slowly as the dough begins to ball. There may still be a tablespoon or so of water left at this point. Only add this if the ball

starts to break up. Once the dough is holding in a ball, continue to process on full speed for about 2 minutes. The dough will be elastic and slightly sticky and, as it begins to adhere to the sides of the processor, switch off. Turn out on a floured surface, knead for 2 minutes, then shape into a ball. Brush a large bowl with olive oil, put in the dough, push down to flatten and brush the surface with more oil. Cover the bowl and leave to rise.

People think yeast needs to be put somewhere hot for dough to prove. This is not true and too hot an environment can be counterproductive. Dough will rise in a cold place, even in the fridge, though this of course takes longer. Somewhere in the kitchen away from drafts and away from direct heat is best. After 90 minutes to 2 hours it will have trebled in bulk and, once you have removed it and knocked it down, you will have a versatile bread mix to experiment with (see above).

Preheat the oven to 220°C/425°F/gas 7. Shape the loaf as you wish and bake for 20 minutes. Reduce the heat to

200°C/400°F/gas 6 and bake for another 15 minutes. Remove the loaf and rap the bottom. If it sounds hollow, it is done. If not give it another 5 minutes. Put to cool on a rack for 30 minutes. This is important. If you put loaves straight from the oven on to a hard surface the base crust will be soggy.

**FOCACCIA**

Divide the dough above, after the first rising, into 2 equal pieces. Don't knock them down, but pull them out into rough rectangles and shake flour on top. Leave, uncovered, to rise for a second time for 1 hour.

Preheat your oven to 250°C/475°F/gas 9. Spray a little water on the inside of the oven, close the door and wait 60 seconds for steam to generate, then put in the loaves as quickly as you can. If they can't both sit on the same shelf you will have to bake them one at a time, which will take about 25 minutes, when you should have a good, crisp brown crust and the loaf will sound hollow when you rap the bottom.

## SOURDOUGH BREAD

Bakers who use traditional methods always save some yeast-fermented dough from the day before to use as the leavening starter for the next batch. In some parts of the world this is called *poolish*, in Italy *biga* and sponge in English. It works in a different way to fresh yeast, giving an unmistakable nutty flavour to the bread.

MAKES 2 LOAVES
**about 725 ml / 25 fl oz hand-warm water**
**15 g / ½ oz dried yeast**
**515 g / 1 lb 2 oz strong white bread flour, plus more for dusting**
**1 tbsp bran flour**
**400 g / 14 oz wholemeal flour**
**1 tbsp sea salt**
**olive oil, for greasing**

Put 125 ml / 4 fl oz hand-warm water in a bowl and add half the yeast. Let stand for a minute, then stir with a wooden spoon until the yeast dissolves. Now stir in 115 g / 4 oz strong white bread flour and the bran flour until you have a thick, smooth batter, adding a little more water if needed. Cover the bowl with cling-film and leave at room temperature for 24–36 hours, when it will be bubbly, risen and smell strongly of yeast.

Transfer this to a large mixing bowl or to the bowl of an electric mixer. Break it up with a wooden spoon, then add a further 600 ml / 21 fl oz hand-warm water, the remaining yeast, 200 g / 7 oz more strong white bread flour, half the wholemeal flour and the sea salt. If using a mixer, turn on the dough hook at slow speed. Check manufacturer's instructions to make sure your machine is up to this task! If the motor burns out, don't say you haven't been warned. Gradually add the remaining white and wholemeal flours. After 5 minutes, increase speed to medium and work for a further 5 minutes, when the dough should be springy to the touch and have a satin sheen.

Remove to a floured surface and continue kneading by hand for a final 5 minutes, shaking on flour if it is too sticky to work with.

Roll the dough into a ball and put it in a bowl lightly greased with olive oil. Brush the surface with a little more oil and cover with a clean damp cloth. Put to rise in a warm place for 2-3 hours, until doubled in volume. The ideal temperature is 23–26°C/74–78°F.

Knock the dough down, turn it over, cover again and leave for 30 minutes.

Turn the dough out, divide into 2 and flatten, then reform into 2 balls. Line two 20-cm / 8-inch bowls or baskets with clean drying-up cloths and flour them heavily. Put the dough into them and dust the tops with flour. Leave to rise again for 2 hours, until almost doubled in volume.

Preheat the oven to 230°C/450°F/gas 8. Turn the bowls upside down to turn the loaves on to a heavily floured board. Slash the tops with a razor blade to a depth of 5 mm / ¼ inch. Spray the insides of the oven with water, close the door and leave for steam to generate for 3 minutes. Ideally you want to slide the loaves on to a baking stone in the centre of the oven. If this is not possible, slide the loaves on to a preheated non-stick Swiss roll tin.

Bake for 10–15 minutes then lower the temperature to 200°/400°F/gas 6 and cook for further 30 minutes. Test by rapping the bottom of the loaves as above.

### WHY FLOUR IS WHITE
*Flour naturally retains the colouring present in the wheat as a pigment. Semolina is completely unbleached hard wheat flour that gives pasta its yellowish colour. What we buy as milled, refined flour has usually been whitened by exposure to chlorine dioxide gas, a harmless process except that it destroys the vitamin E found in wheat.*

*This gas also ages the flour, accelerating a process of improvement in the gluten that takes place automatically during prolonged exposure to the air. It was demonstrated empirically hundreds of years ago that if flour was kept for a few months before use, it had better baking properties. However, it is bulky stuff and takes up expensive space, so food scientists came up with a process to do the job quickly and cheaply. Thus the description 'improved flour' means it has been chemically aged to improve the elasticity of the gluten proteins, which delivers a better rise and a lighter loaf.*

## SODA BREAD

Soda bread is distinguished by its use of baking soda and cream of tartar to generate the carbon dioxide which lightens and lifts the loaf instead of yeast. Buttermilk — originally the slightly sour residue of milk, from which most of the fat has been removed in churning to make butter — is today made commercially from skimmed milk. It gives a rich and distinctive tang to the bread. Health food shops are usually reliable sources of supply, though some supermarkets now stock it. Soda bread is a great Irish tradition and this recipe, handed down from mother to daughter for generations, is from Rose Irwin in Donegal.

MAKES 1 LOAF

**450 g / 1 lb plain flour, plus
more for dusting
1 level tsp sugar
1 level tsp salt
1 level tsp baking soda
1 level tsp cream of tartar
about 350 ml / 12 fl oz
buttermilk**

Preheat the oven to 230°C/450°F/gas 8. Sieve the flour into a bowl with the sugar, salt, baking soda and cream of tartar. Make a well in the centre and pour in the buttermilk, mixing in with one hand and working from the side of the bowl inwards while turning the bowl with the other hand. The dough should be soft, but not too wet and sticky. If it is too dry to hold, add a little more buttermilk.

As soon as it holds, turn out on to a lightly floured surface and knead briefly.

Put the dough into a 20-cm / 8-inch round baking tin with a 4–5-cm / 1½–2-inch rim. Cut a deep cross into the top, taking the cuts all the way down at the edges. Put to bake for 15 minutes, then turn the temperature down to 200°C/ 400°F/gas 6 and continue to cook for 30 minutes, when the bottom of the bread should sound hollow when rapped.

## GUINNESS BREAD

Beer has been used in baking from early Egyptian times, as its natural yeasts work as a raising agent or leaven.

MAKES 2 LOAVES

**600 ml / 1 pt Guinness, or other
stout
1 tbsp muscovado sugar
30 g / 1 oz butter
1 tsp salt
550 g / 1¼ lb strong white bread
flour, plus more for dusting
285 g / 10 oz wholemeal flour
7-g / ¼-oz sachet of easy-blend
yeast
oil, for greasing**

Put the stout in a pan with the muscovado sugar, butter and salt. Bring to the boil, remove from the heat and allow to cool to hand-warm.

Pour into the mixing bowl of a mixer with a dough hook. Switch on at the lowest speed and pour in the flours and yeast. Work for 10 minutes, remove to a floured surface and knead briefly, shaping into a ball. Put this in large oiled bowl and cover the top with cling-film. Leave to prove at room temperature for 2 hours.

Take out, knock down and divide into 2. Put each half into a 1-kg / 2-lb loaf tin. Cover with a cloth and leave to rise again for 30 minutes.

Preheat the oven to 250°C/475°F/ gas 9. Spray the hot oven with water and mist the tops of the loaves. Close the door and allow steam to generate for 60 seconds. Put the bread into the oven on a rack and bake for 15 minutes. Lower the temperature to 200°C/ 400°F/gas 6 and cook for a further 15 minutes, when the bread should be well risen and brown on top. Turn out and rap the bottoms, which should sound hollow. Put on a rack and resist the temptation to slice until cooled to room temperature.

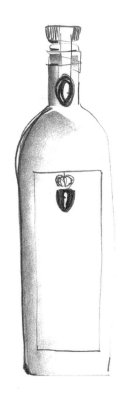

## WALNUT BREAD

MAKE 2 LOAVES
275 g / 10 oz strong white bread
flour, plus more for dusting
275 g / 10 oz wholewheat flour
275 g / 10 oz rye flour
6 g / ¼ oz easy-blend yeast
2 tsp salt
600 ml / 1 pt hand-warm water
1 tbsp clear honey
30 g / 1 oz softened butter, plus
more for greasing
oil, for greasing
225 g / 8 oz halved walnuts

Sift each flour into a bowl with the yeast and salt. Pour the hand-warm water into the bowl of an electric mixer fitted with a dough hook. Add the honey and softened butter, then switch on at low speed. Pour in the flour mixture and work gently for 10 minutes, turning up to full speed and working for a further minute.

Turn the dough out on to a floured surface and form into a ball, then transfer it to an oiled bowl. Cover the top with cling-film and leave to prove for 2 hours at room temperature.

Turn out, knock down and scatter on the halved walnuts. Knead to work these uniformly into the dough.

Butter two 23-cm / 9-inch cake tins. Cut the dough in half, shape it into 2 round loaves and place in the tins. Cover with a damp cloth and leave to rise again for 30–40 minutes. During this secondary proving, preheat the oven to 250°C/475°F/gas 9. Spray the loaves with water and put to bake for 15–20 minutes. Turn down the heat to 200°C/400°F/gas 6 and continue cooking for 30 minutes, when the loaves should sound hollow when tapped on the bottom.

Allow to cool on a rack and do not slice until completely cold.

## BAGELS

The differentiating element in their preparation is a brief scalding in boiling water prior to baking. They should be eaten as soon after they cool as possible, as after only a few hours they become dry and heavy. They do freeze extremely well, however, and can be reheated from frozen by 10 minutes in a moderate oven.

Serve them with the classic combination of smoked salmon (known in Yiddish as *lox*) and cream cheese or with cream cheese and chopped onion. A scrape of cream cheese on its own is called a *schmir*.

MAKES ABOUT 12
300 ml / ½ pt milk
300 ml / ½ pt hand-hot water
2 tsp salt
1 tsp sugar
one 6-g / ¼-oz sachet of easy-
blend yeast
900 g / 2 lb strong white bread
flour, plus more for dusting
2 eggs, separated
60 g / 2 oz melted butter
oil, for greasing

Put the milk and hand-hot water in the bowl of an electric mixer with the salt, sugar and yeast. Turn on the dough-hook at low speed and pour in the flour, whites of the 2 eggs and the melted butter. Work for 8 minutes to a smooth, pliant dough. Turn up the speed to full and beat for 1 minute.

Remove to a floured surface and knead briefly, then roll into a ball. Put in an oiled bowl, cover the top with cling-film and leave to rise at room temperature for 2 hours.

Knock the dough down, then divide it into 30 pieces. Roll these into cylinders and join the ends together to form rings. Cover with a cloth and leave to rise for 45–60 minutes.

Put a large pan of water to boil and preheat the oven to 220°C/425°F/gas 7. Working 2 at a time, put the bagels into the boiling water for 20 seconds, then transfer them to a lightly oiled baking tray. Glaze the tops with the egg yolks beaten with 1 tablespoon of water and bake in batches for 20 minutes, when they will be well risen and a nice shiny golden colour. Allow to cool on a rack.

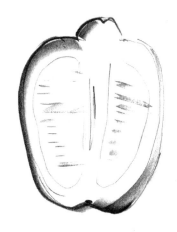

## BUTTERMILK BISCUITS

For the uninitiated, a biscuit in the USA is closest to a savoury scone, while they call our sweet biscuits 'cookies'. American supermarkets sell really good instant biscuit mixes, though they are not difficult to make from scratch.

**MAKES ABOUT 16**
**675 g / 12 oz self-raising flour, plus more for dusting**
**1 tbsp bicarbonate of soda**
**½ tsp baking powder**
**1 tsp salt**
**60 g / 2 oz chilled hard baking margarine, diced**
**60 g / 2 oz unsalted butter, diced, plus more for greasing**
**300 ml / ½ pt buttermilk**

**for the glaze:**
**1 egg**
**1 tbsp milk**

Preheat the oven to 230°C/450°F/gas 8.

Sift the flour into a bowl with the bicarbonate of soda, baking powder and salt. Rub the margarine and butter in gently with your fingertips to achieve a crumb consistency. Stir in the buttermilk with a fork to form a soft dough.

Flour your hands and form the dough into a ball, then transfer to a floured surface. Push it down and out into a circle about 1 cm / ½ inch thick. Use a 5-cm / 2-inch round pastry cutter to cut out as many biscuits as you can, putting them on a lightly greased baking sheet. The dough is very resilient, so squeeze the off-cuts into a ball, push this out into another round and cut out some more biscuits.

Make the glaze: whisk the egg with the milk and brush the tops. Bake for 12-15 minutes, when the biscuits will have risen and become golden brown.

Allow to cool on a wire rack and serve still warm. If it makes life easier, they can be made up to 6 hours in advance. Warm them through in the oven, wrapped in foil, just before serving.

## CORN TORTILLAS

Traditionally, tortillas are made by hand from fresh masa, a dough produced from white field corn that can be bought in Central America and the southern United States from tortillerias, the factories which make tortillas commercially. Alas, no such facilities exist in Britain, so we need to make them from masa harina, force-dried finely ground corn meal. Quaker Oats produce one in the USA which you can buy here by mail order, from Made in America (01249 447558), a very useful supplier of otherwise virtually unobtainable food products, like corn syrup.

The finished dough is not easy to work with since it has none of the elasticity of a yeast dough and dries out very quickly to become unworkable.

**MAKES ABOUT 20**
**300 ml / ½ pt hot water**
**255 g / 9 oz masa harina (see left)**

Put the hot water in the bowl of an electric mixer. Turn on the dough-hook, add the masa harina and knead at slow speed until you have a soft but not sticky dough.

Remove, cling-wrap and leave to rest for 30 minutes at room temperature.

Divide into 15 balls, then roll these out between plastic sheets to a thickness of a 50 p piece or press in a tortilla press between plastic sheets.

Cook in a hot dry frying pan for about 40 seconds on each side, when the bread will have puffed and be speckled brown.

Wrap the tortillas in a cloth and leave them for 15 minutes before serving to allow their steam to soften them slightly.

267

### NAAN BREAD

Naan is a Punjabi bread from the north of India, made from wheat flour and leavened by fermenting yoghurt. A tandoori restaurant cooks its naan bread in tandoor ovens, which are charcoal-fired and shaped like giant clay vases. The dough is slapped skilfully just beneath the lip of the open oven. The weight of the dough pulls it down as it cooks, to give the traditional elongated shape, and it is ready just at the moment when the baked bread would unstick from the oven side and fall down on the coals.

It will never be possible to bake anything exactly like the tandoor naan, but you can make a very good bread using a standard grill and self-raising flour.

MAKES 8

300 ml / ½ pt hand-warm water
4 heaped tbsp natural yoghurt
1 tsp salt
550 g / 1¼ lb self-raising flour

Put the warm water in the bowl of a food mixer with the yoghurt and salt. Turn on at low speed and add the flour. Work for 5 minutes, then remove the sticky dough to a floured surface and knead for a minute or two. Put into an oiled bowl and cling-wrap the top. Leave at room temperature for 2 hours.

Preheat the grill and a metal grill tray. Pull off balls of dough the size of squash balls and roll these out into 23-cm / 9-inch ovals. Put under the grill on the preheated metal tray for 45–60 seconds. As they puff up and spot, turn and give the other side 30–45 seconds.

Keep warm in a low oven, wrapped in a cloth while you cook the rest.

### POORIS

Pooris are deep-fried Indian unleavened loaves.

MAKES 12

60 g / 2 oz besan (chickpea) flour
60 g / 2 oz high-protein white bread flour, plus more for dusting
60 g / 2 oz wholemeal flour
125 ml / 4 fl oz hand-warm water
1 tbsp sunflower oil
1 tsp salt
oil, for greasing and deep-frying

Sift together the three types of flour.

Put the hand-warm water in the bowl of a food mixer fitted with a dough-hook. Add the sunflower oil and salt. Switch on at the lowest speed and pour in the flours. Work for 5 minutes, when you should have a good, smooth and elastic dough. If it is too dry and not balling properly, dribble in more water, 1 tablespoon at a time, until it does.

Turn out on a floured surface, form into a ball and put into an oiled bowl to rest for 60 minutes, covered with a damp cloth.

Heat oil for deep-frying to 190°C/ 375°F. Divide the dough into 12 equal parts and roll them into balls. With a rolling pin and on a floured surface, roll these out into 12.5-cm / 5-inch circles.

Slide one at a time into the oil, pushing it under the surface. It should balloon within seconds. When it does, turn over and cook for another 10 seconds. Remove and drain on kitchen paper. Eat as soon as possible, while still warm.

### GOUGÈRES

*Gougères* are cheese choux pastry puffs, traditionally served in Burgundy with a glass of Beaujolais. A youngish wine with lots of acidity is most appropriate, not that *nouveau* stuff which tastes of bubble gum, but a decent *cru* like a Brouilly, Fleurie or Chiroubles. In southern Burgundy they serve *gougères* between the main course and the pudding instead of a cheese course. Although the choux can be cooked as one large ring in a mould, it is more usual to have individual puffs, which may be served filled or unfilled. Both are nice, but filled with a Gruyère-enriched béchamel is best of all.

MAKES 12-16 INDIVIDUAL GOUGÈRES

salt
100 g / 3½ oz butter, plus more for greasing
freshly grated nutmeg
140 g / 5 oz flour
5 egg yolks
200 g / 7 oz Gruyère cheese, grated
600 ml / 1 pt thick béchamel sauce (page 208)

Preheat the oven to 220°C/425°F/gas 7. In a saucepan, bring to the boil 250 ml / 8 fl oz lightly salted water with the butter and freshly grated nutmeg to taste.

Remove from the heat and immediately beat in the flour, until the mixture forms a ball which pulls away easily from the pan. Return to a low heat and continue to beat for 2 minutes.

Off the heat, beat in the egg yolks, one at a time, to produce a glossy, elastic dough, then stir in 85 g / 3 oz of the grated Gruyère until incorporated. The last two stages may be done in a food processor or mixer.

Grease a baking tray. Use 2 dessertspoons to shape balls of choux: first dip the spoons into boiling water, then turn a piece of dough from one spoon to the other to get a uniform shape about 2.5 cm / 1 inch across. Put these on the baking sheet, allowing room between them because they will puff up about 3 times in size. If you are not filling the gougères, then sprinkle the tops with a little grated Gruyère.

In either case, bake for 10 minutes, then lower the temperature to 200°C/ 400°F/gas 6 for a further 10–15 minutes, when they should be puffed and golden.

Remove, pierce the sides with a skewer and return to the switched-off oven with the door slightly ajar for 5 minutes. Remove to a wire rack and cool. This will keep them crisp.

While they are baking, make the thick béchamel and finish it with the remaining Gruyère. When smooth and amalgamated, cut the tops off the gougères and spoon in this cheese sauce to fill.

Serve hot or at room temperature.

## OATCAKES

For centuries oatcakes were eaten daily in many parts of Britain and Ireland, before wheat bread ceased to be for special occasions only and became commonplace. Different parts of the country had different local variations and the following is based on an old Donegal recipe. Originally they would

have been cooked on an iron griddle, but oven-baking produces good results. Unlike baking bread, which demands a very high temperature, oatcakes are cooked very slowly, more a drying process akin to making meringues. Oatcakes are delicious with cheese or buttered with jam.

MAKES ABOUT 30
450 g / 1 lb fine oatmeal
2 tsp salt
60 g / 2 oz butter
450 ml / ¾ pt boiling water

Put the oatmeal in a large mixing bowl. Put the salt and butter in a measuring jug and add the boiling water. Stir until dissolved, then pour over the oatmeal and mix with a fork to achieve a malleable consistency. It may need a little more water. Cover and leave overnight in a cool place but not in the fridge.

Spoon out on a work surface and press flat as thinly as you can. Using a pastry cutter and working from the edge inwards, cut out circles, transferring these with a palette knife to an ungreased baking tray or trays. Leave to stand for 2 hours in a warm place.

Preheat the oven to 130°C/275°F/ gas 1 and bake the oatcakes for 3 hours. Any leftover can be kept in an airtight tin and reheated when wanted, again at the lowest temperature. If they go soggy from moisture absorption from the air, just return them to a low oven to dry out and recrisp.

## SHORTBREAD

Shortbread is so called because of its high fat content, short being the abbreviation of shortening, which in this rich crumbly biscuit means butter.

MAKE TWO 20-CM /
8-INCH ROUNDS
225 g / 8 oz chilled unsalted butter, plus more for greasing
225 g / 8 oz flour
60 g / 2 oz caster sugar, plus more for dusting
pinch of salt
1 tsp vanilla extract

Dice the butter and put it into a mixing bowl to soften. Sift the flour on top with the caster sugar, a pinch of salt and the vanilla extract. Rub together gently and form into a ball. Alternatively, blitz all the ingredients in a food processor until they ball. The mixture needs no liquid.

Shake some sugar on a surface, put the dough on it and cut in half, shaping into 2 equal balls. Put each into a lightly buttered 20-cm / 8-inch tart tin and gently press the mixture out into an even layer, but slightly thicker at the edges, and crimping between finger and thumb. Prick the surface all over with a fork and incise 4 bisecting shallow cuts from edge to edge, like the spokes of a wheel so that the biscuit can be divided neatly into 8 equal wedges when baked. Refrigerate for 30 minutes to 1 hour.

Preheat the oven to 180°C/350°F/ gas 4 and bake the shortbread for 20–25 minutes, when the surface should be an even golden brown and firm to the touch. Leave in the tins until completely cooled before removing.

## BRIOCHE

Because brioche is made from a very rich dough, it is important to give it a prolonged kneading. The high butter content makes this difficult by hand and a much better result is achieved using a dough-hook in an electric mixer. The goal is an extravagantly buttery flavour, but without its presence being discernible either visually or on the palate. Questions about butter oozing from the dough suggest under-kneading and putting the dough to rise in too warm an environment.

Brioche requires three risings, two at room temperature and the third — the middle one — in the fridge. Room temperature for proving dough should be between 20°C/68°F and 22°C/72°F. Never force matters by standing it next to something hot.

The richest brioches can have equal parts flour and butter, but a good result will be achieved using half the weight of butter to flour. If you have a 24-cm / 9½-inch brioche mould, then use it; otherwise use a loaf tin.

MAKES 1 LARGE BRIOCHE
225 g / 8 oz chilled unsalted
butter, plus more for greasing
5 tbsp hand-warm milk
500 g / 1 lb 2 oz sifted strong
bread flour
6 g / ¼ oz easy-blend yeast
30 g / 1 oz sugar
1 tsp salt
5 large eggs

for the glaze:
1 egg
1 tbsp milk

Cut the chilled unsalted butter into dice and leave on a plate to soften. Put the hand-warm milk in the mixing bowl. Switch on at the lowest speed and add the flour, yeast, sugar and salt.

Whisk the eggs and pour them in, then work for 10 minutes. Turn up the speed to full and gradually add the butter, continuing to beat for 3 minutes, when you will have a glossy and elastic dough.

Turn out into a large bowl, cover the top with cling-film and leave to rise for 2 hours at room temperature, when it should have at least doubled in size. You don't want to knock the dough down aggressively, so just turn it twice, which will break the surface and it will sink. Cover the top again and refrigerate for a minimum of 4 hours, a maximum of 24.

Turn out on a floured surface and shape into a ball. If using a classic, fluted brioche mould, lightly butter it and shake in some flour, upending and tapping to get rid of any excess. Cut off one-third of the dough to form the central rounded top. Reform the larger piece into a ball and place in the mould, making a hole in the middle. Shape the smaller piece into a ball and place snugly in the hole.

Make a glaze by whisking the egg with the milk. Brush this sparingly all over the top, taking care not to allow any to dribble down the inside of the tin as this would affect the rise. Leave at room temperature for 1½–2 hours, when it will again have doubled in size.

Preheat the oven to 220°C/425°F/ gas 7. Brush more glaze on the top and bake for 40 minutes. Turn out and rap the bottom, which should sound hollow; if it doesn't, return to the tin and give it another 5 minutes. Turn out on a wire rack to cool.

### BISCUITS D'ANCHOIS À LA ROYALE

These easy-to-make biscuits are a good nibble with dry sherry or dry white wine.

MAKES ABOUT 30
170 g / 6 oz plain flour
85 g / 3 oz chilled butter, diced
2 egg yolks
2 tsp anchovy essence

for the anchovy cream:
one 60-g / 2-oz can of anchovy fillets, drained
1 shelled hard-boiled egg
60 g / 2 oz butter
3 tbsp double cream
1 tsp cayenne pepper
a few drops of red food dye, such as cochineal (optional)

In a food processor, blitz the flour with the butter until they crumb. Add the egg yolks and anchovy essence and process briefly, adding a little water through the feeder tube until a stiff dough forms. Scrape out on to cling-film, roll up and chill for 30 minutes.

Preheat the oven to 200°C/400°F/ gas 6. Roll the pastry out on a floured surface until about 3 mm / ⅛ inch thick and use a pastry cutter to cut out biscuits. Place them on a baking sheet and bake for 10-15 minutes, or until crisp and golden. Allow to cool on a rack.

Make the anchovy cream: in the food processor, blend the anchovy fillets, egg, butter, cream and cayenne pepper. If you have some red food dye, add a few drops to give a pink colour. If you are feeling tricky, pipe this on to the biscuits; if not, spread thinly with a knife.

### WATER BISCUITS

Few people go to the trouble of baking water biscuits, the crisp savoury crackers most of us automatically buy in packets to serve with cheese. It is an interesting challenge, however, and the ingredients could not be more basic — fat, flour and water. Keeping the fat-to-flour ratio low, at about 1 to 4, makes it easier to roll the pastry very thin. A way of preventing curl is to prick the biscuits all over. You will also get a lighter result by adding a little baking powder to plain flour, which will help create the slightly bubbled surface characteristic of water biscuits. The fat needs to be worked in as cold as possible and this is a pastry which benefits from using a food processor briefly to do the job. If you overwork it, the result will be too elastic, making the pastry difficult to roll out, and the biscuits will be unpalatably chewy.

MAKES 20 BISCUITS
225 g / 8 oz plain flour
1 tsp baking powder
60 g / 2 oz lard, cut into small dice
about 2–3 tbsp ice-cold water
oil, for greasing
sea salt

Preheat the oven to 180°C/350°/gas 4. Sift the flour into a food processor with the baking powder. Add the lard dice and blitz briefly to a crumb, then add just enough of the ice-cold water through the feeder tube, 1 tablespoon at a time, until the pastry balls. Remove, cling-wrap and allow the pastry to rest in the fridge for about 10 minutes.

Roll out thinly (about 3 mm / ⅛ inch) on a floured surface. Prick all over and cut into 10-cm / 5-inch rounds with a pastry cutter. Transfer to a lightly oiled baking sheet, sprinkle with sea salt and bake in the oven for 10–15 minutes, when they will have taken a pale colour. Allow to cool on a rack.

### CHEESE STRAWS

For full-flavoured, melt-in-the-mouth cheese straws you need a high fat content and a strong farmhouse Cheddar.

MAKES ABOUT 20
225 g / 8 oz plain flour, sifted, plus more for dusting
225 g / 8 oz unsalted butter, plus more for greasing
170 g / 6 oz Cheddar cheese, grated
2 tsp cayenne pepper
½ tsp salt
a little grated Parmesan cheese (or more Cheddar), for sprinkling

*Opposite (from the top): Norwegian Apple Cake (page 286), Chocolate Génoise (page 284), Madeira Cake (page 282)*

In a bowl, rub together the flour and butter to a crumb, then rub in the grated Cheddar with the cayenne pepper and salt. Add about 1 tablespoon of cold water and bind. Alternatively, put all the ingredients in a food processor and pulse-chop to a crumb, before adding the water through the feeder tube while running at full speed until the dough balls. Cling-wrap and refrigerate for 1 hour.

Preheat the oven to 180°C/350°F/ gas 4 and grease 2 baking trays with a little butter. Roll out the cheese pastry on a lightly floured surface to a thickness of about 6 mm / ¼ inch and cut into fingers about 7.5 cm / 3 inches long and 2 cm / ¾ inch wide. Sprinkle with a little grated Parmesan or Cheddar, put on the trays and bake for 10 minutes.

Ideally, serve while still warm.

*Opposite (clockwise from the top left): Garlic Mayonnaise (page 295), Tarator (page 294), Blue Cheese Dressing (page 296), Skordalia (page 293), Honey Vinaigrette (page 296)*

## PORK CRACKLING BISCUITS

*Pogacice* are small round yeast-raised biscuits with pork cracklings. This recipe is based on one by Inge Kramarz in *The Balkan Cookbook*. The technique of folding the dough and brushing with fat before three separate rollings has similarities with flaky pastry. Since the whole point is to have the crackling crisp and discernible both visually and texturally, you cannot use a food processor to make the dough because it would mulch the crackling, giving a greasy effect.

MAKES ABOUT 16–20

**175 g / 6 oz pork skin with a layer of fat, cut into 1-cm / ½-inch dice**
**150 ml / ¼ pt milk**
**salt**
**225 g / 8 oz flour, plus more for dusting**
**3 egg yolks**
**6 g / ¼ oz easy-blend yeast**
**about 125 ml / 4 fl oz dry white wine**
**about 85 g / 3 oz fresh lard**

Put the pork skin dice in a large frying pan with the milk. Bubble this down over a high heat, then turn the heat right down and allow the fat to render, stirring from time to time until you are left with crisp brown cracklings. Pass through a sieve, reserving the liquid fat. (This will set as lard and should be refrigerated for use in another dish, for example the Refried Beans recipe on page 203. Do not, for the time being, put it in the fridge as you will need some of the fat later in the recipe.) Drain the cracklings on kitchen paper, seasoning with salt while still hot, and leave to cool.

In a bowl, mix the cracklings with the flour, egg yolks, yeast and just enough dry white wine for the mixture to cohere. Mix into a ball, transfer to a floured surface and knead to a stiff dough, shaking on more flour if too sticky. Put into a clean bowl, cover with a cloth and leave to stand for 45 minutes.

Turn out on to a floured surface and roll into a rectangle 1 cm / ½ inch thick. Brush this with about half the fresh lard and fold the sides into the middle and then fold the bottom and top in over again. Put in the fridge for 30 minutes, then roll out and repeat the process, again brushing with lard. Return to the fridge for a further 30 minutes and repeat yet again, returning to the fridge for a final rest.

Preheat the oven to 220°C/425°F/ gas 7 and roll out the chilled dough to a thickness of about 2 cm / ¾ inch. Use a 5-cm / 2-inch cutter to cut out rounds and place them on a lightly greased baking sheet. Bake for 30 minutes and serve while still hot.

### ROSE WATER BISCUITS

Rose water, which is made from the diluted essence of rose petals, was almost certainly first introduced to Europe from the Middle East as the consequence of some sensible crusader bringing back an Arab cook as a souvenir who, in turn, brought with him a stoppered vial of the stuff. In that part of the world it is still widely used to flavour drinks, puddings and sweet pastries. As with orange blossom water, which is used in the same way, its sweet intensity can be rather sickly in large doses, so add sparingly. Try making these biscuits, *petits soufflés à la rose*. They are a bit fiddly, but are worth the effort.

MAKES ABOUT 16
**225 g / 8 oz caster sugar**
**white of 1 egg**
**2 tsp rose water**
**a few drops of red food**
**colouring**
**icing sugar, for dusting**

Put the caster sugar in the bowl of a food mixer with the egg white and rose water. Beat to a paste, working with the balloon whisk for 8–10 minutes at full speed. Towards the end of this time, add a few drops of red food colouring to give a strong pink colour. Spoon on to clingfilm, roll into a cylinder and refrigerate for 20–30 minutes.

Preheat the oven to 150°C/300°F/ gas 2. Roll the paste out to a depth of 1 cm / ½ inch on a work surface dusted with icing sugar and cut into dice. Moisten your fingers with iced water and roll these into little balls. Flatten them into paper baking cases, again

with a moistened finger. The water stops you sticking to your biscuit and also doubles as a glaze.

Bake on a tray in the oven for 12–15 minutes. They should have risen and be dry on top. If not, give them 2–3 minutes more.

### BRANDY SNAPS

MAKES 12
**75 g / 2½ oz caster sugar**
**30 g / 1 oz butter, plus more for**
**greasing (optional)**
**1 tbsp golden syrup**
**30 g / 1 oz plain flour**
**2 tsp ground ginger**

Preheat the oven to 150°C/300°F/ gas 2. Beat the caster sugar with the butter and golden syrup until light and thick. Sift in the flour and ginger and stir to amalgamate. Divide into 12 equal parts, then roll these into small balls. Put them on a silicone sheet or lightly greased non-stick baking tray or Swiss roll tin and bake for 10–15 minutes, when the balls will have spread into dark brown biscuits.

Allow to cool briefly and then lift them off, one at a time. At this point they will be pliable and bend. Lay them one at a time over the handle of a wooden spoon and roll it around it. They will set hard very quickly. As you go along, should the remaining biscuits have firmed too much to roll, just return them briefly to the oven.

You can eat them as they are — they are excellent, for example, with ice-cream — or fill them with whipped cream.

### GINGER BISCUITS

An electric whisk makes these biscuits very quick and easy to make.

MAKES 16-20
**115 g / 4 oz unsalted butter**
**115 g / 4 oz caster sugar**
**115 g / 4 oz self-raising flour,**
**plus more for dusting**
**1 tbsp ground ginger**

Preheat the oven to 150°C/300°F/ gas 2. In a bowl, beat the butter with the sugar until pale and light. Sift in the flour and ground ginger, then whisk to incorporate.

Use a dessertspoon to scoop out amounts sufficient to make walnut-sized balls, rolling them between floured hands. Put these on a non-stick baking sheet and press them down gently into ovals. As they cook they will spread and set as thin biscuits.

Bake for 50–60 minutes, when they will be crisp and golden brown. Use a spatula to remove them to a wire rack to cool. If given the opportunity, they keep for a week in an airtight tin before going soft, but can be crisped back to life with 10 minutes in a low oven.

## CROSTOLI

Italian fried sweet pastries are called different things depending on the part of Italy in which you are eating them, and may be presented in different shapes — bows, knots, little plaits or simple rectangles. Traditionally they are fried in lard, but perhaps sunflower oil is a better idea. Whatever medium you use to deep-fry, make sure it is fresh for any sweet deep-frying, or it will taint the pastries.

Eat these crostoli with espresso or a strong cup of coffee, and, depending on the time of day, a glass of grappa. This is rather a nice way to conclude a dinner.

SERVES 4–6
**50 g / 2 oz softened butter**
**30 g / 1 oz caster sugar**
**1 egg**
**1 tbsp grated lemon zest**
**5 tbsp sweet red vermouth**
**300 g / 10 oz flour, plus more for dusting**
**oil, for deep-frying**
**icing sugar, for dusting**

In a mixing bowl, cream the softened butter with the sugar and egg. Add the lemon zest and vermouth, then mix in the flour and form a ball of dough.

Flour a work surface and roll the dough out as thinly as pasta (3 mm / $^1/_8$ inch) or use a pasta machine. With a pasta cutter — one of those wheels with a fluted edge — cut it into 20 x 2-cm / 8 x $^3/_4$-inch strips. Tie into bows or knots.

Preheat oil for deep-frying to 190°C/375°F. Fry the crostoli in batches for 2–3 minutes each, until golden brown. Transfer to kitchen paper to drain, then dust with icing sugar.

Eat as soon as possible.

## SCONES

When making scones, precise amounts will help deliver good results, for the proportions of flour to fat to raising agent are critical. Never use more than 60 g / 2 oz butter, block margarine or lard to 225 g / 8 oz flour, with the amount of fat reducing to 85 g / 3 oz for 450 g / 1 lb flour. Unsalted butter gives the best flavour. If you add too much baking soda to plain flour, it will ruin the scones — they will be as tall as houses, but with a bitter chemical aftertaste. So, to be on the safe side, use self-raising.

Handle the dough as little as possible, for hot hands and overworked dough will produce hard, poorly risen scones. A food processor helps and, if possible, make them in a cool place as, unlike yeast doughs — which must have warmth — scones should go cool into the oven, where the sudden exposure to heat encourages rapid air expansion and delivers more lift.

For a richer result, whisk 1 egg into 125 ml / 4 fl oz milk and use this instead of plain milk.

MAKES 8
**225 g / 8 oz self-raising flour, plus more for dusting**
**30 G / 1 oz caster sugar**
**pinch of salt**
**30 g / 1 oz frozen butter, cut into dice, plus more for greasing**
**about 140–150 ml / 4½ fl oz-¼ pt cold milk**

**for the glaze (optional):**
**1 egg, beaten**
**a little milk**

Preheat the oven to 220°C/450°F/ gas 8. Put the flour, caster sugar and salt in a processor and blitz briefly to mix. Add the butter dice and work again until the mixture crumbs. Then add 140–150 ml / 4½ fl oz-¼ pt cold milk in a thin stream through the feeder tube, stopping when the dough balls. It should be quite moist, but not sticking to the sides. If it is too dry, turn on again and dribble in a little more milk.

Turn out on a heavily floured surface, and form into a ball, then press gently into a round 2 cm / $^3/_4$ inch thick. Cut out the scones using a 5-cm / 2-inch round cutter and put on a greased baking tray. To give the tops an attractive colour, if you like, brush the scones lightly with a mixture of milk and egg.

Bake for 12–14 minutes. Remove and allow to cool slightly on a rack, but serve while still warm.

### CHEESE SCONES

Adding cheese always makes achieving a light result more difficult. The dough should be softer than for pastry, but this does not mean sticky. The addition of some mustard in the mix will enhance the flavour. You can use self-raising flour, which already contains raising agents, but try the traditional method of adding bicarbonate of soda and cream of tartar to plain flour.

MAKES ABOUT 6

250 g / 9 oz flour, plus more for
dusting
1 tsp salt
1 tsp bicarbonate of soda
2 tsp cream of tartar
2 tsp Colman's mustard powder
45 g / 1½ oz block margarine,
cut into small dice, plus more
for greasing
100 g / 3½ oz Cheddar cheese,
grated
125–150 ml / 4 fl oz - ¼ pt milk
oil, for greasing (optional)

Preheat the oven to 220°C/425°F/gas 7. Sieve the flour, salt, bicarbonate of soda, cream of tartar and mustard powder into a bowl. Add the margarine and rub in with your fingers to achieve a fine crumb texture. Add the grated Cheddar, followed by the milk, cutting it in with a blunt knife, adding just enough to get it to hold as a soft dough.

Turn out on a heavily floured surface and knead gently to complete the holding process. This is the point where overworking will result in a heavy end-result. Roll out the dough to a depth of 1 cm / ½ inch and cut into scones with a 5-cm / 2-inch cutter. Dust the tops with a little flour.

Put on a lightly oiled or non-stick baking sheet and bake for 10–12 minutes, when they will be nicely risen and golden brown.

Serve within minutes of taking them from the oven, with unsalted butter. If the result is still too heavy, try making them in a food processor, following the same order of procedure but adding the milk through the feeder tube at the end and stopping the instant the dough balls.

### TUILES OR BISCUIT CUPS

MAKES ABOUT 16

45 g / 1½ oz unsalted butter,
plus more for greasing
250 g / 8½ oz caster sugar
45 g / 1½ oz plain flour
whites of 5 eggs

Melt the butter in a pan over a low heat. Mix the caster sugar and flour in a bowl. Add the egg whites and the melted butter and stir to a smooth mixture. Allow to rest for 2 hours.

Preheat the oven to 160°C/325°F/gas 3 and butter a baking sheet. Using a fork dipped in cold water, spread 2 teaspoons of the mixture at a time in 10-cm / 4-inch circles on the prepared sheet. Working in batches or on several baking sheets, do 4 at a time and bake for 10 minutes until pale brown.

Immediately place over the base of 4 upturned tumblers and pull down to make inverted cups. They harden at once into tuiles, which you can slide off. If they go soggy they can be recrisped in a low oven.

### GIRDLE OR GRIDDLE SCONES

A griddle is only a large flat iron plate, so a heavy flat-bottomed frying pan will do the job just as well. Correct temperature rather than utensil is the key to success. If too hot, the scones will burn before the middle is done; if too cool, the batter will not rise enough and the result will be leaden. As with pancakes, it usually takes a few goes before you get it right. Always test the temperature by putting on one small spoonful of batter first. The best way is to put a pan on a moderate heat for 2–3 minutes, then turn it right down. Leave to allow the pan surface heat to stabilize before testing, wiping the base first with oiled paper.

MAKES 20

225 g / 8 oz plain flour
1½ tsp baking powder
15 g / ½ oz caster sugar
½ tsp salt
1 egg, beaten
about 150 ml / ¼ pt full-fat milk

Sieve the flour into a bowl with the baking powder, sugar and salt. Make a well in the middle, put in the egg then the milk and whisk to a thick batter, adding a little more milk if the mixture is too dry (you want the consistency of double cream). Leave to stand for 30 minutes at room temperature before use.

Preheat the frying pan and test, cooking one scone, then cook the rest in batches. One tablespoon of batter will make 1 scone. As the bottom of the scones cook, after about 2 minutes, bubbles will come to the surface. Turn them and cook the other side for 2 minutes.

Keep the scones warm, wrapped in a cloth in a low oven until all are done. Eat while still warm, with butter and jam.

## POTATO PANCAKES

These are equally good with a slice of Cheddar or jam.

**MAKES ABOUT 10**

**170 g / 6 oz plain flour, plus more for dusting**

**2 tsp baking powder**

**1 tsp salt**

**50 g / 2 oz softened butter, plus more for greasing**

**150 g / 5 oz dry mashed potato**

**2–3 tbsp cold milk**

**beaten egg yolk, to glaze**

Preheat the oven to 220°C/425°F/gas 7. Sieve the flour, baking powder and salt into a bowl. Rub in the softened butter, then add the mashed potato and mix with a fork, adding just enough of the cold milk, 1 tablespoon at a time, to bind it to a soft dough.

Turn out on a floured surface and knead briefly, forming into a ball. Roll out to a thickness of 2 cm / ¾ inch and cut into triangles. Put on a lightly greased baking sheet and brush the tops with beaten egg yolk.

Bake for 10–12 minutes, when they should we well risen and golden brown. Serve while still warm.

## CHELSEA BUNS

Chelsea buns are characterized by an egg-enriched yeast dough with a high butter content, which is rolled up before cutting. After baking this creates vertical concentric layers, that can be pulled apart as you eat them.

**MAKES 10–12**

**75 g / 2¾ oz unsalted butter, plus more for greasing**

**150 ml / ¼ pt milk**

**550 g / 1¼ lb sifted strong plain flour, plus more for dusting**

**85 g / 3 oz, plus 1 tbsp sugar**

**6 g / ¼ oz easy-blend yeast**

**pinch of salt**

**4 eggs**

**oil, for greasing**

**85 g / 3 oz currants**

**1 tsp ground allspice**

Melt half the butter in the milk over a low heat to hand-warm, and leave the remaining butter in a warm place to soften.

Put the buttered milk into a food mixer bowl with the dough hook. Switch on at the lowest speed. Add the flour, 45 g / 1½ oz sugar, yeast and salt. Whisk the eggs and add, then work the dough for 10 minutes until smooth, shiny and elastic. Transfer to a large, oiled bowl, cover the top with cling-film and leave to prove at room temperature for 2 hours.

Cream the softened butter with 45 g / 1½ oz sugar and reserve. Turn out on a floured surface and knead, shaking on more flour if too sticky. Shape into a brick. Roll this to a rectangle about the size of a Swiss roll tin. The dough is very elastic, so you will need to use plenty of flour. Spread half the rectangle with the creamed butter and fold the other half over and roll out again. Scatter over the currants and allspice, then roll up like a Swiss roll. Cut across into 3.5-cm / 1½-inch slices.

Grease a baking sheet and put the slices on it, almost touching. Cover with a cloth and leave to rise again for 30 minutes.

Preheat the oven to 200°C/400°F/gas 6. The buns will have risen and will now be touching. Sprinkle the remaining tablespoon of caster sugar on top and bake for 15–20 minutes, when they will have risen further and be golden brown.

Remove to a rack to cool completely before separating the buns.

## CRUMPETS

How crumpets came into being is unknown. The earliest references to them are to be found in the late 17th century, when they were made from buckwheat flour and sound very similar to blinis, the small Russian yeast pancakes served with caviar. Elizabeth Raffald, the eighteenth-century cookery writer, described something very similar to today's crumpets in 1769, by which time they were made from a wheat-flour batter raised with leaven – a piece taken from the day's bread dough – and cooked on a griddle before being toasted before an open fire.

Charles Dickens was certainly partial to crumpets and, in *Nicholas Nickleby*, called an imaginary baker who specialized in them the United Metropolitan Improved Hot Muffin and Crumpet Baking and Punctual Delivery Company, a splendidly mellifluous title.

Their heyday was probably the 1920s and 30s, when afternoon tea would not have been complete without hot buttered crumpets and jam. You can certainly make them, but to do the job properly you will need some 8.75-cm / 3½-inch metal crumpet rings (or straight-sided pastry cutters) to put on the flat metal surface on which you cook them. While this is traditionally a griddle, a heavy frying pan or flat-surfaced non-stick pan will do just as well.

MAKES ABOUT 12

**450 g / 1 lb plain flour**
**1 tsp sugar**
**one 8-g / ¼-oz sachet of dried instant yeast (the small-grained fermipan type)**
**700 ml / 1¼ pt milk**
**1 tsp salt**
**½ tsp bicarbonate of soda**
**butter, for greasing**

Start by sifting the flour into a bowl with the sugar and yeast. Warm the milk to hand-hot and beat this with the flour to form a smooth batter. Cover the bowl and leave to stand at room temperature for 1 hour, when the batter will have more than doubled in size before falling.

Beat in the salt and bicarbonate of soda and leave to rest for 10 minutes, while you heat your griddle or frying pan dry over a low flame. You have now reached the tricky point of determining whether your batter is the right consistency: if too thick, the honeycomb of holes which is the defining point of the crumpet will not occur; if too thin, the batter will run from under the rings. Getting the heat just right is another determining factor of success: if too hot the batter will burn before it is ready to be turned; if too cool, the mixture will rise incompletely and be leaden. Test both with a spoonful of batter before proceeding. If too thick, thin with a little water and if too thin, beat in a little more flour.

Grease the rings and place on the griddle. Put 3 tablespoons of batter into each ring. As soon as the upper surface is set and filled with holes, which takes about 8 minutes, remove the rings with a cloth and turn the crumpets with a palette knife or spatula, cooking for a further 2–3 minutes. The first side should be a chestnut brown, the second only barely coloured and the crumpets about 3 cm / 1¼ inch thick.

Eat at once or toast the pale side and serve with butter and jam or honey.

## DOUGHNUTS

The key to successful doughnuts is a properly proved sweet yeast dough and clean oil at 190°C/375°F — the temperature at which the exterior of the doughnut is sealed, preventing excessive fat absorption and hot enough to cause the carbon dioxide gas trapped inside the dough to expand rapidly, giving the right airy, light texture. Frying dough gives a completely different exterior finish to baking and a lovely uniform golden-brown colour.

Before you begin, change the oil in the fryer and clean the interior. Any neutral-tasting oil, like sunflower, will do. The dough is very hard to work by hand and is best made in a food mixer with a dough hook.

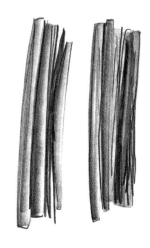

MAKES 20

**275 g / 10 oz high-protein bread flour, plus more for dusting**

**170 g / 6 oz plain flour**

**1 tsp salt**

**one 8-g / ¼-oz sachet of easy-blend yeast**

**175 ml / 6 fl oz hand-warm milk**

**85 g / 3 oz softened butter, cut into dice**

**2 eggs, beaten**

**85 g / 3 oz caster sugar**

**grated zest of 1 lemon**

**1 tsp ground cinnamon**

**oil, for greasing and deep-frying**

**caster sugar, for dusting**

Sift the flours into a bowl with the salt and yeast. Put the hand-warm milk in the mixing bowl and turn on at the lowest speed, then pour in the flour. Add the softened butter dice, a piece at a time. When fully incorporated, add the beaten eggs, one at a time. Add the sugar, lemon zest and cinnamon, and run the machine for 10 minutes, turning it to full speed for the last 2 minutes.

Turn the sticky dough out on a heavily floured surface and finish kneading by hand, incorporating flour until you have a smooth, elastic ball. Brush this with a little oil, place in a lightly oiled bowl and cover with cling film. Leave to rise at room temperature for 2 hours, when it should have at least doubled in size.

Knock down the dough by kneading it lightly, then divide it into 20 equal pieces, and roll them into balls. Make a hole in the centre by pushing your finger through, circling it to enlarge the hole to

about 2 cm / ¾ inch in diameter. Put the rings on a floured tray, cover with a cloth and leave to rise for 40–50 minutes, when again they will have doubled in size.

Heat oil for deep-frying to 190°C/375°F. Fry the doughnuts in small batches, being careful not to overcrowd as this will cause the temperature to drop below sealing point. Fry for 1–2 minutes on the first side, turn and give them a further minute on the other side. When done, drain on kitchen paper.

Put some caster sugar on a plate and turn the doughnuts in this to coat while still warm. Serve as soon as possible. They are best eaten minutes from the pan.

## MADELEINES

It is said that madeleines, small cockleshell-shaped sponge cakes, were invented in the last century by Madeleine Palmier, a Commercy pastry chef, and the town still bakes them in prodigious numbers to export to the rest of France. Few people have read Marcel Proust's *Du Côté de Chez Swann*, but many know of his famous reference to the vivid memory of taking tea with his Aunt Léonie as a child, brought back by the taste of a madeleine dipped in lime blossom tisane.

That instant, '…the old grey house upon the street, where her room was, rose up like a stage set to attach itself to the little pavilion opening on to the garden which had been built out behind it for my parents'.

Clearly a 'Desert Island' dish for Proust, but just another small rich orange-flavoured sponge for the rest of

us. You will need 20–30 madeleine moulds, depending on size, as they are available in small, medium and large. You can buy 20-unit non-stick madeleine moulds for about £15 and, if the kitchen department of your local department store doesn't stock them, by mail order from Nisbets, 01454 855555.

This recipe is taken from Anne Willan's brilliant *French Regional Cooking*, sadly out of print but one of the best books about French food ever written.

MAKES 20–30

**125 g / 4 oz plain flour, plus more for dusting**

**1 tsp baking powder**

**4 eggs**

**125 g / 4 oz caster sugar**

**1 tsp orange flower water or the grated zest of 1 orange**

**125 g / 4 oz melted unsalted butter, plus more for greasing**

Sift the flour into a bowl with the baking powder. In another bowl, whisk the eggs with the sugar until light and frothy, then add the orange flower water or grated orange zest. Fold in the flour in three stages. When the last third is almost amalgamated, pour over the melted butter and fold all together as lightly as possible. A heavy hand at this stage will deliver chewy madeleines. Refrigerate this batter for 30 minutes.

Preheat the oven to 230°C/450°F/gas 8. Butter and flour the moulds (see above), then fill two-thirds full with batter. Bake for 5 minutes, turn down the oven to 200°C/ 400°F/gas 6 and bake 5–7 minutes more, until golden brown.

Turn out on a wire rack to cool. 279

## ECCLES CAKES

These are easily made using frozen puff pastry.

**MAKES 12**

450 g / 1 lb frozen puff pastry
30 g / 1 oz butter
225 g / 8 oz currants
60 g / 2 oz chopped mixed peel
115 g / 4 oz muscovado sugar
grated zest of 1 lemon
1 tsp freshly grated nutmeg
1 tsp ground allspice
1 tsp ground ginger
1 tbsp lemon juice
white of 1 egg, lightly beaten
caster sugar, for dusting

Preheat the oven to 220°C/425°F/gas 7 and roll the pastry to a thickness of 3 mm / ⅛ inch, then cut out 12 rounds 11 cm / 4½ inches in diameter.

Melt the butter in a pan, then stir in the currants, chopped mixed peel, muscovado sugar, the grated lemon zest, nutmeg, allspice, ground ginger and lemon juice. Place equal amounts of the filling in the centre of the rounds.

Brush the edges with water and pull the pastry up, pinching it together in the middle. Turn these balls over and roll gently with a rolling pin until you have discs with the fruit showing through the surface. Make 2 small parallel cuts in the middle of each and put on a baking tray you have brushed with water. Brush the Eccles cakes with the lightly beaten egg white and dust with a little caster sugar.

Bake for 20 minutes, when they will be golden brown, and allow to cool on a rack.

## CHOCOLATE ÉCLAIRS

Éclairs and profiteroles are made from choux pastry, an egg-rich dough which is partially cooked in a pan to give it elasticity and which, when baked, puffs up into crisp, hollow shapes that can be filled with sweet fillings, such as crème pâtissière (confectioners' custard) or, omitting sugar from the dough, savoury mixtures. Éclairs must be baked until dry inside before being filled or they will go soggy.

**MAKES ABOUT 16**

85 g / 3 oz unsalted butter, diced
8 g / ¼ oz caster sugar
pinch of salt
125 g / 4½ oz sifted plain flour
3 eggs
about 300 ml / ½ pint whipped cream or confectioners' custard

**for the chocolate glacé icing:**
115 g / 4 oz icing sugar
1 tbsp cocoa powder
1–1½ tbsp boiling water

Put 200 ml / 7 fl oz water in a pan with the diced butter, caster sugar and pinch of salt. Simmer until the butter melts, then turn up the heat and bring to the boil. Add the sifted flour and beat with a wooden spoon until it forms a dough which comes away from the pan but is still slightly moist and sticky. Return to a low heat and continue to beat for 1 minute to dry to the point where it comes away from the pan in a smooth, elastic ball. This is most easily effected using an electric mixer. Transfer the

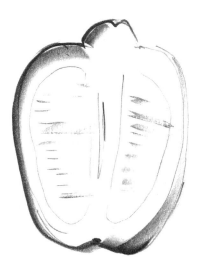

dough to the mixer bowl fitted with a balloon whisk.

In a separate bowl, lightly beat the eggs. When the dough has cooled to warm, switch on the mixer and add the beaten eggs, a little splash at a time, until you have a silky, shining, pipeable paste. It is best used immediately, but if you want to hold the dough for a while, cling-wrap the bowl or the dough will dry out.

Preheat the oven to 190°C/375°F/gas 7. Put the dough into a piping bag fitted with a 1-cm / ½-inch plain nozzle. Twist the end of the bag to compact the dough until it begins to ooze from the nozzle and squeeze out twelve 7.5-cm / 3-inch lines on to a non-stick baking tray, cutting the lengths through with a sharp knife and leaving about 5 cm / 2 inches space between them to allow for expansion. Bake for about 15–17 minutes, when they should be crisp, golden coloured and well risen. Remove, pierce the ends and return to the oven. Switch it off and leave them for 5 minutes. This ensures uniform crispness. Put to cool on a rack.

Using a piping bag, fill through the ends with whipped cream or confectioners' custard.

For a chocolate glacé icing, sift the icing sugar into a bowl and add the cocoa powder mixed to a smooth paste with the boiling water. Stir together to produce a glacé icing thick enough to coat the back of a spoon. Dip the top of each filled éclair in this icing and leave to set. Éclairs should be eaten within 3–4 hours of being filled or the pastry, no matter how crisp at the outset, will go soggy.

## DEVONSHIRE SPLIT

This is another sweet yeast-risen bun which is claimed by Cornwall as its own too. Both counties seem to go about things the same way, which means using proper clotted cream when you fill them.

**MAKES 14**
450 g / 1 lb strong bread flour, plus more for dusting
4 g / ⅛ oz instant fermipan yeast
1 tsp sugar
pinch of salt
30 g / 1 oz butter
150 ml / ¼ pt milk
150 ml / ¼ pt hand-hot water
olive oil, for greasing
icing sugar, for dusting

to serve:
250 g / 9 oz clotted or whipped cream
250 g / 9 oz strawberry jam

Sift the flour into a bowl with the yeast, sugar and salt. Melt the butter and add it with the milk and hand-hot water. Mix to a soft dough. Turn out on a floured surface and knead until silky smooth and elastic. Alternatively put the liquid into a food mixer, turn on and work for 8 minutes, an easier option. Brush with olive oil (not traditional but effective), put into a bowl and cling-wrap the top. Leave to rise at room temperature for 1½ hours.

Knock down on a floured surface and knead with the heel of your hand, turning, for a minute or so. Divide into 14 pieces and roll into neat balls. Put these on a greased baking tray, leaving space between them, cover with a damp cloth and leave to rise until roughly doubled in size.

Preheat the oven to 220°C/425°F/ gas 7 and bake for 15–20 minutes, when they should be a uniform golden brown. Remove from the oven to a rack and immediately dust with icing sugar. Leave to cool covered in a dry cloth to help prevent a crisp crust forming.

Just before serving, split and fill with clotted cream and strawberry jam. If clotted cream is not available, use whipped double cream.

## TEA CAKE

Cakes flavoured with strong tea and dense with fruit are very much in the Celtic tradition, with bannock, barm brack and bara brith being the Scottish, Irish and Welsh variations respectively. Some are baked with yeast, though these days it is more common to use self-raising flour.

**MAKES 12 SLICES**
150 ml / ¼ pt strong cold tea
275 g / 10 oz sultanas
200 g / 7 oz Muscovado sugar
60 g / 2 oz chopped mixed peel
butter, for greasing
275 g / 10 oz self-raising flour, plus more for dusting
1 egg, beaten
butter, to serve

Put the cold tea in a bowl with the sultanas, sugar and chopped mixed peel. Stir, cling-wrap the top and leave overnight.

Preheat the oven to 180°C/350°F/ gas 4. Butter a 20-cm / 8-inch round cake tin, then shake flour into it, turning it to coat well. Turn it upside down and tap sharply to remove any excess flour.

Sieve the self-raising flour into the mixture with the beaten egg and beat together with a wooden spoon.

Turn this mixture into the cake tin and bake for 1¾ hours, when a skewer inserted into the centre should come out clean. Leave in the tin for 10 minutes after you take it from the oven, then turn out on a wire rack to cool.

Serve the tea cake cut into thick slices and buttered.

## BANNOCK

Bannock is a yeast-raised fruit loaf found throughout Scotland.

**SERVES 10–12**
60 g / 2 oz butter, plus more to serve
350 ml / 12 fl oz milk
550 g / 1¼ lb strong bread flour, plus more for dusting
6 g / ¼ oz easy-blend yeast
60 g / 2 oz caster sugar
½ tsp salt
60 g / 2 oz sultanas
30g / 1 oz currants
30 g / 1 oz candied peel
oil, for greasing

for the glaze:
1 egg yolk
1 tbsp milk
1 tsp sugar

Put the butter in the milk and heat to hand warm. Pour into the bowl of a food mixer with a dough hook attached. Switch on at low speed and pour in the flour, yeast, sugar and salt. Work for 5 minutes, then add the sultanas, currants and candied peel, and continue to work for a further 5 minutes.

Remove to a floured surface and shape into a ball, then transfer to a large oiled bowl. Cling-wrap the top and leave to prove for 2 hours at room temperature.

Turn out, flour and knead, shaping into a round. Put on a baking tray, cover with a cloth and leave to rise again for 40 minutes.

Preheat the oven to 190°C/375°F/gas 5. Make a glaze by mixing the egg yolk with the milk and sugar, and brush this on the bannock before baking for about 40 minutes.

Remove to a rack to allow to cool completely before slicing. In Scotland it is always served well buttered.

## WAFFLES

The waffle is not – as many people think – an American invention, to be served automatically with maple syrup, but French and very ancient, dating back to the middle ages. This batter is easy to make and produces lovely light waffles.

**MAKES 6**
225 g / 8 oz plain flour
4 g / ⅛ oz easy-blend yeast
2 eggs, beaten
30 g / 1 oz caster sugar, plus more to serve
3–5 drops of vanilla extract
1 tsp salt
about 350 ml / 12 fl oz milk at room temperature
60 g / 2 oz melted unsalted butter
sunflower oil, for brushing
whipped cream, to serve

Sift the flour into a large bowl. Add the yeast, eggs, sugar, vanilla extract and salt. Gently whisk in 200 ml / 7 fl oz of the milk, then pour in the melted butter. You should have a thick smooth batter, but it is important not to over-whisk or you will have tough, chewy waffles. Cover the bowl and leave to prove for 2 hours.

Preheat the waffle iron. While it is heating, stir a further 150 ml / ¼ pint of milk into the risen batter to achieve a thick but pourable consistency. If it is too thick to pour, add more milk, a tablespoon at a time, stirring, until it will. Pour and scrape the batter into a jug.

Open the waffle iron and brush the surfaces lightly with sunflower oil. Pour in just enough batter to fill the holes, close the lid and cook for 4 minutes or for the length of time specified by the manufacturer. Lift the lid. The first one usually sticks and, as with making pancakes, practice makes perfect. If it sticks, leave it in for another minute and try again.

In Northern France these would be eaten with sugar and whipped cream, but they are also great with jam or maple syrup or ice-cream.

## MADEIRA CAKE

Madeira is a plain cake that was first baked in the eighteenth century, when it was served mid-morning with a glass of Madeira, a sweet fortified wine – hence the name. It is easy to make in a food processor and you could, if you so wish, drink a glass of Madeira while switching it on and off to get into the spirit of the thing.

**SERVES 10–12**
175 g / 6 oz unsalted butter, diced, plus more for greasing
175 g / 6 oz caster sugar
3 eggs
1 heaped tbsp plain flour
30 g / 1 oz ground almonds
grated zest of 1 lemon
200 g / 7 oz self-raising flour
1 tbsp cold milk

Preheat the oven to 180°C/350°F/gas 4. Put the butter in the bowl of a processor with the caster sugar. Blitz to a cream, scraping down the sides. With the machine running, add 3 eggs one at a time through the feeder tube, again scraping down as needed. After the second egg, add the heaped tablespoon of plain flour which will prevent the mixture from splitting. Add the ground almonds and the grated lemon zest. Sift in the self-raising flour and milk, processing to a smooth, creamy batter. Butter a non-stick 20-cm / 8-inch loaf tin and pour and scrape the batter into it.

Bake towards the bottom of the oven for 70–75 minutes. Leave to cool in the tin for 15 minutes before running a palette knife round the cake and turning out on a rack.

When completely cool, wrap in foil or cling-film and put into a tin, steeling yourself not to eat any until the next day, when it will be better than if devoured immediately.

## OLIVE OIL CAKE

**SERVES 12**
**olive oil, for greasing**
**125 g / 4½ oz plain flour, plus more for dusting**
**4 eggs**
**125 g / 4½ oz caster sugar**
**1 tsp grated orange zest**
**1 tsp grated lemon zest**
**2 tbsp sweet wine or sherry**
**3 tbsp extra-virgin olive oil,**
**icing sugar, for dusting**
**soft fruit or whipped cream, to serve**

Preheat the oven to 150°C/300°F/gas 2. Cut a circle of baking paper to fit the bottom of a 25-cm / 10-inch springform cake tin exactly. Brush the sides of the tin with olive oil and dust with flour, shaking off excess.

Sift the flour into a bowl. Combine the eggs and sugar in the bowl of a mixer and beat at high speed until it reaches the ribbon stage, that is, off-white and stiff. Add the orange zest and lemon zest.

Turn the mixer to low and pour in the flour in a steady stream to combine with the egg-and-sugar mixture. Quickly add the sweet wine or sherry and the extra-virgin olive oil. Switch off as soon as you have poured in the oil. It will not be fully incorporated.

Remove the mixer bowl and fold in with a spatula. Do this by stirring gently, starting from the centre at the bottom and working outwards and upwards, while rotating the bowl one-quarter turn. This should be repeated 3 more times, which means the bowl will have been turned full circle.

Working quickly, pour this mixture into the prepared cake tin, using the spatula to scrape the last of it from the mixing bowl. If the mixture collapses when you are folding in the flour, go ahead and bake anyway, though the result will be heavier than it should be.

Put immediately into the centre of the oven and bake for 25 minutes. Do not open the oven door for at least 15 minutes. After 20 minutes, insert a small knife into the centre of the cake. If it comes out clean, the cake is done, so remove it. If the mixture clings to the knife, cook for a further 5–10 minutes,

by which time it should be cooked, but there is no harm in testing again as oven temperatures do vary.

Leave to cool on a cake rack, removing from the tin as soon as you can handle it by running a small sharp knife round the edge before undoing the spring clip to release. Leave the paper on the bottom and return to the rack to cool completely.

To serve, lightly dust with icing sugar then cut into wedges. It is nice with any soft fruit or with whipped cream.

### CHOOSING CAKE TINS
*A sponge baked in a deep tin rises more in the middle than at the sides. This is because the sides effectively block the heat from the centre. The hotter edges cook faster and the centre rises for a longer period, giving a domed effect. This may not matter, but the usual plan with a Victoria sponge is to have more than one layer, and if you want a flat top surface to decorate you will have to cut the top off. No big deal, but that is why a high-sided tin is not ideal.*

*Conversely, if you overfill a shallow baking tin you will get a soufflé effect and the cake will collapse shortly after it comes from the oven. The ideal sponge tin is no more than 3 cm / 1¼ inches deep. Black tins are the most efficient in terms of heat conduction.*

## CHOCOLATE GÉNOISE

In Britain, learning to make a Victoria sponge has always been an essential part of what used to be called domestic science, which may be why people have both conceptual and functional difficulties when addressing a génoise for the first time. If you have an electric whisk you can easily achieve a consistent and light result. If your early attempts tend to be on the dry and heavy side, rescue is to hand in the shape of a bottle or rum or whisky. Spoon some over to moisten the cake and serve with whipped cream or ice-cream and nobody will complain. Génoise sponges are best baked the day before they are needed as they will slice better after a night's rest in a cake tin. They also freeze well.

> SERVES 12
> 5 eggs
> 125 g / 4½ oz caster sugar
> 60 g / 2 oz unsalted butter, plus
> more for greasing
> 125 g / 4½ oz plain flour, plus
> more for dusting
> 60 g / 2 oz cocoa powder

Preheat the oven to 150°C/300°F/gas 2. Cut baking paper to fit the bottom of a 25-cm / 10-inch loose-bottomed cake tin. Grease the paper and insides of the cake tin, then dust lightly with flour and shake off any excess.

Put the eggs and caster sugar into a mixing bowl and beat at a medium speed for 5–10 minutes, when the incorporated air will make it rise and you achieve a ribbon consistency, that is, when the mixture is stiff and an off-white colour.

Melt the butter over a low heat. Sieve the flour and cocoa powder together, then add to the egg mixture in the bowl, folding in gently with a spatula. A heavy hand at this point will guarantee a leaden cake. Now fold in the butter.

Spoon the finished mixture into the prepared cake tin and bake for between 20 and 30 minutes. After 20 minutes, test the cake is done by inserting a small clean sharp knife or skewer into the centre of the sponge. If it comes out clean, then the cake is done; if moist bits of sponge adhere to it, bake for another 5 minutes and test again. Repeat one more time if necessary. When satisfied, remove to a wire rack to cool.

As soon as you can handle the tin, unclip and unmould the sponge, which should have doubled in volume.

## SLY CAKES

Traditional English sly cakes are not cakes at all, but squares or fingers of puff pastry stuffed with a mixture of dried fruits and chopped apples. If the sultanas and currants have been given a preliminary soaking in brandy, rum or whisky the end result will be even nicer, but this is optional.

> 450 g / 1 lb puff pastry
> 2 cooking apples
> 60 g / 2 oz butter, plus more for
> greasing
> 60 g / 2 oz muscovado sugar
> 225 g / 8 oz sultanas or currants
> 60 g / 2 oz mixed peel
> 2 tsp ground allspice
> 1 egg yolk, beaten, to glaze
> icing sugar, for dusting

Preheat the oven to 200°C/400°F/gas 6. Roll out the puff pastry to a thickness of 1 cm / ½ inch, then trim and cut into 2 equal rectangles. Put one of them on a lightly greased non-stick baking tray.

Peel, core and dice the cooking apples, then fry them in the butter. When golden and starting to soften, add the muscovado sugar and toss to coat. Remove from the heat and stir in the sultanas or currants, mixed peel and allspice.

Spread the mixture on the pastry rectangle on the baking tray. Put the other rectangle on top and press down gently. Cut a neat cross-hatch with a scalpel or sharp knife, then cut almost all the way through the top pastry to make 16 squares and brush with egg yolk.

Bake for 15–20 minutes, when the pastry will be well risen and golden brown. Transfer to a rack to cool, before cutting along the indentations into squares. Finish by dusting with icing sugar.

## CARROT CAKE

All questions concerning cakes should really be addressed to Mary Berry, whose *Ultimate Cake Book* was where we found a delicious and easy carrot cake recipe.

SERVES 12

225 g / 8 oz self-raising flour
150 g / 5 oz muscovado sugar
115 g / 4 oz grated carrots
60 g / 2 oz chopped walnuts
2 ripe bananas, mashed
2 eggs

150 ml / ¼ pt sunflower oil, plus more for greasing
2 tsp baking powder

for the topping:
175 g / 6½ oz low-fat cream cheese
115 g / 4 oz icing sugar
60 g / 2 oz soft margarine
4 drops of vanilla extract
walnut halves, to decorate

Preheat the oven to 180°C/350°F/gas 4. Grease the base of a 20-cm / 8-inch round cake tin and line it with greased greaseproof paper.

Put the flour, muscovado sugar, grated carrots, chopped walnuts, mashed bananas, eggs, sunflower oil and baking powder in a large bowl. Mix thoroughly until blended and smooth. Turn into the prepared cake tin and smooth the top. Bake for 50–60 minutes, when the cake will be well risen and shrinking from the sides. Leave to cool in the tin for 5 minutes before turning out on a wire rack. Leave to cool completely.

Make the topping by putting the cream cheese, icing sugar, margarine and vanilla extract in a food processor and blitzing until smoothly incorporated. Spread over the top of the cake with a spatula and decorate with halved walnuts.

Refrigerate the cake for about 2 hours before serving and keep in the fridge as the topping softens at room temperature.

## SPANISH SPONGE

*Pan de spagna* is characterized by a high proportion of eggs to flour and a cooking technique which seems odd when compared to, say, making a Victoria sponge.

MAKES TWO 18 X 25-CM / 8 X 10-INCH SPONGES

60 g / 2 oz butter
8 eggs
170 g / 6 oz caster sugar
170 g / 6 oz fine plain flour

Preheat the oven to 180°C/350°F/gas 4. Non-stick cake tins work best here; if you don't have them, grease two 18 x 25-cm / 8 x 10-inch sponge tins lightly with butter. Melt the butter in a pan and reserve.

Over a low heat, whisk the eggs with the caster sugar until just warm. Remove from the heat and beat vigorously until trebled in volume. An electric whisk makes this job quick and painless.

Sift in the flour, then fold in the melted butter. Divide this mixture between the cake tins and bake for 16–20 minutes.

### CHOCOLATE BROWNIES

A good brownie is a rich chocolate experience, but how good it tastes will depend on the quality of the chocolate. An electric mixer is essential, because this recipe will not work with a food processor. For a real treat, serve your brownies with some good-quality vanilla ice-cream.

**MAKES ABOUT 20**
**115 g / 4 oz best confectioner's chocolate, broken into pieces**
**115 g / 4 oz butter**
**115 g / 4 oz caster sugar**
**1 egg plus 1 extra yolk**
**1 tsp vanilla extract**
**115 g / 4 oz flour, sifted**
**2 tbsp cocoa powder**
**¼ tsp baking powder**
**pinch of salt**

Preheat the oven to 160°C/325°F/gas 3. Put the chocolate to melt in a bowl set over hot water, making sure it does not come into direct contact with the water. Put the butter and sugar in the bowl of a mixer and work at high speed with the paddle-type beater (as distinct from the whisk or dough hook) until a smooth creamed consistency is achieved. This takes about 7 minutes.

Add the egg and extra yolk and the vanilla extract, continuing to beat until smooth, then incorporate the melted chocolate. Finally beat in the flour, cocoa powder, baking powder and salt.

Line a rectangular baking tin with non-stick baking paper and spoon the mixture into it, then bake for 30 minutes before testing with a skewer, pushing deep into the centre. It should be moist and squidgy in the middle and will continue cooking after you remove it from the oven. The cake will have risen, but will fall soon after you take it out of the oven.

Leave it to cool in the tin before turning out on a rack for at least an hour before serving.

### NORWEGIAN APPLE CAKE

This is a very rich, buttery cake which is best made with Bramleys, our finest cooking apple. It should be baked in a roasting tin rather than a cake tin and for the following amounts you will need a 30 x 20-cm / 12 x 8-inch tin.

**SERVES 12**
**140 g / 5 oz unsalted butter, plus more for greasing**
**200 g / 7 oz plain flour, plus more for dusting**

**4 large Bramley apples**
**juice of ½ lemon**
**3 eggs**
**250 g / 9 oz caster sugar**
**200 ml / 7 fl oz single cream**
**3 tsp baking powder**

Preheat the oven to 200°C/400°F/gas 6. Butter the roasting tin (see above), dust with flour and set aside.

Peel and core the apples, cut into slices and sprinkle with lemon juice to prevent discoloration.

Whisk the eggs with 225 g / 8 oz of the sugar until the mixture creams and stiffens so that threads fall back from the whisk when it is lifted from the bowl. Put the butter with the cream in a pan and bring to the boil. Pour this into the egg mixture while whisking. Sift in the flour and baking powder, and fold in carefully with the whisk to make sure there are no lumps.

Pour this batter into the prepared roasting tin, then arrange the apple slices overlapping on the top. Sprinkle the remaining caster sugar on the top and bake for 25 minutes, when it will have risen and be golden brown round the edges. Leave to cool in the tin.

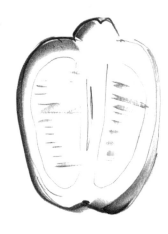

### GLAZING FRUIT TARTS
*For red fruits, melt redcurrant jelly and brush it on. For white, yellow or green fruits, melt apricot jam with a little lemon juice and water. Put through a sieve before brushing it over.*

## PASTRY FOR PIES

When you think that pies historically preceded plates as a means of getting hot food to the table you can see that the pastry crust continues to exist on the pie for cosmetic and nostalgic effect rather than culinary necessity.

For a hot dish, like steak and kidney, there are no objective benefits to be had from cooking the pastry on top of the meat and gravy, and there are strong arguments for making the filling in a casserole dish on top of the hob and baking the pastry separately. Steam and puff or flaky pastry are not good friends, but shortcrust is more forgiving. For those who insist on a traditional construction it is important not to bake at too low a temperature; 200°C/400°F/gas 6 for puff pastry is about right.

For those wanting to present a whole pie in the dining room, one solution is to bake a piece of glazed puff pastry on a metal sheet the same shape and size as the pie dish from which it is to be served, simply sitting it hot and crisp from the oven on top of the dish before taking it to the table. This is a more sophisticated variation on the institutional approach of serving 500 with a meat-and-gravy dinner, complete with individual pastry pieces for every inmate.

## ONION TART

SERVES 8–10
900 g / 2 lb onions, sliced
60 g / 2 oz butter
60 g / 2 oz flour
salt and pepper
freshly grated nutmeg to taste
300 ml / ½ pint milk
3 eggs, separated

for the shortcrust pastry:
125 g / 4½ oz plain flour
75 g / 2¾ oz chilled unsalted butter, cut into dice
1 egg yolk
pinch of salt

First make a shortcrust pastry by putting the flour in a food processor with the chilled butter dice. Whiz to a crumb consistency then add the egg yolk, salt and 1-2 tablespoons of cold water. Work briefly until it balls. Remove, cling-wrap and refrigerate for 1 hour.

Preheat the oven to 200°C/ 400°F/ gas 6. Roll the rested pastry out and use to line a 23-cm / 9-inch tart tin, with a double thickness round the edges, pricking the base and pinching the pastry up above the level of the tin to allow for shrinkage. Line with baking paper, weight with beans then bake blind for 10 minutes. Remove from the oven.

Sweat the onions in the butter until soft. Add the flour and cook for 2 minutes. Season with salt, pepper and nutmeg, and pour over the milk. Cook over a low heat for 20 minutes, stirring at regular intervals. Off the heat, beat the yolks into this mixture.

Whisk the egg whites until stiff and fold them into the onion custard. Spoon into the pastry shell, put into the oven, lower the temperature to 190°C/ 375°F/gas 5 and bake for 15–20 minutes, until golden and risen. Serve immediately.

# SAUCES, RELISHES AND OTHER BASICS

**W**hile this section tends to cover well-worn ground, with the inclusion of absolute start points like the making of stock — without which food is reduced and made insubstantial — they also address the things which go with other things, giving them the necessary extra dimension that allows them to expand and become memorable. Here you will find sauces, relishes, chutneys and pickles, opportunities to give new angles to old favourites, reminders of delicious old friends and new taste departures from other lands.

## SAUCES

### STOCK-BASED GRAVIES

A chicken-based gravy will work with any meat but, conversely, other meats will be too dominant in a cross-fertilization. Imagine how nasty a lamb gravy would be with chicken.

Whenever you cook a chicken you have a carcass to make stock. Simply cover with cold water, bring to the boil, lower the heat as scum forms, then skim carefully. Add an onion in its skin (the skin deepens the colour), a carrot, a bay leaf and 8 or 10 peppercorns, and simmer at the barest possible simmer for several hours, occasionally topping up with more cold water, bringing back to the boil and skimming each time before lowering the heat. The water should tremble, never boil during the long period when flavour will leach out from

the bones and residual flesh to deliver a perfect clear broth. Boil it and the stock will be tainted by deep extraction from the bones, making it rank, gluey and cloudy.

If you start the process last thing at night you will wake up next day to a finished stock which then only needs to be strained through a muslin-lined sieve into a clean pan and reduced at a fast boil until the flavour is as intense as you want it. This is a gravy in its own right or can be beaten into a butter and flour roux to make a velouté sauce.

Without stock, gravy can be made very quickly with the caramelized pan juices and fat from any roast meat. Simply pour or spoon off excess fat and put the roasting dish over a high heat on the hob. Add a glass of red or white wine and boil vigorously, scraping and stirring. When reduced, taste and sea-

son if needed, then whisk in 30 g / 1 oz butter. Gravy, alors!

Classic French cooking demands a range of base stocks and sauces. These include *fonds brun* (beef and veal), *fonds blanc* (chicken and veal), *fonds de gibier* (game) and *fumet de poisson* (fish). A *glace*

*Opposite (clockwise from the top left): Maitre d'Hôtel Butter (page 291), Sauce Vièrge (page 291), Gooseberry Sauce (page 292), Sweet-and-sour Chilli Sauce (page 292), Salsa Rossa (page 290), Roast Tomato Sauce (page 293)*

*de viande* is made from a reduction of *fonds brun.* Put 600 ml / 1 pt of well-flavoured clear beef stock in a pan and reduce it at a rapid boil by two-thirds, skimming from time to time. Pass through a fine sieve into another pan, lower the heat to very low and continue reducing until the glaze holds on the back of a metal spoon in a glossy dark coating. Do not attempt to make a meat glaze from stock cubes. The result would be too ghastly to contemplate.

## SAUCE BERCY

In restaurants, sauce bercy is based on veal stock but, in reality, it can be made using any meat *jus* other than lamb, *jus* describing the intensely flavoured jelly which you find set in a roasting tin after cooking a piece of beef or chicken. You could, of course, use lamb *jus* to serve with lamb. A *jus* can also describe a stock reduced to the point where it sets as a jelly. Sauce bercy is very good with a steak or pan-fried chicken breast.

*Opposite (clockwise from the left): Hot Chocolate Sauce (page 297) on Profiteroles (page 280), Butterscotch Sauce (page 297) on chocolate ice-cream, puréed raspberries on Vanilla Ice-cream (page 249)*

SERVES 4

**4 shallots, finely diced**
**100 ml / 3½ fl oz dry white wine**
**3 tbsp meat jelly (see above)**
**30 g / 1 oz butter, cut into small pieces**
**squeeze of lemon juice**
**1 tbsp chopped flat-leaved parsley**

Put the shallots in a small pan with the wine and reduce over a high heat to about 3 tablespoons.

Add the meat jelly and bubble through, then whisk in the butter, a few pieces at a time. Add a squeeze of lemon juice and the parsley... et voilà, sauce bercy!

## REFORM CLUB SAUCE

Traditionally served with grilled lamb cutlets.

SERVES 4

**1 egg**
**6 shallots, diced**
**3 tbsp red wine vinegar**
**30 g / 1 oz caster sugar**
**1 tbsp coarsely crushed black peppercorns**
**300 ml / ½ pt chicken stock**
**115 g / 4 oz cooked beetroot, cut into matchsticks**
**85 g / 3 oz cooked ham, cut into matchsticks**
**4 small gherkins (cornichons), cut into wafer-thin slices**
**salt and pepper**

Hard-boil the egg, refresh in cold water, shell and reserve.

Put the shallots in a pan with the red

wine vinegar, sugar and crushed black peppercorns. Cook over a moderate heat, until the vinegar has evaporated and the shallots are soft.

Add the chicken stock, bring to the boil and skim. Lower the heat and simmer for 10 minutes, then pass through a sieve into a clean pan.

Add the cooked beetroot, ham and gherkins, and stir in with the diced white of the egg (use the yolk to make Salad Cream, page 295). Season.

## GREEK YOGHURT AND CHEESE SAUCE

A robust mixture of lemon, olive oil, cheese and yoghurt, this sauce goes well with sausages or kebabs.

SERVES 4

**4 egg yolks**
**4 tbsp olive oil**
**5 tbsp lemon juice**
**1 tbsp Dijon mustard**
**salt and pepper**
**115 g / 4 oz full-fat cottage cheese**
**300 ml / ½ pt thick Greek-style yoghurt**

In a bowl set over simmering water, whisk the egg yolks, olive oil, lemon juice, Dijon mustard and salt and pepper. Then beat in the cottage cheese and yoghurt. Cook gently, stirring, until the mixture forms a thick savoury custard.

Serve at once hot, or allow to cool and serve at room temperature.

## SAUCE SOUBISE

Soubise is an onion béchamel which makes the perfect accompaniment to lamb. Classically the sauce is made in three stages, with the onion first blanched in boiling water, before being sweated in butter then added to a béchamel and simmered for 15 minutes. It is then sieved and has double cream added. The process can be simplified as below.

MAKES ABOUT 600 ML / 1 PT

**1 onion, finely chopped**
**60 g / 2 oz butter**
**60 g / 2 oz flour**
**850 ml / 1½ pt full-fat milk**
**salt and pepper**
**freshly grated nutmeg to taste**
**2–3 tbsp double cream (optional)**

Sweat the onion in the butter until soft and translucent, but don't allow it to brown. Stir in the flour and cook to a roux for 2 minutes.

Pour in the milk and simmer, stirring occasionally, for 20–30 minutes, when it should be thick and creamy and reduced to about 600 ml / 1 pt. Season with salt, pepper and grated nutmeg.

Purée in a food processor or blender. Pour back into a clean saucepan, taste and adjust the seasoning if necessary. You can add a few tablespoons of cream if you like.

Reheat gently before serving.

## SAUCE NORMANDE

This goes brilliantly with any firm-fleshed white fish.

MAKES ABOUT 850 ML/ 1½ PINTS

**85 g / 3 oz unsalted butter**
**85 g / 3 oz onion, diced**
**30 g / 1 oz flour**
**600 ml / 1 pint dry cider**
**salt and pepper**
**freshly grated nutmeg, to taste**
**300 ml / ½ pint crème fraîche**
**½ tablespoon lemon juice**

Melt one-third of the butter in a heavy-based pan and sauté the diced onion in it, stirring until it becomes translucent.

Add another third of the butter and stir in the flour. Cook, stirring, over a low heat for 2 minutes.

Whisk in the cider and bring quickly to a boil. Lower to a simmer, season with salt, pepper and grated nutmeg, and cook for 10 minutes.

Add the crème fraîche, raise the heat and bubble. Immediately remove from the heat and whisk in the remaining butter in little bits. Finish with the lemon juice. Don't attempt to reheat or your beautifully coherent sauce will disintegrate.

## SALSA ROSSA

Usually a simple accompaniment for boiled or grilled meats, salsa rossa also makes a great pasta sauce. Once filmed with oil to make an airtight seal, it keeps well in a screw-top jar in the fridge for up to a month. You can ring the changes by adding clams to the finished sauce and bubbling it through until they open. If so, don't serve any Parmesan.

SERVES 4

**4 red peppers**
**4 onions, diced**
**4 tbsp olive oil**
**2 small hot red chillies, deseeded and cut into thin strips**
**2 garlic cloves, smashed and chopped**
**450 g / 1 lb chopped tinned tomatoes**
**2 tbsp tomato ketchup**
**salt and pepper**
**1 tsp freeze-dried oregano**
**handful of torn basil leaves**

Grill the red peppers until blackened, put into a bowl and cover. Leave to steam for 15 minutes, remove and peel. Cut in half, scrape out the pips and discard along with the skin. Cut the peppers into pieces and put in a food processor.

While the peppers are steaming, in a heavy-based pan fry the diced onions gently in the olive oil, stirring from time to time, until soft and translucent. Add the chillies to the pan, together with the chopped garlic. Continue to cook, stirring, for 2 minutes, then add the tomatoes with their liquid and the tomato ketchup. Turn up the heat and cook at a fast bubble to reduce slightly, stirring from time to time. Season with salt and pepper to taste and add the oregano.

Add to the processor with the basil leaves and blitz to a purée. Use the salsa at once to sauce spaghetti, with plenty of freshly grated Parmesan, or store as described.

## ITALIAN SAUCE

This is very good with poached chicken or cod. For the wine, something bone-dry, like an Orvieto Classico, would be suitably Italian.

SERVES 4

4 shallots, thinly sliced

30 g / 1 oz butter

115 g / 4 oz button mushrooms, thinly sliced

150 ml / ¼ pt dry white wine (see above)

1 tbsp lemon juice

2 tbsp chopped flat-leaved parsley

freshly grated nutmeg, to taste

1–2 tbsp double cream (optional)

for the béchamel:

45 g / 1½ oz butter

45 g / 1½ oz flour

850 ml / 1½ pt milk

First make a basic béchamel: melt the butter over a gentle heat. Stir in the flour and cook to a roux for 2 minutes. Pour in the milk and simmer, stirring occasionally, for 20–30 minutes, when it should be thick and creamy and reduced to about 600 ml / 1 pt. Season to taste.

Sweat the shallots until soft in the butter. Add the mushrooms and continue to fry gently for 5 minutes or so.

Pour over the wine, turn up the heat and bubble down quickly, until almost evaporated.

Stir in the béchamel, lemon juice, parsley and nutmeg to taste. Simmer for 3–4 minutes. Just before serving, stir in a few tablespoons of double cream if you like.

## MAÎTRE D'HÔTEL BUTTER

This is no more than lightly salted butter amalgamated with parsley and lemon juice, though other herbs like chervil and tarragon may also be included. Serve it on steaks, chops or grilled fish instead of a sauce or gravy.

Experiment, making different flavoured butters like anchovy, garlic, shallot, chilli or mixed fresh herbs. Flavoured butters will freeze for up to a month. They don't go bad after that time but the flavour starts to deteriorate.

MAKES ABOUT 350 G/12 OZ

225 g / 8 oz lightly salted butter

85 g / 3 oz flat-leaved parsley, finely chopped

juice of ½ lemon

Soften the butter and put it into a mixing bowl. It needs to be soft enough to beat with a wooden spoon. Finely chop the parsley and add to the butter with the lemon juice. Cream to mix evenly.

Scrape out on to cling-film, roll into a neat cylinder and chill. Remove from the fridge or freezer just before you need it, cut across into rounds.

## SAUCE VIÈRGE

Sauce viärge is a combination of fresh herbs, tomatoes and olive oil. It goes well with cold poached salmon, salmon trout and any non-oily fish and may be served cold or hot.

MAKES ABOUT 450 ML / ¾ PINT

3 large ripe tomatoes

½ garlic clove, finely chopped

2 tbsp chopped flat-leaved parsley

2 tbsp chopped chervil

1 tbsp chopped coriander

1 tbsp chopped tarragon

200 ml / 7 fl oz extra-virgin olive oil

salt and pepper

Blanch the tomatoes in boiling water for 30 seconds, refresh in cold water and peel. Cut in half and scrape out the seeds and watery centre, then cut the flesh into 5-mm / ¼-inch dice.

Put into a bowl with the garlic, parsley, chervil, coriander and tarragon. Add the oil, season and stir. Leave to mature for an hour or so.

Stir again before serving. To serve hot, warm gently over the lowest heat for 10 minutes, but do not allow it to boil or you will lose the fresh intensity of the herbs.

## SHALLOT SAUCE

This sauce is spooned, while still hot, over cold meat like roast lamb. This means lamb at room temperature, never please straight from the fridge.

SERVES 4

225 g / 8 oz shallots, diced

4 tbsp olive oil

2 tbsp fresh breadcrumbs

2 tbsp white wine vinegar

16 small gherkins

Fry the shallots gently in the olive oil until soft and translucent.

Stir in the breadcrumbs and vinegar. Lower the heat and cook, stirring, for 3 minutes. Stir in the gherkins and spoon over the lamb.

## GOOSEBERRY SAUCE

Gooseberry sauce is often served with mackerel, its astringent clean taste setting off the rich, oily flesh to perfection. Since it is little more than a purée with flavour-enhancing additions, that may include lemon juice and chives, freeze the berries on their own as a purée which you can then use for other things like tarts, fools or sorbets, or as the fancy takes you.

MAKES ABOUT 300 ML / $^1/_2$ PINT

450 g / 1 lb gooseberries
30 g / 1 oz butter
30 g / 1 oz caster sugar
juice of 1 lemon
1 tbsp chopped chives

Remove any remaining element of stalk from the gooseberries and put them in a pan with 250 ml / 8 fl oz cold water and the butter. Bring to the boil, immediately lower the heat and simmer gently until the gooseberries are soft.

Put them into a food processor and whiz until puréed. Push them through a sieve with a wooden spoon to extract any skins. The purée can now be held in the fridge for a day or two, or frozen.

If proceeding immediately, put the purée into a clean saucepan with the caster sugar and heat gently. Add the lemon juice and chopped chives.

Serve with grilled mackerel or herring and with plain boiled new potatoes.

## RÉMOULADE SAUCE

Rémoulade is a forcefully flavoured, cold mayonnaise-based sauce, like gribiche or tartare, which is most often served with fish or shellfish. All of these sauces are very easy to make and can be reduced in calorie content by the incorporation of thick natural yoghurt without detriment to the flavour.

In Louisiana, rémoulade is a popular part of both Creole and Cajun cooking, where it is quite heavily spiced. Try this New Orleans oyster house variation as a dip to have with crab claws or prawns.

MAKES ABOUT 600 ML / 1 PINT

6 spring onions
2 anchovy fillets
2 hot red chillies, deseeded
1 tbsp capers
2 tbsp chopped flat-leaved parsley
2 tbsp chopped chives
1 tbsp Dijon mustard
3 tbsp tomato ketchup
juice of 1 lemon
1 tbsp Worcestershire sauce
350 ml / 12 fl oz thick mayonnaise
Tabasco sauce (optional)

Chop the spring onions, anchovy fillets, chillies and capers. In a bowl, mix with the parsley, chives, mustard, tomato ketchup, lemon juice and Worcestershire sauce. Add the mayonnaise and stir together.

This will be quite spicy, but if you want to feel more Bourbon Street than Bond Street, it can be made hotter by the addition of some Tabasco to taste.

## GUBBINS SAUCE

Nathaniel Gubbins — aka Edward Spencer — concocted a spicy grill sauce dedicated to himself. It is very easy to make in a double boiler or in a bowl set over hot water, and is actually delicious.

Grilled chicken wings make the ideal foil for Mr Gubbins tasty hot dressing. Perish the thought, but if you wanted to do something entertaining with a turkey leg then Gubbins sauce is also the very thing.

SERVES 4

60 g / 2 oz butter
1 tbsp freshly made Colman's mustard
1 tbsp tarragon vinegar
4 tbsp double cream
2 tsp chilli flakes
$^1/_2$ tsp salt
1 tsp freshly ground black pepper

In a bowl set over simmering water, melt the butter then stir in the mustard, tarragon vinegar, double cream, chilli flakes, salt and black pepper. Whisk until warmed through and amalgamated.

While your chicken wings are still very hot, pour Mr Gubbins' sauce over them.

## SWEET-AND-SOUR CHILLI TOMATO SAUCE

SERVES 4–6

100 g / 3$^1/_2$ oz sultanas
3 garlic cloves, chopped
4 hot red chillies, deseeded and chopped
2 tbsp white wine vinegar
225 g / 8 oz tinned chopped tomatoes
3 tbsp sunflower oil
4 tbsp tomato ketchup
1 tsp salt
1 tsp pepper
Tabasco or other chilli sauce (optional)

Put the sultanas, garlic, chillies, vinegar and tomatoes (with their liquid) in a saucepan with the sunflower oil. Bring to the boil, lower the heat and simmer gently for 15 minutes.

Add the tomato ketchup, simmer for another 5 minutes, then transfer to a food processor. Season with the salt and pepper, and whiz to a purée.

Taste and adjust the seasoning if desired. If it is not fiery enough, add some Tabasco or other chilli sauce then leave to cool before serving.

## ROAST TOMATO SAUCE

Preheat your oven to 190°C/375°F/gas 5 and lightly oil a roasting tin. Fill with halved tomatoes, cut side up and tightly packed, then sprinkle them with salt, pepper and a little sugar. Dress them with olive oil and roast for 20 minutes.

Dice 225 g / 8 oz onion, 4 garlic cloves and 1 hot red chilli and scatter over the tomatoes. Dress with more oil and return to the oven for 20–30 minutes, when the tomatoes will have shrunk and the onions browned. Check at regular intervals during this second roasting period that they are not burning. If you allow them to burn you will make the sauce bitter and unpleasant.

Remove from the oven and, when cool, purée and sieve before packing in jars and filming the surface with oil to store.

You can ring all kinds of changes at the puréeing stage. Try adding anchovies or stoned, black olives or basil.

## SKORDALIA

Made traditionally with a pestle and mortar, skordalia is a simple garlic sauce that may be thickened either with bread or mashed potato and is usually served with sliced fried vegetables, such as aubergines, with fried fish and with poached chicken. It has close affinities with aïoli and, with the addition of weak chicken broth or water, becomes the Spanish cold soup *gazpacho blanco*.

MAKES ABOUT 850 ML / 1 ½ PINTS
**450 g / 1 lb potatoes, peeled**
**salt and pepper**
**8–10 garlic cloves, finely chopped**
**300 ml / ½ pt olive oil**
**about 100 ml / 3½ fl oz milk**

Cook the potatoes in boiling salted water until just tender. Drain well.

While the potatoes are still warm but not hot, put them in a food processor with the garlic. Season with salt and pepper, then blitz to a purée.

With the machine still running, pour the olive oil through the feeder tube in a thin stream, followed by just enough milk to give the consistency of mayonnaise. Adjust the seasoning.

## PESTO

Pesto is a magical basil-based raw sauce that is made in seconds in a food processor, but tastes really sensational. It is classically served with a dried pasta like spaghetti, but is also delicious in a bean soup or as an addition to other sauces. It can also be added to mashed potatoes or baked on half tomatoes in the oven with fresh breadcrumbs to make a light and delicious gratin.

If you don't use it all immediately, it will keep in a kilner jar in the fridge for at least a month without deterioration, if the surface is covered in a thin film of olive oil and as long as the jar was sterile and the pesto packed down with the back of a clean metal spoon to make sure there are no air pockets.

The precise percentage of one ingredient to another is not absolute. You can use more or less of anything, except the basil which is of course the whole point. The Parmesan may be replaced wholly or in part by Pecorino romano.

You vary this theme by substituting a different herb for the basil, for example, mint or coriander.

SERVES 4
**85 g / 3 oz basil leaves**
**45 g / 1½ oz flat-leaved parsley**
**75 g / 2½ oz Parmesan, grated**
**55 g / 2 oz pine nuts**
**4 garlic cloves, chopped**
**200-300 ml/ 7 fl oz-½ pt extra-virgin olive oil**
**salt and pepper**

Tear the basil and parsley leaves away from the stalks, discarding the stalks. Cut the Parmesan into chunks that will go down the processor feeder tube.

Turn the machine on and drop the cheese into it, a piece at a time, until you achieve a uniform coarse crumb. Add the pine nuts and garlic and process again briefly, then add the herbs, followed by the olive oil in a thin stream until you have a coarse paste. Taste and season. Process once more, adding any remaining oil. You should have a spoonable but quite runny consistency. Check the seasoning one last time.

Unless storing in jars as above, use within two or three days.

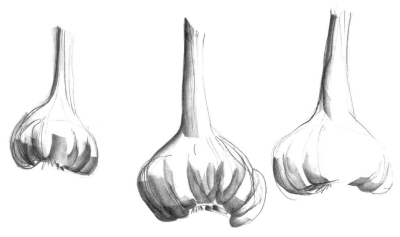

## TARATOR

You find different variations on pine nut sauces in Egypt, the Lebanon and Syria. They are usually thinner than the Turkish tarator sauce, which is thick like a mayonnaise. Tarator is also made using walnuts and is very easy to produce using a food processor. Tarator also makes a nice dip for raw vegetables.

SERVES 4–6

85 g / 3 oz pine nuts
3 garlic cloves, smashed and
finely chopped
1 tsp salt
½ tsp freshly ground black
pepper
2–3 tbsp extra-virgin olive oil
juice of 1 lemon

Grind the pine nuts to a coarse powder in a coffee grinder (not forgetting to clean it first). Put the garlic into a food processor with the ground pine nuts, salt and black pepper.

With the machine running at full speed, add the olive oil through the feeder tube, then the lemon juice. If necessary, add a little more oil to achieve a thick, spoonable sauce. Taste, adding more lemon juice if you think it needs it. The nuts are very rich and need quite a lot of lemon to ameliorate this if the sauce is not to be sickly.

Serve the tarator in a bowl for people to help themselves as with sauce tartare.

## HORSERADISH SAUCE

Originally, horseradish was used as a natural medicine, considered to be good for cleansing the blood. It is not widely sold in root form these days, which is a shame because there is nothing like the pungent hot flavour it delivers when freshly grated.

Since it grows anywhere with the tenacity of the worst kind of weed, you could grow it yourself to ensure a supply, though you will need a garden to do so, for it produces a long cylindrical root and is not, therefore, suitable for pot cultivation. When you do find some to buy, choose roots which are as straight as possible and which are woody and dry. These will keep in a plastic bag in the fridge for a month.

It is volatile in both the sense of inflammatory and inconstant; hot enough to take your breath away when just grated, yet rapidly losing its power when exposed to heat.

To make horseradish cream, peel as much of the end of a root as you want and grate about 2 tablespoons into a bowl. Add 1 tablespoon of lemon juice, ½ teaspoon of caster sugar, 1 teaspoon of freshly made English mustard and a little salt and pepper. Stir to mix. In another bowl whisk 150 ml / ¼ pint double cream until it just begins to thicken, then fold in the horseradish mixture.

Alternatively, use crème fraîche straight from the tub or thick Greek-style yoghurt. It should be served chilled, so refrigerate for 1–2 hours before using as a classic accompaniment for rare roast beef, though it is equally good with a steak or sausages and excellent with smoked salmon. Once made, it will keep for up to a week in the fridge.

For people addicted to horseradish, offer it freshly grated at the table. For a milder effect, serve it heated by adding it just before serving to a white sauce. A heaped tablespoon of horseradish to every 300 ml / ½ pt of white sauce and a few drops of balsamic vinegar is quite delicious.

## MAYONNAISE

Mayonnaise has a kind of alchemy about its construction when emulsification is successful, an infuriating conspiracy when it fails. Precisely who thought about adding oil slowly to raw egg yolks while stirring with a wooden spoon is not known, though it was almost certainly in France and probably in the 18th century.

A whisk is better than a spoon and an electric balloon whisk perhaps the most reliable and quickest way of getting a good result every time. The ingredients should neither be too cold nor too hot. If you keep your eggs in the fridge, then you should remove them well in advance and bring to room temperature before attempting to make the mayonnaise.

If the mayonnaise curdles you can usually bring it back by whisking the curdled mess into a fresh yolk in a clean bowl though it is better to start the yolk with fresh oil, only adding the curdled mayonnaise when this has started to cohere.

The ratio of oil to egg is not the major issue some recipes suggest. One egg yolk will happily hold 600 ml / 1 pt of oil and experiments have proved that one yolk will emulsify up to 6 gallons of oil! Although the original mayonnaise was made with olive oil only, equal parts olive and sunflower oils produces a less strident result — which is also less expensive. Season the yolks with salt and pepper before you begin to add the oil, but do not add lemon juice or white wine vinegar until after you have a very thick sauce.

The salmonella issue with using raw eggs in mayonnaise remains a vexing one. The law forbids the use of raw eggs in restaurant kitchens, but at home you can evaluate the risk for yourself. As a general rule do not feed raw eggs to the elderly, sick or pregnant, or to young children. Otherwise we are old enough to live dangerously at our tables if we wish.

## SALAD CREAM

Salad cream is the British version of mayonnaise. It is made using hard-boiled rather than raw egg yolks and may combine cream and oil in the mixture or use cream alone.

MAKES 450 ML / ³/₄ PINT
**2 hard-boiled egg yolks**
**2 tsp made English mustard**
**salt and pepper**
**3½ tbsp neutrally flavoured oil, such as sunflower**
**1 tbsp white wine vinegar**
**150 ml / ¼ pt double cream**

Push the hard-boiled egg yolks through a sieve into a bowl, then beat in the mustard, salt and pepper.

Whisk in the oil, a few drops at a time. When smoothly amalgamated, whisk in the vinegar, again a few drops at a time. Finally, beat in the cream. Taste and adjust the seasoning.

## GARLIC MAYONNAISE

Garlic mayonnaise is popular in France, Spain and Portugal. It is perhaps best known as the dipping sauce in a Provençal *grand aïoli*, a great party extravaganza of cold cod, snails, boiled eggs and raw vegetables that is invariably washed down with masses of rosé. Although aïoli is traditionally made only with olive oil, it is less heavy if made with equal parts olive and sunflower oil.

MAKES 600 ML / 1 PINT
**4 garlic cloves**
**2–3 egg yolks**
**1 tsp salt**
**1 tsp freshly ground black pepper**
**300 ml / ½ pt olive oil**
**juice of ½ lemon**
**300 ml / ½ pt sunflower oil**

Crush the garlic cloves to a pulp using some suitably heavy implement and put into a bowl with 2 of the egg yolks.

Whisk in the salt and pepper, then start to add the olive oil in a thin stream. After you have used half of it, add the lemon juice. Now beat in the sunflower oil. If it becomes too thick, add a tablespoon of warm water.

Repeat the process, using the rest of the olive oil, Drip in water if it gets too thick. The consistency should be heavy, a dipping rather than a pouring thickness. If it becomes too thick, add a tablespoon of warm water. If it should separate, just put a third egg yolk into another bowl and beat the curdled glop into it, a little at a time, until it holds again.

Taste and adjust the seasoning and lemon balance as necessary. The garlic, being raw, will continue to gain in strength for several hours, but then this is supposed to be an emphatic sauce.

## HOLLANDAISE SAUCE AND VARIATIONS

Hollandaise is one of the great classic sauces of the French kitchen, a simple and very rich emulsion of melted butter flavoured with lemon juice and bound with egg yolks. It is usually served with poached fish or vegetables and forms the basis for a number of variations, such as béarnaise, choron, mousseline and moutarde. Usually served with grilled meat, these are more strongly flavoured because they include a reduction of wine vinegar, shallots and herbs, and other defining ingredients. Traditionally all are made in a double boiler or in a bowl set over simmering water, but the easiest method uses a food processor.

## BÉARNAISE SAUCE

SERVES 4
115 g / 4 oz unsalted butter
60 g / 2 oz finely chopped shallots
4 tbsp white wine vinegar
1 tsp coarsely crushed peppercorns
2 egg yolks
$\frac{1}{2}$ tsp salt

Melt the butter in a pan over a low heat.

At the same time, boil the shallots with the vinegar and peppercorns until reduced to about 1 tablespoon.

Pass through a sieve into a food processor and add the egg yolks and salt. Turn on at full speed and slowly pour the butter through the feeder tube.

Transfer to a bowl set over simmering water and whisk until a spoonable consistency is achieved.

## MICHEL GUÉRARD'S NOUVELLE TOMATO BÉARNAISE SAUCE

Delicious as these emulsion sauces are, calorie-conscious readers often ask whether there is a way of making them with less saturated fat.

Michel Guérard was the first great chef to address the area of healthy eating, with low-calorie gourmet food at his hotel attached to the health spa at Eugénie-les-Bains in South-west France, and this is his diet version of béarnaise sauce.

SERVES 4
60 g / 2 oz shallots, finely chopped
1 tbsp chopped tarragon
1 tsp coarsely crushed black peppercorns
4 tbsp white wine vinegar
about 6 ripe plum tomatoes
2 egg yolks
2 tbsp extra-virgin olive oil
100 ml / 3½ fl oz chicken stock
1 tsp tomato purée
1 tsp chopped chervil
salt

Put the chopped shallots in a small saucepan with the chopped tarragon, crushed peppercorns and white wine vinegar. Bring to the boil and reduce, stirring, to a moist purée. Sieve to remove the pepper and return to the pan.

Blanch, peel, deseed and chop the tomatoes to produce 200 g / 7 oz of pulp. Boil this down in a second pan until the liquid has almost evaporated.

Add the egg yolks and 1 tablespoon

of water to the shallot reduction and whisk over a moderate heat until you have the consistency of a creamy mousse, with each stroke of the whisk leaving its trace on the bottom of the pan.

Remove from the heat and add the extra-virgin olive oil in a thin stream, whisking in. Then slowly add the chicken stock, whisking all the time. Stir in the cooked tomato pulp, tomato purée, chopped chervil and season with a little salt to taste.

Keep warm and serve with all kinds of grilled meat, chicken and fish.

## HONEY VINAIGRETTE

This is particularly good with warm salads and has an affinity with duck, ham or barbecued pork. It also functions well as a marinade for chicken.

MAKES ABOUT 150 ML / $\frac{1}{4}$ PINT
2 tbsp clear runny honey
5 tbsp extra-virgin olive oil
2 tbsp balsamic vinegar
2 tbsp lemon juice
$\frac{1}{2}$ tsp chilli powder
salt and pepper

Put the honey in a food processor with the olive oil, vinegar, lemon juice, chilli powder, salt and pepper. Blend to a homogenized dressing.

## BLUE CHEESE DRESSING

Danish Blue is fine, Roquefort is best of all, but you can use any blue cheese. You can make the dressing less rich by using equal parts of mayonnaise and thick plain yoghurt.

MAKES ABOUT 450 ML / ³/₄ PINT

300 ml / ½ pt mayonnaise

3 tbsp crème fraîche or sour cream

2 tsp Worcestershire sauce

1 tsp Tabasco

1 tbsp lemon juice

½ tsp black pepper

2 celery stalks, including leaves

3 spring onions

small bunch of chives

115 g / 4 oz blue cheese (see above), broken into small pieces

Put the mayonnaise into a bowl with the crème fraîche or sour cream and whisk in the Worcestershire sauce, Tabasco, lemon juice and black pepper. Finely chop the celery stalks, including leaves, the spring onions and chives, and add.

Finally, stir in the cheese, but not too thoroughly or it will break up and turn the dressing a weird colour.

## CRÈME ANGLAISE

One of the few things which proudly carries an English name tag in international cooking, this refined and slightly runny custard is delicious with any fruit or in sweet pastries, and is very easy to make.

SERVES 4

600 ml / 1 pint single cream

1 vanilla pod, split

5 egg yolks

175 g / 6 oz caster sugar

Put the cream and vanilla pod in a pan over a low heat and bring to the point where it is just below boiling.

While it is heating, whisk the egg yolks with the caster sugar until you have a pale amalgam which will fall in ribbons from the whisk.

Off the heat, slowly whisk in the hot cream. Pour into a bowl set over simmering water and cook, stirring with a wooden spoon, until it forms a custard thick enough to coat the back of a spoon (about 10–12 minutes).

Pour and scrape into a bowl, remove the vanilla pod and leave to cool. Rinse the pod, dry and keep for another time.

## BUTTERSCOTCH SAUCE

It is worth making enough for eight as here, as it keeps in the fridge for 2–3 weeks.

MAKES 500 ML / 16 FL OZ

400 g / 14 oz soft brown sugar

4 tbsp liquid glucose

200 ml / 7 fl oz double cream

140 g / 5 oz unsalted butter, diced

Put the soft brown sugar in a pan with the liquid glucose and 300 ml / ½ pint cold water. Place over a low to moderate heat and stir until the sugar has dissolved, then turn up the heat slightly. Put in a sugar thermometer and bring the syrup to 120°C/250°F, when the caramel will have coloured from a light blond to dark brown, the 'soft ball' stage, so called because if you put a small spoonful in cold water it should form a malleable ball when rolled between thumb and finger.

Remove the pan from the heat and gradually add the double cream. Start with a spoonful at a time as the mixture will rise dangerously when the cold cream hits the volcanic caramel.

When all the cream has been incorporated, gradually stir in the butter dice, until you have a smooth, creamy sauce.

You can use the sauce at once or allow to cool, then refrigerate for up to 2 weeks. Reheat gently, only returning to the boil after the butterscotch is hot.

## HOT CHOCOLATE SAUCE

MAKES ABOUT 400 G / 14 OZ

225 g / 8 oz best-quality dark chocolate, broken into pieces

60 g / 2 oz caster sugar

100 ml / 3½ fl oz double cream

Put the chocolate in a pan with 350 ml / 12 fl oz water and the caster sugar. Bring to the boil, stirring. The instant it bubbles, turn down the heat to very low and simmer for 15 minutes.

Stir in the cream and immediately pass through a sieve. You can serve this hot or cold, as it will not solidify.

> PREVENTING BUTTERSCOTCH SAUCE FROM GOING GRAINY
> *Butterscotch sauce often goes grainy because the sauce contains butter and cream which tend to crystallize sugar. The addition of liquid glucose, which you will find in the baking section of your supermarket, counteracts this.*

## RELISHES, CONDIMENTS AND PICKLES

### HARISSA

Harissa is the fiercely hot chilli paste of North Africa, where it is used in small amounts to lift dishes with its aromatic fire. It is also used in rouille, the spicy orange mayonnaise served with Mediterranean fish soups, and in the making of merguez sausages. It is an excellent hot relish to add to many dishes, and the more you eat it the more you are seduced by it, for what starts out startlingly hot seems to get milder as you grow accustomed to its bite. Despite its natural heat, harissa is not impervious to bacterial contamination, so take all the usual hygiene precautions and sterilize the jar and lid in boiling water.

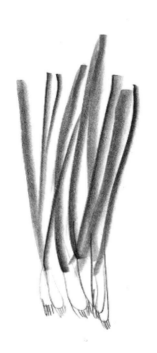

MAKES ABOUT 225 G / 8 OZ

115 g / 4 oz dried hot red chillies
10 garlic cloves
1 tbsp coriander seeds
1 tbsp black peppercorns
½ tbsp caraway seeds
½ tbsp salt
4–5 tbsp olive oil

Put the chillies in a pan, pour over 600 ml / 1 pt water and bring to the boil. Boil for 60 seconds, remove from the heat and leave to soak for 30 minutes. Don't throw away this water.

Destem the chillies and put them a food processor. Peel and chop the garlic cloves and put with the chillies.

Toast the coriander seeds, peppercorns and caraway seeds in a dry pan over a low heat. Grind in a coffee grinder and add to the processor with the salt and olive oil. Whiz to a thick paste. If too thick, add a couple of tablespoons of the cooking water.

Spoon into a sterilized jar, packing down to eliminate air pockets and film the surface with olive oil.

Once opened it should keep for 2 weeks if refrigerated.

### TOMATILLO SALSA

You find this sauce on the tables of neighbourhood restaurants and cafés throughout Mexico. Eat with any savoury dish, or as a dip for corn chips.

SERVES 4

500 g / 1.25 lb tomatillos
4 hot green chillies
3 garlic cloves

1 tsp caster sugar
2 tsp salt
15 g / ½ oz coriander leaves and stalks, coarsely chopped
½ Spanish onion, diced
juice of ½ lemon
salt and freshly ground pepper

Husk the tomatillos and put in a pan with the destemmed chillies, garlic, caster sugar and salt. Pour over 750 ml / 1.25 pint cold water and bring to the boil. Lower the heat and simmer for 5 minutes. Drain through a colander, reserving 150 ml / ¼ pint of the poaching liquid.

Put this in a food processor with the tomatillos, chillies and garlic and blitz briefly to a coarse purée. Transfer to a serving bowl and leave to cool.

Stir in the coriander leaves and stalks, onion and lemon juice. Taste and season with freshly ground pepper and a little more salt if you think it is needed.

### KIMCHEE

Kimchee, a pickle of sour-tasting fermented Chinese cabbage and garlic, is a Korean national institution, served with every and any meal from breakfast to dinner. It is produced there in huge amounts in wooden tubs, but it works well on a smaller scale.

SERVES 8–10

1 Chinese cabbage
450 g / 1 lb daikon (white radish)
3 tbsp salt
7.5-cm / 3-inch piece of root ginger

**8 garlic cloves**
**6 spring onions, thinly sliced**
**2 tsp chilli flakes**
**2 tsp caster sugar**

Cut the Chinese cabbage in half lengthwise and then cut the halves across into 5-cm / 2-inch sections. Peel the daikon, cut it in half lengthwise, then cut the halves across into 5-mm / ¼-inch thick slices. Put into a bowl.

Dissolve the salt in 1.75 litres / 3 pints cold water and pour this over the vegetables. Cover the top with a cloth and leave at room temperature overnight.

Finely chop the ginger and garlic. Put in a large bowl with the sliced spring onions, chilli flakes and caster sugar, mixing together with a spoon. Remove the soaking vegetables from the brine with tongs or a slotted spoon and add to the ginger-and-garlic mixture. Don't throw away the brine!

Pack the vegetables into a 2.25-litre / 2-quart jar, leaving a 3-cm / 1¼-inch space at the top. Pour over enough reserved brine to cover. Don't put on the lid, but cover with a cloth — the pickle needs air to ferment.

Leave at room temperature for 3 days, then taste a piece. If it is sour enough to your taste then it is ready, but the precise time will depend on the ambient temperature. The warmer it is, the quicker it works. If it is cool, then it may take as long as 7 days.

To serve 4, remove about a cupful and put it in a bowl on the table for people to help themselves. In Korea, spoonfuls of the pickling liquid are added to soups.

## MINT JELLY

Cooking apples form the base for this preserve, their natural pectin providing the setting agent for the jelly. The efficiency of the set will however depend on a number of factors, notably the balance between the pectin, acid and sugar.

**MAKES ABOUT 450 G / 1 LB**

**1.8 kg / 4 lb cooking apples**
**60 g / 2 oz chopped mint, including the stalks, plus 2 tbsp more finely chopped mint leaves, to finish**
**grated zest and juice of 1 lemon**
**1 tbsp white wine vinegar**
**675 g / 1½ lb caster sugar**

Chop the apples coarsely, including the cores, and put in a pan with the 60 g / 2 oz chopped mint, including the stalks, the lemon zest and juice, and vinegar, and barely cover with about 1.1 litres / 2 pints of cold water. Bring to the boil, turn down the heat and simmer gently for 45 minutes.

The proper piece of kit for the next stage is a jelly bag, but if you don't have one you could improvise. Line a colander with a double thickness of fine muslin and scald with boiling water to sterilize. Put this over a bowl and pour the contents of the pan into it and leave to drip overnight. Don't try and hurry this process by pushing with a spoon or squeezing the bag, as this will force solids through and make the jelly cloudy.

Measure the juice and put into a pan with 450 g / 1 lb caster sugar per 600 ml / 1 pt of apple juice. Bring to the boil slowly, then increase the heat and boil rapidly for about 8 minutes. Continue to boil for another 2 minutes, when the right amount of water will have evaporated and the frothing boil will have changed to a thicker rolling boil, with fat bubbles plopping noisily to the surface. At this stage setting point should have been reached.

Remove from the heat, pour through a sieve into a warmed jug and then stir in the 2 tablespoons of finely chopped mint leaves. Test by putting a spoonful of the mix on a cold plate. The surface should set as it cools and will wrinkle when prodded. Pour immediately into warm sterilized jars. Don't tilt them until set. Put on sterilized lids and keep in a cool cupboard.

Once opened, keep in the fridge. Once you have made a batch successfully, you may like to make a larger amount when cooking apples are cheap, to give as presents. If so, use the same relative amounts. You should get about 4.5 kg / 10 lb jelly from every 2.7 kg / 6 lb sugar used.

## NUOC CHAM

Nuoc cham is a chilli-hot lime-based dipping sauce that is as easy to make as vinaigrette. How hot you make it is up to you and it can be made with red or green chillies. The recipe calls for nuoc mam, Vietnamese fish sauce, but you could use nam pla, Thai fish sauce, without discernible difference.

**SERVES 4**
**3 hot red chillies**
**3 garlic cloves, finely chopped**
**juice of 5 limes**
**3 tbsp nuoc mam or nam pla**
**fish sauce**
**3 tbsp sugar**
**2 tbsp shredded carrot**

Cut the chillies into tiny dice and put in a bowl with the seeds from the chillies and the garlic. Cover with the lime juice and leave to marinate for 30 minutes.

Add the fish sauce, sugar and shredded carrot. Mix together and leave for another 10 minutes before using.

It will keep in the fridge for a week without deterioration.

## PICKLING VINEGAR

Supermarkets sell pickling vinegar in large jars, suitable for the onions or whatever you want to preserve, but it is easy to make. You can use either white spirit vinegar or malt vinegar for the base liquid.

**MAKES ABOUT 675 G / 1 1/2 LB**
**1.75 litres / 3 pints vinegar (see above)**
**7.5-cm / 3-inch piece of root ginger, sliced**
**15 g / 1/2 oz cloves**
**1 cinnamon stick**
**15 g / 1/2 oz allspice berries**
**3 bay leaves**
**20 black peppercorns**

Put the vinegar in the top part of a double boiler. If you don't have one, sit a bowl with a lid over a pan of gently simmering water. You should find one of your saucepan lids to fit.

Add the ginger, cloves, cinnamon stick, allspice berries, bay leaves and peppercorns. Put over a low heat for 2 hours.

Pass through a muslin-lined sieve and you are ready to start pickling.

## SWEDISH GREEN TOMATO PICKLE

If you can't get green tomatoes, pick out unripe ones in the supermarket and they will work just as well. It would be much more difficult to find ripe tomatoes, come to think of it. The pickled tomatoes are excellent with cold meats or cheese.

**3 kg / 6 1/2 lb green tomatoes**
**300 ml / 1/2 pt malt vinegar**
**150 ml / 1/2 pt red wine vinegar**
**900 g / 2 lb caster sugar**
**12 cloves**
**2 hot chillies, diced**

Prick the tomatoes here and there with a needle and put them in a large heatproof bowl or pan.

Boil 600 ml / 1 pint water with the malt vinegar. Pour it over the tomatoes and leave to stand overnight.

Put the red wine vinegar in a large saucepan with the caster sugar, cloves, diced chillies with their seeds and 600 ml / 1 pint water. Bring to the boil and stir. When the sugar has dissolved, drain the tomatoes in a colander and add to the syrup. Simmer gently for 20 minutes.

Using a slotted spoon, take out the tomatoes and pack carefully in sterilized Kilner jars. Do not force too many in or they will burst.

Turn up the heat under the poaching liquid and reduce it until it is a thick syrup, then pour this over the tomatoes to cover.

Leave for at least 2 weeks before eating. They will keep unopened for months.

## CUCUMBER PICKLE

**MAKES ABOUT 1.35 KG / 3 LB**
**2 large cucumbers**
**1 large Spanish onion**
**1 green pepper**
**2 tbsp sea salt**
**225 g / 8 oz muscovado sugar**

1 cinnamon stick
1 tsp allspice
2 bay leaves
2 cloves
450 ml / ¾ pt white wine vinegar

Use a mandoline to slice the unpeeled cucumbers and peeled onion into the thinnest slices. Cut the green pepper in half, deseed and cut into the thinnest strips possible.

Mix the cucumber, onion and pepper together and spread them out over a large flat dish. Scatter over the sea salt and leave at room temperature for 2 hours.

Rinse thoroughly in a colander and reserve, allowing excess moisture to drain off.

Put the muscovado sugar, cinnamon stick, allspice, bay leaves and cloves in a pan with the vinegar. Bring slowly to the boil, turn down the heat and simmer for 5 minutes.

Add the sliced vegetables. Turn down the heat to its lowest setting and continue to cook for 2 minutes, but do not allow it to boil.

Remove from the heat and pour and spoon into sterilized jars. Put lids on when cold and keep for 3–4 weeks before eating. Once opened, keep in the refrigerator.

## HARVY-SCARVY

Harvy-scarvy was originally a pungent Norfolk speciality, made from apples, onions and malt vinegar.

The recipe below is for a more subtle variation on the theme. Use it with any cold meat, though it is particularly good with pork.

MAKES ABOUT 350 G / 12 OZ
125 g / 4 oz tart eating apples
125 g / 4 oz red shallots
125 g / 4 oz celery
salt and pepper
5 tbsp extra-virgin olive oil
4 tbsp cider vinegar

Dice the unpeeled apple, shallots and celery into a bowl. Season with salt and pepper and pour over the oil and cider vinegar. Stir, cling-wrap and leave to let the flavours develop for 2 hours.

Stir again before serving.

## HILLOSIPULIT

Finnish pickled onions are milder and sweeter than ours.

MAKES ABOUT 900 G / 2 LB
75 g / 2½ oz sea salt
675 g / 1½ lb peeled baby onions
600 ml / 1 pt white spirit vinegar
30 g / 1 oz peeled ginger root, cut into julienne strips
175 g / 6 oz brown sugar
¼ tsp ground mace
10 white peppercorns

Bring 600 ml / 1 pt of water to the boil with the sea salt and pour it over the baby onions in another pan or heat-proof bowl. Put a plate on the top to keep them covered by the brine and leave overnight.

Put the vinegar in a saucepan with the ginger, brown sugar, mace and peppercorns. Bring to the boil, lower the heat and simmer for 3 minutes. Drain

the onions and add to this mixture, continuing to simmer for 4 minutes.

Remove the onions to sterilized jars with a slotted spoon, then sieve in pickle to cover. Put on lids, allow to cool, then refrigerate for a week before eating.

## ONION MARMALADE

This popular relish is made from sugared onions which are stewed slowly to a syrupy consistency. Start with a lot of onions as they cook down to a tiny part of their original watery bulk.

MAKES ABOUT 450 G / 1 LB
1.8 kg / 4 lb brown onions, thinly sliced
100 ml / 3½ fl oz olive oil
salt and pepper
170 g / 6 oz caster sugar
150 ml / ¼ pt red wine
5 tbsp red wine vinegar

Put the onions in a big heavy-based pan with the oil and stir to coat. Season and cook over a moderate heat, stirring, for 5 minutes. It is important not to let the onions brown at this point or the end-product will be bitter.

Lower the heat to its lowest setting, put on a lid and cook for 20 minutes.

Remove the lid, scatter over the sugar, wine and vinegar. Continue to cook, stirring from time to time, until most of the liquid has evaporated and you are left with a thick, jammy residue. This will take 20–30 minutes.

Put into sterilized jars, cover the surface with olive oil, put on lids and keep in a cool cupboard for a month before use. Once opened, keep refrigerated.

## INDIAN MINT CHUTNEY

Although it is called a fresh chutney, this delicious yoghurt dipping sauce bears little resemblance to the sweet preserves we usually call by that name. It is most often served with samosas and pakoris, and is eaten immediately because no preservative ingredients or cooking are used.

MAKES ABOUT 300 ML / ½ PINT

**2 big handfuls of coriander**
**handful of coarsely chopped mint leaves**
**1 hot green chilli, chopped but with seeds**
**juice of ½ lemon**
**1 tsp salt**
**150 ml / ¼ pt thick plain yoghurt**

Chop the coriander and put into a food processor. Add the chopped mint leaves, chilli, lemon juice and salt. Blitz to a fine mulch, scraping down the sides of the bowl from time to time.

Add the yoghurt and work to combine evenly.

## BATTERS

Batters are not technically difficult, but can be overworked. Only beat them to the point where all the ingredients are incorporated to a smooth coating consistency. Here are 5 different formulae to try. Amounts given will coat four 225-g / 8-oz fish fillets.

**1** In the classic English version, whisk together 115 g / 4 oz sifted plain flour, 1 egg, 150 ml / 5 fl oz milk and 1 tsp salt, then leave it to stand for 30 minutes. It should be smooth and creamy.

**2** For a tasty light beer batter: sift 115 g / 4 oz plain flour, add 1 tbsp olive oil, then whisk 200 ml / 7 fl oz cold beer into 125 g / 4 oz plain flour. Leave to stand for 1 hour. Whisk the whites of 2 eggs to soft peaks, then fold them in just before coating the fish fillets.

**3** For a substantial thick batter that holds up well if the food is not served immediately: sift 225 g / 8 oz plain flour into a bowl and add 4 g (⅛ oz, ½ sachet) easy-blend yeast, 1 tsp salt and 300 ml / ½ pt hand-warm water. Whisk together. Cover and leave to stand at room temperature for 90 minutes. Stir before use.

**4** For one of the lightest and crispest of batters: sift 200 g / 7 oz self-raising flour with 1 tsp salt and ½ tsp baking powder into a bowl and whisk in 300 ml / ½ pt cold water to a smooth batter. Leave to stand for 1 hour. Whisk again before use.

**5** For a crisp batter: whisk an egg in a bowl with 450 ml / ¾ pt of milk at room temperature, a sachet (8 g / ¼ oz) of easy-blend yeast and ¼ tsp caster sugar. Sift 175 g / 6 oz plain flour and 115 g / 4 oz cornflour into another bowl with ½ tsp salt. Whisk the milk mixture into this to make a thick batter. Cling-wrap the top and leave for 2 hours when it will have increased in volume by about a half.

### WHISKING EGG WHITES FOR SAVOURY DISHES
*When whisking egg whites to add to other ingredients, do not salt them as it will cause them to split and liquid to exude.*

## BREADCRUMBS

Remove the crust from a white loaf, slice it and leave the slices uncovered at room temperature for about 24 hours. Only then are they ready to be turned into fresh crumbs. Once this would have been done by rubbing through a sieve, today a food processor does the job effortlessly. The resulting crumbs still have a high moisture content and will go mouldy if put into a jar.

The next stage is to dry them, either on a tray in an oven at the lowest setting, with the door slightly ajar, or laid out on a tray in a warm place. When dried, they will keep in an airtight container for several weeks.

Another approach is to put slices of bread on a baking tray, crusts on, and bake them in a moderate oven (180°C/350°F/gas 4) until golden-brown, then blitz them in a food processor to a crumb. This produces the finest crumb, technically called raspings, which are best for coating fish cakes or any food which is to be egged-and-crumbed, then deep-fried. They hold better than fresh crumbs.

It is a good idea to give a double coating of raspings to food which is to be deep-fried.

If you want to fry breadcrumbs to serve with game, then these need to be the fresh variety, which are shallow-fried over a low heat with butter until crisp and golden.

A final variation is to make olive oil crumbs from bread brushed with oil and baked until crisp. These are excellent with grilled or baked vegetables, but need to be used the same day or they go rancid.

## CORNICHONS

Few French restaurants would think of putting a coarse-textured terrine on the table without a crock of cornichons — baby pickled cucumbers — complete with little wooden tongs to remove them to the plate. They are as automatic an accompaniment as bread. The only difficult bit is finding them fresh in this country. They should be unripe and firm, no larger than 3.5 cm / 1½ inches long and, from a cosmetic point of view, it is nice if they still have some stem attached.

European ones are available in late spring or early summer, though you sometimes see them in Asian markets at other times of the year. It is worth asking your greengrocer when he can get hold of them.

This recipe is given by Richard Olney in *Preserving*, one of the *Time Life Good Cook* series. There is no absolute about the type of vinegar to use, though it should have an acidity of at least 6 per cent. White wine, champagne or cider vinegar would all be appropriate.

**MAKES ABOUT 1.5 KG / 3 LB**

**1.5 kg / 3 lb cornichons**
**about 850 ml / 1½ pints vinegar (see above)**

Pick over the cornichons, discarding any that are blemished. Pack them into one large sterilized 3-litre/ 5-pt earthenware crock or jar. Pour the vinegar into the filled jar or jars to cover the cornichons by 2–3 cm / 1 inch.

Empty the vinegar into an enamelled pan (since a metal one would react

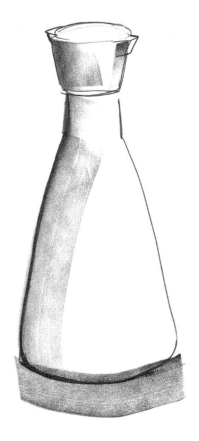

with the vinegar). Add another 125 ml / 4 fl oz of the vinegar, bring to the boil and immediately pour it over the cornichons. Cover the top and leave for 24 hours.

Repeat the process, pouring the vinegar from the jar into the pan, adding another 125 ml / 4 fl oz vinegar. Boil and pour over. Leave for a further 24 hours and repeat for a third time.

When cool, put on the lid and store in a cool dark place for 6 weeks before eating. If needed, top the crock up with more vinegar as it is important to keep them covered. Unexposed to the air, they will keep for ages.

### FLAVOURED OLIVE OIL

In Italy, olive oil is so much a part of culinary life its absence from the daily diet would be unthinkable. Today, with the large-scale importation of olive oil to this country, we too are able to buy a selection of good olive oils in any supermarket and it is odd to think that not so many years ago olive oil was something you only bought in Boots the Chemist to treat earache or to rub into sore muscles.

Indeed, 20 years ago the majority of Britons had never tasted olive oil and found the idea of its widespread use in cooking little short of repugnant, as package holidaymakers returning from the Mediterranean made clear.

As our appreciation grows for *olio santo*, sacred oil, as it was known to Etruscans and Romans 2,000 years ago, so we seek to change and adapt it. When adding raw organic solids to oil as a flavouring, however, you will find that although the process of decomposition is slowed by the absence of oxygen it is not stopped completely. Some additions work better than others and there are good arguments not to make garlic oil at all, since the principal joy of garlic is the pungency of its fresh, just peeled state. When old, it develops a rancid, stale taste.

One flavoured oil worth making is still referred to as *olio santo* in Tuscany, the home of much of Italy's finest olive oil. Cleanliness is vital, while tossing the flavouring ingredients in lemon juice increases the acidity, which helps prevent bacterial contamination. Your hands should be scrubbed clean before handling the flavouring ingredients and the jar should be sterilized. It is also important to fill the jar right to the top, to allow as little exposure to the air as possible.

MAKES ABOUT 600 ML / 1 PINT
**20 dried hot red chillies**
**juice of 1 lemon**
**20 coarsely crushed black peppercorns**
**10 washed and dried fresh basil leaves**
**about 600 ml / 1 pint olive oil**

Pour boiling water over the dried chillies in a bowl and leave for 20 minutes. Strain through a sieve, dry on kitchen paper, then toss in lemon juice with the peppercorns and basil leaves. Put them into a sterilized jar and fill with olive oil.

Close the jar tightly and put somewhere cool and dark, but not the fridge as the oil solidifies at low temperature and the flavours and chilli spice heat will not pass into the oil. Leave for 2 weeks, before passing through a fine sieve into another clean jar or bottle, discarding the leaves (which will have turned black and slimy). The chillies may be returned to the oil if you want it to get hotter.

This oil can now be used for frying to add spice to your cooking, or simply added by the spoonful to chicken broth at the table as it is in Tuscany.

### RASPBERRY VINEGAR

Use 600 ml / 1 pt red wine vinegar to each 450g / 1 lb raspberries. Blitz the fruit to a purée in a food processor and transfer to a bowl. Pour the appropriate amount of vinegar over, cling-wrap the top and leave to macerate at room temperature for a week.

Put into a saucepan and bring to the boil. Lower the heat and simmer for 15 minutes. Pass through a muslin-lined sieve. Bottle and keep in a cupboard (as exposure to light results in a more rapid loss of fruit flavour). It will not keep for ever and is best used within six months.

Use it to finish sautéed meat dishes.

### THAI GREEN CURRY PASTE

Two of the essential ingredients of *gaeng kiow wan* — green curry paste — are kaffir lime leaves and galangal. There is no single recipe for a curry paste and you can change the balance and emphasis by, for example, adding more or less chillies, garlic, shallots or galangal. When made with a pestle and mortar, a true paste results, which keeps for a long time in an airtight container. On the other hand, a processor produces quite a wet purée which will not keep as well. The whole point, however, is the impact of the fresh ingredients and, when made in a food processor, the job takes minutes. Packed in jars and filmed with oil, fresh processor-made paste will keep in the fridge for a month. It may also be frozen in ice-cube trays and stored in the freezer in zip-lock bags.

MAKES ABOUT 675 G / 1½ LB

- 4 tsp belacan (shrimp paste)
- 2 tsp cumin seeds
- 2 tsp coriander seeds
- 1 tsp black peppercorns
- 10 small hot green chillies, chopped, with their seeds
- 3 long green milder chillies, stems removed
- 10 Thai red shallots, chopped
- 10-cm / 4-inch piece of galangal, scrubbed and grated
- 2 lemon grass stalks, outer leaves removed and sliced
- 115 g / 4 oz coriander, including stems and roots
- 60 g / 2 oz Thai holy basil
- 5 garlic cloves, chopped
- 8 chopped lime leaves (if you don't have any, substitute 2 tbsp fish sauce)
- oil, for filming

Wrap the belacan in foil and grill until fragrant. In a dry pan and over a low heat, toast the cumin seeds, coriander seeds and peppercorns for 2–3 minutes until they give off an aroma.

Grind to a powder in a coffee grinder and put into a food processor with the chopped small hot green chillies and their seeds, long green milder chillies, shallots, galangal, lemon grass, coriander, basil, garlic, belacan and chopped lime leaves or fish sauce. Blitz, adding 1 or 2 tablespoons of water through the feeder tube and stopping from time to time to scrape down the sides until you have a thick purée.

Store in a sterilized jar, filmed with oil, in the fridge, where it will keep for

weeks. Use 1 tablespoon per 4 servings when frying the other curry ingredients. The precise amount will depend on the heat of the chillies and you really must judge this by taste.

## RED CURRY PASTE

Called *gaeng pet* in Thai, when using stir a tablespoon into sweated onions and fry for a minute, stirring, before adding the other ingredients.

MAKES ABOUT 675 G / 1½ LB

- 4 tsp belacan (shrimp paste) or 2 tbsp fish sauce
- 8–10 hot red chillies
- 2 tsp each toasted ground cumin, coriander seeds, peppercorns (as above)
- 8–10 red shallots, chopped
- 3 lemon grass stalks, thinly sliced
- 8 lime leaves, chopped
- 10-cm / 4-inch piece of galangal, grated

- handful of coriander stems and roots, chopped
- 5 garlic cloves, chopped

Wrap the belacan in foil and grill until fragrant.

Put all the ingredients into the food processor and blitz to a purée as for green curry paste.

## PRALINE

Praline is made from blanched almonds coated in caramel and is easy to make. Use to fold into ice-creams and chocolate desserts.

MAKES ABOUT 400 G / 14 OZ

- 225 g / 8 oz caster sugar
- 175 g / 6 oz blanched almonds
- butter, for greasing

In a heavy-based saucepan, dissolve the caster sugar in 100 ml / 4 fl oz water over a moderate heat, stirring with a wooden spoon until the syrup boils, then reduce the heat and continue to cook, uncovered and without stirring, until it is a pale caramel colour.

Tip in the blanched almonds and swirl the pan to coat them, then pour and scrape on to a buttered baking tray and leave until cold and set.

Break this up into pieces and put into a food processor. In a blender, crush to a uniform coarse texture. You have just made praline, which will keep in an airtight container for up to three weeks.

# SOME ENTERTAINING IDEAS

The secret to successful party food is to make items small enough to make one mouthful, as this eliminates the need for individual plates. Things like:

- Miniature pizzas with a variety of toppings, including pieces of Home-dried Tomato (page 183) and mozzarella, pesto, spring onion and shaved Cheddar, sweet grilled pepper and anchovy. You can use thinly rolled shop-bought puff pastry for the base if you are too busy to make a proper pizza dough. Use a pastry cutter to cut out bite-sized rounds.

- Puff pastry can also be glazed with egg yolk and simply topped with a spoonful of creamy scrambled egg.

· Little pies made in a tart pan and filled with Bolognese Sauce (page 103) are always popular.

- Meat eaters also love real ham sandwiches made from slices cut fresh off the bone. Use fresh made English mustard and unsalted butter on good, white bread, but with the crusts cut off and the sandwiches sliced into bite-sized squares.

- Crudités like sticks of carrots, celery, cauliflower florets, strips of sweet peppers and other crisp vegetables with a hot dipping sauce made from 20 anchovy fillets, 115 g / 4 oz butter, 300 ml / $\frac{1}{2}$ pint single cream and 8 large garlic cloves, smashed and chopped, all heated together in a pan until they combine into a smooth purée.

- Tiny Scotch Eggs (page 248) can be made with quails' eggs and lean, spicy sausagemeat. The sausagemeat can be made more interesting by mashing into it finely diced chilli and garlic and chopped coriander or flat-leaved parsley.

- Finally, finger sandwiches made from smoked salmon never go amiss, nor do cubes of best mature farmhouse Cheddar.

**SOME MORE PARTY IDEAS:**

**1 GRILLED SPATCHCOCKED POUSSINS.**

Spatchcock the birds (see Umbrian Lemon Poussin, page 137 ) and marinate them overnight in lemon juice and ginger juice, with chilli flakes and lots of pepper. They must not be aggressively char-grilled, as this makes them bitter when cold, but cooked under a medium-hot overhead grill, after being brushed with olive oil, and turned frequently until the skin is crisp and golden. Cook about 15 cm / 6 inches from grill for about 20–25 minutes.

**2 COLD RACKS OF LAMB WITH CHINESE SPICE.**

Each rack will yield 5 to 6 cutlets. Trim them well and rub each rack with 1 teaspoon of Chinese five-spice powder, lots of coarse ground pepper and some salt just before going into a very hot (250°C/475°F/gas 9) oven for 15 minutes. Slice into cutlets at the last minute and mound on a plate with some quartered limes.

**3 GRILLED TIGER PRAWNS.**

Brush them with mirin and soy sauce, then grilled on bamboo skewers, one to a skewer with the prawn pulled out straight. Serve hot or cold with a coriander Pesto (page 293) as a dip.

## 4 ROAST TINY YORKSHIRE PUDDINGS.

Make them in bun tins (104), served with a piece of rare beef and a teaspoon of Horseradish Sauce (page 293) in the indentation. These are excellent hot or cold.

## 5 DEEP-FRIED CHICKEN WON-TONS.

To make 30, put 500 g / 1 lb lean cubed chicken in a food processor with a 4-cm / 1½-inch piece of ginger, peeled and chopped, a handful of coriander leaves, 1 tablespoon soy sauce, 1 tablespoon mirin or dry sherry, white of 1 egg and salt and pepper. Pulse-chop to a purée and fill the won-ton wrappers with a heaped teaspoon on each. Wrap up and seal with a little cornflour mixed to a paste with water. Deep-fry at 190°C/375°F for about 6 minutes. Drain on paper towels and serve with Sweet-and-sour Chilli Tomato Sauce (page 292).

## 6 SMOKED SALMON SUSHI.

Sticky rice, smoked salmon and wasabi paste rolled in toasted nori and cut in bite-sized rounds.

## 7 POTATOES DELUXE.

Cubed potatoes coated in olive oil, roasted and topped with slices of black truffle or caviar.

## 8 INDIVIDUAL BOLOGNESE TARTS.

Line a bun tin with shortcrust pastry, fill with Bolognese Sauce (page 105) and put on lids, brushing the edges with milk and pinching shut. Glaze the tops with beaten egg and bake for 20–25 minutes at 200°C/400°F/gas6.

## 9 PUFF PASTRY CHEESE STRAWS.

Defrost frozen puff pastry and roll out thinly. Cover one half with grated mozzarella and thin rings of green chilli. Fold over, glaze with egg and shake over sesame seeds. Cut into strips and bake on a tray at 200°C/400°F/gas 6, until puffed and golden brown.

## 10 BRIE AND SAFFRON FILO TARTLETS.

For 12 tartlets: warm 2 tablespoons dry white wine and put about 24 saffron threads to soak in it for 15 minutes. Brush 2 sheets of filo with melted butter and cut them into 7.5-cm / 3-inch rectangles. Press a rectangle into each depression of a buttered bun tin and put a second buttered rectangle on top with the corners at angle to the first sheet. Divide 350 g / 12 oz diced firm brie between the tarts and drizzle the saffron and soaking liquid over each. Mill plenty of coarsely ground pepper over and bake at 200°C/400°F/gas 6 for 15 minutes or until the pastry is crisp and brown round the edges and the cheese bubbling hot.

## 11 SHREDDED CANTONESE ROAST DUCK.

Make as described on page 153, roll in pancakes with hoisin sauce, cucumber and spring onion.

## 12 CRUMBED CRISP FRIED HERRING ROES.

## 13 SCRAMBLED EGG TARTLETS.

For 12 tartlets: roll out 1/2 recipe-quantity savoury short-crust pastry (page 287) and cut out 12 circles 1 cm / ½ inch larger in diameter than the depressions of a bun tin. Lay the pastry in the buttered depressions, gently pressing in with your fingertips. Put a sheet of foil on top, pressing it down to touch each of the pastry cups and weight each depression. Bake blind at 190°C/375°F/gas 5 for 10 minutes. Remove the foil and weights and return to the oven for another 10 minutes or until the pasty starts to colour. Turn out on a rack. Melt 30 g / 1 oz unsalted butter in a heavy-based pan over the lowest heat. Whisk 6 eggs with 2 tablespoons milk and season with salt and pepper. Add to the butter and cook, stirring constantly until the eggs just set in creamy curds. Immediately remove from the heat and stir in 2 tablespoons of double cream to stop the cooking. Put the pastry shells on a plate and divide the scrambled egg between them.

## 14 VEGETABLE CRUDITÉS WITH BAGNA CAUDA (PAGE 185).

## 15 GRISSINI WITH CHILLI-DUSTED PARMA HAM.

Grissini are feather-light Italian breadsticks. Wrap 30 of them (one box) in Parma or Serrano ham (you'll need about 450 g / 1 lb) and you have a quickly made canapé. Have the ham sliced on the thinnest setting, number 1. Put 2 teaspoons chilli flakes and 2 tablespoons brown sugar in a food processor and work briefly to mix. Scatter on a Swiss roll tin. Wrap a slice of ham round each breadstick in a spiral. Roll them in the chilli sugar to give them a light dusting and arrange (not touching) on a rack over a roasting tray. Bake for 10 minutes at 180°C/350°F/gas 4 and leave on a rack to cool. The bread will have softened, but leave it for 10 minutes and it will firm up again. Serve at room temperature.

**16 ANCHOVY BISCUITS (BISCUITS D'ANCHOIS, PAGE 272) WITH SCRAMBLED EGGS.**

**17 HUMMUS (PAGE 202), SERVED ON BATONS OF TOASTED PITTA.**

**18 MOORISH OLIVES.**
Toast 1 tablespoon sesame seeds in a pan over a low heat, stirring for 2 minutes, when they should give off a nice aroma. Set aside. Drain a large can of brined green olives and put them in a bowl. Wash an orange thoroughly, scrubbing gently under cold, running water. Dry it and carefully peel off the zest without any white pith. Cut the zest into the thinnest strips you can manage and add to the olives. Cut the orange into segments, again without pith, and add these. Coarsely crush 1 teaspoon black peppercorns with the sesame seeds. Stir this into 4 tablespoons extra-virgin olive oil with 12 chopped mint leaves (not spearmint!). Toss the olive mixture in this and put to marinate in the fridge for 2 hours before serving.

**19 FRITTATA (PAGE 243).**

**20 DISHES OF SALTED NUTS, DUKKAH (PAGE 225), OLIVES, RADISHES, HARD-BOILED EGGS AND CORNICHONS (PAGE 303).**

**21 HORIATIKI.**
Serve this Greek salad on skewers: wedges of ripe plum tomato, stoned kalamata olives, cubes of feta and chunks of sweet red onion. Dress with olive oil and lemon juice. Scatter over flat-leaf parsley to present.

**22 CHICKEN TERIYAKI (PAGE 147).**

**23 FISH GRATIN TARTLETS.**
Fish pie mixture (page 92) in pastry shells baked in bun tins, tops dotted with breadcrumbs and butter.

**24 BANDERILLAS (TAPAS ON COCKTAIL STICKS).**
Wrap cubes of Gallia or Honeydew melon in serrano ham, then secure with a toothpick, adding a quarter of fresh fig to the end. To make 12 takes about 115 g / 4 oz ham and 3 ripe figs.

Try spearing a piece of asparagus, 3 capers and a piece of tuna canned in olive oil or skewer a gherkin, cocktail onion and a pitted black olive with a raw floret of cauliflower or a piece of canned pimiento.

Wrap a cube of Idiaz†bal smoked cheese with an anchovy fillet and add a cherry tomato, fixing them together with a cocktail stick. You will need about 170 g / 6 oz cheese and 140 g / 5 oz tomatoes to make 12.

Gildas are a combination of rolled anchovy fillets, pitted olives and pickled green chilli.

**25 PUMPKIN SEEDS.**
For 6, preheat the oven to 200°C/400°F/gas 6. Put 200g / 7 oz dried pumpkin seeds in a single layer on a Swiss roll tin and bake for about 8–10 minutes, when they will have darkened. Any longer and you risk burning them. While they are baking, chop a garlic clove as finely as you can and put into a serving bowl with 1 tsp flake sea salt. Add the hot seeds and toss to coat. Leave for 1–2 hours for the flavour to permeate before eating.

# INDEX

## ACKNOWLEDGEMENTS

The publishers would like to thank Divertimenti, of Fulham Road and Wigmore Street in London, and Maison Blanc for their help in supplying items for photography.

    Thanks also to Steve Aland, Bob Cramp and Maria Moore for their assistance with the photography.

    The author would like to thank Cutty Catering Specialists for their supplies of fish and meat and George Allans for their fruit and vegetables.

# NOTES

# NOTES